The Papers of Dwight David Eisenhower

THE PAPERS OF DWIGHT DAVID EISENHOWER

THE PRESIDENCY: KEEPING THE PEACE XVIII

EDITORS

LOUIS GALAMBOS DAUN VAN EE

EXECUTIVE EDITOR

ELIZABETH S. HUGHES

ASSOCIATE EDITORS

JANET R. BRUGGER ROBIN D. COBLENTZ

JILL A. FRIEDMAN

ASSISTANT EDITOR

NANCY KAY BERLAGE

THE JOHNS HOPKINS UNIVERSITY PRESS

BALTIMORE AND LONDON

This book has been brought to publication with the generous assistance of the National Endowment for the Humanities, the National Historical Publications and Records Commission, the Eisenhower World Affairs Institute, and the France-Merrick Foundation.

Printed in the United States of America on acid-free paper

The Johns Hopkins University Press, 2715 North Charles Street,
Baltimore Maryland 21218-4363
www.press.jhu.edu

All illustrations in this volume are from the
Dwight D. Eisenhower Library, Abilene,
Kansas, unless indicated otherwise.

Library of Congress Cataloging-in-Publication Data

Eisenhower, Dwight D. (Dwight David), 1890–1969.
The papers of Dwight D. Eisenhower.

Vol. 6 edited by A. D. Chandler and L Galambos;
v. 7– , by L. Galambos.
Includes bibliographies and index.
Contents: v. 1–5. The war years.—[etc.]—
v. 10–11. Columbia University.—v. 12–13. NATO and the
Campaign of 1952.
1. World War, 1939–1945—United States. 2. World War,
1939–1945—Campaigns. 3. United States—Politics and
government—1953–1961. 4. Presidents—United States—
Election—1952. 5. Eisenhower, Dwight D. (Dwight David),
1890–1969. 6. Presidents—United States—Archives.
I. Chandler, Alfred Dupont, ed. II. Galambos, Louis, ed.
III. United States. President (1953–1961 : Eisenhower)
IV. Title.
E742.5.E37 1970 973.921'092'4[B] 65-027672
ISBN 0-8018-1078-7 (v. 1–5)
ISBN 0-8018-2061-8 (v. 6–9)
ISBN 0-8018-2720-5 (v. 10–11)
ISBN 0-8018-3726-x (v. 12–13)
ISBN 0-8018-4752-4 (v. 14–17)
ISBN 0-8018-6638-3 (v. 18)
ISBN 0-8018-6684-7 (v. 19)
ISBN 0-8018-6699-5 (v. 20)
ISBN 0-8018-6718-5 (v. 21)

Published in cooperation with
The Center for the Study of Recent American History
at The Johns Hopkins University

We dedicate these four concluding volumes of *The Papers of Dwight David Eisenhower* to the Board of Advisors of the Eisenhower Papers and to the Board of Trustees of the Johns Hopkins University, who together made it possible for us to complete this grand project.

Contents

Acknowledgments

The compilation, annotation, and publication of The Papers of Dwight David Eisenhower's Second Administration involved the dedicated efforts of an experienced and talented editorial team, as well as the support of a large number of other individuals and institutions. Eisenhower would have appreciated the collaborative effort necessary to complete the publication of twenty-one volumes of his papers.

All of the staff contributed to the annotations. Executive editor Elizabeth S. Hughes trained and supervised our research assistants, prepared the index, copyedited the manuscript, and guided it through the publication process. Associate editor Robin D. Coblentz conducted research at the Dwight D. Eisenhower Library in Abilene, Kansas, and the British Public Record Office in Kew, England, and drafted most of the foreign-policy annotations. Associate editor Janet R. Brugger performed a wide variety of technical and administrative tasks, researched and drafted notes, and assisted in many other ways throughout the production process. Associate editor Jill A. Friedman drafted annotations on the administration's domestic policy and also helped search the files in Abilene. Assistant editor Dr. Nancy K. Berlage researched and drafted notes across a wide range of fields. The editorial team continued to rely on the assistance provided by several hardworking graduate and undergraduate students, including Michael Cavino, Frances M. Clarke, Lynn K. Gorchov, Sol Rhee Kwon, Rebecca Jo Plant, Michael Rossi, Kelly R. Schrum, and Jayesh Shah. Their contributions were crucial, and we deeply appreciate the seriousness with which they conducted their work.

The Johns Hopkins University Board of Trustees, which in 1963 launched this enterprise, has sustained us through the years. We are especially grateful to Chairman Michael R. Bloomberg, to former Chairman Morris W. Offit, to Aurelia S. Garland Bolton, and to Walter D. Pinkard Jr., of the France-Merrick Foundations. Johns Hopkins President William R. Brody, Interim President Daniel Nathans, and former presidents William C. Richardson and Steven Muller have supported the project, as have Provost Steven Knapp, Dean Richard E. McCarty, Associate Dean Gary Ostrander, former Provost and Vice-President Joseph Cooper, and Vice-Presidents Robert R. Lindgren and Ross Jones. In the Office of Homewood Research Administration, Associate Dean Cheryl-Lee Howard, Dr. Milton T. Cole, Susan S. Doane, Holly A. Benze, Janet M. Palmer, Eugene Rutter, Patty Donahue, and Gwen Patterson provided enthusiastic assistance. Others at Hopkins have been similarly helpful. In the history department, the chair, Gabrielle Spiegel, former chairs John Russell-Wood, Richard Goldthwaite, and Dorothy Ross, the department administrator, Sharon A. Widomski, and administrative assistant Shirley Hipley have continued to aid us in numerous ways.

The staff of the Milton S. Eisenhower Library, where we were housed, has provided valuable support. We would like to thank Dean of University Libraries and Sheridan Director James G. Neal, Interim Sheridan Director Stephen G. Nichols, James E. Gillispie, Thomas M. Izbicki, Cynthia H. Requardt, and Deborah Slingluff, as well as Charles A. Baughan III, Bettie G. Cook, Allan H. Holtzman, Zachary Jaffe, Lynn Mathieu, Mary Jane Miller, Sharon Morris, Edith Overstreet, and Lynne Stuart.

Aiding in the research conducted in England were Keeper of Western Manuscripts at the Bodleian Library Mary Clapinson and John Wood and his staff in the Reader Services Department of the Public Record Office in Kew. Helen M. Carrier provided valuable assistance in the research conducted at the PRO.

Continued assistance from the federal government has made this undertaking possible. A great deal of that help has been financial. The National Endowment for the Humanities, headed by William R. Ferris, has provided significant grants to sustain our work. We are especially indebted to Margot Backas and Steve Veneziani for their guidance. At the National Historical Publications and Records Commission, also a granting agency, we have been helped over the years by Roger A. Bruns, Timothy D. W. Connelly, Mary Giunta, J. Dane Hartgrove, Ann W. Newhall, and former head Gerald W. George. We are also indebted to Archivist John W. Carlin at the National Archives, an important source of records in our research.

We are deeply indebted to the staff of the Dwight D. Eisenhower Library and to Director Daniel D. Holt and Assistant Director Martin M. Teasley. We are most appreciative of the efforts on our behalf of Thomas W. Branigar, Barbara J. Constable, James W. Leyerzapf, Stacey Meuli, Linda K. Smith, Dwight Strandberg, Hazel O. Stroda, and Kathleen A. Struss. Special thanks go to David J. Haight, Bonita B. Mulanax, and Herbert L. Pankratz, who continued to provide us with invaluable research assistance as we edited the documents of President Eisenhower's second administration. Stewart Etherington, of the Eisenhower Foundation, and Dennis H. J. Medina, of the Eisenhower Museum, also have continued to help us in significant ways.

Additional assistance came from Steven D. Tilley at the National Archives, Kathryn I. Dyer at the Central Intelligence Agency, Carol Hegemen and James C. Roach at the Gettysburg National Historic Site, Darwin H. Stapleton and Harold W. Oakhill at the Rockefeller Archive Center, Marie-Louise Kragh in the Special Collections Department at the University of Virginia Library, Judith A. Gray at the Library of Congress, Mary Haynes at the U.S. Army Center of Military History, and Barbara Spencer at the Augusta National Golf Club.

As we completed the final manuscripts and began the publication process, we were fortunate to work with an experienced, enthusiastic, and skillful staff at the Johns Hopkins University Press. Director James Jordan, former Director Willis G. Regier, and Director Emeritus Jack G. Goellner were extremely supportive, as were Joanne S. Allen, Douglas M. Armato, Eric F. Halpern, Barbara B. Lamb, and Henry Y. K. Tom. Acquisitions editor Robert J. Brugger and senior production editor Carol Zimmerman guided the manuscript through to publication.

Computer assistance in preparing the manuscript was provided by Peter A. Batke, David R. Chesnutt, James Cawley, Brian Elefant, Vincent LaMonte, Scott Franch, Greg S. Little, and Louise Miller-Finn.

Since this project has received federal matching grants, we have continued to look to the private and nonprofit sectors for financial support. The Eisenhower World Affairs Institute and Center for Political and Strategic Studies was especially helpful in these efforts. We are particularly indebted to Rocco C. Siciliano, president of the board of directors, and to Susan E. Eisenhower, Institute president. We are also most grateful for the support given us by Brigadier General Carl W. Reddel, Paul T. O'Day, Jane L. Kratovil, Dr. Elliott Converse, and Eugene T. Rossides.

Our special thanks to the members of our project's board of advisers, who stepped in to help us at a particularly crucial period. These include John S. D. Eisenhower, D. David Eisenhower II, Anne B. Evans, Jack G. Goellner, General Andrew J. Goodpaster, Douglas R. Price, W. James Price IV, Raymond J. Saulnier, and Ray Scherer. Others who deserve thanks are Janet E. and Edward K. Dunn Jr.,

Robert M. Evans, and Louise G. Sleichter. Every development effort needs at least two spark plugs. Ours were Anne B. "Shiny" Evans and Douglas R. Price, neither of whom ever seemed to be on vacation.

The Eisenhower family, especially General John S. D. Eisenhower, Susan E. Eisenhower, and D. David Eisenhower II, have continued to support us and ensure that our volumes met the standards set by President Eisenhower at the beginning of this project. Douglas R. Price, formerly of the Eisenhower White House staff and now a member of our editorial board, has supported the research for these volumes in countless ways. Through him we were able to call upon the memories of former members of the Eisenhower White House staff, including General Andrew J. Goodpaster Raymond J. Saulnier, Edward A. McCabe, and H. Roemer McPhee Jr. We were privileged to meet with others whose lives touched Eisenhower's in meaningful ways, including the late Ray Scherer and the late Wallace C. Strobel.

Introduction

President Dwight David Eisenhower may not have planned to make foreign affairs, in particular the effort to preserve the policy of containing communism, the central feature of his second administration. On January 20, 1957, as he took the oath of office in a private Sunday ceremony, Ike knew that he still had unfinished items on his agenda dating from his first four years in office, when he had launched a balanced attack on foreign and domestic problems. He could be excused a strong sense of satisfaction with what had been accomplished. He had, with impressive success, met the major challenges that he faced. As the world's most dominant leader, he had ended the bloody, stalemated war in Korea, replaced threatening leftist governments in Guatemala and Iran, eased the Soviets out of Austria, brought Germany into the NATO alliance, salvaged at least half a country from communism following a French debacle in Indochina, and restored order after his allies had launched their ill-advised invasion of Egypt's Suez Canal region. On the domestic scene, he had tamed the military and reformed America's defense posture, defanged, at last, the dangerous Joe McCarthy, initiated a revolutionary program of federal interstate-highway construction, opened the Midwest to ocean traffic through the St. Lawrence Seaway, brought an out-of-control federal budget into balance, and engineered a sound, growing economy. In the political realm, where he was an admitted novice, he had crushed his Democratic opponent in an election even more lopsided than his first decisive triumph four years earlier. The theme of successful crisis management was mirrored in his personal life. He had survived a heart attack and emergency surgery for a serious intestinal ailment. Recovering swiftly, he had won the assurances of his doctors that he could take control of his own health and serve out another full term.

The next four years would, however, destroy the illusion of political control, force him to devote most of his energy to foreign affairs, and thoroughly test his ability to lead the effort to defend the frontiers of the capitalist world. The assumption that the course of history can be controlled has been very strong in American presidents of the twentieth century, and Dwight David Eisenhower was no exception. But the notion that Eisenhower and the United States could shape the world to their liking turned out to be difficult to sustain in the second administration. A case in point was the Middle East, where the ceasefire Eisenhower had imposed by leaning on his allies—Britain, France, and Israel—had left the charismatic Egyptian leader Gamal Abdul Nasser in power and pan-Arabism gaining strength as the Soviets threatened to extend their influence in the oil-rich region. Fortified by bipartisan acceptance of the basic policy expressed in the Eisenhower Doctrine, the President worked quietly and methodically to prevent any renewed outbreak of hostilities. He forced the Israelis to withdraw their troops from the territory they had occupied during the 1956 Suez Crisis. Working through the United Nations whenever possible, he was able to broker an uneasy peace that featured renewed Western access to Middle Eastern oil, a reopened Suez Canal, and international passage through the Straits of Tiran up to the Israeli port of Eilat.

A lasting settlement proved far more elusive. "The basic reason for our Mid East troubles is Nasser's capture of Arab loyalty and enthusiasm throughout the region," he wrote former Secretary of the Treasury George Humphrey. Seeking a counterweight, Eisenhower attempted to forge a personal relationship with the deeply religious king of Saudi Arabia, ibn Abd al-Aziz Saud, whom he felt could "lead most of the Arab world toward the Western camp" even though he was "so patently a dictator." Given the persistence of religious conflict between Moslems and Jews, this strategy had its limitations, and Eisenhower eventually abandoned it after the king's own family stripped him of power. In 1958 Eisenhower was forced to go beyond his usual diplomatic and internationalist approaches when two other potential allies in the region, Lebanon and Jordan, were menaced by Nasserite subversion. Moving swiftly after a coup in Iraq threatened to destabilize the area, he dispatched a joint Army-Marine force to Beirut and aided the British in their almost simultaneous troop deployment to Jordan. Eisenhower's largely symbolic actions prevented a further deterioration in the Middle East, but the basic problem of Arab-Israeli conflict remained long after his military forces were withdrawn. This was, indeed, the type of fundamental conflict that made the era of the cold war so trying to the patience of Americans and so threatening to the peace of the world. Eisenhower provided steady leadership, looking always to contain a still expansive communism by bolstering the U.S. system of alliances and stabilizing regimes that promised to support that overriding goal.

One very important cold-war tool that Eisenhower employed against the Communists in the Middle East and elsewhere was foreign aid. This assistance was, he said, an "effective way of helping to defeat that kind of socialism (Imperialistic Communism) which the nations of the world, unaided, could not successfully withstand." Often, his best efforts were frustrated by domestic reluctance to provide U.S. resources to foreigners. Congress was particularly unwilling to fund the mutual-assistance program at a time when the Eisenhower Administration was trying to cut back on domestic spending for the good of the economy. The President lashed out at what he saw as short-sighted thinking, the unbridled "stupidity of the opponents of the program." Since the United States was in actuality supplying foreign countries with the means to buy its goods and services, he argued, "our mutual security operations represent America's best investment." Eisenhower labored continuously to convince Congress that foreign aid was an inexpensive way to defend our country, but he was frequently forced to accept serious funding cuts.

Equally frustrating was his effort to control events in the Far East. The Communist government of the People's Republic of China threatened to reclaim Quemoy and Matsu, the small offshore islands held by the Formosa-based regime of Chiang Kai-shek, an American client. Eisenhower believed that if the Sino-Soviet alliance took the islands "by armed assault," then it could capture Formosa and "'expel' the United States from the West Pacific and cause its Fleet to leave international waters and 'go home.'" His freedom of action was constrained by the significant domestic and allied opposition to risking a nuclear war over two valueless pieces of real estate. Chiang complicated matters further by refusing to modify his rigid, confrontational stance. In the end, the Communists backed down and partially lifted the blockade. Sporadic shelling of the islands continued, and here as elsewhere the United States and its allies had to play the nerveracking, waiting game central to containment. Eisenhower's confidence in that strategy never wavered. But he often felt discouraged when his support wavered as the struggle ground on and the Communists appeared to be winning the contest for global supremacy.

Looming over each of these crises was the threat of nuclear conflict, Eisenhower's greatest concern. He wrote a friend that "atomic war could mean the end of all civilization, including our own," and he believed that it was in the power of the United States, "along with those others who possess nuclear weapons to put an end to the fear and horror which the possibility of their use imposes." The basic problem, for Eisenhower, was that the other major superpower, the Soviet Union, refused to agree to the specific American solutions to the dilemma. Suspicious of "Communist imperialism" and "its announced purpose of world revolution and the Kremlin's control of the entire earth," he insisted that any disarmament agreement contain provisions for inspection and verification.

The most promising area in which to begin a diplomatic journey toward nuclear disarmament seemed to be the elimination of atomic testing, which was threatening the health of all the world's peoples. "I am convinced," Eisenhower wrote, "that a cessation of nuclear weapons tests, if it is to alleviate rather than merely to conceal the threat of nuclear war, should be undertaken as a part of a meaningful program to reduce that threat." But how could he get the Soviets to agree upon a program for inspections and inspection stations? The President and hardline Secretary of State John Foster Dulles were willing to make concessions to the Soviet suspicions about inspection by outsiders. Others in the Administration insisted that American flexibility was dangerous because the Soviets could never be trusted. Eisenhower decided to move ahead toward banning the tests, and in August 1958 he offered to cease testing if the Soviets would do likewise. Khrushchev agreed, and in October of that year test-ban talks began. At last it seemed as though the first small steps toward a reduction in tensions had begun.

But almost immediately the Soviets stirred up a new round of trouble and disrupted Eisenhower's dream of orderly progress toward a more peaceful world. Khrushchev announced that by the end of May 1959 he was going to make a separate peace with the Communist East Germans unless the United States and its allies agreed to Soviet proposals regarding the two Germanies. This step threatened the West's beleaguered outpost in Berlin. Allowing East Germany control over access rights to Berlin would jeopardize the West's ability to remain in the symbolic city and would make the reunification of Germany far less likely. Khrushchev had precipitated an "artificial crisis," Eisenhower complained. The United States could not think of risking its "honor by accepting, under the threat of force, conditions which would undermine our ability to fulfill our commitment to the people of Berlin. Our rights are clear." The President, who realized that the city could not be held by conventional forces in the face of overwhelming Soviet ground strength, refrained from provocative actions and proclaimed himself "completely ready to negotiate where there is any possible negotiable ground." Here too patience trumped provocation, and the Soviets eventually allowed the ultimatum to lapse without incident. But the threats to containment appeared to be mounting, and no long-term settlement was on the horizon in Berlin, the Far East, or the Middle East.

Each dangerous flash of conflict increased the media's demands and the popular yearnings for a four-power summit of Western and Soviet leaders. Eisenhower distrusted summits. In his view, they were all too likely to provide the Communists with a propaganda platform and to raise false hopes. He wrote that "to go back to the world with no more specific accomplishment" than had followed the 1955 Geneva meeting would "sound the death knell of much of the stirring hope that is discernible in the world." He insisted that before heads of government met, there first had to be progress at meetings between foreign ministers; "unless most careful preparations precede a summit meeting," he said, "such a conference would end in failure." Lower-level discussions continued to deadlock, however, and Eisenhower decided to hold out an additional inducement: the prospect of a personal visit to the United States by the Soviet leader, with a reciprocal visit to the Soviet Union by Eisenhower. Khrushchev, as expected, leapt at the chance to come to America, and his trip dominated the headlines in September 1959. There were few substantial diplomatic results, but the Soviets agreed to forgo any more ultimatums regarding Germany and the status of Berlin. This concession was enough to prompt Eisenhower to drop his insistence on progress at the foreign ministers' level as a precondition for a summit. The meeting, which was expected to produce an agreement banning atomic tests, was scheduled for May 1960.

Eisenhower set to work bringing his own administrative house into better order so that he could deal effectively with the Soviets. The Defense Department and the Atomic Energy Commission opposed disarmament deals with the Communists, and Eisenhower knew that the Democrats were poised to take advantage of any moves that might be seen as weakening the nation's security. The President had one great advantage, although it was not one about which he could speak publicly. Since 1956 the CIA had been flying over the Soviet Union in sophisticated, high-altitude reconnaissance planes. These flights had revealed the enemy's shortcomings in delivery systems for their nuclear weapons. Eisenhower later explained that this daring aerial-reconnaissance program was but "one phase of an intelligence system made necessary for defense against surprise attack on the part of a nation which boasts of its capability to 'bury' us all—and one which stubbornly maintains the most rigid secrecy in all its activities."

On the eve of the summit conference disaster struck. Eisenhower granted permission for one more overflight, the results of which he could use to overcome opposition within the ranks of his administration. On May 1, however, the Soviets shot down a U-2 spy plane deep within their own territory. Even worse, they captured the pilot, along with sufficient evidence to give the lie to the U.S. cover story that the flight's purpose had been weather research. Professing outrage at the opening of the Paris Summit, Khrushchev demanded that Eisenhower apologize. When the President declined, Khrushchev abruptly terminated the meeting and crushed any hope that these two powerful leaders would be able to make the world less threatening. Dismayed, Eisenhower blamed the debacle on the Soviet leader, who he said had "embarked on a calculated campaign, even before it began, to insure the failure of the conference and to see to it that the onus for such failure would fall on the West, particularly the United States." In truth, however, all of the blame belonged to the hazards of fortune and the overconfidence that had prompted Eisenhower and the CIA to push their luck at the worst possible time.

While weathering the wave of shock and dismay that followed, Eisenhower could take some consolation from the manner in which the crisis bolstered the Western alliance. America's staunchest friends, the British, were led by Prime Minister Harold Macmillan. He and Eisenhower were "old wartime comrades and friends of long standing" dating back to World War II, and the American President was usually confident that they would remain united in the "more difficult job of waging the peace." In accord concerning most aspects of the cold war, they both believed in the NATO concept of collective security as a means of stopping Soviet aggression. As in all such relationships, a number of relatively minor conflicts had to be worked out. Eisenhower was far less eager than Macmillan for a summit, but he eventually agreed to hold it. Macmillan in turn agreed to Eisenhower's requests for suitable berthing facilities for U.S. missile submarines in the United Kingdom. The President could not grant every one of Macmillan's pleas for the United States to open its doors to British imports, but he was glad to lend a sympathetic ear and was steadfast in his largely successful attempts to remove barriers to trade. As the letters in these volumes show, Eisenhower took care to consult his principal ally on every major matter in which the British had a substantial interest.

Another wartime associate, Charles de Gaulle, proved to be less receptive to American leadership. For years Eisenhower had longed for a strong figure to take charge in France. He once asked Dulles, "The trick is—how do we get the French to see a little sense?" In 1958 he got his wish. De Gaulle took power as a revolt in the French territory of Algeria threatened to disrupt not only the French nation but the nascent American ties to the emerging Moslem nations in North Africa as well. For the most part the United States supported the French as they groped their way toward a resolution of the bloody conflict, a resolution that would eventually end in complete independence for Algeria, but de Gaulle often aggravated

Eisenhower by challenging the fundamental premises on which the North Atlantic alliance was based. De Gaulle's desire to modify NATO's power relationships did not mean that he was leaning toward neutralism or the Soviet bloc. During the Paris Summit his firm pro-Western support in the face of Khrushchev's threats heartened Eisenhower in one of his darkest hours. Eisenhower responded, "Certainly the word 'ally' has for me now an even deeper meaning than ever before."

Eisenhower's strongest ally within the U.S. government had been unable to support him at the Summit. From the outset of his administrations Secretary of State John Foster Dulles had been an almost ideal adviser and subordinate, and the President had praised "his wisdom, his knowledge in the delicate and intricate field of foreign relations, and his tireless dedication to duty." These two strong men had their differences. The lawyerlike Dulles was often inclined toward an adversarial approach to world affairs at inappropriate times. He was also quick to give moralistic lectures when tolerant persuasion was needed. Dulles lacked some of Eisenhower's vision and flexibility, especially in such matters as admitting Soviet students to the United States in order to give them a taste of life in a free society. Their differences had to do with tone and tactics rather than fundamentals, however, and Dulles remained loyal and effective throughout the first six years of Eisenhower's presidency. When Dulles succumbed to illness in the spring of 1959 Eisenhower was devastated. The new Secretary of State, former Congressman Christian A. Herter, was seasoned and capable, but Eisenhower would never be as close to him as he had been to Dulles.

Unlike Dulles, Herter was supportive of the kind of initiative that Eisenhower now launched in the cold-war struggle for worldwide public opinion. The President reasoned that he could employ his enduring personal popularity by visiting a number of foreign nations as an antidote to Communist propaganda. He explained: "I have found from experience that there is no substitute for personal contact in furthering understanding and good will." The trip that he most wanted to take, to the Soviet Union, was a casualty of the U-2, and domestic unrest forced the Japanese government to request cancellation of the President's visit to that important American ally. But in country after country Eisenhower drew large and enthusiastic crowds, and he found the results gratifying: "Everywhere there is evidence that they look to America as a sort of father-nation, and that they feel we will be able to help them achieve the fulfillment of their desires." As Eisenhower sensed, democratic capitalism, with or without American help, had widespread appeal even during the years when the Communist empires seemed to be growing ever stronger. In dealing with Latin America, where he had tried to foster friendlier relationships, he was shaken by the hostile reception given to Vice-President Richard M. Nixon during a 1958 trip to Venezuela and Peru. Even worse was to come. Cuba's Fidel Castro, whom the President regarded as a "little Hitler," had come to power and was threatening to hand his country over to the Soviet Union "as an instrument with which to undermine our position in Latin America and the world." By July 1960 Eisenhower was tactfully explaining to Harold Macmillan that American patience had been exhausted and that he had begun "creating conditions in which democratically minded and Western-oriented Cubans can assert themselves and regain control of the island's policies and destinies." President John F. Kennedy would employ the resources Ike had started to create in an ill-planned and tragically unsuccessful armed invasion of the island by American surrogates.

During Eisenhower's final year in office two other hot spots developed, in Africa and Asia. In the Congo, Belgium's reluctant decolonization efforts had resulted in chaotic factionalism and territorial secession of a province rich in mineral resources. Fearful of opportunistic Soviet penetration into Africa, Eisenhower was able to bring about at least a modicum of stabilization by using U.N. peacekeeping troops. In Laos, the President was even more apprehensive that Communist forces from North Vietnam were threatening to upset the uneasy status quo that prevailed after the 1954 Geneva accords had halted a dangerous and bloody conflict. He told India's Prime Minister Jawaharlal Nehru that he was "deeply troubled by the renewal of fratricidal warfare in this small and weak but strategically important Kingdom, whose only 'offense' is geographical: it lies in the path of Communist expansionist intent in Asia, and is perhaps the most vulnerable spot on the entire periphery of the communist-controlled Eurasian land mass." Matters came to a head in January 1961, as he was preparing to turn power over to the Democrats and was powerless to affect events except by warning President-elect Kennedy that another nation was threatening to fall to the Communists. The domino theory and the assumption that global communism was a unified force were still playing a powerful role in shaping U.S. foreign policy.

The world had clearly become a more dangerous place in the four years of Ike's second term. Nuclear weapons were a greater threat than ever, and increasing hostility between the United States and the Soviet Union was exacerbating cold-war tensions. The Soviet Union had gained its first foothold in the Western Hemisphere, and Southeast Asia seemed to be on the verge of collapse. Although de Gaulle had brought a measure of stability to the French republic, he had started to challenge American leadership and threatened to withdraw his country's support from the alliance. Neutral nations, led by Nehru's India, had resisted Eisenhower's assiduous courting and continued to act in ways that injured American interests. The newly emerging nations of Africa faced overwhelming problems and were vulnerable to Communist influence even as Congress grew ever more reluctant to provide economic support overseas. The future looked stark.

But in reality, the explosive combination of Communist imperialism and national socialist revolutions would never be stronger than it was when Eisenhower left office. He had guided the U.S. system of alliances through the worst stage of a threatening era and had kept intact the containment policy that would ultimately bring about the astonishing collapse of the Soviet empire and the rapid retreat of communism as an ideological and political force. He had done so while preventing the bitter rivalry between the United States and the Soviet Union from exploding into a general war. As ideologically driven conflicts erupted, Eisenhower and his allies had been able to keep these struggles localized. The great powers had not gone to war over Quemoy, Suez, Lebanon, the Congo, or the access routes to Berlin. The cold war continued, but the soldier-president had kept the peace through the world's most dangerous years.

International relations was Eisenhower's strength as a national leader, but while in office he improved his skills in handling domestic affairs. By 1957 he had learned, for example, how to work with Congress even when it was controlled by the Democratic opposition. He forged personal ties with House and Senate leaders in both parties and cultivated a loose alliance between Republicans and conservative Democrats. These measures, coupled with a judicious use of his veto power, were usually effective in preventing what he felt were liberal excesses.

Eisenhower wanted to maintain a sound economy by means of an equally sound fiscal policy. He was convinced that a balanced budget was necessary to keep the economy healthy over the long term. Eisenhower wrote to a businessman friend that the enemy was inflation: "With this thief and robber stalking across the country, we can easily have an <u>apparent</u> prosperity for a time, but not for long. Inflation must be avoided, and this means that the Federal government must not only live within its means but must, in times of prosperity, begin reducing the nation's debt." His determination was put to the test after the Soviets launched their Sputnik, the world's first earth satellite, in October 1957. This was bad news for two reasons. First, it meant that the Soviets had, or soon would have, the capability to reach the United States with long-range missiles armed with atomic weapons. The United States was losing an important element of its continental security. Second, Eisenhower's domestic foes were certain to take advantage of the crisis atmosphere to attempt to push higher defense expenditures through Congress. Since the Administration's balanced budget was predicated upon reducing military spending, the President's economic programs were placed in jeopardy. Eisenhower tried to hold down the increased funding for missiles while reassuring the American people that even though "a purely materialistic dictatorship" had accomplished an impressive technological feat, he still retained the "complete conviction that the American people can meet every one of these problems and these threats if we turn our minds to it." His prestige as a military leader was enough to keep the lid on a potentially runaway defense budget, but he paid a political price for this successful effort to control the sense of panic that followed Sputnik.

Meanwhile, Eisenhower continued his efforts to reform the nation's military structure so as to reduce interservice rivalry and to bring the Pentagon under tighter civilian control. As he wrote U.N. Ambassador Henry Cabot Lodge in April, "I am, if I may use the expression, 'going to town' on the issue of Defense Reorganization." Energetic in his campaign to overcome entrenched congressional opposition, Eisenhower won the necessary support by marshaling a cadre of influential businessmen. He argued that the military establishment had to adopt modern business and organizational practices in order to meet the challenges of rapidly advancing technology: "All of us know that the competition faced by the Defense Department is the sternest in the world, that provided by the military might of the Soviet Union. The single objective of the Defense Department is the nation's security; in this it must be successful." The resulting bill, which Eisenhower signed into law in August 1958, simplified command structures and consolidated power in the hands of the Secretary of Defense at the expense of the individual military services.

While these positive results were being achieved, Eisenhower was resisting congressional pressure to act on another front. In 1957 the economy had gone into recession due in large part, the President believed, to "the 1955 inflationary splurge by certain automobile companies," which had increased production of new cars far out of proportion to consumer demand. Whatever the cause, consumer spending fell and unemployment rose. Politicians, labor officials, and even some business leaders urged the White House to cut taxes and increase spending for public-works programs. Eisenhower was very reluctant to take steps that he thought would throw the nation back into a New Deal frame of mind. He feared that tax cuts and spending increases could not be repealed after the economic difficulties were over, and that a ruinous inflation would result. By formally requesting such measures, he would "open flood gates in the Congress that will never be closed." Freely wielding his veto against recovery bills he felt were unwise, Eisenhower refused to heed the calls for drastic action. The economy, as he predicted, slowly recovered, but the President found himself "tagged as an unsympathetic, reactionary fossil." Both he and the Republican party suffered a loss of political prestige for refusing to yield their long-range objectives to a quick economic fix.

Eisenhower also came under fire for his attempts to manage public policies dealing with three specific sectors of the economy. Particularly controversial were the farm policies that he and his Secretary of Agriculture, Ezra Taft Benson, employed in their efforts to reduce federal subsidies and agricultural surpluses. The problem seemed insoluble. "Every suggested cure seems to bring additional problems in its wake," he complained to a Kansas dairy farmer. He tried to get Benson to show more flexibility in trying to secure acceptable legislation, but he was forced to alienate Farm Belt residents and politicians by vetoing Congress's attempt to raise farm subsidies in 1958. In the field of transportation, Eisenhower tried in vain to reverse the continuing decline of the nation's railroad systems. He was able to remove certain federal restrictions, but this only resulted in limited relief. The development of the Interstate Highway System also caused the President concern. He attempted to accelerate construction of the great roadway net, but his efforts ran aground on the reluctance to raise taxes and the insistence that expensive projects through urban centers should be added to the original concept. Finally, Eisenhower's energy policy, which was predicated upon encouraging the freest possible market for petroleum products, was thwarted by political forces determined to foster and protect domestic oil producers. Attempting to find a middle way between consumer and producer interests, he imposed voluntary and then mandatory quotas on imported oil. Eisenhower took these steps reluctantly, for they alienated America's cold-war allies and slowed progress toward free trade in the world economy.

The most explosive domestic issue in Eisenhower's second term—civil rights—was only tangentially related to economic concerns. In deciding the best course to take in response to the growing demands of African Americans, Eisenhower discovered that the middle-way strategy that had served him so well in the realms of politics and the economy would not prevent conflict. Although he sympathized with the plight of white Southerners, he saw that the advocates of racial progress had justice on their side, most particularly in their quest for minority enfranchisement. He set forth his convictions in a letter to a supporter: "A President of all the people must defend the rights of all citizens, most especially he must do all he rightfully can to make sure that the basic right to vote is not denied any citizen entitled to it." He disliked "rigidly conceived laws" to protect civil rights, however, favoring instead a gradual, constitutional approach that would not risk tearing the fabric of Southern society. In 1957 he patiently cajoled the Congress to enact the first civil-rights legislation since Reconstruction, a measure that established the U.S. Civil Rights Commission and allowed the federal government to take limited steps to protect voting rights for African Americans. In 1960 he successfully pushed for amendments that strengthened the law by giving federal authorities greater enforcement powers.

The movement for social change and equality was, however, too powerful and too deeply grounded to be satisfied by these measures. The issue of school desegregation, which was far more volatile than even the question of voting rights, stirred mixed feelings within the President. He privately grumbled to a confidant that "no other single event has so disturbed the domestic scene in many years as did the Supreme Court's decision of 1954 in the school segregation case." He disliked the idea of "undesirable social mingling" and counseled a young African American girl to be patient in the face of injustice, explaining that "progress, to be lasting, must be steady and sometimes painfully slow." But in the fall of 1957 even his noted ability to be patient gave way when Arkansas Governor Orval Faubus defiantly obstructed a federal court's desegregation order in Little Rock. Faubus's actions provoked mob violence against African American students attempting to attend a segregated high school, and the President took decisive measures: "Failure to act in such a case would be tantamount to acquiescence in anarchy and the dissolution of the union." He placed the Arkansas National Guard, which had been used to prevent compliance with the federal court's order, under federal control and sent in units of the elite 101st Airborne Division to restore order and enforce the court's rulings. These dramatic actions provoked widespread resentment in the South, and a few school districts tried to evade the inevitable by closing their public-school systems before federal judges could issue integration orders. But the process of creating a new order in the South would continue and accelerate in the following decade.

Although Eisenhower told a friend that "political problems—and by this I mean internal political problems—are the most wearing in this difficult job," he took his role of party leader seriously. After the 1956 election confirmed the widely held impression that voters liked Ike better than the Republican Old Guard, Eisenhower tried to bring more young people into the party and to remold it in his own Modern Republican image. Progress in recasting the party was slow, but by early 1958 Ike nevertheless hoped to regain control of the legislative branch: "If a Republican Congress could be elected it would be the neatest trick of the week." Two factors appear to have undermined his hopes: his reluctance to take fiscally irresponsible measures to alleviate the economic distress caused by the lingering effects of the recession; and a scandal involving one of his closest associates, Sherman Adams, the Assistant to the President, in reality a powerful White House Chief of Staff. It was revealed that Adams had accepted favors from, and performed services for, a shady New England businessman. Eisenhower, who believed that Adams typified "sturdiness, forthrightness and integrity," was dismayed. "Nothing that has occurred has had a more depressive effect on my normal buoyancy and optimism than has the virulent, sustained, demagogic attacks made upon him." Taking a political beating in the press, Eisenhower accepted Adams's resignation after warnings that Adams's presence would drag the party down to certain defeat.

Dumping Adams did not help. In November 1958 the GOP lost thirteen seats in the Senate and forty-seven in the House of Representatives. The Democrats also won twenty-six of the thirty-four gubernatorial elections. One of these was in California, where Eisenhower had focused his attention and energy on the task of electing outgoing Senate Majority Leader William Knowland. Among the few bright spots was the dynamic Nelson Rockefeller's victory in his bid to be New York's governor, a victory that encouraged the President "to believe that people have decided that 'moderate government' when properly explained by a personable, intelligent candidate is still a goal of the majority of Americans." Rockefeller's triumph also marked him as a likely contender for the next Republican presidential nomination, a position on which Vice-President Nixon had seemed to have a lock.

Eisenhower found it difficult to choose and develop a successor. As the campaign intensified, he became grumpy about some of the proposals Nixon and Rockefeller were making. New initiatives seemed to imply criticisms of his efforts over the past eight years. For reasons of temperament and ideology he found it impossible to commit absolutely to Nixon. On the other hand, Rockefeller's dynamism seemed to break too decisively with the Middle Way. Ike continually daydreamed about men who in fact had no chance to win the Republican nomination, including Democrats like Ohio Governor Frank Lausche and Treasury Secretary Robert Anderson. In the end, Nixon won the nomination because of the careful groundwork he had done in the Republican party.

Once Nixon, with Eisenhower's U.N. Ambassador Henry Cabot Lodge as his running mate, started to campaign, the President entered the fray. But he did so in a constrained way. "Many people," he explained to a supporter, "seem to forget that I am seventy years old." He was, he said, avoiding overexposing himself on the stump so as to steer clear of "Mamie's wrath." Realizing that Nixon would have to appear as his own man in the campaign, he doubted "the wisdom of any president appearing in the role of mentor or sponsor of the individual he hopes to be his successor." These doubts and "Mamie's wrath" notwithstanding, Eisenhower hit the campaign trail in a last-minute effort to push Nixon over the top. It was not enough to keep Kennedy and the Democrats from capturing the White House. At first, Eisenhower wrote, he felt as though he had been "hit in the solar plexus with a ball bat," and he wondered whether his eight-year effort had been in vain. His "normal optimism" soon reasserted itself, however, and he began making plans for the presidential transition and an active retirement.

Throughout Eisenhower's second administration, it was not only Mamie who was concerned about Eisenhower's health. Given his two serious illnesses in 1955 and 1956, the President's health was indeed a matter of both personal and public concern. In November 1957 he suffered a cerebral occlusion—a stroke—that temporarily incapacitated him while he was working at his desk in the White House. He wrote a close friend from Abilene that "never at any time" did he "feel ill," and he minimized the event in a letter to Macmillan by telling him that he had experienced merely "a marked 'word confusion,' with, also, some loss of memory of words alone." Deciding that he could not continue in office if he were not physically capable of withstanding the demands of the office, Eisenhower set for himself, and passed, a rigorous personal test by attending the meeting of NATO heads of government three weeks after the onset of his illness. He made, virtually, a full recovery, and his health remained good for his final years in the presidency.

As the documents in these volumes show, Eisenhower's family played a significant role in his life from 1957 until January 1961. The saddest event of those years was the death of Arthur Eisenhower, whose ill-health had been a source of filial concern and whom he had described to a cabinet officer as "our 'big' brother—always dependable and always devoted." The President also continued his lively correspondence with Edgar Eisenhower, a conservative lawyer who never hesitated to criticize his famous brother whenever he detected deviation from Republican orthodoxy. As Dwight told another brother, Earl, who had worried that intra-family disagreements might become public knowledge, "all the Eisenhower brothers have fought for nearly sixty years—and loved every minute of it!" The President's youngest brother, Milton, had no such concerns. He continued to advise the President on a number of matters and to serve as special representative to the troubled nations of Latin America. As Ike explained to a friend, Milton had for many years been one of his "most respected and trusted counsellors and associates." The President and Mamie also delighted in the growing family of their son, John, who held an important national-security position in the

White House. While Mrs. Eisenhower mentored and played with her three granddaughters, the President took great pleasure in paying special attention to the upbringing of his grandson, David. John and his family had even more opportunities to see the First Family after June 1959, when they moved to Gettysburg and settled in a location close to the Eisenhowers' cherished cattle farm.

Letters to Eisenhower's widespread network of friends are abundant in this collection. In addition to showing a warm and hidden side to this rather formal man, these writings also reveal new information about his ideas regarding public policy. Secure in the knowledge that his friends would not pass his letters along to the media, Eisenhower frequently expressed himself in a candid manner. The President suffered a blow when his favorite correspondent, Edward Everett "Swede" Hazlett, died late in 1958. Hazlett, a boyhood friend from Abilene, had been one of the few people to whom he could vent the full range of his emotions, and he told Hazlett's widow that his old friend's death had left "a permanent void" in his life. Eisenhower also asked his friends for help in such matters as fundraising for political and charitable causes and support for initiatives stalled in Congress. The materials presented here also testify to the fact that Eisenhower lived in a less suspicious age, when, despite the Sherman Adams scandal, public men could still receive gifts from their close friends with little thought of impropriety.

Eisenhower also corresponded with his friends from World War II. These letters were often characterized by warm remembrances and nostalgia, but they took on a more acerbic tone after his wartime associate Field Marshal Bernard Law Montgomery published a memoir that slighted Eisenhower's accomplishments. Although he told a friend that he "never allowed such matters to disturb me more than momentarily," few things enraged the President as much as the criticisms of a man he privately referred to as a "very small magpie." Although forced to abandon his plans to orchestrate a definitive joint reply to Montgomery, Eisenhower prompted a reunion of Allied leaders that revalidated his unspoken claim to have been a primary architect of the victory over Germany.

As 1961 approached, the President turned his attention to his impending retirement. He decided to accept an affiliation with Gettysburg College, which had offered to provide him with office space and facilities to conduct the business of an ex-President. Choosing among many competing offers, Eisenhower selected publishers for his memoirs and made arrangements to house his papers in a suitable repository. Resentful of the worshipful attention given to the President-elect, he nevertheless dutifully met with Kennedy and in the course of his briefing handed over, in effect, the problems he had not been able to solve during his eight years. Eisenhower acknowledged his many debts to staff members, colleagues, and subordinates as he made his final farewells. The most important of these was, of course, to the American people in a thoughtful farewell address, in which he repeated the themes that had characterized his stewardship and warned his fellow citizens about the dangers of both a military-industrial complex and a scientific-technological elite.

At the end of his presidency Eisenhower remained convinced that the basic course he had chosen for the United States had been correct. As he told a classmate from his days at West Point, "The middle-of-the-road is still the only constructive policy for dealing with human concerns of vast proportions." He had achieved a balanced budget and overall economic health without dislocating the economic system or unnecessarily burdening the population. He had ended one war, avoided another, and taken the first steps toward a peaceful accommodation with America's ideological enemies—all of this without surrendering either America's principles or her allies. As he told his old wartime colleague Hastings Ismay, "The verdict on my efforts will of course be left to history, and I don't have to worry about it now." Several generations of historians have ground away at that task, and their verdicts, while far from unanimous, have gradually become more positive, more enthusiastic about Eisenhower's leadership in foreign affairs and more appreciative of his efforts to shape a domestic order that followed the middle way. Each reader of these documents will be able to debate that verdict, an intellectual process that we hope will continue for many decades to come.

SELECTION AND ANNOTATION

We are fortunate in this, our final set of volumes, to have been able to maintain continuity of our basic editorial policies regarding selection and annotation of documents. Our focus has remained on Eisenhower the man and not on the presidential office. Accordingly, we have selected for publication only documents that he wrote, dictated to a secretary, redrafted, or was closely involved with in some other way. We have excluded such routine correspondence as the large number of declinations sent out over his signature. These selection criteria were necessary given the amount of time and support available; they have also served to make manageable the overwhelming volume of material generated by the Chief Executive and his principal assistants.

As in Eisenhower's first administration, staff members drafted many of his letters. Our task was to determine the level of Eisenhower's involvement in the creation of the document. Using memorandums of conversation, lists of items signed by the President, diary entries, congressional mail summaries, records of telephone conversations, calendars, routing sheets, emended drafts, handwritten postscripts, and Presidential Secretary Ann C. Whitman's own detailed notes, we were almost always able to make an informed judgment on whether or not a particular letter was a true "Eisenhower" document. We excluded items prepared by the staff and merely signed by the President with minimal involvement on his part. In our annotations we have continued to identify the aide or, in some cases, the executive department or Cabinet official who drafted the letter or cable for Eisenhower. Readers may safely assume that unless otherwise noted, Eisenhower himself prepared, or caused to be prepared, the first draft. (For a relatively small number of personal items that we have selected, Ann Whitman drafted correspondence for the President, often at his express direction.) During Eisenhower's First Administration many of these drafts were saved; in the 1957–61 period most of the drafts were deliberately destroyed. All the evidence that we have seen indicates, however, that every significant letter that left the White House with Eisenhower's signature was, in the largest sense, Eisenhower's own.

Since it was the practice in the White House during these years to make multiple copies of letters and memorandums, we often had a choice of files from which to obtain Eisenhower documents. We have selected the best available copy as the source of our text. Frequently, however, we were able to locate a number of identical copies of the same Eisenhower document. Although in such cases we have cited those files that were most convenient for us, often the location where we first found the document or the folder containing the relevant supporting material, we have also tried to cite a variety of files in order to assist those doing research in the original sources. Our annotations will guide readers to the collections containing incoming and backup correspondence. Foremost among these, of course, are the Eisenhower Manuscripts, which we have abbreviated as "EM." Citations to the richest subset of EM, the Ann Whitman File, are given as "AWF," and we cite the almost equally valuable White House Central Files as "WHCF" (see the note on primary sources in vol. XVII).

As we stated in the introduction to volumes XIV–XVII, one other aspect of our editorial apparatus requires explanation. In his correspondence with foreign leaders Eisenhower often dictated letters or edited State Department drafts for dispatch via diplomatic pouch. When rapid communication was called for, as it often was, the State Department usually cabled the text of Eisenhower's letter to the appropriate American embassy for hand delivery. Occasionally both means of transmission were used for the same letter. In such cases we have normally taken the letter rather than the cable version as our source text. We have also noted any variations between the letter and cable versions.

We have tried to remain consistent in our editorial policies regarding annotations as well as document selection. Since we do not publish incoming letters and reports in their entirety, we have continued to provide a summary of the contents of the incoming letters or reports. Our aim, as always, has been to give the reader a context for understanding what prompted Eisenhower to dictate, draft, or approve his document. We have also provided thumbnail sketches of Eisenhower's correspondents and information concerning the formulation of specific documents. Of special importance have been the deletions the President made to earlier versions of his communications, which were often even more important than the additions. Whether the changes were made to his own dictations or to staff-drafted letters and cables, these editorial alterations provide, we feel, a glimpse into the decision-making process in the presidency of Dwight David Eisenhower.

Louis Galambos
Daun van Ee

The Papers of Dwight David Eisenhower

The Presidency: Keeping the Peace

New Beginning, Old Problems

JANUARY 1957 TO MAY 1957

1

The Mideast and the Eisenhower Doctrine

1

EM, AWF, Name Series

TO EDGAR NEWTON EISENHOWER

January 21, 1957

Secret and personal

Dear Ed:[1] Yesterday afternoon (Sunday), we had a partial reunion, limited only to brothers and their wives. Naturally all of us felt its incompleteness due to your absence.

The only real piece of news is the ill health of Arthur.[2] This is something that apparently they have tried to keep secret at the insistent desire of Louise, who, as you probably know, is a Unitarian. I think that this sect believes in "faith healing" or maybe it is that with right thoughts you never get sick.[3]

In any event, the story, as I got it from Arthur, runs something like this: He went to New York last November and had a very trying trip with the result that he felt excessively tired. As quickly as he got back to Kansas City, he went to a hospital and they diagnosed his difficulty as an "enlarged heart" and told him to take it very easy from then on. When he told me this he said, "Please do not let on to Louise that you know this because she is very anxious that no one hear of it." However, a little later, when the ladies were absent from the room, he blurted out the same story to all the rest of the boys and failed to give the same caution to them that he had to me. As a result, when Louise rejoined the group, one of the boys spoke about this enlarged heart and she seemingly hit the roof.

Here in one of our government hospitals is probably one of the finest cardiologists in the world. In that hospital there is reserved always for the President a very splendid suite; in fact, I know of few hotel suites that are so attractive. I promptly offered to put Arthur out in this suite (he now has nothing demanding his time) and get my cardiologist friend to give him a thorough going-over. Of course there is nothing that can be done to bring him back to the condition he was in, but he is apparently completely without advice from doctors as to what kind of a life he should lead. He is uncertain in his talk and actions and looks very old indeed. I think most of us were really astonished, if not shocked, at his appearance.

My offer was indignantly rejected by Louise, who said several times, "If he will do just like I tell him, he will be all right."

I tell you all this merely as information—there is nothing whatsoever to do about it. For example, Arthur had told me personally that he would like to accept my offer. When it was repeated in Louise's presence, she turned on him and demanded in a shrill voice, "Do you want to go?" Then she frankly stated that she would neither stay here in a hotel nor go out to the hospital with him. He immediately backed off and said, "Oh no, of course not; really I feel fine."

All this conversation was brought on by the fact that he had gone yesterday afternoon to the airport to meet his grandson who was coming in. To each of the brothers there is an aide assigned, and his aide found suddenly that Arthur was showing every sign of weakness and fatigue—virtual collapse. He sat him down and rushed to a telephone to call a doctor to meet him. When they returned from the airport Arthur was feeling well enough to insist on going straight to his hotel. So the doctor never did see him.

There are some more distressing details, largely of a financial character, that Milton told me, but none of us knows whether there is any truth in them so I do not repeat them.[4] The crux of these statements (as Milton understands) was that for some legal reason Arthur long ago put all his property in Louise's name and that his pension from the bank is a very meager one, out of which he has to pay alimony to his first wife.[5] However, I notice that Arthur has kept his directorship on two or three companies, so I assume that he is in no financial straits at the moment. And of course it is always possible that the woman will play square with him, but I was shocked when I heard her say yesterday in such certain terms that she would merely go back to Kansas City if he should go to the hospital for three or four days.

I hope that you will not repeat any of this to Arthur or to anyone else. I merely give you as accurate a picture as I can of the impressions we got yesterday so that you will not expect too much of Arthur if you should happen to pass through Kansas City.

He apparently spends his mornings at home and his afternoons are given to bridge at the Mission Hills Club.

Today is the Inauguration and the only part about it that I really dread is the viewing of the parade that will certainly last from 2¼ to 2½ hours. I gave orders to hold it down to two hours, but of course everybody wants to get his face into the thing if he possibly can.[6]

The other part that gives me a little pause is that again today I swear to do my best for another four years in working at a job that at times is nothing but frustration. We have never successfully got across to America as a whole the cold war requirements in fighting Communism. Some people simply will not wake up to the great danger inherent in inflation and most want more services from government with lower taxes.

Of course some phases of this life have their amusing aspects. For example, I hear directly or indirectly from some newspaper writers or commentators that I have gotten over resenting the duties of the office and now enjoy them. Moreover, they say that I am no longer nervous or ill at ease with the press, that I have learned to get along with them.[7]

As to the first of these, I have always made it a point to like my work. Even when I get angry (which I am prohibited by the doctors from doing) it is not an anger at the job but at some stupidity that creates a problem which never had to occur.[8] As far as my attitude toward the job itself is concerned, it is no different than it was in 1953—indeed, before that, because I had a very accurate idea of what was involved when I finally agreed to stand for the nomination.

As for the newspaper people, they simply kid themselves. I have been meeting the press since 1941 and from the beginning I have never been conscious of any "fear" of press conferences. As a matter of fact, most of the meetings are very poor. The average newspaper man likes to ask questions about individuals and personalities, rarely does he want to talk philosophy. There is no story in that.

There are five or six individuals of the working press that I admire and respect very much. Also there are quite a few publishers that I count as my good friends.[9] But I find that the average writer is more "New Dealish" in his sentiment than almost anyone else. Consequently one merely gets rather tired meeting and talking to them.

The only reason that I rather resent signing on to do my best for the next four years is that there are so many things Mamie and I have wanted to do for so long, and this time it is more difficult for me than it was in 1953 to believe that I personally had the duty of standing again for this office. Possibly I am like a woman convinced against her will.[10]

Yesterday morning I saw Janis and her husband when they attended the private swearing-in at the White House.[11] The families and family connections, numbering about 75 or 80, stayed around a while in the State Dining Room where we had coffee and cakes of various kinds. It was a very pleasant occasion.

Give my love to Lucy, and of course I do hope that the improvement in your condition, reported to me recently by Lucy, continues steadily and surely.[12] *As ever*

[1] Eisenhower's older brother Edgar was a senior partner in the law firm Eisenhower, Hunter, Ramsdel and Duncan, in Tacoma, Washington. For background on the Eisenhower brothers see *The Papers of Dwight David Eisenhower* (Baltimore, 1970–); vols. I–V, *The War Years*, ed. Alfred D. Chandler, Jr. (1970), hereafter cited as Chandler, *War Years*; vol. VI, *Occupation, 1945*, ed. Alfred D. Chandler, Jr., and Louis Galambos (1978), hereafter cited as Chandler and Galambos, *Occupation*; vols. VII–IX, *The Chief of Staff*, ed. Louis Galambos (1978), hereafter cited as Galambos, *Chief of Staff*; vols. X–XI, *Columbia University*, ed. Louis Galambos (1983), hereafter cited as Galambos, *Columbia University*; vols. XII–XIII, *NATO and the Campaign of 1952*, ed. Louis Galambos (1989), hereafter cited as Galambos, *NATO and the Campaign of 1952*; vols. XIV–XVII, *The Presidency: The Middle Way*, ed. Louis Galambos and Daun van Ee (1996), hereafter cited as Galambos and van Ee, *The Middle Way*. See also Bela Kornitzer,

The Great American Heritage: The Story of the Five Eisenhower Brothers (New York, 1955).
[2] Arthur Bradford Eisenhower, the eldest of the five brothers, was vice-chairman of the board of the Commerce Trust Company, Kansas City, Missouri. Louise Sondra Grieb was Arthur's second wife.
[3] Eisenhower was apparently confusing Unitarians with Christian Scientists. Unitarianism stresses the oneness of God, the humanity of Jesus, the perfectibility of human character, and the ultimate salvation of all souls. Unitarians, who reject the doctrine of the infallibility of the Bible, emphasize individual freedom of belief, democratic principles, and hospitality to the methods of science in seeking truth. The Church of Christ, Scientist, holds that disease is "a mental concept which can be dispelled by active Christian discipleship, spiritual regeneration, and application of the truths to which Jesus bore witness" (Frank S. Mead, *Handbook of Denominations in the United States,* revised by Samuel S. Hill [Nashville, 1985], pp. 80–83, see also pp. 239–45; John C. Godbey, "Unitarian Universalist Association," in *Encyclopedia of Religion,* vol. 15, edited by Mircea Eliade [New York, 1987], pp. 143–47, and Stephen Gottschalk, "Christian Science," in *Encyclopedia of Religion,* vol. 3, edited by Mircea Eliade [New York, 1987], pp. 442–46.
[4] Milton Stover Eisenhower, the youngest Eisenhower brother, had been president of Johns Hopkins University since July 1956.
[5] Arthur had been married to Alida B. Eisenhower from 1906 until 1924. In December 1957 the first Mrs. Arthur Eisenhower would sue for $3000 in back alimony (*New York Times,* Jan. 27, 1958).
[6] The President would be sworn to a second term of office at 12:23 P.M. on this same date. The inaugural parade would last from 2:30–5:15 P.M. (*New York Times,* Jan. 21, 1957; see also the following document and no. 11 below).
[7] For background see Craig Allen, *Eisenhower and the Mass Media: Peace, Prosperity, & Prime-Time TV* (Chapel Hill, 1993), pp. 49–55.
[8] In the aftermath of his September 1955 heart attack, Eisenhower had been advised by his physicians to avoid situations that produced annoyance, irritation, frustration, or any kind of tension (see Galambos and van Ee, *The Middle Way,* no. 1703).
[9] Eisenhower's extensive observations and criticisms of the press, as well as his comments on reporters he held in high esteem, can be found in *ibid.,* especially no. 669; for his friends in newspaper publishing see, for example, nos. 410, 477, 898, and 934.
[10] On Eisenhower's ambivalence regarding a second term, see, for example, *ibid.,* no. 1766.
[11] Edgar's daughter Janis was married to William Oliver Causin. For more on the private and public swearing-in ceremonies see no. 2; on the reception following the private ceremony see *New York Times,* Jan. 21, 1957.
[12] Edgar's wife, Lucille Dawson Eisenhower. Edgar would respond on January 29 (same file as document) saying that although he found Eisenhower's letter "disturbing," he could not write Arthur since he was not supposed to know about his condition. "I am qualified to give him some advice," he would write, "but have learned no one will take it unless they have to pay for it—So—." Edgar had experienced a slipped disc and nervous collapse in November 1956 (see Galambos and van Ee, *The Middle Way,* no. 2092; for developments see no. 4).

2

EM, AWF, DDE Diaries Series

TO EARL WARREN

January 22, 1957

Dear Mr. Chief Justice—My special thanks for 'swearing me in,' twice in two days.[1] *Sincerely*

[1] United States Supreme Court Justice Warren (J.D. University of California 1914) had administered the oath of office to Eisenhower in a private White House ceremony on Sunday, January 20, and again in a public ceremony on January 21. To date, Eisenhower is the third U.S. President to have taken the private oath on Sunday; the two others were Rutherford B. Hayes in 1877, and Woodrow Wilson in 1917. Relatives, close friends, and high-ranking officials were among the nearly eighty persons who attended the private ceremony (*New York Times*, Jan. 13, 21, 22, 1957).

At noon on Monday, January 21, thousands watched the President take the oath of office. In his thirteen and one-half-minute Inaugural Address Eisenhower pledged U.S. aid to impoverished nations and honored the aspirations of those countries under foreign domination. He went on to call upon Americans to build "peace with justice in a world where moral law prevails" (*Public Papers of the Presidents of the United States: Dwight D. Eisenhower, January 1, 1957 to December 31, 1957* [Washington, D.C., 1958], pp. 60–65). Following the ceremony, Eisenhower reviewed the inaugural parade and attended four inaugural balls (*New York Times*, Jan. 21, 22, 1957).

3

EM, AWF, Administration Series: Budget 1958

TO PERCIVAL FLACK BRUNDAGE

January 22, 1957

Memorandum for the Director, Bureau of the Budget:[1] Recently I had a long talk with General Bragdon, my Special Assistant for Public Works Planning.[2] The conversation to which I referred was an amplification of a memorandum he sent to me on November fifteenth.[3] Not knowing that you have a copy of this memorandum, I send my own herewith, but with the request that when you have studied it you return it to me.

I completely concur in the very great desirability and, in some cases, necessity of Federal, State and Municipal authorities executing the work to which General Bragdon refers. The guarantees of which he speaks, he informs me, are relatively small. But I do have some qualms about the lack of any assurance we might have that the States and Municipalities actually would perform the work, even though they have some financial help from the Federal Government. Work such as this will be valueless unless conducted according to the highest professional standards and with the greatest possible administrative efficiency.

Would you please consult with General Bragdon as to *how* we would be assured that we "got our money's worth."

Another point that would occur to all of us is how long such a program would have to be continued. We do not want to get into another endless "grant-in-aid" affair. It might be better to do it on a one-shot basis if such were practicable.

In any event, after you have talked to General Bragdon, please give me a memorandum on the whole matter.[4]

[1] Eisenhower had appointed Brundage as Director of the Bureau of the Budget on April 2, 1956 (see Galambos and van Ee, *The Middle Way*, no. 1692).

[2] Major General John Stewart Bragdon had been Special Assistant to the President for Public Works Planning since August 15, 1955 (see *ibid.*, no. 1699).

[3] Bragdon had written the President on November 15, 1956, to propose "A New Concept in Public Works Planning," offering "comprehensive and coordinated long-range planning based on measured needs and relative urgencies for all types of works at all levels of government" (WHCF/OF 141). The plan sought to overcome the difficulties encountered in earlier planning efforts by formulating a new methodology for measuring "needs," by integrating planning at all levels, by promoting intergovernmental collaboration, and by eliminating duplication in programs. Bragdon urged Eisenhower to seek legislation providing for grants-in-aid to the states in order to finance his proposal.

During a November 15 conversation with Bragdon, Eisenhower said that "greatly improved coordination, on an over-all basis, is urgently needed" and deplored "congressional and other tendencies to oppose these efforts at coordination, since they tended to take the 'pork' out of the barrel" (Goodpaster, Memorandum of Conversation, Nov. 15, 1956, AWF/D; see also Bragdon, Memorandum of Conference, Nov. 16, 1956, Bragdon Papers). In a November 17 letter to Bragdon, Eisenhower wrote, "Your plan to give greater emphasis at this time to the coordination of public works planning by the Federal agencies seems to me correct. I also concur with your findings as to the desirability and necessity of having the Executive departments and agencies intensify their planning efforts and that the stimulation of State and local public works planning be increased" (Bragdon Papers).

[4] Brundage would reply to Eisenhower on February 5, 1957, disapproving Bragdon's proposal (WHCF/OF 141). Brundage felt that "the initiative for planning of State and local public works should remain with those governments closest to the people." Bragdon's plan, moreover, would "give undue emphasis to construction planning" as opposed to functional program areas such as education, health, water resources, and transportation. Noting that other federal agencies disliked the proposal, Brundage expressed concern over the tendency for such programs to perpetuate themselves.

4 *EM, AWF, DDE Diary Series*

TO EDGAR NEWTON EISENHOWER *January 23, 1957*

Dear Ed: The other morning I wrote you a letter when I was in a state of great disgust because of what seemed to me to be the unreasonable attitude of one of our in-laws.[1] I just received word this minute that Arthur is coming back to Washington this weekend, and while he is here I will seize the opportunity to have my cardiologist look him over.[2] What Arthur needs, of course, is advice as to how he should conduct his life from here on out. This apparently he has not had.

In any event, this news reassures me, as I hope it will you.[3]

Give my love to Lucy and tell her that I received the note she wrote to me the day you were having the big snow. By this time I hope you are on the way down to Southern California, and I shall send this letter to the Paradise Inn at Phoenix, to be held until you reach there.[4] *As ever*

[1] On the morning of his public Inauguration (see no. 2) Eisenhower had written about Arthur Eisenhower's heart condition and the unwillingness of his wife, Louise, to have him undergo a complete medical checkup. (The letter is no. 1.)

[2] Arthur had telephoned the President at 11:05 A.M. (Telephone conversations, AWF/D). On January 31 (AWF/D) Eisenhower would tell Edgar that Arthur had been examined at the Walter Reed Army Hospital and given the name of a good Kansas City cardiologist. "Louise," the President added, "was very cooperative through it all."

[3] On February 27 Arthur would be admitted to the Johns Hopkins Hospital in Baltimore, Maryland, for treatment of an eye ailment. The following day he would be transferred to the heart clinic. Eisenhower would tell his brother that he agreed with the doctors' decision to make certain that Arthur was "in the best possible condition before they engage in any operation, even a relatively minor one" (Feb. 28, 1957, AWF/N). Following a series of tests Arthur would be diagnosed with arterial sclerosis and weakened heart muscles. He would be released from the hospital on March 11 (see Milton Eisenhower to Eisenhower, Mar. 4, 1957, AWF/N, and *New York Times*, Feb. 28, Mar. 12, 1957).

[4] Edgar's wife Lucille had written on January 19 (AWF/N) that it was snowing in Tacoma. Due to Edgar's poor health, she said, the couple planned to visit Sacramento and then drive to Phoenix to spend "an indefinite time" in the "Southern sunshine" (for background on Edgar's health see Galambos and van Ee, *The Middle Way*, no. 2168).

5 *EM, AWF, Administration Series, Brundage Corr.*

[NOTE] *[January 24, 1957]*[1]

Making F.C.D.A. a "Department" would tend to create a public feeling that Fed. Govt. would do it all. This would defeat F.C.D.[2]

[1] According to the Ann Whitman Diary, Eisenhower wrote his note about Federal Civil Defense on this date (see Ann Whitman memorandum, Jan. 24, 1957, AWF/AWD).

[2] The President was responding to a memorandum (Jan. 22, 1957) from Bureau of the Budget Director Percival F. Brundage (AWF/A) about converting the Federal Civil Defense Administration (FCDA) into an executive department. In July 1956 Eisenhower had written to FCDA Administrator Val Peterson expressing his concern that the "destructive capabilities of potential enemies have been outpacing our non-military defensive measures" (see Cabinet meeting minutes, Jan. 9, 1957, AWF/Cabinet; see also *Public Papers of the Presidents of the United States: Dwight D. Eisenhower, January 1 to December 31, 1956* [Washington, D.C., 1958], pp. 598–602). The federal civil defense law, which had been written before the advent of the hydrogen bomb, needed to be "realistically revised," the President said (for background on the FCDA see National Archives and Records Service, *United States Government Organization Manual 1957–1958* [Washington, D.C., revised June 1, 1957], pp. 361–64). The Federal Civil Defense Administration needed "authority to carry out necessary pre-attack preparations" and "must be enabled to assure adequate participation in the civil defense program." Eisenhower said that the agency "must be empowered to work out logical plans for possible target areas which overlap state and municipal boundaries" and "must have an organization capable of discharging these increased responsibilities." In an effort to increase the "prestige and effectiveness" of the FCDA, the President asked that the administrator now participate in Cabinet meetings. The Cabinet had approved FCDA recommendations for modifying the 1950 Civil Defense Act on January 9, with the understanding that the administrator would proceed "conservatively" (Cabinet meeting minutes, Jan. 9, 1957, and further correspondence in AWF/Cabinet).

In his memo to the President, Brundage had stated that making the Federal Civil Defense Administration an executive department would not, on balance, increase FCDA's ability to coordinate the civil defense activities of other federal departments—one of its central responsibilities. Upgrading this small agency would also reduce the President's flexibility in composing his Cabinet and suggest that the nation would be "permanently under conditions of threatening atomic disaster" (see also Peri E. Arnold, *Making the Managerial Presidency: Comprehensive Reorganization Planning 1905–1980* [Princeton, N. J., 1986], pp. 218–25).

6

EM, AWF, Administration Series: Army

To Maxwell Davenport Taylor — *January 24, 1957*

Personal

Dear Max: Recently Andy Goodpaster brought to me a summary of my son John's efficiency record. He gave me to understand that this had been prepared at your direction.[1]

I am grateful to you for your thoughtfulness and on two counts I am delighted that you had it done. First, I have been curious for some time as to whether the traits that I think I see in John are shared by people with whom he works. Secondly, I was highly pleased to see his record shows a steady climb over the last five or six years, to a point where he is classed among the first ten percent of his group.[2]

I hope that your physical difficulties have largely disappeared as a result of your trip to Puerto Rico.[3] Please take it easy and remember that you can always come for a swim in the pool without bothering to send any advance notice whatsoever.

With warm regard, *Cordially*

[1] The summary, dated December 28, 1956, is in AWF/M: OF, John Eisenhower Corr. Taylor would reply on January 28 that the performance record was compiled without "knowledge of its intended use" (AWF/A: Army). For background on Taylor see *Eisenhower Papers*, vols. I–XVII; on his appointment as Army Chief of Staff see Galambos and van Ee, *The Middle Way*, no. 1620. Brigadier General Andrew Jackson Goodpaster, Jr., was Eisenhower's Staff Secretary (see *Eisenhower Papers*, vols. XII–XVII).
[2] According to the report Major John Sheldon Doud Eisenhower was "highly efficient," with "excellent command and leadership qualities" and was an "excellent writer." John had an "excellent chance of selection" for the Armed Forces Staff College in 1958 and would be eligible for War College level training the following year. For background on the President's interest in his son's career see Galambos and van Ee, *The Middle Way*, nos. 888, 1073, and 2143; for developments see no. 121.
[3] On December 31 Taylor had gone to Puerto Rico to recuperate from a back ailment. He would report on January 28 that he was close to full recovery (AWF/A: Army; see also *New York Times*, Jan. 1, Mar. 15, 27, 1957).

7

EM, AWF,
Administration Series

To George Magoffin Humphrey — *January 24, 1957*

Dear George: The dates I am now trying to hold out for our Thomasville visit are as follows: to leave on Friday, the eighth, and return on Sunday, the sixteenth. How would that strike you?[1]

I mentioned these dates to Jock and he thought these would fit their situation perfectly.[2] As long as Jock is there, I imagine he would be quite content to put up anybody we would like to include in our bridge. I think we could ask Bill or Pete[3]—and we might ask the Gruenthers.[4] Actually if we got rained or snowed in, we would even like a fifth, so as to have someone to cut in. If you have any thoughts on the matter, let me know, and I will call both Jock and the people we want. I doubt that either Bill or Gruenther shoots and, of course, Gruenther being on a new job, may feel that he cannot spare a week.

We could also, if we wanted, ask George and Mary Allen, who are always fun to have around.[5] *As ever*

[1] Treasury Secretary Humphrey (LL.B. University of Michigan 1912) and his wife, the former Pamela Stark, owned Milestone Plantation, located near Thomasville,

Georgia. For background on the Eisenhowers' visits to Milestone for bridge-playing and turkey and quail shooting see *Eisenhower Papers*, vols. XII–XVII. The Eisenhowers would visit the Humphreys from February 8–19. Eisenhower's February 26 thank-you letter to the Humphreys is in AWF/D.

[2] John Hay ("Jock") Whitney, newly appointed U.S. Ambassador to Great Britain, and his wife, the former Betsey Cushing Roosevelt, would accompany the Eisenhowers. For background on the Whitneys see *Eisenhower Papers*, vols. X–XVII, esp. vol. XVI, nos. 1580 and 1662.

[3] Coca-Cola Company President William Edward Robinson would travel with the President's party. William Alton ("Pete") Jones, chairman of the board of Cities Service Company, would not go to Thomasville. (For background on Robinson see *Eisenhower Papers*, vols. VI–XVII; on Jones see *ibid.*, vols. X–XVII.)

[4] Former NATO Supreme Allied Commander, Europe, Alfred Maximilian Gruenther had become president of the American Red Cross on January 1 (see Galambos and van Ee, *The Middle Way*, no. 2008; see also *Eisenhower Papers*, vols. I–XVII). His wife was the former Grace Elizabeth Crum. As it turned out, the Humphreys would invite another couple, and the President would apologize to Gruenther for asking him to hold that "period for a possible invitation" (Feb. 4, 1956, AWF/D).

[5] Washington, D.C., lawyer and business executive George Edward Allen and his wife, the former Mary Keane, were old friends of the Eisenhowers (for background see Dwight D. Eisenhower, *At Ease: Stories I Tell to Friends* [Garden City, N.Y., 1967], pp. 282–87, 360–61; and *Eisenhower Papers*, vols. I–XVII). The Allens would join the Eisenhowers at Humphrey's plantation.

8 — *EM, AWF, Administration Series*

To Harold Edward Stassen — *January 28, 1957*

Dear Harold:[1] Thank you very much for your letter of the 26th, telling of recent developments in the United Nations on the disarmament matter.[2] I assume that you are making to the Secretary of State such official report as may be appropriate.[3]

I realize that formulation of disarmament policies that will conform to the best interests of the United States is in itself an intricate process; to achieve any measure of agreement by other nations to such policies is even more difficult. There is, however, no alternative to continuation of the effort, with all the intelligence and patience that we can bring to bear on the matter. I am grateful for what you have contributed in the furthering of this great effort.[4]

With warm regard, *Sincerely*

[1] A draft of this letter with Eisenhower's handwritten emendations is in AWF/A. For background on Harold Edward Stassen, Eisenhower's Special Assistant for Disarmament since March 1955, see Galambos and van Ee, *The Middle Way*, nos. 8, 1318, and 1348.

[2] As Stassen had explained, the United Nations General Assembly's Political Committee had voted to refer all disarmament discussions to the Disarmament Commis-

sion, giving special consideration to Eisenhower's proposal for the exchange of military blueprints and aerial inspection. The committee also agreed that equal consideration should be given to Soviet Premier Nikolai Bulganin's proposal for the establishment of ground inspection posts at strategic centers. Stassen wrote: "Divisive voting on all measures adverse to US policy, such as the proposal for the cessation of nuclear tests, was avoided; a favorable reference for the Eisenhower plan was included in a unanimous resolution; and the stage was set for a renewed effort to reach a sound first step agreement in this field" (Jan. 26, 1957, AWF/A; for background on Eisenhower's proposals made at the July 1955 Geneva Summit Conference see Galambos and van Ee, *The Middle Way*, no. 1523). On Bulganin's inspection plan see *ibid.*, no. 2151; for United Nations discussions see U.S. Department of State, *Foreign Relations of the United States, 1955–1957*, 27 vols. (Washington, D.C., 1985–92), vol. XX, *Regulation of Armaments; Atomic Energy* (1990), pp. 449–55; see also Whitman to Bernau, January 29, 1957, AWF/D-H; and *New York Times*, January 26, 1957.

[3] On January 25 Stassen had told Brigadier General Andrew Goodpaster, Eisenhower's Staff Secretary, that he had been unable to reach Secretary Dulles but would call him before the end of the day (Goodpaster, Memorandum, Jan. 25, 1957, WHO/OSS: Subject [Alpha], Disarmament).

[4] For developments see no. 171.

9 — *EM, AWF, Name Series*

To George Catlett Marshall — *January 28, 1957*

Dear General Marshall:[1] On February seventh Mamie and I have scheduled a Reception for the Judiciary and the Military, and I am enclosing with this note a formal invitation to you and Mrs. Marshall.[2] I write to assure you that under no circumstances should you consider coming to Washington for the affair, much as we should like to see you. I am sure you know just how exhausting and frustrating such affairs can be. On the other hand, I did not want to overlook sending you an invitation, if there was the slightest chance you might like to come.[3]

With warm personal regard, *As ever*

[1] For background on Eisenhower's long and cordial relationship with former Secretary of State and Secretary of Defense Marshall see *Eisenhower Papers*, vols. I–XVII.

[2] We have been unable to locate a copy of the invitation in EM. Mrs. Marshall was the former Katherine Boyce Tupper Brown.

[3] On January 30 (WHCF/OF 101-B-1) Marshall would thank the President for the "personal . . . invitation." He would, however, decline.

10 *EM, AWF, Gettysburg Series*

To Arthur Seymour Nevins *January 28, 1957*

Dear Art: George and I spent some time with Mr. Hartley on Friday and Saturday.[1] A number of interesting things came up, among which there was one that I wanted to tell you about.

Mr. Hartley said certain of the heifer calves that we are now raising are not of the quality that we should keep on our farm. He said that most of them were "above average" but not up to the standard of our cow herd.

Instantly I told him that so far as my own heifers were concerned, he could get rid of them at once at any age that he thought the most economical and beneficial from the standpoint of labor, feed and income.[2]

However, since we had our talk I have been thinking over something else. Our combined herd is gradually growing. We are not yet certain as to the total number of brood cows we can profitably maintain on the combined farms, including George's.[3] I am assuming, however, that our number is still well below the maximum that we can take care of without buying feed.

So long as this condition prevails, why do we not take the heifers who do not meet our strict standards and segregate them from the others. We could use them as sort of a beef herd—using with them a bull that we are not trying to reserve for our very best stock. For example, we could use the young Sunbeam or Rodgate bull, or even the Essar, as long as he is there.[4] Such a herd should require very little care and would live entirely on grass until just before any particular animal would be marketed. At, say, 60 to 90 days in advance of marketing, the animal could be penned up and fed grain and so on.

An advantage of this system is that the farm operator would derive some income from the raising of beef for sale to the market, and the ground of all the farms would get the benefit of having a capacity number of cattle living on it. Under this system we could continue to use George's farm largely for quarantine and for production of winter hay.

Since such a herd would be carefully segregated from the certified animals, they could be treated almost as range cattle, thus minimizing the cost. I doubt that they would even have to be given the ordinary tests and vaccinations, except as we chose to do so to protect ourselves from any contagion getting started.

In any event this is a point that occurred to me. If you think well enough of it, please talk it over with Mr. Hartley and then use your own judgement.[5]

I am sorry we didn't get to see you, but I know that you had an interesting time at the Ankony sale.[6] I heard that their total revenue was $212,000 for the day.

Incidentally, I have just been offered a heifer that the donor thinks is a very unusual one.[7] However, one of her progenitors is Prince Sunbeam 29th, concerning which animal we heard tales, I think from the Ewings.[8] Will you ask Hartley what he thinks of her, based upon the attached pedigree?[9] I tried to get Dr. Purdy on the phone today, but he is in Texas. I may get to talk to him later.[10]

Give my love to Ann and, of course, warmest regard to yourself.[11]
As ever

[1] In late 1950 Eisenhower had hired Brigadier General Nevins to manage both his and George E. Allen's Gettysburg, Pennsylvania, farms (see *Eisenhower Papers*, vols. X–XVII). Robert S. Hartley was the herdsman on the Eisenhower-Allen farms (for background on Hartley see Galambos and van Ee, *The Middle Way*, no. 1929; on the partnership with Allen see *ibid.*, no. 892). See also Arthur S. Nevins, *Gettysburg's Five-Star Farmer* (New York, 1977).

[2] For background on removing undesirable cattle from the farm see Galambos and van Ee, *The Middle Way*, no. 1460.

[3] Allen and another partner owned sizeable farms in Gettysburg (see Galambos and van Ee, *The Middle Way*, no. 1155; and Nevins, *Five-Star Farmer*, p. 126).

[4] Bulls from these families were largely responsible for the dwarfism that was beginning to appear in many Angus herds (see Bratcher to Stuart, Oct. 29, 1956, AWF/Gettysburg; and Nevins, *Five-Star Farmer*, p. 126).

[5] On February 2 Eisenhower would approve Nevins's plans to dispose of the inferior heifer calves along with the bull calves (AWF/D).

[6] See no. 15.

[7] *Ibid.*

[8] William Francis Cochran Ewing and his wife, the former Emily Fordyce Dodge, owned the Duncraggan Ranch in Sonoma, California (for background see Galambos and van Ee, *The Middle Way*, no. 1244).

[9] The pedigree is further discussed in no. 15.

[10] Herman R. Purdy, a professor at Pennsylvania State University, was a specialist in beef cattle. He had been advising Eisenhower since November 1954 (see Galambos and van Ee, *The Middle Way*, no. 1168). The President would speak to Purdy the following day (see Telephone conversations, Jan. 29, 1957, AWF/D). For developments see no. 55.

[11] Ann Louise Stacy Nevins was Nevins's wife.

11 — *EM, AWF, Administration Series*

To Richard Milhous Nixon — *January 29, 1957*

Dear Dick: While I am always hesitant to impose additional burdens on you, especially during the time the Congress is in session, your ready willingness to assume them makes me dare to make an additional suggestion.

I would appreciate it very much if you could find it possible to head the United States delegation to the Gold Coast Independence Ceremonies, to be held March 6, 1957.[1] I understand that two members of the Congress would also be included in the special delegation.[2]

Would you give the matter your earnest consideration and let me, or the Secretary of State, know your decision?[3]

With warm regard, *As ever*

[1] The Gold Coast, part of the British colonial empire, would become the independent country of Ghana and a member of the British Commonwealth of Nations.

[2] Representatives Adam Clayton Powell, Jr. (Dem., N.Y.) and Charles Coles Diggs, Jr. (Dem., Mich.) would attend the ceremony.

[3] On this same day Secretary Dulles had told Eisenhower that Vice-President Nixon would head the delegation if the President thought his attendance was important (Memorandum of Conversation, Jan. 20, 1957, Dulles Papers, White House Memoranda Series). Nixon would include the ceremonies in a tour of African countries.

Eisenhower would write to the governor of the Gold Coast on February 28, saying that the United States had an "abiding interest" in the new country. He would also commend the cooperation and understanding that the British had shown to the colony in its move toward independence (Eisenhower to Arden-Clarke, Feb. 28, 1957, AWF/A, Nixon Corr.).

12 — *EM, AWF, Administration Series*

To Henry Robinson Luce — *January 29, 1957*

Dear Harry:[1] Your note reminds me that toward the end of last week I had an opportunity to talk to Sid Richardson.[2] I had to interrupt his moaning about the situation of the independent in the oil business today in order that I might present my idea to him.[3] I told him that you were in charge of raising money for the National Presbyterian Church and that you would be approaching him—and that I wanted him to know of my interest.[4]

Incidentally, I pointed out to him that if he was actually stopping drilling, as he told me he was, then his taxable income would go up rapidly because of his inability to charge off drilling expenses. This should make it possible for him to give quite large sums, out of income, with almost no cost to himself.

This seemed to startle him, but he then replied about as follows: "My full gift possibilities are mortgaged for the next three years, but I would be glad to talk to Mr. Luce on the basis of what I could do at that time."

In spite of this, I think it is possible you could present the case in such a way that he might be able to rearrange his plans and begin to help immediately. I am sure he will be glad to talk to you.[5]

You know how enthusiastically I support your effort.

My warm greetings to Clare and, of course, all the best to yourself,[6] *As ever*

[1] Luce, founder, owner, and publisher of *Time* and *Life* magazines, had written to Eisenhower on January 26 (AWF/A; for background on Luce see *Eisenhower Papers,* vols. VI–XVII).

[2] Eisenhower had seen his old friend, Texas oil tycoon Sidney Williams Richardson, on January 25 (Telephone conversation, Eisenhower and Allen, Jan. 24, 1957, AWF/D; and President's daily appointments). For background on Richardson see *Eisenhower Papers,* vols. X–XVII.

[3] The blocking of the Suez Canal in November had forced the United States to supply oil to Europe. In addition to tanker shortages, the crisis pointed up the inadequacy of the nation's pipelines for moving crude oil from interior fields to the coast. While the nation had built up a large reserve, it was useless without the necessary pipelines (see Dwight D. Eisenhower, *The White House Years: Waging Peace, 1956–1961* [Garden City, N.Y., 1965], pp. 80, 95–98; Richard H. K. Vietor, *Energy Policy in America Since 1945: A Study of Business-Government Relations* [Cambridge, 1984], pp. 105–8; *New York Times,* Jan. 1, 4, 6, 1957; for background on the Suez crisis see Galambos and van Ee, *The Middle Way,* nos. 2027 and 2057).

[4] Luce had written that he was "engaged in drafting a 'prospectus' for the National Presbyterian Church." The Church was seeking money to provide facilities for congregational activities and to develop a national center on the Church's present site at Connecticut Avenue and N Street, NW, in Washington, D.C. (see Galambos and van Ee, *The Middle Way,* no. 308). The Eisenhowers had joined the National Presbyterian Church in 1953.

[5] On February 20 Luce would write "Your 'follow-through' on the matter of the National Presbyterian Church puts me to shame." He said he was not in a position, however, to "tackle Sid" at this time. For developments see no. 133.

[6] Luce's wife was Clare Boothe Luce, former U.S. Ambassador to Italy (for background see *Eisenhower Papers,* vols. I–XVII).

13

EM, AWF, Dulles-Herter Series

DIARY

January 31, 1957

Top secret

The King started off by saying that he wanted to talk to me mainly about very secret, confidential things, some of them really personal.[1] At the same time he said there were others that I could discuss with my advisers. However, I failed to get any clear understanding of which ones he considered absolutely secret (except for the last subject which I shall mention later), and which ones were of a lesser sensitivity. Consequently, I write this paper only for my own use and for the personal use of the Secretary of State. I have no objection if the Secretary of State permits a maximum of three other individuals in his Department to read it, should he believe that by doing so they would be helped in any way.

I. Relations with the British

The King's first subject was his relationships with the British. He spoke at length and rather bitterly.

The King said that dating back into his father's reign, the Arab policy had been to trust the British and to work with them in the advancement of their own country. He said this policy was practically forced upon them because the only alternative was to seek help from the Soviet Government; and they have always been anti-Communistic. Long before his father died, the relationships between Arabia and Britain had become strained and very unsatisfactory to the Arabs. Because of this the British had a deliberate policy of keeping the Arabs weak; that is, denying them any arms—at least in amounts that would be satisfactory to any self-respecting nation. Because of their weakness he said the Arabs had suffered many indignities, to say nothing of encroaching upon their borders and the flouting of their government in critical areas. Because of this weakness, the Arabs have also suffered indignities from the Israeli and they have been helpless to reply. This situation has grown steadily worse over the years. His people have become more and more restless, more demanding that he do something, and there has arisen a strong element in his country demanding that he even deal with the Soviets in order to get the necessary arms.

The King said that in spite of all these provocations, the basic tenet of his policy continued to be refusal to have anything whatsoever to do with the Kremlin.

About seven years ago the Arabs started an intensified campaign to obtain some arms. He encountered nothing but failure. Finally, about a year and a half ago, the Soviets approached him with what he said were wide open and very enticing offers.

The Soviets told him that they would provide any amount of arms he desired, together with adequate training teams to bring his forces to a good state of readiness. They offered to do this at a cost that would be "lower than that of anyone else." He still refused.

Now, he says, the question has gotten to be a most sensitive one in his country. He simply must do something about the matter. He referred repeatedly to the demands of his people and the strength of public opinion. He talked about such matters far more than one would expect from a ruler who is so patently a dictator.

In reply I said that this matter of armaments was not as simple as it appeared and that he should proceed very cautiously in making up his mind as to how much he wanted. I told him that we had helped to arm certain nations which had demanded far too much in the way of armaments, and as a result their economies were showing strains, and in some cases proved unequal to the task of maintaining their forces. I told him that I thought the best military policy for any nation which had a great problem of economic development facing it was to seek such arms as would assure the maintenance of internal order and freedom from subversive activities, together with a small reserve that would give it reasonable protection against small raiding attacks against its borders. Beyond this point I argued that any country in this position should depend largely upon its friendship with the other free nations of the world. I maintained that the United Nations was set up to preserve weak nations from unjustified and unprovoked aggression and that he could always count upon help in such a case. However, I did admit that the self-respect of a nation did demand arms to the level I had roughly described, and asked him how much he thought would be necessary in his case.

The King replied in a rather devious way about as follows: "My country has 900,000 square miles and *at least* 12 million people. The British are nibbling at a number of my borders and have been particularly aggressive in the case of Buraimi and the Empty Quarter.[2] The Israeli have raided us a number of times and now Iran has committed an aggression against us. (Later he spoke about this incident at some length.) He finally said that he had a program for armament which had been approved by American training teams in his country."[3] (It is possible I misunderstood this particular statement, but this is what I thought he said.)

He did repeat, "I know that Britain would attempt to oppose our acquisition of armaments from you." He feels that we would long ago have agreed to let him have arms except for British opposition.

He then remarked that his military program would take up half of his national budget and so he would need economic help. To this I made little reply except to say that it had been our experience that the first thing that undeveloped nations needed was technical help because otherwise they spent money uselessly.

II. Economics

The King said he had been working very hard at building new schools, hospitals, roads and communications. He said their five-year progress had been remarkable but it was, of course, still far too meagre. All his public expenditures had gone into these activities and he remarked, "All the money I have received has been wisely spent and for these good purposes."

The King remarked that the Bedouins were in a particularly deplorable state economically and had so little in the way of resources that they were practically living on a dole. This dole he furnishes from his private purse. (He did not tell me the distinction between private and public purses in Arabia.) But he said beyond the things just mentioned, Arabia could do no more by itself and they need desperately to have economic assistance.

In reply to this, I repeated my assertion that technical help should probably come first. I pointed out that schools were no good without teachers; that irrigation systems were of little use except where there were people who knew how to make economic use of water on land. I pointed out that this same observation applied almost in everything that was economic in character.

I emphasized that money alone could not make a country prosperous or raise its level of industrialization. It took investment, brains, experience in organization and professional matters, and a provision for balance among the various segments of the economy. I pointed out that purchasing power had to go along with the production of goods. Most of this was lost on him, but at least he did not express to me any thoughts of rushing into "big business" and he seemed to be responsive to the idea when I told him that small village and household industries were far more important to a country with very low living standards than were heavy goods industries.

Finally, I told him that our staffs would study both the military and the economic matters very sympathetically in cooperation with his staffs, but I did want to point out that it was progress all across the board that was sought, not an imbalance that would do no good at all for his country.

I thought that possibly the King felt that I was being too pessimistic in my attitude toward his desires and ambitions, for he remarked to me, "When we get this strength it will always be *with yours.*" He wanted to make clear that whatever strength we built up for him would always be available to us. He said over and over again, "We are your friends and we want to be even better friends."

III. Islands

The next matter that the King wanted to talk about were two islands in the Persian Gulf—Farasan and one named, I think, Arabi, or Aribi.[4] The modern political history of these islands as given to me by the King is as follows: For some years the ownership of the islands has been claimed by both Kuwait and Arabia. No other nation has asserted any claim to the islands, although of course Britain has supported the Kuwait claim.

A short time ago an Iranian force suddenly moved into the islands, seized them and is now occupying one.[5] The Arabs regard this as rank aggression. The King's Government has protested to Iran, but to no avail. Iran has not attempted to establish any historical claim—rather it has depended completely upon the power of possession. In this situation the Arabian Government has proposed two possible solutions to the Iranians:

(1) The Iranians to go home and leave both islands unoccupied, and the Arabs and Iranians thereafter to meet in negotiations to work out an agreed ownership.

(2) The Iranians to occupy one island and to recognize Arab ownership of the other.

The Iranians have refused to accept either suggestion. In fact, the suggestions have simply been ignored.

Again, the King said, a tense situation has developed in his country. This has reached a point where he believes he will have to cancel the planned visit of the Shah to Arabia, which was to take place in early March.

The King is at a complete loss to understand the developments since he says the Shah and he are great personal friends and "I have liked and admired him very much." He indicated that the Shah could be embarrassed very badly if he should come to Arabia at present. This subject was left with the intimation that he would appreciate our support wherever it was possible to give it in reaching a satisfactory solution to this question.

In reply I merely told him I would have the matter studied. I said that it was one thing that had escaped my attention.[6]

IV. Cairo Meeting

The next subject was his meeting with some of the other Arab chieftains at Cairo.[7] The King said that reports of the leanings of Nasser and the President of Syria toward the Soviets have been greatly exaggerated. Each of these men told the King that if the Soviets made any move that implied an attempt to interfere in their internal governmental activities, they would instantly cease all dealings with the Soviets. My impression is that he believes that these rulers can take from the Soviets anything they please, but still retain their own power of decision and control over all internal affairs. (I refrained from commenting, but of course it is this type of naive thinking that is so alarming.) In any event, the King twice repeated a statement about as follows:

> "I told my associates very plainly and flatly—I am with you in Arab cooperation and in opposition to Israel, but I will not go one step with you in working with the Soviet Union—I shall have nothing to do with the Soviets."

The King did not discuss plans for opening the Canal beyond saying that this subject had already been mentioned at the preceding conference.[8] He did, however, take up the Israeli question and said that, as he explained in his letter of some time ago, he believed that we must take the status quo for the present and wait for feelings to calm down before we could do much in the way of constructive work. Of course the status quo for him involves a withdrawal of all Israeli forces inside the armistice line.

He repeated at some length the familiar complaints that the Arabs have against Israel, although he did tacitly agree that Israel, as a nation, is now an historical fact and must be accepted as such. He tried to put all the blame for border troubles on the Israelis, even though occurring a long time before the attacks of last fall.[9] The Arab activities along the border he said were mostly those of civilians who had been dispossessed from their homes and who were hungry and starving—and just across the border they see their old properties being exploited by the Jewish communities. In desperation they try to go back at times and get some of the food and things of which they have been deprived. The Israeli use these small incidents as excuses to put on big raids, killing lots of Arabs. The King remarked that any fair settlement of the Jewish-Arab problem would give these border villages back to their former owners.

The King therefore felt that the Israeli should retire immediately from the Port of Agaba and from the Gaza Strip and cease all of their border raids.[10] He repeated that in the relatively quiet state that would result from such Israeli movements, we could then begin to hope to find the solution of the bigger and broader problem. This, of course, was a very one-sided presentation and so I told him that I would bring up some of the complaints brought to me by Jewish sympathizers.

I said, first, that because of the Egyptian embargo on Israeli shipping in the Canal, the Israelis had a good excuse to keep the Port of Agaba and make it a useful and workable one.

Also, they have had so much trouble with raids originating in the Gaza Strip that they would under no circumstances permit Egypt to reoccupy it, arguing that in any case the Strip had never been a part of Egypt. I referred also to the Israeli complaints against the Fedayeen and their purpose of retaining partial mobilization to conduct retaliatory raids at any time they suffered a Fedayeen attack.[11]

The King took each of these up in turn.

First, he said that the Egyptians in his opinion would not permit the Israeli shipping to transit the Canal, but after discussing it a little while longer, he said he did believe this was a negotiable item and that in return for other concessions, they would probably do so.

I immediately told him that unless the Egyptians would permit such transitting, then they would defeat in advance any attempt to settle the Canal issue on the six principles of the United Nations because they would stand in violation of the 1888 Treaty even before they started to confer.[12]

The King repeated that he thought they might yield on this point.

He next stated that the Egyptians would never consent to the internationalization of the Gaza Strip. He said it was Arab, and internationalization of the Strip would mean inevitably that it was partly occupied by Arab enemies. I gained the distinct impression that the King thoroughly approved of the Egyptian stand on this point.

I replied that if the Israelis refused to turn over the Gaza Strip and the Egyptians refused to allow even an international force to occupy it, then we were at an impasse and any hope of reducing Arab-Israel tensions was gone.

Consequently, I asked him what would he think of establishing the Gaza Strip as an independent principality, somewhat like Yemen. He replied that this might provide an answer, although I told him that I was merely asking a question—that I did not know whether such an idea would be acceptable to either the Arabs or the Israeli or anyone else—but I was simply trying to find out whether there was some point of negotiation and flexibility rather than rigidity in the situation.

The King then went to the question of the Fedayeen. He declared that there had been only one raid by the Fedayeen in many weeks (I forget its exact date), and all other border disorders were not of their making. I felt sure, * * * * * that the King was completely misinformed, but that he implicitly believed what Nasser told him.[13] So I did not pursue the subject further.

* * * * *

Finally, the King took up a subject which he said was completely personal and had not been mentioned to him by anyone, nor by him to anyone other than me.

It was the suggestion that I should ask Nasser and the King of Syria to visit me. He said that he believed great good could come of such visits. He did not say that either knew of his suggestion—he intimated the contrary.

I had not expected this one and so I stalled a little bit, saying that of course I would think the matter over. He hastened to interject that he was certain these people did not lean nearly so much toward the Soviets as we had thought and they would like to re-establish their ties with the West.

I then remarked that, of course, I could not ask the two people he suggested immediately after the King himself had made a visit here without causing difficulty with our relationships with Israel. I asked him what he would think of my asking the head of the Jewish State. This he said would be quite all right and satisfactory.

In discussing this subject at some length, the King was rather vague and I am not quite certain what he thought would come out of it, but he did urge that it be treated on a top secret basis.

The King concluded with a little talk that showed he knew something about our political situation, at least that we had a lot of Jewish voters in this country. He maintained a very pleasant attitude throughout the conversation and seemed quite happy that I had given him an hour and three-quarters to get all of these matters off his chest.

He ended up by saying that in the Cairo meeting he had urged his associates to look upon American efforts in the region as motivated by genuine friendship and a desire to help—and not a desire to conquer. He repeated that he thought a face-to-face talk with both Nasser and the President of Syria would be very valuable.[14]

[1] King ibn Abd al-Aziz Saud of Saudi Arabia had begun a state visit to Washington on January 30. Accompanied only by an interpreter, he had met with Eisenhower for one hour and forty-five minutes that afternoon. The President dictated this memorandum "largely from memory" on the following day. For background on U.S.-Saudi Arabian relations and the complications relating to the King's visit see Galambos and van Ee, *The Middle Way*, no. 2147; see also Memorandum of Conversation, January 11, 1957; and Notes on Meeting, January 29, 1957, both in Dulles Papers, White House Memoranda Series; U.S. Department of State, *Foreign Relations of the United States, 1955–1957*, vol. XIII, *Near East: Jordan-Yemen* (1988), pp. 413–23; and Eisenhower, *Waging Peace*, pp. 114–20. King Saud's memorandum on Saudi Arabian relations with the United States and Middle Eastern affairs is in Dulles Papers, Subject Series: Visit of King Saud.

[2] For background on the Buraimi controversy see Galambos and van Ee, *The Middle Way*, nos. 245 and 1744. The Empty Quarter (Rub al Khali) was located in the southeastern portion of the Arabian peninsula.

[3] The Saudi Arabian government had requested armaments for two complete infantry divisions, one hundred planes of different types for the Saudi air force, and the development of a navy for coastal defense (see State, *Foreign Relations, 1955–1957*, vol. XIII, *Near East: Jordan-Yemen*, pp. 433–35, 451–53).

[4] Eisenhower was referring to the islands of Farsi and Arabi.

[5] Iran had occupied the island of Farsi in September 1956 and had dislodged Saudi forces on Arabi in November.

[6] The President would bring the Persian Gulf island issue to the National Security Council (NSC) on February 7. Secretary Dulles said that the issue probably could be presented to the Iranians, "but he doubted very much whether anything could be accomplished prior to the departure of King Saud" (see NSC meeting minutes, Feb. 8, 1957, AWF/NSC). In a subsequent meeting (Feb. 8), Eisenhower would tell King Saud that the United States would offer help to solve the frontier and island problems, but "the United States was trying to be friends with all of these other countries and would not wish them to feel that it was discussing their problems without their consent or in their absence" (State, *Foreign Relations, 1955–1957*, vol. XIII, *Near East: Jordan-Yemen*, p. 483; see also Draft Communiqué [Feb. 8, 1957], AWF/D-H).

[7] On January 18 and 19 the heads of state from Egypt, Syria, and Jordan had met with the Saudi Arabian monarch in Cairo. They had asked King Saud to convey their viewpoints on Middle Eastern problems to President Eisenhower (State, *Foreign Relations, 1955–1957*, vol. XIII, *Near East: Jordan-Yemen*, pp. 421, 447; see also *New York Times*, Jan. 20, 21, 1957).

[8] Egyptian President Gamal Abdul Nasser had closed the Suez Canal on November 4 (see Galambos and van Ee, *The Middle Way*, no. 2078). Immediately preceding this meeting, King Saud and his advisers had met with Eisenhower, Secretary Dulles, and other State Department officials. Dulles had told King Saud that the canal should be operated with full respect for Egyptian authority but must always remain an international waterway. Neither Egypt nor any other nation, Dulles said, should be able to control canal traffic unilaterally. He assured the King that control of the canal need not be taken away from Egypt if other countries were confident that the canal would always be open to them (State, *Foreign Relations, 1955–1957*, vol. XIII, *Near East: Jordan-Yemen*, pp. 419–20).

[9] Eisenhower is probably referring to the Israeli attacks on Egyptian bases on October 29 and 30 (see State, *Foreign Relations, 1955–1957*, vol. XIII, *Near East: Jordan-Yemen*, pp. 844–47.

[10] A*q*aba.

[11] The Egyptian government had mobilized the Fedayeen, commando units of the Egyptian Army, to carry out attacks on Israeli territory.

[12] On the United Nations principles see Galambos and van Ee, *The Middle Way*, nos. 2057 and 2068.

[13] These words were deleted from the source text.

[14] For developments see no. 25.

14

EM, AWF, Administration Series: Budget 1958

To Percival Flack Brundage — *January 31, 1957*

Dear Percy: The attached paper deals with a project that has long had a strong personal appeal for me, the establishment of an American Armed Forces Institute. The matter has been studied before, by General Pershing and a group under him in 1923.[1] Later, in 1946, a small private group headed by David Finley made a report to President Truman on the project.[2]

Recently, I have had a small group of civilians making a preliminary study for me, which I send along to you with this memorandum, as well as a copy of the report by the 1946 Committee.[3] I should like for you to study the matter and give me a report on it at your convenience.

I am not interested in a mere Museum type of operation that shows the kind of buttons worn by the Revolutionary soldier and the kind of musket he shot. But I am interested in some exhibit that gives to us an indication of what the Continental soldier—and his successors in 1812, 1845, 1865, 1898, 1917, 1942 and 1950—have contributed to our civilization. By this I mean what they have done to give us the life we enjoy today.

In the same way, I am not interested merely in some antiquated field order of Nathanael Greene or Nathan Forrest.[4] But I am interested in documents and literature that show us why wars have been fought, how we have organized our democracy to fight them, and what have been their destructive effects on our financial structure and indeed our whole economy.

Finally, I am not interested in gazing on modern weapons of destruction, just to express horror of the destructiveness of war. But I am interested in a display that can help Americans understand what war means today and how necessary it is, if our type of economy and civilization is to endure, that we—all of us—put our hearts and souls into the job of bringing about a more stable peace which can justify disarmament step by step until these destructive weapons will be unknown.

I merely tell you this to show you that far from a mausoleum type of development, I am thinking of something dynamic and educational.

Of course there are many obstacles—one of which is money—even if you and other trusted advisers would agree that it is desirable to go ahead with such a project. There would have to be a preliminary Commission that could outline the whole project and its possibilities in detail, so that there could be built up logical organization and plans. Legislation authorizing such a project could possibly be secured from the Congress, say, within a year (assuming the Congress has any interest in the matter), and thereafter the annual appropriations—assuming a gross outlay of some $45–50 million—would probably range between a very small amount in the first year up to $20 million each for the year of completion.

However, in spite of all these things, I should like, provided my principal associates agree with me, to get the thing started during my Administration.[5] *Sincerely*

[1] Eisenhower was referring to General of the Armies John Joseph Pershing (see Galambos, *Columbia University*, no. 119).

[2] David Edward Finley was chairman of the U.S. Commission of Fine Arts, National Trust for Historic Places. From 1938 to 1956 he had been director of the National Gallery of Art (see Galambos and van Ee, *The Middle Way*, no. 864).

[3] For background on the proposal to establish an Armed Services Memorial Museum see Galambos and van Ee, *The Middle Way*, no. 1741. On January 30, 1957, a small group headed by long-time Eisenhower friend Major General Kenyon Ashe Joyce (for background see *Eisenhower Papers*, vols. I–XIII) had submitted a report to the President, recommending the creation of a "National Museum of Peace and War" in Washington as an independent institution within the Smithsonian (Joyce *et. al.* to Eisenhower, Jan. 30, 1957, AWF/A: Budget 1958). The group further recommended

that Eisenhower establish a presidential commission to look into the matter and prepare the necessary legislation in coordination with the White House staff and the Bureau of the Budget.

[4] As commander of the Southern Department during the American Revolutionary War, Nathanael Greene (1742–1786) so weakened British forces that by the latter part of 1781 their only secure position was at Charleston. Confederate cavalry leader Nathan Bedford Forrest (1821–1877) was one of the most successful Southern generals during the Civil War.

[5] Brundage would respond to the President on February 5 (AWF/A: Budget 1958). The Secretary would report that he had been advised that the Smithsonian Museum of History and Technology "would provide excellent facilities for what you have in mind," since "military history can best be understood as part of an overall coherent picture of progress which also sets forth the civilian developments of the same age and time." Although Eisenhower would appoint a committee, headed by Chief Justice Earl Warren, in January 1958 to study comparable European military museums, no separate museum would be established (see Paul H. Oehser, *The Smithsonian Institution* [New York, 1970], pp. 101–4, and 193–94).

15

EM, AWF, Gettysburg Series

To Allan A. Ryan

January 31, 1957

Dear Allan: Thank you very much for your letter. I am most deeply appreciative of your offer to let us keep Ankonian for a while.[1] I should really like to have every good heifer on the place have at least one by him.

This spring Mamie and I are planning to spend quite a few week ends at the farm. If things work out that way, possibly we can have both of you down for a couple of days. We could then go over the herd very thoroughly.[2]

You might be interested in some late developments. First a couple of good Republicans over the country have each transferred a young heifer to me, to be delivered in the spring.[3] One is a Black Beauty Zara heifer, sired by a Bandolier bred bull.

Another is one named "Mamie of Shadow Isle."[4] One of her grandsires is your Eileenmere 1032. Different animals in her background are a Barbarian of Rosemere, a Barbara Corneller and Ankonian 3216. She is a Blackcap heifer.

Recently there arrived at my farm a Scottish heifer, bred to a Scottish bull.[5] Since arrival she has dropped a bull calf. Both the dam and the calf look fine but I am not sufficiently well acquainted with the Scottish families and blood lines to make it worthwhile to try to tell you anything about her.

I am buying two heifers soon.[6] One is a granddaughter of Homeplace Eileenmere 999–35; the other is a daughter of Bardoliermere

H 55. He is a full brother to the 1953 International Champion. Both of these will be bred to O. Bardoliermere 32nd, a brother of the bull who sired both the International male and female champions this year.

We got rid of the Bandolier bull, and since he was in the name of the "Eisenhower Farms" I just sent him to the meat market.[7] I wouldn't take any chance of his carrying my name in some consignment sale.

I have not checked up to find out when we will have some of the Ankonian calves on the ground. I will ask Art Nevins to let you know. I have not yet had his report on your sale, except an indirect word that he said it was a "huge success."[8] More power to you.

Please remember me kindly to Mr. Leachman,[9] and, of course, my greetings to your lovely bride.

With warm regard, *Sincerely*

[1] Ryan, chairman of the board of Royal McBee Corporation and owner of Ankony Farms in Rhinebeck, New York, had written on January 29 (for background see Galambos and van Ee, *The Middle Way*, no. 1746). In a letter of January 24 Eisenhower had discussed returning Ankonian 3551, a Black Angus bull of high quality.

[2] Ryan said he and his wife, the former Grace M. Amory, hoped to visit the President's farm and "inspect the calves by 3551." In his February 19 reply Ryan said he would look over the herd at Eisenhower's convenience.

[3] For the names of the donors see Whitman to Nevins, Feb. 2, 1957; and undated memo to Mr. Ryan.

[4] See no. 69.

[5] The Eisenhower Farm had acquired the heifer in October (for background see Galambos and van Ee, *The Middle Way*, no. 2049). For developments on the bull calf see no. 228.

[6] For developments see no. 55.

[7] The bull had developed a weakness in his hind quarters (see Galambos and van Ee, *The Middle Way*, no. 2140).

[8] The calves were expected in April or May (see Nevins to Whitman, Feb. 26, 1957). Ryan had seen Nevins at the Ankony Farms sale on January 26 (see no. 10). Two days later, in a telephone conversation, Nevins told Ryan that he had sent a brief report to Eisenhower (see Nevins to Eisenhower, Jan. 11; Ryan to Eisenhower, Jan. 29, 1957). We have been unable to find Nevins's report in AWF. All correspondence is in AWF/Gettysburg.

[9] Leland L. Leachman was a partner in the Ankony Farms enterprise (for background see Galambos and van Ee, *The Middle Way*, no. 1661).

16

EM, AWF, Name Series

To Michael Doud Gill

Personal and confidential

January 31, 1957

Dear Michael: Possibly you have already made up your mind with respect to the new job offer you have, and if so, this letter can be consigned to the waste basket without further reading.

I have been thinking over the things you told me the other night and I have come to this conclusion.[1] You should take a job for the next several years that keeps you either in Washington or in some other American city where you can attend night school. You explained to me the great handicap under which you suffer is lack of an education. That you should, and you can easily, procure.

Almost every worth while university now has good night schools, and my idea would be that you would take the job that would give you the most time to devote to your studies. You could earn your B.S. or B.A. in three or four years, and then go on to take a Masters' in Business Administration or some other subject of your own choosing. Or—what would be almost as satisfactory—you could major in Economics during a B.S. or a B.A. course.

In any event, I have gone far enough in my thinking that I believe that in a four-year college course you should take the following without fail:

1 year General History
1 year American History
2 years Mathematics
1 year of any Science that you might choose—
chemistry or physics preferred

I think it would be most important to take at least one year of a course that would acquaint you completely with the development of American government. Just what it might now be called I am not sure, but you could easily identify the proper course. It might possibly be called Civics. Along with all the above I think you should take other courses based upon what you believe you will want to do when you finish. If you want to stick in business, then I would take a good bit of Economics and possibly a year of Business Law.

If the job you are contemplating is such that you could discharge its duties and responsibilities effectively and still go to school steadily without interruption, then I think you might well take it. On the other hand, you know that as long as you are working for Gordon, he would always give you a day off to study, if necessary, for a special examination.[2]

I can summarize my entire thinking on the matter by saying that you should simply take the job that will facilitate your correcting the deficiency you feel in your education.

I am writing this letter personally and confidentially in the hope that you will show it to no one, except possibly Corky.[3] It represents my very earnest conviction.

In any event, love to Corky and the best to yourself. *Sincerely*

[1] Gill was Mamie Eisenhower's nephew (for background see *Eisenhower Papers,* vols. I–XVII). On January 20 he had attended the private inaugural ceremony at the White House and the reception following (see no. 2).

[2] George Gordon Moore, Jr., was Gill's stepfather (for background see *Eisenhower Papers,* vols. I–XVII).

[3] Corky was Gill's first wife. We have been unable to locate further correspondence on this matter in EM.

17 — *EM, AWF, Administration Series*

To Charles Erwin Wilson — *February 1, 1957*

Dear Charlie: To my astonishment, not to say chagrin, I find that newspapers are trying to make a lot out of what they call my "rebuke" of you at last Wednesday's press conference.[1] I think a reading of the text will dispel any thought that such was my intention.

It is true that I remarked that anyone who enlisted in the National Guard could not be called a draft dodger because he was obeying the law of the land. I said that I knew you were not pointing the finger at any individual—and certainly I was not.

Having disposed of what I thought was the unimportant part of your original statement, I then launched into a defense of your position in demanding the proper training for the Guard. I frankly stated that without six months' prior training, I saw no hope of getting the kind of Guard that we need.[2] This I assumed to be the crux of the whole matter.

If my mere observation that I thought your particular words of description concerning the Guard were unwise seemed to you to be a "rebuke," then all I can say is that I hope you will realize that such was not my intention.[3]

We have worked long and hard together in this business of developing an adequate defense at the lowest possible cost; I have been most deeply appreciative of all you have done and hope that so long as you may care to stay in your post you will continue to discharge your official responsibilities and duties in exactly the same way you have in the past. *As ever*

P.S. I tried to call you this afternoon, but I understand you have been entertaining the King.[4]

[1] For background on Secretary of Defense Wilson see Galambos and van Ee, *The Middle Way*, nos. 7 and 23. In a January 28 statement to the Armed Services Committee of the House of Representatives, Wilson had accused the National Guard of "harboring youthful draft dodgers during the Korean conflict" (*New York Times*, Jan. 29, 1957). Asked about the Secretary's comment during his January 30 news conference, Eisenhower had replied that Wilson "was shortcutting and making a very, I think, unwise statement, without stopping to think what it meant, because these men have not been slackers when they have entered the military service in accordance with the law." Eisenhower's comment made headlines as "President Calls Wilson 'Unwise' in Guard Dispute" (*ibid.*, Jan. 31, 1957; see also *Public Papers of the Presidents: Eisenhower, 1957*, p. 102). Privately, Eisenhower had deplored Wilson's statement, saying that Wilson "could do more to ruin himself than any man" (Jan. 30, 1957, AWF/AWD).

[2] In his statement before the Armed Services Committee, Wilson had advocated a program that would require National Guard enlistees without basic military training to serve six months on active duty. The Army had previously required only an eleven-week, active duty program (*New York Times*, Feb. 3, 1957). The National Guard, fearing a cut in enlistments in the 17–18½ year age group because of school and job obligations, opposed the new policy. On February 26 the Guard and Army would agree to delay the start of the six-month active duty policy until January 1, 1958 (see Legislative Leadership meeting supplementary notes, Jan. 23, 1957, and Memorandum of Conference with the President, Feb. 6, 1957, both in AWF/D; see also *New York Times*, Feb. 27, 1957).

[3] The Secretary's wife, the former Jessie Ann Curtis, had responded to calls for Wilson's resignation from members of Congress and others by saying that her husband should quit the Cabinet because the President was not supporting him as much as he supported John Foster Dulles. Speculation about a rift between Eisenhower and Wilson would die down after the Wilsons flew with the President to Augusta on their way to a vacation in Florida (Ann Whitman memorandum, Feb. 1, 1957, AWF/AWD, and *New York Times*, Feb. 3, 1957).

[4] On the visit of King Saud see no. 13.

18

EM, AWF, DDE Diaries Series

To Sherman Adams
Memorandum

February 1, 1957

It occurs to me that we have some new officials in executive positions in government who might not be aware of my strict instructions regarding no favoritism for friends or relatives of mine. Will you please see that everyone is acquainted with the policy that this government hires no one except on their own merits—and not on the basis of any connection with the president's family or friends.[1]

[1] On Eisenhower's actions in this regard see, for example, Galambos and van Ee, *The Middle Way*, nos. 237, 819, and 940. See also Dwight D. Eisenhower, *Mandate for Change, 1953–1956* (Garden City, N.Y., 1963), p. 120. The President's memorandum was undoubtedly prompted by the possibility of personnel changes at the beginning of the Second Administration.

To David Ben Gurion *February 3, 1957*
Cable. Confidential

Dear Mr. Prime Minister:[1] I attach the greatest importance to the efforts of the United Nations to resolve the situation brought about by the recent hostilities in Egypt.[2] In my message to you of November 7, 1956 I emphasized our belief that it was essential that Israel forces be withdrawn to the General Armistice line, in accordance with the United Nations General Assembly Resolution of November 2. I was gratified at your reply on the following day which stated that upon conclusion of satisfactory arrangements with the United Nations in connection with the international force entering the Suez Canal area, Israel would willingly withdraw its forces.[3]

Nearly three months have passed. British and French forces have been withdrawn from Egypt. Israel withdrawal to the General Armistice line has not yet been completed.[4] This delay in implementation of pertinent resolutions of the United Nations General Assembly has resulted in continuing tension in the Near East and has impaired efforts to work toward the achievement of lasting solutions to the problems which provoked the Near East crisis.

On February 1, 1957 there were tabled in the United Nations two further resolutions addressed to the situation in the Near East. The first of these calls again upon Israel to withdraw its forces behind the general Armistice line. The second calls for scrupulous observance of the 1949 Armistice Agreement and recognizes that withdrawal by Israel must be followed by action which would assure progress toward the creation of peaceful conditions. Provision is made for the placing of the United Nations Emergency Force on the Egyptian-Israel armistice demarcation line and the implementation of other measures as proposed in the Secretary General's report of January 25, 1957, with a view to achieving situations conducive to the maintenance of peaceful conditions there. It is recalled that the Secretary General indicated useful measures which might be developed in the case of Gaza and Sharm el Shaikh.[5]

Other nations deeply and directly interested in the establishment of peaceful conditions in the Near East have joined the United States in sponsoring these resolutions. We believe that the measures set forth in the Secretary General's report, which these resolutions are designed to implement, lay a sound foundation for the establishment of peaceful conditions in the former area of hostilities, the prevention of further outbreaks, and the solution of the problems of Gaza and Sharm el Shaikh.

The essential first step must be the completion of the withdrawal of Israel forces behind the General Armistice line. It is my earnest hope that this withdrawal will be completed without further delay. You know how greatly our nation values close and friendly relations with yours, and we wish to continue the friendly cooperation which has contributed to Israel's national development. We like to feel that our friendly sentiment is reciprocated by Israel. Therefore, I feel warranted in urging most seriously that Israel should not continue an ignoring of the United Nations Resolutions which, taken as a whole, mark, I believe, an important step toward bringing tranquility and justice to your and neighboring lands. Such continued ignoring of the judgment of the nations, as expressed in the United Nations Resolutions, would almost surely lead to the invoking of further United Nations procedures which could seriously disturb the relations between Israel and other member nations including the United States.

The United States Government has made great exertions to promote constructive United Nations action and I greatly hope that your Government will make its own indispensable contribution.[6]

I was distressed to learn of your recent illness but am happy to hear reports that you are mending rapidly.[7]

With best wishes, *Sincerely*

[1] David Ben Gurion had been Israel's Minister of Defense since February 1955 and Prime Minister since November 1955. On the preceding day Secretary Dulles had discussed the State Department draft of this cable with Eisenhower, who was vacationing in Augusta, Georgia. Dulles said that he would not send the message unless the U.N. General Assembly passed the two resolutions referred to in the text. This happened later that evening (see Telephone conversation, Eisenhower and Dulles, Feb. 2, 1957, Dulles Papers, Telephone Conversations; Eisenhower, *Waging Peace*, p. 184; and *New York Times*, Feb. 3, 1957).

[2] For background on the closing of the Suez Canal and the Anglo-French and Israeli invasions of Egypt see Cole C. Kingseed, *Eisenhower and the Suez Crisis of 1956* (Baton Rouge and London, 1995); see also Galambos and van Ee, *The Middle Way*, nos. 2051, 2057, and 2068.

[3] See *ibid.*, no. 2077, for Eisenhower's letter, the General Assembly resolution, and Ben Gurion's response.

[4] The British and French had withdrawn their troops in December. Israel continued to maintain forces in the Sharm el Sheikh area at the mouth of the Gulf of Aqaba and in the Gaza Strip (see State, *Foreign Relations, 1955–1957,* vol. XVI, *Suez Crisis July 26–December 31, 1956* [1990], pp. 1238–40; and State, *Foreign Relations, 1955–1957,* vol. XVII, *Arab-Israeli Dispute, 1957* [1990], pp. 5–7, 12–14, 35).

[5] United Nations Secretary General Dag Hammarskjöld had called for a broader implementation of the armistice agreement. Any possible claim of belligerent rights, he said, should be exercised with restraint on all sides and should be limited to clearly non-controversial situations. He recommended the stationing of the United Nations Emergency Force (UNEF) in Sharm el Sheikh to preserve the Straits of Tiran and the Gulf of Aqaba as international waterways. The International Court of Justice, he said, should determine the legal status of the Gulf of Aqaba. Hammarskjöld also recommended deployment of the UNEF in the Gaza Strip to prevent the area from be-

ing used as a base for raids against Israel. The Secretary General's report is in *U.S. Department of State Bulletin* 36, no. 921 (February 18, 1957), 275–80; see also State, *Foreign Relations, 1955–1957*, vol. XVII, *Arab-Israeli Dispute, 1957*, pp. 45–47. On the two United Nations resolutions see *ibid.*, pp. 58–61, 67–82; and *U.S. Department of State Bulletin* 36, no. 922 (February 25, 1957), 325–28.

[6] Ben Gurion would reply (Feb. 8) that Israel was prepared to withdraw its forces from Sharm el Sheikh if freedom of passage through the Straits of Tiran and the Gulf of Aqaba was assured. He would promise to evacuate Israeli troops from the Gaza Strip as soon as a civil government was established to work with a United Nations force. "In the last resort the solution of the problems of the area depends on whether the Egyptian Government is prepared to end its belligerency against Israel as required by United Nations resolutions" (State, *Foreign Relations, 1955–1957*, vol. XVII, *Arab-Israeli Dispute, 1957*, pp. 109–12; see also Lawson to Dulles, Feb. 3, 1957, AWF/I: Israel; Telephone conversation, Eisenhower and Dulles, Feb. 9, 1957, Dulles Papers, Telephone Conversations; and Isaac Alteras, *Eisenhower and Israel* [Gainesville, 1993], pp. 246–62). For developments see no. 40.

[7] Ben Gurion had been confined to his home with pneumonia.

20 — *EM, AWF, DDE Diaries Series*

To Moretta Hinkle Skinner — *February 4, 1957*

Dear Mrs. Skinner: This will acknowledge your letter of January twenty-eighth.[1] I am told that when you applied for a position at the Republican National Committee some years ago, Mrs. Eisenhower endorsed you on the basis of a long-time acquaintanceship.

I am sure that your services have proved satisfactory to the Committee, but I feel that any application for promotion or transfer of duties that you may have should be directed to Mr. Alcorn in person.[2] The record of your service and your qualifications is undoubtedly on file, and will be helpful to him in making his decision. I cannot possibly interfere in a matter that is obviously one of office management within the headquarters of the Republican National Committee.

I am grateful for your good wishes and trust you will understand why I cannot provide you with a personal endorsement for a specific position within the Committee's office. *Sincerely*

[1] Mrs. Skinner was a receptionist in the Administration Division of the Republican National Committee. She had written to ask the President to endorse her for "one of the many vacancies coming up (as assistant to the chairman) on a local basis" (AWF/D).

[2] Hugh Meade Alcorn, Jr., (A.B. Dartmouth College 1930, LL.B. Yale 1933) had been elected chairman of the Republican National Committee on January 22 (*New York Times*, Jan. 23, 1957).

21

EM, AWF, Administration Series

To Marion Bayard Folsom

February 4, 1957

Memorandum for the Secretary of Health, Education and Welfare:[1] Attached is a note from General Mark Clark, my long time friend and recently national campaign chairman for the American Heart Association.[2]

Will you please study the memorandum carefully and give me a draft on which to base a reply?

Incidentally, with respect to his final paragraph in which he mentions that a former President who had been a victim of polio initiated the great March of Dimes, I think it is more accurate to say that this was done by friends of the President and not by him personally.[3] In other words, if I am to have any special connection with a program of attack upon heart and related diseases because I myself had a coronary occlusion, then it would appear that while I might support the matter, I should not be in the forefront of the project. To do so would seemingly give it a touch of self-interest.[4]

This, of course, is more of a personal matter. What I should expect from you is an analysis of the money now available, the money needed, the sources from which it should come, and the availability of scientific personnel to make use of more money—and so on.[5]

[1] Folsom had been appointed Secretary of Health, Education and Welfare in August 1955 (see Galambos and van Ee, *The Middle Way*, no. 1513).

[2] General Mark Wayne Clark, president of The Citadel and former commander of U.N. forces in Korea, had been national campaign chairman for the American Heart Association since 1954 (see Galambos and van Ee, *ibid.*, no. 7). Clark's January 29 note thanked Eisenhower for meeting with him on December 20; he also enclosed a memorandum outlining the Heart Association's plans for attacking heart disease (AWF/A, Folsom Corr.). See also Oglesby Paul, *Take Heart: The Life and Prescription for Living of Dr. Paul Dudley White* (Boston, 1986), pp. 114–30.

[3] Clark had written that "the experience of a former president with polio became the dramatic focal point of a fight which has already saved thousands of lives. . . . It would be splendid if you would give at this time your personal leadership to a similar attack on diseases of the heart and related diseases." The Georgia Warm Springs Foundation, from which the National Foundation for Infantile Paralysis grew, had initially been a private philanthropy established by President Franklin D. Roosevelt in 1927. The decision to use the proceeds from the first nationwide fund-raising campaign of 1933, the President's Birthday Ball, to support a national organization resulted in part from Roosevelt's 1930 proposal for "'one vast national crusade against infantile paralysis'" (David L. Sills, *The Volunteers: Means and Ends in a National Organization* [Glencoe, Ill., 1957], pp. 42–45).

[4] At the time of Eisenhower's September 24, 1955, heart attack, the White House had rejected linking a fund drive for the American Heart Association with the President's illness and sixty-fifth birthday (see *New York Times*, Sept. 30, 1955). Nonetheless, the publicity surrounding the President's heart attack had brought the Association to the fore as the authoritative source of information on heart disease.

Contributions to the Association had increased by thirty-nine percent in 1956 and by 1957 would pass the twenty million dollar level (William W. Moore, *Fighting for Life: The Story of the American Heart Association 1911–1975* [Dallas, Tex., 1983], pp. 71–75). On Eisenhower's heart attack see Galambos and van Ee, *The Middle Way*, no. 1595.

[5] Folsom would respond to the President on February 19 (AWF/A). The Secretary would suggest that the Heart Association's promotional efforts to stimulate wider public interest in heart diseases and to raise funds was "fitting as a private endeavor, but not as an undertaking of the Federal Government." Folsom would support Clark's suggestion to establish a group to explore broader questions relating to medical research and would plan to establish a Committee on Medical Research. Eisenhower would respond to Clark on February 19 (AWF/A, Folsom Corr.), informing him of Folsom's answer. Eisenhower would add that while he felt "quite strongly that private giving for medical research must be sustained and increased," any role that he might play in such an effort "would have to be most carefully considered."

22 — *EM, AWF, DDE Diaries Series*

Diary — *February 5, 1957*

Almost four years ago, the Attorney General and I agreed that except for the position of Chief Justice, we would confine our selections for the Supreme Court to people who had served on either minor Federal benches or on the Supreme Courts of various States.[1] We also agreed that so far as possible, we would try to get a balance on the Court between Democrats and Republicans. In working toward this balance (the Court was 8 to 1 Democratic when I was first inaugurated), I have appointed two Republicans and one Democrat.[2]

Yesterday I saw in the paper quite a squib concerning the qualifications of Herb Brownell himself for the Supreme Court.[3] While I was certain the article was not "inspired," I did have a short talk with the Attorney General last evening. I mentioned the article and asked him whether he was still of the opinion that we should stick to our plan of selecting Supreme Court judges from sitting judges on the lower courts, always with the rule, too, that they be under 62 years of age. He agreed. He did say, however, that our rule should not be inflexible, in the event we did discover some outstanding attorney who we should like to put directly on the Supreme Court. I told him that if he had any ambitions to go on the Court, that we should appoint him immediately to the vacancy now existing on the Appellate Court in New York and then when and if another vacancy occurred on the Supreme Court, I could appoint him to it.

He said he thought we should just let things go as they were.

It is entirely possible that he would like to be on the Supreme Court. But I think that on the balance he prefers to go back to private practice some day and earn some money for himself and his family.[4]

[1] See Eisenhower, *Mandate for Change*, pp. 226–29, and Galambos and van Ee, *The Middle Way*, no. 457. Herbert Brownell, Jr., served as Attorney General from January 21, 1953, to November 8, 1957.

[2] During his first Administration, Eisenhower had appointed Republicans Earl Warren and John Marshall Harlan, and Democrat William Joseph Brennan to the Supreme Court (see *ibid.*, nos. 1386 and 2009).

[3] We have been unable to identify the article to which Eisenhower was referring. At the President's news conference on February 6, 1957, a reporter would make reference to "recurrent speculative reports" that Brownell might be under consideration for the Supreme Court opening (*Public Papers of the Presidents: Eisenhower, 1957*, p. 123).

[4] Brownell would return to private practice in November 1957 (see Herbert Brownell with John P. Burke, *Advising Ike: The Memoirs of Attorney General Herbert Brownell* [Lawrence, Kans., 1993], pp. 176–85, 329–30).

23

EM, AWF, Administration Series: Atomic Energy Commission

To John Foster Dulles, Charles Erwin Wilson, and Lewis Lichtenstein Strauss

Secret

February 5, 1957

Memorandum for the Secretary of State, the Secretary of Defense, and the Chairman of the Atomic Energy Commission:[1] I have determined that the recent amendments to the agreements for cooperation with Canada and the United Kingdom which authorize exchange of Restricted Data on military propulsion reactors with those countries constitute binding obligations on our Government and that it is in the best interest of the United States to go forward under them.[2] Accordingly, I hereby direct:

(*a*) That implementation be initiated of the amendment to the Agreement for Cooperation with the United Kingdom which authorizes the exchange of Restricted Data with respect to reactors for the propulsion of naval vessels, aircraft or land vehicles for military purposes.

(*b*) That, upon exchange of notes necessary to make effective the amendment to the Canadian Agreement, implementation be initiated of the amendment to the Agreement for Cooperation with Canada which authorizes the exchange of Restricted Data with respect to reactors for the propulsion of naval vessels, aircraft or land vehicles for military purposes.

(*c*) That, at present, no additional agreements for cooperation with any other nation be negotiated insofar as the exchange of such information is concerned until the position of Congress in this regard has clarified.[3]

[1] For background on Atomic Energy Commission Chairman Strauss see Galambos and van Ee, *The Middle Way*, no. 295. Secretary of State Dulles recommended that a copy of this memorandum be sent to Attorney General Herbert Brownell, Jr.
[2] On the exchange of atomic information with the United Kingdom see *ibid.*, nos. 1640 and 2026; see also State, *Foreign Relations, 1955–1957*, vol. XX, *Regulation of Armaments; Atomic Energy*, p. 371.

In June 1956 Eisenhower had approved amendments to agreements with the United Kingdom and Canada, providing that "classified information on development, design, construction, operation, and use of military package power reactors and reactors for the propulsion of naval vessels, aircraft, or land vehicles, for military purposes shall be exchanged to the extent and by such means as may be agreed" (Memorandum to the President, [Jan. 29, 1957], AWF/A: AEC; see also *U.S. Department of State Bulletin* 35, no. 889 [July 9, 1956], 84; and *ibid.*, no. 893 [August 6, 1956], 250). In July, however, the Joint Committee on Atomic Energy (JCAE) had recommended the suspension of any portion of the agreements with the United Kingdom and Canada that allowed for the exchange of this kind of restricted data. Although the agreements had been authorized by a "valid, strict, and legal interpretation" of the Atomic Energy Act of 1954, the committee was opposed to the exchanges and believed that Congress had not envisioned these agreements when the act was adopted. The JCAE feared that data on nuclear-powered guided missiles, aircraft, and submarines would be released to these two allies (Anderson to Eisenhower, July 27, 1956, AWF/A: AEC; Memorandum to the President, [Jan. 29, 1957]; and Strauss to Eisenhower, July 31, 1956, both in AWF/A: AEC).

An ad hoc committee, composed of Secretaries Dulles and Wilson, Attorney General Brownell, and AEC Chairman Strauss, had studied the issues raised by the report and recommended the action outlined in the President's memorandum. Although the JCAE was considering amendments to the relevant portions of the Atomic Energy Act, Dulles told Eisenhower, "We do not believe that fulfillment of our existing agreement with Canada and the United Kingdom should be further delayed pending conclusion of the Committee study" (Jan. 29, 1957, AWF/D-H). With the draft of this directive, Dulles enclosed the draft of a letter explaining the decision to Carl T. Durham, Chairman of the JCAE (see Eisenhower to Durham, Feb. 5, 1957, AWF/A: AEC).
[3] For developments see no. 628.

24 — *EM, AWF, International Series: Canada*

To Louis St. Laurent — *February 5, 1957*
Cable. Confidential

Dear Prime Minister:[1] Since Governor Adams' letter to you of January fifteenth, he proceeded with the course of action there outlined to evaluate for me the problem about which you wrote to me concerning the impact of our surplus disposal program on your western wheat producers.[2] An oral report has been given to your Ambassador here for transmittal to you.[3]

A review of the transactions involving our foreign sales of wheat last year and those projected for this year has been made and has been discussed with me.[4] In turn, I have given instructions to communicate my deep concern in the matter to United States representatives who participate with Canadian officials in periodic conferences on wheat export problems. In addition, my recognition of the complex nature of this problem is being brought to the attention of our Council on Foreign Economic Policy.[5]

Needless to say, I am keenly interested in working toward our essential goals in this field with the fullest possible consideration of its impact on Canada. It may be unreasonable to hope that disagreement will be eliminated from all areas in which Canada is affected by our emergency surplus disposal program, but I want you to know that it is the intention of all of us here to reduce to a minimum the points at which our respective interests diverge.

We shall continue to keep your representatives informed through normal channels of developments in our surplus disposal program and will, I assure you, be prepared to review with Canadian officials those aspects of our policy which appear to jeopardize Canadian interests.[6] *Sincerely*

[1] St. Laurent had been Prime Minister of Canada since November 1948. The State Department would cable the text of this letter to the U.S. embassy in Ottawa on February 7.

[2] The Agricultural Trade and Development Assistance Act (passed on July 10, 1954) had established guidelines for the disposal of surplus agricultural commodities through both sales and barter (*Congressional Quarterly Almanac*, vol. X, *1954*, pp. 121–24). Transactions under the law had seriously affected the commercial sales of these commodities by traders from several countries. St. Laurent had told Eisenhower that the pace of U.S. wheat surplus disposal "had been stepped up rather than moderated" since Canadian officials had met to discuss the problem with Secretary of Agriculture Ezra Taft Benson in September 1955. "In one way or another," the Prime Minister wrote, " . . . your wheat is being made so attractive to importing countries that they reduce their purchases from Canada and other exporting countries, which cannot afford to subsidize on such a tremendous scale." St. Laurent said that the proposed expansion of U.S. wheat sales to France and Poland would further harm Canadian wheat producers. Sherman Adams had told St. Laurent that the Administration would review the impact of U.S. wheat sales on Canada (see *Foreign Relations, 1955–1957*, vol. XXVII, *Western Europe and Canada* [1992], pp. 857–62, 877–79; State, *Foreign Relations, 1955–1957*, vol. IX, *Foreign Economic Policy; Foreign Information Program* [1987], pp. 217–19; and Ezra Taft Benson, *Cross Fire: The Eight Years with Eisenhower* [New York, 1962], p. 270).

[3] Arnold D. P. Heeney had been Canadian ambassador to the United States since 1953.

[4] We have been unable to locate any record of this review and discussion.

[5] For background on the council see Galambos and van Ee, *The Middle Way*, no. 975.

[6] St. Laurent would tell Eisenhower that he was confident the United States would implement the disposal program in a way that would be "the least disturbing to normal grain marketing operations" (St. Laurent to Eisenhower, Feb. 12, 1957, AWF/I: Canada).

At Cabinet meetings on April 12 and June 17 Secretary Dulles and Under Secretary of State Christian A. Herter would both note the Canadian apprehension over any future U.S. agreements involving surplus wheat. On August 13, 1957, however, the legislation would be extended for another year (State, *Foreign Relations, 1955–1957*, vol. IX, *Foreign Economic Policy; Foreign Information Program*, pp. 225–29, 231–34, 246–48, 250–53, 258–59, 267–74; see also *Foreign Relations, 1955–1957*, vol. XXVII, *Western Europe and Canada*, pp. 888–901).

25

EM, AWF, International Series: Saudi Arabia

TO IBN ABD AL-AZIZ SAUD

February 5, 1957

Your Majesty: I have had the impression that the military program we are proposing is a substantial one.[1] However, in reply to your letter I assure you that I shall look further into the details at once.[2]

I do hope you will not minimize in your own mind the importance of the training function. This is a long, even tedious, process. To perform this part of the work necessary to the development of an army, reconditioned equipment should be as good as the most expensive. I believe it would be to your advantage to avoid wear and tear on combat equipment while the troops are learning fundamentals.[3]

With great respect, *Sincerely*

[1] For background see no. 13. The U.S. aid package, which stressed loans rather than outright grants, provided technical assistance. The proposal included $50 million over a five-year period for an air force and army training program; engineering surveys and loan assistance for economic projects; plus an agreement to sell the Saudis $110 million in arms (State, *Foreign Relations, 1955–1957*, vol. XIII, *Near East: Jordan-Yemen*, pp. 464–65).

[2] In his letter King Saud had expressed dissatisfaction with the U.S. proposals. Military instructors and renovated equipment did not fulfill his country's need to create a strong army, King Saud said. Only with the "latest methods and the most modern equipment" could he maintain his country's integrity and independence (Saud to Eisenhower, Feb. 5, 1957, AWF/I: Saudi Arabia). Eisenhower had told Deputy Secretary of Defense Reuben Buck Robertson, Jr., that the King believed the United States was "just going through the same old drill, saddling off on them reconditioned equipment." He asked Robertson to confer with State Department officials about revising the proposal. "The program now seems to be the same as was discussed before the King came here," Eisenhower said; "he cannot go back & report that he has done nothing better" (Telephone conversation, Eisenhower and Robertson, Feb. 5, 1957, AWF/D).

[3] In a subsequent conversation, Secretary Dulles would tell Robertson that the Administration wanted "to hold a little back" because the Saudis were "great traders. But in the end the Pres will have to throw something into the kitty" (Feb. 5, 1957, Dulles Papers, Telephone Conversations). For developments see no. 77.

26

EM, AWF, Administration Series

To Lucius Du Bignon Clay

February 5, 1957

Dear Lucius:[1] Before the Inauguration Tom Stephens told me that you had—since you were a highly intelligent man—decided against coming down to Washington for the ceremonies.[2] I agreed completely and with envy to your decision, but the fact remains that I haven't had an opportunity to talk with you in a long time.

I'm going to try to get away to Georgia on Friday for a week or ten days, but sometime after my return, when you are planning to be in Washington on business, won't you give my office a ring.[3] I have nothing particular on my mind, but I have missed seeing you of late.

Give my love to Marjorie and, as always, the best to yourself.[4] *As ever*

[1] General Clay, Eisenhower's old friend and political adviser, was chairman of the board and chief executive officer of Continental Can Company. For background see *Eisenhower Papers*, vols. I–XVII.

[2] On the Inauguration see no. 2. Thomas Edwin Stephens had been Eisenhower's appointments secretary in his 1952 campaign and in his first Administration (see *Eisenhower Papers*, vols. XII–XVII).

[3] The Eisenhowers would vacation in Thomasville, Georgia, from February 8–19 (see no. 7). Clay would visit the White House on May 27.

[4] Clay's wife was the former Marjorie McKeown.

27

EM, AWF, DDE Diaries Series

To Carl F. Marsh

February 6, 1957

Dear Mr. Marsh:[1] A day or so ago I sent you an acknowledgment of your letter of January nineteenth.[2] But my mind has gone back so persistently to some of your observations that I decided to write you again.

First of all, you say, "We in Nebraska have always looked askance at Foreign Aid." The trouble with this whole problem is its name. Fundamentally, this is a program to help ourselves.

It would not be possible here to write a long exposition of the background of this problem, but I think I can sum up the reasons pretty well by taking a specific incident.

Therefore, consider for a moment the Mid East. To preserve this region from Communism is essential to the continued existence of America as a free nation. This is true because we must keep Western Europe from going Communistic. Yet without the opportunity to purchase fuel from the Mid East, Western Europe cannot live as a group of free nations. But, if all of the productive facilities and skilled labor of Western Europe should pass under the control of Moscow and International Communism, we would have to transform ourselves into an armed camp.

The first result of this would be vastly increased military expenditures—possibly 80 to 100 billion dollars per year. We would have a strictly controlled economy—all power centralized in Washington. If global war should then break out—and under these circumstances its likelihood would multiply one hundredfold—the northern hemisphere would soon become a desert. Certainly the free institutions and civilization that we have, and are defending, would no longer exist.[3]

* * * * *

You referred to the size of the Budget.[4] The figure of almost 72 billion of course deeply disturbs almost every thinking American. But even today the Congress has many people who are insistently demanding that we spend billions more upon our armed forces. Well over half of our national budget is devoted to the single question of national security,[5] and, as I said, if we ceased the program that you call "foreign aid" and nation after nation began falling under the domination of Communism, our defense budget would be increased by a far greater sum than we could possibly save.

* * * * *

Finally, with respect to the statements of the Secretary of the Treasury, George Humphrey, you obviously have overlooked his original statement, which was *about* as follows:

"No one has worked harder to reduce Federal expenditures than the President. He and I have worked together on this. Moreover, many devoted men in government have worked months and months to reduce our expenditures to the minimum. *This is the best that all of us, working together, can do.* But in the long term, it is not good enough. To continue indefinitely to spend at this rate will bring great trouble."[6]

With all of this I agree word for word and thought for thought. But the reason that Secretary Humphrey said "This is the best that we can do" is because he recognizes the terrible consequences, as of *now,* of providing inadequately for our security or for refusing to follow programs that give promise of keeping vital areas of the world out from under the rule of Communism.

All of the remainder, aside from these security measures, including Mutual Aid, is set up to provide for the requirements of the public or for the services which the public demands. For example, your own letter mentions the terrible drought that Nebraska is now experiencing. Great sections of our country are undergoing that drought, while some others suffer floods. In all of these instances, people turn to the Federal Government for help and it is promptly given. It is this kind of thing, multiplied in a hundred different directions, that accounts for the size of our budget.

The one way—under present circumstances—left to us to make economies is through perfection of administrative measures. In this line we have made tremendous improvements and have saved many millions. Counting both military and civilian workers, there are more than five million people now employed by the Federal Government. Consequently, to avoid duplication, to keep organizations streamlined and efficient, is a tremendous task, but one on which people like Secretary Humphrey, Secretary Wilson[7] and many, many others are always working.

Real savings are going to be possible only when we have made noticeable progress toward a peace in which we can be confident. To promote such a peace is one of the reasons that I meet so many people from abroad and work so hard through the United Nations and elsewhere to advance understanding among nations. Until that is done, I am very much afraid that the United States will have to carry a very large annual budget, in spite of all the savings that may otherwise be made.[8] *Very sincerely*

[1] Marsh, of McCook, Nebraska, was owner of the Carl F. Marsh real estate agency. White House aide Gabriel Hauge probably drafted this letter.

[2] Both letters are in WHCF/OF 114.

[3] See also no. 60.

[4] Marsh had expressed shock at the size of the budget, which, he said, would "increase inflation and take from those on a fixed income . . . money they simply can not afford to lose" (Marsh to Eisenhower, Jan. 19, 1957). On February 5 Eisenhower had told Marsh that in the past year economic pressures had "resulted in some advance in the average level of prices. We are seeking to abate that pressure," the President wrote, "by overbalancing the budget and using the small surplus to retire some of the debt by holding expenditures down in the face of tremendous demands that they be sharply increased in many areas" (for Eisenhower's budget message see *Public Papers of the Presidents: Eisenhower, 1957,* pp. 38–59).

[5] The federal government expended over $81.7 billion in 1957. National defense and international relations expenditures that year were $45.8 billion.

[6] At a news conference on January 15 Secretary of the Treasury Humphrey had in-

advertently set off a storm of speculation that he was at odds with the President over Eisenhower's budget request. After making a prepared statement designed to express support of the budget, Humphrey had said that if the government could not reduce the tax burden on the country there would be "a depression that will curl your hair" (see *New York Times,* Jan. 17, 1957; Eisenhower, *Waging Peace,* pp. 127–32; George M. Humphrey, *The Basic Papers of George M. Humphrey as Secretary of the Treasury, 1953–1957,* ed. Nathaniel R. Howard [Cleveland, 1965], pp. 236–83; and Raymond J. Saulnier, *Constructive Years: The U.S. Economy Under Eisenhower* [Lanham, Md., 1991], pp. 102–6. For more on the perception of differences between Eisenhower and Humphrey over the record-setting budget see Richard E. Neustadt, *Presidential Power: The Politics of Leadership* (New York, 1976), pp. 132–48; Fred I. Greenstein, *The Hidden-Hand Presidency: Eisenhower as Leader* (New York, 1982), p. 121; and John W. Sloan, *Eisenhower and the Management of Prosperity* (Lawrence, Kans., 1991), pp. 98–104.

[7] Secretary of Defense Charles Erwin Wilson.

[8] Marsh would tell Eisenhower that his letter had helped him "'see' and understand for the first time the meaning of Foreign Aid." He wished that the people of Nebraska could understand it as well (Marsh to Eisenhower, Feb. 9, 1957). All papers are in WHCF/OF 114.

28

EM, AWF, Dulles-Herter Series

To John Foster Dulles

February 6, 1957

Secret

Dear Foster: While I think this needs no reply, I felt that you might like to read the personal opinions of Dr. Schweitzer.[1] Because of the earnest request he made upon Norman Cousins for secrecy in this communication, I ask that you do not show it to anyone else in your Department.[2]

As perhaps you know, I was asked about this letter at my press conference this morning. I understand that the New York Times had an inquiry from their Paris office about it.[3] *As ever*

P.S. Please return the letters to me.

[1] Dr. Albert Schweitzer (M.D. University of Strasbourg 1913), missionary surgeon, clergyman, musicologist, and winner of the 1952 Nobel Peace Prize, was founder of the hospital in Lambaréné, French Equatorial Africa. He had written Eisenhower regarding an African-Asian resolution on Algeria soon to be brought before the United Nations. The resolution supported Algerian self-determination and called for immediate French-Algerian negotiations. "Would you forgive me," Schweitzer wrote, "for speaking of the grave consequences that would follow for the French Government if, not having the support of America, it sustained a defeat in the United Nations. The situation would be so compromised that it does not seem likely that it could continue in office" (Jan. 27, 1957, AWF/D-H). For background on the Algerian situation see Galambos and van Ee, *The Middle Way,* nos. 1792 and 2108.

[2] Norman Cousins, editor of *The Saturday Review,* had sent Schweitzer's letter to Eisen-

hower after returning from a visit to Lambaréné. According to Cousins, a French government official had "made a special rush trip" to persuade Schweitzer to write to the President. Such a message, Cousins said, represented the "violation of a basic operating principle" of Schweitzer's life—not to involve himself in political affairs—and he was "absolutely firm in his opposition to public release of the letter" (Cousins to Eisenhower, Feb. 4, 1957, AWF/D-H; see also Telephone conversation, Eisenhower and Dulles, Feb. 6, 1957, Dulles Papers, Telephone Conversations; and Eisenhower, *Waging Peace*, p. 106).

[3] Eisenhower had told his questioner that although he had not yet seen a letter from Dr. Schweitzer, he thought the humanitarian was "a very knowledgeable, wise man" and that he was interested in his views (*Public Papers of the Presidents: Eisenhower, 1957*, p. 130; see also *New York Times*, Feb. 6, 1957).

On February 13 the First Committee of the General Assembly would—with U.S. support—reject the resolution. Subsequently the General Assembly would unanimously adopt a resolution calling for a peaceful and democratic solution to the Algerian question through measures appropriate and consistent with the United Nations Charter (State, *Foreign Relations, 1955–1957*, vol. XVIII, *Africa* [1989], pp. 258–62; see also *U.S. Department of State Bulletin* 36, no. 924 [March 11, 1957], 421–23). For developments see no. 67.

29

EM, AWF, Dulles-Herter Series

To John Foster Dulles

February 6, 1957

Dear Foster: I should like to reply to the attached letter from the President of Lebanon in a sympathetic vein.[1] Would you pass it down to some staff officer who could whip up a draft? While I should like to generalize a bit on our readiness and anxiety to help, I don't, of course, want to be specific or say anything that might tie our hands later.[2] *As ever*

[1] Dr. Charles Malik, Lebanese Foreign Minister, had delivered President Camille Nimr Chamoun's letter to Eisenhower earlier on this same day. Chamoun emphasized the close relationship between Lebanon and the United States and commended Eisenhower for his firm stand during the Suez crisis. "I believe the United States commands now a position of moral authority which is the envy of friend and foe alike," Chamoun wrote. "In the development of the Near East the United States is virtually now an arbiter" (Chamoun to Eisenhower, Jan. 1, 1957, AWF/I: Lebanon).

[2] In his February 11 answer Eisenhower would thank Chamoun for support of U.S. policies in the Middle East and express optimism for peace in the area (State, *Foreign Relations, 1955–1957*, vol. XIII, *Near East: Jordan-Yemen*, p. 207). For developments see no. 124.

To Margaret Louise Coit *February 6, 1957*

Dear Miss Coit: While I would like to be helpful to you with regard to the biography you are writing of Bernard Baruch, I cannot give you permission to quote from my personal letters to him. So long as I am in my present position—and because both Mr. Baruch and I are alive—I could not consent to the use of any extracts taken from my private correspondence. The list of people with whom I correspond is a considerable one, and to establish such a precedent would put me eventually in an impossible position. I am confident of your understanding.[1]

On the other hand, I see from the file that over a period of time you have sought a personal interview with me. I assure you I would be glad to see you to talk of my association with my friend Mr. Baruch.[2] It would have to be understood, of course, that I had your previous assurance that you would not use in direct quotation or attribution anything I might say.

With best wishes, *Sincerely*

[1] Journalist Coit (A.B. University of North Carolina 1941), who had won the 1950 Pulitzer Prize for her biography of John C. Calhoun, had written Eisenhower on January 2. She was writing an authorized biography of financier Bernard Mannes Baruch, Eisenhower's old friend and veteran public servant, and had asked permission to use quotations from Eisenhower's letters. In subsequent correspondence Coit sent the quotations she wished to use and requested an interview with the President. Noting that she was a "Republican party worker," a "former Town Committee vice-chairman," and had interviewed former President Truman, Coit complained that she had not had "access to the President, whose relationship with Mr. Baruch was so much closer than Mr. Truman's was with him." She added, "I hate to have Mr. Truman loom bigger in the book."

[2] Coit would meet with Eisenhower for a half-hour on April 8, 1957. In a subsequent thank-you letter, Coit would write that it meant "a lot to an American, trying to do a serious job, to know that the President of the United States will take time out of the most crowded schedule in the country to help guarantee that the job be a good one." In her published study, Coit would refer to, but not quote from, the Eisenhower letters in Baruch's files (see Margaret L. Coit, *Mr. Baruch* [Boston, 1957], pp. 676–88). Baruch, who had in the meantime quarreled with Coit, would publish the first volume of his own autobiography (*Baruch: My Own Story* [New York, 1957]) in this same year. All correspondence is in same file as the document; see also *New York Times*, November 21, 24, 1957.

31

EM, AWF, Name Series

To Sigurd Stanton Larmon

February 7, 1957

Dear Sig:[1] I forgot to write you that a few nights ago Al Gruenther was sitting in my house and I gave him the "problem."[2] After a very few tries he solved it. The whole key to the thing, of course, is the discard of a diamond instead of a club so as to give a chance to come back to your own hand twice by trumping clubs. This provides two discards for the ace and king of diamonds.

Today I have a note from your nephew, sending the solution along.[3] I am sorry he was put to the trouble but appreciative of his thoughtfulness.

Personally after looking at it that first evening, I just decided lazily that it could not work and I let it go at that—but once you have the key play it is simple enough.

Have a good vacation![4] *As ever*

[1] Larmon, a New York advertising executive and a member of the U.S. Advisory Committee on Information, was among the select group of friends who from time to time accompanied the President on vacations. For background see *Eisenhower Papers,* vols. XII–XVII.

[2] Gruenther had visited Eisenhower's Gettysburg, Pennsylvania, farm on January 25 and 26. The "problem" involved bridge, one of Eisenhower's favorite games.

[3] Park Larmon Brown's February 5 letter is in AWF/N.

[4] Larmon had gone to Jamaica (see *ibid.*).

32

EM, AWF, Name Series: Columbia Miscellaneous

To Harry James Carman

February 8, 1957

Dear Harry: Your letter reached me just as I was preparing to take off for the South for a week's recreation.[1] I have had no chance to consult my colleagues, so I don't know what will be the attitude of the Vice President and the Cabinet Members toward your proposition.[2]

In many ways the idea is most appealing, but for myself the question of precedent almost compels a negative answer. I am invited to participate in so many different types of public discussions that to accept your invitation would create for me very great embarrassment.

However, as soon as I return from the South, I shall get in touch with the Vice President, discuss the matter with him, and see whether he could get together a group that would meet your requirements. As you know, our Vice President has been better acquainted than any of his predecessors with all the activities of government. You would find his participation in a panel discussion very satisfactory indeed.[3]

Of course I deeply regret that I cannot comply with a request of such an old and good friend as yourself, to do something that would give me great personal satisfaction, but I hope you will understand the reasons that I have merely hinted at above.

With warmest personal regard, *Sincerely*

[1] Carman, dean emeritus of Columbia College, was a professor of history at Columbia University (for background see *Eisenhower Papers*, vols. X–XVII). He had written on February 4 to invite Eisenhower and the Cabinet members to serve on a panel discussion at the annual dinner of the Citizens Union of the City of New York. The Union, a non-partisan organization formed in 1917, was composed of business and civic leaders and represented New Yorkers in local, state, and federal matters.

Later this day the President would travel to Thomasville, Georgia (see no. 7).

[2] Carman had suggested that if Eisenhower could not attend "perhaps Vice President Nixon could honor us . . . " (see also Carman to Eisenhower, Mar. 4, 1957). On February 13 Carman would thank the President for offering to "intercede with the Vice President on our behalf."

[3] As it turned out, Nixon could not "arrange his schedule in order to participate" (Eisenhower to Carman, Mar. 4, 1957). Carman's March 25 thank-you letter to the President and all correspondence are in AWF/N: Columbia Miscellaneous.

33 *EM, AWF, Name Series, Nielsen Corr.*

To Vernon Bigelow Stouffer *February 9, 1957*

Dear Mr. Stouffer:[1] A week or so ago Aksel Nielsen wrote me that you were sending to the White House some of the unusual foods for which you have developed a successful freezing method, and the other day, just before we left Washington, I was handed a list of the other various items that had arrived.[2] Both Mrs. Eisenhower and I are eager to try each one of them, especially on Aksel's enthusiastic recommendation. I know that everything from spinach souffle to apple cobbler will be delicious, and I am indeed grateful for your thoughtful kindness.[3]

Although I would not want to impose on you, I am also appreciative of your suggestion that you would like to keep our Gettysburg deep freeze stocked, and we may possibly take you up. Unfortunately, our visits up there have been much too few of late, and what you have already sent us will last quite a while.[4]

With my thanks and best wishes, *Sincerely*

[1] Stouffer (B.S. University of Pennsylvania 1923) was president and chairman of the board of United Airlines.

[2] Nielsen was president of the Title Guaranty Company in Denver, Colorado. For background on Eisenhower's long friendship with him see *Eisenhower Papers*, vols. I–XVII. Nielsen had written on January 31 (AWF/N; see also Nielsen to Whitman, Feb. 1, 1957, AWF/N, Nielsen Corr.). Eisenhower wrote this letter while vacationing in Thomasville, Georgia (see no. 7).

[3] "I have never tasted anything better," the President would write Nielsen on April 17. He went on to ask Nielsen to "quietly get . . . a price list" of the available dishes and to determine where they might be found in the Washington area. Eisenhower said he was thinking of his daughter-in-law and some of her "household problems." "I could always order them through . . . some other third person," he wrote, to "avoid the embarrassing possibility" that Stouffer would think he was asking for a "'donation.'" Nielsen would send the list on April 29 (see also Eisenhower to Nielsen, May 6, 1957, all in AWF/N).

[4] In June arrangements would be made for Stouffer to install an electric oven at the Gettysburg farm (see Whitman to Nevins, June 18, 1957, AWF/N).

34 *EM, AWF, Administration Series: Army*

To Dorothy Mills Young *February 11, 1957*

Dear Dorothy: I brought along to Thomasville your letter of the third, to attempt to explain to you my own feelings about the recent Army order regarding military funerals.[1]

I, too, felt more than a little sad when I was informed as to the decision. But the passing of time creates changes in the customs of the past and we simply have to go along with them. Uniforms, weapons, regulations, means of transportation, and even some traditions all change with time. From sentiment I want to rebel at some of the things that must be done, but intellectually I know I must go along.

At any rate, I do want to thank you for writing to me as you did.

With affectionate regard, *Sincerely*

[1] Mrs. Young was the wife of Brigadier General Gordon Russell Young (for background see Galambos, *Chief of Staff*, no. 1581). She had written to ask Eisenhower to intervene, on behalf of the bereaved in opposition to the "motorization" of military funerals. She had "learned firsthand," she wrote, of the "comfort and pride . . . that the old rituals give" (AWF/A: Army). On Eisenhower's Thomasville, Georgia, vacation see no. 7.

The military had for some time been considering this change in an effort to reduce costs. Widespread military and public disapproval would, however, force the government to drop the matter (Telephone conversation, Tom Sherlock, Office of the Historian, Arlington National Cemetery, Aug. 17, 1995, EP; see also Goodpaster to Young, Feb. 16, 1957, WHCF/PPF 1881; and B. C. Mossman and M. W. Stark, *The*

Last Salute: Civil and Military Funerals 1921–1969, Department of the Army [Washington, D.C., 1971]).

35 *EM, AWF, Name Series*

TO PHILIP YOUNG *February 11, 1957*

Dear Phil: It is with a deep feeling of loss that I view your resignation later this month as Chairman of the Civil Service Commission and as my Adviser on Personnel Management.[1] All during the past four years I have been reassured by the knowledge that you were devoting your many abilities to the strengthening of the civil service and the entire personnel structure of the Federal Government. I am certain that all who have participated in our frequent discussions of these matters will share my regret at your departure.[2]

As you so well know, it has been the constant purpose of this Administration to improve the conditions of government service and attract to it those well-trained, dedicated, intelligent people who are so essential to the proper conduct of public affairs. Through the many programs you have helped to develop, and particularly through your own full devotion to the highest principles of public service, you have contributed immeasurably to the achievement of our purpose.[3] Government personnel at all levels, indeed the nation as a whole, will long recognize your outstanding service.

You have my heartfelt thanks for your strong support during these four years. I am grateful, too, that you are willing to be of further service in the future.[4]

With warm personal regard, *Sincerely*

[1] Young, a member of the Eisenhower Administration since March 23, 1953, had submitted his resignation on February 8 (see *Eisenhower Papers*, vols. X–XVII; see also Eisenhower, *Mandate for Change*, p. 120). Eisenhower would write a number of similar letters in response to personnel changes at the start of the new Administration (see, for example, Eisenhower to Herbert Hoover, Jr., Jan. 28, 1957, AWF/A; Eisenhower to Arthur S. Flemming, Jan. 28, 1957, AWF/A; and Eisenhower to Robert Tripp Ross, Feb. 14, 1957, AWF/D).

[2] Young had cited the accomplishments of the commission from 1953 to 1957. Under Eisenhower's leadership, he wrote, "For the first time effective coordination of personnel policies has been achieved at the top levels of Government" (see *Public Papers of the Presidents: Eisenhower, 1957*, pp. 142–44).

[3] On civil service reform see, for example, Galambos and van Ee, *The Middle Way*, no. 90; on health insurance for federal employees see *ibid.*, no. 1266.

[4] Young would be confirmed as U.S. Ambassador to the Netherlands on March 28, 1957 (see Young to Eisenhower, Mar. 30, 1957, AWF/N; see also *New York Times*, Mar. 29, 1957).

36

EM, AWF, Name Series

To [Ann Cook Whitman]

[February 12, 1957]

Please send this to Mr. Dulles. It represents, I think, a biased, but fairly intelligent, statement of the Israeli's position—from the Jewish viewpoint.[1]

[1] Eisenhower wrote this notation at the top of a letter he had received from Leonard Finder, vice-president of the Universal Match Company. For background on Finder see Galambos and van Ee, *The Middle Way*, nos. 113 and 797. He had told the President that although the Eisenhower Doctrine (*ibid.*, no. 2155) was "a positive step forward" in Middle Eastern diplomacy, American foreign policy had dismayed a large number of people in the United States. He asked Eisenhower why Israel was not entitled to the same safeguards for its citizens as any nation. The United States, he said, insisted that Israel return territory taken only to prevent Egypt's "raiding aggression." Although the United Nations had given Israel "a flat ultimatum," it had merely passed resolutions regarding the aggressions of countries like the Soviet Union and India. "Justice cannot be one thing for the strong and another for the weak," Finder wrote; "firmness becomes harshness when manifested only against those most dedicated to the ideals of the United Nations." The United States had remained "relatively silent" regarding the "flagrant abuses" of Egypt, a country that "has no regard for the individual, supports a military dictatorship, has no sincere international loyalties, and has played with Russia when it saw fit" (Finder to Eisenhower, Feb. 7, 1957, AWF/N).

In a brief note of acknowledgment Eisenhower would tell Finder that he would give his opinions "personal and earnest consideration" (Eisenhower to Finder, Feb. 12, 1957, *ibid.*; see also Telephone conversation, Eisenhower and Dulles, Feb. 13, 1957, Dulles Papers, Telephone Conversations).

37

EM, AWF, International Series: Saudi Arabia

To ibn Abd al-Aziz Saud
Cable. Secret

February 14, 1957

Your Majesty:[1] During your recent visit to Washington we discussed a wide range of subjects relating to the Middle East.[2] We also agreed that, as future circumstances might require, we would communicate with each other regarding matters of importance. One of these matters—the question of Israeli withdrawal from Gaza and the area of the Straits of Aqaba—has come to the fore in the United Nations since your departure.[3]

Accordingly, we have been giving fresh consideration to this important matter. Our ideas have been discussed with the Secretary General of the United Nations, and are known to the representatives of Egypt and of Israel. The subject also has been discussed recently with Your Majesty's Deputy Foreign Minister and Ambassador.[4]

Current press accounts have been misleading, and to avoid any misunderstandings I want to reassure Your Majesty concerning our attitude. We stand first and foremost in favor of immediate Israeli withdrawal from Gaza and the Straits of Aqaba. Our efforts are designed to achieve this end and to do so urgently. Also we do not think that Israel should gain advantages from its invasion or that Egypt should have to make fresh promises to Israel to assure Israeli withdrawal.

At the same time, as was indicated to Your Majesty in Washington, we hold and have always held that the waters of the Gulf of Aqaba have an international character. We understand that this view is shared by Egypt as indicated in the Egyptian Government's memorandum in 1950 to the American Ambassador wherein it stated that the Egyptian occupation of the two islands, Tiran and Sanafir, at the entrance of the Gulf of Aqaba was only to protect the islands themselves against possible damage or violation and that "this occupation being in no way conceived in a spirit of obstructing in any way the innocent passage through the stretch of water separating these two islands from the Egyptian coast of Sinai, it follows that this passage, the only practicable one, will remain free as in the past, in conformity with international practice and recognized principles of the law of nations."[5]

In all of our consideration and discussions of this matter we have emphasized that in the use of this passage by any nations, it is of utmost importance that there should be fully respected the passage of pilgrims on religious missions.

It is our belief that the United Nations General Assembly has no authority to require either of Egypt or of Israel a substantial modification of the Armistice Agreement, which now gives Egypt the right and responsibility of occupation of the Gaza strip. Accordingly, we believe that Israeli withdrawal from there should be prompt and unconditional, leaving the future of the Gaza strip to be worked out through the efforts and good offices of the United Nations. We believe that the United Nations General Assembly and the Secretary General should seek that the United Nations Emergency Force, in exercise of its mission, move into the area and be on the boundary between Israel and the Gaza strip. The United States will use its efforts to assure these results, which we believe are contemplated by the two General Assembly resolutions of February 2, 1957.[6]

Our discussions subsequent to your departure have reflected no change in the position taken here with Your Majesty, although a contrary impression undoubtedly has been given in erroneous press stories.[7] Stated simply, we believe that Israel should immediately withdraw in accordance with the United Nations resolutions, after which we believe that the rules of international law should apply to the shipping of all nations in the Gulf of Aqaba. Of course, as to this, we would consider any decision of the International Court of Justice to be binding, if such a decision is involved. Thus we believe that Israel would obtain no rights or privileges to which it is not entitled by international law.

I am communicating with you on this important matter in furtherance of my desire to consult with you on problems of mutual interest and in the light of full and frank discussions which we had. These discussions were a source of great pleasure and profit to me. Privately and officially I value highly the friendship that we established.[8]

I hope that Your Majesty is well and is enjoying the visits to other friendly countries enroute to your kingdom.[9] *Sincerely*

[1] The State Department drafted this cable and sent it to the U.S. embassy in Madrid for delivery to King Saud, who was en route from Washington to Saudi Arabia.

[2] See no. 13.

[3] See no. 19.

[4] Secretary Dulles had discussed the points Eisenhower raises in this letter with Deputy Foreign Minister Sheikh Yusuf Yasin and Ambassador Sheikh Abdullah al-Khayyal on February 7 (State, *Foreign Relations, 1955–1957*, vol. XIII, *Near East: Jordan-Yemen*, pp. 468–69).

[5] See U.S. Department of State, *Foreign Relations of the United States, 1950*, 7 vols. (Washington, D.C., 1976–81), vol. V, *The Near East, South Asia, and Africa* (1978), p. 711.

[6] On the resolutions see no. 19.

[7] Eisenhower may have been referring to a report on the preceding day that the United States was attempting to end Egypt's monopoly over maritime traffic between the Red Sea and the Mediterranean by establishing an alternate route from the Middle East oil fields to the Mediterranean (*New York Times*, Feb. 13, 1957).

[8] Eisenhower had directed Secretary Dulles to add this sentence to the original State Department draft (Telephone conversation, Eisenhower and Dulles, Feb. 14, 1957, Dulles Papers, Telephone Conversations).

[9] In his response (Feb. 16) King Saud would reaffirm the significance of the Strait of Aqaba to the safe passage of religious pilgrims visiting their holy lands (AWF/I: Saudi Arabia). For developments see no. 40.

38

EM, AWF, Administration Series

To Isidor Schwaner Ravdin

February 14, 1957

Dear Rav: When you are next in Washington perhaps I could talk to you about the suggestions in your letter of the twelfth to Mrs. Whitman.[1] My offhand reaction is that I could not possibly give *two* talks before medical groups in one year simply because, silly as it sounds,

I would be accused of favoritism and deluged with similar requests from physicists, atomic scientists, and the like!

But before I come to any decision, I would like to talk the matter over with Howard Snyder and Bobby Cutler—and you, if you are going to be in Washington sometime in the next two or three weeks.[2]

The weather here has been delightful, and I feel no urge at all to return to the dampness and cold that I understand still prevails up there.[3] I've had only fair success with golf, but a couple of lucky days in the field.

With warm regard, *As ever*

[1] Ravdin, professor of surgery at the University of Pennsylvania School of Medicine, was chairman of the Board of Regents of the American College of Surgeons (for background see Galambos and van Ee, *The Middle Way*, no. 1912). He had written to Eisenhower's personal secretary Ann Cook Whitman asking that the President address both the Students of the American Medical Association and the American College of Surgeons. These two occasions, he wrote, would "provide the opportunity for the President to express himself on matters of tremendous importance to American medicine" (AWF/A, Ravdin Corr.). For background on Whitman see *Eisenhower Papers*, vols. XII–XVII.

[2] Eisenhower would meet with his personal physician Howard McCrum Snyder, Special Assistant to the President for National Security Affairs Robert Cutler (to whom Ravdin had also written) and Ravdin on February 25 (for background on Snyder see *Eisenhower Papers*, vols. VI–XVII; on Cutler see *ibid.*, vols. X–XVII). For developments see no. 160.

[3] See no. 7.

39 — *EM, AWF, Name Series*

To Harry S. Truman — *February 15, 1957*

Dear Mr. Truman: I would like to express my appreciation of the views about the Middle East Joint Resolution that you expressed in your syndicated column of yesterday, particularly urging prompt Congressional action on the Resolution.[1] I feel that your attitude is in the high tradition of non-partisanship on foreign policy matters of grave national concern.[2]

With best wishes, *Sincerely*

[1] Secretary Dulles had told Eisenhower that former President Truman had written "a very helpful piece urging prompt action on the plan." An expression of appreciation, Dulles said, would "highlight his recommendation." Eisenhower agreed but told Dulles that the letter "should not be too personal." The message was dictated to Ann Whitman at Thomasville, Georgia, where Eisenhower was vacationing (Telephone conversation, Feb. 15, 1957, Dulles Papers, Telephone Conversations; see also Dulles to Truman, Jan. 14, 1957, Dulles Personal Papers). For background on the

joint resolution, known as the Eisenhower Doctrine, see Galambos and van Ee, *The Middle Way,* no. 2155.

[2] "As you know," Truman would answer, "I have always been in favor of a bi-partisan foreign policy and have never myself made any statements or actions which would make a partisan matter out of foreign policy" (Truman to Eisenhower, Feb. 19, 1957, AWF/N).

40

EM, AWF, International Series: Israel

To David Ben Gurion
Cable. Secret

February 20, 1957

Dear Mr. Prime Minister:[1] I know Ambassador Eban is reporting fully to you the views of the United States Government concerning the withdrawal by Israel behind the Armistice lines in accordance with the pertinent resolutions of the United Nations.[2] The views expressed to Ambassador Eban by Secretary Dulles, as well as those set forth in our Aide Memoire of February 11, are fully shared by me.[3] These are designed to give our national assurances reenforcing the assurances of the United Nations with reference to the future of the Gulf of Aqaba and the Gaza Strip.[4] It has been our earnest endeavor, in supporting fully the United Nations in this matter, to explain our attitude and future policies regarding certain future aspects of the problem. This we hoped would encourage you to comply with the resolutions.

Acting upon the request of your representatives, and upon the request contained in your letter of February 18 to Secretary Dulles, the United States has supported the postponement of further General Assembly consideration of measures to be taken to achieve implementation of its resolutions on withdrawal.[5] I understand now that the Assembly plans to consider this matter again on February 21 and that further postponement is probably impracticable. Thus, in the absence of an immediate and favorable decision by your Government, there can be no assurance that the next decisions soon to be taken by the United Nations will not involve serious implications. It continues to be my earnest hope that you will announce your intention immediately to comply with the withdrawal resolution and, in the words of the public statement which I authorized on February 17, "rely upon the resoluteness of all friends of justice to bring about a state of affairs which will conform to the principles of justice and of international law and serve impartially the proper interests of all in the area."[6]

I would greatly deplore the necessity of the United States taking positions in the United Nations, and of the United Nations itself having to adopt measures, which might have far-reaching effects upon Israel's relations throughout the world. Our position must, however, conform with the principles for which we have firmly stood in relation to these tragic events. I have been in touch with leaders of the Congress. I plan again to speak tonight to the American people with respect to this matter by radio and television.[7] I also feel that at this time I should express again to you the sincere hope that your Government will accede to the wishes of the overwhelming majority of the members of the United Nations.[8]

Believe me, Mr. Prime Minister, that this message is sent in the spirit of the traditional friendship between our countries,—a friendship which we zealously seek to preserve and develop.[9] *Sincerely*

[1] To speed communication, the minister of the Israeli embassy telephoned the substance of this letter, which had been delivered to him by hand, to the Prime Minister (see Shiloah to Rountree, Feb. 20, 1957, AWF/D-H; see also Telephone message, Arthur Dean, Feb. 20, 1957, Dulles Papers, Telephone Conversations).

[2] For background see no. 19. Abba Eban, the Israeli ambassador to the United States, was also the Permanent Representative at the United Nations.

[3] Dulles and Eban had conferred, probably by telephone, on February 18. In an aide-mémoire, the State Department had endorsed the United Nations order of urgency for the withdrawal of Israeli invasion and occupation forces. After the prompt and unconditional withdrawal from Gaza, the statement said, the United Nations Emergency Force would occupy the boundary between Israel and the Gaza Strip to prevent its use as a base for terrorist attacks against Israel. The United States would join other countries in protecting the right of free passage through the Gulf of Aqaba (State, *Foreign Relations, 1955–1957*, vol. XVII, *Arab-Israeli Dispute, 1957*, pp. 132–34, 202; see also Eisenhower, *Waging Peace*, pp. 184–87; and Draft of text resolution, Feb. 21, 1957, AWF/D-H).

[4] Eisenhower added this sentence in the course of a telephone conversation with Secretary Dulles (Feb. 20, 1957, Dulles Papers, Telephone Conversations).

[5] Ben Gurion had asked Secretary Dulles to obtain a postponement of United Nations discussions and to send a committee of representative states to Israel and Egypt to reach a settlement. "Withdrawal under the present circumstances," he wrote, "will spell disaster for us" (State, *Foreign Relations, 1955–1957*, vol. XVII, *Arab-Israeli Dispute, 1957*, p. 200).

[6] Eisenhower's statement is in *Public Papers of the Presidents: Eisenhower, 1957*, pp. 144–46.

[7] See *ibid.*, pp. 147–56.

[8] In a message on the following day, Ben Gurion would tell Dulles that the Israeli government had "bent all efforts" to reach a position on the points raised by the President, but that there was too little time to reach a decision before the United Nations debate scheduled for February 22. He asked that the United States exert its influence to postpone the discussion until Monday (Feb. 25). Repeating his request for a postponement in his letter to Eisenhower on February 22, Ben Gurion said "it is our most ardent wish to cooperate to the fullest in seeking a solution" (Ben Gurion to Dulles, Feb. 21, 1957, AWF/D-H; and Ben Gurion to Eisenhower, Feb. 22, 1957, AWF/I: Israel; see also Abba Solomon Eban, *An Autobiography* [New York, 1977], pp. 243–48; and Alteras, *Eisenhower and Israel*, pp. 263–73). Eisenhower and Dulles agreed that the message was "bad news." "This stubborn attitude finally gets

you down," Eisenhower told the Secretary, who said that "he would have bet odds in favor of their giving in" (Telephone conversation, Feb. 21, 1957, Dulles Papers, Telephone Conversations). For developments see no. 56.

[9] Secretary Dulles had suggested that Eisenhower add this sentence (Telephone conversation, Eisenhower and Dulles, Feb. 20, 1957, Dulles Papers, Telephone Conversations).

41

EM, AWF, Name Series

To Edward Everett Hazlett, Jr.

February 20, 1957

Dear Swede: My underground sources tell me that you are getting along fine, although you have had a recurrence of those bad headaches that used to plague you.[1] I do hope that the doctors will succeed in eliminating them soon—and in keeping your blood pressure under control.

I promised myself to come out to see you at Bethesda, but with one thing and another I haven't made it.[2] At any rate these flowers bring you, as always, my warm regard.[3] *As ever*

[1] Hazlett had entered Bethesda Naval Hospital on January 9 for a series of gastrointestinal tests. During his hospitalization Hazlett was treated for recurring "histamine headaches" and high blood pressure. Currently, his blood pressure was responding favorably to treatment (Hazlett to Eisenhower, Jan. 10 and Mar. 2, 1957, and related correspondence in AWF/N; and Memorandums, Jan. 19, 25, 1957, AWF/N, Hazlett Corr.).

[2] In the margin of this paragraph Eisenhower placed an asterisk and added: "Also, now a mild but irritating case of bronchitis. D." Hazlett would reply, "Your expressed wish to come out here to see me is enough for me. Please dismiss it from your mind, and don't attempt it" (Mar. 2, 1957, AWF/N).

[3] The President would continue to send flowers to his old friend throughout his hospitalization (Hazlett to Eisenhower, Jan. 10, Mar. 2, 1957, and Eisenhower to Hazlett, Feb. 26, Mar. 13, 1957, all in AWF/N).

For developments see no. 105.

42

EM, AWF, Name Series

To Chester Bowles

February 21, 1957

Dear Mr. Bowles:[1] Thank you for your letter of January twenty-sixth on the problems facing India in carrying out its Second Five Year Plan for economic development. Having recently discussed these problems with Prime Minister Nehru in Washington, I was interested to receive your views on this situation.[2]

It has been, of course, our conclusion along the same lines which has led us to increase materially United States assistance to India over the past months. In addition to the technical and developmental aid programs with which you are familiar, we have recently concluded a Public Law 480 agreement with India on surplus agricultural commodities, valued at $360,000,000 which India may repay in local currency on easy terms over a long period.[3] Further, in the same general pattern, we have also given our full support to India's request to draw up to $200,000,000 from the International Monetary Fund, the main burden of which transaction will rest ultimately on the United States. The question of whether we should do more to help India meet its needs is, of course, constantly under study.

I do agree with you that successful development is of great importance to India, not only for economic progress but for continued political stability.

With best wishes, *Sincerely*

[1] For background on Bowles, former U.S. Ambassador to India, see Galambos and van Ee, *The Middle Way*, no. 38.

[2] Bowles had told Eisenhower that the Second Five-Year Plan, scheduled for completion in 1961, was "almost certain to fail without assurance of substantial American assistance in the next few months." India had devised the plan to keep pace with the development of both industry and agriculture in Communist China. Bowles said that repayment of previous U.S. loans to India, a wartime agreement to pay the United States treasury 180 million ounces of silver, rising prices in Western nations, and increases in costs due to the Suez crisis all strained India's ability to finance the plan (AWF/N). For background on Prime Minister Nehru's visit see *ibid.*, no. 2139.

[3] See *Congressional Quarterly Almanac*, vol. XII, *1956*, pp. 489–92.

43 *EM, AWF, DDE Diaries Series*

To Herbert Brownell, Jr. *February 21, 1957*

Dear Herb: I understand you have already received a copy of Senator Bricker's letter to me of February thirteenth.[1] When you have completed your comments on it, won't you communicate directly with Senator Bricker? I really think it is senseless to use me merely as a post office in transmitting messages that are by their very nature extremely technical in character.

My own views on this subject have not changed since the whole matter was first explained to me.[2]

In spite of the above, I hope you will report to me on the results of your conversations with Judge Orie Phillips.[3]
With warm regard, *As ever*

[1] Eisenhower was referring to a February 13 letter from Senator John W. Bricker (AWF/D) regarding the Senator's latest efforts to limit the treaty-making power by amending the Constitution. The Senator had expressed disappointment with the Justice Department's "blanket condemnation" of the text of a proposed revision to the controversial amendment (see Galambos and van Ee, *The Middle Way*, no. 2150). He said that he had asked Judge Orie L. Phillips to analyze the Justice Department's arguments. Bricker further suggested that he was in "full accord with the three objectives stated in your letter of September 25" (*i.e.*, that no treaty should be valid if it conflicts with the Constitution; that treaties should be used in the conduct of foreign relations and not as a subterfuge to enact domestic law; and that no amendment should hamper the president's power to conduct foreign affairs; see *ibid.*, no. 1995). "Why not," he asked, "have your legal and diplomatic advisers draft a constitutional amendment strictly limited to the three basic principles on which we are agreed? Such a draft might open the way for fruitful discussions. I just can't believe," he wrote, "that the English language is so inflexible that the three principles . . . are incapable of constitutional expression." On February 18 Eisenhower had acknowledged Bricker's letter and promised that when he returned to Washington from his Thomasville vacation, he would discuss the matter with Attorney General Brownell (AWF/D).

[2] For Eisenhower's opposition to the Bricker amendment see Galambos and van Ee, *The Middle Way*, nos. 59, 741, and 1824. For more on the Bricker amendment see Duane Tananbaum, *The Bricker Amendment Controversy: A Test of Eisenhower's Political Leadership* (Ithaca, 1988), pp. 203–9, 227.

[3] On Orie Leon Phillips, former Chief Judge of the Tenth Circuit Court of Appeals, Denver, see Galambos and van Ee, *The Middle Way*, nos. 415 and 1725.

44

EM, AWF, Name Series

To Arthur Krock
Personal

February 21, 1957

Dear Arthur:[1] I remember well the incident to which you refer in your column of February nineteenth.[2]
With respect to government controls, I have pondered the matter long and seriously, and always end up with the decision that a "controlled" economy would mean the end of our present private enterprise system. And I don't believe our system *is* outmoded.[3]
With warm regard, *Sincerely*

[1] Eisenhower was responding to a February 19, 1957, note written by *New York Times* columnist Arthur Krock to White House Press Secretary James C. Hagerty (AWF/N).

[2] Krock had enclosed a copy of his February 19 *New York Times* column, "In the Na-

tion," which discussed inflation. He had written Hagerty that "Even if I were fatuous enough to assume that the President keeps in touch with my pieces, I would still retain enough sense to realize he has more important matters on his mind these days. But the enclosure has a connection with an incident in December, 1947, to which he usually refers when I see him." Krock's article referred to Eisenhower's 1947 proposal to control inflation by persuading the United States Steel Corporation to announce that it was maintaining prices for a year in the hope that this would inspire "labor, farmers, government and the rest of the population" to act in a similar fashion (see Galambos, *Chief of Staff*, no. 1926).
[3] In Eisenhower's draft of this letter—originally a note to Hagerty—the President had written that he had "pondered" the question of government controls "long and seriously, but I always end up with a 'controlled' economy. This means the end of our system. It's hard for me to believe the system is outmoded—at least as yet." For background on Eisenhower's efforts to control inflation during his first Administration see Galambos and van Ee, *The Middle Way*, nos. 172, 348, 1805, and 2060.

45 *EM, AWF, Name Series*

To Henry Agard Wallace *February 22, 1957*
Personal

Dear Mr. Wallace: It is indeed humbling to realize that anyone so widely read as yourself should find similarities in the characters of President Washington and myself.[1] Of one thing I assure you—at this moment I am very much in need of the wisdom, faith, and strength that he possessed.

My sense of pride is all the greater because I've never been able to agree with those who so glibly deprecate his intellectual qualities. I think that too many jump at such conclusions merely because they tend to confuse facility of expression with wisdom; a love of the limelight with depth of perception. His Newburgh Address to his officers must have been largely his own;[2] and so far as I know, everyone agrees that he substantially corrected, and possibly re-wrote, Hamilton's draft of his Farewell Address.[3] I've often felt the deep wish that The Good Lord had endowed me with his clarity of vision in big things, his strength of purpose and his genuine greatness of mind and spirit.[4]

Thank you very much for sending me a copy of your talk.

With personal regard, *Sincerely*

[1] Wallace, a former Vice-President of the United States (1941–1945) and Progressive party candidate for President (1948), had written Eisenhower on February 19 (AWF/N) to forward a copy of his recent talk on "George Washington as a Statesman and Religious Man." Stressing the postwar difficulties faced in both American revolutionary and contemporary times, the talk drew comparisons between Washington and Eisenhower. Wallace stated that he believed the likeness between Eisenhower

and Washington was "more than superficial." "You both have a combined military-agricultural background," he wrote. "But above everything you both have a profound faith in God, innate in your own natures and bequeathed to you by God-fearing ancestors." Wallace also expressed the hope that his talk would give the President "renewed strength." For background on Wallace see Galambos and van Ee, *The Middle Way*, nos. 88 and 2125.

[2] In his March 1783 Newburgh Address, Washington had sought to diffuse the anger of officers who had demanded back pay from the government. While assuring his men that he would do everything in his power to help, he pleaded with them not to challenge the nascent authority of Congress. Washington's extemporaneous opening remarks are the most often quoted lines from this famous speech: "Gentlemen, you will permit me to put on my spectacles, for I not only have grown gray but almost blind in the service of my country." See George Washington, *Basic Writings of George Washington*, ed. Saxe Commins (New York, 1948), pp. 455–60; Douglas Southall Freeman, *George Washington: A Biography*, 7 vols. (New York, 1948–57), vol. V, *Victory with the Help of France* (Fairfield, N.J., 1981), pp. 428–37, vol. VII, *First in Peace*, by John Alexander Carroll and Mary Wells Ashworth (1957); and John E. Ferling, *The First of Men: A Life of George Washington* (Knoxville, Tenn., 1988), pp. 309–12.

[3] Washington's Farewell Address is perhaps best known for his warning against entangling alliances ("Tis our true policy to steer clear of permanent alliances, with any portion of the foreign world"). See Washington, *Basic Writings*, pp. 627–44, and Carroll and Ashworth, *George Washington*, vol. VII, *First in Peace*, pp. 402–7.

[4] On Eisenhower's respect for Washington, see, for example, Galambos, *NATO and the Campaign of 1952*, no. 379, and Galambos and van Ee, *The Middle Way*, nos. 1192 and 2141.

46 — *EM, AWF, International Series: Macmillan*

To Harold Macmillan — *February 23, 1957*

Cable. Secret

Dear Harold:[1] Thank you for your note. As I read it, I am impressed by a feeling that we are not far apart in our thinking. Certainly Foster and I have struggled to be fair and have done our utmost to assure the Israeli of the things we would do and the support we would give as soon as they agreed to the major proposition of withdrawal.[2]

Of course any prediction as to the details of future United Nations action is largely guess work. I agree that as of this moment, a simple condemnation of Israel and vote of sanctions would be wrong. I think that a single Resolution could properly combine both withdrawal orders and important assurances to Israel along the lines of my address.[3] But I suspect that things have gone far enough that no Resolution can command the required votes unless it also includes some intimation of consequences to Israel if she refuses to comply.

We are anxious, in this as in all other important matters, that you and ourselves should stand together. I devoutly hope that we can work this one out.[4]

With warm regard, *As ever*

[1] Harold Macmillan had been Foreign Secretary and Chancellor of the Exchequer before being named Prime Minister of Great Britain on January 10, 1957; for background see Galambos and van Ee, *The Middle Way*, nos. 2124 and 2164. The State Department drafted this cable.
[2] For background see no. 40. Macmillan had told Eisenhower that British public opinion strongly favored a fair settlement. "Of course we want the Israeli forces to be withdrawn so that all the efforts of the world can be directed to forcing Nasser to a reasonable settlement of the Canal in the short and in the long term. On the other hand, public opinion here will not allow us to do what they think is inequitable." Macmillan said that he understood Israel's hesitancy, "since Egypt has been in default over the resolutions dealing with Israeli shipping in the Canal for many years without any real action being taken against her" (Macmillan to Eisenhower, Feb. 22, 1957, AWF/I: Macmillan).
[3] In Eisenhower's February 20 address to the nation he had supported Israel's claim that the Gulf of Aqaba was an international waterway. He also said that the United States would work to assure that the Gaza Strip "could no longer be used as a source of armed infiltration and reprisals" (*Public Papers of the Presidents: Eisenhower, 1957*, pp. 147–56).
[4] For developments see no. 56.

47 — *EM, AWF, Name Series*

To Hugh Roy Cullen — *[February 23, 1957]*

Dear Roy:[1] Thank you for your letter about the natural gas legislation.[2] The bill that was drafted by the group representing the three segments of the industry—producers, pipelines, and distributing utilities—is presently being reviewed within the Executive Branch. When I have the comments of the interested agencies, I will then be in a position to determine what course to pursue.[3]

With best wishes, *Sincerely*

[1] Hugh Roy Cullen, Texas oil millionaire and philanthropist, was president of Quintana Petroleum Corporation (see Galambos, *Columbia University*, no. 602). White House aide Gerald D. Morgan drafted this letter for the President.
[2] Cullen had written Eisenhower on February 21, 1957 (AWF/N), to urge support for the natural gas legislation pending in Congress. Cullen favored the bill because it was "*a compromise of the views of all branches of the industry*" and afforded the consumer "*maximum protection.*" The new bill needed Eisenhower's active support if it was to be passed, Cullen wrote, saying that only a "strong statement" from the President in support of the bill "can prevent it from becoming a political football." Enactment of the legislation would "benefit the nation," Cullen said, by leading to the

development of additional reserves of natural gas "when the chaotic conditions arising from the present utility type regulation of the production of gas are corrected." Eisenhower had recommended new legislation to Congress following his veto of the Harris-Fulbright natural gas bill in 1956 due to the scandalous efforts by the oil industry to influence the Senate vote (see Galambos and van Ee, *The Middle Way*, no. 1763, 1748, and 1767).

In January 1957 the President had told Congress that "Legislation freeing gas producers from public utility-type regulation is essential if the incentives to find and develop new supplies of gas are to be preserved and sales of gas to interstate markets are not to be discouraged. . . . " The new gas legislation followed the 1956 bill in exempting independent producers and gatherers of natural gas from federal rate-of-return regulation, while empowering the Federal Power Commission (FPC) to regulate producer rates directly through approval of pipeline costs (see *Public Papers of the Presidents: Eisenhower, 1957*, p. 56; see also *Congressional Quarterly Almanac*, vol. XIII, *1957*, pp. 665–66; M. Elizabeth Sanders, *The Regulation of Natural Gas: Policy and Politics, 1938–1978* [Philadelphia, 1981], pp. 105–6; and Edith T. Carper, "Lobbying and the Natural Gas Bill" in *Case Studies in American Government*, Edwin A. Bock and Alan K. Campbell, eds. [N.J., 1962], pp. 175–222).

[3] For developments see no. 169.

48

EM, AWF,
Administration Series

TO NELSON ALDRICH ROCKEFELLER — *February 23, 1957*
Personal

Dear Nelson: Because she knew of my interest, Mrs. Whitman showed me the exchange of correspondence you had with a mutual friend of ours.[1] While I have never read the article referred to, I am familiar with its contents. I am delighted that you are continuing to take a friendly interest in an individual who, regardless of anything in the past, is obviously a sensitive character, devoted to his country and well informed in the international field.[2]

I personally think that the advice you gave him in your letter represents the wisest course, provided he finds it possible to follow it.[3]

For my part, I am truly grateful to you for being helpful in this situation, as you are in so many others.

With warm regard, *As ever*

[1] For background on former White House aide Rockefeller, see Galambos and van Ee, *The Middle Way*, no. 1203. Eisenhower was referring to Rockefeller's contacts with Arthur H. Vandenberg, Jr., son of the late Republican Senator Arthur H. Vandenberg. For background on the younger Vandenberg, who had served as the national chairman of the Citizens for Eisenhower Committee in 1952, see *ibid.*, no. 1183.

[2] Vandenberg, who had previously served as a consultant to Nelson Rockefeller in the International Basic Economy Corporation, had written Rockefeller in mid-

January (AWF/A, Rockefeller Corr.) stating that his life had been "grievously upset" following a "smear" in *Confidential* magazine. Vandenberg explained that he had felt compelled to resign from his position as instructor in international relations at the University of Miami due to the "nearly ruinous impact" of the affair on his "nerves and health." Furthermore, he now found himself financially obliged to sell his house at a loss. See also *New York Times*, September 26, 1956.

[3] Rockefeller had responded to Vandenberg (Jan. 17, 1957, AWF/A) that "few people have as good a background as do you" in international affairs. He suggested that Vandenberg attempt to return to the university. "You might also consider publishing some of your lectures," Rockefeller wrote, and "do more in the way of writing articles commenting on current events." Rockefeller suggested that Vandenberg would have greater security in the long run if he sold the house and moved "into an apartment in one of the new attractive buildings which seem to be going up all over Miami." Vandenberg would not, however, return to the university; he worked as a public relations consultant until his death on January 18, 1968 (*New York Times*, Jan. 19, 1968).

49 *EM, AWF, Name Series*

To Lucille Dawson Eisenhower *February 25, 1957*

Dear Lucy: Thank you for your very fine explanation of Edgar's present condition and attitude.[1] I was interested in Dr. Baldwin's statement to the effect that Edgar can be helped only through his own good sense and actions.[2]

As to this matter of rest, I am not sure whether you are talking about seclusion for days at a time or for a certain period each day. If the latter is the case, I will give you a little personal experience.

After the doctors dismissed me from the hospital in November of last year, following upon my coronary occlusion, I was instructed to rest, flat on my back, for at least thirty minutes in the middle of each day.[3] The preferable period was one hour. This was to be done before lunch rather than after. The reason for this last instruction is more mental than physical, because when one is merely waiting for lunch he is not thinking of the appointment back at his office or the papers on which he wants to get to work.

When I first started this habit I found it more than irksome. It seemed to me that lying flat for one hour was not only a sheer waste of time, but was most irritating. But because I felt I owed it to my position to follow the doctors' orders, I stuck with it religiously, and the strange thing is that now I find it no chore at all. I really feel I profit from it and far from resenting it, I would rather miss my lunch than miss my noon day rest. I frequently go to sleep and when I get up, I eat the very lightest of luncheons. For example, I have a small bowl of cottage cheese ground and whipped up in a Waring mixer until it is like ice cream, and a bowl of fruit salad. The point of reciting this is that it is not too difficult to train oneself, even at Ed's age and mine, to a new custom.

Incidentally, my doctors also told me that if I had started this habit ten years ago, I never would have had a heart attack.

I thoroughly understand your problem in trying to get Edgar to do anything that is good for him. Like other Eisenhowers, he is both stubborn and somewhat emotional, but I do hope he is not falling prey to the terrible disease of self-pity. If he could just find a doctor that he trusted implicitly and put all his present worries on the doctor's shoulders, he probably would have little trouble in adjusting himself to necessary habits.

As far as Walter Reed is concerned, I could, of course, have him go into that hospital for a check-up and advice.[4] It is a very fine institution. On the other hand, I could not put him in there for any long treatment—that would be unethical, if not illegal.

I can promise you, though, that while there he would get the finest possible care and the best advice that could be given him. I am not certain whether they have an outstanding man in the neurological area, but they are certain to have a competent one.

I am delighted that you had a chance to meet Howard Pyle and Edgar to meet Ben Fairless.[5] Both are my warm friends, individuals that I admire a lot.

I have been suffering with a very annoying and irritating bronchitis, which the doctors now describe as "chronic."[6] This scares the living daylights out of me because it sounds as if I would have to go through something like this every once in a while. If I do, I will surely be in an awful fix because at times I cough until my face gets purple.

Mamie went to Walter Reed three or four days ago for an examination and has stayed there for a rest the past three days, but I think she is coming home today.[7] Fortunately the doctors found she was in her customary health. As you know, her heart is not a good one but at least she is no worse.

You might remind Ed that he once told me when I was dealing with legal things to consult a lawyer and, presumably, follow his advice. If he would now do the same with the doctors, he would probably be better off.

Give my best to him and, of course, affectionate regard to yourself. *As ever*

[1] The President's sister-in-law had written on February 23 (AWF/N). For background on Edgar's health see no. 4. Lucy Eisenhower explained that Edgar suffered from braxial neuritis, a painful, but temporary condition. "Edgar's other problem," she wrote, "is his nerves. He is tense to the point of breaking, and it's impossible for me to get him away from people for the rest he should have."

[2] We have been unable to identify Dr. Baldwin.
[3] Eisenhower had suffered a coronary thrombosis in September 1955. On his hospitalization and convalescence see Galambos and van Ee, *The Middle Way.*
[4] Mrs. Eisenhower said they would travel to New York City in mid-April. Perhaps, she suggested, the President would encourage Edgar to "come to Washington, and *enter Walter Reed.*" The Edgar Eisenhowers would visit Washington, D.C., April 16 and 17 (see the President's daily appointments). For developments see no. 117.
[5] Former Governor of Arizona Howard Pyle had been Deputy Assistant to the President since 1955 (for background see *Eisenhower Papers,* vols. XIV–XVII). Mrs. Eisenhower had met him while lunching and playing golf at a club in Phoenix, Arizona. U.S. Steel President Benjamin Franklin Fairless was coordinator of the President's Citizens Advisors on the Mutual Security Program (for background see *Eisenhower Papers,* vols. XII–XVII). Edgar and Fairless had met by chance, Mrs. Eisenhower wrote, and "they immediately formed a mutual admiration society."
[6] The bronchial condition would persist until spring. For developments see nos. 84 and 105.
[7] The First Lady had entered the hospital on February 22 for a routine checkup (*New York Times,* Feb. 23, 24, 26, 1957).

50 — *EM, AWF, Name Series*

To Howard McCrum Snyder, Sr. — *February 26, 1957*

Dear Howard: My friend, Mr. William E. Robinson, tells me that you are to take part in the Diamond Jubilee Convocation of the University Hospital of the New York University-Bellevue Medical Center, on March fourth and fifth.[1] I hear that your topic will be "The Conservation of Human Resources," a subject that we have discussed many times over a span of more than ten years.

When our wartime experience was still fresh and stark in memory, you and I started talking on the urgent need for a thorough study of America's human resources and for a comprehensive approach to their conservation.[2]

In time, with the help of many others equally concerned about minds and skills wasted or neglected or ill-used, we were able to do one thing that has proved realistic and far reaching—the establishment of the Conservation of Human Resources project at Columbia University.[3]

As you review its development, you can report great progress in our knowledge of the mistakes we have made heretofore and in our understanding of what must be done to correct and to use better all the talents of our people, for the good of the individual himself and of the Republic.

A substantial start has been made. But an ever sharper awareness is needed that our nation's strength is rooted in the minds, in the creative talents, in the ingenuity and genius of our people. This mighty resource we dare not waste; rather we must use it fully and wisely, if we are to continue prosperous and strong, able to work for peace.

The theme of the Convocation—"The Hope of Mankind—Health and Peace"—crystallizes our talking and thinking of more than ten years ago. I know that in your discussion of Human Resources within that framework, you will increase the consciousness of an important national responsibility, and the will, among our people, to discharge it.

With best wishes to all who are participating in this important Convocation, and warm personal regard, *As ever*

[1] Eisenhower had written Coca-Cola Company President Robinson on February 2, saying that he would "be glad to write a note to Howard Snyder concerning the Conservation of Human Resources Project," presumably for use at the convocation (AWF/D). White House Special Assistant Kevin McCann drafted this letter for the President.

[2] See, for example, Galambos, *Chief of Staff*, no. 1882.

[3] Eisenhower's concern about this issue stemmed from the critical manpower shortages faced during World War II. The military had rejected many potential soldiers as unfit for service, and the resulting shortages had been aggravated by combat-induced psychological breakdowns. Shortly after assuming the presidency of Columbia University, Eisenhower met with economist Eli Ginzberg and appointed him director of what would become the Conservation of Human Resources Project (for background see Galambos, *Columbia University*, nos. 155, 300, 481, and 945). Snyder, Eisenhower's personal physician, had been senior adviser to the project.

51 — *EM, AWF, Administration Series*

To Hugh Meade Alcorn, Jr. — *February 27, 1957*

Dear Mr. Alcorn: I am delighted to know of the plans you are formulating to conduct a series of regional meetings of Republican Party leaders and workers. It is truly encouraging to know that your basic purpose is to get personally acquainted with local Party leaders and to make certain that the hopes, aspirations and ideals of the Republican Party as expressed by the workers and members in the field will be accurately reflected in all Party plans and programs.[1]

This direct contact with the individuals who make up the Republican Party throughout the nation will assure that the Voice of the People is truly the voice of the Republican Party. This will be an auspicious start in the all-important task of electing a Republican Senate and a Republican House of Representatives in 1958.[2]

Your program has my warmhearted endorsement and I wish you and every participant in each conference all possible success.

With warm personal regard, *Sincerely*

[1] Recently elected Republican National Committee Chairman Alcorn had addressed the Cabinet on February 8 concerning his hope to use such groups as Citizens for Eisenhower-Nixon to strengthen the party organization prior to the 1958 elections (see Cabinet meeting minutes, Feb. 8, 1957, AWF/D). Alcorn had also conferred with Eisenhower for almost an hour on February 27. Plans for six regional fact-finding conferences to launch the 1958 congressional election drive would be announced on March 11 (*New York Times*, Mar. 12, 1957).

[2] In fact, the Democrats would sweep the 1958 congressional elections. For developments see no. 942.

52 — *EM, AWF, Dulles-Herter Series*

To John Foster Dulles — *February 27, 1957*

Dear Foster: Mr. Wright Morrow, of Texas, came to my office today to request consideration for appointment as Ambassador to Mexico in the event that that office should become vacant. Mr. Morrow is a successful Texas businessman and at one time was National Committeeman of the Democratic Party from that State.[1] In both the 1952 and 1956 elections, he publicly supported me for the Presidency—and because of this was dropped as Democratic National Committeeman. Because of these circumstances I had assumed that Senator Lyndon Johnson would personally object to any appointment of Mr. Morrow requiring Senatorial confirmation. Mr. Morrow assures me that this is not now the case.[2]

He has spent much time in Mexico and says that some years ago he was offered the Ambassadorship to Belgium or Holland, but has not previously held an Ambassadorial post.

He is of the personal belief that he would be particularly acceptable to President Ruiz Cortines and to other Mexican officials.

I merely told him that I did not know whether we expected a vacancy to occur soon or not, but that I would convey to you his aspirations and feelings in the matter.[3]

I will talk further to you about this when I see you. *As ever*

[1] For background on Morrow see Galambos, *NATO and the Campaign of 1952*, no. 313; and Galambos and van Ee, *The Middle Way*, no. 1029.

[2] Johnson, a Texas Democrat, was the Senate Majority Leader and Chairman of the Democratic Policy Committee.

[3] For developments see no. 62.

53 EM, AWF, Administration Series

To William Fife Knowland February 28, 1957

Dear Senator Knowland: I appreciate your request for my views on the amendment which would strike economic and military assistance provisions from the Middle East Resolution.[1]

Elimination of these features would gravely impair our ability to help these nations preserve their independence. The Resolution is directed against two dangers, direct armed aggression and indirect subversion. To counter one and not the other would destroy both efforts.

This I emphasize once again: We cannot wage peace with American arms alone. We must understand other national needs. We must respond to human wants. We must help nations and peoples satisfy those needs and wants in order to wage peace successfully.

The pending amendment ignores the danger of subversion. This we must not do. These nations need effective security forces. Their peoples need hope for improving economic conditions. The present Resolution serves these ends. Thus economic and military assistance provisions are more than desirable. They are essential to our efforts to bring peace to this area.

I trust it is clearly understood that these provisions do not make available one additional dollar. They simply authorize us to adapt these funds to the new conditions resulting from recent military action in the area and its economic consequences. It is hardly reasonable to insist that these funds, which are already appropriated, be spent only for programs approved before such drastic changes occurred.

And this I consider even more serious—the world-wide interpretation of such action. Approval of the amendment would suggest that our country wants only to wage peace in terms of war. This is neither the purpose nor the spirit of our nation's foreign policy. I should deplore any action by the Senate that could give the world a contrary impression.[2] *Sincerely*

[1] For background on the resolution for military and economic aid to Middle Eastern nations (the Eisenhower Doctrine) see Galambos and van Ee, *The Middle Way*, no. 2155. Congressional conflict had arisen over an amendment proposed by Senator Richard Brevard Russell (Dem., Ga.) that would have eliminated an authorization to sustain the program with $200 million in previously appropriated funds (*Congressional Quarterly Almanac*, vol. XIII, *1957*, pp. 573–79; see also George to Dulles, Jan. 23, 1957, Dulles Personal Papers). On the preceding day Senate Minority Leader Knowland (Rep., Calif.), who supported the original resolution and opposed the amendment, had told Secretary Dulles that a "well-written letter" from the President to Knowland "might make the difference" in the upcoming vote. The Secretary subsequently drafted this letter (Telephone conversation, Dulles and Knowland, Feb. 27,

1957, Dulles Papers, Telephone Conversations; see also Telephone conversations, Dulles and Johnson, Feb. 26, 1957; Dulles and Persons, Feb. 27, 1957; Dulles and Harlow, Feb. 28, 1957, *ibid.*; and Ann Whitman memorandum, Feb. 27, 1957, AWF/AWD).

[2] On March 2, after hearing this letter read, the Senate would defeat the Russell amendment and pass the resolution. Eisenhower would sign the legislation on March 9.

54

EM, AWF, International Series: Saudi Arabia

To ibn Abd al-Aziz Saud — *February 28, 1957*

Cable. Secret

Your Majesty:[1] As Your Majesty knows, we have continued since your departure from Washington to exert every effort to achieve the withdrawal of Israel behind the Armistice line.[2] As I informed you, and as I reaffirmed in my address to the Nation on February 20, we have been prepared to support the United Nations in bringing pressure upon Israel to withdraw.[3] At the same time we have endeavored to persuade the Israeli Government that it should avoid the necessity of such United Nations action by deciding itself to comply with the resolutions. We have had in mind that even with a United Nations resolution imposing sanctions, the withdrawal might be long delayed. In this connection, you will recall that the United States made public on February 20 its Aide Memoire of February 11 setting forth its attitude concerning various aspects of the matter in the hope that Israel would, without receiving gains from her invasion, proceed with this withdrawal.[4]

I am pleased that Israel has stated today its intention to announce to the General Assembly tomorrow that it will withdraw immediately.[5] As we understand it, the withdrawal will be unconditional and Israel will state that the decision was made on certain assumptions and expectations. These we understand, relate to the role of the United Nations in the Sharm el Shaikh and Gaza areas in accordance with pertinent resolutions of the General Assembly and reports of the Secretary General. We also understand that Israel will state its inherent right under Article 51 of the Charter to protect its interests with respect to incursions from Gaza and armed interference with the international use of the Straits.

I am asking the Secretary of State to pass on to Your Majesty further information as the situation unfolds, as I want you to be fully informed concerning developments and our attitude regarding them. I want to reassure you that our position is as Secretary Dulles and I described it to you, and as the United States government has stated publicly. We continue to be disturbed by reports from the Middle East which indicate some misunderstanding of our attitude. We are making every effort to make the truth known and hope Your Majesty will continue your own efforts in this direction. I am hopeful that, after long delays since the military operation against Egypt began, the continued occupation by Israel of territory beyond the Armistice line will now be ended. It will of course be incumbent upon all of us then to work towards solutions of other difficult problems.

May I take this opportunity to express to Your Majesty my sincere appreciation for the position which you took at the Cairo conference, as you kindly explained to the American Ambassador.[6] It is indeed gratifying that our common interests are so well understood by Your Majesty and that this understanding manifests itself in your relationship with the other Arab states.

With kindest personal regards and great respect,[7] *Sincerely*

[1] The State Department drafted this letter for the President. Secretary Dulles asked Eisenhower for the authority "to send it as soon as the situation firms up, with such minor modifications as intervening events make appropriate" (Dulles to Eisenhower, Feb. 28, 1957, AWF/I: Saudi Arabia; see also State, *Foreign Relations, 1955–1957*, vol. XVII, *Arab-Israeli Dispute, 1957*, p. 310).

[2] For background on King Saud's visit see no. 13; on the Israeli withdrawal see no. 40.

[3] Eisenhower had written to King Saud on February 14 (see no. 37). His address is in *Public Papers of the Presidents: Eisenhower, 1957*, pp. 147–56.

[4] On the aide-mémoire see no. 40.

[5] Prior to a meeting in Secretary Dulles's office, Ambassador Abba Eban had announced that the Israeli delegation would make the statement. Eban reviewed the text of the Israeli declaration with Dulles and other State Department officials, who made a number of modifications and corrections, including a clarification of the United Nations Emergency Force's function (State, *Foreign Relations, 1955–1957*, vol. XVII, *Arab-Israeli Dispute, 1957*, pp. 311–17; see also Telephone conversation, Dulles and Lodge, Feb. 28, 1957, Dulles Papers, Telephone Conversations).

[6] At a conference of the leaders of Egypt, Syria, Jordan, and Saudi Arabia, King Saud had reported that during his recent talks with President Eisenhower and Administration officials he had found the United States more tolerant of neutralism and more willing to concede that there were two sides to the Arab-Israeli dispute than he had previously believed (*New York Times*, Feb. 26, 1957). Raymond Arthur Hare had been U.S. Ambassador to Egypt since September 1956.

[7] The President added the preceding three words to the original draft (Whitman to Bernau, Feb. 28, 1957, AWF/I: Saudi Arabia).

55 *EM, AWF, Gettysburg Series*

To Herman R. Purdy *March 1, 1957*

Dear Dr. Purdy: General Nevins sent to me your letter of the 26th, and since he is leaving on a trip of some two or three weeks, I am replying to you directly.[1]

I would like to purchase the three heifers mentioned, and I am enclosing with this note two checks: (1) to W. L. Henning, for $1,500, in payment for the granddaughter of Homeplace Eileenmere 99935.[2] General Nevins and Bob Hartley are appreciative of your suggestion that you keep her until after she calves and then re-breed her to your 32nd bull.[3] (2) Check for $1,000 in payment of the Blackbird heifer #279 and the daughter of Bardoliermere H55. This check is made payable to The Pennsylvania State University.

I assume that you will be in touch with Bob Hartley about the necessary papers; incidentally, the cows should be re-registered in the name of "The Eisenhower Farms."[4] And once again I am indebted to you for the interest you take in my Angus herd.

With warm regard, *Sincerely*

P.S. I am delighted you had the opportunity to see my apartment at Culzean Castle.[5]

[1] Purdy had written to Eisenhower's farm manager. Nevins was traveling to Asheville, North Carolina; Tyler, Texas; and Carthage, Illinois (see Nevins to Whitman, Feb. 27, 1957, and undated memo, both in AWF/Gettysburg).

[2] For background on the heifers see nos. 10 and 15. Pennsylvania Secretary of Agriculture W. L. Henning owned Nittany Farms.

[3] Purdy had suggested that Nevins consult with Hartley, who was Eisenhower's herdsman (see Purdy to Nevins, Feb. 26; Nevins to Whitman, Feb. 27; and Nevins to Purdy, Feb. 27, 1957, all in AWF/Gettysburg).

[4] On March 14 (*ibid.*) Henning would notify the President that the Eileenmere heifer was registered to the Eisenhower Farms. For developments see no. 70.

[5] In 1945 the National Trust for Scotland had presented a portion of Culzean Castle in Ayrshire, Scotland, to General Eisenhower as a token of Scotland's admiration and appreciation for his wartime leadership (for background see Chandler and Galambos, *Occupation, 1945*, no. 444; and *Eisenhower Papers*, vols. VI–XIII).

56 *EM, AWF, International Series: Israel*

To David Ben Gurion *March 2, 1957*
Cable. Confidential

My dear Mr. Prime Minister: I was indeed deeply gratified at the decision of your Government to withdraw promptly and fully behind the Armistice lines as set out by your Foreign Minister in her address of yesterday to the General Assembly.[1] I venture to express the hope that the carrying out of these withdrawals will go forward with the utmost speed.

I know that this decision was not an easy one.[2] I believe, however, that Israel will have no cause to regret having thus conformed to the strong sentiment of the world community as expressed in the various United Nations Resolutions relating to withdrawal.

It has always been the view of this Government that after the withdrawal there should be a united effort by all of the nations to bring about conditions in the area more stable, more tranquil, and more conducive to the general welfare than those which existed heretofore. Already the United Nations General Assembly has adopted Resolutions which presage such a better future. Hopes and expectations based thereon were voiced by your Foreign Minister and others. I believe that it is reasonable to entertain such hopes and expectations and I want you to know that the United States, as a friend of all the countries of the area and as a loyal member of the United Nations, will seek that such hopes prove not to be vain.[3]

I am, my dear Mr. Prime Minister, *Sincerely*

[1] On March 1, during the 666th plenary meeting of the General Assembly, Israel's Foreign Minister Golda Meir had announced the withdrawal. See no. 54 for background.

[2] Prime Minister Ben Gurion had called Meir less than three hours before the scheduled announcement, asking for a delay because of the delicate situation. According to Israeli officials, Meir told Ben Gurion that his proposal, which had been motivated by internal political pressures, "was just not in the cards" (State, *Foreign Relations, 1955–1957,* vol. XVII, *Arab-Israeli Dispute, 1957,* p. 337; see also Alteras, *Eisenhower and Israel,* pp. 273–81).

[3] For developments see no. 72.

57

EM, AWF, DDE Diaries Series

DIARY

March 5, 1957

Phoned Harold Macmillan (see note from Secretary Dulles dated 3/5/57).[1] He expressed the belief that the matter (of the reduction of British forces in NATO) would not be finally determined by the British government until after the Bermuda meeting, but that he could not at this time reverse his position. The plan is to reduce the British force on the continent from 80,000 to 50,000 over a period of two years.[2] Macmillan implied that Norstad had approved of this plan.[3]

[1] Dulles had told Eisenhower that a "critical situation" had developed because of "British insistence on a sharp and early reduction of their NATO forces" to numbers far below the commitment they had made in 1954. Dulles had suggested that Eisenhower ask Prime Minister Macmillan to postpone a final decision until the two men could discuss the matter during their meetings in Bermuda (Dulles to Eisenhower, Mar. 5, 1957, AWF/I: Macmillan). On the Bermuda meetings, which would begin on March 21, see no. 78.

[2] Eisenhower told Macmillan that such an announcement would give him problems "because the US participation in NATO is based on the so-called Fair Share formula, and there are people in this country—there is always a section here—that is totally against such participation, and always wants to cut down." Although Macmillan said that the troop reduction "was necessary because they were not solvent," he agreed not to "push the matter" (Telephone conversations, Eisenhower and Macmillan, and Eisenhower and Dulles, Mar. 5, 1957, AWF/D; see also State, *Foreign Relations, 1955–1957*, vol. XXVII, *Western Europe and Canada*, pp. 694–96; on Britain's economic problems see Galambos and van Ee, *The Middle Way*, nos. 2106 and 2124A).

[3] For background on General Lauris Norstad, Supreme Allied Commander in Europe since November 1956, see Galambos and van Ee, *The Middle Way*, nos. 954 and 1832. According to Secretary Dulles, Norstad had indicated that in light of the magnitude of the reductions, he was not certain he could carry out his duties (Telephone conversation, Eisenhower and Dulles, Feb. 5, 1957, AWF/D).

Hoping to clear up any misapprehension, Macmillan cabled Eisenhower later on this same day. Claiming that he was "up against a rigid timetable," he said that he had to prepare both a defense white paper and the budget before leaving for Bermuda. Macmillan also noted that the British government had tried to address General Norstad's concerns by spreading out the reductions over a two-year period. "I earnestly hope," the Prime Minister concluded, "that in these circumstances it will be possible for the United States Government at least not to query our proposals. I am sure that this will make all the difference to our chances of getting a quick and satisfactory conclusion on which our whole economy depends" (AWF/I: Macmillan). For developments see no. 98.

58 *EM, AWF, Administration Series*

To Herbert Brownell, Jr. *March 6, 1957*

Memorandum for the Attorney General: I have two questions with respect to the attached:[1]

(*a*) Section 2 and Section 3 declare that the President must state certain things "in writing." Under the conditions visualized in Section 2, it could well be that the President could not actually write.[2]

(*b*) In the attached explanation it states on page two, "The first covers a case in which the President himself declares his inability, and the second applies to a case in which he is unable to declare his inability." I can find nothing whatsoever in any of the Sections or the proposed article that relates to the second of these cases. I cannot even find that it is implied, although I am aware that you assure me it was so implied.[3]

[1] Brownell had first discussed the question of presidential disability with Eisenhower following the President's heart attack in September 1955 (for background see Galambos and van Ee, *The Middle Way*, no. 1595). During a meeting at Fitzsimons Army Hospital in Denver, the President had asked Brownell what would happen under the Constitution if his illness were prolonged and emergencies arose requiring immediate action (see Brownell, *Advising Ike*, p. 274). Brownell prepared a preliminary study of a constitutional amendment and presented it to Eisenhower upon his return to Washington. Congressional hearings on the matter began shortly thereafter, but no action would be taken before the end of the Eighty-Fourth Congress (see *Congressional Quarterly Almanac*, vol. XII, *1956*, p. 591).

On January 25, 1957, Brownell had submitted to Eisenhower the "final form" of his recommendations for a Constitutional Amendment on Presidential Disability (AWF/A). He proposed that the Vice-President should be "Acting President" only during the period the President was ill; that the President himself ought to be able to declare in writing his inability to exercise the powers of his office; and that the President should be able later to declare in writing his ability to resume his duties. Because a situation in which the President would be physically unable to declare himself disabled presented greater legal complexities, the Justice Department delayed reaching a conclusion on procedures (Cabinet meeting minutes, Feb. 8, 1957, AWF/D). We have been unable to locate in AWF the particular version of the amendment on which Eisenhower was commenting.

[2] Section 2 of the proposed constitutional amendment as presented to Congress (see Statement of the Attorney General on Presidential Inability, April 1, 1957, AWF/A) stated that "If the President shall declare in writing that he is unable to discharge the powers and duties of his office, such power and duties shall be discharged by the Vice-President as Acting President." Section 3 stated that "If the President does not so declare, the Vice President, if satisfied of the President's inability, and upon approval in writing of a majority of the heads of executive departments who are members of the President's Cabinet, shall discharge the powers and duties of the office as Acting President." Section 4 stated that "Whenever the President declares in writing that his inability is terminated, the President shall forthwith discharge the powers and duties of his office." For further background see Herbert L. Abrams, "Shielding the President from the Constitution: Disability and the 25th Amendment," *Presidential Studies Quarterly*, vol. XXIII, no. 3 (Summer 1993), pp. 533–53.

[3] For developments see no. 107.

59 *EM, AWF, Name Series*

To William Edward Robinson *March 6, 1957*

Dear Bill: Today I had a "surprise party" at the south entrance to the White House. Mamie seemed to be master of ceremonies, but the guest of honor was the old Cadillac that I started using in England in the spring of '44 and finally was forced to abandon to the Army in the summer of '52.[1] Mr. Heller of the Abilene Museum was at the party to take charge of the car and put it in a suitable showcase at the Museum.[2]

For all of this I am told you are responsible—that you started the quest many months ago and had to follow it persistently before you finally got hold of the original car and could buy it from the Army.[3]

I cannot tell you how touched I am by this additional evidence of your continued concern for me and my welfare—even my whims. I am truly grateful.

Incidentally, you will be glad to know that the Cadillac Company did a wonderful job of refurbishing the car to put it back in the condition it was when I first used it, during the war. It is in the original O.D.[4] color, with the five stars front and rear, and the flags of the United States, Britain and France decorating the radiator cap. The inside has been completely rebuilt and I imagine the car could start out on a fifty thousand mile trip right now with every prospect of finishing it successfully.[5]

Some day perhaps you and I can go out together and look over the Museum and see the car in its "permanent" home.

With warm regard, *As ever*

[1] Eisenhower had received the 1942 Cadillac sedan at his European headquarters in October 1944. He had used the car while serving as Army Chief of Staff, President of Columbia University, and Supreme Commander, Allied Forces, Europe. In 1952 Eisenhower had retired from the Army in order to participate in Republican preconvention activities (see Chandler, *War Years*, no. 2082; Galambos, *NATO and the Campaign of 1952*, no. 952; see also Ann Whitman memorandum, Mar. 6, 1957, AWF/AWD, and *New York Times*, Mar. 7, 1957).

[2] Sam Raymond Heller, a local business executive, served as president of the Eisenhower Foundation from 1951 until 1969.

[3] Robinson and "anonymous friends" had purchased the car from the U.S. Army motor pool at an auction in Germany (see Schulz to Snyder, Feb. 7, 1957; Snyder to Schulz, Feb. 14, 1957; and Gruenther to Wilson, Feb. 13, 1957, all in WHCF/PPF 42-A).

[4] Olive drab.

[5] On March 9 (AWF/N) Robinson would reply that the car was in "perfect mechanical condition." Eisenhower's thank-you letters to the Cadillac executives and others who assisted in obtaining the car are in AWF/N, Robinson Corr.

60 — *EM, AWF, Administration Series*

To Paul Gray Hoffman — *March 8, 1957*

Dear Paul:[1] I read your study carefully and then sent it to George Humphrey for comment.[2] I will be interested in his reaction.

Fundamentally, there is now going on in our country a great struggle between two schools of thought. One holds that, regardless of reasons, government is spending far too much money, requiring a taxation rate that is unbearable and not consistent with the need for accumulating capital to provide new jobs. This particular school stoutly maintains that *all* government spending should be curtailed on the theory that if carried on at the present rate, we are certain to end up with a controlled economy—some form of socialism. Consequently we would lose what we are trying to defend.[3]

The other school of thought maintains that this is a very critical time in the world's political history and that if we fail to do all those things which will tend to bind the free world more tightly together in firm opposition to Communistic effort, we will eventually be destroyed. All the defense experts belong to this school, as do countless others. However, this particular group is divided into two parts. On the one hand are those who want to put a lot of extra money in the organisms of war; the other is a school that wants to spend more and more for humanitarian reasons both at home and abroad.[4]

A day or so ago the President of the United States Rubber Company—for the moment his name slips my mind—made a speech representative of the thinking of the economy-minded boys. It was a bitter speech, charging the Administration with outdoing the New Dealers in the spending of people's money and so on and so on.[5]

Frankly, I classify myself with those that oppose the kind of government spending in which we are now indulging, but I get very tired of reading such criticisms when they are, at the same time, barren of specific recommendations as to where appropriations should be cut. Our money goes for interest on the public debt, for veterans, for farmers, for a myriad of grants-in-aid to States for humanitarian purposes, and for aid to other nations. Aside from this, almost the whole goes into security activities.

Politically the critics seem to be afraid to tackle the farmers, the veterans and the welfare activities—but they are frightened to suggest real cuts in the defensive arrangements. So they have only one target—"foreign aid."

You and I have been over this subject time after time.[6] We are agreed that there is much short-sightedness and a deal of demagoguery apparent in the attitudes of "isolationists." But the fact is that people engage in demagoguery only when they *think* their words will be publicly acclaimed.

So—we must:

(*a*) Be sound, sensible and clear in every proposal we make.

(*b*) Organize to show the people of the United States how sound and sensible investment in foreign economies helps us both in the short-term and in the long-term sense.

(*c*) Do the same to show how such expenditures increase our national security and the prospects of peace more than do *excessive* expenditures on armaments.

(*d*) Avoid useless or wasteful foreign expenditures like the plague.

(*e*) Have the courage to postpone desirable, but not immediately necessary, projects until implementation does not tend to push up prices in a tight money market.[7]

For everything we do, we must have broad, simple, easily understood plans. The whole problem is complicated by needless difficulties in the international world. For example, the recent closing of the Canal and the blowing up of the pipe lines across Syria have imposed upon us great burdens. Knowing that to allow the British pound to deteriorate markedly would endanger the economy of the free world, we have had to do the things necessary to bolster it. It is a real burden; and the whole affair need never have happened.[8]

At the same time we, with large military commitments abroad, have to keep large forces and to make great expenditures in Europe, an area which because of its population, culture and intellectual level of its people, should now need no help from abroad.

There are many other instances where it would appear that with better cooperation in the world, needless expenditures could be cut down and make greater amounts available for constructive purposes.

What I am trying to say is that both at home and abroad political and emotional factors often play too large a part in complicated problems where fact, logic and good sense should be controlling.

That is enough of all this—most of it you have studied over and over again.[9]

With warm regard, *As ever*

[1] Hoffman, a long-time friend and political adviser to Eisenhower, had been chairman of the board of the Studebaker-Packard Corporation, a former president of the Ford Foundation, and a member of the U.S. delegation to the United Nations from 1956–1957 (see Galambos and van Ee, *The Middle Way*, no. 61).

[2] Hoffman had written the President on February 25 (AWF/A) to forward a copy of his February 17 *New York Times* article entitled "Blueprint for Foreign Aid." Drawing on Eisenhower's Inaugural Address, Hoffman had set forth a program that he hoped would enable "one-third of all mankind" to achieve "a new freedom: freedom from grinding poverty" (see *Public Papers of the Presidents: Eisenhower, 1957*, pp. 60–65). Proposing a new "Marshall" plan for the underdeveloped areas of the world, Hoffman wrote, "The plan is practical because it calls for no funds in addition to those already requested for foreign aid in 1958." The program would, moreover, substantially increase U.S. prestige in the United Nations while also "strengthening the position of the United Nations with the member states." Hoffman cautioned Eisenhower that it would be necessary to engage in a substantial educational campaign to sell the plan to Congress. On March 7 Eisenhower had sent the article to Secretary of the Treasury Humphrey saying, "Although I know you have some reservations about the judgment of the author of the attached article, I hope that you will read it. I believe that it represents a very good case for the general principle of economic aid to under-developed areas, even though you need not necessarily agree in detail with the suggested approach" (AWF/A).

[3] See, for example, Galambos and van Ee, *The Middle Way*, no. 1861.

[4] For more on this issue see *ibid.*, nos. 977 and 1147, and Eisenhower, *Waging Peace*, pp. 127–36.

[5] Harry Elmer Humphreys, Jr., president of U.S. Rubber since 1949, had criticized the Administration's tax and spend policies in a speech (Mar. 7) before the annual meeting of the Associated Business Publications (*New York Times*, Mar. 8, 1957). Charging the Administration with reverting to "'the taxing and spending philosophy and policies of the past,'" Humphreys stated that big government with "'its excessive spending, huge national debt, inflation, runaway welfare plans, threatened controls and progress-stifling back-breaking tax load, is still with us.'"
[6] See, for example, Galambos and van Ee, *The Middle Way*, nos. 404 and 1870.
[7] In his March 7 news conference the President had rejected the idea of trimming the federal budget by cutting foreign aid or abandoning other projects the Administration considered vital. Concerned over the rising cost of living, Eisenhower had suggested that the government "vary the speed" of its expenditures in order to "take that much pressure off this rising curve" of inflation (*Public Papers of the Presidents: Eisenhower, 1957*, pp. 174–75, and *New York Times*, Mar. 8, 1957).
[8] See Galambos and van Ee, *The Middle Way*, nos. 2057, 2078, 2106, and 2124A.
[9] Hoffman would respond on March 22, 1957 (AWF/A). Thanking the President for the "consideration" he was giving to the proposal, Hoffman further stressed that "there literally is no way in which federal expenditures can be reduced to a comfortable level until world tensions are so lessened that military expenditures can be sharply cut." What was needed was to "force a change of policy on the part of the Russians," a goal Hoffman believed we now "have a historic opportunity to start toward." Hoffman again emphasized the problem of organizing public opinion in support of a program of economic aid for the "underdeveloped" countries, since "economic aid as an abstraction is unsalable."

61 — *EM, AWF, Dulles-Herter Series*

To Christian Archibald Herter — *March 8, 1957*

Memorandum for the Acting Secretary of State:[1] Herewith a copy of a letter I have just received from the Prime Minister of Holland, handed to me this morning by the Ambassador from that country.[2] In addition to the statements made in the letter, the Ambassador verbally made the point that Holland was a very good customer of America's and has an annual trade deficit of some three hundred million dollars with us. He said also that Holland was going to great lengths to carry out her obligations in NATO, even increasing her defense expenditures this year by some twelve to fifteen percent. This, he said, is being done in the face of a very threatening inflation.

Because Holland has an annual trade deficit in the exchange of goods, it is necessary that it perform services to the world. One of its most important is in the operation of KLM.

The Dutch government is very hopeful that we will take all of these factors into consideration when our negotiating teams meet on March 19th and that we will not allow ourselves to be influenced too much by factors exclusively pertaining to civil aviation. He made the additional point that the German, British and Scandinavian Airlines enjoy privileges in our country of the type that Holland seeks.[3]

[1] For background on Herter, Under Secretary of State since February 21, see Galambos and van Ee, *The Middle Way,* no. 933. Secretary Dulles was in Australia for the South East Asia Treaty Organization (SEATO) Council meeting.

This letter was also sent to Attorney General Herbert Brownell, who would tell Eisenhower that the Justice Department had not been asked to participate in the negotiations. At the top of his response, telling Eisenhower that the issue was "exclusively in the hands of the State Department," Ann Whitman had written "all my fault" (Brownell to Eisenhower, Mar. 8, 1957, AWF/A).

[2] Dr. Willem Drees, Prime Minister of the Netherlands, had asked that Eisenhower give "special attention" to the negotiations between his country and the United States that were scheduled to begin in Washington on March 19. The Dutch were trying to replace a temporary arrangement regulating air routes between the two countries with a permanent civil air agreement. They also sought the expansion of KLM Royal Dutch Airline service in the United States to include stops in Los Angeles, Miami, and Houston. "The special geographic and demographic situation of my country, its limited natural resources," Drees said, "require that the Netherlands maintain its historic position as a world carrier, if it is to pull its weight as a sound member of the Western Alliance" (Drees to Eisenhower, Feb. 28, 1957, AWF/I: Netherlands; see also State, *Foreign Relations, 1955–1957,* vol. IX, *Foreign Economic Policy; Foreign Information Program,* p. 461). Dr. Jan Herman van Roijen was the Netherlands' ambassador to the United States.

[3] On April 3 the two countries would agree to give KLM permission to begin service to Miami and Houston. The Dutch proposal to fly the Los Angeles route, which the Netherlands regarded as the most significant of the three, was rejected (see *U.S. Department of State Bulletin* 36, no. 928 [April 8, 1957], 579–80; no. 932 [May 6, 1957], 746–50; and *ibid.,* no. 939 [June 24, 1957], 1013; see also *Public Papers of the Presidents: Eisenhower, 1957,* pp. 226–27; and *New York Times,* Mar. 11, 22, Apr. 1, 4, 6, 1957).

Attempts by the Netherlands to negotiate a route to the West Coast would continue until the end of Eisenhower's Administration (see [Luns] to Eisenhower, Oct. 7, 1960; and de Quay to Eisenhower, Jan. 6, 1961, both in AWF/I: Netherlands).

62 *EM, AWF, Diaries Series*

To Wright Francis Morrow *March 8, 1957*

Dear Mr. Morrow: Following your visit to me the other day I had a long talk with Secretary Dulles about the Ambassadorial post in Mexico.[1]

As of this moment, there are no specific plans for supplanting Mr. White in that post.[2] On the other hand, it is a fact that as a general proposition we prefer to avoid keeping any individual in any Ambassadorial post for longer than four years.

With respect to a possible successor, the State Department is no longer concerned as to the State in which an appointee might have his residence.[3] They are, however, convinced that the next man selected for the Mexican post, whenever such a change may be made, should have had extensive State Department experience. Supporting this decision are sound reasons with which I agree and which I am sure would be persuasive to you.

I know that this will be personally disappointing to you, but I assure you that neither in the Secretary's judgment nor in mine does it reflect in any way upon your own personal qualities and abilities, all of which we much admire and respect. I regret that I cannot send you a more encouraging letter.

Incidentally, while I was dictating this, your letter of March fourth reached my desk. Certainly I agree with you that merely because an individual claims Texas as his native State, it presents no disqualification for this particular post.[4]

With warm personal regard, *Sincerely*

[1] See no. 52.

[2] For background on White, U.S. Ambassador to Mexico since March 1953, see Galambos and van Ee, *The Middle Way*, no. 149.

[3] Morrow had criticized the State Department's consideration of an ambassador's home state as a criterion for making appointments. "It is hard for me to understand," he said, "why we have Good Neighbor Commissions and reciprocal trade obligations and still want to 'bar the gate' to the people most familiar with Mexico" (WHCF/OF 204).

[4] Disappointed that he did not receive the appointment, Morrow would write Eisenhower on March 27. "I do have the consolation, however, of offering my services to the President of my country in a capacity for which I believed I was best qualified" (WHCF/OF 204; see also Dulles to Eisenhower, Mar. 29, 1957, *ibid.*).

Robert Charles Hill, former U.S. Ambassador to El Salvador and Assistant Secretary of State for Congressional Relations, would become Ambassador to Mexico in June (see Morrow to Adams, Apr. 26, 1957; and Adams to Morrow, May 1, 1957, both in *ibid.*).

63 — *EM, AWF, Administration Series*

To James Prioleau Richards — *March 9, 1957*

Dear Mr. Ambassador:[1] I asked Congress on January 5, 1957, to join with me in a program for economic and military cooperation with the states in the general area of the Middle East. I said that I intended promptly to send a special mission to the general area of the Middle East to explain the cooperation the United States is prepared to give. The Congress, by Joint Resolution adopted on March 7, 1957, endorsed the program.[2]

I am now asking you as a Special Assistant to the President, with the personal rank of Ambassador, to undertake the mission to the Middle East as soon as possible. In charging you with this responsibility, I wish to express again my complete trust and confidence in your carrying out of this difficult assignment. You will be given full support by the various Government Departments and Agencies concerned. I know you will wish to consult closely with our Chiefs of Mission in the field.

I believe it will be desirable for you to visit each independent nation in the general area of the Middle East which expresses an interest in discussing the program. You will, of course, be speaking directly for me and the Secretary of State.

You are entrusted with a fourfold task:

1. To convey to the Middle East Governments the spirit and purposes of my Middle East proposals as endorsed by the Joint Resolution of the Congress.
2. To determine, after consultations with the Governments concerned, which countries in the area wish to avail themselves of the United States offer of assistance and to participate in all or part of the program.
3. To make commitments for programs of economic and military assistance, within the provisions of the Joint Resolution and within the limitation of funds appropriated by the Congress, which you deem to be essential and urgent to accomplish the purpose of the program.

   I assume you will keep me informed, through the Department of State, in regard to any commitments which you contemplate. This authorization, of course, does not extend to any question regarding the employment of the armed forces of the United States, which I alone must decide.
4. To report to me your findings and to recommend further appropriate measures to accomplish the purpose of the program either under the Joint Resolution or otherwise.

More detailed guidance with respect to your first three responsibilities will be provided by the Secretary of State on my behalf.[3] In connection with your report and recommendations, I shall value any observations you may wish to make regarding intra-area problems and measures that may facilitate their solution.

I know you share my personal conviction of the importance of this mission to the welfare of the United States and to the cause of world peace to which we are all dedicated. I wish you all success.[4]

With warm regard, *Sincerely*

[1] For background on retired Congressman James Richards, former Chairman of the House Foreign Affairs Committee, see Galambos, *NATO and the Campaign of 1952,*

no. 284; see also Galambos and van Ee, *The Middle Way*, no. 1901. In January Eisenhower had appointed Richards to a new position (with the rank of Ambassador) in which he would help implement Middle East policy. The State Department drafted this letter (see Dulles to Eisenhower, Mar. 4, 1957, AWF/D-H; see also Goodpaster memorandum, Mar. 7, 1957, AWF/D; and Telephone conversations, Dulles and Macomber, Dulles and O'Connor, and Dulles and Barnes, Mar. 6, 1957, AWF/D).

[2] For background on the Eisenhower Doctrine see Galambos and van Ee, *The Middle Way*, no. 2155.

[3] On this same day Dulles would tell the Ambassador that the basic purpose of the program was "to help the states in the general area of the Middle East, at their request, to maintain their national independence against the encroachments of international communism" (State, *Foreign Relations, 1955–1957*, vol. XII, *Near East Region; Iran; Iraq* [1991], pp. 454–57).

[4] Richards would leave on March 12 and return on May 8, having visited fifteen countries (see Richards to Eisenhower, May 28, 1957, AWF/A). For developments see no. 154.

64

EM, AWF, Administration Series

To James Paul Mitchell

March 11, 1957

Dear Jim:[1] I was highly interested in reading your presentation concerning the wisdom of developing the high level manpower resources of under-developed nations.[2]

As I told you the other day, I think that on the whole you have brought up some admirable ideas. Concerning it I have one question.

You rightly point out that if we industrialize countries without developing high level human resources, there could very easily evolve a rapid trend toward totalitarianism in such countries. You make a good case on this point.[3]

You therefore stress the need for development of human resources. But there is one danger here that I think your paper overlooks. If we develop human resources without providing opportunities for logical employment of educated or trained people, then we can be promoting unrest, frustrated ambitions and resentment.

It would seem to me that we must develop high level manpower resources in some kind of coordination with the development of opportunity in the same country. If we train a machinist, there should be a machine for him to run. If we train a teacher in the Social Sciences, there should be schools where he can teach Social Science. To be lacking in either of these efforts would seem to me running the risk of failure in the whole effort. Is this not correct?[4] *Sincerely*

[1] Former Assistant Secretary of the Army for Manpower and Reserve Affairs, Mitchell had been Secretary of Labor since October 1953.

[2] Mitchell had met with the President on March 8, 1957, to discuss his ideas on "Labor Aspects of Economic Aid" (Mitchell to Eisenhower, Mar. 8, 1957, WHCF/OF 116-B-5). Arguing that economic and political pressures were impelling the underdeveloped countries of the world to industrialize as rapidly as possible, Mitchell had stated that it was imperative to find some means to "*enable the underdeveloped countries to industrialize without sacrificing human values and political democracy on the altar of economic progress.*" It would be "folly," Mitchell had written, to assume that American interests would be "automatically advanced" through the industrialization and economic development of "backward countries." Industrialization and economic development, by themselves, might not offer any guarantee of social progress or general economic welfare and might "even provide ready excuses for wholesale disregard of human values in the pursuit of the overriding goals of totalitarian rulers." Eisenhower underlined many sections in Mitchell's report.

[3] Mitchell had argued that the United States had "no legitimate interest in helping countries to industrialize unless we can influence the course of their economic development." This, he believed, should be done through the "development of managerial, labor and educational institutions, for these institutions will determine in large measure the course of economic and political growth of the countries in question."

[4] Mitchell would respond on March 12 (AWF/A), saying that Eisenhower had raised a crucial point regarding the need to relate development of skills to present or potential employment opportunities in undeveloped nations. Stating that the United States must be "alert to the danger that in helping people to help themselves, we do not compound old problems nor create new ones," Mitchell proposed an initial inventory of skill requirements. This inventory would be based upon the "foreign countries' own realistic appraisal of the skills and resources needed and those which are available, to meet its current and anticipated industrial and agricultural programs." On April 12, 1957, Assistant to the President Sherman Adams would send Mitchell a memorandum (WHCF/OF 116-B-5) informing him that Eisenhower wished to act upon Mitchell's suggestion to set up a "small task force" responsible for implementation. For background see nos. 50 and 90.

65 — *EM, AWF, Dulles-Herter Series*

To John Foster Dulles — *March 11, 1957*

Dear Foster: I am delighted that things are going well with you and do hope that you feel repaid for the long trip you have made to attend the meeting.[1] You are, of course, correct in giving our friends reassurance that under existing circumstances we shall not vary our policy toward Communist China.[2]

I think that my difficulty is gradually disappearing, but I am still anxious for a few days of sun.[3] I am considering the possibility of taking a cruise to Bermuda during which trip I could make a swing to the southward. If I do so, I shall leave the Columbine here to pick up you and the necessary staffs to come on directly to Bermuda where I will meet you.[4] If I follow this plan, I think I would leave Norfolk about the evening of the fourteenth.

Please give my warm regard to any of my old friends at the Conference and of course all the best to yourself.[5]

[1] Secretary Dulles was in Canberra, Australia, to attend the council meeting of the South East Asia Treaty Organization.
[2] Dulles had told Eisenhower that friendly Asian countries were exhibiting "considerable concern" regarding the repeated stories of a forthcoming change in the U.S. policy of nonrecognition of Communist China. He was planning to make a statement reaffirming U.S. policy of support for the Nationalist Chinese Republic, nonrecognition of Communist China, and continued opposition to seating the Communist regime in the United Nations. "I hope," he said, "this will allay the present nervousness" (Dulles to Eisenhower, DULTE 4, Mar. 11, 1957, AWF/D-H).
[3] Eisenhower had been suffering from a persistent case of bronchitis.
[4] On Eisenhower's plans for a cruise see the following document. The Bermuda Conference between Eisenhower and Britain's Prime Minister Harold Macmillan would begin on March 21 (see no. 78).
[5] Dulles would tell the President that he had restated the American position and had received "highly favorable reactions from the Philippines and Vietnam where there had developed serious concern as to our policy" (Dulles to Eisenhower, DULTE 6, Mar. 12, 1957, AWF/D-H).

66 — *EM, AWF, Dulles-Herter Series*

To Harold Macmillan — *March 11, 1957*

Dear Harold: In order to get two or three days in the sun, which the doctors advise me to do to get rid of my persistent cough, I am thinking of taking a sea voyage to Bermuda, starting three or four days ahead of time so as to proceed leisurely on a circuitous route leading through the warmer regions to the south of us. Would it cause you any inconvenience? It would mean that I would land at the seaport instead of the airfield, and I should like to know whether this would mean any considerable change in your plans. I would, of course, land at the same hour previously proposed for arrival by air. I would be grateful for an early reply.[1] *With warm regard*

[1] Eisenhower's plans would be "entirely agreeable" to Macmillan, who hoped that a few days at sea would be beneficial (Macmillan to Eisenhower, Mar. 12, 1957, AWF/D-H). The President would meet Macmillan in Bermuda for a three-day conference beginning on March 21 (see no. 78).

67

EM, AWF, Name Series

To Norman Cousins
Personal

March 11, 1957

Dear Mr. Cousins: I am distressed that Dr. Schweitzer is upset over the "leak" of his last letter to me.[1] Won't you please tell him that I understand only too well how such things occur and that, of course, I appreciate his motives in writing as he did.

My admiration and respect for Dr. Schweitzer and his work are unbounded, and I hope you will be good enough to convey my sentiments to him when next you write to him.[2]

With warm regard, *Sincerely*

[1] For background see no. 28. Cousins had told Eisenhower that Dr. Schweitzer was "saddened and discouraged" that French officials had not followed his instructions regarding the transmission of his letter and had released its contents in Paris without his permission. Dr. Schweitzer was "especially unhappy," Cousins wrote, "that he may have lost standing in your eyes as a result of a seeming presumption" (Cousins to Eisenhower, Mar. 6, 1957, AWF/N).

[2] Cousins had asked Eisenhower's permission to tell Dr. Schweitzer that the President's respect for him was "unimpaired, despite the matter of the Algerian letter."

68

EM, AWF, Name Series

To Milton Stover Eisenhower

March 11, 1957

Dear Milton: I had a chance to read the talk you made before the Grand Masters.[1] I think it is very fine indeed and I have one suggestion only.

You speak of the "Judiac-Christian heritage."[2] I would suggest that you use a term on the order of "religious heritage"—this is for the reason that we should find some way of including the vast numbers of people who hold to the Islamic and Buddhist religions when we compare the religious world against the Communist world.

I think you could still point out the debt we all owe to the ancients of Judea and Greece for the introduction of new ideas. *As ever*

[1] Eisenhower's brother, Milton, had addressed the Conference of Grand Masters of the Masons on February 20, 1957 in Washington, D.C. (see *Congressional Record*, 85th Cong., 1st sess., 1957, Appendix: A1723–25, 103). Milton had written Ann Whitman on March 7 (AWF/N) saying that the President had suggested he "make a talk or talks before certain groups. Knowing of his interest, I think he might like to read the enclosed." An accompanying handwritten note explained, "Since my brother is

the best critic I know, I'd like to have him see the enclosed when he has a free moment" (AWF/N).
[2] Milton's speech had addressed the "fundamental moral and intellectual differences" between freedom and communism. Eisenhower's comment regarding the "Jud*aic*-Christian heritage" referred to Milton's statement that "Communism poses not only a military, economic and political challenge to the free nations; it strikes at the very heart of the ideology of freedom—the Judaic-Christian heritage which forms the basis of Western civilization."

69

EM, AWF, Gettysburg Series

To Armand Hammer

March 11, 1957

Dear Dr. Hammer:[1] After talking with Senator Smith, I have come to the conclusion that I should not accept your more than kind offer to present to me "Mamie of Shadow Isle."[2] She is a valuable animal and, quite frankly, she would be a fine addition to my little herd of Angus. However, should I accept, I would find myself in an embarrassing position because of some other similar suggestions of gifts that I have had to decline.

I assure you that this negative answer in no way affects the very real sense of gratitude I have for your thoughtfulness—a fact that I am sure Senator Smith, when he next talks to you, will also emphasize.

With my thanks and best wishes, *Sincerely*

[1] On January 18 petroleum magnate Hammer, who owned a stock farm in New Jersey, had offered Eisenhower an Aberdeen Angus heifer (AWF/Gettysburg). For background on Hammer and his efforts to provide Black Angus cattle for Eisenhower's Gettysburg farm see Galambos, *NATO and the Campaign of 1952*, no. 270.
[2] Eisenhower had met with H. Alexander Smith (Rep., N.J.) on March 9. On the heifer see no. 15.

70

EM, AWF, Administration Series

To George Edward Allen

March 13, 1957

Dear George: Herewith a letter from Billy Byars. He may have talked to you about this same subject. Personally I have no objection at all to all these cattle being put in the name of the "Eisenhower Farms" and of course what Billy has to say about artificial breeding is not only true but this has many advantages, as you know.[1]

However, it would have to be understood that in this event there could be no sale conducted under the name of the "Eisenhower Farms" until I was in a position to participate.[2] This would likely not be earlier than January, 1961.

While I think that none of us will have a sufficient number of heifers to want to conduct a sale before that time, if you two should want to get rid of some of your stock before I would feel in a position to go along, it would obviously be necessary to transfer the animals you wanted to sell back to the name of the Allen-Byars partnership in order to dispose of them.

Except for this one remote possibility I have no objection and you can so notify Art Nevins. I will leave it up to you to talk to Billy—and then the two of you can go ahead in any way you please. *As ever*

[1] Texas oil tycoon Billy G. Byars had written Eisenhower on March 11 (AWF/Gettysburg) about transferring the cattle from the Allen-Byars partnership to the Eisenhower Farms in order to "relieve a lot of complications" and breed the cattle artificially. For background on Byars and on the Allen-Byars partnership see Galambos and van Ee, *The Middle Way*, no. 1101.

[2] For background see no. 55.

71

EM, AWF, DDE Diaries Series

To Michael D. O'Connell

March 13, 1957

Dear Monsignor O'Connell: When I visited the Carmel Mission last August, I tried to find some colored pictures from which I could attempt a small painting of the mission.[1] Later a number of individuals kindly sent me colored photographs and slides, but none of them was quite right. Fortunately, however, I found in a magazine a very nice view of the edifice and one that was in sufficient detail that I could make out the principal features.

In any event, from this photograph I painted a small picture, which I should like to present to the Mission, to yourself and to the Sisters who so kindly greeted Mrs. Eisenhower and me the day we visited there.

The painting is, of course, the work of a rank amateur and deserves no place of prominence, but because the subject itself involves all of you, I thought you might like the result of my efforts. It will arrive by railway express within a very short time.

With warm greetings to all of you and, of course, personal regard to yourself, *Sincerely*

[1] Following the Republican National Convention, the Eisenhowers vacationed at the Cypress Point Club in Monterey, California (see Galambos and van Ee, *The Middle Way*, no. 1916). On August 26 they visited the Franciscan Mission San Carlos Borromeo (see *New York Times*, Aug. 27, 1957, and President's daily appointments). On the mission see Paul H. Kocher, *California's Old Missions: The Story of the Founding of the 21 Franciscan Missions in Spanish Alta California 1769–1823* (Chicago, 1976), pp. 138–40.

72

EM, AWF, International Series: Mollet

To Guy Mollet
Secret

March 14, 1957

Dear Mr. President:[1] I fully share the concern expressed in your letter, which I received through your Ambassador late March 13, regarding the situation between Israel and Egypt.[2]

I can assure you that I am making great efforts to the end that the objectives which we seek of peace and tranquility in the area will be achieved. We are in constant touch with both parties to the dispute, with the Secretary General, and with other friendly governments. Our purpose has been to avoid precipitate action by Egypt or by Israel which might result in a deterioration leading to a renewal of hostilities, thus undoing all that has been accomplished, with consequences of a most grave character.

We must realize, of course, that the current difficulty stems from problems of long standing which require the greatest patience and perseverance in their solution. I am sure you will agree that the Governments of both Israel and Egypt should be urged to exercise the utmost restraint.

The United States, along with other powers, stated in the United Nations its attitude regarding the international character of the Straits of Tiran, and expressed its view that United Nations forces should be deployed at Sharm el-Sheikh following the Israeli withdrawal. It endorsed the Secretary General's statement of February 28 regarding notice to the United Nations before the Emergency Force would be withdrawn from that area.[3] Further, the United States set forth its views concerning United Nations functions in the Gaza Strip following Israeli withdrawal. I assume that the statement of our respective positions regarding these matters made in the UN Assembly is what you mean by our "accord commun."[4] We continue to stand by these positions, although it is of course obvious that these matters are not for the United States alone to decide.

As you know, it is our belief that the arrangements for the administration of the Gaza Strip can only be within the legal framework brought about by the Armistice Agreement. While that Agreement gives Egypt certain rights with respect to Gaza, it is our expressed hope that Egypt will not exercise those rights but will permit the United Nations, pending some suitable agreement or settlement, to continue responsibilities in Gaza along the lines of the Secretary General's report of February 22.[5] If, notwithstanding our efforts to achieve this in its entirety, Egypt should exercise its legal rights and insist upon a return to Gaza of some Egyptian personnel, we would not feel that would create a situation in which Israel would be justified in taking military action. We made our attitude on this latter point clear to Israeli officials prior to the Israeli decision to withdraw behind the Armistice lines. It is our position, however, that if there should be any recurrence of hostilities or violation by either party of its international obligations, including those of the Armistice Agreement, a situation would be created for United Nations consideration. The United States would consult with other members of the United Nations to consider appropriate action which they or the United Nations might take.

In view of the seriousness of this matter our two Governments should, of course, continue close consultation as the situation develops.[6] *Sincerely yours*

[1] A past president of the Consultative Assembly of the Council of Europe and Secretary-General of the French Socialist Party, Mollet had been President of the French Republic since February 1956 (see Galambos and van Ee, *The Middle Way*, no. 2123). Eisenhower approved and signed the State Department draft of this message, which we have used as our source text. The State Department cabled the text of this letter to the American embassy in Paris on this same day (AWF/I: Mollet).

[2] For background on the withdrawal of Israeli troops from the Gaza Strip and Sharm el-Sheikh see no. 56. Fearing that the civilian situation in the Gaza Strip had become dangerous, Egyptian President Nasser had appointed an administrative governor and staff to oversee conditions in the area. Israel believed that Egypt intended to reoccupy the territory and had urged the United States to intervene. In his letter Mollet told Eisenhower that if the Egyptian attitude did not change, Israel would be justified in redeploying its forces. "In this eventuality, [the] effort which we have achieved in common would prove to be [in] vain and [the] situation [in the] Middle East would be gravely compromised" (AWF/I: Mollet; State, *Foreign Relations, 1955–1957*, vol. XVII, *Arab-Israeli Dispute, 1957*, pp. 396–406, 415–16).

[3] We have been unabie to locate a statement regarding this issue made by Hammarskjöld on February 28. Two days earlier, however, he had assured the Israeli government in writing that any proposal to remove United Nations troops from the area would first come before the General Assembly (*ibid.*, p. 314; see also *New York Times*, Feb. 27, 1957).

[4] "We are ready, on our part," Mollet had said, "to urge moderation and patience on Israel if the situation evolves within the framework of our common accord."

[5] According to Secretary General Hammarskjöld, Egypt desired a safe and orderly takeover of the Gaza Strip by the U.N. forces and would work with the United Na-

tions in assisting the Arab refugees. Egypt would also cooperate in ending all incursions and raids across the border from either side (*U.S. Department of State Bulletin* 36, no. 927 [April 1, 1957], 544).

[6] Charles Woodruff Yost, Minister-Counselor of the U.S. embassy, personally delivered this message to Mollet on the following day. Although the French President told Yost that he "would counsel restraint and prudence upon [the] Israelis to the best of his ability," he said that he was shocked by Egyptian President Nasser's dictatorial moves (Yost to Dulles, Mar. 15, 1957, AWF/I: Mollet). For developments see no. 74.

73

EM, WHCF, Confidential File: Defense Department

To Charles Erwin Wilson

March 14, 1957

Memorandum for the Secretary of Defense: This morning when we discussed the Cordiner studies and your memorandum of March eighth, I told you I would try to give you my comments before leaving today.[1]

We would be well advised, I think, to pinpoint—insofar as we possibly can—the proposals for compensation adjustment on the retention of those hard-to-train technicians and specialists (especially enlisted personnel) who are now leaving the service at an undesirable rate, with consequent heavy cost both in money and in operating effectiveness.[2]

In like manner, the proposals regarding officers ought to be focused on meeting the problem at the particular points where officers are leaving the service with comparable adverse consequences.[3]

I recognize that other features might also be desirable, but in present circumstances, it strikes me that these must be very few if the proposals to meet the most serious situations are to have any prospect of success.

While there would be no objection to your sending your proposals as currently developed to the Bureau of the Budget, provided it is made clear to all concerned that the whole matter is still under consideration, I am sending the Bureau a copy of this letter for its use in its analysis both of your current proposals and of proposals you may develop in response to this memorandum.[4]

[1] Eisenhower had met with Secretary of Defense Wilson following the NSC meeting to discuss Wilson's response to the recommendations of the Cordiner Committee on Modernization of the Pay Structure for the Members of the Armed Services. (Wilson's March 8 memorandum is in same file as this document; the March 14 meeting is summarized in Goodpaster, Memorandum of Conversation, Mar. 14, 1957,

AWF/D.) The Defense Department had established the Cordiner Committee, technically known as the Defense Advisory Committee on Professional and Technical Compensation, in May 1956 (see *Congressional Quarterly Almanac*, vol. XIII, *1957*, p. 636). The committee's chairman, Ralph Jarron Cordiner (B.S. Whitman College 1922) had been president of the General Electric Company since 1950. Eisenhower would leave Washington that afternoon to attend the upcoming conference in Bermuda (see no. 78).

[2] The Cordiner report proposed to make skills and proficiency, rather than seniority, the basis for military pay scales. In a March 4 meeting with Cordiner and Wilson, Eisenhower had expressed his dismay that more attention had not been paid to the true "hard skills," the lack of which, he believed, were hurting the armed forces (Goodpaster, Memorandum of Conversation, Mar. 5, 1957, AWF/D).

[3] During the March 4 meeting the President had expressed his opposition to any program which proposed substantial increases in the pay of generals without concomitant pay raises for privates; such a program, he thought, would probably generate criticism. Eisenhower also expressed concern that any change in military pay scale would put pressure on the governmental pay scale, and probably on the general economy as well.

[4] On May 8 Secretary Wilson would approve a proficiency pay system for 350,000 skilled technicians in the armed forces. Legislation to implement the Cordiner Committee recommendations would be introduced in the Senate in June 1957. For developments see no. 226, and *New York Times*, May 9, 1957.

74

EM, AWF, International Series: Israel

TO DAVID BEN GURION

March 15, 1957

Cable. Secret

Dear Mr. Prime Minister: I have received your message of March 13 delivered through Ambassador Eban. I want you to know that we are following recent developments affecting Gaza with concern and are working hard to the end that the objectives of peace and tranquility in the area will be achieved.[1]

The United States has made clear its hopes with respect to the situation which should prevail following the Israeli withdrawal.[2] We shall continue to strive to see to it that those hopes materialize. It is, of course, obvious that this will involve many difficulties and will raise questions which the United States alone cannot decide. The problems with which we are confronted have been for a long time in the making, and patience and forbearance are required in our task of seeking a solution to them. I am sure you will agree that it is of the utmost importance that the greatest restraint be exercised by all concerned and that there be avoided any precipitate action which might result in a deterioration of the situation and a risk of undoing all that has been accomplished.

My personal interest in the establishment of stability and tranquility in the area continues deep. I look forward to continuing close consultation with your Government on the problems involved.[3]

With kind regard. *Sincerely yours*

[1] For background on Egypt's plan to install a military governor in the Gaza Strip see no. 72. Israel's ambassador to the United States, Abba Eban, had given Ben Gurion's letter to Acting Secretary of State Herter. Ben Gurion had informed Eisenhower that fedayeen guerrilla units had begun operations against Israeli settlements. "At the same time," the Prime Minister said, "Cairo Radio has officially announced that Egypt will not permit any ship, Israeli or other, including American tankers, to exercise the right of free passage through the Straits of Tiran." Ben Gurion added that the area could be "cast in the throes of a most grave crisis" and asked for Eisenhower's assurance that Israel would have no cause to regret its withdrawal (AWF/I: Israel; see also State, *Foreign Relations, 1955–1957,* vol. XVII, *Arab-Israeli Dispute, 1957,* pp. 423–24, 433–41).

[2] See, for example, no. 56; see also State, *Foreign Relations, 1955–1957,* vol. XVII, *Arab-Israeli Dispute, 1957,* pp. 422–23.

[3] Upon receiving the President's letter, Ben Gurion stated that Israel would "take no precipitate action" and would "do nothing to contribute to [the] deterioration of the situation" (State, *Foreign Relations, 1955–1957,* vol. XVII, *Arab-Israeli Dispute, 1957,* pp. 429–30). For developments see no. 77.

75

EM, AWF, Administration Series

TO CLARENCE BELDEN RANDALL

March 17,[1] 1957

Dear Clarence:[2] I agree with your recommendations on each point.[3]

So far as the letters were concerned I found something interesting in each, but believe I was more in accord with State and Committee of Economic Advisers than with the others.[4]

Gene Black made some pungent comments.[5] However I think that, in a way, he was unfair to Fairless Committee. That committee undoubtedly assumed—possibly too much so—a rather extensive knowledge of problems involved on the part of readers of the report.[6] This gives validity to Mr. Black's criticisms, and frankly, I'd like to see more analysis of the several problems in the different countries.

This gives me the idea that, for our Congressional presentations, we should attempt short, succinct descriptions of each country or area in which we have a major interest. These could form part of the raw material out of which we fashion our recommendations. I would avoid, like the plague, long dissertations. I'm thinking of something like 150 words in each important case.

Thanks for a fine job of pointing up the questions.

With warm regard. *Sincerely*

[1] Eisenhower noted that this handwritten letter had been composed "Sunday—(at sea)." The President was aboard the U.S.S. *Canberra,* en route to the conference in Bermuda (for background see no. 78).
[2] Randall, Special Assistant to the President on foreign economic policy since July 10, 1956, had served as Chairman of the Commission on Foreign Economic Policy in 1953–54. For background see Galambos and van Ee, *The Middle Way,* nos. 170 and 1307.
[3] Eisenhower was referring to Randall's March 14 report on the work of a special advisory group on foreign aid and collective security. The President's Citizen Advisors on the Mutual Security Program, chaired by former president and chairman of the board of the United States Steel Corporation, Benjamin Franklin Fairless, had presented its report to Eisenhower on March 1, 1957 (*ibid.*, no. 1849). Randall's report, presenting the twenty-three recommendations of the Fairless Committee, the position of ten concerned government agencies, and Randall's own recommendation on each point, can be found in State, *Foreign Relations, 1955–1957,* vol. X, *Foreign Aid and Economic Defense Policy,* pp. 146–70. In general, the Fairless report (see n. 6 below) had recommended that the United States should be more businesslike and less liberal in providing assistance to foreign countries. Randall, in most cases, had concurred. He had disagreed, however, with a few of the most restrictive provisions, including one calling for a fixed limit on the total amount of collective security expenditures abroad.
[4] Randall had obtained written statements from such concerned agencies as the State, Defense, Treasury, and Commerce Departments, the Bureau of the Budget, and the Council of Economic Advisors (CEA). For a summary of their positions see *ibid.*, pp. 147–70. Both State and the Council of Economic Advisors had taken a position strongly supporting mutual aid.
[5] Eisenhower was referring to Eugene Robert Black, president and chairman since 1949 of the International Bank for Reconstruction and Development (the World Bank). In a March 11 letter to Randall, Black had criticized the Fairless Committee for failing to consider the purposes of foreign aid, for neglecting the differing development needs of various countries and regions, and for overemphasizing the strategic necessity of all aid (see *ibid.*, pp. 141–44; and Burton I. Kaufman, *Trade and Aid: Eisenhower's Foreign Economic Policy, 1953–1961* [Baltimore, 1982], p. 99. See also Jochen Kraske, *Bankers with a Mission: The Presidents of the World Bank, 1946–91* [New York, 1996], pp. 75–112, and Louis Galambos and David Milobsky, "Organizing and Reorganizing the World Bank 1946–1972: A Comparative Perspective" in *Business History Review* 69 [Summer 1995], 156–90.
[6] The Fairless Committee had released its report on March 5. Although it had called for limits on the amount of assistance given, the committee had also concluded that both military and economic aid programs had been successful in countering Soviet expansion and should be continued. The current level of overseas economic support were seen as adequate. While the group expressed the hope that foreign aid spending might decline over time, it warned that the United States "must resolve to stay the course and must abandon the false hope that collective security costs are temporary" (see Report to the President by the President's Citizen Advisers on the Mutual Security Program, Mar. 1, 1957, AWF/A: Mutual Aid 1957; *New York Times,* Mar. 6, 1957; and Russell Edgerton, *Sub-Cabinet Politics and Policy Commitment: The Birth of the Development Loan Fund* [Syracuse, 1970], pp. 67–114).

76

EM, AWF, Administration Series

To Clarence Belden Randall
Memorandum

March 17, 1957

With respect to specific actions of some immediate importance.[1]

a. That relating to inclusion of mil. aid in our own mil. budget—and placing ICA *inside* State.[2]

We've been over this every year since my first Inauguration . . .[3] I have the feeling that whatever decision is reached should not be implemented this year. We should present the case to Congress under *present* adm organization with statement that this will again be analyzed and report made to Congress at next Session. (If Congress insists on action this year, I'm sure we can by cooperation reach some satisfactory answers. I'm not too impressed by details of org. as panaceas for serious ills—if any.)

b. With respect to 2 year authorizations. No use! [(]We've tried before—and I think the best we can get is continuation of Emergency or contingency funds.)[4]

c. With respect 6,7,8, and 11.[5] I think we can probably come somewhat closer than we have to meeting Fairless conclusions, but the progress will be only gradual. I realize that some (head of I.C.A.) believe in "soft" loans, even to Korea.[6] I don't say they are entirely out the window, but in that type of case have little, if any, application.

[1] This handwritten memorandum from Eisenhower to Randall was an addendum to the President's letter regarding the Fairless Committee report (no. 75; see also State, *Foreign Relations, 1955–1957,* vol. X, *Foreign Aid and Economic Defense Policy,* p. 175).

[2] The Fairless Committee had recommended that: "For the administration of economic activities, the International Cooperation Administration (ICA) should be integrated into the Department of State, and merged with the existing economic activities within the Department, as soon as practicable (see Report to the President by the President's Citizen Advisors on the Mutual Security Program, March 1, 1957, AWF/A, Mutual Aid 1957). Eisenhower had established the ICA (May 9, 1955) as a semiautonomous agency associated with the Department of State. For background see Galambos and van Ee, *The Middle Way,* nos. 1402 and 1849; Kaufman, *Trade and Aid,* p. 52; and *Congressional Quarterly Almanac,* vol. XI, *1955,* p. 304.

The Fairless Committee had also recommended that there should be "a separation between economic and military contributions to the collective security program." Funding for the so-called "military assistance" and "defense support" portions of the mutual security program should be included as a separate title within the regular Defense Department budget. The Committee further recommended that nonmilitary assistance—to be justified and administered by the Department of State—should be submitted separately and labeled as economic assistance. The Council on Foreign Economic Policy recommended support of this position "with the understanding that the military portion of defense support would be charged to the Department of Defense budget but would be administered by ICA" (State, *Foreign Relations, 1955–1957,* vol. X, *Foreign Aid and Economic Defense Policy,* p. 163).

[3] The ellipsis is in Eisenhower's document.
[4] The Fairless Committee had recommended that "both the military and economic assistance programs be presented to each Congress for approval rather than to each session of each Congress."
[5] Fairless Committee recommendations 6, 7, 8, and 11 concerned the conditions for making loans and grants. In general, the Committee sought to tighten the conditions under which the United States made loans. Recommendations were made to end loans repayable in inconvertible currencies and loans in situations where there was "grave doubt of the ability of the borrower to repay." Grants should be made only to those countries which had joined in the collective security system, and "where it is clearly in the national interest to do so."
[6] John Baker Hollister, Director of the ICA since 1955, had taken a position in support of the Fairless Committee's recommendation that in certain cases the United States should make "soft dollar loans" on more "liberal terms than those of the established public banks with respect to interest rates and periods of repayment." For developments see no. 109.

77

EM, AWF, International Series: Saudi Arabia

TO IBN ABD AL-AZIZ SAUD
Cable. Secret

March 18, 1957

Your Majesty: Thank you for your messages of February 28 from Cairo and of March 4 from Riyadh and for your courtesy in sending me the memorandum on the proceedings of your recent meetings.[1]

Events have moved swiftly since these messages were received. I know you will share with me gratification that the withdrawal of Israel from Gaza and Aqaba has now been completed.[2] Other serious problems lie ahead. I hope that the Governments of Saudi Arabia and the United States can continue to work closely together to support those measures which may be required, particularly in the United Nations, to meet these problems and to establish that state of quiet which we both desire.

Your Majesty may rest assured that in all of our recent efforts to meet this crisis no part of our recent conversations has been forgotten. The positions of this government which were expressed to you during these conversations and in our recent exchange of messages on Aqaba and Gaza remain the same.[3] We agree with Your Majesty on the importance of the establishment of peaceful conditions in Gaza and share your desire for a tranquil border between Israel and Gaza. We hope that the presence of the United Nations Emergency Force in the area will ensure these conditions.

In considering our position with respect to the Gulf of Aqaba, the territorial integrity and security of your Kingdom and the requirement that there be no interference with the travels of pilgrims to the Holy Places are, we recognize, considerations of great importance.[4] As you know, however, we believe that ships of all nations should be able to proceed in free and innocent passage through the Gulf in accordance with the accepted principles of international law, as stated by the Government of Egypt in its memorandum to the American Ambassador on January 28, 1950.[5]

During the course of our recent discussions, we agreed that the establishment and maintenance of close and friendly relations between the United States and the nations of the area must depend upon mutual confidence and trust. Your Majesty expressed appreciation for our explanations of problems which have arisen in our relations with certain other Arab states. We in turn appreciated the manner in which Your Majesty has conveyed these to the other Arab leaders. I hope our exchange of memoranda has served, in part at least, to develop a better understanding.

From the latest Cairo memorandum it would appear there are still differences between us on certain of these issues. Most of these have been covered in our previous exchanges and in our reply to the earlier Four-Power memorandum.[6] Your Majesty will recall, I am sure, our reviewing with you the history of our discussions with Egypt in the matter of arms purchases in the United States. I can assure you that there has never been a refusal on our part to supply arms to Egypt.

In the months to come, the United States will continue to hope for a more complete understanding with the Arab states on many of the matters raised in this exchange of memoranda and on others. The United States Government desires close and friendly relations with all of the Arab states on the basis of full recognition of the integrity and sovereignty of independent nations. In our efforts to move forward toward a close relationship with these states and to achieve an era of stability, I am pleased that we can count on Your Majesty's friendship and understanding. Your Majesty may be assured, on our part, that the United States Government will keep the Government of Saudi Arabia appropriately informed of any important developments which may arise or be contemplated in order that we may be continually aware of each other's views on issues of vital importance to the area.

Your Majesty's oral invitation to the Vice President to visit Saudi Arabia is very much appreciated. I regret that his very full schedule and the necessity for him to return to his duties here as soon as possible will not permit him the privilege of partaking of your hospitality.[7]

May God have you in His safekeeping. *Your sincere friend*

[1] State Department officials drafted this letter (see Herter to Eisenhower, Mar. 15, 1957, AWF/I: Saudi Arabia). The Saudi Arabian monarch, Jordan's King Hussein, Syrian President Quwatly, and Egyptian President Nasser had recently completed their second series of meetings in Cairo (see n. 5 below; and no. 54; Herter to Eisenhower, Mar. 15, 1957, AWF/I: Saudi Arabia; and State, *Foreign Relations, 1955–1957*, vol. XVII, *Arab-Israeli Dispute, 1957*, pp. 310, 323). In his letter, written on February 27, King Saud had told Eisenhower that he had assured the other Arab nations at the Cairo meeting that the United States wanted to improve its relations with the Arab states and would respect their sovereignty and independence. King Saud had later thanked the President for his role in Israel's declared intention to withdraw from Gaza and the Gulf of Aqaba. He did, however, condemn Israel for numerous acts of aggression against its Arab neighbors (Saud to Eisenhower, Feb. 27, 1957, and Mar. 3, 1957, both in AWF/I: Saudi Arabia).

[2] The Israelis had withdrawn the last of their troops by March 7; see no. 56.

[3] On King Saud's visit see no. 13. Eisenhower's previous letters regarding these issues are nos. 37 and 54.

[4] The cities of Mecca and Medina are the Holy Places of Islam.

[5] Eisenhower had quoted a portion of the Egyptian statement in his cable of February 14; see no. 37.

[6] On January 18–19 the leaders of Egypt, Jordan, Syria, and Saudi Arabia had met in Cairo. On January 30, during his visit to Washington, King Saud had given Eisenhower a memorandum of the meetings. The U.S. reply to the memorandum (Feb. 7) stated that the Palestine issue and the Suez Canal problem were two areas the United States considered "'harmful' to the security and stability of the Middle East" (see no. 13; and State, *Foreign Relations, 1955–1957*, vol. XIII, *Near East: Jordan-Yemen*, pp. 421, 441–43, 447, 468–77). The memorandum of the later Cairo meeting had emphasized the unconditional withdrawal of Israeli forces beyond the armistice lines and the prohibition of Israeli ships in the Gulf of Aqaba (Saud to Eisenhower, Feb. 27, 1957, AWF/I: Saudi Arabia).

[7] Vice-President Nixon had represented the United States at the independence ceremonies in Ghana on March 6 and would visit six other African countries before returning to the United States on March 21.

78 *EM, AWF, DDE Diaries Series*

DIARY *March 21, 1957*
Secret

BERMUDA CONFERENCE[1]

The principals attending the meeting today were the President, Prime Minister Macmillan, Secretary of State Dulles and Foreign Minister Selwyn Lloyd.

Each side was represented at the table by three other individuals and a few staff officers were behind this delegation.

I. The meeting was by far the most successful international meeting that I have attended since the close of World War II. This had three causes:

(*a*). The pressing importance of the problems discussed and the need for reaching some kind of definite answer rather than merely referring the problems to a study group, as is so often done in international conferences;[2]

(*b*). The atmosphere of frankness and confidence that was noticeable throughout the day; this possibly resulted, in part, from the fact that Harold Macmillan and I are old wartime comrades and friends of long standing;

(*c*). The obvious fact that each side was well informed on the several subjects taken up. Consequently conversations were far more definite and to the point than is normally the case when generalizations and protestations of good will take the place of informative exchanges.

II. We discussed all phases of the Mid East problem and it was apparent that there was a very large measure of agreement on most of the matters that have filled the pages of the public press for the past many weeks. Some of the items that came in for very special and searching investigation were:

A. The question of our future relationships with Nasser and a satisfactory arrangement for the future use of the Suez Canal.

Here, very early in the conversation, the Foreign Minister, Mr. Lloyd,[3] delivered a tirade against Nasser, saying that he was not only an evil, unpredictable and untrustworthy man, but was ambitious to become a second Mussolini. He thought also that in pursuing his ambitions he would probably, just as Mussolini became the stooge of Hitler, become the stooge of the Kremlin.[4]

This was followed up by a presentation by the British of the need for obtaining promptly a satisfactory arrangement for the use of the Canal. They felt the matter of tolls was probably the most important single consideration in such an agreement. They were quite clear that if we should fail to get a satisfactory arrangement, we should not later dodge the issue and pretend that it was at least a half-victory and one with which we could live. Rather, they believe we should under these conditions denounce the whole affair, including the intransigence of the British government. But they re-emphasized their need both economically and politically for obtaining a truly satisfactory agreement and this very quickly.

I immediately pointed out to them the inconsistencies in their approach to these two problems. If we were at this moment to begin an attack on Nasser (and we admit that he is far from an admirable character) and do everything in our power overtly and covertly to get rid of him, then the hope of getting an early and satisfactory settlement on the Canal would be completely futile.

They quickly saw the point of this and while earnestly retaining the hope that Nasser would come to some bad end, quickly agreed that we should first stick with the task of getting a satisfactory agreement on the Canal operation.

B. Gaza and Aqaba. We found ourselves largely in agreement on these two subjects and the consensus was that we must do our best to prevent extreme action by either side in the region. We believe that if we can have a period of tranquility during which time these two regions will be largely under the control of the United Nations, that we can probably work out satisfactory answers.[5]

C. The question came up of maintaining oil production in the Mid East and satisfactory access to it through pipe lines and otherwise. This subject again brought out some very plain talk and I think much was done to clarify our thinking.

Harold Macmillan pointed out that Kuwait was really the key to a satisfactory answer. This is for the reason that even in a region where many areas are great producers of oil, Kuwait is by far the greatest of these and in itself can produce oil enough for all Western Europe for years to come.[6]

Along with this fact was brought up the British difficulties in Burami involving the Arabs, and difficulties in Aden, Jordan, Egypt and Syria.[7]

To each of these difficulties the British had certain proposals to make.

On our side we pointed out that so many different considerations apply in each of these problems that the only logical approach was to take our principal purpose or objective and subordinate all other purposes to a successful solution of this principal one.

This principal purpose is, of course, that of retaining access to Kuwait and an adequate flow of oil therefrom, for one of the requirements for success in this is to achieve better relationships with the surrounding areas, the principal one of which would be Arabia. Yet the second important purpose mentioned by the British involves Burami, an object of bitter dispute between the British and the Arabians. I pointed out that the pursuit of both of these objectives simultaneously could very well endanger attainment of the important one. They had a number of reasons—all of which they felt were unselfish—for retaining their hold upon Burami, but I am sure that as a result of the conversation they are going to take a second look at their activities in the region and try to establish priorities that will keep first things first.[8]

D. We agreed to put off discussion of the Baghdad Pact for

a day or so. This was because of our own commitment to keep confidential our plans in this connection for a few days.[9]

E. The British mentioned the existence of a secret Egyptian plot for executing a coup to dispose of Nasser. They apparently thought we knew a great deal about it and wanted us to make some public statement against Nasser in the hope that this would encourage the dissident Egyptians. Manifestly anything the British said against Nasser would only make him stronger in the area.

This was a matter on which neither the Secretary nor I had any worthwhile information, but during the day we secured an evaluation from Washington. Our appraisal was that the dissidents didn't stand much chance. Again we brought out that if the United States had to carry the burden for the Western world of negotiations with Nasser for a Canal settlement, we had better keep our mouths shut so far as criticism of him was concerned, at least for the moment.

III. The Prime Minister outlined the major factors in the whole Cyprus problem.[10] They are quite complicated and he asserts that Britain wants nothing more to do with the island except to keep its base there, but any action that the British can suggest up to this moment antagonizes either the Greeks or the Turks. The British believe that the antagonisms that would be created by dropping the British responsibility in the island might even lead to war between the Turks and the Greeks.

I told them that I had certain important messages, particularly from the Greeks, asking me to urge upon Macmillan the importance of freeing Archbishop Makarios.[11] I told them that in my opinion I didn't believe they were gaining much by keeping him prisoner, so I would just turn him loose on the world. At the very least this would prove to the world that the British were trying to reach a solution to this problem. My impression is that they are probably going to turn him loose, but subject only to his agreement not to go back to Cyprus and to abjure violence.[12]

[1] Eisenhower had first suggested a Bermuda meeting with British Prime Minister Harold Macmillan in January 1957. For background on the conference see State, *Foreign Relations, 1955–1957*, vol. XXVII, *Western Europe and Canada*, pp. 682–83, 693–94, 697–99, 704–5; see also no. 57; and Macmillan to Eisenhower, January 23, 25, 1957, AWF/I: Macmillan. For appraisals of the meetings see Eisenhower, *Waging Peace*, pp. 121–25; and Harold Macmillan, *Riding the Storm 1956–1959* (London, 1971), pp. 249–58.

[2] Items scheduled for discussion between the two men included NATO and related defense matters, British association with Europe, relations with the Soviet Union, Anglo-American cooperation in the Middle East, Cyprus, China, East-West trade, and atomic energy.

[3] Sir John Selwyn Brooke Lloyd, former Minister of Defense, had been Great Britain's Secretary of State for Foreign Affairs since December 1955.

[4] For earlier references to Egyptian President Nasser as "a second Mussolini" see Galambos and van Ee, *The Middle Way*, nos. 2024 and 2128A.
[5] Eisenhower and Macmillan agreed that the United Nations Emergency Force should remain in the Sharm-el-Sheikh area until "the chance of renewal of clash was eliminated." Both men were concerned about Israel's intention to reoccupy Gaza if Egypt took over the area; this action, they decided, would call for convening the U.N. General Assembly. The discussions are recorded in State, *Foreign Relations, 1955–1957*, vol. XVII, *Arab-Israeli Dispute, 1957*, pp. 454–56.
[6] Prior to the Suez invasion, Kuwait produced sixty million tons of oil per year. Saudi Arabia, Iraq, and Iran together produced a total of 109 million tons (Diane B. Kunz, *The Economic Diplomacy of the Suez Crisis* [Chapel Hill, 1991], p. 199; see also State, *Foreign Relations, 1955–1957*, vol. XII, *Near East Region; Iran; Iraq*, pp. 464–65; and vol. XXVII, *Western Europe and Canada*, p. 713.
[7] For background on the Anglo-Arabian conflict over the Bura*i*mi Oasis see Galambos and van Ee, *The Middle Way*, nos. 245 and 1875. Foreign Secretary Lloyd had cited Aden as an example of a "Free World outpost" which was "being menaced by the Soviets through assistance to Yemen, with additional help from Saudi Arabia" (State, *Foreign Relations, 1955–1957*, vol. XXVII, *Western Europe and Canada*, pp. 713, 714, 720).
[8] For the Buraimi discussions see *ibid.*, pp. 713–14.
[9] For background on the Baghdad Pact, signed by Turkey, Iraq, Great Britain, Pakistan, and Iran in 1955, see Galambos and van Ee, *The Middle Way*, nos. 1681, 1774, and 2147. The British had long pressed the United States to join the alliance. Later on this same day Secretary Dulles would ask U.S. Ambassador John Hay Whitney to tell Macmillan and Lloyd that the United States would join the Baghdad Pact Military Committee if invited to do so by the members. Dulles had decided to inform the British at this time because the information had leaked to the press (State, *Foreign Relations, 1955–1957*, vol. XII, *Near East Region; Iran; Iraq*, pp. 463, 466–69; *ibid.*, vol. XXVII, *Western Europe and Canada*, pp. 721–22).
[10] For background on the conflict over Greek and Turkish claims to Cyprus see Galambos and van Ee, *The Middle Way*, nos. 1031, 1785, and 1900. Macmillan had stated that the British were beginning to doubt the strategic value of the island, and with the increasing range of aircraft, he wondered whether it was "worth the risks" (State, *Foreign Relations, 1955–1957*, vol. XXIV, *Soviet Union; Eastern Mediterranean* [1989], pp. 464–65).
[11] In March 1956 the British had arrested the Cypriot archbishop on suspicion of inciting terrorism and had deported him to the Seychelles. King Paul of Greece had written to Eisenhower (Mar. 13) urging the release of Makarios (*ibid.*, pp. 459–60).
[12] For developments see no. 91.

79

EM, AWF, International Series: Brazil

To Juscelino Kubitschek de Oliveira — *March 21, 1957*
Secret

Excellency:[1] I was very happy to meet with Ambassador Peixoto on March 12, 1957, and to receive from him your gracious letter of February 11, 1957, as well as the welcome assurances of friendship, support and collaboration which you asked him to convey in behalf of yourself and of the people of Brazil.[2] You may be assured that these sentiments are warmly held and fully reciprocated by the people of the United States of America, and by myself.

The conclusion of an agreement to establish a guided missiles tracking station on Fernando de Noronha Island was most gratifying to me and I sincerely appreciate the personal actions you took to bring this negotiation to a prompt and mutually satisfactory conclusion.[3] As you are aware, this installation will play an important role in the development of weapons vital for the defense of Brazil and the United States, as well as of the entire free world. Its establishment on Brazilian territory is an important step toward realization of this great purpose. You may be confident that in connection with further negotiations you have entrusted to Ambassador Peixoto, he will find on the part of representatives of the United States Government the same good will and spirit of cooperation which have always been fundamental in our approach to relations with Brazil.

Please accept, Excellency, assurances of my highest regard, and best wishes for your personal well being, and for the continued progress and prosperity of the people of Brazil. *Sincerely*

[1] Kubitschek de Oliveira, a physician and former president of the Brazilian Society of English Culture, had been President of Brazil since January 1956.

[2] At the top of the translation of President Kubitchek's letter (AWF/I: Brazil) Eisenhower had written: "Mrs. Whitman. Pls give following to Gen. Goodpaster 'Before filing, ask State whether we should make any reply. While this is really only an answer to a former message of mine, we *might* want to keep open this channel for the moment.' D.E." (see also Herter to Eisenhower, Mar. 6, 1957; and Memorandum of Conversation, Mar. 12, 1957, both in *ibid.*). A response to President Kubitschek, Dulles said, "would support our interests in negotiating other defense facilities" mentioned in the Brazilian president's letter; he enclosed a State Department draft, which Eisenhower approved (Dulles to Eisenhower, Mar. 19, 1957, *ibid.*). Erani do Amaral Peixoto, former leader of the Social Democrat party, had been Brazilian ambassador to the United States since July 1956.

[3] The Air Force had first expressed interest in a guided missiles tracking station in Brazil in 1952. Although upheavals in the Brazilian government had prevented the conclusion of a military facilities agreement, Defense Department officials had conducted site surveys on the island of Fernando de Noronha in 1954 and 1955. In December 1956 the State Department had advised Eisenhower of further negotiation delays by the Brazilian government. On December 14 Eisenhower had urged Kubitschek to "find means to assure that the construction of these essential facilities will be allowed to begin without further delays, so as not to imperil the testing of intercontinental ballistic missiles." The United States and Brazil had signed an agreement establishing the missiles facility on January 21, 1957 (Eisenhower to Kubitschek, Feb. 14, 1956, AWF/I: Brazil; see also Galambos and van Ee, *The Middle Way*, no. 1925; and State, *Foreign Relations, 1955–1957*, vol. VII, *American Republics: Central and South America* [1987], pp. 713–37, 747–55). The text of the agreement is in *U.S. Department of State Bulletin* 36, no. 922 (February 25, 1957), 316–17.

80 *EM, WHCF, Official File 99-Z*

To Barak Thomas Mattingly *March 21, 1957*

Dear Barak:[1] The idea in your letter of the fourteenth interests me far too much for relegation to that "circular filing cabinet."[2] As a matter of fact, Tom Stephens and I have discussed something similar—specifically with the dual purpose of keeping "Citizens" alive by giving them *now* assignments with reference to current legislation.[3] When I get back to Washington, I shall talk to him further about the whole idea. Certainly I do not want to neglect a single suggestion that might help secure favorable action by the Congress on certain of the proposals now before them.

With thanks and warm regard, *Sincerely*

[1] Mattingly, a St. Louis attorney and chairman of the board of Ozark Airlines, had been active in the effort to draft Eisenhower as the Republican presidential nominee in 1952 (see Galambos, *NATO and the Campaign of 1952*, no. 726).

[2] Presidents since George Washington, Mattingly had written, had problems with Congress which they attempted to solve "by various and sundry means." He suggested that Eisenhower ask his "many many loyal supporters in all the States of the Union" to write their congressional representatives "criticizing their actions or asking them to be for or against a particular bill." The response to such a campaign, he predicted, "would be nothing short of miraculous," and would, with some newspaper support, be sufficient to "kill or pass such legislation as you desire." Mattingly recommended that if Eisenhower did not think his idea had merit, he should throw the letter in the waste basket, that is "the circular filing cabinet" and then "forget it" (same file as document).

[3] Stephens, who had resigned as the President's appointments secretary on February 19, 1955, had remained an active participant in Republican party politics and would return to his post in the White House in March 1958 (*New York Times*, Jan. 27, Feb. 19, 1955, Mar. 24, 1958). Eisenhower had met with Stephens and others on February 27, 1957, to discuss efforts to promote "grass-roots" activity in the Republican party (see AWF/AWD, Feb. 27, 1957). For background on the Citizens for Eisenhower committees see Galambos and van Ee, *The Middle Way*, nos. 324 and 1133. For developments see no. 278.

81 *EM, AWF, Name Series*

To Mamie Geneva Doud Eisenhower *March 21, 1957*

Dearest: We arrived here on schedule last evening.[1] I feel somewhat better but am possibly a little more optimistic than General Snyder.[2]

Plan to leave here Sunday morning but am not yet sure how I shall come home. If weather is excellent so that we can maintain zero altitude pressure in cabin, I shall probably come in the Columbine, otherwise by ship.[3]

Do hope that you and Min are having a fine time with the children.[4] I would certainly like to be with you. *Love to all of you*

[1] The President had left Washington, D.C., on March 14 to travel aboard the U.S.S. *Canberra* to Bermuda for a conference (see no. 78 and *New York Times*, Mar. 15, 1957).
[2] Earlier this month Eisenhower had suffered an ear infection and tracheitis (*New York Times*, Mar. 8, 1957).
[3] See the following document.
[4] Mrs. Eisenhower, her mother, Elivera Carlson Doud, and the Eisenhower grandchildren had been staying at the Eisenhowers' Gettysburg farm (*New York Times*, Mar. 16, 17, 1957).

82

EM, AWF, International Series: Macmillan

To Harold Macmillan — *March 23, 1957*
Top secret

[*Dear Harold:*] I have your memorandum dated March twenty-second[1] to which there are four attachments dealing with the subjects of:

I. AQUATONE[2]
II. Tripartite Alert Procedure[3]
III. Nuclear Weapons for R.A.F. bombers
IV. Nuclear bomb release gear for R.A.F. bombers

The first two items mentioned in the attachments are completely satisfactory to the United States Government, and I should like to add that we are pleased that you found your way clear to allow United Kingdom bases to be used for AQUATONE if it should at some time become necessary.

With respect to Item III, "Nuclear Weapons for R.A.F. bombers," I have a couple of additions to the phraseology submitted, merely to make certain that the meaning of the paper conformed to the requirements of United States law. The item as revised would read as follows:

"The United Kingdom Government welcome the agreement to co-ordinate the strike plans of the United States and United Kingdom bomber forces, and to store United States nuclear weapons on R.A.F. airfields under United States custody for release subject to decision by the President in an emergency.[4] We understand that for the present at least these weapons will be in the kiloton range. The United Kingdom forces could obviously play a much more effective part in joint strikes if the United States weapons made available to them in emergency were in the megaton range, and it is suggested that this possibility might be examined at the appropriate time."

With respect to Item IV, "Nuclear bomb release gear for R.A.F. bombers," I agree of course that you shall probably have to make some statement in order to prevent speculation in the press that might prove not only inaccurate but damaging.[5] However, as I explained to you verbally, the United States would prefer not to be a party to a public statement which might give rise to demands upon us by other governments where we should not be in a position to meet the requests. Consequently I suggest the possible adequacy of a unilateral statement by yourself or by the British Defense Minister to the effect that Canberras are now being equipped to carry atomic bombs.[6] *With warm regard*

[1] Macmillan's memorandum is in PREM 11/1763. Eisenhower wrote this note while attending the Bermuda Conference (see no. 78).

[2] In November 1954 the United States had initiated a secret project, code-named AQUATONE, to build a high-altitude reconnaissance plane that could penetrate Soviet air defenses. Former British Prime Minister Anthony Eden had authorized the lease of Lakenheath, a Strategic Air Command (SAC) base northeast of London, as the launch point for these U-2 spy planes, but in early 1956 the fears of worsening British-Soviet relations had dampened British enthusiasm for the cooperative venture. Royal Air Force (RAF) pilots trained in the United States had nevertheless manned U-2s on several flights over the Soviet Union (Ann Whitman memorandum, Nov. 22, 1954, AWF/AWD; Eden to Eisenhower, May 17, 1956, AWF/I: Eden; Richard M. Bissell, Jr., *Reflections of a Cold Warrior: From Yalta to the Bay of Pigs* [New Haven, 1996], pp. 92–117; Michael R. Beschloss, *Mayday: Eisenhower, Khrushchev, and the U-2 Affair* [New York, 1986], pp. 81–94, 105, 112, 116, 121–22, 146–47; Stephen E. Ambrose, *Eisenhower*, 2 vols. [New York, 1983–84], vol. II, *The President* [1984], pp. 227–28, 340–41).

[3] For more on U.S.-Canadian coordination of alert measures see no. 206.

[4] For background on the program to modify RAF planes in order to use atomic weapons see Galambos and van Ee, *The Middle Way*, no. 2026; and Eden to Eisenhower, Oct. 5, 1956, AWF/I: Eden; see also Eisenhower to Adams and Hauge, Feb. 15, 1954, and other supporting documents in AWF/A, Wilson, and AWF/I: Great Britain, Plan K.

Eisenhower had added the words "under United States custody" and "subject to decision by the President" to Macmillan's memorandum (Macmillan to Eisenhower, Mar. 22, 1957, AWF/I: Macmillan).

[5] RAF Canberra bombers had been fitted with special nuclear weapons release slips manufactured in the United States. "Although this work has been treated with the utmost secrecy," Macmillan had written, "Canberras with these fitments are now coming into squadron service, and the danger of a leakage of this news or speculation is inevitably growing." He suggested the release of a joint public statement (*ibid.*).

[6] In a handwritten note at the bottom of Macmillan's memorandum Eisenhower had

written to Dulles: "Foster—regarding this point—I suggested possibility—and adequacy—of mere unilateral statement of British Defense that 'Canberras are now equipped to carry atomic *bombs*'" (*ibid.*).

On April 4 British Defense Minister Duncan Sandys would include this statement, as amended by Eisenhower, in his announcement of changes in British defense policy (Macmillan, *Riding the Storm*, pp. 263–64; *New York Times*, Apr. 5, 1957).

83

EM, AWF, Name Series

To Mamie Geneva Doud Eisenhower — *March 23, 1957*

Dearest: As yet cannot decide whether I shall return by cruiser or by Columbine. Will inform you Sunday morning.[1]

I do hope you are having pleasant weather at the farm. My thoughts turn constantly to you, to Min and the children. I believe that Barbie and Johnnie are now with you so I know that with almost all the family present you are having a most enjoyable time.[2]

To all of you my love

[1] The President was attending a conference in Bermuda (see nos. 78 and 81). The following morning he would return via the presidential plane *Columbine* (*New York Times*, Mar. 25, 1957).

[2] Eisenhower was referring to his son John Eisenhower and his daughter-in-law, the former Barbara Jean Thompson. See no. 81.

84

EM, AWF, Name Series

To Edgar Newton Eisenhower — *March 25, 1957*

Dear Ed: Until I received your letter I did not know there was an impending vacancy on the Securities and Exchange Commission.[1] I am turning over your recommendation to Sherman Adams who, in the case of the Independent Agencies, has the task of investigating personal records to determine suitable appointments to these posts. This morning he tells me that he has been looking over the records of several men—all recommended by Secretary Humphrey of the Treasury Department.[2]

Sherman will look into the matter thoroughly—but I do suggest that when you know of a man who might fill a government position with distinction you should submit your suggestion at the earliest possible moment. In that way we can sometimes give greater consideration because of the fact that decisions are not already in the crystallizing stage.

As to health, I am delighted that you are better. I saw George Allen last evening who had met you as you were going back to Tacoma. He thought that so far as appearance was concerned you were perfectly wonderful.[3]

For myself, I have not yet completely shaken off my bronchial cough. This morning I had an hour's session with a whole flock of doctors. They apparently think it is just a stubborn case of bronchitis and nothing serious, but I must say that at times it really gets me down.[4]

Give Lucy my love. I am especially grateful to her for her faithfulness in writing to me so often about your condition while you were in Arizona. Also, of course, my warm greetings to Janis and her family. *As ever*

[1] Eisenhower's brother Edgar had written on March 20 saying he had just heard that the chairman of the Securities and Exchange Commission was about to resign. He urged Eisenhower to appoint New York attorney Abraham N. Davis, Edgar's friend, to the position (AWF/N). On April 16, 1957, Eisenhower would nominate J. Sinclair Armstrong (LL.B. Harvard 1941), SEC chairman since 1955, to be Assistant Secretary of the Navy (see *New York Times*, Apr. 17, 1957).

[2] Edward Northrup Gadsby (J.D. New York University 1929) would be named a member of the SEC in July, and chairman on August 31, 1957 (see *ibid.*, Sept. 1, 1957).

[3] On Edgar's health see no. 1. Eisenhower had spoken by telephone with his friend George E. Allen on March 24.

[4] For background on Eisenhower's bronchitis see no. 81.

85

EM, AWF, Administration Series, Brownell Corr.

TO CHARLES AUGUSTINE CASE — *March 25, 1957*

Dear Charley:[1] All the recommendations made to me for appointments in the Federal Courts come through the Attorney General. I charge the Attorney General with investigating the record, professional standing, character and connections of every possible candidate, and thereafter make the choice of the man who appears to be best suited for the job.[2] One of the important features is invariably the recommendation of the American Bar Association.

Consequently, I have turned your letter over to Attorney General Brownell who will give to Governor Arn's case very thorough and exhausting consideration.[3]

That is all I can promise, as I am sure you will understand.[4]

It was good to hear from you. I hope that you are well. Remember me to your children when you write to them, and especially to Maude Hurd when next you see her. Of course you will also run into some of my friends around town, like Sam Heller and Emmett Graham and others—give them my best.[5]

With warm personal regard, *As ever*

[1] Case, who was a long-time friend, was vice-president of the Eisenhower Foundation.

[2] For more on Eisenhower's "deep personal interest in the appointment of Federal Judges" see no. 593. See also Galambos and van Ee, *The Middle Way*, no. 1254.

[3] Case had written Eisenhower on March 22, 1957, to recommend the appointment of former Kansas governor (1951–1955) Edward F. Arn to an anticipated opening on the Tenth U.S. Circuit Court of Appeals (AWF/A Brownell Corr.). Arn, a Republican who was now practicing law in Topeka, had written to Eisenhower on March 23 to express his interest in the judicial vacancy; see Eisenhower to Arn, Mar. 28, 1957, AWF/D. For background see Galambos and van Ee, *The Middle Way*, no. 1160.

[4] Eisenhower would send Attorney General Brownell a note on March 25 (AWF/A, Brownell Corr.) stating that "Mr. Case is a very old & fine friend—but I do not know how much he appreciates the qualifications of a Fed. Judge." For further developments see no. 299.

[5] Sam Raymond Heller and Emmett Schwedner Graham, friends of Eisenhower from Abilene, had also written in support of Arn's judicial appointment. Their letters of March 28 and April 1, 1957, are in AWF/D. For background on Heller see no. 59. Graham was secretary of the Eisenhower Foundation (see Galambos and van Ee, *The Middle Way*, no. 47). Maud Rogers Hurd was also a long-time friend of Eisenhower from Abilene (see *Eisenhower Papers*, vols. I–XVII).

86 — *EM, AWF, Name Series*

TO JOYCE CLYDE HALL — *March 25, 1957*

Dear Joyce:[1] When I was in Bermuda I mentioned to Harold Macmillan your suggestion of inviting Sir Winston to bring or send to America an exhibition of his paintings.[2] The Prime Minister thinks the exhibition is a splendid idea, as do I. However, he feels that it would be wise not to invite Sir Winston to come with his collection because his strength would probably not permit him to make such a trip without adverse effects and to have to refuse on such grounds might be embarrassing to him.

I do not know how far your negotiations have gone with Sir Winston, but I do know that you have a good contact through his daughter Sarah.[3] You could either quote me to her saying I believe it would be a very nice idea if the collection could be brought over here for exhibition in some of our good galleries or, of course, if you think it necessary I would write Sir Winston a short note to express this fact.[4]

With warm regard, *Sincerely*

[1] For background on greeting card manufacturer Hall see Galambos and van Ee, *The Middle Way*, no. 587.

[2] On the Bermuda Conference see no. 78. On February 25 Hall had telephoned Eisenhower to relate a conversation he had had with the "top man in British art." At a meeting with the President on March 6 Hall had repeated the proposal (see Telephone conversation, Eisenhower and Hall, AWF/N; Hall to Whitman, Mar. 14, 1957, AWF/N, and President's daily appointments).

[3] Sarah Churchill, Lady Audley, was a British actress and painter. Following a telephone conversation with Churchill's daughter, Hall would report that she wanted her father to accompany his paintings. She said she thought "it would be good for him" because "he feels left out of things" (Telephone conversations, Hall and Eisenhower, July 10, 1957, AWF/N).

[4] On April 16 Eisenhower would invite Churchill to provide paintings for a travelling exhibition in the United States. "I am certain it would serve in a very definite way to strengthen the friendship between our two countries," he wrote (AWF/I: Churchill). Hall would deliver the letter to Churchill on June 23. In his June 24 reply Churchill would say that he was "much complimented" by Eisenhower's proposal, and that he would make thirty paintings available for the exhibit (AWF/I: Churchill; see also Telephone conversations, Hall and Eisenhower, July 10, 1957, AWF/N). For developments see no. 222.

87 *EM, AWF, Administration Series*

To Charles Douglas Jackson *March 25, 1957*

Dear C. D.:[1] When I returned from Bermuda, I found awaiting me the beautifully bound volume of LIFE's series on the World's Great Religions that you so kindly sent me. Incidentally, have *you* made any plans for shifting recently?[2]

This 1957 Conference was profitable and pleasant, but we missed you and the excitement of the return trip from the 1953 affair.[3]

With warm regard, *As ever*

[1] Jackson, publisher of *Fortune* magazine, had been a special assistant to the President from January 1953 until April 1954. For background see Galambos and van Ee, *The Middle Way*, no. 8.

[2] In a letter accompanying the specially bound copy of the book Jackson had written: "If, as the months go by, the Christians seem to be too impossible, you will find in this book the basic information on which to base a shift at any time" (Mar. 21, 1957, AWF/A). Eisenhower may have been referring to the possibility of Jackson's return to a job in the White House (see Galambos and van Ee, *The Middle Way*, no. 881).

[3] On the recently completed Bermuda Conference with Britain's Prime Minister Harold Macmillan see no. 78. In early December 1953 Eisenhower had met in Bermuda with British Prime Minister Winston Churchill and French Premier Joseph Laniel at his first Western summit conference (see Galambos and van Ee, *The Middle Way*, nos. 589 and 597). He had taken with him the draft of the "Atoms for Peace" speech he was to deliver before the United Nations on December 8, the day of his departure from Bermuda. After conferring with Churchill, Eisenhower and Dulles agreed to modify two phrases in the speech that the Prime Minister thought would weaken its constructive purposes. With the help of Jackson and AEC Chairman Lewis Strauss, Eisenhower and Dulles made the changes during the flight to New York. According to the President, the plane circled New York for half an hour, enough time for his personal secretary Ann Whitman to type the final draft. "It was amusing," Eisenhower wrote, "to see the Secretary of State, the Chairman of the Atomic Energy Commission, and my principal adviser on 'propaganda' help run the mimeograph machine and do the stapling" (Eisenhower, *Mandate for Change*, pp. 251–52; see also Robert J. Donovan, *Confidential Secretary: Ann Whitman's 20 Years with Eisenhower and Rockefeller* [New York, 1988], p. 51; for background on the speech see Galambos and van Ee, *The Middle Way*, no. 598).

88

EM, AWF, International Series: Macmillan

TO HAROLD MACMILLAN
Eyes only

March 26, 1957

Dear Harold: I enclose herewith a copy of the article to which I referred today in my cable, sent to you at Bermuda. I likewise send a copy of that cable.[1]

The part of the article that disturbs me so deeply appears in the first two columns. Here is practically a verbatim account of the detailed incidents and events surrounding the elimination of the words "intelligence and planning" from the draft of the communique. The writer, of course, did not know the background that led to the original suggestion, that is, your thought that Canada, yourselves and ourselves should coordinate our efforts to detect any hostile move on the part of the Russians in periods of tension.

Of course the writer himself proves that he did not have the good of either your country or ours in mind in writing the article because he gives the logical reason for its elimination in the two sentences "The announcement was eliminated from the final draft of the document by Secretary of State Dulles. It is understood Mr. Dulles felt this evidence of a more intimate British-United States relationship would offend other allies of the United States, notably France." In other words, he cared nothing for the soundness of the national reasons, only for a story.

This article came out this morning, after Foster and I had held a meeting with our Congressional leaders last evening in which we outlined the general character of our talks, carefully avoiding, however, operational or planning details which could, if publicized, cause embarrassment to either or both of us. Nevertheless we made the truthful assertion that no "secret agreements" were arrived at.[2] This morning some of them may be wondering!

I am sure, of course, that you share my disappointment at such an occurrence, with its implication that even the members of such friendly governments as yours and ours cannot talk frankly and freely with one another without the danger of serious leaks to the public press. I earnestly hope that both of us may be successful in preventing things like this in the future so that there may be no interruption of the close communion and coordination that we consider so important to our future security and welfare.[3]

With warm personal regard, *[As ever]*

[1] On March 26 the *New York Times* had published, as their lead article, a report by its chief London correspondent Drew Middleton regarding the recently completed Bermuda Conference (see no. 78 for background). According to Middleton, Eisenhower had suggested to Britain's Prime Minister Macmillan that the two countries reestablish their "intimate wartime cooperation, including joint intelligence and planning systems, to meet international problems." Secretary Dulles had removed the announcement from the final communiqué, Middleton wrote, because of his concern that the agreement would offend other U.S. allies (*New York Times*, Mar. 26, 1957; see also "Secretary Dulles' News Conference of March 26," *U.S. Department of State Bulletin* 36, no. 929 [April 15, 1957], 595).

Eisenhower had immediately cabled Macmillan that the publication of the item disturbed him "mightily" and that the leak created doubt in his mind that he and Macmillan could "talk frankly to each other in confidence on matters of import . . ." (Eisenhower to Macmillan, Mar. 26, 1957, AWF/I: Macmillan).

[2] See Bipartisan Congressional Meeting, March 25, 1957, AWF/D.

[3] For developments see no. 93.

89 — *EM, AWF, Dulles-Herter Series*

To John Foster Dulles — *March 26, 1957*

Dear Foster: Upon request of the Department of State, I have just signed a photograph for the Argentine Ambassador.[1] Is it possible that we might be starting a precedent that could become quite a burden? Of course I do not mind signing one or even a very few pictures for this purpose, but I would rather dread having to keep the entire procession of Ambassadors that go through this capital supplied with autographed photographs.[2] *As ever*

[1] Adolfo Angel Vicchi had been ambassador since October 1956 (see Buchanan to Whitman, Mar. 18, 1957, AWF/D-H).

[2] As Dulles would tell the President, the number of requests had been few, "probably not more than four or five a year." He would recommend that Eisenhower forward the photograph to the ambassador; he would also ask the State Department Protocol Office to notify him of any marked changes in the number of requests (Dulles to Eisenhower, Mar. 28, 1957, *ibid.*).

90

EM, AWF, DDE Diaries Series

To George Magoffin Humphrey

March 27, 1957

Dear George: The Americans went into the Philippines in 1898. For the ensuing forty years we tried to do everything for that country that an enlightened, civilized nation could do for another. We established schools, sanitation systems, roads and communication nets, and in every way tried to inculcate in that Asiatic people a respect for our system of personal liberty and national independence based upon an economic system of free enterprise.

Forty years later I was serving in the Philippines and my work took me into all the provinces and principal villages of the country.[1] Over the years the word "independencia" had become a great watchword in the islands—promoted and exploited by shrewd politicians who saw that if they could become independent of United States supervision they themselves would have far greater opportunity to exploit the masses. To promote their own interests (and I do not mean to say there were not among them some few real patriots), they promised to the people all sorts of things, including a much higher living standard when independence should arrive. And so the word "independencia" began to mean to the peasants in the countryside something to eat and something to wear—in other words, material betterment. That is what I found in the Philippines after forty years under the stewardship of the United States government.

I quote this experience merely to show that in this complicated question of striving for mutual security there is no simple answer ready to hand, one that will meet all the requirements of a world in crisis.

Personally I feel that the things argued in your letter to Paul Hoffman would have had particular application during the first decade and a half of this century and to the period between the two world wars.[2] Both of those periods were for us and for much of the world years of relative calm and peace. The Russo-Japanese War was remote from our shores and only a few men were able to discern, as Henry Stimson[3] did, critical situations that were building up all over the world and which were certain one day to cause us the worst kind of trouble. Nevertheless, could those years of peace been continued indefinitely, I do believe that education—education alone—supported by word, by precept and example could have gradually brought about the same respect, in most places in the world, that we hold for individual liberty and free enterprise.

Today such an educational effort is not, by itself, sufficient. This I believe because[4] the circumstances and conditions that allowed a few men to put a steel plant in a corn field and another successful one in a marsh are as different from today's conditions in most of the Afro-Asian countries as day is from night. A country that has reached the saturation point in population long before its people understand or, indeed, even hear of the terms "personal rights" and "personal freedom" presents far different problems from those Americans faced in the first half of this century.

Just two other thoughts. The first is that few individuals understand the intensity and force of the spirit of nationalism that is gripping all peoples of the world today. They obtain, from a realization of their ambitions for national independence, fierce pride and personal satisfaction regardless of the individual's status within his own government. It is my personal conviction that almost any one of the newborn states of the world would far rather embrace Communism or any other form of dictatorship than to acknowledge the political domination of another government even though that brought to each citizen a far higher standard of living.

The other is a fact, which all of us know to be true, that a country such as ours could not exist, alone, in freedom were we surrounded by a sea of enemies, which all would be if they were Communist-dominated—and we would soon see our island of freedom take on a far different form. Many values that we have prized highly would disappear.

It is such thinking as all this that leads me to the conclusion that *protection of our own interests and our own system* demands and requires that we not only pursue diligently a plan of education and proselyting such as you outline in your long letter to Paul, but that we must at the same time understand that the spirit of nationalism, coupled with a deep hunger for some betterment in physical conditions and living standards, creates a critical situation in the underdeveloped areas of the world. Unless we have the fortitude and courage and stamina to meet the situation, we are not going to emerge unscathed from the struggle. Communism is not going to be whipped merely by pious words, but it can be whipped by a combination of the broadest and most persistent kind of education, coupled with a readiness on the part of ourselves—helped at least to some minor extent by the other free nations of the West—to face up to the critical phase through which the world is passing and do our duty like men.

What you have to say about collective planning resulting generally in unilateral payments and multilateral disposal of the money strikes a very responsive chord in my soul. In fact, I think that all I am trying to say is that neither education or mutual aid is in itself sufficient. Only in their unity will we find the strength necessary to do what we need to do.[5]

With warm regard, *As ever*

[1] For background see Eisenhower, *At Ease*, pp. 223–32; and Ambrose, *Eisenhower*, vol. I, *Soldier, General of the Army, President-Elect, 1890–1952* (1983), pp. 101–18.

[2] Eisenhower friend and political adviser Paul Hoffman had written the President (Feb. 25) to forward a copy of his article, "Blueprint for Foreign Aid." Eisenhower had sent the article to Treasury Secretary Humphrey for comment (see no. 60). On March 26 Humphrey had responded to the President and enclosed a copy of his letter to Hoffman (AWF/A). Humphrey argued against Hoffman's call for a new "Marshall Plan" for underdeveloped areas, saying that, "Conditions for the Marshall Plan were entirely different than the conditions in underdeveloped countries that we are talking about today." "Buying friendship is of very questionable lasting value," Humphrey maintained. "Discouraging the association of other countries with Russia over a period of time will be determined only by mutually advantageous and sound economic conditions and not by gifts from us. To assure their lasting support, we must instill in underdeveloped people a true desire for individual freedom that will be strong enough to persuade them permanently to our way of life rather than to communism." Humphrey believed that too much emphasis had been placed on support to big governments and government-owned property at the expense of private investment and the preservation of individual incentives. Comparing the situation to the development of steel towns by private entrepreneurs in the United States, Humphrey thought that the United States "would be making far greater progress toward assuring ourselves of a growing devotion to our way of life, which will stand the test of time and provide friends when they are needed, if we spend more effort on inducing governments to provide laws to encourage individual initiative and effort and the protection of private property as its reward and finance fewer governmental activities that compete with individual enterprise."

[3] On Stimson see Galambos, *Columbia University*, no. 747.

[4] Eisenhower had crossed out the words "in spite of the fact that" and substituted "because" in the draft of this letter.

[5] Humphrey had written that he was "opposed to multilateral ventures because our experience almost without exception has been that in the end all proposals finally suggest that we provide the money and they provide for spending it. It is far better, more effective, and more useful for us to give by ourselves, whatever we do decide to give, without entangling alliances." For more on Eisenhower's views on the importance of mutual aid see nos. 27 and 76.

91

EM, AWF, International Series: Macmillan

To Harold Macmillan
Cable. Secret

March 29, 1957

Dear Harold: I have noted with great interest your decision to release Archbishop Makarios.[1] I know that this entailed great difficulty for you. I earnestly hope that his release will bring about a substantial improvement in the atmosphere relating to Cyprus, with greater prospects for a satisfactory settlement of this problem.

I want you to know that we will do all we can to encourage others concerned to approach the matter in a constructive and conciliatory manner so that the opportunities afforded by this action on your part will not be lost.[2]

With kind regard, *Sincerely*

[1] For background on the Cyprus situation and the imprisonment of the Greek Cypriot archbishop see no. 78. On March 20 the British government had presented Makarios with a proposal that would end his detention on conditions that he publicly renounce violence and not return to Cyprus. He was released on March 28 (State, *Foreign Relations, 1955–1957,* vol. XXIV, *Soviet Union; Eastern Mediterranean,* pp. 462, 467–68; *New York Times,* Mar. 29, 1957).

[2] Macmillan would tell Eisenhower that the decision "was not taken without loss to the Government. I do not believe," he said, "that the Archbishop has changed his views in the Seychelles; he is the Bourbon of Cyprus." The Prime Minister asked Eisenhower for his help "in persuading all concerned to face reality." He cautioned, however, that private pressure would be better than public statements (State, *Foreign Relations, 1955–1957,* vol. XXIV, *Soviet Union; Eastern Mediterranean,* pp. 469–70). For developments see no. 209.

92

EM, AWF, International Series: Greece

To Paul I, King of the Hellenes
Cable. Secret

March 29, 1957

Dear King Paul:[1] I would like to tell you that I very much appreciated your letter of March 15, 1957. Your views on the Cyprus problem, especially with respect to Archbishop Makarios, were of great value to me and my associates at Bermuda and during the Conference I took the opportunity of urging that the Archbishop be released.[2]

It is encouraging to learn that the Archbishop has recently been offered the opportunity of leaving the Seychelles.[3] His release presents a great opportunity and, as you stated in your letter, marks 'a definite step toward a possible solution of this thorny problem'. I sincerely hope that with your advice and encouragement the Greek Government will do everything possible to use this opportunity for the purpose of creating an atmosphere which will lead to constructive negotiations between the leaders of the Cypriot communities and the British authorities.

Further, I would urge you to consider the possibility that NATO could at the same time play a useful role in considering the international aspects of this question.[4] If the domestic and international aspects of the problem could be more clearly separated, and if they are approached with courage and resourcefulness, I believe that this painful problem can gradually but certainly be solved in accordance with the principles of the Charter of the United Nations.[5]

Thank you again for your letter. Please accept the best wishes of myself and Mrs. Eisenhower and convey our greetings to Queen Frederika. *Sincerely*

[1] Secretary Dulles probably drafted this letter, which the American ambassador would deliver to King Paul on March 31. (see State, *Foreign Relations, 1955–1957,* vol. XXIV, *Soviet Union; Eastern Mediterranean,* p. 468). Eisenhower had also written to Greek Prime Minister Constantine Karamanlis regarding U.S. interest in the Cyprus situation (see Eisenhower to Karamanlis, Mar. 21, 1957, AWF/I: Greece).

[2] For background on the political struggle over Cyprus, the detention of Archbishop Makarios, and the Bermuda Conference, see no. 78. King Paul had written that Makarios was the only "personality or authority that could be found in Cyprus or Greece, under present circumstances, to take any decisions that could ever be accepted by all concerned." According to the American ambassador, King Paul "noted with obvious relish" that Eisenhower had supported the release of the archbishop (AWF/I: Greece, King Paul; see also State, *Foreign Relations, 1955–1957,* vol. XXIV, *Soviet Union; Eastern Mediterranean,* pp. 459–60, 468).

[3] The British had released Makarios on March 28 (see the preceding document).

[4] The dispute between Greece and Turkey over Cyprus had threatened the unity of the NATO alliance. A weakened NATO, Dulles believed, would expose the Mediterranean area to the threat of Communist penetration, and he had raised the possibility of a role for NATO in future negotiations. Greek officials, preferring that the issue be handled in the United Nations, had been reluctant to consider NATO intervention. Earlier in March the Greek government had rejected an effort by the NATO Secretary General to appoint three outstanding citizens to formulate procedures for settling the dispute. NATO involvement, according to Prime Minister Karamanlis, would lead to discussions that would include Turkey, whereas U.N. guidelines required negotiations only between Great Britain and the Cypriots (see Galambos and van Ee, *The Middle Way,* no. 1900; and State, *Foreign Relations, 1955–1957,* vol. XXIV, *Soviet Union; Eastern Mediterranean,* pp. 289–90, 356–57, 360–61, 388–92, 447, 449–50, 461–64).

[5] For developments see no. 209.

93 *EM, AWF, International Series: Macmillan*

To Harold Macmillan *March 29, 1957*
Cable. Top secret

Dear Harold: As I should have told you before, I initiated immediately upon the appearance of the Middleton story the same kind of inquiry here as you did in Bermuda and with the same negative results. I believe with you that we should drop the matter and give our attention to the future, as you suggest in your last paragraph where you say 'the embarrassment of this article will not make us lose faith in the need for us to talk frankly and with confidence to each other.'[1]

With warm personal regard, *As ever,*

[1] For background on the controversy surrounding the article by Drew Middleton, London correspondent for the *New York Times*, see no. 88. After prodding from State Department officials, *New York Times* editors had learned from Middleton that the press director of the British Foreign Office had given him the story. "I cannot doubt the correctness of this fact," Secretary Dulles told Eisenhower. "Indeed I assumed it in any event because (1) Drew Middleton has for long been the semi-official mouthpiece of the British Foreign Office; (2) there was no American left in Bermuda who could have given the information, with the possible exception of Jock Whitney "[John Hay Whitney, U.S. Ambassador to Great Britain]"; (3) it was the UK Delegation which evidenced a very strong desire to put in the communiqué language about combined intelligence and planning, and the US which wanted it out, so that there was demonstrable motivation for a UK leak and none for a US leak" (Dulles to Eisenhower, Mar. 27, 1957, Dulles Papers, White House Memoranda Series; see also Telephone conversations, Dulles and Hagerty, Mar. 26, 27, 1957, and Dulles and Elbrick, Mar. 26, 1957, Dulles Papers, Telephone Conversations).

Eisenhower had called Ambassador Whitney when the latter had returned from Bermuda, asking him if he had any idea who had disclosed the information. Whitney did not know "but pointed out it was datelined Bermuda" (Telephone conversation, Mar. 26, 1957, AWF/D).

In his letter Macmillan had denied that his public relations people had leaked the information. He admitted that Foreign Secretary Selwyn Lloyd had spoken with Middleton but claimed that Lloyd had "stuck closely to the words" used by Dulles in his earlier talk with British correspondents. "Much of the article could be based on intelligent guess-work," he wrote (Macmillan to Eisenhower, Mar. 29, 1957, AWF/I: Macmillan).

Whitney later told Eisenhower that the British were "professing high-and-mighty injured feelings that they were accused of the Drew Middleton leak." Middleton was "very sore at their denial, but must, of course, protect his source." Whitney also told Eisenhower that Macmillan "was just as mad" as the President "and that is why the innocent faces all around" (Whitney to Eisenhower, Apr. 13, 1957, AWF/A).

94 *EM, AWF, DDE Diaries Series*

To Arthur Krock *March 29, 1957*
Personal and confidential

Dear Arthur: When I saw your column this morning, I was perfectly certain that you had misquoted me when you reported me as having said, "To say you are going to save a few millions here and a few millions there is the poorest kind of economy we can find." Upon looking up the text of my press conference, I find you are absolutely correct.[1]

When I made the statement quoted in your column of today, I was talking, as you probably realize, about mutual aid. In this field I believe that we must look at what we are trying to do; we must think in terms of objectives and of needs. So when I was talking about piecemeal savings, I was applying it to this one program only. Elsewhere in the press conference you will find that I mentioned that the Defense Department had already found the possibility of saving money through further shortening of lead time and through a better use of accumulated spare parts.[2] I also pointed out in another place that some savings could be made in flexibility of programs.[3] But I do decry any effort to save money in the mutual aid area by merely saying that we will cut this country ten million, that one five million and the next a different figure, and so on.

I send you this note merely to make clear to you my own meaning. I do not expect or desire to influence in any way what you may find it proper to say about this budgetary situation.[4] It is because I want to keep this on a purely personal basis that I so mark this letter.

With warm regard, *Sincerely*

[1] Eisenhower was referring to *New York Times* columnist Arthur Krock's March 29 editorial comments regarding the President's March 27 news conference (see *Public Papers of the Presidents: Eisenhower, 1957*, pp. 218–23, and *New York Times*, Mar. 29, 1957). The President had spent a large part of the conference defending his program on foreign aid. Asked what the Administration had done specifically to help its foreign aid program through Congress, Eisenhower had responded that "I am afraid you have opened up yourself for a little speech." Stating that since foreign aid had no pressure group in any district in the United States, it became the "fair target" of anyone who wanted to save money. However, Eisenhower continued, "I say to you there are no dollars today that are being spent more wisely for the future of American peace and prosperity than the dollars we put in foreign aid." The President indicated his awareness of the limitations of foreign aid ("I don't believe you can buy friendship"), stating that he saw foreign aid as only one part of a many-sided program. "You are trying to teach respect for individual liberty and rights to people who never heard the words. And while you are going along with that, you have got a critical problem. They are proud of their national existence, but they are also suffering under the lowest standards of living. . . . That is the thing you are up against; and, therefore, to say

you are going to save a few millions here and a few millions there, I think is the poorest kind of economy we can find." For background see nos. 75 and 76.
[2] Eisenhower had said: "I am told by the Defense Department they found they can make probably some savings for one year by shortening up still further their carryovers, which has been a point of some argument for some years."
[3] The President had said: "I think the more flexibility, the longer term it is, the more you can save, because the more efficiently you can plan."
[4] For more on the budget and foreign aid see also no. 27.

2

Foreign Aid

95

EM, AWF, Administration Series

To Lauris Norstad

April 1, 1957

Dear Larry: Many thanks for your fine letter. I hasten to send you a short reply because I very much want you to continue giving me your impressions of individuals, governments and conditions in the NATO region.[1]

Another reason for writing you immediately is because there will soon arrive in Paris, as the American Ambassador, my good friend Amory Houghton. He is a fine type of American businessman and will work seriously at his job.[2]

I told him that you could often be of great help to him because of your long familiarity with the personalities of the region, and I would appreciate it if you would make some arrangement for meeting him promptly after he arrives. I assure you that it will not be long before you like him immensely.

Give my warm greetings to Isabelle[3] and, of course, all the very best to yourself. *As ever*

[1] General Norstad, Supreme Allied Commander, Europe, had written Eisenhower regarding British plans to reduce their NATO forces (for background see no. 57). Norstad had been "particularly worried about the dangers of a definite split between the Nato members on this question." The decision by the Western European Union to study the issue of force levels, he said, would give the organization "a little more time to work out the answer"; however, the issue would take "some rather delicate handling to avoid even a more serious difference of opinion in the fall."

Norstad had just completed visits to the NATO capitals and had told Eisenhower about meetings with Portuguese Prime Minister Antonio Oliviera Salazar in Lisbon and German Chancellor Konrad Adenauer in Bonn. Norstad reported that Salazar, who had been concerned that U.S. action in the Middle East had damaged the NATO alliance by destroying the prestige of Great Britain and France, had accepted his argument that the over-all strength of the alliance was more important than the individual strength of any of its members.

Adenauer had declared his "firm friendship" with the United States and was optimistic about his chances for reelection in September (Norstad to Eisenhower, Mar. 29, 1957, AWF/A; see also State, *Foreign Relations of the United States, 1955–1957*, vol. IV, *Western European Security and Integration* [1986], pp. 165–66).

Eisenhower would send Norstad's letter to Secretary Dulles on this same day. "I do this," the President wrote, "not so much because it provides anything particularly new (except possibly for the paragraph on Salazar) but because it gives you some idea of the calibre and character of Norstad" (AWF/D).

[2] Amory Houghton (A.B. Harvard 1921) was chairman of the board of the Corning Glass Corporation (see Galambos, *Chief of Staff*, no. 1304). Eisenhower had named Houghton U.S. Ambassador to France on February 25.

[3] Norstad's wife was the former Isabelle Helen Jenkins.

To Arthur Seymour Nevins *April 1, 1957*

Dear Art: I send you herewith a memorandum from Admiral Strauss giving information on the matter of a school on artificial insemination that Bob Hartley might like to attend.[1] If he should like to go to this particular school, you can see from Admiral Strauss' memorandum that he must act promptly in submitting his application. If he does not desire to do so, I should like to have immediate notification so that I can inform the Admiral.

Because of the importance of the time factor, I am sending a copy of this part of my letter directly to Bob Hartley. I understand that you are temporarily absent from Gettysburg and my thought is that if Bob Hartley wants to attend, he can notify my office and we will have Admiral Strauss put in the application.[2]

I have been thinking about the location of the new fitting barn and sales theatre. I talked to Pete about the matter and he is quite clear in his mind that it being a fixed feature on his land, he should be the one to pay for it.[3] In this way there can be no possible complication in the event he should want to dispose wholly of his farms.

One location I should like to have you consider is one just to the south of the entrance to the Brandon farm. You will recall that there were a number of trees cut out that provide a good view of our house from certain spots on Highway 15. If we should place a good looking structure on that location, I suggest that we might find it would be the best possible shield from the curiosity of people on the highway.

You might find, of course, that there are certain objections to using the site for this purpose, or I may be mistaken in my assumption that such a structure would actually serve the additional purpose I suggest. In any event, there is no rush about this particular matter, but you and Hartley could study it over.[4]

* * * * *

Incidentally, I hope you understand that Pete is very anxious that you immediately get the workmen on the job to finish up the top of the old schoolhouse. He seemed to be disappointed that we had not done so in the very beginning, but when I explained that we stopped because of Mamie's feeling in the matter he understood—but again requested that we get at it at once. Since I want to bring Pete there again in a matter of a few weeks, I hope that you can get the men working on it without delay.[5] *As ever*

[1] Atomic Energy Commission Chairman Strauss had written on this same day offering to make arrangements for Eisenhower's herdsman to attend the course at Virginia Polytechnic Institute.

[2] Hartley would enroll in the course, which commenced on April 22 (Strauss to Eisenhower, Apr. 3, and Nevins to Eisenhower, Apr. 8, 1957). See also telephone conversations, Eisenhower and Strauss, April 1, 1957, AWF/D.
[3] The show barn and smaller barns, erected at W. Alton ("Pete") Jones's expense, would be located on the Brandon and Redding Farms (see Nevins, *Five-Star Farmer,* p. 131). For background on Jones's purchase of these farms see Galambos and van Ee, *The Middle Way,* nos. 1229 and 1297.
[4] As it turned out, five large evergreen trees would be planted to shield the farm from curious onlookers (see Nevins, *Five-Star Farmer,* p. 117).
[5] Jones had visited the farm the preceding day. For background on the Pitzer schoolhouse, purchased by Jones in 1955, see Galambos and van Ee, *The Middle Way,* no. 1576. Apparently Mrs. Eisenhower had stopped progress on the cottage "pending the proposed inspection by John or Barbara or both this weekend" (Nevins to Eisenhower, Apr. 8, 1957). The Eisenhowers and their children and grandchildren would visit the new house on April 13 (President's daily appointments). On April 30 Nevins would report, "The work on the second floor of the school cottage is progressing well. . . ." In July Major John Eisenhower and his wife Barbara would purchase the property and cottage from Jones; see John S. D. Eisenhower, *Strictly Personal,* (Garden City, N.Y., 1974), pp. 230ff; Nevins, *Five-Star Farmer,* p. 131; and *New York Times,* July 8, 9, 21, 1957. All correspondence is in AWF/Gettysburg.

According to the President's daily appointments calendar, Jones would not return to Gettysburg until July 5.

97

EM, AWF, Name Series

To Clifford Roberts

April 1, 1957

Dear Cliff: I'm afraid some of the White House reporters, if ever they hear about the plaque you have sent me, would not quite agree with the designation of "most even tempered golfer of the year."[1] But I think Howard Snyder will be proud that I have earned it, at least in your opinion.[2]

Not that I am ungrateful, but if you were going to stretch the truth at all why could I not be "the most improved golfer of the year" or something like that?

I am looking forward—with impatience and yearning—to Augusta on the eighteenth.[3]

With warm regard, *As ever*

[1] Eisenhower's long-time friend Roberts had sent the 7½ by 10½ inch walnut plaque depicting a golfer in bas-relief on tinted bronze metal. The inscription read: "Awarded to Dwight D. Eisenhower For Most Even Tempered Golfer Of The Year" (see gift card, Roberts, Mar. 29, 1957, WHCF/Gift File, and correspondence list, Apr. 1, 1957, AWF/D). For background on Roberts see Galambos and van Ee, *The Middle Way,* no. 29. In a recent news conference Eisenhower had become angered when questioned about his alleged plan to use helicopters to fly from the White House to the golf course (see no. 104).

[2] Following Eisenhower's September 1955 heart attack, his physician had urged him to control his anger by avoiding situations that may cause irritation or frustration (see Galambos and van Ee, *The Middle Way*, no. 1772, and no. 1 in these volumes).
[3] The Eisenhowers would vacation in Augusta, Georgia, from April 18–30. For background on their traditional April trip to Augusta see Galambos and van Ee, *The Middle Way*, no. 680; see also Eisenhower to Roberts, April 5, 1957, AWF/D.

98

EM, AWF, International Series: Macmillan

To Harold Macmillan *April 2, 1957*
Secret

Dear Harold: Thank you for your letter of March twenty-third enclosing a memorandum concerning cooperation within the Western European Union in armaments research, development and production.[1]

As I indicated when we discussed this subject at Bermuda, we recognize the political considerations underlying your interest in strengthening WEU, and the economic and military benefits which might be derived from a cooperative effort within WEU with respect to the research, development and production of armaments. I am generally sympathetic to the broad purpose which your Government has in mind.

There are of course several important practical considerations which must be taken into account and which I am sure you fully appreciate. These considerations arise from the necessity of maintaining essential safeguards on the security of military information and of protecting the proprietary rights of United States citizens and business concerns with respect to items of military equipment or technical information which might be involved.

As I believe the memorandum attached to your letter recognizes, the question of your making available to other WEU countries armaments information containing data restricted by security agreements between the United Kingdom and the United States, or among the United Kingdom, Canada and the United States, will in the final analysis have to be looked at on a case-by-case basis. Therefore, I think that the only general statement that can usefully be made at the present time in response to your question (*a*) is that we will give such case-by-case requests our most prompt and careful consideration.

With respect to your question (*b*), I think it is implicit that, within the arrangements already in effect, including the security agreements, and within the procedure under which our two Governments would examine items which you may wish to release to WEU countries, there would be no prejudice to existing United States-United Kingdom cooperation.

It is my understanding that NATO would be kept informed of this coordination within WEU and that the arrangements contemplated in your memorandum would be without prejudice to comparable arrangements for exchange of information in the NATO forum.

I concur in the suggestion that specific lists of projects which you wish to discuss with us be communicated to the Department of State through normal diplomatic channels. The Departments of State and Defense can then give the matter their attention.[2]

With warm regard, *As ever*

[1] On March 22 at the Bermuda Conference Eisenhower had asked Prime Minister Macmillan for this memorandum (see no. 78; and State, *Foreign Relations, 1955–1957*, vol. XXVII, *Western Europe and Canada*, pp. 724–28). The State Department drafted this response (see Eisenhower to Macmillan, Mar. 25, 1957, AWF/D-H; and Dulles to Eisenhower, Apr. 1, 1957, *ibid.*). On April 5 the State Department would cable the text of this letter to the American embassy in London for delivery to Macmillan (AWF/I: Macmillan). The signed original would be sent by diplomatic pouch on the following day.

Britain's purpose, Macmillan had written, was "to prove our resolve to co-operate with Europe, to give greater reality to the concept of a united Europe, and to offset the effects of our force reductions." Aware of the security considerations involved, Britain had made it clear to the WEU that cooperation "must be without prejudice" to Britain's association with the United States. Although atomic matters would be excluded from discussion, the British planned exchanges that would incorporate some information, obtained from the United States, about new weapons projects. Macmillan asked specifically if (*a*) the United States would "adopt a liberal attitude towards the release of information" and (*b*) would give an assurance that Britain's association with the WEU would not prejudice the release of further information (Macmillan to Eisenhower, Mar. 23, 1957, AWF/I: Macmillan).

[2] "We are very conscious of the practical considerations mentioned in the third paragraph of your letter," Macmillan would write, and he assured the President that security safeguards would be maintained (Apr. 27, 1957, AWF/I: Macmillan).

99

EM, AWF, International Series: Saudi Arabia

To ibn Abd al-Aziz Saud
Cable. Secret

April 4, 1957

Your Majesty, My Great and Good Friend: Pending opportunity to make full and studied reply to your cable of March 31st, I send you this message.[1] As Your Majesty is aware, we are currently discussing with

President Nasser the Egyptian position with respect to arrangements for the Suez Canal. We have given to the Egyptian Government our comments upon its draft statement which we understand it proposed unilaterally to make. While I have not yet received a report of Egypt's formal reactions to these comments, I believe I should tell you that preliminary indications are not encouraging.[2]

Our great concern is that the arrangements to be made should be such as would give assurance to the users of the Canal that it will be a dependable channel for trade. I know, of course, of your own interest in this regard, as indeed the dependability of the Canal is of vital importance in the movement of products of Saudi Arabia and thus it is of vital importance to the welfare of your nation. It is our belief that unless the Egyptian proposal is amended substantially along the lines we have suggested, the reliability of the Canal will be seriously undermined. We fear that the users would find it imprudent to place great reliance upon it in the future, and would then turn increasingly to other means of meeting their fuel requirements.

It would indeed be regrettable if Egypt, which in its recent crisis benefitted so much from the support of the world community, should now, apparently looking to the Soviet Union for advice and support, disregard world opinion and reject the Resolution of the United Nation's Security Council of October 13 which set forth the principles upon which arrangements for the Canal should be based. I earnestly hope that Your Majesty will see fit to counsel the Egyptian Government not to destroy the present opportunity for a fair, just and peaceful solution of this problem which is of such deep concern to the free world.

Referring again to the matter of the pilgrims, may I remind you of my pledged word that I shall never agree to any arrangement that will in the slightest degree impede the passage of pilgrims to the Holy Places of Islam.[3]

I am glad that our advisors have at last found satisfactory language to express the Agreements which we arrived at in principle when you were here and that the Agreements have been signed this week.[4]

May God have you in his keeping.

With warm personal regard, *Sincerely*

[1] The State Department drafted this message for Eisenhower. After making some changes, the President returned it to Secretary of State Dulles for transmission (see Memorandum of Conversation, Apr. 4, 1957, Dulles Papers, White House Memoranda Series). In his letter, written on March 26, King Saud had told the President that Saudi Arabia would consider free passage of Israeli ships through the Gulf of Aqaba "a violation of recognized international rights, and an aggression against Islamic sanctuaries." He also believed that the United States and Egypt could elimi-

nate the obstacles which prevented the resumption of commercial and economic relations (AWF/I: Saudi Arabia).

[2] In anticipation of the reopening of the Suez Canal, scheduled for mid-April, the Egyptian government had delivered a draft communiqué to the American embassy in Cairo on March 18. According to the communiqué, which established guidelines for the administration of canal operations, Egypt had proved its ability to manage navigation in the canal and had reaffirmed its determination to abide by the Constantinople Convention of 1888. The old system of levying canal dues would continue; the question of compensation and claims would be settled through arbitration; and a special fund for improvements to handle increasing traffic would be established. On March 26 the Egyptian government had released a more detailed statement of its position (State, *Foreign Relations, 1955–1957*, vol. XVII, *Arab-Israeli Dispute, 1957*, pp. 430–31, 469–72; on the 1888 convention see Galambos and van Ee, *The Middle Way*, no. 1946).

Dulles, disappointed in the Egyptian declaration, said that the document was a unilateral statement of intention subject to change at any time. It failed to implement the principles agreed upon by the U.N. Security Council on October 13, 1956, and did not provide for organized cooperation between the Egyptian government and the users of the canal. The State Department had sent its counterproposals to the U.S. embassy in Cairo on March 30. Although the United States had not received a formal report of Egyptian reaction, on April 2 the Egyptian foreign minister had told the American ambassador that his government could not accept some of the U.S. proposals. The U.N. principles were "vague and unfortunately worded," according to the Egyptians, who thought that their own declaration provided "specific substantive provisions" that would solve the problem. Egypt refused to allow other governments to veto its programs and declared that it could not be bound by outside decisions (*ibid.*, pp. 473–74, 477–80, 485–88, 496–98, 502–4; on the principles adopted by the Security Council see State, *Foreign Relations, 1955–1957*, vol. XVI, *Suez Crisis July 26–December 31, 1956*, pp. 718–19).

[3] See no. 77.

[4] On King Saud's visit see no. 13. On the agreements, signed on April 2, see *U.S. Department of State Bulletin* 36, no. 931 (April 29, 1957), 680–81.

Saud would tell Eisenhower that although he had not seen the U.S. comments to the Egyptian proposals, he had conveyed the President's concerns to the Egyptian leader and told him that he was confident that "his wisdom and initiative" would lead to a just solution (Saud to Eisenhower, Apr. 7, 1957, AWF/I: Saudi Arabia). For developments see no. 154.

100

EM, AWF, DDE Diaries Series

To Arthur William Radford

April 4, 1957

Dear Raddy: Today General Goodpaster brought to my attention the question you raised as to the basis for selecting Chiefs of MAAGS—with special reference to those for Italy and Western Germany.[1]

I believe that there are capable officers in all services and that the nature of the work of a MAAG is not such as to imply a need for an official from any particular branch of the service. If, in spite of that conviction, the services find any occasion on which they cannot agree, the Secretary of Defense should make a decision forthwith.

With warm regard, *Sincerely*

[1] Radford had been Chairman of the Joint Chiefs of Staff (JCS) since 1953 (for background see Galambos and van Ee, *The Middle Way*, nos. 166 and 194). Brigadier General Andrew Goodpaster, Eisenhower's Staff Secretary, had met briefly with the President prior to the National Security Council meeting on the morning of April 4. Military Assistance Advisory Groups (MAAGs) were a component of the Mutual Defense Assistance Program's supervisory machinery.

[2] Each recipient country under the Mutual Defense Assistance Program was assigned its own MAAG, headed by an officer nominated by the Joint Chiefs of Staff. The MAAGs also prepared recommendations for the Joint Chiefs regarding further assistance. After June 1955, when the functions of the Foreign Operations Administration were transferred to the International Cooperation Agency (in cooperation with the State Department), the Department of Defense retained the responsibility for defining military assistance responsibilities. The MAAGs continued to recommend fiscal year military assistance programs for their respective areas and implement the approved programs (see U.S., Joint Chiefs of Staff, *The History of the Joint Chiefs of Staff*, 6 vols. to date [Wilmington, Del., 1979–80; Washington, D.C., 1986–], vol. V, *The Joint Chiefs of Staff and National Policy, 1953–1954*, by Robert J. Watson [1986], pp. 201–3; and vol. VI, *The Joint Chiefs of Staff and National Policy, 1955–1956*, by Kenneth W. Condit [1992], pp. 240–41. For background see no. 76).

101 — *EM, AWF, DDE Diaries Series*

To Charles Edward Potter — *April 4, 1957*

Dear Charlie:[1] I like a lot what you have to say in giving a definition of "Modern Republicanism." Of the terms you were experimenting with I think I like "perspective" the best.[2]

A sense of perspective, while respecting basic principles, adjusts methods and means to the inescapable problems of the place and time.

With warm regard, *Sincerely*

[1] Potter, Republican Senator from Michigan since 1952, had written Eisenhower on March 28, 1957 (WHCF/OF 138-C-12) to inform the President that *U.S. News & World Report* was polling Republican senators on their concept of "modern republicanism." "Knowing your deep interest in this subject," Potter wrote, "I am taking the liberty of sending you a copy of the remarks I have today sent to the magazine. I shall be pleased to receive any comment you are inclined to make on the views I have stated." (See editor David Lawrence's article "'Modern Republicans' and 'Modern Democrats,'" in *U.S. News & World Report*, Apr. 5, 1957, pp. 35–36.)

[2] Eisenhower defined "modern republicanism" as the "application of Republican principles to the problems of today." For the specifics see Eisenhower, *Waging Peace*,

p. 375, and Galambos and van Ee, *The Middle Way*, nos. 2095 and 2098. Potter had written that "Like charm in a woman or age in a man, 'modern Republicanism' is a state of mind. Perhaps a better word for it is 'perspective,' a perspective best understood, not in terms of pat definitions, but in the light of cumulative, concrete results." "Flexibility" and "heart" were also terms Potter had suggested as ways of defining modern republicanism: "Each would be true," he wrote, "but something less than the whole truth."

102

EM, AWF, Administration Series

TO GEORGE MAGOFFIN HUMPHREY *April 4, 1957*

Dear George: This morning the Baltimore Sun has a preposterous story concerning you. I send you this information as quickly as possible because it strikes me that you may want to sue them for, say, something like $8,025,000. The story is to the effect that you are pleading with Congress to restore a cut in the amount above named to the Treasury budget.[1] This is like saying that George Washington didn't chop down a cherry tree or that Lincoln never split a rail. I think you should demand retraction, sue them for libel, challenge them to a duel at forty paces, and—all in all—just set the record straight.[2]

Love to Pam, *As ever*

[1] The April 4 *Baltimore Sun* had reported that Secretary of the Treasury Humphrey had asked restoration of an *$8,205,000* cut made by the House in the Treasury's budget despite a previous agreement to accept the reduction. The *Sun* reminded its readers of the "fiscal storm" set off by Humphrey in January when he stated that unless the government reduced the country's tax burden there would be a depression that would "curl your hair" (see no. 27 and *New York Times*, Jan. 17, 1957).

[2] Humphrey would respond on April 8 (AWF/A). Deploring the "degenerating times when even you are deceived by a newspaper headline," the Secretary of the Treasury would quote from his testimony before the Senate Subcommittee in order to clarify his position to Eisenhower. Humphrey reported that the $8,205,000 represented the cost of replacing Coast Guard aircraft, an item that had been omitted from the original budget request (see also U.S. Congress, Senate Subcommittee of the Committee on Appropriations, *Treasury and Post Office Departments Appropriations, 1958: Hearings on H.R. 4897*, 85th Cong., 1st sess., 1957, pp. 18–19). Humphrey concluded that he had been "as we all have been increasingly of late, the victim—by newspaper duplicity or partisan design—of false innuendo with no decent regard for protection of the truth or honest statement of the facts. Either a lawsuit or a duel would be far more fun but I guess, as usual, I just have to grin and bear it." For developments on the budget see no. 128.

103

EM, AWF, DDE Diaries Series

To Edwin Palmer Hoyt

April 4, 1957

Personal

Dear Ep: Thanks for your cooperation in a recent item involving the Army. Its publication could well have caused us great national embarrassment.[1]

With warm regard, *As ever*

[1] An April 1, 1957, Special Staff Note (AWF/D) states that, "At the suggestion of Assistant Secretary of Defense Snyder, the *Denver Post* has voluntarily killed a story with extensive pictures (all cleared by Army) concerning nerve gas manufacture at Denver Arsenal which might have supplied the Communists with propaganda material." Eisenhower's letter to *Denver Post* editor Palmer Hoyt (A.B. University of Oregon 1923), a long-time friend, presumably refers to this incident.

104

EM, WHCF, Official File 101-W-1

To Charles McElroy White

April 4, 1957

Dear Charlie: Many thanks for your note and for your (and the Cleveland Plain Dealer's) defense of my "right" to use a helicopter to go to Burning Tree if I desire.[1] What with such a story, plus the "speeding" business, and then the one on my poor caddy, Cemetery, I have decided that this is the silly season for reporters and there is nothing at all to be done about it.[2]

But I do thank you for writing.

With warm personal regard, *Sincerely*

[1] White, president of Republic Steel Corporation, had written on March 29 (same file as document). With his note he included an editorial in the *Cleveland Plain Dealer* of that same date. White and the editors endorsed the use of helicopters to transport Eisenhower to the Burning Tree Club or anywhere else. "If there is any way that your time can be saved, whatever it is," White had written, "you should take advantage of it, regardless of a cheap press or cheap politicians." In a recent news conference, a member of the press had angered the President by questioning the use of helicopters to fly from the White House to the golf course (see no. 97; *Public Papers of the Presidents: Eisenhower, 1957*, pp. 214–15; and *New York Times*, Mar. 28, 1957). The issue would continue to surface throughout the second administration (see Adams to Scrivner, May 15, 1957; Roller to Wheaton, June 4, 1958; and Wheaton to Roller, June 9, 1958, all in same file as document).

[2] On March 29 Maryland State Police had intercepted the presidential motorcade and press cars en route to the Eisenhowers' farm in Gettysburg. Although the police allowed the motorcade to continue at high speed, the press vehicles were required to adhere to the posted speed limit (*New York Times*, Mar. 30, 31, 1957).

Willie Frank Parteet ("Cemetery"), had caddied for Eisenhower at the Augusta National Golf Club since 1951. But the fifty-one-year-old caddy had recently lost his job to a younger man who could keep up with the President's vigorous pace around the course (*New York Times*, Apr. 2, 1957).

105 — *EM, AWF, Name Series*

To Edward Everett Hazlett, Jr. — *April 5, 1957*

Dear Swede: I cannot tell you how much I regret that a combination of bronchitis, work, and a trip to Bermuda prevented me from coming occasionally to the hospital to see you while you were here.[1] I truly had looked forward to an opportunity for a couple of real visits.

There is one thing that I have found out concerning the relative rank of leaders. Every time you climb a rung, you become the boss of more people but you become likewise less and less the boss of your own time. You are constantly the slave of people, events and circumstances.

Today the weather is a mere continuation of all the vile experiences we have had since mid winter. To be cold, disagreeable and rainy in Washington on April fifth is almost unbelievable but it is absolutely true.

Recently I consented (I assure you in a weak moment) again to sit for a sculptor who was determined to make a bust of me.[2] I resent even sitting for a painter in spite of the fact that I love to see a portrait develop and I am particularly interested in the techniques a true painter uses to get the effects he sees. But to sit for a bust to my mind is about the dreariest experience a man can have and it always takes longer than does a portrait. Having learned this lesson so clearly in the past, I do not know why I again fell victim to the arguments of the artist and one or two "friends(?)."

This morning I gave the sculptor an additional half hour and as I did so I began to ponder about people, particularly the Presidents, who have undoubtedly had the same experience in the past as I am now undergoing. Friends convinced them that they "owed it to posterity" to leave a likeness in bronze or marble and they, resenting every minute of the process, consented. Now, in 1957, I looked back, as I sat in front of the sculptor, and tried to evaluate in my own mind just what those individuals actually did for this generation.

I decided that the only bust that meant much to me was the famous one of Washington.[3] Statues and busts of Lincoln were not made until after he died, if for no other reason than while he was alive he was far more vilified than admired. While here and there I have seen busts of other Presidents—even including a head of Truman—there is no single one of them that has ever provided me with any feeling of satisfaction, much less inspiration. All of which convinces me that again I have sworn off sitting for sculptors for ever and ever, amen! So if in the future I ever write to you a new complaint on this score, please remind me that I am a weak, vacillating and easily swayed individual.

The Mid East continues to be the central factor in my thinking, in spite of the fact that the newspapers are trying to make the budget the most important item in the world today. If we could ever get a concession from Egypt that could to some degree satisfy Britain, France and Israel, I think I could regain what many people once regarded as a cheerful disposition.[4]

The Bermuda Conference was very interesting and some day, when I have an hour or two completely to myself, I will try to give you an account of it. Macmillan is, of course, one of my intimate wartime friends and so it is very easy to talk to him on a very frank, even blunt, basis.[5]

Right now I am off with Mamie to the farm, to be back on Sunday afternoon. The weather, as I said, is abominable, but at least it provides a change of scenery and we love the place—both its interior and the surroundings. I have had bad luck on the weather at the farm, illustrated by the fact that although I have had a skeet range there for well over a year, I have never yet fired a shot.[6]

Give my love to Ibby and, of course, all the best to yourself, in all of which Mamie joins.[7] *As ever*

P.S. Of course I do most sincerely hope that those wretched headaches of yours have disappeared and that you are feeling much more like yourself.[8]

[1] Hazlett had entered Bethesda Naval Hospital in January (see no. 41). On Eisenhower's bronchitis see no. 111; on the Bermuda Conference see no. 78.

[2] In 1958 the bust would be exhibited in the U.S. pavilion at the World's Fair in Brussels.

[3] The well-known bust of George Washington by Jean Antoine Houdon remains at Washington's Mount Vernon, Virginia, estate.

[4] The preceding day, the *Baltimore Sun* had reported a disagreement between Eisenhower and Treasury Secretary Humphrey over budget cuts; the paper gave crises in the Mideast secondary treatment (see nos. 102 and 99, respectively).

[5] On Eisenhower's wartime relationship with British Prime Minister Harold Macmillan see Chandler, *War Years.*

[6] For background on the skeet range see Galambos and van Ee, *The Middle Way*, no. 1899.

[7] "Ibby" was Hazlett's wife, Elizabeth.

[8] For developments see no. 457.

106

EM, AWF, Administration Series

To John Hay Whitney

April 5, 1957

Dear Jock: I think the only reason for this note is that Mamie and I miss you and Betsey so constantly. We do hope that you are well and both enjoying the experience that is yours.[1]

With respect to the matter that I mentioned to you on the telephone when you were at Idlewild, I will give you the full story one day. We were able to get an authenticated account of it at this end. I can scarcely give it to you in this letter but it is quite interesting.[2]

As you know, many of the treasured items that come into the possession of Mamie and me find their way to the little Abilene Museum in which, of course, I am most interested. However, the "Sitting Lincoln" that you gave us last Christmas seems to me definitely to belong to the Gettysburg farm which after all claims an intimate association with Lincoln.[3] My problem is to find the exact spot where it should go. Mamie and I are going up there this weekend and I hope that I can work it out.

We have played almost no bridge since you left but a week ago George Allen found a partner with whom he challenged Al and me to a set game.[4] He had a grand time moaning and groaning and complaining. I think he is still awaiting news on the "horse deal" that you and he were cooking up.[5]

Slats Slater seems to be improved, and recently I have seen Bill Robinson (right now he is in Caracas). Pete Jones spent part of a weekend with us—and I have seen also a few others of our Augusta group.[6] Yesterday was the first day of the Masters and winds were so high that scores were pretty bad. Only one man, Jackie Burke, broke par—and he by only one stroke. Middlecoff had 79 and Hogan 76.[7] What the weather is down there today I don't know, but I hope very much it is improved because they had a very large advance sale of tickets this year.

Day before yesterday I tried my first nine holes on a golf course since my Thomasville experience.[8] I was not good.

Give my love to Betsey and, of course, all the best to yourself. *As ever*

[1] Whitney was U.S. Ambassador to Great Britain.

[2] See no. 93.

[3] On the Abilene Museum see Galambos and van Ee, *The Middle Way*, no. 760. The bronze statue depicts Lincoln seated on a bench. Eisenhower's December 23 thank-you letter and Whitney's December 29 reply are in AWF/A.

[4] The bridge partner was probably Walter Robert Tkach (M.D. University of Pittsburgh 1945), assistant physician to Eisenhower from 1956–1960. "Al" was Eisenhower's favorite bridge partner, General Alfred M. Gruenther.

[5] On the "horse deal" see no. 130.

[6] In December Ellis Dwinnell ("Slats") Slater, president of Frankfurt Distillers Corporation, had broken his arm in a New York subway (see Galambos and van Ee, *The Middle Way*, no. 2127; for background on Eisenhower's friendship with Slater see *Eisenhower Papers*, vols. X–XVII). William E. Robinson had met with Eisenhower at the White House on March 26. W. Alton ("Pete") Jones had been a guest at Eisenhower's Gettysburg farm on March 30. For a complete list of the President's visitors see the Chronology.

[7] As it turned out, neither Jack Burke, Cary Middlecoff nor Ben Hogan, all professional golfers, would win the Masters Golf Tournament. The victory this year would go to Doug Ford (see *New York Times*, Apr. 8, 1957).

[8] In February the Eisenhowers had vacationed in Thomasville, Georgia (see no. 7).

107

EM, AWF, DDE Diaries Series

To Milton Katz
Personal

April 9, 1957

Dear Milton: In your letter you voice doubts that plagued both the Attorney General and me while we were considering the question of the Vice President substituting for the President during any period of disability on the part of the latter.[1]

Because of these doubts, we decided to attempt to provide in our suggestion for only two of the possible contingencies that could arise.

We decided first that we would not attempt to handle a case where the President might insist that he was able to discharge the duties of his office while at the same time the Vice President was alleging that the President was unable to do so. We avoided entering into this kind of a controversy by stating that whenever the President should think that he was capable of reassuming his duties, no matter through what means he had ceased performing them, he would be the final judge. We believe that if a President should become mentally deranged and should insist upon retaining his office when he was manifestly incapable of doing so, he would be certain to do things that would expose him to impeachment proceedings.

Therefore, the first case we considered is where a President voluntarily decides he is incapable of discharging his duties. The second would be where the President, by reason of coma due to accident or stroke or something of that nature might be *unable* to declare his own inability.

This case might also apply, I should think, while a President was temporarily out of touch, let us say, in transoceanic flight. But again the suggested amendment requires that immediately that the President declares his ability to resume his duties, he forthwith do so.

In the past there were two basic reasons why, even with the best of intentions on the part of all concerned, it was always highly undesirable to allow a Vice President to take over the duties of President, as long as the latter was alive.

First: great controversy has raged over the question of the exact status of the Vice President during his period of "Acting President." Some authorities have held that the moment he takes over because of the disability of the President, he becomes in fact *President for the remainder of the term.* Others hold, of course, that he does not. (I belong to this school so far as my in-expert understanding of the Constitution provides me with an opinion). Nevertheless this question never has been decided and unless some extraordinary emergency should arise, far more serious than the cases of Garfield and of Wilson were, at the time, judged to be, probably never will be decided until too late.[2]

A second point that has been in great doubt is the method by which the President would resume his duties.

Actually, you see, we have based our simple solution on the theory that the men involved would be honest—more than likely, good friends. But the provision enabling a President to take back the full functions of his office the second he himself announced his ability to do so would, we felt, protect against any such contingency as you suggest.

Finally, with respect to the Cabinet, it has long since been accepted that the President is not compelled to keep in his Cabinet a single individual that does not enjoy his full confidence. Interference by the Congress in this matter—which brought about the law called, I believe, the "Tenure of Office Act"—could scarcely be attempted today.[3]

We were guided all the way through by the idea that the President is elected by all the people and that the office must be protected against indignities and carping partisan efforts at annoyance, as well as against the development of any means whereby he could be acutely embarrassed in discharging his Constitutional duties. What we therefore wanted to do was to make it possible for men of good will to understand exactly what would be their responsibility and authority in the two cases that seem most likely to occur and to rely on existing Constitutional authority to take care of any case that degenerated into actual malfeasance, or gross incompetence due to mental deterioration, while in office.

All this is poorly expressed, but I am merely reviewing for you in some detail why our suggestion refuses to concern itself with every conceivable kind of contingency that could arise, but does make some provision for continuity of authority in this atomic age when immediate decisions could be vital to our very existence.[4]

With warm regard, *Sincerely*

P.S. Some have argued that because we have existed since 1789 as a going Republic, there is no need for the kind of Constitutional change we suggest. The difficulty with that kind of reasoning is that the existence of new and fearful weapons multiplies very greatly the risks to us of an inability to act promptly in certain types of emergency. When I say promptly, I mean *instantly*.

[1] Katz, Henry L. Stimson Professor of Law at Harvard since 1954 and director of the National Conference of Christians and Jews, had been director of the Economic Cooperation Administration (Marshall Plan) from 1950–1951 (see Galambos, *NATO and the Campaign of 1952*, no. 16). Katz had written the President on April 3 (AWF/D) to caution against certain aspects of the proposed constitutional amendment on presidential disability (for background see no. 58). Saying that he was "troubled" by reports that "a majority of the Cabinet, acting on their own motion or on the initiative of the Vice President," could "declare a President of the United States unable to perform the duties of his office," Katz suggested that this action "might entail a grave risk of loss of public confidence in the succession" as well as create a "danger to the stability of the Presidency" and the possibility of Cabinet intrigue. Katz contended that only the Supreme Court should determine the question of presidential inability. Such a course of action, however, would pose dangers to the stability of the Supreme Court and its ability to command public confidence. Katz concluded that since the difficulties posed by the "existing constitutional position" were "less serious than the disadvantages of attempts to eliminate them," the proposed amendment should be "limited to the provision which would authorize the President to declare himself temporarily unable to perform his duties, subject to his right to resume his office when he should judge himself fit to do so."

[2] On the debate over this issue see, for example, U.S. Congress, House, Committee on the Judiciary, *An Analysis of Replies to a Questionnaire and Testimony at a Hearing on Presidential Inability*, 85th Congress, 1st sess., March 26, 1957, and Brownell, *Hearings Before the House Judiciary Special Subcommittee on Study of Presidential Inability*, 85th Congress, 1st sess., April 1, 1957. President James A. Garfield was shot on July 2, 1881, and died of the wound on September 19; Woodrow Wilson, President from 1913 to 1921, suffered a massive stroke on October 2, 1919.

[3] The Tenure of Office Act, which Congress passed on March 2, 1867, sought to prevent President Andrew Johnson from using his patronage power against his political enemies during Reconstruction. It provided that "a civil office holder, appointed with the consent of the Senate, was to serve until a successor had been nominated by the President and approved by the Senate." The act further stipulated that Cabinet members were to hold office during the term of the President by whom they were appointed and for one month afterward (U.S. *Statutes at Large*, vol. 14, p. 430; see Edward McPherson, ed., *The Political History of the United States of America During the Period of Reconstruction* [1875. Reprint: New York, 1969], pp. 176–77; Michael Les Benedict, *A Compromise of Principle: Congressional Republicans and Reconstruction 1863–1869* [New York, 1974], pp. 293–96, 309; Harold M. Hyman, *A More Perfect Union: The Impact of the Civil War and Reconstruction on the Constitution* [Boston, 1975], p. 500; and Kenneth M. Stampp, *The Era of Reconstruction, 1865–1877* [New York, 1966], pp. 147–50). Johnson's alleged violation of the act formed the legal basis for his impeachment.

[4] For developments see no. 566.

108

EM, AWF, Administration Series: Army

TO WILBER MARION BRUCKER
Personal and confidential

April 9, 1957

Dear Governor Brucker:[1] By no means do I want to appear as interfering in your business. However, you have coming up a vacancy to fill in the Army and I understand that one of the men under consideration is an individual who served under me throughout almost the entire period of the War, both in Africa and in Europe.

The vacancy is that of Quartermaster General in the Army and the individual to whom I am referring is General McNamara.[2] My own direct contact with General McNamara was, of course, slight, but his reputation for character, efficiency and leadership was well known to me.

I strongly commend him to you for consideration in filling this vacancy.[3]

I think I have never previously sent to you or to anyone else in the Army a communication of this character.[4] I do so in this case because of the outstanding war record of this man and because of my continuing interest in the welfare of the Army. I understand, of course, that the recommendations of Selection Boards under the Chief of Staff are properly considered almost final in such cases. However, I feel sure that General Taylor[5] would agree with my own very high opinion of General McNamara.

With warm regard, *Sincerely*

[1] Eisenhower had appointed Brucker Secretary of the Army in July 1955 (for background see Galambos and van Ee, *The Middle Way,* no. 1594).

[2] Major General Andrew Thomas McNamara (USMA 1928) was Assistant Chief of Staff, G-4, with the United States Army in Europe. He had served with the Quartermaster Corps since 1937 and had been Quartermaster General of the First and Second Army Corps (*New York Times,* Apr. 23, 1957). He would replace Quartermaster General Kester Lovejoy Hastings, who had announced his retirement on March 22.

[3] For further developments see no. 110.

[4] Actually, Eisenhower had written a similar letter to Brucker's predecessor on December 30, 1953, recommending the appointment of Hastings as Quartermaster General (see Galambos and van Ee, *The Middle Way,* no. 642).

[5] Army Chief of Staff Maxwell Davenport Taylor.

109

EM, AWF, DDE Diaries Series

To Percy Maxim Lee

April 10, 1957

Dear Mrs. Lee:[1] Many thanks for your kind letter of April third telling me of the activities of the League of Women Voters in furthering public understanding of the role of economic aid in our foreign policy.[2]

I believe there is a growing awareness that the safety and material well-being of our country are closely bound up with that of other free nations. As the globe is shrunk by modern means of communication and transportation and by modern weapons and their advanced means of delivery, it must be clear that the fate and future of our land are linked more tightly than ever with the free world community. The concept of a common defense, for example, is now well established, as evidenced by the fact that we have collective defense treaties with forty-two other nations. The Middle East Resolution authorizes a further widening of this area of common defense.[3]

But, as your letter properly points out, there is a vital economic development aspect to this whole matter.[4] Undergirding a common defense must be a sound and growing economic base which affords the peoples in the nations of the free world a chance to realize their hopes and aspirations. In many parts of the world, old peoples are becoming new nations. In these developing nations there is a surging movement to better the lot of the people, to telescope in time the development of their economies. Now, of course, economic development is not a product for export, to be acquired from the United States or any other economically advanced nation. Economic development is a homespun product; it is the product of a people's own work. Our opportunity is to help through sound technical and, where necessary through financial assistance, the people of these developing lands in their own endeavors. Within prudent limits, such activity on our part is clearly in the best interest of all concerned.[5]

I encourage you and your associates in widening the understanding among our people of these basic facts.[6] *Sincerely*

[1] Percy Maxim Lee (Mrs. John Glessner Lee), former president of the Farmington, Connecticut, and Connecticut chapters of the League of Women Voters, had been national president of the League since 1950. Eisenhower had directed Presidential Aide Gabriel Hauge to draft this letter.

[2] Lee had written on April 3, 1957 (WHCF/OF 116-B) to inform the President that the League of Women Voters had been conducting nationwide community discussions of foreign policy. Meetings had been held in more than six hundred communities across the United States, and "Public interest and participation has been overwhelming."

[3] See no. 63.

[4] Economic aid was "a profoundly important element in our foreign policy," wrote Lee, and could "be effective only if it is designed to serve long-range as well as short-range objectives."

[5] For background see no. 60.

[6] Eisenhower would meet with Lee and members of the National Council of the League of Women Voters in the Rose Garden at the White House on May 1. In an effort to broaden popular support for the Mutual Security Program, Eisenhower would address the League, saying: "Foreign aid, my friends, is something that is being conducted to keep the United States secure and strong. It is preventing the isolation of the United States as a prosperous, rich, powerful country. There would be isolation if the United States refused to participate in the realization by underdeveloped countries of their proper ambitions for nationalization, for national independence and for the economic base that will support that individual independence" (see *Public Papers of the Presidents: Eisenhower, 1957*, pp. 315–21; *New York Times*, May 2, 1957). For developments see no. 137.

110

EM, AWF, Administration Series: Army

To Wilber Marion Brucker
Personal

April 10, 1957

Dear Governor Brucker: I was extraordinarily pleased to receive your letter of yesterday concerning General McNamara.[1] My satisfaction did not derive principally from the fact that your judgment agreed with mine regarding General McNamara (who, as I explained to you, I know mainly because of the character of his war service). But it was a most enjoyable experience to read of the detailed consideration you give to such appointments and the high standards you have set for yourself and your associates in making them.[2] While on this matter I have had no doubts, it was fine to have such an eloquent recitation of the actual processes you use to insure satisfaction in making appointments of this kind.

With warm regard, *Sincerely*

[1] Secretary of the Army Brucker had written the President on April 9, 1957 (AWF/A: Army) in response to Eisenhower's request of the same day regarding the appointment of Major General Andrew T. McNamara as Quartermaster General (see no. 108). Brucker had stated that, "As you did not know when you wrote your letter, the Selection Board appointed to consider this matter has recommended General Andrew T. McNamara." Thus, Eisenhower's "high recommendation of him, coming at this time, was therefore very opportune and most helpful." With the support of both Brucker and Army Chief of Staff Maxwell Taylor, Eisenhower would nominate McNamara to the position on April 22 (see *New York Times*, Apr. 23, 1957).

[2] Brucker had explained that since "the recommendations of Selection Boards carry great weight," he personally considered and approved each member of these boards. In the case of this particular selection board, Brucker had included several senior

officers "who would have in mind the qualities of aggressive leadership, great integrity and truly outstanding administrative ability" which he believed to be the essential characteristics of a Quartermaster General. Brucker explained that his "concern in this regard stems from grave dissatisfaction with many of the procurement and administrative practices of the Quartermaster Corps." Because of recent scandals involving the activities of some of the suppliers to the Army, Brucker was convinced of the "urgent need for a Quartermaster General with sufficient drive, determination and ability to reverse a trend of apparent long duration" (for background see, for example, David Frier, *Conflict of Interest in the Eisenhower Administration* [Baltimore, 1970], pp. 130–44; *New York Times*, Feb. 1, 10, Mar. 21, Apr. 9, 1957).

111

EM, AWF, Administration Series: Fitzsimons

To Edythe P. Turner

April 11, 1957

Dear Colonel Turner: I am delighted to know that you are finding your tour of duty at Tripler Hospital as interesting and satisfying—and the climate in Hawaii as pleasant—as you had anticipated.[1] That combination ought to make the next years about as nice for you as possible.

The principal complaint that we have had around here has been the disagreeable weather that we have had since you were here.[2] I've been fighting a cold and a cough since then and matters have not been helped by the dreariness of constant low temperatures and rain. There are signs that there may be a break soon, but we still have to encounter a real spring day. However, I am going to Augusta toward the end of next week, where I hope the sun and exercise that I get there will bring me back to par.[3]

With the hope that you continue to enjoy your assignment, and warm personal regard, *Sincerely*

[1] On April 5, 1957, Lieutenant Colonel Turner, former chief of the nursing service at Fitzsimons Army Hospital, Denver, Colorado, had written about her new position as chief nurse at Tripler Hospital, Honolulu, Hawaii (AWF/A: Fitzsimons). Turner had attended the President in the fall of 1955, while he recovered at Fitzsimons from a coronary thrombosis. Following his return to the East, the President continued to correspond with members of the Fitzsimons Army Hospital staff (see, for example, Eisenhower to Knox, Apr. 8, 1957, AWF/A: Fitzsimons). For background on Turner see Galambos and van Ee, *The Middle Way*, no. 2100; on Eisenhower's heart attack, see *ibid.*, no. 1595.

[2] Turner had been in Washington for the Inauguration (see Eisenhower to Turner, Dec. 19, 1956, AWF/D).

[3] As it turned out, Eisenhower's health would improve during his stay in Augusta, Georgia (Apr. 18–30), where the weather was milder (*New York Times*, Apr. 23, 1957; see also see no. 97).

112

EM, AWF, DDE Diaries Series

To Josephine Ogden Forrestal
Personal

April 11, 1957

Dear Jo:[1] It was nice to hear from you again and I am grateful to you for writing as frankly as you did. I only wish I had the opportunity to discuss with you personally the sensible suggestions you present.[2]

At this long distance I am afraid I can only paraphrase what I said in a press conference yesterday on the subject of your letter. I have the utmost faith in Secretary Dulles' wisdom and integrity, and I am certain he would not recommend as the American Ambassador to Ireland a man who would not prove to be sympathetic and interested, and understanding both of the problems of the people of Ireland and the demands made all over the world today upon our own country.[3]

My bridge, too, has suffered of late, though now that Al Gruenther is back in the States I do find time for an occasional game.[4]

With affectionate regard, and again my thanks for taking the trouble to write me, *Sincerely*

[1] Josephine Ogden Forrestal was the widow of James Vincent Forrestal, the first Secretary of Defense (for background see Galambos, *Chief of Staff*, vols. VII–IX, and *Columbia University*, vols. X–XI).

[2] We have been unable to locate Forrestal's letter in EM.

[3] On April 9 Eisenhower had nominated the controversial R. W. Scott McLeod, a former Federal Bureau of Investigation agent and head of the State Department's Bureau of Security and Consular Affairs, as U.S. Ambassador to Ireland. While at the State Department, McLeod had sought to purge security risks within the department and had received criticism for allegedly damaging State Department morale (*Congressional Quarterly Almanac*, vol. XIII, *1957*, p. 726; and *New York Times*, May 4, 1957).

In his April 10 news conference Eisenhower had said that he was not well acquainted with McLeod and had accepted Dulles's recommendation (*Public Papers of the Presidents: Eisenhower, 1957*, pp. 281–82). On April 23 Secretary Dulles would comment that he and McLeod had not always seen "eye-to-eye" about everything in the early days of the Administration but that McLeod had "grown in stature and understanding; his knowledge of world affairs is very considerable." "I think he would be a good ambassador" (*U.S. Department of State Bulletin* 36, no. 933 [May 13, 1957], 770–71; see also Telephone conversation, Dulles and Bridges, Apr. 18, 1957, Dulles Papers, Telephone Conversations; for background on McLeod see Galambos and van Ee, *The Middle Way*, no. 490; see also McLeod to Dulles, Apr. 23, 1957, Dulles Papers).

On May 1 McLeod would tell the Senate Foreign Relations Committee that at one time Secretary Dulles had been authorized to discharge him "as a security risk" because of a leak of information to a Washington newspaper. But the secretary, McLeod said, had decided against it (U.S. Congress, *Senate Committee Hearings*, 85th Cong., vol. 1220, 1957, pp. 62–63).

The Senate would confirm McLeod on May 9.

[4] The former Supreme Allied Commander, Europe, had become president of the American Red Cross in January.

113

EM, AWF,
Administration Series

To Christian Archibald Herter
Secret

April 12, 1957

Memorandum for the Acting Secretary of State: I have seen a memorandum from the State Department, the subject of which is "Conversations at Bermuda regarding Kashmir."[1] Paragraph two of that memorandum purports to give the gist of the reports I made to Prime Minister Macmillan concerning certain statements made to me by Mr. Nehru when he visited me here in Washington. The paragraph does not accurately state the thoughts I expressed.[2]

Actually Mr. Nehru said to me that the outstanding problems between India and Pakistan were not in themselves impossible of solution. He named four, of which I recall three were the Kashmir problem, the water problem and the refugee problem. Mr. Nehru did not give me any reason why he objected to a plebiscite; in fact I said to Prime Minister Macmillan that the one thing I failed to ask Mr. Nehru was why he was opposed to a plebiscite in spite of the fact that Mr. Nehru said that the vast majority of the people in Kashmir wanted to belong to India.[3]

The statement to the effect that the Kashmir problem ought to be settled on the basis of the status quo with other problems negotiated directly between India and Pakistan is roughly correct. In this connection Mr. Nehru did say that in the refugee problem there were theoretically large sums due to India from Pakistan. He indicated that India would be willing to forego a considerable proportion of these claims.

Whether or not there is any necessity for clarifying this matter in the mind of Prime Minister Macmillan I leave to your judgment.

[1] We have been unable to locate this memorandum.

[2] Eisenhower had reported his conversations with Indian Prime Minister Nehru to Macmillan in Bermuda on March 23 (State, *Foreign Relations, 1955–1957,* vol. XXVII, *Western Europe and Canada,* p. 754; for background on the Bermuda Conference see no. 78). Nehru had visited Washington and Gettysburg in December 1956 (see Galambos and van Ee, *The Middle Way,* no. 2139).

[3] Conflict between Hindu India and Moslem Pakistan over the territory of Kashmir dated from 1947. Under U.N. auspices the two countries had agreed to temporary areas of control, but had not executed a subsequent U.N. resolution calling for a plebiscite. After intensive discussions in the Security Council during January and February 1957, the United Nations had passed a resolution to send the council president to the subcontinent to explore possibilities for settling the dispute (for background see Galambos and van Ee, *The Middle Way,* no. 104; see also State, *Foreign Relations, 1955–1957,* vol. VIII, *South Asia,* pp. 103–29).

The fourth problem may have involved the continuing migration of the Hindus from East Pakistan into India. Nehru had told Eisenhower that the only problem that could not be settled without difficulty was Kashmir; India would, he said, take a tolerant attitude toward the others (see Galambos and van Ee, *The Middle Way*, no. 2139; see also Telephone conversation, Eisenhower and Dulles, Dec. 19, 1956, AWF/D). For developments in the Kashmir situation see no. 443.

114 *EM, AWF, International Series: Adenauer*

To Konrad Adenauer *April 12, 1957*

Secret

Dear Mr. Chancellor: I have received your letter of March 25, 1957 with regard to the German contribution to the costs of supporting American forces in the Federal Republic. I appreciate your having gone into the matter personally and am glad that you have written me on the subject.[1]

I can understand that this problem involves difficulties for you. Frankly it also involves serious political difficulties for my Administration. Our defense budget is now being considered by the Congress. As you probably know, we ran into substantial difficulty with the Congress last year regarding the amount of financial support which the Federal Republic gave to our forces. The Congress was very critical of the agreement which we made with you last year, and there has been increased criticism this year of the arrangements which your Government has proposed to us.[2]

The criticism stems basically from the fact that our Congress does not feel that the Federal Republic has been carrying its fair share of the burden of defending the Atlantic Community, either in financial terms or as regards the actual contribution of forces. Our figures indicate that the defense burden borne by the Federal Republic has been substantially less than that of the average for other European NATO countries and far less than the burden being carried by the United States. While I recognize that the buildup of military forces by the Federal Republic is now under way, progress has been considerably slower than we had been led to expect by earlier statements by the Federal Government. Our agreement to the current level of support for our forces was based in large measure on the increased burden to the Federal Republic that was expected to result from a rapid buildup of military forces, which has not materialized. Moreover it is not clear to us that steps are being taken which will in fact lead to the creation of the forces which we understood as recently as the conversation between Defense Minister Strauss and Admiral Radford in December 1956 would be established.[3]

At the same time, as you are aware, the already heavy burden of our defense budget has been rising and we are encountering increasing difficulty in meeting fully all of the varied military requirements which our own position in the world imposes upon us. The current level of DM[4] support covers only a fraction of the total cost of equipping and maintaining the United States Forces in Germany, and any further reduction in the level of support would directly increase our already rising defense costs. These circumstances create a political problem for us which I can assure you is a very genuine one.

I have been glad to learn from your letter of the importance which you attach to the arrangements which you have worked out with the British. I hope that these arrangements, and those which you have made with the French, can be brought to a final conclusion as soon as possible. Prime Minister Macmillan mentioned to me at Bermuda his concern regarding this matter. I see no reason why the conclusion of these arrangements should be held up by our negotiations.[5]

When we concluded the arrangements on this subject with your Government last year, our negotiators made it clear that our agreement to the amount of support which you offered for our forces was premised on our expectation that the buildup of German forces would proceed rapidly. It was understood we were free to raise the issue of further support in the future if, in our judgment, the circumstances warranted.

In view of our respective political problems, it occurs to me that we might approach the matter on somewhat the same basis as that employed last year. This might permit us to accept the lump-sum payment which your government has offered us. It would be regarded as a payment "on account" so that the entire subject could be reviewed again in six months' time. This suggestion might provide the way out of our immediate problems. Meanwhile, your forthcoming trip to Washington will give us an opportunity to discuss all these problems personally.[6]

With kindest personal regards,[7] *Sincerely*

[1] On February 23, 1957, the United States government had asked the German Federal Republic to increase its payments toward the costs of maintaining U.S. troops in Germany. In October 1954 the two countries had negotiated an agreement regarding support costs in connection with the restoration of West German sovereignty (see Galambos and van Ee, *The Middle Way*, nos. 1084 and 1340). The German government had offered $77 million, half the amount contributed for 1956. Adenauer had emphasized that the Federal Republic was no longer obligated to pay support costs and that under the NATO agreements, measures taken regarding mutual aid were considered voluntary. Diverting additional funds from the defense budget, Adenauer said, "would considerably slow down the speed of German rearmament." Asking for an increase in his defense budget was not possible, since during an election year his defense policies were "particularly exposed to debate and controversy" (Ade-

nauer to Eisenhower, Mar. 23, 1957, AWF/I: Adenauer; see also State, *Foreign Relations, 1955–1957,* vol. XXVI, *Central and Southeastern Europe* [1992], pp. 90–93, 102–3, 221–22; and *New York Times,* June 8, 29, 1956).

[2] For deliberations regarding the defense budget, signed by Eisenhower on July 2, 1956, see *Congressional Quarterly Almanac,* vol. XII, *1956,* pp. 609–16; see also *U.S. Department of State Bulletin* 34, no. 869 (February 20, 1956), 279–80; and NSC meeting minutes, June 18, 1956, AWF/NSC; on congressional opinion regarding the German proposal for 1957 allocations see Goodpaster, Memorandum of Conference, April 4, 1957, AWF/D.

[3] The Western European Union, however, only had required twelve full divisions from Germany. According to JCS Chairman Radford, five divisions of 80 percent strength were scheduled for June 1957, with two more by the end of the year. Radford and Franz-Josef Strauss had met on December 10, before the beginning of the North Atlantic Council Ministerial Meeting held in Paris (State, *Foreign Relations, 1955–1957,* vol. IV, *Western European Security and Integration,* pp. 104, 123–33, 157, 253–54; and Goodpaster, Memorandum of Conference, Apr. 4, 1957, AWF/D; see also Galambos and van Ee, *The Middle Way,* no. 2134).

[4] Deutsche mark.

[5] British plans to reduce its forces in Germany posed a "grave threat not only to the Federal Republic but to the entire Western Defense Community," Adenauer had said. To help Britain with the financial difficulties posed by maintaining its forces on the continent, Germany had agreed to increase its allocation to the British. The negotiations would, however, be "placed in jeopardy," Adenauer said, if the United States did not accept the reduced defense allocations proposed by the Federal Republic (Adenauer to Eisenhower, Mar. 23, 1957, AWF/I: Adenauer; see also State, *Foreign Relations, 1955–1957,* vol. IV, *Western European Security and Integration,* pp. 151–52; on British force reductions see *ibid.,* pp. 165–66; no. 57; and State, *Foreign Relations, 1955–1957,* vol. XXVII, *Western Europe and Canada,* pp. 722–23, 749–51; see also Macmillan, *Riding the Storm,* pp. 245–48, 262; on the Bermuda Conference see no. 78).

Dulles had told Eisenhower that the Anglo-German agreement would not be finalized until and unless the United States accepted the German offer. "Any increased payment to us," Dulles said, "would probably be at the expense of the United Kingdom and would have a serious impact upon the whole matter of stationing United Kingdom troops on the continent" (Dulles to Eisenhower, Mar. 27, 1957, AWF/D-H).

[6] Although the Defense Department, according to Secretary Dulles, wanted to press the Federal Republic for an increase in its appropriation, the State Department felt "quite clearly that the political price of getting more would be excessive." Adenauer would have difficulty in asking for additional funds, and relations with the United Kingdom would suffer if the United States received German funds previously earmarked for the British (*ibid.*; see also Telephone conversations, Eisenhower and Dulles, Mar. 28, 1957, Dulles Papers, Telephone Conversations and AWF/D).

Eisenhower had met with State and Defense Department officials on April 2 to discuss U.S. response to the German proposal. Dulles believed that the United States should acquiesce to the Federal Republic's planned contribution to the British and "should try to get the Germans to accept the British arrangement as definitive." After the President suggested that Adenauer be told that the German proposal would be reviewed at the end of the year, Dulles agreed to collaborate with the Defense Department in drafting this reply to the German chancellor (Goodpaster, Memorandum of Conference, Apr. 4, 1957, AWF/D; and Ann Whitman memorandum, Apr. 2, 1957, AWF/AWD).

[7] Dulles would discuss this letter with Adenauer and German Foreign Minister Heinrich von Brentano in Bonn on May 4. The German government would not accept

an agreement with such a reservation as the words "on account" implied, the foreign minister stated, and his government could not be expected to approve a contribution larger than the previous year (State, *Foreign Relations, 1955–1957*, vol. XXVI, *Central and Southeastern Europe*, pp. 241–42).

Eisenhower and Adenauer would discuss the language of the agreement during the chancellor's visit to Washington (May 24–29), and on June 7 officials from both governments would exchange notes that provided for the contribution of $77 million from the Federal Republic to support U.S. forces in Germany. The U.S. note reserved the right to raise the question of additional aid at a later time (State, *Foreign Relations, 1955–1957*, vol. XXVI, *Central and Southeastern Europe*, pp. 284–85, 296). The texts of the notes are in *U.S. Department of State Bulletin* 37, no. 942 (July 15, 1957), 129–30. On Adenauer's visit see no. 186.

115

EM, AWF, International Series: Macmillan

To Harold Macmillan
Cable. Secret

April 15, 1957

Dear Harold: During our conversation at Bermuda, I assured you that we would continue to support in every appropriate way the purchase by Germany of Centurion tanks, which, as you know, is a policy we have long pursued.[1]

We have recently received definite indications, following the recent exhaustive military tests of the Centurion, and the U.S. models M-47 and M-48, that a German decision to purchase the model M-48 is probable. Such a situation has long been recognized as a possibility, as I pointed out to Anthony Eden in my letter of last September.[2]

In the circumstances, if the Germans do request the opportunity to purchase a specific number of our tanks which are clearly available to meet their requirements, it would be extremely difficult to refuse to sell them. A flat refusal to sell these tanks would most certainly expose us to German charges of lack of cooperation in assisting the Germans in meeting their NATO commitments.

Pending notification of a firm governmental decision by Germany, we shall continue to avoid urging the purchase of our equipment. Considering your lower price and long-range logistical convenience, it seems to me that the German government may decide to procure all or part of its needs from the United Kingdom. I hope so.[3]

With warm regard, *As ever*

[1] On the Bermuda Conference (Mar. 21–23) see State, *Foreign Relations, 1955–1957*, vol. XXVII, *Western Europe and Canada*, pp. 704–67; see also no. 78. After discussing Britain's economic problems with Eisenhower on March 22, Macmillan told the Pres-

ident that the balance of payments in the United Kingdom could be strengthened by selling British armaments to other countries. Macmillan had learned that the Federal Republic was contemplating the purchase of Centurion tanks "acknowledged to be a superlative weapon" and asked that Eisenhower encourage the Germans to make the purchase (Macmillan to Eisenhower, Mar. 22, 1957, AWF/I: Macmillan). The State Department would send this message to the American embassy in London on April 16.

[2] On April 5 the Federal Republic had informed the United States of their decision to select the M-48 over the Centurion because of the ease in procuring spare parts, servicing, and maintenance (see Robertson to Eisenhower, [Apr. 2, 1957], and other supporting material in WHCF/CF: State Department; see also *New York Times*, Mar. 24, 1957). For Eisenhower's letter to the former British Prime Minister see Galambos and van Ee, *The Middle Way*, no. 1991.

[3] For developments see no. 166.

116

EM, AWF, International Series: Argentina

To Pedro Eugenio Aramburu
Cable. Secret

April 17, 1957

Dear Mr. President:[1] Your letter of March 25, 1957, was delivered to me on April 10 by Dr. Alberto Gainza Paz, who is, of course, widely known and admired in the United States.[2]

During the course of a most interesting conversation, Dr. Gainza Paz conveyed to me Your Excellency's reflections on the situation in Argentina and on current relations between our two countries. I, in turn, took the liberty of suggesting that he discuss some of these problems further with various officials of the United States Government.[3] For my part, I am very pleased to have had the opportunity of discussing these matters with Dr. Gainza Paz, and I wholeheartedly agree with you that such a personal exchange of views is decidedly helpful. You may be sure that we here in Washington will continue to give the closest attention to problems of mutual interest to our two governments.[4]

I reciprocate the kind wishes contained in your letter, and assure you of my warm personal regard for both you and the people of Argentina. *Sincerely*

[1] Aramburu had become chairman of Argentina's ruling military junta and provisional president in November 1955. Eisenhower had asked Acting Secretary of State Herter to draft this reply to Aramburu on a "top secret basis" (Eisenhower to Herter, Apr. 10, 1957, AWF/D; and Herter to Eisenhower, Apr. 15, 1957, AWF/I: Argentina; see also Ann Whitman memorandum, Apr. 10, 1957, AWF/AWD).

[2] Gainza Paz, owner and editor of *La Prensa*, the Argentinian newspaper published in Buenos Aires, had met with Eisenhower and Acting Assistant Secretary of State

Roy R. Rubottom, Jr., in Washington on April 10. Aramburu's letter said that he considered Gainza Paz's visit a "direct and personal contact" and that he would be pleased to receive any message from his "responsible intermediary" (Aramburu to Eisenhower, Mar. 25, 1957, AWF/I: Argentina). For background on U.S. relations with Argentina and that country's previous takeover of *La Prensa* see Galambos and van Ee, *The Middle Way*, no. 523.

[3] Gainza Paz had gone to Washington because Argentina was at a point in its history where democracy could be permanently restored by general elections scheduled for February 1958. According to Gainza Paz, his country was recovering from the "economic shambles" left by the Perón dictatorship and badly needed economic assistance, particularly to rebuild the public transportation system and power plants. He also said that Aramburu had wanted Eisenhower to know that Argentina was prepared to enter into a military defense agreement with the United States (State, *Foreign Relations, 1955–1957*, vol. VII, *American Republics: Central and South America*, pp. 456–60). For subsequent discussions with officials of both countries see *ibid.*, pp. 460–72.

[4] On June 3 the two countries would sign a General Agreement for a Program of Technical Cooperation (*U.S. Department of State Bulletin* 37, no. 940 [July 1, 1957], 42. For developments see no. 658.

117

EM, AWF, Name Series

TO MILTON STOVER EISENHOWER

April 17, 1957

Dear Milton: In a letter from Ed Bermingham he says that he has sent to you a copy of what he wrote to me.[1] The second and third paragraphs of that letter seem to contain material that the State Department should know about.[2] Rather than send them a copy of my letter from him, won't you undertake to give them an account of the statements made in those two paragraphs when next you have a chance?

* * * * *

This morning at press conference I was asked about Ed's criticism of me. I merely replied "Ed has been criticizing me since I was five." I hope that settles that.[3] *As ever*

[1] For background on Edward John Bermingham, a retired investment banker who frequently wrote Eisenhower regarding U.S.-Mexican affairs, see Galambos and van Ee, *The Middle Way*, no. 34.

[2] Bermingham reported what he called "scuttle-butt stuff" regarding Mexican President Adolfo Ruiz Cortines's disappointment in the U.S. State and Commerce Departments' reversal of a decision that would have sanctioned the Mexican purchase of $25 million in surplus corn from the United States.

Bermingham had also told Eisenhower about a meeting between Mexican Senator Antonio J. Bermudez and Deputy Under Secretary of State for Economic Affairs C. Douglas Dillon, regarding the possibility of private American loans for the support of Pemex (Petróleos Mexicanos), the national oil company of Mexico. Dillon had been "brutally frank," according to Bermingham, saying that "Pemex must adjust its huge tax load, rid itself of subsidy prices and obtain a fair return on its overall sales" (Bermingham to Eisenhower, Apr. 14, 1957, AWF/N; for background on loans to Mexico see Galambos and van Ee, *The Middle Way*, nos. 1324 and 1472; on the corn purchase see State, *Foreign Relations, 1955–1957*, vol. VI, *American Republics: Multilateral; Mexico; Caribbean* [1987], pp. 746–47, 751–52).

[3] Edgar Eisenhower, the President's brother, had criticized federal spending under the Administration's budget and the liberal influence of Milton Eisenhower and the Assistant to the President Sherman Adams. According to Ann Whitman, "The President laughed it off in press conference, not so in private. However, he was not nearly as disturbed as Dr. Milton" (Ann Whitman memorandum, Apr. 17, 1957, AWF/AWD). Eisenhower's comments are in *Public Papers of the Presidents: Eisenhower, 1957*, p. 284; see also *New York Times*, April 17, 1957.

On this same day Eisenhower would thank Bermingham for his letter and for sending a copy to Milton (Eisenhower to Bermingham, April 17, 1957, AWF/N).

118

EM, AWF, Name Series: Eisenhower Exchange Fellowships

To Thomas Bayard McCabe — *April 17, 1957*

Dear Tom:[1] For some time Mr. Barnes has been negotiating with my secretary for something that could be used in the new home for the Eisenhower Exchange Fellowships, Inc. that you provided in Philadelphia. As a temporary measure, I believe some photographs were sent to him.[2]

Meantime I searched my mind for something that I thought would be suitable for the splendid headquarters you have so generously given to the Fellowships. Finally it occurred to me that you might like to have a painting of "The Towers of Riga," by Ludolfs Liberts given to me some years ago by the American Latvian Association, Inc.[3] It has hung in my office since late in 1953 and is a picture that I have found very interesting. (You may, as a matter of fact recall it.)

If you think there is a proper place for it in Philadelphia—and if the idea appeals to you—I shall see that it is sent along.

With warm regard, *Sincerely*

P.S. The picture bears a brass plate of dedication to me, which gives it a certain personal character.[4]

[1] McCabe was chairman of the board of trustees of the Eisenhower Exchange Fellowships, Inc., and president of Scott Paper Company in Chester, Pennsylvania. In 1952 he had served on the sponsors' committee for the National Committee for Eisenhower. For background see Galambos, *NATO and the Campaign of 1952*, no. 652, and Galambos and van Ee, *The Middle Way*, no. 1021.

[2] Newspaper publisher J. Hampton Barnes, the executive director of the Eisenhower Exchange Fellowships, had written Ann Whitman (Feb. 7) to make arrangements to pick up several photographs of Eisenhower with world dignitaries. On February 10 Whitman asked Barnes to notify her in advance of his arrival so that the photographs could be marked and prepared (both in AWF/N: Eisenhower Exchange Fellowships). The program's headquarters had moved from New York City.
[3] Liberts, a Latvian refugee who formerly taught in Riga's Academy of Fine Arts, was a landscape painter. "The Towers of Riga," was an impressionistic picture of the skyline of Latvia's capital. In 1954 the American Latvian Association had purchased the painting as a gift to the President (see *New York Times*, Mar. 16, 1959).
[4] McCabe would thank Eisenhower for his "thoughtful and generous" gift on April 24. The board of trustees expected to meet in May, McCabe wrote, and at that time he would "notify the members of your gift and your great interest in our new building" (AWF/N: Eisenhower Exchange Fellowships, and telephone conversation with Rosemary Ranck, Eisenhower Exchange Fellowships, Inc., Mar. 19, 1996).

119 — *C. D. Jackson Papers*

To Charles Douglas Jackson — *April 18, 1957*

Dear C. D.: The delay in acknowledging your letter of the eleventh means simply that we have been studying earnestly your proposals for enlisting support for the mutual aid program.[1] I like very much your suggestion for a citizens' group, and Sherman Adams is currently exploring ways and means of forming such an organization. I believe, as I am sure you do, that it would be best if it did not appear to have a professional—or White House—character.[2]

At any rate, I do want, in the few hurried moments I have before leaving for Augusta,[3] to thank you for your support for the program—support that is manifested in more ways than I could possibly enumerate.

With warm regard, *As ever*

[1] Jackson had written on April 11 (AWF/A) to propose that Eisenhower bolster Secretary of State John Foster Dulles's recent speech on mutual security with a statement of his own (see *New York Times*, Mar. 9, 10, 1957). Dulles had called for a fundamentally altered Mutual Security Program, which would feature a special economic development fund with multi-year funding authorization, and which, by bracketing military aid into the regular budget of the Defense Department, would remove the necessity of seeking annual military aid authorization from Congress. Jackson believed that Dulles's speech should be seen as "only a beginning." "The words were all there," he wrote, "but of necessity there was not much music; and a certain amount of well orchestrated music is going to be necessary if this is going to be made to come alive and start generating its own dynamic so that Congress will sit up and take notice." Jackson suggested that the President launch a campaign "using your Second Inaugural as a springboard, and moving on from there." "It is essential," Jackson emphasized, "that you be publicly and strongly identified with this proposal beyond a

press conference endorsement. This one needs Presidential 'launching' just as much as did Atoms-for-Peace." (For background on Eisenhower's commitment to the mutual security program see nos. 60 and 90. For Eisenhower's Second Inaugural Address see no. 2 and *Public Papers of the Presidents: Eisenhower, 1957*, pp. 60–65; on Atoms for Peace see Galambos and van Ee, *The Middle Way*, no. 598.)

[2] Jackson had suggested that the Administration enlist the support of the "large national citizens' organizations." Stating that "the people are way ahead of the Congress on this subject," Jackson proposed a White House Conference as "the quickest way to get national organization leaders educated and fired up. Properly interested and stimulated," he wrote, "I am quite sure that most of them would be eager to undertake a quick program of local education throughout their membership. I am convinced that such grassroots education would meet great popular receptivity, which would rapidly combine to produce the kind of articulate national psychology which this program needs after all the kicking around it has received for so many years." For developments see no. 137.

[3] On Eisenhower's Augusta vacation see no. 97.

120 *EM, WHCF, President's Personal File 1494*

To David Lawrence *April 18, 1957*
Personal

Dear Mr. Lawrence:[1] This morning I read your column in the Herald Tribune, which served to remind me of an editorial I had read last evening in the April nineteenth issue of your magazine.[2] Both of these show such a clear understanding of our problems abroad, such a keen appreciation of the thoughtful, earnest and serious way we must approach those problems, that I could not refrain from writing you a note to express my admiration.[3] Without claiming perfection for any process of government, I think we can still maintain that in this great field that you touch upon in these two pieces, we are at least on the right track.[4]

With personal regard, *Sincerely*

[1] David Lawrence (B.A. Princeton 1910) was the president and editor of *U.S. News & World Report* and a syndicated columnist.

[2] Lawrence's editorial, "Peoples Above Governments," in the April 19, 1957, *U.S. News & World Report*, strongly endorsed the Administration's recently announced foreign aid program. "The main idea," Lawrence wrote, "is to grant funds for strictly military defenses erected in the free world and to handle economic aid so far as possible on a public as well as a private loan basis." Lawrence called the foreign aid program "business-like and sensible." He exhorted the American people to support the program as an opportunity to "form and maintain friendships with other peoples. For it is the people everywhere who decide whether there shall be war—they alone must do the fighting. And it is the people in every country who alone must decide whether they wish to enjoy the fruits of peace." For background see no. 119. For developments see no. 137.

[3] For Lawrence's earlier thinking on foreign aid see Galambos and van Ee, *The Middle Way*, no. 1761.
[4] Lawrence would write on April 18 to thank the President for his comments (same file as document).

121

EM, AWF, DDE Diaries Series

To John Sheldon Doud Eisenhower *April 18, 1957*

Dear John: I had a talk with Chief Baughman this morning, explaining accurately, I think, your feeling about Mr. Barton.[1] He told me that in order to achieve permanent civil service status, Mr. Barton had only to do a short tour of field service in some line of work other than on the White House Detail.

While I suppose you should not tell Mr. Barton until Chief Baughman speaks to him, the Chief said that his plan was to put Mr. Barton on field service during the month of July. Immediately after that he would return him to his present duties because of the complete satisfaction you have with his services. Incidentally, he was delighted to have such a fine report on Mr. Barton who the Chief himself believes to be a very fine man in the Secret Service.

Mamie told me that she had asked Barbie and the family to stay on the third floor, if you care to, during the period you will be on temporary duty here at the White House. It just occurred to me that you might like to have the opportunity to go back and forth as you choose. By this I mean that you might feel like staying here during the week and spending the weekends at your own home—or vice versa.[2]

In any event, please feel free, both of you, to do the thing that would most suit your convenience. *Devotedly*

[1] Urbanus Edmund Baughman was the Chief, United States Secret Service. Bill Barton managed the Eisenhower grandchildren's secret service detail.
[2] Major Eisenhower, his wife, and their children were stationed at Fort Belvoir, Virginia. On June 3 he would join the White House staff for a period of temporary duty as liaison representative for national security affairs in the office of the staff secretary. In late summer John would be assigned to the Pentagon in the Joint War Plans Branch, Plans Division, Office of the Deputy Chief of Staff for Operations. As it turned out, the John Eisenhowers would live in Alexandria, Virginia (see John S. D. Eisenhower, *Strictly Personal*, pp. 190–93; and *New York Times*, June 1, 4, 1957).

122

EM, AWF, DDE Diaries Series

To Priscilla Allen Slater

April 20, 1957

Dear Priscilla: Last night we had a small gathering of the clan in "Mamie's Cottage" to celebrate three important events in American history. In chronological order they are: the Battle of Lexington, Pete Jones' birthday, and Priscilla Slater's birthday.[1] Incidentally one of the hits of the evening—especially for hungry and frustrated golfers—was the magnificent cake of brie that you sent down by Slats.

This note is to tell you that we missed you very much, but all of us drank a toast to your health and happiness in good California wine provided by Charlie Jones.[2]

The weather here has turned really hot—the first welcome relief I have had from cold, chilly weather in months.

With affectionate regard in which Mamie joins, *Sincerely*

[1] Mrs. Slater, the wife of Ellis D. ("Slats") Slater, had missed this "gathering" because she remained at the Slater farm in Spartanburg, South Carolina, to close it up for the summer. "Mamie's Cottage," the Eisenhowers' home at Augusta National Golf Club, had been built on the edge of the golf course in 1953. For background see Galambos and van Ee, *The Middle Way*, no. 480; Ambrose, *Eisenhower*, vol. II, *The President*, p. 94; and Ellis D. Slater, *The Ike I Knew* (Baltimore, 1980), pp. 151–54. W. Alton Jones, who attended the dinner party, was born on April 19, 1891, the same date that the Revolutionary War battle at Lexington was fought in 1775.

[2] Charles S. Jones, a member of the board of directors of Douglas Aircraft Company (see Galambos and van Ee, *The Middle Way*, no. 1543), was among the dinner guests.

123

EM, AWF, DDE Diaries Series

To Barry Morris Goldwater

[*April 24, 1957*]

Dear Barry:[1] The speech you sent me, and which I have now read, surprised and disappointed me.[2]

The Party's 1956 Platform I consider a binding commitment on every responsible Republican.[3] Those Party pledges to the American people I will keep on doing my best to fulfill. I am sorry that our efforts to that end seem so distasteful to you. *Sincerely*

[1] Presidential Assistants Bryce N. Harlow and Gerald Morgan drafted this undated letter for Eisenhower.

[2] Eisenhower was referring to a speech that Arizona Senator Goldwater had delivered to the Senate on April 8 (see *Congressional Record*, 85th Cong., 1st sess., 1957, 103, pt. 1:5258–65, and *New York Times*, Apr. 9, 1957). The Republican Senator had

charged the President with breaking his 1952 campaign promises by submitting a budget whose "abominably high" expenditures would subvert the American economy because they were "based on high taxes, the largest deficit in history, and the consequent dissipation of the freedom and initiative and genius of our productive people, upon whom the whole structure of our economic system depends for survival." In addition to attacking the Administration's "big budget concept," Senator Goldwater assailed Eisenhower's philosophy of "modern Republicanism."

[3] See Kirk H. Porter and Donald Bruce Johnson, comps., *National Party Platforms, 1840–1968* (Urbana, 1970), pp. 545–62.

124

EM, AWF, International Series: Lebanon

To Camille nimr Chamoun *April 25, 1957*
Secret

Dear Mr. President:[1] I have studied with care your impressive message of April 24, 1957 and share your belief that present developments in Jordan are of great importance to free peoples everywhere.[2] The independence and integrity of Jordan are of deep concern to the United States and I entirely agree that this is a situation where those who love freedom must join together to strengthen that cause.

We are following developments in Jordan closely and have conveyed to King Hussein our encouragement and support.[3] In our close consultation with King Saud, we have expressed to him our appreciation for the very effective measures he has taken to support King Hussein.[4] We have also been in touch with the Government of Iraq, and share the belief of the Iraqi Government that the deployment of Iraqi forces on Iraqi territory in a manner in which they can be quickly available to King Hussein is a wise precautionary measure.[5]

The Government of Israel has been told of our firm view that Israel should exercise the greatest restraint in the present crisis in Jordan. Israel seems to display a constructive attitude.[6]

Units of the United States Sixth Fleet, with United States Marines aboard, are moving into the Eastern Mediterranean. Ambassador Heath is being instructed to ask the Government of Lebanon for permission for a call by ships of the Fleet at Beirut for approximately three or four days beginning April thirtieth. This could of course be extended if considered desirable by our two governments in the light of circumstances.[7]

We are keeping in close touch with other friendly Governments.[8] I am gratified at your expression of Lebanon's deep concern in this matter of our common interest, and at reports indicating measures which Lebanon is taking to assist King Hussein. Perhaps you might wish to consider further steps such as a public expression of support for King Hussein and private consultation with friendly Governments in the area with regard to steps they might take to assist the King.

You may be certain that you and I share the same purpose, and I would greatly appreciate any further views or suggestions which you might have.[9] *Sincerely*

[1] Chamoun, former head of the Lebanese delegation to the United Nations, had been President of Lebanon since September 1952. Eisenhower, who was vacationing in Augusta, approved this message, which State Department officials had drafted; it was sent by cable to the American embassy in Beirut (see Whitman to Eisenhower, [Apr. 25, 1957], AWF/I: Lebanon).

[2] See Galambos and van Ee, *The Middle Way*, nos. 1681 and 2038 for background. Although King Hussein had publicly taken a strong anti-Communist stand, the Eisenhower Administration had long been concerned with the economic and military instability of Jordan. In December 1955 rioters had protested British pressure on Jordan to join the pro-Western Baghdad Pact, and in October of 1956 Arab nationalists had taken control of parliament. The new government recommended the abrogation of the Anglo-Jordanian mutual defense treaty of 1948, an action that the State Department feared would allow Egypt, Syria, and the Soviet Union to fill the resulting void with economic and military assistance. The newly elected Jordanian officials also recommended establishing diplomatic relations with the Soviet Union and Communist China.

At an April 11 meeting Central Intelligence Agency (CIA) Director Allen Dulles had told the National Security Council that the situation in Jordan was "extremely critical." A government reorganization had left power largely in the hands of the army, whose allegiance to Hussein was uncertain. Pro-Communist demonstrators had denounced the United States, the Eisenhower Doctrine, and the Baghdad Pact. On April 13 King Hussein had thwarted an attempted coup by pro-Egyptian, pro-Syrian, and leftist factions and had formed a new cabinet thought to be favorable to his pro-Western policies. Twelve days later Hussein had tried to control this volatile situation by placing Jordan under martial law and imposing curfews in designated areas (State, *Foreign Relations, 1955–1957*, vol. XIII, *Near East: Jordan-Yemen*, pp. 49–113; NSC meeting minutes, Apr. 12, 19, 1957, AWF/NSC; Eisenhower, *Waging Peace*, pp. 194–95; Matthew F. Holland, *America and Egypt: From Roosevelt to Eisenhower* [Westport, Conn., 1996], pp. 137–38; and *New York Times*, Apr. 25, 26, 1957; on the Eisenhower Doctrine see Galambos and van Ee, *The Middle Way*, no. 2155; and Eisenhower, *Waging Peace*, pp. 178–83).

In his letter of April 24 Chamoun had told Eisenhower that "if Jordan falls to international communism or to its puppets or allies, then that might start a chain reaction in our area whose sombre consequences can not be foretold." Collective action by all countries opposed to the communistic system would, Chamoun believed, save Jordan and "win it to our camp." The moment required "swift and decisive action almost at any cost," and Eisenhower, Chamoun said, was "the one most clearly indicated both to act and to lead" (Heath to Dulles, Apr. 24, 1957, AWF/I: Lebanon).

[3] In a message that had reached the State Department through intelligence channels King Hussein had promised to "take a strong line in Jordan, including martial law on the West Bank, suspension of constitutional rights and a strong statement regarding the activities of Egypt and Syria in Jordan." He had asked if the United States would support him if Israel or the Soviet Union intervened. After consultation with

Eisenhower, Secretary Dulles had told Hussein that Israeli intervention "would involve a strong adverse reaction on the part of the United States." Overt Soviet intervention would be a challenge to the Eisenhower Doctrine, Dulles said, and would prompt the United States to intervene militarily at Jordan's request (State, *Foreign Relations, 1955–1957*, vol. XIII, *Near East: Jordan-Yemen*, pp. 106–7, 112–13; see also Telephone conversation, Eisenhower and Dulles, Apr. 24, 1957, Dulles Papers, Telephone Conversations and AWF/D).

[4] On this day Secretary Dulles had requested that the U.S. ambassador to Saudi Arabia review the situation in Jordan with King Saud and ask the King publicly to express his willingness to provide forces for Hussein if he should request them. On April 27 King Saud would tell the U.S. ambassador that Saudi forces were already in Jordan under Hussein's command (State, *Foreign Relations, 1955–1957*, vol. XIII, *Near East: Jordan-Yemen*, pp. 96, 111–12).

[5] Iraq would announce its support of U.S. policy regarding Jordan and would state that King Hussein should request Iraqi troops in writing if he wanted them. The Iraqi Prime Minister would also tell Secretary Dulles on April 26 "that what you have been doing and propose to do is all to the good, but up to now you have been working only on the tail and leaving the head intact. The head is Nasser and in the last analysis, it is Nasser who is the source of all the disturbances in the Middle East" (*ibid.*, pp. 110–11; see also State, *Foreign Relations, 1955–1957*, vol. XII, *Near East Region; Iran; Iraq*, p. 1048).

[6] On April 24 Secretary Dulles had told the Israelis that the United States wanted to give Jordan a fair chance to resolve the situation and if that country were physically threatened, the United States would respond very strongly. The Israelis replied that they would avoid any move that played into Nasser's hands and were aware of the need for caution (State, *Foreign Relations, 1955–1957*, vol. XIII, *Near East: Jordan-Yemen*, pp. 104–6; see also Eban, *An Autobiography*, p. 261; and Alteras, *Eisenhower and Israel*, pp. 306–7).

[7] Donald B. Heath had been U.S. Ambassador to Lebanon since March 1955. Six ships of the fleet would arrive in Beirut on April 30; on May 3 the fleet would sail westward to join NATO allies in maneuvers off the Italian coast (State, *Foreign Relations, 1955–1957*, vol. XIII, *Near East: Jordan-Yemen*, pp. 107–9; see also Telephone conversations, Dulles and Radford, Apr. 24; Eisenhower and Dulles, Apr. 25; Dulles and Rountree, Apr. 26, 1957, Dulles Papers, Telephone Conversations; and *New York Times*, May 1, 4, 1957).

[8] For Eisenhower's letter to Britain's Prime Minister Harold Macmillan regarding the Jordanian situation see no. 132.

[9] On April 29, after the political turmoil in Jordan had subsided, the United States, in response to a Jordanian request, would offer that country $10 million in economic assistance under the Mutual Security Act (State, *Foreign Relations, 1955–1957*, vol. XIII, *Near East: Jordan-Yemen*, p. 118). For developments see no. 277.

125 — *EM, AWF, DDE Diaries Series*

To George Magoffin Humphrey — *April 25, 1957*

Dear George: I saw a note in the paper that you support the Senate's proposal of investigating our whole financial structure. I hope this does not mean that you do not support the Administration plan for a broad scale inquiry by experts, together with a certain group of Congressmen.[1] *As ever*

[1] On April 12, 1957, Democratic Senator from Virginia Harry Flood Byrd had unexpectedly launched a Senate Finance Committee investigation to study the nation's money and credit system. Byrd's action may have been in response to Eisenhower's January 1957 State of the Union Address, in which he had stated that "the time has come to conduct a broad national inquiry into the nature, performance and adequacy" of the financial system (see *Public Papers of the Presidents: Eisenhower, 1957*, pp. 23–24). The President had called for Congress to authorize a commission of "able and qualified citizens" to develop proposals "for the purpose of improving our financial machinery." Byrd's move had led the House Banking and Currency Committee to drop efforts to launch its own investigation (see *Congressional Quarterly Almanac*, vol. XIII, *1957*, pp. 789–90). Announcing that the Senate's study would be "'one of the broadest investigations ever undertaken by Congress,'" Byrd pledged to examine government revenue, debt and debt financing; and the effect of the debt on credit, interest rates and the nation's economy and welfare (*New York Times*, Apr. 13, 1957). For Humphrey's reaction see no. 128.

126

EM, AWF, DDE Diaries Series

To Charles H. Gibboney

April 25, 1957

Dear Mr. Gibboney: Thank you very much for your cordial note of the twenty-second. Mrs. Eisenhower and I always derive inspiration from the services at the Reid Memorial Church. Easter Sunday was no exception, and our feelings were fully shared by Secretary and Mrs. Humphrey.[1]

As to your invitation to play golf, I have had to make an inflexible rule not to leave the Augusta National grounds, while vacationing in this city, except for the one purpose of attending Church.[2] If it were not for this rule I am afraid I would, through discrimination, hurt the feelings of many kindly and friendly people who have invited me to participate in some enjoyable activity. But if I should accept all, I would have to cease coming to this beautiful place. I am certain that you will understand why I cannot come to the Country Club.

With respect to the Miami meeting, I am, of course, always glad to know of this kind of a convention. In this particular case I have a special interest, but I am indeed doubtful that I shall find it possible to be there in person.[3]

In response to your invitation to come to the Church next Sunday morning, I am sure that, except for some unforeseen circumstance, we shall be delighted to accept.[4]

With best wishes, *Sincerely*

[1] Gibboney was minister of the Reid Memorial Presbyterian Church in Augusta, Georgia. His note is in WHCF/PPF 53-B-1. On the Eisenhowers' vacation (Apr. 18–30) see no. 97. On the Humphreys' visit see no. 131.
[2] Gibboney had invited Eisenhower to join him in a round of golf at the Augusta Country Club.
[3] For developments in regard to the Presbyterian Men's Convention see no. 264.
[4] The Eisenhowers would attend services at Reid Memorial on April 28.

127

EM, AWF, Name Series: Guided Missiles

To Charles Erwin Wilson
Secret

April 26, 1957

Memorandum for the Secretary of Defense: I understand that actions have recently been initiated which would add project "Polaris," with a top priority rating, to the IRBM/ICBM programs presented to the NSC on March 28 (NSC action number 1690).[1]

Before authorization is given for expenditures under this project, I would like to be furnished:

a. The specific details of the proposed funding of this project, identifying the component elements and their costs;

b. An indication of the extent to which this project is included in, or will take the place of, IRBM/ICBM programs previously proposed for funding, and specifically how much additional funding, if any, this project would require if approved.[2]

[1] In 1956 the Navy's Special Projects Office had begun development of a sea-launched system for the Jupiter intermediate range ballistic missile (IRBM). Searching for ways to overcome the difficulties involved in launching a large liquid-fueled rocket, Navy scientists had conceived Polaris, a smaller, submarine-launched, solid-fuel missile with the range and destructive power of the liquid-fuel missiles under development by the Army and Air Force (Kenneth W. Condit, *History of the Joint Chiefs of Staff,* vol. VI, *The Joint Chiefs of Staff and National Policy 1955–1956* [Washington, D.C., 1992], p. 70; for background see Wyndham D. Miles, "The Polaris," in *The History of Rocket Technology,* Eugene M. Emme, ed., [Detroit, 1964], pp. 162–75; Charles D. Bright, *The Jet Makers: The Aerospace Industry from 1945 to 1972* [Lawrence, Kans., 1978]; and Walter A. McDougall, *The Heavens and the Earth: A Political History of the Space Age* [New York, 1985], pp. 128–29).

NSC Action No. 1690, issued at the March 28, 1957, National Security Council meeting, had authorized the Department of Defense "to achieve initial operational capability" for the IRBM and ICBM programs Thor, Atlas, and Titan, "at the earliest practicable date" (State, *Foreign Relations of the United States, 1955–1957,* vol. XIX, *National Security Policy* [1990], pp. 455–56). Although Eisenhower had earlier issued a directive to give the highest priority to both the research and development of the IRBM and ICBM programs, Secretary of Defense Wilson had informed the President in February that the Polaris program was "being prosecuted at a priority which, while high, is not as high as that assigned to the ICBMs or other IRBMs" (Wilson to Eisenhower, Feb. 26, 1957, AWF/N: Guided Missiles; see also Galambos and van Ee, *The Middle Way*, no. 1663).

[2] Eisenhower's memo reflected his continuing concern about the costs of missile development and the interservice rivalries that led to duplication of research efforts (for background see Galambos and van Ee, *The Middle Way*, no. 1663; see also Memorandum of Conference with the President, Mar. 14, and Apr. 1, 1957, AWF/D). While there is no record of a response to Eisenhower's memorandum by Secretary Wilson, the President's concerns would be addressed in the July 3, 1957, National Security Council meeting (for developments see no. 229).

128

EM, AWF, Administration Series

To George Magoffin Humphrey

April 27, 1957

Dear George: I have your note explaining the matter of the "Financial Resolution."[1] I suppose you are right that we should not press for action this session of Congress, but it seems obvious that if I am questioned about the matter at any press conference I have no recourse except to maintain that I am still for our scheme.[2] *As ever*

[1] Secretary of the Treasury Humphrey had replied on April 26, 1957 (AWF/A) to Eisenhower's April 25 letter regarding Senator Harry Byrd's announcement that the Senate Finance Committee would launch an investigation of the nation's money and credit system (see no. 125). Humphrey reported that "After Byrd took his action, I told him on the telephone that of course the Treasury would cooperate with his investigation in every way, which is the position we always take with any Committee of the Congress."

[2] The Treasury Secretary had stated that at a meeting in his office "attended by Hauge, Persons, and all the others that we could find who were interested," it had been decided that "for the present at least and certainly until after the vacation, no Administration position should be pushed as we were not in a position to stop the Byrd investigation and it was thought best to let the thing settle and see how the land lay before determining whether or not a further move should be made on the Administration's suggestion." Humphrey added that he personally believed that "it would be a mistake to push the Administration's program in this session" of Congress. The Byrd Committee was "the best forum in this hostile Congress that we can have," he said "to prevent the emergence of bad legislation. . . ." This was the case, Humphrey said, "even though it will be a platform for a lot of demagoguery." For developments see no. 216.

129

EM, AWF, Name Series

To William Alton Jones

April 27, 1957

Dear Pete: Last evening someone told me that you have had a perfectly terrible time with your teeth. It was my impression, when you left here, that you were anticipating only some fairly routine treatment and might even be back for the weekend.[1]

It seems that everybody around here, except me, knew that you had run into some difficulty. I found it out only by asking whether you were going to come back last evening.

In any event, my sympathies are with you. I know what it is to be in the hands of the doctors and to have painful ailments, and I do hope that you will soon escape their clutches.

Take care of yourself and if you should be coming to Washington and feel like a homeless waif, just drop in and there is always a room (complete with toothbrush and pajamas) awaiting you.

Mamie had a rather severe asthmatic attack just after you left, but now seems quite well again.[2] She joins me in affectionate regard and the hope that you will remember us both warmly to Nettie.[3] *As ever*

P.S. As I sit in my office to write this, I realize that I might be surer of getting hold of you if I used the telephone, but it is my feeling that anyone with a jaw swollen out of shape, as I am sure yours is, doesn't want to be bothered with an instrument which at the very best is fairly devilish.[4]

[1] The Eisenhowers would vacation in Augusta, Georgia, from April 18–30. Jones would share golfing, bridge, and dining with the Eisenhowers at Augusta during this period (see, for example, no. 122; see also President's daily appointments, Apr. 18–30).

[2] As a result of her ongoing problem with asthma, Mamie would return to Washington before the President (see President's daily appointments, Apr. 27, 1957, and Slater, *The Ike I Knew*, pp. 151–54).

[3] Jones's wife was the former Nettie Marie Marvin.

[4] For developments see no. 140.

130

EM, AWF, Administration Series

To George Edward Allen

April 27, 1957

Dear George: The other day I had a note from Jock Whitney, written in response to a letter I had sent him a couple of weeks ago. He told me that his trainer had orders to sell you a good horse. Jock says the trainer reported "The horse may not win no Derbies but he is some horse."[1]

I suppose that all you have to do in the circumstances is to get in touch with the Greentree Stables.[2]

Mamie and I expect to be home Monday—or Tuesday at the latest.[3] *As ever*

[1] Ambassador Whitney had written on April 13 (see no. 136).

[2] Whitney owned the Greentree Stables at Manhasset, Long Island.

[3] The President would return to Washington, D.C., on Tuesday, April 30 (see also the preceding document).

131

EM, AWF, Administration Series

TO PAMELA STARK HUMPHREY AND GEORGE MAGOFFIN HUMPHREY

April 27, 1957

Dear Pam and George: Much as we enjoyed your notes, it is for us, rather than for you, to be writing bread-and-butter notes about our all too short stay together at the Augusta National. We are really grateful that you found time to come down; we enjoyed every minute of your visit.[1]

I have only one concern. I am afraid with George back in Washington, he will decide once more that he is "busy" and the all-important subject of his golf swing will be neglected.

After you left Mamie had an asthmatic attack one evening and for the next day or so stayed in bed to rest up. Once more she seems fine.[2]

We are looking forward to seeing you when we get back, possibly Monday.[3]

With affectionate regard, *As ever*

[1] The Humphreys had spent a few days with the Eisenhowers (on vacation from April 18–30) in Augusta, Georgia, before returning to Washington on the afternoon of April 23 (see Slater, *The Ike I Knew*, p. 152). We have been unable to find their notes.

[2] See no. 129.

[3] The President would meet Humphrey on Wednesday, May 1.

cordance with right and justice, the problems that plague us in the region. I know that Foster is working closely with Harold Caccia and your Foreign Office people in all these matters.[7]

The Vice President's recent trip to most of the North African countries proved to be very informative.[8] He found a great reservoir of good will toward the West, but he concluded that a modest amount of technical and economic aid was badly needed in each of the countries visited. He feels that if the West does not find ways of supplying some of this help, these countries will be forced to turn to the Soviets. That would be tragic.

The Vice President is convinced that we have a need for a better relationship between the French and some of the North African regions and that we must help achieve this relationship without hurting the interests of either. This will mean walking a tight rope, but, again, I think we can pull through if we work together—and do not expect the impossible. It seems clear that several of these countries are growing fearful of Egypt's influence among their populations and are searching for ways and means to combat that influence which, they rightly believe, is inspired by the Soviets.[9]

I share your disappointment that Lord Salisbury resigned because of the release of Makarios.[10] While I think that the latter is far from a statesman and can probably stir up quite a bit of mischief, still I think that Britain, as a great country, is in better position in the matter than she was with him as a prisoner. Certainly you have taken away from demagogues one of their chief arguments against you. I have heard that one of our ambitious governors has invited the Archbishop to come to this country.[11] One is frequently tempted to ask "How stupid can you get?" To conclude—I hope that Lord Salisbury comes back into the fold.

I am delighted that Anthony is successfully through his operation. Foster had asked to see him in Boston on his own and my behalf. But apparently he is forbidden to have visitors before he leaves for Canada.[12]

Please write to me whenever the spirit moves you. I am sending this from Georgia, where I am spending a few days. I should like to call it a vacation, but I am frequently reminded that a man cannot take a vacation from his own thoughts.[13]

With warm regard, [*As ever*]

[1] On April 15 Prime Minister Macmillan had written Eisenhower about strikes in both the engineering and shipbuilding industries; about his budget, including some "modest but encouraging" tax cuts; and about Britain's economy, which had "survived Suez and other troubles with extraordinary resilience" (State, *Foreign Relations, 1955–1957*, vol. XXVII, *Western Europe and Canada*, pp. 768–71; see also Macmillan, *Riding the Storm*, pp. 211–12, 255–68, 346–49; and Telephone conversation, Eisenhower and Dulles, Apr. 26, 1957, Dulles Papers, Telephone Conversations).

[2] On Britain's announced reduction in its NATO forces because of budget constraints see nos. 57 and 95. Not only would force reductions save money and manpower, Macmillan said, but the policy would enable Britain to return to career men for their forces, which would provide a better contribution to NATO "than we have now with this continual movement in and out. . . ."
[3] Macmillan compared his efforts to resolve the canal issue to the water jump at the Grand National Steeplechase: "I do not honestly think that we can make a very glorious showing over this. Indeed we may well fall in; but I think we can pull the horse out all right on the other side, struggle somehow into the saddle, and ride on."

For background on Egypt's Suez Canal Declaration, setting forth guidelines for the administration of canal operations see no. 99. In order to ensure that the principles established by the U.N. Security Council would be included in the declaration and to establish guidelines for cooperation between Egypt and the user nations, the United States had continued talks with the Egyptian government. On April 26 the Security Council had discussed the Suez situation but had made no recommendations (see State, *Foreign Relations, 1955–1957*, vol. XXVII, *Western Europe and Canada*, pp. 479–88, 492–98, 500–504, 509–51, 559–74; and Macmillan, *Riding the Storm*, pp. 230–34). On the Bermuda Conference see no. 78.
[4] The words: "live with some patience with the interim arrangement. To look forward" were apparently typed in error at this point in the source text (see State, *Foreign Relations, 1955–1957*, vol. XVII, *Arab-Israeli Dispute, 1957*, p. 575).
[5] See no. 124.
[6] For two years Syria's government had been dominated by a group of Arab nationalists whose membership, largely unknown, was held together by its opposition to Western imperialism and its desire to strengthen relations with the Soviet bloc. Continuing conflict in the Syrian army between right and left wing elements had threatened to erupt into violence in March 1957. Some civil authorities had attempted to weaken the military by transferring out of the country those officers thought to support closer ties with the Soviet Union. Anticipating elections to be held on May 4, conservative newspapers had launched written attacks on the Arab Socialist Resurrection (Baath) Party and its desire for closer relations with the Soviet Union (see Galambos and van Ee, *The Middle Way*, no. 2147; State, *Foreign Relations, 1955–1957*, vol. XIII, *Near East: Jordan-Yemen*, pp. 618–19, 674–80; and *New York Times*, Mar. 19, 22, 24, and Apr. 2, 20, 1957).
[7] Sir Harold Anthony Caccia, former Deputy Under Secretary of State for Foreign Affairs, had been British Ambassador to the United States since November 1956. For discussions between U.S. and British officials see State, *Foreign Relations, 1955–1957*, vol. XII, *Near East Region; Iran; Iraq*, pp. 504–15; and State, *Foreign Relations, 1955–1957*, vol. XVII, *Arab-Israeli Dispute, 1957*, pp. 492–95, 539–40, 550–51.
[8] Nixon had left on February 28 to attend independence ceremonies in Ghana. Before returning on March 21, he visited Ethiopia, Liberia, Libya, Morocco, the Sudan, Tunisia, and Uganda (see no. 11; and State, *Foreign Relations, 1955–1957*, vol. XVIII, *Africa*, pp. 57–66, 339–45, 374–78, 397–401, 467–72, 561–64, 610–12, 633–39, 660–63).
[9] Libya, Tunisia, and Morocco were exploring cooperative ways to combat Nasserism, Nixon had reported, and Ethiopia and the Sudan were "taking the first cautious steps for cooperation among themselves toward the same end" (*ibid.*, p. 59).
[10] Britain had released the controversial Cypriot Archbishop Makarios from detention on March 28 (see nos. 78 and 91 for background). "I am bound to say I don't much like letting him out," Macmillan said, "and he will be a great nuisance when he gets to Athens, and still more when he comes to London. I expect he will turn up in New York and Washington too" (State, *Foreign Relations, 1955–1957*, vol. XXVII, *Western Europe and Canada*, pp. 769–70; see also Macmillan, *Riding the Storm*, pp. 228–29). For background on the Marquess of Salisbury, leader of the House of Lords and

Lord President of the Council, see Galambos and van Ee, *The Middle Way*, no. 297. Salisbury's resignation, Macmillan said, was "a great grief."

[11] Governor Averell Harriman had written Makarios on April 12, saying that he hoped the state of New York would have the opportunity to extend Makarios "hospitality and warm welcome." The archbishop would arrive in New York City on September 12 to press the case for Cypriot independence before the U.N. General Assembly (*New York Times*, Apr. 19, May 2, Sept. 13, 1957).

[12] Former British Prime Minister Anthony Eden had undergone surgery for a bile duct obstruction on April 6. He would leave New England Baptist Hospital on April 29 for a week's recuperation in Milton, Massachusetts, before leaving for Ottawa on May 8.

[13] Eisenhower had been in Augusta since April 18. He would return to Washington on April 30.

133

EM, AWF, Administration Series

To Henry Robinson Luce

[April 28, 1957]

Telegram

Dear Harry: Following is a short message I have been thinking of sending you for the brochure for the National Presbyterian Church.[1] Does it strike you as okay? If not what are your suggestions?[2]

"The Great Presbyterian Church proposed for the Nation's Capital, a noble and worthy house of worship, will bear witness to the religious faith within us; to the civil freedom we possess because of our forebears' faith; to the vigilant responsibility that, as citizens, we must constantly demonstrate by words and by works if we hope to preserve both faith and freedom.

This is a proposal that should excite to purposeful and persevering action all who cherish the Reformed and Presbyterian heritage. By the building of this Church, they will testify that they are true to our long and heroic traditions of dedication to God and country." *With warm regard*

[1] Luce, the publisher and director of Time, Inc., was leading the fund-raising campaign for the National Presbyterian Church (see no. 12). Reporting to Eisenhower on his efforts, he wrote: "No money yet, but at least we're getting our lines out. . . . Some day not too far off I hope I can have the thrill of telling you that we've got that first million" (Apr. 17, 1957, AWF/A).

[2] In his April 29 thank-you letter Luce would say that the message "cannot be improved upon" (see also Luce to Weaver, May 3, 1957; both letters are in AWF/A).

134

EM, AWF, International Series: Adenauer

To Konrad Adenauer

April 29, 1957

Dear Mr. Chancellor:[1] A review of the question of vested German properties and of war claims of American nationals against Germany, in anticipation of Congressional hearings on this subject, had been under way for some weeks when your letter of March 26, 1957 arrived.[2] After a full study of the entire problem, including the considerations stated in your letter, it was decided to recommend again to the Congress the program for a limited return of vested assets outlined to your Government in 1955.[3] If this program is carried into effect, it will be possible to make a full return as a matter of grace to approximately 90 percent of the individuals whose property was vested. This would in particular afford relief to the hardship cases for which I expressed sympathy in my letter to you of August 7, 1954.[4]

Your request that I should not raise objection to a broader return program which might find favor with the Congress gives rise to the difficulties I mentioned in that letter. In this connection I am enclosing a memorandum which explains the situation more fully.[5]

With warm personal regard,[6] *Sincerely*

[1] The State Department drafted this letter, which went to the Chancellor through the American embassy in Bonn.

[2] At the end of World War II the United States and seventeen other nations had agreed to retain German assets held within their jurisdictions and to subtract the proceeds of the sale of confiscated property from reparation claims against Germany. Although Congress had confirmed these provisions when it passed the War Claims Act of 1948, pressure from Adenauer and Eisenhower's own desire to resolve the issue had prompted a reexamination of the agreement (see Galambos and van Ee, *The Middle Way*, no. 1190; and State, *Foreign Relations, 1955–1957*, vol. XXVI, *Central and Southeastern Europe*, pp. 120, 229–30).

[3] Adenauer had explained the bad effects that the continued holding of assets would have on the German economy and asked that the U.S. government reconsider its policy. The issue, he wrote, could also damage him politically. "Its fundamental aspects unceasingly engage the attention of the German public and the German business community, that is even more so in a year in which political consciousness is particularly acute" (Adenauer to Eisenhower, Mar. 26, 1957, AWF/I: Adenauer).

The 1955 proposal provided for a limited return of German assets, including individual payments of up to $10,000, and the satisfaction of the remaining American war claims. Because funds from the sale of the assets would not cover both kinds of payments, the Administration desired to authorize the spending of $100 million in public funds to execute the policy. Congress, however, took no action on the proposal.

On April 4, 1957, the Senate Judiciary Committee's Trading with the Enemy Subcommittee had begun hearings on bills that would dispose of $600 million of foreign assets, without the use of public funds. Again the legislation failed to reach a vote in Congress (Cabinet meeting minutes, Jan. 7, 1955; and Rabb to Eisenhower, July 11, 1957, both in AWF/Cabinet; and *Congressional Quarterly Almanac*, vol. XIII, *1957*, pp. 673–74).

[4] Adenauer had called particular attention to the large number of aged persons, without other means of support, who had small amounts of money vested in pensions, life insurance policies, and other holdings in the United States. "I am hopeful that it may be possible to take some remedial action in such cases," Eisenhower had written, "and at the same time provide some measure of compensation to those American nationals who incurred losses arising out of the war, with resultant hardship in many cases" (Both letters are in *U.S. Department of State Bulletin* 31, no. 791 [August 23, 1954], 269–70).

[5] Using German assets as a source for payment of the claims of American citizens had enabled the German economy to progress without a reparations burden, Eisenhower had told Adenauer. "In considering the problem of the vested assets, it is necessary therefore to take into account legitimate claims on the part of American citizens arising out of the war for which some provision should be made, if the original approach is reversed" (*ibid.*). The memorandum that accompanied this letter stated, "It might have been possible to consider a different approach to the question . . . if the Federal Government had found some alternative method for satisfying the claims of American nationals" (AWF/I: Adenauer).

Secretary Dulles had recommended that this letter be kept confidential. "It would not be helpful to the Chancellor in the current election campaign" (Dulles to Eisenhower, Apr. 26, 1957, AWF/I: Adenauer).

[6] Eisenhower would discuss the issue with the German Chancellor during the latter's visit to Washington at the end of May. After Cabinet deliberations in July, the President would state that the Administration intended to submit a supplementary plan to Congress early in 1958. "It is contemplated that this plan would provide for the payment in full of all legitimate war claims of Americans against Germany and would permit, as an act of grace, an equitable monetary return to former owners of vested assets" (see no. 186; Dulles to Eisenhower, May 24, 1957, AWF/I: Adenauer; Memorandums of Conversation, May 28, 1957, *ibid.*; State, *Foreign Relations, 1955–1957*, vol. XXVI, *Central and Southeastern Europe*, pp. 248, 254–55, 258, 284, 303–7; *Public Papers of the Presidents: Eisenhower, 1957*, pp. 585–86; and *U.S. Department of State Bulletin* 37, no. 947 [August 19, 1957], 306).

Although Eisenhower's July statement indicated that the issue might be resolved in 1958, the Germans, objecting to some provisions, would ask that the bill be withheld. For developments see no. 1412.

135

EM, AWF, Administration Series

TO EMMET JOHN HUGHES

April 29, 1957

Dear Emmet:[1] This is in no sense an acknowledgement of your letter of the eighth (I would not dare in view of your dire threats). But I do at least want to tell you that I am glad to have your explanation of why the Administration is to be deprived of your contribution—and to tell you, too, that I understand thoroughly the decision you reached.[2]

Don't ever feel badly that you are, for the present at least, not to be working on a day-to-day basis for the government and for our country. You have already given so freely of your talents that I would not dare to ask you to make further sacrifices to continue to do so; and I have never promised, have I, to refrain from calling upon you for a particularly sensitive and demanding job?[3]

I have had the best possible vacation in the best possible weather,[4] and as of tomorrow return to do battle with the Congress on appropriations and legislation. Keep your fingers crossed.

Give my best to your charming bride,[5] and, of course, warm personal regard to yourself, *As ever*

[1] An editor of *Fortune Magazine*, Hughes (A.B. Princeton 1941) had served as a speechwriter for Eisenhower during both his presidential campaigns and had drafted both of Eisenhower's inaugural addresses.

[2] Hughes had written Eisenhower on April 8 (AWF/A) "with the tacit understanding between us that you *never* take the time to reply." Hughes had explained why he had "almost returned to Government work some weeks ago." He said that while he had been initially very interested in the positions discussed with him by Sherman Adams (Ambassador to London, Assistant Secretary of State for Public Affairs, or Assistant Secretary for European Affairs), he realized that there was only "*one* diplomatic post" for which he "would instantly and gladly renounce my journalistic life for good—and this was the post at the U.N." When Secretary of State John Foster Dulles offered him instead a position on the Policy Planning Staff, Hughes had responded that Dulles "had happened to define his proposal in precisely the terms that I could *not* accept—namely the acquiring of experience in a kind of high-level apprenticeship," a position which would not justify leaving Time Inc. (For another perspective on this letter see William Bragg Ewald, Jr., *Eisenhower the President: Crucial Days: 1951–1960* [Englewood Cliffs, N.J., 1981], pp. 223–40.)

[3] Eisenhower would call upon Hughes for help with his televised address on mutual security in May 1957 (see Emmet John Hughes, *The Ordeal of Power: A Political Memoir of the Eisenhower Years* [New York, 1963], p. 233; *Public Papers of the Presidents: Eisenhower, 1957*, pp. 385–96). In a May 22 letter to Hughes, Eisenhower would write, "I literally do not know how we could have been able to whip the speech last night into shape without your help" (AWF/A).

[4] On Eisenhower's Augusta vacation see no. 97.

[5] Eisenhower was referring to Hughes's second wife, Eileen Lanouette Hughes.

136 — *EM, AWF, Administration Series*

To John Hay Whitney — *April 29, 1957*

Dear Jock: I thoroughly enjoyed your delightful letter of the thirteenth, and brought it down here to Augusta with me with every expectation of answering it immediately.[1] But somehow or other the pressing "business" hereabouts intruded, and has thwarted my best intentions.

That business has been, in two major departments, much beyond anything I could have anticipated. My golf has been pretty good—

I am proud, for instance, of five pars on the last nine yesterday. And the other day I had two, repeat two, birdies, which, of course, pleased me immensely.

Even the bridge picked up. A couple of men were here from Chicago (I don't know whether you know them or not—Doug Casey and John Ames).[2] They challenged Cliff and me to a set game one evening.[3] The result was an evenly-paired, challenging session, and one that we continued for, I believe, three evenings.

The weather has been perfect. I don't think I have ever known such a continued spell of delightful days. I have soaked up the sun on every opportunity, and my cough is almost gone.[4]

Of course the official duties go on and I am never completely out of touch with Washington. Foster and I have conferred daily, mostly about the situation in Jordan. I have developed a great deal of respect for the young King's courageous stand, and hope that it will be possible for him to form a stable government. If by some miracle stability could also be achieved in Syria, I think we could congratulate ourselves that we have come a long way in an effort to establish peace in that troubled area.[5]

George and Pam Humphrey came down for a few days, and after a great deal of prodding George took a few golf lessons and even played a few holes.[6] Ed reported that he did surprisingly well, but whether or not George will continue to practice once he is back in the Washington treadmill, I cannot be sure.[7] We all missed you and Betsey very much.

Tomorrow I fly back to Washington, and to the inevitable battle with the Congress on appropriations for foreign aid, for the State Department and for USIA.[8] I definitely do not relish the prospect.

Please write to me whenever the spirit moves you; I like to hear from you. And give Betsey my affectionate regard, in which I know Mamie joins.

With all the best, *As ever*

[1] Whitney's letter, containing news about family, bridge, golf and horses, is in AWF/A.

[2] Douglas Casey, an investment banker and president of A. C. Allyn & Company, Inc., was a member of the Augusta National Golf Club. John Dawes Ames, a partner at Bacon, Whipple & Company, was a member of the executive committee of the U.S. Golf Association.

[3] Clifford Roberts.

[4] The President had suffered an ear infection and tracheitis in March (see no. 81).

[5] See no. 124.

[6] On the Humphreys' visit see no. 131.

[7] Ed Dudley was the golf pro at the Augusta National.

[8] See no. 137.

To Charles Douglas Jackson *April 30, 1957*

Dear C. D.: Your letter just came to my desk and of course I am delighted that you are taking such a positive interest in the fight to support the M.S.A. program.[1]

In your opposition to the "mixing of apples and oranges" you overlook the fact that the entire opposition to mutual aid has a financial base. I believe that if we are to get these things into proper perspective before the American people, we have to show that the money we are spending on farm programs, school building, road construction and even the health of our people, could all be wasted unless they are supported, in the international field, by policies and procedures that create the proper kind of atmosphere in which America can be safe and prosperous.[2]

Demagogues have appealed to the American people on the proposition of "Why give millions to Timbuktu when you won't give fifty dollars' worth of cottonseed meal to a distressed farmer in Texas?"

As you know I have for many years talked mutual security, one part of which is necessarily the economic development of less fortunate countries. I have made my argument on the basis of principle and moral law, but even more than this, on the basis of the best interests of the United States. I am convinced that we must get this matter down to the housewife and her working husband on the basis of "What am I buying with this amount of money? How important is it to me? What will happen to me if we eliminate this item from the budget?"[3]

It is such questions as these that must be answered. I have lost all interest, as far as the present critical battle is concerned, in making speeches on the basis of the high destiny and responsibility of the United States in world leadership. We have got to get down to cases and, without calling names, get over to the average family the clear conviction that those who are opposing foreign aid and saying that by eliminating this item we will have a tax cut—which of course everybody wants—are not only penny-wise and pound-foolish, but are actually risking the security and safety of the country and of all its citizens.

Coming up from Augusta today in the airplane a guest kept inquiring into this matter by lumping the two items together, budget and mutual security.[4] Finally I said to him in effect:

> "The United States, with its budgetary and security problems, could be likened to the individuals in this airplane, if collectively we owned it. All of us pay the costs of its operation and

we think that those costs are too high. We want to make savings so that we can have more money for ice cream sodas and ball games when we get to the end of the run.

"Now everything on that plane has been put there because it helps to give the kind of service that the passengers have wanted. But since, now, we want to save on the operation we decide that we can do without one of the stewards. Moreover, we say that we are no longer going to demand that the airplane be prepared to operate in all kinds of weather. So we take out one of the men in the forward compartment by making the copilot double as navigator—we don't intend to fly in bad weather. On this basis, we also get rid of a bit of splendid but expensive radar equipment, keeping only the bare minimum.

"Now up to this point we have made savings by agreeing that there are certain kinds of services we could readily do without, but we are still unhappy about the amount the operation costs us. So a group among us alleges that it is easy enough to save more money. We will merely cut out one of the engines! The pilot—and everyone of any sense on the plane—immediately argues that the margin of safety provided by the engine should not be sacrificed because now if another one goes out all of us crash. In other words, we will have no reserve for emergency. We are not prepared to meet the normal vicissitudes of flying and we are risking our own lives.

"This is the kind of economy that urges the drastic cutting of the M.S.A. appropriations."

Now, this is not necessarily a very apt analogy, but I got over my point to my friend. That point is that you simply have got to confine budget cutting to those programs that represent some greater convenience, greater comfort or greater protection against the normal vicissitudes of living; you cannot, logically, possibly apply them against the things that keep our ship of state safe and sound in this turbulent world. The mutual security program is a very important engine.

Having said all this, I am perfectly willing to make two speeches provided that the relationship between the two subjects is not lost in the division, and if in my own mind—and this is a big if—someone can show me a draft of two speeches, each of which will be crowded with the actual facts of today's existence so that the case will be proved by recitation of those facts and will not rest upon a mere exhortation to nobler performance of duty on the part of the American people.[5]

I am ready to do a solid job of work to get the thing across, just as I have been doing for so many years, but I am entirely unwilling to devote time to treating the whole matter as a philosophical exercise rather than as down-to-earth, sink-or-swim, survive-or-perish.

With warm regard, *As ever*

[1] Jackson had written on April 29 (C. D. Jackson Papers) to discuss developments in the effort to enlist support for the Mutual Security Administration (MSA). At the request of Secretaries Dulles and Herter, he had persuaded Owens-Corning Fiberglas president Harold Boeschenstein to "head up a private citizens' group to go into immediate action." Jackson also reported that "the lists have been organized, the Committee for Economic Development has agreed to swing into action, the Business Advisory Committee is also enlisted and the American Assembly . . . has agreed to have this as the major positive item on its agenda" (for background see nos. 119 and 135).

[2] Jackson had heard that Eisenhower planned to make a speech that would address both the budget battle and the mutual security program. "May I," he wrote, "with all respect and deference, but with great emphasis, say that this could be disastrous for the Mutual Security project. It is mixing apples and oranges; it will inevitably link in the public mind a nasty political fight—the budget—with an imaginative, positive, 'happy' program."

[3] See also Eisenhower, *Waging Peace*, pp. 132–36.

[4] The President had returned from a two-week vacation in Augusta on that day (see no. 97).

[5] Eisenhower would make separate speeches on the budget (May 14), and on mutual security (May 21); on the budget see *Public Papers of the Presidents: Eisenhower, 1957*, pp. 341–52; on mutual security see *ibid.*, pp. 372–85. For developments see the following document.

138

EM, AWF, Administration Series

To George Magoffin Humphrey — *April 30, 1957*

Dear George: After you left Augusta, a number of my friends began, first by gentle hints and then by gradually increased shoving and pushing until it finally became a battle, to urge upon me the need for my making a speech.[1] The purpose of the speech was to show:

(*a*). That the budget is merely a bill presented to the American people in advance for services for which they have expressed a desire or for which there is an inescapable need;[2]

(*b*). That you and I have been in the same stable, combatting what we consider to be excessive requests in several different departments, and that our attitude toward governmental spending is identical;[3]

(*c*). That mutual security funds are essential; to slash them would be far worse than cutting off a like amount in any other item, no matter what.[4]

Finally the pressure took a slightly different turn as this problem was considered and argued from time to time, and it was urged that I should make one, possibly two, speeches, on the budget and mutual security and the relationships I have with you, and *you* should make at least one.[5]

Some of this gives me almost a sense of frustration. It would appear that enough had been said to allow any man of intelligence, who is interested in governmental affairs, to understand exactly what our individual and collective opinions are. But the point that impresses me is that if these people, admittedly well educated and generally informed in business matters, and supposedly well read, are so confused as to the true state of affairs, then it must be clear that the taxicab driver, the farmer, the miner, the carpenter, the barber and all their wives, must be in a state of utter bewilderment.

In any event when we have a chance I should like to talk to you about some of these things.[6] *As ever*

[1] Secretary of the Treasury Humphrey had joined the President April 19–23 during his Augusta vacation (for background see no. 97).

[2] For background on the $71.8 billion 1958 budget, which represented the largest peacetime budget in U.S. history to date, see, for example, no. 27. See also *New York Times*, January 17, 1957; *Congressional Quarterly Almanac*, vol. XIII, *1957*, pp. 49–54; and Sloan, *Eisenhower and the Management of Prosperity*, pp. 99–102.

[3] On the perception of differences between Eisenhower and Humphrey over the budget see no. 102.

[4] See the preceding document and also no. 94.

[5] On plans for Eisenhower to make separate budget and mutual security speeches see the preceding document. Humphrey would speak to Republican leaders at a dinner in Des Moines, Iowa, on May 7, 1957 (see Humphrey, *Basic Papers*, pp. 286–92).

[6] The President would meet with Humphrey for one hour the following afternoon, May 1.

139

EM, AWF, Gettysburg Series

To Arthur Seymour Nevins

May 1, 1957

Dear Art: I want to assure you that I never had any particular interest in the land between the creek and the Redding farm.[1] It is nothing but a wild tangle and I thought could possibly be bought for a very low price. It apparently has never been used.

Actually the only land I was ever really interested in was the acre or so across from the schoolhouse, but as long as the man owning the house will not divide his property, I have little interest in that either.[2]

We will probably be up at the farm this weekend. I do not know exactly when Mamie will come, but I should get there Friday evening. I think it would be a good idea now to take the cattle out of the six acre field and then when you get a good chance, have them run that new chain harrow over it.[3]

Love to Ann. *As ever*

P.S.: I am enclosing a copy of a letter I have written to Pete about the land.[4]

[1] Nevins had reported on plans to purchase more land for Eisenhower's Gettysburg farm (Apr. 30, 1957, AWF/Gettysburg), explaining that the owners of the land in question wanted a total of $22,000 for two separate parcels. He also wrote that the property was not worth that amount, and that the owners should "keep their properties, at least until they get a more reasonable idea of their value."

[2] The owner of the nearly four acres of wooded creek near the school cottage had refused to sell a portion of his property. On Eisenhower's interest in the schoolhouse see no. 96.

[3] Nevins said that they were pasturing the six-acre field east of the house, and that he had purchased a rotary mower to clip pastures that were "plagued with a good deal of mustard."

[4] Nevins also had written to W. Alton Jones about the property. Eisenhower's letter to Jones is the following document.

140 — *EM, AWF, Name Series*

To William Alton Jones — *May 1, 1957*

Dear Pete: I just had some information from Art Nevins telling about the fantastic prices quoted for the land just across the road from the old school house. I urgently hope that you will have nothing to do with any purchase as long as these people are so unrealistic in their demands.[1] We do not need the property. We can simply plant a high hedge on that side of the yard and they can do as they please with their miserable acreage.

Since you left Augusta I have had only one report on you and that to the effect that your tooth problem was really a serious one. I wrote you a note but have heard nothing further. I most sincerely hope that you have gotten the difficulty cleared up and are well on the road to normalcy.[2]

With warm regard, and, of course, love to Nettie. *As ever*

[1] See the preceding document. On Jones's purchase of land adjacent to Eisenhower's farm see Galambos and van Ee, *The Middle Way*, nos. 1229 and 1297. In his May 6 reply (AWF/N), Jones would agree to follow the President's advice. "It seems fantastic," he wrote, "when you think of the prices people attach to land near your farm but, in a way, this is a compliment to you."

[2] Jones was among the close friends who visited the Eisenhowers during their Augusta, Georgia, vacation (see no. 122). Eisenhower's note to him is no. 129. Jones would explain that his dental condition was improving each day (May 6, 1957, AWF/N).

141 — *EM, AWF, Administration Series*

To Kevin Coyle McCann — *May 2, 1957*

Dear Kevin: I am thinking of addressing the Fordham student body at their commencement on June twelfth. It is the forty-second anniversary of my graduation from West Point.[1]

If I could get hold of a rough draft of a talk that, after the usual opening remarks, would launch into an explanation of America's position in the world and her responsibilities therein, to be followed by a clear explanation of the need for some mutual security aid in terms of military, technical and economic assistance, I would be very much disposed to accept the invitation.[2]

I have the feeling that the Congress may still be arguing over foreign aid at that time.

Any such talk would, of course, take into consideration the force of the spirit of nationalism now rampant in the world. The spirit of nationalism is stronger than communism; unfortunately, it is also stronger than anti-communism.

In other words, to live in the pride of political independence, people seem ready to embrace any kind of political philosophy which makes the struggle for the allegiance of the under-developed peoples critical. Since all of them desperately need an economic base on which their political independence may rest, and they can attain this only with sizeable sums of investment money from others, they will in the long run be forced to turn to those people who will assist them sympathetically.[3]

If the majority turn to the Soviets we face a very bleak and desperate future, one that will demand many more billions from us in the effort to remain secure and free.

I should like to have your draft within the next two or three days.

With warm regard, *As ever*

[1] On Eisenhower's June 1915 graduation from West Point see Ambrose, *Eisenhower*, vol. I, *Soldier, General of the Army, President-Elect*, pp. 43–55.

[2] Although he would not speak at Fordham, the President would incorporate many of these ideas in an address to Congress and a televised speech on the need for mutual security (see *Public Papers of the Presidents: Eisenhower, 1957*, pp. 372–96). Eisenhower would remind the American people that mutual aid was "not a new policy nor

a partisan policy," but had its roots in postwar aid to Greece and Turkey. The lessons of Greece and Turkey, Eisenhower would say, had recently been repeated in Vietnam, where U.S. military and economic assistance "saved" Vietnam for freedom. The President would explain that the mutual security program had three key purposes: to help equip and support the armed forces of friendly nations; to provide the sustained support that would enable countries to develop freedom as their way of life; and to meet emergencies and special needs affecting America's national interest. Eisenhower would describe each of these three aims at length and would conclude by warning the American people that "to cripple our programs for Mutual Security in the false name of 'economy' can mean nothing less than a weakening of our nation. To try to save money at the risk of such damage is neither conservative nor constructive. It is reckless." (For background on the speech see no. 135; for developments see no. 147).

[3] See nos. 60 and 90.

142

EM, AWF, Dulles-Herter Series

TO JOHN FOSTER DULLES

May 2, 1957

Cable. Top secret

Dear Foster: Many thanks for the report of your initial talks.[1] I agree with what you told Lloyd concerning the Suez problem. It appears that Nasser is having real difficulties both at home and with his neighbors.[2]

Regarding the point Martino raised with you, I would be inclined to support something in NATO that would give Italy a chance to have a little added prestige, if you can think of something appropriate.[3] *As ever*

[1] Dulles was in Bonn, Germany, to attend the ministerial meeting of the North Atlantic Council. On the preceding day he had emphasized to West German Chancellor Konrad Adenauer the important role in world affairs that Germany could play under his leadership.

[2] Foreign Secretary Selwyn Lloyd had told Dulles that the British wanted to bring the current arrangement for administering the Suez Canal before the Security Council (see no. 132 for background). "I counselled against this," Dulles said, because President Nasser "in his present rather ugly mood" could use such an approach as a reason to defy Western powers, particularly the British, who were economically dependent on the canal. Dulles had suggested that "a future Security Council meeting was a good bit more valuable as a threat than as a reality" (Dulles to Eisenhower, DULTE 1, May 1, 1957, AWF/D-H; see also State, *Foreign Relations, 1955–1957*, vol. IV, *Western European Security and Integration*, pp. 167–71).

CIA Director Allen Dulles had told the National Security Council that although alleged plots in Egypt against Nasser had not materialized, there was, nevertheless, "evidence that Egyptian dissatisfaction with Nasser had been growing." Having "already alienated the middle class and the shopkeepers," Nasser now faced "a division of view in the armed forces." Allen Dulles also told the council that King Saud had asked Nasser to stop his propaganda campaign against Jordan's King Hussein (NSC

meeting minutes, May 2, 1957, AWF/NSC; see no. 124 for background on the Jordanian political crisis).
[3] Italian Foreign Minister Gaetano Martino was "greatly worried," Dulles told Eisenhower "that the 4-power working group of US, UK, France and Germany on German reunification should develop into a kind of 'directorate' for Europe and NATO with Italy left out." Martino had suggested that NATO create a series of working groups on the issues of German reunification, disarmament, and European security. "I am not sure that this is the correct answer," Dulles said, "but I did give him assurance that . . . the 4-power working group . . . would not develop into a 'directorate'" (Dulles to Eisenhower, DULTE 1, May 1, 1957, AWF/D-H).
For developments see the following document.

143 — *EM, AWF, Dulles-Herter Series*

To John Foster Dulles — *May 3, 1957*

Dear Foster: I appreciate your informative report on your further discussions.[1] If you think that President Heuss would be just as content to come in 1958 as this year, that solution would suit me fine, since we already have two or three Chiefs of State lined up this year. On the other hand, if he should wish strongly to come this year, I would of course have no objection.[2] *As ever*

[1] Dulles had reported from the NATO ministerial meeting in Bonn that British Foreign Minister Selwyn Lloyd was "still in a stew about the Security Council meeting on Suez" (see no. 142). "He is clinging to the rather desperate hope that something good might come out of it to relieve their domestic position. To me it seems like keeping the bidding open when you hold a Yarborough [a poor bridge hand, with no card higher than a nine]."

Disagreeable issues that before had been "gingerly avoided" were more openly discussed, Dulles said, such as the jealousy between Germany and Italy over NATO roles (see no. 142) and the use of atomic weapons (Dulles to Eisenhower, DULTE 4, May 3, 1957, AWF/D-H; see also State, *Foreign Relations, 1955–1957*, vol. IV, *Western European Security and Integration*, pp. 578–86).
[2] Illness had forced West German President Theodor Heuss to cancel his visit to Washington, scheduled for March 6–8. He would begin a three-day state visit to Washington on June 4, 1958. Ngo Dinh Diem, President of the Republic of Vietnam, Britain's Queen Elizabeth and Prince Philip, and King Mohamed V of Morocco would also visit the United States during the year.

144

EM, AWF, Name Series

To Edgar Newton Eisenhower

May 6, 1957

Dear Ed: The appointment with Mr. Maxwell is all fixed up.[1]

I hope you are playing golf again. My own experience at Augusta was in a sense frustrating. My muscles over the last two years had time to become too flabby and weak to be completely corrected in just twelve days' exercise.[2] The best I can say is that my golf was spotty. Each day I would have a few holes that were almost better than I know how to play; the others were mostly bogies and triple bogies.

Love to Lucy. *As ever*

[1] The President's brother, Edgar, had written on May 3 (AWF/N) to request that David F. Maxwell (LL.B. University of Pennsylvania 1924) be permitted to pay a courtesy call on the President on May 20 or 21. Maxwell was president of the American Bar Association and a partner in the Philadelphia law firm Edmonds, Obermayer & Redmann. The meeting would take place on the morning of Tuesday, May 21 (President's daily appointments).

[2] The Eisenhowers had vacationed in Augusta, Georgia, April 18–30 (see no. 131). In Edgar's May 8 (AWF/N) reply he also expressed concern about being physically unfit to play golf. He had, however, shot a 77 in a recent game.

145

EM, AWF, Name Series

To Edward Lee Roy Elson

May 6, 1957

Dear Dr. Elson:[1] The reason Mrs. Eisenhower and I have not been to your Church for some weeks is because we have been so persistently out of town.[2] We will be gone again next week due to a visit from Field Marshal Montgomery who is anxious to go up to the farm.[3]

With warm regard, *Sincerely*

P.S. The autographed picture is on its way to you.[4]

[1] Elson, pastor of the National Presbyterian Church in Washington, D.C., since 1946, had served as chaplain of the XXI United States Army Corps in Europe during World War II (for background see *Eisenhower Papers*, vols. XII–XVII). On April 30 (AWF/N) he had invited the Eisenhowers to a May 11 service which would feature the cadet choir of the Virginia Military Institute.

[2] The President had attended the Bermuda Conference March 14–24, and had vacationed in Augusta, Georgia, April 18–30 (see nos. 78 and 97). The Eisenhowers had spent the remaining weekends at their Gettysburg farm. As it turned out, the Eisenhowers would continue to spend weekends at their farm and would not attend services at the National Presbyterian Church until June 2.

[3] Eisenhower's wartime colleague Field Marshal Bernard Law Montgomery ("Monty")

To Harold Macmillan *April 28, 1957*
Secret and personal

Dear Harold: Your letter of some ten days ago was filled with interest for me. I follow reports of your government's activities and progress almost as intensely as I do our own.[1]

As you know, I have agreed that you were wise in making important technical changes in the character of your military forces; my only fear was that populations at large, particularly in Europe, would erroneously regard some of the consequences as indicative of British loss of interest in NATO and find in it an excuse for doing less, themselves, in the anti-Communistic effort.[2]

So far as the Canal is concerned, I agree with you that there is in sight no completely satisfactory solution. From the beginning that has seemed to me to be an ill-starred affair, and I did my very best to keep it from developing as it did. But we have done everything, as we agreed at Bermuda, to obtain the best possible "interim" agreement.[3]

If, in the Mid-East, one could completely separate the problems of the Canal from the age-old Israel-Arab dispute and deal with each of these individually, I am certain that we could reach a satisfactory arrangement in the lesser one, and make considerable progress toward improving the chronic one. To believe that such might happen soon is, of course, nothing but wishful thinking. In spite of this, I remain confident that we shall eventually secure a fairly satisfactory Canal agreement, if we can[4] live in some patience while the constructive effort goes on. To look forward with confidence to such a result it is necessary that we improve and solidify the Western position—specifically yours and ours—in the whole Mid East area.

Right now the young King of Jordan seems to be waging a gallant fight to eject subversive elements from his government and country.[5] Of course whatever support he gets from the West must be carefully handled because he could be ruined if his enemies falsely spread abroad the charge that he is acting as a puppet. He seems to be a courageous young man and I am sure that if he succeeds in establishing a stable government in that country, completely independent of Communistic domination, the position of the West will be immeasurably strengthened. Incidentally, I've often wondered why Western propaganda does not refer, constantly to our Mid East enemies in terms that are truthfully descriptive, that is, as puppets of the Kremlin.

In Syria, there is another internal struggle for power.[6] If, in both of these countries, the spirit of freedom and independence could be successful, we should have a very great start on solving, in ac-

of Alamein, Deputy-Supreme Allied Commander, Europe, would visit Eisenhower's farm on May 11 and 12. (For background on Montgomery, and Eisenhower's relationship with him, see *Eisenhower Papers*, vols. I–XVII.) On both days the two generals would inspect the Gettysburg battlefield (see also no. 148). On their comments regarding the battle and the commanding generals see Glenn LaFantasie, "Monty and Ike Take Gettysburg," *MHQ: The Quarterly Journal of Military History*, vol. 8 (Autumn, 1995), pp. 67–73, and *New York Times*, May 8, 11, 12, 13, 1957; see also no. 184).
[4] Elson had asked for an autographed photograph to hang in his "personal den at the manse."

146

EM, AWF,
Dulles-Herter Series

To Christian Archibald Herter and Sherman Adams
Memorandum

May 7, 1957

Subject: Telegram from Secretary Dulles, DULTE 10, May 5th.[1]

I do not know what occasioned this particular telegram from Secretary Dulles. I know of no suggestion that we should desert the "development fund concept." I strongly endorsed Secretary Dulles' statement of April 8th before the Congressional Committee.[2]

[1] On May 5 Secretary of State Dulles had cabled Under Secretary Christian Herter to state how "deeply disturbed" he was by Herter's cabled suggestion that it would be necessary to accept annual appropriations as the price of economic support for the proposed "development fund" concept (AWF/D-H). Dulles stated that the United States must "break away from the cycle of annual authorizations and appropriations" and "eliminate advance allocations by countries." "Economic development is a continuing process," the Secretary had pointed out, "not an annual event. Present annual appropriations have resulted in procedures which do not allow either us or the receiving countries to make the most efficient use of the resources which we are providing. The best way to achieve this greater efficiency is, we believe, the establishment of an economic development fund to provide assistance through loans on terms more favorable than are possible through existing institutions."

Dulles told Herter, "If we now ask for operation of the fund through annual appropriation this will involve a major retreat. I think that the political consequences of such a retreat would be disastrous. It would dismay our friends in Congress and in the country who are building their hopes and efforts on my presentation of April 8 and it would enable the opponents of economic aid to portray us as vacillating and without conviction, and wedded to a system which we ourselves had condemned." Herter's suggestion had been prompted by continuing opposition to the fund concept from the Department of the Treasury, the Bureau of the Budget and the ICA, which feared further congressional and media attacks on the budget (see Edgerton, *Sub-Cabinet Politics and Policy Commitment: The Birth of the Development Loan Fund*, pp. 134–42; for background see nos. 75 and 76). See also *New York Times*, Apr. 9, 1957; W. W. Rostow, *Eisenhower, Kennedy, and Foreign Aid* [Austin, Tex., 1985], pp. 121–38; and Kaufman, *Trade and Aid*, pp. 103–4).

[2] Meeting with Eisenhower and Herter on May 7, Dulles would explain to the President the inter-departmental conflicts over the development fund proposal. Dulles reiterated his own belief that the fund should, insofar as possible, "be financed through borrowing from the Treasury with specific authorizations carried forward over at least a three-year period." Eisenhower agreed and said that he would "communicate at once with Secretary Humphrey and with Director of the Budget Brundage" (Herter, Memorandum of Conversation, May 7, 1957, Dulles Papers, White House Memoranda Series). For developments see the following document.

147 *EM, AWF, DDE Diaries Series*

To George Magoffin Humphrey *May 7, 1957*

Dear George: It seems that some misunderstanding has arisen about a project in mutual security to which I am completely dedicated and committed. It is the securing of a foreign development fund of some $500 million for the first year (out of sums now included in the budget) and $750 million for each of the two succeeding years, without the necessity of going before the Appropriation Committee with detailed plans for each of these three years.[1]

As you know, I have long studied our situation abroad. I am convinced that unless we can, often in unforeseen emergencies, act promptly and effectively in meeting some of the more crying needs of under-developed countries, we will very shortly have to raise our already swollen military budgets far beyond any savings we could ever hope to accomplish in the mutual security field.

To operate effectively, we must have greater flexibility, particularly as to time as well as in spending our money to meet our own best interests according to the needs of the *particular moment and situation.* To go annually before the Appropriation Committee, with a description of projected plans, is merely to notify every country therein mentioned that it has a vested right in the appropriated moneys. This hamstrings us and is far more costly than it should be.

The Secretary of State presented to a Senate Committee on April eighth an applicable plan in a document which I studied carefully before presentation.

Now I understand that on the technical levels, some in the Administration have advanced objections to the plan.

I would very much appreciate it if you would meet with Foster in an effort to find a way in which my basic purpose can be accomplished, including its presentation in the most persuasive form possible to the Congress.

In this concept, not one cent more is contemplated for expenditures than is now planned by the Administration. We are merely trying to adopt a businesslike method to a very complicated problem, and one which in the long run should save us a great deal of money and advance our national interests immeasurably.

I am sending a copy of this immediately to the Bureau of the Budget. *As ever*

P.S.: I tried to phone this to you, but found that you were out of town.

[1] For background see the preceding document. See also *Congressional Quarterly Almanac,* vol. XIII, *1957,* pp. 601–10. For developments see no. 155.

148

EM, AWF, Gettysburg Series

To Eric Harlow Heckett

May 7, 1957

Dear Mr. Heckett: I called in my pilot to ask him about the condition of airfields in and around Gettysburg.[1] For the DC-3 he suggests the use of the Harrisburg airport. While it is true that DC-3's have occasionally used the Hanover airport, he thinks it is not a particularly wise thing to do unless necessary.

Of course Mrs. Heckett could go to Gettysburg at any time of greatest convenience to herself, and always be sure of a warm welcome from General Nevins. He would be glad to take her all through our farm operation. Quite naturally, however, I should like to be present if possible just for the pleasure of greeting her and chatting with her about the Angus breed and the great success the two of you have achieved in its development.[2]

As I told you last evening, either Saturday or Sunday afternoon would be perfectly agreeable so far as I am concerned.[3] I should like to have about 24 hours' advance notice, because I am having a week end guest—Field Marshal Montgomery—and he is very anxious to make a tour of the battlefield, on which I shall have to accompany him.[4]

If by chance you find yourself able to accompany Mrs. Heckett, that would give me an added pleasure.

It was fine to see you looking so well after the terrible siege of sickness you have been through.

With warm regard, *Sincerely*

[1] Eisenhower had met with his pilot, Colonel William Grafton Draper, at 3:20 P.M. (for background on Draper see Galambos and van Ee, *The Middle Way,* no. 1036).
[2] Heckett was president of Heckett Engineering, Inc., and a member of the American Aberdeen Angus Breeders Association. He and his wife, Greta Shield Heckett,

owned and operated Heckmeres Highlands farm in Valencia, Pennsylvania, where they raised Angus cattle. The President had begun correspondence with them in 1955 regarding import-export regulations on cattle (see Galambos and van Ee, *The Middle Way*, nos. 1301 and 1586).

[3] Heckett had been seated next to the President during a May 6 stag dinner at the White House. In a letter dated May 9 he would thank Eisenhower for a "most delightful" evening and discuss further arrangements for the trip to Gettysburg (AWF/Gettysburg).

[4] The Hecketts would visit the Gettysburg farm on May 11. Field Marshal Bernard Law Montgomery would accompany the Hecketts and the President on a tour of the Eisenhower farm (on Montgomery and his trip to Gettysburg see no. 145). Mrs. Heckett's May 16 thank-you note to Eisenhower is in AWF/Gettysburg.

149 — *EM, AWF, Gettysburg Series*

To John Christian Gall — *May 7, 1957*

Dear John: I was glad to get from you, last evening, at least the essentials of the story concerning the presentation to me of the Angus heifer by the newspaper women more than a year ago.[1] Someday I hope we can have the time together so that I may hear the remainder.

Incidentally, I remember one statement you made to the effect, "Don't sell 3551 short."[2] If I said anything to indicate a failure to admire that animal, almost extravagantly, then my words did not convey my meaning. All I was talking about was the great ambition of every stock man to raise, someday, his own topflight bull.

It was fine to have you with us.

With warm regard, *Sincerely*

[1] Gall, a Washington, D.C., lawyer and owner of Amandale Farm in Upperville, Virginia, had attended a May 6 stag dinner at the White House (for background on Gall see Galambos and van Ee, *The Middle Way*, no. 1888). The Women's National Press Club had presented a heifer to the President in May 1955 (see Rayburn to Eisenhower, May 20, 1955; Eisenhower to Johnson, May 20, 1955; Eisenhower to Kain, May 20, 1955; Eisenhower to Carpenter, May 20, 1955; Carpenter to Eisenhower, March 23, 1955; and Barbara to Shanley, May 23, 1955). All correspondence is in AWF/Gettysburg.

[2] For background on Ankonian 3551, a herd sire on loan to the Eisenhower Farm, see no. 15.

150 *EM, WHCF, Official File 148*

TO GEORGE MAGOFFIN HUMPHREY *May 9, 1957*

Dear George: Here is one of those who, hating taxes as much as any of the rest of us, refuses to join the pack in yelling for indiscriminate cuts.[1] *As ever*

[1] Eisenhower had forwarded to Treasury Secretary Humphrey a letter and newspaper clipping from Boston financier Richard S. Robie, a director of the Hertz Corporation. Robie had written Assistant to the President Sherman Adams on May 3 in support of the President's mutual security program. Complaining about an article by Bill Cunningham in the April 14 issue of the *Boston Sunday Herald*, Robie had stated that it was "about time some of our so-called friends in the Chamber of Commerce realize it is better to spend dollars and have peace than to spend American lives." "I don't like to pay taxes any more than anyone else," Robie had written, "but neither do I like war. Of the two I prefer to pay taxes." In his response (May 9) Adams told Robie that he was so delighted with his letter that he had passed it on to "the boss." "He, too, was pleased at your understanding of the tough problems we are facing." (All correspondence is in same file as document; see also nos. 141 and 147).

151 *EM, WHCF, Official File 14*

TO WILLIAM MCCHESNEY MARTIN, JR. *May 9, 1957*

Dear Bill: Yesterday in my Press Conference I inadvertently used the word "Government" when I meant "Administration" in connection with an answer on financial matters.

The statement I made was, "The monetary policy of this Government is mine, and no one underneath me is going to change my policy." Naturally, I did not mean to imply that I was usurping the powers of the Federal Reserve System—I was simply talking about the Executive Department itself.[1] *Sincerely*

[1] During the May 8 news conference, *El Paso Times* correspondent Sarah Newcomb McClendon had asked the President whether he would appoint Robert Anderson to replace Secretary of the Treasury George Humphrey, who would announce his resignation at the end of the month. She also asked whether the new Secretary would "change monetary policy now and perhaps use his influence to bring about some lowering in interest rates" (*Public Papers of the Presidents: Eisenhower, 1957*, p. 326; see also no. 175). Eisenhower had responded that any announcement of a nominee would be made to the Senate before being made public, and that he had not proceeded sufficiently in the selection process to answer the question. At that time the President also made the statement quoted above, which White House aide Gabriel Hauge mentioned in a May 8 note to Eisenhower (same file as document).

Martin would respond (May 10, same file as document) that he was aware that Eisenhower had "been at pains on several occasions to stress the independent status of the Federal Reserve System within the Government so that no one here at the Board had any misgivings whatever on this score." For more on the independence of the Federal Reserve and its chairman, William McChesney Martin, see Donald F. Kettl, *Leadership at the Fed* (New Haven, 1986), pp. 82–92 and A. Jerome Clifford, *The Independence of the Federal Reserve System* (Philadelphia, 1965), pp. 300–322. See also Galambos and van Ee, *The Middle Way*, nos. 464, 650, and 2005.

152 *EM, AWF, DDE Diaries Series*

TO MARY JANE MCCAFFREE[1] *May 9, 1957*
Memorandum

The following is a list of guests for the President Coty dinner[2] (8 P.M., Monday, June 3rd) provided me by the State Department—less a number that I have eliminated from their recommendations, but adding both the Attorney General and the Postmaster General with their wives, as well as Governor Adams and Mr. Shanley and their wives.

(2) The President and Mrs. Eisenhower
(1) President Coty
(12) Members of President Coty's Party
(12) *The Department of State*:
The Secretary and Mrs. Dulles[3]
The Under Secretary and Mrs. Herter[4]
Deputy Under Secretary and Mrs. Douglas Dillon[5]
Mr. and Mrs. Elbrick[6]
Mr. and Mrs. Buchanan[7]
Ambassador *and Mrs.* Houghton[8]
(6) *The Cabinet*:
The Secretary of the Treasury and Mrs. Humphrey
The Attorney General and Mrs. Brownell[9]
The Postmaster General and Mrs. Summerfield[10]
(16) *The Congress*:
Senator and Mrs. Johnson[11]
Senator and Mrs. Knowland[12]
Senator and Mrs. Mansfield[13]
Senator and Mrs. Dirksen[14]
(Senator and Mrs. Hayden)—Why?[15]
Congressman Rayburn[16]
Congressman Martin[17]
Congressman and Mrs. McCormack[18]
Congressman and Mrs. Arends[19]

(2) *The Supreme Court*:
Chief Justice and Mrs. Warren[20]
(4) *Staff*:
Governor and Mrs. Adams[21]
Mr. and Mrs. Shanley[22]
(2) *The French Embassy*:
Ambassador and Mme. Alphand[23]
(6) *Others*:
General and Mrs. Gruenther
President of Lafayette College and Mrs. Hutchison[24]
Mr. and Mrs. Andre Kostelanetz (Lily Pons)[25]
Alternates:
Mr. and Mrs. David Rockefeller[26]
Mr. and Mrs. Philip Bedard (President of France-America Society)[27]
Admiral and Mrs. Radford[28]
Lt. Gen. and Mme. Platte (French Representative, Standing Group)[29]

It is obvious that the dinner must run over 60, the maximum size for which the gold chairs are used. I think, therefore, that we should include as many at this dinner as is possible.

With regard to the State Department list, the last couple named, Mr. and Mrs. Andre Kostelanetz, is Lily Pons and her husband. I believe I would not invite them unless she has been selected as the artist for the evening.

I believe this list totals 63, and I think you are able to accommodate, with small chairs, about 82. For whatever vacancies we may have, plus any that may be produced by declinations, I suggest the following be taken roughly in the order named. Assuming that all cannot be accommodated at this dinner, please keep them on your list to invite when another state dinner comes around.

Mr. and Mrs. Allan Ryan
Mr. and Mrs. Theodore Ryan[30]
Mr. and Mrs. Eric Heckett
Mr. and Mrs. Ellis Slater
Mr. and Mrs. Taylor Chewning[31]
Mr. and Mrs. Walter Bicknell[32]
Mr. and Mrs. William Ewing
Mr. and Mrs. John Gall
Mr. and Mrs. Samuel James Campbell[33]
Mr. and Mrs. Leland L. Leachman[34]
Mr. and Mrs. Richard Garlington[35]
Mr. and Mrs. John Ames[36]
Mr. and Mrs. John O. Chiles[37]
Admiral and Mrs. Lewis Strauss[38]

Governor and Mrs. Thomas Dewey[39]

I think the invitations should be sent out as soon as possible so that you can take advantage of any declinations received.

P.S. General and Mrs. Charles Lindbergh[40] should go on the Heuss dinner list without fail.

[1] McCaffree, Mrs. Eisenhower's personal secretary, had assisted in planning the Eisenhowers' social events since 1953. See, for example, Galambos and van Ee, *The Middle Way*, no. 1568.

[2] President René Coty of France was expected to visit the United States from June 3–10 (see Dulles to Eisenhower, Apr. 30, 1957, AWF/I: France). The trip would be indefinitely postponed, however, because of the French Cabinet crisis. In a message to the French president Eisenhower would express the hope that Coty could make the visit at a later date (see Coty to Eisenhower, May 24, 1957; Dulles to Eisenhower, May 24, 1957; and Eisenhower to Coty, [May 24, 1957], all in *ibid.*). For background on President Coty see Galambos and van Ee, *The Middle Way*, no. 632. For developments see no. 520.

[3] John Foster Dulles and his wife, the former Janet Pomeroy Avery.

[4] Christian A. Herter and his wife, the former Mary Caroline Pratt.

[5] C. Douglas Dillon and his wife, the former Phyllis C. Ellsworth.

[6] Charles Burke Elbrick, Assistant Secretary of State for European Affairs, and his wife, the former Elvira Lindsay Johnson.

[7] Wiley Thomas Buchanan, Chief of Protocol, Department of State, and his wife, the former Ruth Elizabeth Hale.

[8] Amory Houghton, U.S. Ambassador to France, and his wife, the former Laura DeKay Richardson.

[9] Mrs. Herbert Brownell was the former Doris A. McCarter.

[10] Arthur Ellsworth Summerfield, Sr., and his wife, the former Miriam W. Graim.

[11] Mrs. Lyndon Baines Johnson was the former Claudia Taylor.

[12] Mrs. William Fife Knowland was the former Helen Davis Herrick.

[13] Michael Joseph Mansfield, Democratic Senator from Montana and Assistant Majority Leader, and his wife, the former Maureen Hayes.

[14] Everett McKinley Dirksen, Republican Senator from Illinois, and his wife, the former Louella Carver.

[15] Carl Trumbull Hayden, Democratic Senator from Arizona, and his wife, the former Nan Downing.

[16] Samuel Taliaferro Rayburn, Democratic Congressman from Texas and Speaker of the House.

[17] Joseph William Martin, Jr., Republican Congressman from Massachusetts and Republican Leader of the House.

[18] John William McCormack, Democratic Congressman from Massachusetts and House Majority Leader, and his wife, the former M. Harriet Joyce.

[19] Leslie Cornelius Arends, Republican Congressman from Illinois, and his wife, the former Betty Tychon.

[20] Mrs. Earl Warren was the former Nina P. Myers.

[21] Mrs. Sherman Adams was the former Rachel Leona White.

[22] Bernard Michael Shanley, President Eisenhower's Appointments Secretary, and his wife, the former Maureen Virginia Smith.

[23] Hervé Alphand, French Ambassador to the United States, and his wife, Merenda Nicole Alphand.

[24] Ralph Cooper Hutchison, president of Lafayette College, and his wife, the former Harriet Sidney Thompson.

[25] Orchestra conductor Andre Kostelanetz and his wife, opera singer and film actress Lily Pons.
[26] David Rockefeller, vice-president and chairman of the board of directors of the Chase Manhattan Bank, and his wife, the former Margaret McGrath.
[27] We have been unable to identify Mrs. Bedard.
[28] Mrs. Arthur William Radford was the former Mariam J. McMichael.
[29] We have been unable to identify the Plattes.
[30] Theodore Ryan owned and operated Mole's Hill Farm in Sharon, Connecticut. We have been unable to identify Mrs. Theodore Ryan.
[31] Edmund Taylor Chewning, clay products producer, and his wife, the former Caroline Cupler Mosher, owned Tacaro Farm, in Tracy's Landing, Maryland.
[32] *Warren* Bicknell, Aberdeen Angus cattle breeder, owned Sinkola Plantation in Thomasville, Georgia. We have been unable to identify Mrs. Bicknell.
[33] Samuel James Campbell, printer and publisher, and his wife, the former Ileen Bullis, raised Angus cattle at Argyll Terrace in Mount Carroll, Illinois.
[34] We have been unable to identify Mrs. Leland L. Leachman.
[35] Thomas Richard Garlington was a member of the Augusta National Golf Club. We have been unable to identify Mrs. Garlington.
[36] We have been unable to identify Mrs. John Dawes Ames.
[37] We have been unable to identify the Chileses.
[38] Mrs. Lewis Lichtenstein Strauss was the former Alice Hanauer.
[39] Thomas Edmund Dewey, former Republican governor of New York and presidential nominee, and his wife, the former Frances E. Hutt.
[40] Charles Augustus Lindbergh, first aviator to fly a nonstop trans-Atlantic route, and his wife, the former Anne Spencer Morrow. On the visit of West German President Heuss see no. 142.

153

EM, AWF, International Series: Macmillan

To Harold Macmillan
Confidential

May 10, 1957

Dear Harold: I have read with the greatest interest your letter of April twenty-sixth and its voluminous enclosure containing Bulganin's views on a wide variety of subjects. I fully understand your feeling that you bear a considerable responsibility in framing a substantive reply and appreciate your thoughtfulness in giving me an opportunity to comment.[1]

The letter seems to me to combine several purposes in a skillful manner. Obviously it is a part of the current Soviet effort to stir up issues which will tend to lead people to forget, if not forgive, their actions in Hungary.[2] They would probably like their foreign relations to resume the earlier lines resulting from the liberalizing aspects laid down at the Party Congress last year.[3] The conciliatory tone is well adapted to carry out this purpose. They would of course like to put the Western alliance in the awkward position of appearing to reject genuine efforts to improve the situation.

Second, there is the clear effort to establish a special position in relation to the United Kingdom, such as they periodically seek with the United States. The references to trade, the favorable comments on force reduction and on Britain's position generally are all calculated to have this effect.[4]

There may, however, be a third aspect. In the context of their other recent actions in the Disarmament Committee and elsewhere, the letter seems to betray a genuine concern about the nuclear situation.[5] There is reason to believe that they probably are worried by the prospect of the spread of nuclear weapons around their borders, the coming of ballistic missiles, the possibility of German and other forces having nuclear weapons, and the recognition of the inherent instability in the satellites and East Germany. In addition there are signs that the burden of their military forces is weighing heavily on them. Thus there may be a chance that they are thinking in serious terms about ways in which some of these trends might be dealt with or revised. Their first effort is naturally the negative one reflected in the notes to Denmark, Norway and Germany, and the other propaganda moves.[6] And their note to you, while less threatening, does not suggest any immediate readiness to make major concessions in order to obtain relief from the concerns they may have.

I suggest that it might be helpful if your reply took account of these various themes in the Soviet note. Perhaps it could include a reasoned explanation of the British and Western point of view on the principal issues raised in his letter. Of course it should correct some of the misstatements and allegations in the letter but could, perhaps, avoid the tone of a purely debating reply. It might point out the avenues for real progress toward correcting the present situation.

Specifically, in regard to the Middle East, you might recall that in the talks with Bulganin and Khrushchev in London the United Kingdom made very clear its vital interest in the Middle East and that the Soviets had nonetheless gone ahead to stir up trouble and create friction in ways not compatible with the sweet friendliness they now profess.[7] Similarly in regard to control of nuclear weapons, you might point out the persistent Soviet refusal to talk seriously about methods of control and safeguards. Also I urge you consider whether it is not essential to stress the consequences of Soviet refusal to unify Germany and to relax their control of the satellites. Surely, this is the most explosive situation of all. Finally, I think it worth while to point out that the West is united in its basic policies and for collective security and that efforts to split off one or another country are not the fruitful way to improve conditions.

In short, it seems to me that over all the reply could usefully give the impression that the West is prepared to talk seriously of resolving the existing sources of tension and instability whenever the Soviets are ready to consider seriously the revisions of their policy which this would entail. We are not asking for unconditional surrender or the sacrifice of legitimate Soviet interests and we share their concern regarding the nuclear problem and some of the areas of instability. But they will have to raise their bid if progress is to be made.

A few more detailed suggestions are in the enclosed memorandum prepared by the State Department.[8]

Again, let me express my appreciation to you for giving me this opportunity to comment on your letter from Bulganin. Foster and I stand at your disposal in case we can be of further assistance to you in this matter.[9]

With warm regard, *As ever*

[1] Macmillan was planning to send the Soviet Premier a formal acknowledgment, but, he told Eisenhower, "to be quite frank, I am not sure what to do next." "Since it seems that I have been singled out for this honour I feel a considerable responsibility about it all" (Macmillan to Eisenhower, Apr. 26, 1957, AWF/I: Macmillan; see also Macmillan, *Riding the Storm*, pp. 289–91, 296–97. Bulganin's eighteen-page letter is in AWF/I: Macmillan).

Secretary Dulles had recommended that Eisenhower respond to Macmillan and submitted a State Department draft that commented "only on the most important of the points raised by the Soviets" (Dulles to Eisenhower, May 9, 1957, AWF/D-H).

[2] For background on the Hungarian uprising in October 1956 see Galambos and van Ee, *The Middle Way*, no. 2044.

[3] The Twentieth Congress of the Communist Party of the Soviet Union had been held in Moscow in February 1956. Among the ideas proposed were the importance of collective leadership, the emphasis on peaceful coexistence rather than on the inevitability of war, and the peaceful transition to socialism through parliamentary procedures (State, *Foreign Relations, 1955–1957*, vol. XXIV, *Soviet Union; Eastern Mediterranean*, pp. 56–60, 63–65, 72–82; see also Galambos and van Ee, *The Middle Way*, no. 1813).

[4] The century-old trade ties between the Soviet Union and Great Britain that had not been "properly used" could be substantially expanded, Bulganin had told Macmillan. "There is no doubt that the expansion of mutually beneficial trade would have a favourable effect on the economy of Great Britain as well as the Soviet Union and would at the same time serve as a solid basis for improving relations between them." Bulganin had also praised both the British decision to reduce the force levels of troops stationed in the German Federal Republic and the role Britain continued "to play in the international field as a great industrial, trade and sea power."

[5] The Subcommittee of the United Nations Disarmament Commission had been meeting in London since March 18. The head of the Soviet delegation had indicated the possibility of reaching a limited agreement on the production of nuclear weapons and the establishment of more liberal guidelines for the inspection of their territory.

For conciliatory statements made by the Soviet delegation see State, *Foreign Relations, 1955–1957*, vol. XX, *Regulation of Armaments; Atomic Energy*, pp. 471–76, 486–87, 492–96.

[6] On March 21 and 28 Bulganin had sent notes to the prime ministers of Norway and Denmark respectively, warning them against the stationing of NATO troops equipped with atomic weapons in their countries (State, *Foreign Relations, 1955–1957*, vol. XXVII, *Western Europe and Canada*, p. 499). The Soviet note to Chancellor Adenauer (delivered on May 4) cited a previous statement by the government of the Federal Republic that it did not possess atomic weapons. Such a statement was unsatisfactory, the note said, unless it meant that the Federal Republic would not permit atomic weapons on its soil (State, *Foreign Relations, 1955–1957*, vol. XXVI, *Central and Southeastern Europe*, pp. 238–39, 243).

[7] Bulganin and Party Secretary Nikita Khrushchev had visited London in April 1956 (see Galambos and van Ee, *The Middle Way*, nos. 1828 and 1862).

[8] According to the State Department memorandum, the Western countries should not accept the Soviet claim that they had "an inherent right to participate in all major decisions affecting the Middle East area." This would "open the door to far greater difficulties and turmoil for the West in that area even than those caused by the present 'unrecognized' role of the Soviet Union. It could impede our efforts to fight Communism in the Middle East and discourage those Near Eastern countries which have taken an active and courageous stand against the Communists."

The memorandum also clarified the U.S. position regarding Bulganin's desire for more cultural and scientific exchanges between the Soviet Union and Great Britain. "The US does not intend to engage in exchanges which are clearly to the Soviet's propaganda advantage, nor respond to Soviet overtures calculated to create an aura of respectability" (AWF/D-H).

[9] Macmillan would reply to Bulganin on June 13 (see no. 180; see also Macmillan to Eisenhower, May 17, 1957, AWF/I: Macmillan; and Macmillan, *Riding the Storm*, pp. 305–6).

154

EM, AWF, International Series: Saudi Arabia

To Ibn Abd al-Aziz Saud

May 11, 1957

Cable. Secret

Your Majesty, My Great and Good Friend: This past month has been a significant and critical time in the Middle East. I have during this period appreciated receiving the several messages from Your Majesty. I have, at the same time, followed closely events in the area and been grateful for the opportunities which you gave to Ambassador Wadsworth to deliver various urgent messages from the United States Government.[1]

I should like to address myself, first, to your message of April 15 and to express my thanks for the prompt attention which you gave to my suggestion regarding an approach to the Government of Egypt with respect to the current Suez Canal problem. I am confident your expression of interest was helpful in the discussions which Ambassador Hare had with the Egyptian officials.[2]

We have been during these days, also, following closely the events in Jordan. I know we share with Your Majesty deep admiration for King Hussein in his courageous efforts to preserve the independence and territorial integrity of his Kingdom. The wise and constructive course Your Majesty pursued during these days was of great assistance in the course of events in Jordan.[3]

The events in Jordan illustrate, for all who wish to see, the threats which the agents of international communism pose to an independent country. The firm intentions of the United States to support the territorial integrity and independence of the free nations of the Middle East have been made clear.

Since the receipt of your letter of March 26, I have also been giving thought to the many aspects of the problem of the Gulf of Aqaba.[4] I now have Your Majesty's recent message, delivered to the White House by Ambassador al-Khayyal on May 7, and will withhold further comment on this matter until after careful study of your latest report. Meanwhile, I assure Your Majesty that we recognize the importance of the issue. I shall be in further communication with you on this matter in the very near future.[5]

Ambassador Richards returned and has given me a full report of his very pleasant stay in Saudi Arabia. I appreciate the hospitality which was extended to him and to his colleagues and the opportunity which you gave for a further full and frank exchange with him on matters of common interest.[6]

I have, also, been gratified to learn from my staff of the successful visit of Dr. Mastellone and his associates to Saudi Arabia and can assure Your Majesty that we will continue to make every effort to assist in the treatment of Prince Mashur, whom we were so pleased to have with us during your recent visit.[7] I hope Your Majesty will greet the Prince most fondly for me.

May God have you in His safekeeping. *Your sincere friend*

[1] Eisenhower approved the State Department draft of this letter after consultation with Secretary Dulles (see Telephone conversation, Eisenhower and Dulles, May 11, 1957, Dulles Papers, Telephone Conversations). George E. Wadsworth had been U.S. Ambassador to Saudi Arabia since 1954.

[2] Eisenhower had suggested that the Saudi Arabian monarch use his influence to persuade the Egyptian government to support the establishment of equitable guidelines for the use of the canal (see no. 99). For Hare's consultations with Egyptian officials see State, *Foreign Relations, 1955–1957*, vol. XVII, *Arab-Israeli Dispute 1957*, pp. 532–38, 541–43, 559–61, 568–69. King Saud had told Eisenhower that Egyptian President Nasser hoped to reach a settlement on the canal issue "on the basis of not establishing for Israel any right of passage through the Canal or the Aqaba Gulf, and of cooperating with the Canal users in a manner not prejudicial to Egyptian sovereignty" (Saud to Eisenhower, Apr. 15, 1957, AWF/I: Saudi Arabia).

[3] For background on the Jordanian political crisis see no. 124. Saud had sent Saudi Arabian forces to Jordan to be placed under King Hussein's command.
[4] For King Saud's March 26 letter see no. 99. See also State, *Foreign Relations, 1955–1957*, vol. XVII, *Arab-Israeli Dispute 1957*, pp. 498–99; and no. 156 in these volumes.
[5] Saud's letter, written on May 6, expressed the King's concern at the alleged movements of Israeli warships into the mouth of the Gulf of Aqaba (AWF/I: Saudi Arabia). For Eisenhower's response see no. 156.
[6] For background on the mission of Ambassador James P. Richards, former chairman of the House Foreign Affairs Committee, see no. 63. Richards had been in Saudi Arabia on April 9 and 10 and had met with Eisenhower on May 9. For his assessments of the Saudi Arabian political and economic situation see State, *Foreign Relations, 1955–1957*, vol. XIII, *Near East: Jordan-Yemen*, pp. 491–94.
[7] King Saud's partially paralyzed three-year-old son had been fitted with a corrective brace and shoes at the Walter Reed Medical Center during his father's visit to the United States in January (see no. 13). Lieutenant Colonel Aniello F. Mastellone, chief of the physical and medical service at Walter Reed, had led a three-man team to Saudi Arabia to treat the young prince and train Saudi physicians to care for him (*New York Times*, Feb. 13, 1957).

155 — To Ellis Dwinnell Slater

EM, AWF, Name Series

May 14, 1957

Dear Slats: Many thanks for your letter regarding the favorable reports you have had on various of the foreign aid operations.[1] I was so impressed that I read the entire letter to the legislative leaders at a meeting we had this morning.

I shall bear in mind your suggestion that we might be able to "use" these men; certainly we need all the articulate proponents of the program that we can find.[2]

With warm regard, *As ever*

[1] Eisenhower's friend Slater had written the President on May 6, 1957 (WHCF/OF 116-B). Stating that some of the criticism of the USIA stemmed from "a lack of understanding of just what is being accomplished," Slater said that a number of business executives who had recently returned from trips to Asia had reported that the ICA, the USIA, and other government agencies were "doing a necessary and wonderful work in that part of the world." Foreign aid, Slater added, was "winning a battle" and needed only "minor modifications" in order to "continue to do a big job." For background see nos. 27, 60, and 137.
[2] Slater had suggested that Eisenhower might use the "judgment and opinions" of Harold Holmes Helm, chairman of the board of the Chemical Corn Exchange Bank; Charles Latimer Stillman, executive vice-president of Time Inc.; and Bromwell Ault, vice-president of Interchemical Corporation, as willing "witnesses and spokesmen" in the "battle of the budget." Eisenhower would instruct Ann Whitman to add the names of Helm, Stillman, and Ault to the list of individuals to be invited to a future stag dinner.

156

EM, AWF, International Series: Saudi Arabia

To Ibn Abd al-Aziz Saud
Cable. Secret

May 15, 1957

Your Majesty: I have read with deep interest your message of May 7 delivered by Ambassador Al-Khayyal to the White House. I have given this the most urgent and studied consideration and it has been reviewed extensively within the United States Government.[1]

We appreciate the fact that Your Majesty, in the spirit of cooperation which has so characterized our relations, has consulted with us on the difficult issue of the Gulf of Aqaba. We appreciate, also, that Your Majesty has, as in other matters, followed the line of peaceful pursuit in the resolution of such issues. We sincerely trust the means can be found in which we can work together to resolve this and other issues which affect the peace and stability of the Middle East.

Your message of May 7 addresses itself immediately to the problem of the passage of Israeli warships through Saudi Arabian territorial waters in the Gulf of Aqaba. We note that Your Majesty has brought this matter to the notice of the Security Council and is awaiting our views before taking further action. Our attitude with regard to consideration of the question in the United Nations would depend in part on the approach and action contemplated by your Government. Further discussions between us may therefore be desirable, perhaps with Your Majesty's representatives in this country.

In these discussions we could review with Your Majesty's representatives various aspects of the problem of raising this question in the Security Council. We recognize that there may be advantages to its consideration by the Security Council. We also recognize that such consideration might result in debate which would exacerbate the situation in the area and give opportunity for further disruptive action by the Soviet Union and the forces of international communism.

During such further discussions as we may have with your representatives we might also review the question of the status of the Gulf of Aqaba and the Straits of Tiran to which you referred in your message of March 31.[2] As Your Majesty knows, different states hold varying views of the applicable law regarding this matter. We realize that the views of the United States, which were explained by Secretary Dulles and myself when you were here and which were set forth in an Aide-Memoire dated February 11, 1957, published February 17, 1957, differ from those of Your Majesty, but I hope that we can discuss this difference in the spirit of friendship and cooperation that has characterized our relations in the past.[3] We have recognized that this question might be referred to the International Court of Justice by a government or by the United Nations. Should that be done, the Government of the United States would of course take into account the decision or opinion of the Court in relation to the area.

In our consideration of these matters, we have had continually in our minds our strong friendship for Saudi Arabia and our desire to avoid any action that would result in a threat to the territorial integrity or independence of Your Kingdom. We appreciate the concern expressed in your message. In our relations with the states in the area, we shall continue to counsel moderation and prudence and avoidance of any provocative or aggressive action, particularly any action which might involve the Holy Places of which Your Majesty is guardian.[4]

We shall keep you informed of any developments which come to our attention in connection with the problems Your Majesty has raised. In the meantime, we are keeping in close touch with your representatives in the United States.[5]

May God have you in His safekeeping. *Your sincere friend*

[1] For King Saud's message, which referred to the alleged movements of Israeli warships in the Gulf of Aqaba, see no. 154; see also State, *Foreign Relations, 1955–1957*, vol. XVII, *Arab-Israeli Dispute 1957*, p. 607. Eisenhower approved the State Department draft of this message, which had been transmitted to the White House on the preceding day (see *ibid.*, p. 615).

[2] The Saudi Arabian government considered the Straits of Tiran and the Gulf of Aqaba to be closed Arabian waterways with no international characteristics (see *ibid.*, p. 607; and no. 154 in these volumes). The Israeli government considered them international waterways that could thus not be closed.

[3] The aide-memoire stated the U.S. position that the gulf and the straits leading to it constituted international waters and that no nation could forcibly prevent free and innocent passage through them (State, *Foreign Relations, 1955–1957*, vol. XVII, *Arab-Israeli Dispute 1957*, p. 133; on King Saud's visit see no. 13.

[4] Eisenhower had wanted to assure King Saud in his May 11 letter of his support for the protection of pilgrims traveling to the Holy Places. Secretary Dulles, however, had advised him to wait until State Department officials had formulated a "comprehensive position" on the issue (Memorandum of Conversation, May 11, 1957, Dulles Papers, Telephone Conversations).

[5] Secretary Dulles and other State Department officials would meet with Abdul Rahman Azzam Pasha, special representative of King Saud, on June 12 and 17 (State, *Foreign Relations, 1955–1957*, vol. XVII, *Arab-Israeli Dispute 1957*, pp. 636–41, 648, 656–59).

King Saud would reiterate his position on the Gulf of Aqaba and cite additional acts of alleged Israeli aggression in his May 25 response. To give Israel navigation rights in the gulf, Saud said, would incite the Arabs and Moslems and allow "partisan and seditious propaganda to undermine our efforts to calm the situation and open up a new era of stability and peace in this region" (AWF/I: Saudi Arabia). For developments see no. 220.

157

EM, AWF, DDE Diaries Series

To Sherman Adams

May 15, 1957

Memorandum for Governor Adams: President Hoover had several strong recommendations, and a few complaints, concerning the Hoover Commission Reports.[1] He made statements along the following lines:

(*a*) Mr. Kestnbaum will approve recommendations involving administrative action.[2] Thereafter, he sends the matters to the Bureau of the Budget, but he says that certain people in the Budget staff, as well as all the Departments, block progress.

Recommendation: That I issue a directive requiring from the Budget a report every thirty days on *accomplishments* under these recommendations.

(*b*) The part of the recommendations involving legislative programs have been allowed to die on the vine. He is principally concerned about one involving accounting in the government. He says this has passed the Senate once, and has been recommended to the Congress three times by me.[3] Yet Admiral McNeil of the Defense Department has been actively lobbying against the bill on the Hill. He thinks that Admiral McNeil should be fired and that we should not allow this kind of sabotaging of our plans.[4]

Specific recommendations:

(1) That the Defense Department be required to support the bill.

(2) That I send a special message to Congress urging adoption of all the Hoover recommendations that require legislative action.

(*c*) He is quite upset about failure to reform the Civil Service Commission, particularly of our failure to include a promotion for merit provision in regulations and law. He says the Civil Service Commission itself has been the chief opponent. I informed him that we have a new Commissioner and that possibly something would be done. I told him we would follow up on this point.[5]

(*d*) He says that sometime back he sent me a personal message on legislative proposals which he thought I should send to the Congress. But the "channels" stopped the message along the line, and nothing has been done about it. He is now going to send to me personally a message which I will take up with you after it arrives.[6]

Of all the above, he seems to be most incensed about the Defense Department officials, particularly McNeil, in openly lobbying against the White House proposals before the Congress.

I will be available whenever you want to arrange a meeting with the Budget, Mr. Kestnbaum and yourself.[7]

[1] In September 1953 Eisenhower had established a new Commission on the Organization of the Executive Branch of the Government. This so-called second Hoover Commission had undertaken a broad study of government functions, policy, and organization, and had submitted its final report to Congress in June 1955 (see Galambos and van Ee, *The Middle Way*, nos. 341 and 666; U.S. Commission on Organization of the Executive Branch of the Government, *Final Report to the Congress* [Washington, D.C., 1955]; and Neil MacNeil and Harold W. Metz, *The Hoover Report: 1953–1955* [New York, 1956]). Eisenhower had met with former President Herbert Hoover on May 15.

[2] Presidential Special Assistant Meyer Kestnbaum had been appointed by Eisenhower in October 1955 to oversee the evaluation and possible adoption of the Hoover Commission recommendations (see Galambos and van Ee, *The Middle Way*, no. 1797; Arnold, *Making the Managerial Presidency*, p. 198; and *New York Times*, Oct. 11, 1955).

[3] In his 1957 Budget Message Eisenhower had again requested that Congress follow the Hoover Commission recommendation to enact legislation that would place government appropriations on an accrued expenditure basis (the cost of both services and goods estimated to be received during any given fiscal year) (*Public Papers of the Presidents: Eisenhower, 1957*, p. 58). Although the Senate would pass such legislation on June 5, the House would fail to take action on the bill during the Eighty-fifth Congress (see *Congressional Quarterly Almanac*, vol. XIII, *1957*, p. 682; see also MacNeil and Metz, *Hoover Report: 1953–1955*, pp. 48–64).

[4] Wilfred James McNeil, Assistant Secretary of Defense and Comptroller of the Department of Defense since 1949 (see Galambos, *NATO and the Campaign of 1952*, no. 130), reportedly had approved the bill's objective but opposed its implementation (*Congressional Quarterly Almanac*, vol. XIII, *1957*, p. 682).

[5] Philip Young, Chairman of the Civil Service Commission since 1953, had resigned in February 1957 (see no. 35). In April former Congressman Harris Ellsworth (Rep., Ore.) had been appointed to chair the Commission (*New York Times*, Apr. 19, 1957). On the Hoover Commission recommendations for the Civil Service see MacNeil and Metz, *Hoover Report: 1953–1955*, pp. 29–47.

[6] Eisenhower would forward Hoover's message to Adams on May 20 (AWF/A), and suggest that a meeting with the Director of the Bureau of the Budget Brundage, Kestnbaum, and Adams be held as soon as possible in the President's office. "I am anxious to give Mr. Hoover some kind of a reply as quickly as possible," he would write.

[7] There is no record of a meeting between Eisenhower, Adams, Kestnbaum, and Brundage.

158

EM, AWF, Name Series

To James Frederick Gault

May 15, 1957

Dear Jimmy: Since this letter has to do with the apartment in Culzean Castle, I am sending a copy to Mr. Gray.[1]

Two of my best friends are the American Ambassador in London and his wife Betsey Whitney. They feel it is possible that they might go to Scotland for a week or ten days in August, and if they do I would hope that they could stay in the apartment.[2] If it is not too much trouble for you, I would appreciate your contacting the Ambassador as soon as possible to make certain that on whatever date and for whatever time they may like to occupy the place, we have not given permission to anyone else to be there.

In the event you are prevented for any reason—out of the country, or preoccupation—from taking care of the matter, would you please arrange to notify Mr. Gray at Culzean so that he may communicate directly with the Ambassador?

Incidentally, I should like for you also to invite the Ambassador to go back up during October, or whenever is the best month for the pheasant and partridge shooting. As I recall, I have been there twice in October when we had good shooting, but it may be that some other period is slightly better.[3]

I am sorry to tell you there has been no improvement whatsoever in my golf. I am trying hard to play more often than before, but I am very erratic and uncertain. I hope you are shooting all pars.[4]

With warm regard, *As ever*

P.S. To ensure against the possibility that you may be travelling in Europe, I shall ask Mr. Gray to wait a reasonable time before receipt of instructions from you, after which he should contact the Ambassador by letter.[5]

[1] Retired Brigadier General Gault had served as personal assistant to Eisenhower when he was Supreme Allied Commander in Europe (1943–1945). For background see Chandler, *War Years*, no. 1403; Galambos, *Chief of Staff*, no. 1157; and Galambos, *NATO and the Campaign of 1952*, no. 962. On the President's apartment in Culzean Castle in Ayrshire, Scotland, see no. 55. James T. Gray managed the estate and Eisenhower's apartment. Eisenhower's May 15 letter to him and Gray's May 20 reply are both in AWF/N, Gault Corr.

[2] Mrs. John Hay Whitney had written to Eisenhower on May 8 (AWF/A).

[3] On Eisenhower's visits to the castle in September 1946 and October 1951 see Galambos, *Chief of Staff*, no. 1120; and *NATO and the Campaign of 1952*, no. 401.

[4] Gault would reply that he had not played golf due to "a recurrence of an old knee injury from a bad fall out fox-hunting" (May 22, 1957, AWF/N).

[5] Gault would contact Whitney and report that plans for the visit were underway. He also planned to vacation in Scotland at the end of May and would "call in at Culzean to see that all is well" (Gault to Eisenhower, May 22, 1957, AWF/N). See the following document.

TO JOHN HAY WHITNEY *May 15, 1957*

Dear Jock: Enclosed are copies of two letters, one written to Sir James Gault who has been my friend for many years and normally acts as my representative in handling visitors to Culzean Castle. It is possible, however, that he may be out of the country, and so you will see that I have written also to Mr. Gray who is the Scottish manager of the estate and of the apartment assigned to Mamie and me.[1]

At Culzean, I think you will find none of the August grouse shooting, but I know from experience that the late fall pheasant and partridge shooting is a very great sport.[2]

Mr. Gray himself is a fine gentleman and a very well read historian of the region. Locally it is called the "Robbie Burns country," as his home was in the neighborhood.[3] Prestwick is nearby, and I understand that the city boasts several good golf courses.[4] I have never played there.

A letter I received a day or so ago from Betsey says that her brother-in-law, Jim Fosburgh, paid a compliment to the so-called painting that I gave to you two.[5] This relieves me mightily because, having heard that you displayed it somewhere in the Embassy, I have had my moments of keen embarrassment when I pictured some art lover gazing at this part of the "Whitney collection."

The other day George raced "Banned," the horse that he secured from you. He ran third—I know nothing at all as to the character of the opposition—and George seemed very pleased, and expects him to win the next time out.[6] George has two mares that he says are very well bred, both of which have just foaled. One of them, an Argentine horse who apparently had a very fine record, will have nothing to do with her foal. They have had to purchase a nurse mare. The mother is really a mean horse.

My love to Betsey, and of course all the best to yourself. *As ever*

[1] See the preceding document.

[2] On May 18 (AWF/A) Whitney would reply: "Curiously enough, we were only this week talking about going to Culzean." He added that he was planning to visit Scotland on May 20 and had arranged to "meet the people concerned. . . . With your letters I will really be in fine favor."

[3] Scottish poet Robert Burns (1759–1796) lived in Ayrshire County in southwestern Scotland.

[4] Prestwick was a tourist resort with noted golf courses.

[5] Mrs. Whitney had written on May 8 (AWF). In January Eisenhower had given the Whitneys his painting of a mountain lake scene (see Whitman to Whitney, Dec. 24, 1956, Whitney to Eisenhower, Jan. 16, 22, 29, Feb. 4, 1957, all in AWF/A). James Whitney Fosburgh (M.A. Yale 1935) was an artist. According to Mrs. Whitney, Fosburgh had said that the President's painting "was much better than most of the paintings he had seen yesterday in the Royal Academy exhibition."

[6] For background on George Allen and his horse see no. 130; for developments see no. 173.

160

EM, AWF, DDE Diaries Series

To Daniel Collier Elkin

May 16, 1957

Dear Dr. Elkin:[1] I am deeply grateful to you and the Board of Regents of the American College of Surgeons for inviting me to deliver this year's Martin Memorial Lecture in Atlantic City.[2] I assure you, first of all, that this is one thing I should really like to do.

My difficulty is not in the time involved in making the trip; rather, it is the time and work in preparing any address suitable to deliver before such a distinguished body. Since I am one of those individuals who can neither, in public, complacently read the thoughts evolved and put on paper by someone else, nor, on the other hand, prepare what I consider to be a worthwhile talk in an hour or two of dictation, the kind of engagement you propose really places a considerable burden upon me.

This causes what I believe to be a justifiable hesitancy on my part to say that I can come. Nevertheless, because you and other good friends have been so kind as to put some urgency in your invitations, could you give me some idea of the final date on which your program scheduling would allow me to make a definite decision?

It would seem to me that, if I did not have to give you a fixed answer before about September first, there would be a much greater chance that I could favorably consider the prospect than if I should be required to give such a reply at this moment.

Quite naturally, I do not want to embarrass you by keeping you hanging in mid-air, so if you cannot wait for an answer, as I suggest, I will thoroughly understand. In this latter case, I would feel it best for me to decline.[3]

With warm personal regard, *Sincerely*

[1] Elkin (A.B. Yale 1916, M.D. Emory 1920), the president of the American College of Surgeons, had retired in 1954 as chair of the Department of Surgery in Emory University's School of Medicine.

[2] For background on the invitation see no. 38.

[3] Special Assistant to the President for National Security Affairs Robert Cutler would deliver Eisenhower's address to the American College of Surgeons in Atlantic City on October 14, 1957 (*Public Papers of the Presidents: Eisenhower, 1957*, pp. 743–45). The President, who would apologize for delivering his speech by proxy, would exhort his audience to "take your part in preserving and strengthening the kind of society that has made America's past and present possible." "The waters of liberty flow from one

source: voluntary initiative and effort," Eisenhower would state. "In these complex modern days, too often we find the spring drying up for want of volunteers. Too much dependence on the arm of Government. Too much turning to taxation to supply what initiative once sought out. . . . In a free democracy like ours, less and less, not more and more, should devolve on Government. All citizens—the leaders in surgery like the leaders in other walks of life—should be vigilant to find ways—outside of Government—to carry foward their essential services to man."

A delegation from the American College of Surgeons would present Eisenhower with an honorary fellowship on February 6, 1958.

161

EM, AWF, International Series: Macmillan

To Harold Macmillan — *May 17, 1957*

Cable. Secret

Dear Harold: Foster has just been talking to me about the China trade situation and the message which he is sending to Selwyn Lloyd in reply to Selwyn's memorandum which he gave to Jock Whitney on the evening of May 13th.[1]

Our military advisors are strongly of the opinion that many of the items which you would take off the China list will in fact appreciably help the Chinese Communists to build up the military potential which threatens us in this area and which we have the primary responsibility to resist. Our Congress, although less well informed on the technical details, feels strongly on this issue. As Foster is saying to Selwyn we do not feel confident that increasing the list will really help your trade very much. May it not mean merely that China's trade with you will consist of the more strategic rather than less strategic items?[2]

We are, however, giving some new discretion to our representatives in Paris and hope very much that you will try to meet us as it would be unfortunate in many respects if we should split publicly on this issue.[3] *Faithfully yours*

[1] The United States and Great Britain had held many discussions regarding the type and quantity of items that were restricted in trade between the Western nations and Communist China and the countries of the Soviet bloc. Although Eisenhower had asked (Apr. 1956) for a relaxation of restrictions on all but the most highly technical items, no substantial modifications in East-West trade policy had been introduced. In September 1956 the State Department had announced an interim position that would relax some trade controls if a substantial number of items applying only to China (the so-called "China differential") were retained. The United States also asked that the participating countries within the China Committee of the Paris Consultative Group (CHINCOM) exercise restraint in the use of exception procedures allowing the shipment of some embargoed items to Communist China.

In March 1957 the British had argued that additional controls on trade with Communist China over and above those imposed on the countries of the Soviet bloc were "illogical and ought to be abolished." Economic pressures demanded a greater concentration on exports, they maintained, and additional controls were an unnecessary burden. In a National Security Council discussion of the political implications of a relaxation of trade controls with Communist China, Eisenhower pointed out that if the United States did "not propose to put severe obstacles in the way of our allies trading with Communist China, it seemed to him rather foolish to put such obstacles in the way of our own U.S. trade with Communist China."

After lengthy discussions between legislative leaders and State and Defense Department officials, Eisenhower authorized the implementation of NSC 5704/1, which, in effect, eliminated the special China embargo list but placed those items considered to be particularly strategic on the two remaining international lists (see Galambos and van Ee, *The Middle Way,* nos. 782 and 1854 for background; see also State, *Foreign Relations, 1955–1957,* vol. X, *Foreign Aid and Economic Defense Policy,* pp. 385–96, 418–19, 428–31, 440–42, 445–46; and NSC meeting minutes, Mar. 7, 1957, AWF/NSC).

The U.S. delegation to CHINCOM had presented the U.S. proposals at the committee's opening meeting in Paris on May 7. At the same time, the French delegation submitted a proposal calling for the abolishment of all special controls on trade with China. In a subsequent conversation, Foreign Secretary Selwyn Lloyd had told Secretary Dulles that the British Board of Trade thought that the U.S. proposal was "no good." The United States had obviously made an effort, Lloyd said, but the items that really counted were still on the embargoed list. Lloyd's memorandum to U.S. Ambassador Whitney had explained that "any proposal merely to add certain items from the China list to the Russian list would not, in the United Kingdom view, obtain general acceptance." Lloyd stressed the pressure that he felt from the House of Commons and the "widespread resentment in the United Kingdom at the absence of a satisfactory solution to this problem" (State, *Foreign Relations, 1955–1957,* vol. X, *Foreign Aid and Economic Defense Policy,* pp. 450–52).

In the meeting earlier on this same day, Dulles had told Eisenhower that only a substantial reduction of the "China differential" would bring agreement with the United Kingdom. He suggested that some items could be cleared for sale to Communist China after advance notification to CHINCOM; the United States could then object "if this seemed desirable and feasible." Perhaps, he said, the British and those countries that agreed with them should "go it alone," although a split between the United States and these countries over the issue "would obviously have undesirable implications." Eisenhower approved Dulles's proposal, and the State Department draft of this letter, although, as he said, "basically Communist China and Soviet Russia should be treated alike" (*ibid.,* pp. 455–56; and Memorandum of Conversation, May 17, 1957, Dulles Papers, White House Memoranda Series).

[2] Dulles would tell Lloyd that the United States wanted to avoid added strain on U.S.-British relations by coming to an agreement; but, he would add, it could not "go all the way . . . and in effect wholly abolish the differential." A bad reaction would develop in the United States, Dulles said, if Great Britain were unable to continue cooperation in this area. "We shall do our very best to hold those reactions to a minimum," Dulles told Lloyd, "but we cannot give any assurance that it will not have troublesome consequences" (State, *Foreign Relations, 1955–1957,* vol. X, *Foreign Aid and Economic Defense Policy,* p. 458).

[3] The U.S. delegation would present a modified proposal that would retain an embargo on seventy-eight items on the two international lists; the other participating countries would, however, reject the U.S. proposition (*ibid.,* pp. 458–59). For developments see no. 168.

162 *EM, AWF, Dulles-Herter Series*

To John Foster Dulles *May 20, 1957*

Personal

Dear Foster: Herewith two notes from Harold Macmillan, together with a copy of a letter he sent to Chancellor Adenauer.[1] I send them to you for your reading, and I have no objection if you show them to your Under Secretary and to your Assistant Secretary for European Affairs.[2] When you have read them, will you return them to my office?

I am puzzled by one expression in Harold's letter about the tanks. At the top of page two of that letter he says, "I think you would probably agree with this."[3] I have assured him in every possible way I can that I am very much in favor of Britain becoming one of the munition sources of the free world. Moreover, I recognize their need for foreign exchange. In a recent letter to him I stressed the fact that I had always hoped that the Germans would buy Centurions and was most regretful that they were seemingly making a decision in favor of our T-48s.[4] Nevertheless, there seems to be a lingering doubt in his mind that we are really sincere in this matter. He seems hard to convince—but there is a suspicion that underneath us somewhere there is somebody who is taking a very narrow view about this whole matter of the munitions supply of the free world. I think I shall take an occasion at some meeting of the Security Council when all the Chiefs of Staff are present to re-emphasize my conviction on this point.[5] *As ever*

[1] For the British Prime Minister's letter regarding his reply to Soviet Premier Bulganin see no. 153. Macmillan had written to Adenauer regarding British disappointment about reports that the Federal Republic intended to buy the American M-48 tank (see no. 115 for background). "If no final decision has yet been taken," Macmillan wrote, "may I ask you to give full weight to the fact that for us to obtain a substantial order from you for Centurions would help us politically in demonstrating to industrial and other circles in the United Kingdom the benefits of European cooperation?" (Macmillan to Adenauer, n.d., AWF/I: Macmillan).

[2] Christian A. Herter was Under Secretary of State; Charles Burke Elbrick (A.B. Williams College 1929), former General Deputy Assistant Secretary of State, had become Assistant Secretary of State for European Affairs in February 1957.

[3] Macmillan had written: "I know how keen the professional military people are on their own weapons, but in fact these decisions are of first political importance for us and the rest of Europe. Both for the sake of European co-operation, and in order to lessen the need for dollar end-item aid, it is most desirable that some of these defence requirements should be supplied by Britain." The next sentence in his letter is the one quoted by Eisenhower (Macmillan to Eisenhower, May 17, 1957, *ibid.*).

[4] Eisenhower's April 15 letter to the British Prime Minister is no. 115.

[5] The National Security Council meeting minutes do not indicate that Eisenhower discussed the issue. For developments see no. 168.

163

EM, WHCF, Official File 154-N-2

To Anna Eleanor Roosevelt

May 20, 1957

Dear Mrs. Roosevelt:[1] Thank you for sending me your comments both on the situation of Hungarian refugees in Austria and on Moroccan developments.[2]

While we have not established a specific total for the number of Hungarian refugees to be admitted to this country, we are of course proud of the fact that the number of refugees that have been brought to our shores now approaches 33,000—approximately 20% of all resettled.

It is apparent that the emergency needs for the program initiated last November are coming to an end, as is indicated by the reduced number of refugees now in camps in Austria. Contrary to the belief that some of the refugees have held, we have not terminated the program. It continues with concentration on hardship cases involving refugees who have a close relationship to American citizens or to refugees already in the United States, and those who have special skills and talents. This program will provide for continuing admissions on what we believe is a fair and just basis.

It is important, too, that everything possible be done to achieve approval of immigration legislation that has been pending for quite some time before House and Senate Committees.[3]

In regard to your other comments, Secretary Dulles and I have been giving earnest attention to developments throughout that entire area. Even now, we are studying the food problems to which you referred in your letter, and active conversations are in progress with the Moroccans on these and a wide range of other matters.[4] Your interest is of course closely related to my own concern with the need for approval by the Congress of a Mutual Security program sufficient to the requirements for waging peace.[5]

I am truly appreciative of the trouble you took to inform me of your observations. *Sincerely*

[1] Staff Secretary General Andrew Goodpaster may have drafted this letter, which he submitted to Eisenhower after discussing it with other White House officials (Goodpaster to Eisenhower, May 17, 1957, same file as document).

[2] For background on the Hungarian uprising in October 1956 see Galambos and van Ee, *The Middle Way*, no. 2044. In November Eisenhower had directed that extraordinary measures be taken to process quickly the visa applications of thousands of Hungarian refugees who had fled into Austria after the Soviets had moved to crush the rebellion. In order to coordinate efforts among the various voluntary and government agencies involved in the resettlement, he had also created the President's Committee for Hungarian Refugee Relief (see *ibid.*, no. 2131).

Mrs. Roosevelt, widow of the late president, had written Eisenhower after visiting three Hungarian refugee camps in Salzburg, Austria. Her tour had been at the invitation of the High Commissioner for Refugees to the United Nations. The refugees had called a hunger strike to protest the limit of 32,000 placed on immigration into the United States; they had expected that the figure would be 35,000. "It seems a pity," Roosevelt wrote, "to have all that you have done clouded and besmirched by their feeling of disappointment." If the United States would "let in just these three thousand more," she said, "I think we would greatly increase the appreciation for our generous attitude which you brought about by your original action" (May 14, 1957, same file as document; for more on the President's committee and the resettlement program see Eisenhower to Voorhees, Feb. 28, 1957, WHCF/OF 154-N-3; and Eisenhower to Knowland, Apr. 12, 1957, same file as document).

[3] In a January 1957 message to Congress on immigration matters Eisenhower had asked for prompt action in revising the 1952 Immigration and Nationality Act (*Public Papers of the Presidents: Eisenhower, 1957*, pp. 110–17). On September 11 Eisenhower would sign a bill that he called "a disappointment" since it did not include a revision of the quota system for admitting immigrants (*Congressional Quarterly Almanac*, vol. XIII, *1957*, pp. 670–71; see also no. 417).

[4] After a ten-day visit to Morocco in March, Mrs. Roosevelt had publicly expressed concern that starvation would soon envelop that country if the United States did not send surplus food immediately. She told Eisenhower that U.S. efforts to forestall these conditions could be "too little too late." "Perhaps you could spur the proper authorities on a little," she wrote, "because I think this is a situation which the Soviets will exploit and if we delay they will come with a little relief. Then we will try later to draw the Moroccans back, but the harm will have been done, which we could avoid if we move quickly now."

In June shipments of milk, cheese, and cornmeal would reach Morocco under a program organized by the National Catholic Welfare Conference (*New York Times*, Mar. 18, Apr. 29, and June 6, 1957). For discussions between U.S. and Moroccan officials regarding military bases and economic and technical aid see State, *Foreign Relations, 1955–1957*, vol. XVIII, *Africa*, pp. 564–77.

[5] For background on the Mutual Security Bill and the congressional debates it provoked see *Congressional Quarterly Almanac*, vol. XIII, *1957*, pp. 602–12; see also no. 147; and Kaufman, *Trade and Aid*, pp. 136–38. In a message to Congress and a televised address to the nation on the following day Eisenhower would vigorously defend his foreign aid program as essential to the security of the American people and to world peace (*Public Papers of the Presidents: Eisenhower, 1957*, pp. 372–96).

164 — *EM, AWF, Administration Series*

TO HERBERT BROWNELL, JR. — *May 20, 1957*

Dear Herb: As you know, this whole matter of the Federal Government interfering in the relationships between automobile companies and their dealers has worried me a great deal.[1] I have today a note from my young friend, Arthur Summerfield, Jr.[2] He encloses a memorandum which I think deserves very careful study in your Department. It is a copy of the "Motor News Analysis."[3] Will you please let me know the position of the Justice Department on the several points made in that memorandum?[4]

With warm regard, *As ever*

[1] For more on Eisenhower's involvement with this issue see Galambos and van Ee, *The Middle Way*, nos. 829, 1843, and 1848.
[2] Arthur ("Bud") Ellsworth Summerfield, Jr., was an automobile dealer in Flint, Michigan, and son of Postmaster General Summerfield; see *ibid.*, nos. 1545, 1589, and 1657.
[3] Summerfield had written on May 15—enclosing a copy of the trade publication (not in EM)—to call the President's attention to "the true concern that is felt by the ever-growing number of automobile dealers in this country today" (AWF/A; Brownell Corr.). He criticized "the interpretation of the anti-trust laws by the Justice Department." Justice was continuing its efforts to block a plan by the National Automobile Dealers Association to revive the exclusive territorial security franchise rights for auto dealers that had been outlawed by legislation in 1949 (for background see Galambos and van Ee, *The Middle Way*, no. 1848). The Automobile Dealer Franchise Act of 1956 had sought to alter the balance of power between manufacturers and dealers by giving dealers the right to sue manufacturers for forcing unwanted cars, parts and accessories upon them or for exercising undue control over their capital investment, sales, service facilities, and business policies. Nevertheless, dealers now believed that they needed territorial franchise security in order to relieve the stress of an uncertain market for automobile sales. (See *Business Week*, Feb. 2, Mar. 23, Apr. 6, July 13, 1957, and Jan. 18, 1958. See also *U.S. Statutes at Large*, vol. 70A, pp. 1125–26; U.S. Congress, House Committee on Judiciary, Subcommittee on Antitrust, *Automobile Dealer Franchises*, 84th Cong., 2d sess., July 2, 1956, pp. 3–4, 128–29; Roger J. Weiss, "The Automobile Dealer Franchise Act of 1956—An Evaluation," *Cornell Law Quarterly*, vol. 48, 1962–63 [Ithaca, 1963], pp. 711–53; and "The Automobile Dealer Franchise Act: A 'New Departure' in Federal Legislation?" *Northwestern University Law Review*, vol. 52, no. 2, May—June 1957, pp. 253–83. See also Stewart Macaulay, *Law and the Balance of Power: The Automobile Manufacturers and Their Dealers* [New York, 1966], pp. 43–71).
[4] There is no further correspondence on this matter in AWF. In future cases, however, the Justice Department adhered to its interpretation of the antitrust laws insofar as automobile dealers and manufacturers were concerned. See Brownell, *Advising Ike*, p. 330, and *New York Times*, Dec. 19, 1966.

165 — *EM, AWF, Administration Series*

To Herbert Brownell, Jr. — *May 20, 1957*

Dear Herb: I hear you are in New York City, to be back tomorrow night. When you get into your office Wednesday morning, will you give me a ring? I want to talk to you about a visit I just had from Dick Mellon.[1]

The subject concerns what he believes to be a woeful lack of coordination between governmental responsibility in connection with the Anti Trust Act and the methods pursued in carrying out these responsibilities.[2]

I should prefer a meeting in my office, but if that is inconvenient, I would be glad to talk to you on the phone.[3]

With warm regard, *As ever*

[1] Financier Richard King Mellon, chairman of the Mellon National Bank and Trust Company, had served as a director of numerous large corporations, including Gulf Oil Corporation, the Aluminum Company of America (ALCOA), and the Pittsburgh Plate Glass Company.
[2] Mellon had met with Eisenhower on May 20 to complain about various actions taken by the Justice Department. One issue was the Department's actions in the antitrust suit against ALCOA, which Mellon said was about to be resolved after twenty years of litigation. Meanwhile, however, Justice was investigating the merger of Gulf Oil Corporation and Warren Petroleum Corporation—companies Mellon said had never been competitive. He complained, as well, about the government's "persecution" of Pittsburgh Plate Glass Company (Ann Whitman memorandum, May 20, 1957, AWF/AWD; for background see Galambos and van Ee, *The Middle Way*, nos. 487 and 833; Merton J. Peck, *Competition in the Aluminum Industry 1945–1958* [Cambridge, Mass., 1961], pp. 8–14; Charles C. Carr, *ALCOA: An American Enterprise* [New York, 1952], pp. 217–36); and George David Smith, *From Monopoly to Competition: The Transformation of Alcoa, 1888–1986* [Cambridge, 1988], pp. 250–307).
[3] Eisenhower would meet with the Attorney General on May 23 to discuss Mellon's complaints (AWF/AWD). For developments see no. 194.

166 — *EM, AWF, Dulles-Herter Series*

To John Foster Dulles — *May 20, 1957*

Dear Foster: I have no objection to meeting the Methodist Council of Bishops, particularly since the date is as far off as the spring of 1959.[1] By that time I hope I may be doing a bit of "coasting."[2]

I suppose at the proper time I shall get a specific request from Bishop Oxnam.[3] *As ever*

[1] In a May 16 memorandum (AWF/D-H) Secretary Dulles had recommended that the President meet with the Methodist Council of Bishops during their conference in Washington, D.C., in April 1959 (see also Dulles to Oxnam, May 16, 1957, Dulles Papers, White House Memoranda Series). Dulles explained that the Methodists comprised "the largest Protestant denomination and also the religious group which concerns itself most actively with public affairs." As it turned out the President would meet with the bishops on the morning of April 14, 1959 (see *New York Times*, Apr. 15, 1959).
[2] The President was anticipating the end of his second term in office when he hoped that the pace of work would slow and he could prepare for retirement. For more on the President's thoughts about retirement see Galambos and van Ee, *The Middle Way*, nos. 31 and 2064.
[3] On this same day Dulles would write Garfield Bromley Oxnam (A.B. University of Southern California 1913; S.T.B. Boston University 1915), Bishop of the Washington, D.C., area Methodist Church, of the President's favorable response. President Eisenhower would expect, Dulles added, a "specific request" from the Bishop (Dulles Papers, White House Memoranda Series). We have been unable to locate further correspondence on this matter.

167

EM, AWF, Name Series

TO JACQUELINE COCHRAN

May 23, 1957

Dear Jackie: I am delighted that you enjoyed the experience of being a representative to the Inauguration of President Somoza.[1] From two or three sources I have had reports that you were truly the "belle of the ball."

Thank you, too, for telling me of the esteem in which the Ambassador and Mrs. Whelan are held.[2] In these days, particularly when so many of our representatives abroad are under attack (unjustly in 99% of the cases, I am convinced), it is encouraging to me to have a first hand report of this character from someone whose judgment I trust implicitly.

With warm regard to you and Floyd, *Sincerely*

[1] On May 1 aviator Jacqueline Cochran, wife of financier Floyd Bostwick Odlum and co-owner of the Cochran-Odlum ranch in Indio, California, had attended the inauguration of President Luis A. Somoza Debayle in Managua, Nicaragua (see *New York Times*, May 2, 1957). Her May 17 letter thanking Eisenhower is in AWF/N. For background on Cochran see Galambos and van Ee, *The Middle Way*, no. 1221.

[2] Thomas E. Whelan had been U.S. Ambassador to Nicaragua since 1951. His wife was the former Maybell Stewart. "Probably the greatest thrill of all," Cochran wrote, "was the response of the people of Nicaragua to our American flag and our American Ambassador. . . . Ambassador and Mrs. Whelan are obviously held in high esteem. . . ."

168

EM, AWF, DDE Diaries Series

TO HAROLD MACMILLAN
Top secret

May 24, 1957

Dear Harold: I have been trying to follow in a general way negotiations going on between the several countries on the Russian-Chinese trade differential.[1] As an individual I agree with you that there is very little of profit in the matter either for your country or for any other. Commercially, it affects this nation not at all, for the simple reason that we have a total embargo on Chinese trade. However, many of our people think that the free nations could make a terrific psychological blunder in this matter and possibly even lose all the areas of the Southeast that have strong Chinese minorities.[2]

We understand your predicament and even though we may be compelled, in the final result, to differ sharply in our official positions, I think that each of our Governments should strive to prevent the possible popular conclusion in its own country that we are committed to going "separate ways."[3]

Regarding the German tank purchase, I am extremely disappointed if that Government has finally decided on our Model 48.[4] This is not merely because I know of your great need for exports; mine is a more military conviction based upon experience in World War II. The free world simply must have more than one major source of ordnance supply. Peacetime sales and purchases should reflect this need. I should like to see more countries arming themselves with their own or your hardware instead of ours.[5]

There is one top secret subject that we mentioned at Bermuda which I raise here once more, so that there can be no misunderstanding of our attitude. It involves the possibility of an American visit by the Queen and her husband. I merely want to make certain that you realize that nothing could give me greater satisfaction both personally and officially—a satisfaction that I know would be shared by the Government and our people. Please understand that I am by no means pressing you for an immediate reaction of any kind. But I do feel that there must be no incorrect interpretation about our feelings in the matter.[6]

With warm personal regard, *As ever*

[1] For background on the difference in the trade restrictions the Western powers were applying to the Soviet Union and the People's Republic of China see no. 161.

[2] Macmillan had written Eisenhower on May 21 that the China trade affair had become "almost as much an obsession" with the British as it had with the U.S. Congress. "Quite between ourselves as old friends," he said, "I do not think there is much in it." Persuading the British that the Chinese were more dangerous than the Russians was difficult, Macmillan said, and if a compromise were not possible, he would "have to stick to the line shared by that large number of countries, including the great majority of Europe, who would want to bring the Russian and the Chinese List together" (PREM 11/2529).

[3] Macmillan would respond to Eisenhower on May 29, thanking him for understanding Britain's "special difficulty" regarding the trade question. Because the commercial interests of the United States and Great Britain were not alike, Macmillan said, he had decided to make a statement to Parliament on the following day terminating the controls limited to trade with the Chinese. "Of course we shall stress that we mean to continue cooperating with you and our allies in controlling trade with both the Soviet bloc and China in the interests of our mutual security. I trust that this will be made clear also in the United States" (*ibid.*). For developments see no. 180.

[4] See no. 166 for background.

[5] The Germans would choose the American tank over the British Centurion (see no. 205).

[6] On the Bermuda Conference see no. 78; on the Queen's visit (Oct. 16–21) see no. 188.

169

EM, AWF, Name Series

To Sidney Williams Richardson

May 24, 1957

Dear Sid: I am getting more than slightly irritated by continuing confusion—with complaints from all sides—in the effort to formulate a gas bill that will be fair and just to producer and consumer alike.[1]

For the past year, individuals thoroughly familiar with the whole problem have been negotiating all over the place—that is, with distributors, producers, consumers and Congressmen—in an effort to develop something that would be considered fair by everyone except those who are extremists on one side of the question or the other. I was delighted when I heard that Congressman Harris had introduced a bill that seemed to meet these requirements.[2] Quite naturally, it has to be one that strikes the majority of the people as fair, or it will be impossible to enact any kind of legislation. As you know, I would never approve anything that did not seem to me to be fair.

With respect to the two amendments that are discussed in the editorial you sent me, I understand they were proposed by a lawyer in the Office of Defense Mobilization who felt that it was not inconceivable that in some cases costs might be a factor in arriving at a "fair market price."[3] Certainly I can conceive of cases where producers might wish to show to the Commission that costs had gone up.

I understand the other amendment dealt with the right of the Commission to approve existing contracts with fixed escalation clauses.[4]

No one put these suggestions forward as fixed conclusions of the Administration. They were simply submitted as suggestions to the Congressional Committee for study and for decisions they saw fit.

I do not believe for one second that any individual is trying to regulate *gas production* on a public utilities basis, and I think the man who wrote the editorial is either ignorant or completely off his rocker.[5]

I still have every hope that a satisfactory gas bill will be written—but I assure you that if it is to be approved, it has got to be one that strikes me as fair and just to everybody concerned.[6]

Ever since the court decision in the Phillips case, I have insisted that we needed such a law and all I asked was that it satisfy the demands of fairness.[7] Certainly I am not so stupid as to think the interests of the United States will be served by choking off exploration and production.

I do hope that you continue to improve in health and I am sorry that your most recent illness seemed to be caused by something you must have picked up on your latest visit to Washington. Don't let that fact keep you from coming back again when the spirit moves you.

With warm regard, *As ever*

P.S. I should have said above that I understand thoroughly how differently everybody has interpreted every move and action that has taken place in this whole gas bill development and the account above gives you my personal understanding of what has happened. I am getting used to this kind of prejudiced complaint.

A few days ago the Advisory Council of the Democratic Party charged that mine is a pro-business Administration and that under its policies the rich are getting richer and the poor are getting poorer.[8] On the other hand, certain business groups have charged recently that mine is a New Deal-Fair Deal Administration which is bent on spending our nation into bankruptcy. Even the Republican State Committee of Texas recently passed a Resolution to this effect. Anyone sitting here must develop a large amount of indifference to such complaints.[9]

[1] For background on the Administration's efforts to enact natural gas legislation see no. 47, and Galambos and van Ee, *The Middle Way*, nos. 1748, 1763, and 1767. Oil magnate Richardson had written his friend, the President, on May 17, 1957 (AWF/N), to call Eisenhower's attention to the lead editorial in that week's issue of *Petroleum Week*. The magazine had accused the Administration of not wanting a natural gas bill "that would be acceptable to producers." "I think this statement is unfair," Richardson wrote. "Nevertheless, I thought you would be interested in seeing this editorial because it pretty well outlines the basic problems."

[2] For background on Congressman Oren Harris (Dem., Ark.), one of the sponsors of the 1956 natural gas legislation, see Galambos and van Ee, *The Middle Way*, no. 1748. Harris had introduced H.R. 6790 on April 10, 1957. Although the bill accepted the principle of direct federal controls over producers, it proposed a regulatory regime that would base controls on a flexible "reasonable market price" for the gas being sold (*Congressional Quarterly Almanac*, vol. XIII, *1957*, pp. 665–66).

[3] Eisenhower was referring to Charles H. Kendall, general counsel for the Office of Defense Mobilization (ODM) since 1953. Kendall, who had testified before the House Interstate and Foreign Commerce Committee on May 7th, claimed he was speaking for the Administration. He said that certain changes were necessary to bring the bill sponsored by Harris into line with the President's desire to balance producer and consumer interests. Kendall had suggested that the committee remove the ban against FPC consideration of production costs in determining a "reasonable market price" (see *New York Times*, May 8, 1957, and U.S. Congress, House Committee on Interstate and Foreign Commerce, "Natural Gas Act: Regulation of Producers' Prices," 85th Cong., 1st sess., *Committee Hearings*, Senate Library, vol. 1605 [1957], pp. 29–55).

[4] Kendall had also suggested an amendment to continue the commission's authority to review price increases resulting from pricing clauses in existing contracts, when "such increases do more than reflect additional or increased taxes" (*ibid.*, p. 31).

[5] *Petroleum Week* had written that an amendment allowing the Federal Power Commission the right to use cost of production as a factor in setting gas prices for producers "would make it a public utility bill, pure and simple. And justifiably, the lead-

ing producer associations say that such regulations in any natural gas legislation would make it totally unacceptable to them."

[6] Although Eisenhower would urge passage of a natural gas bill, with or without the Administration amendments, Democratic leaders would decide not to take the bill before the House in 1957 (*Congressional Quarterly Almanac*, vol. XIII, *1957*, pp. 665–66; see also *New York Times*, Aug. 7, 1957). For another view see Sanders, *The Regulation of Natural Gas*, pp. 94–106, and Carper, "Lobbying and the Natural Gas Bill," in *Case Studies in American Government*, ed. Bock and Campbell, pp. 175–222.

[7] For background on the Supreme Court's ruling in the Phillips Petroleum case that the Federal Power Commission had the authority to regulate the field prices of independent producers see Galambos and van Ee, *The Middle Way*, no. 1748.

[8] On May 5, 1957, the Advisory Council of the Democratic National Committee had issued three declarations concerning economic policy, foreign policy, and right-to-work legislation. The Democrats had scored the Eisenhower Administration's fiscal policies saying, "The failures of the Eisenhower fiscal policies are apparent. The burden of these failures rests heavily on the average American family. The rich are getting richer and the poor are getting poorer" (*New York Times*, May 6, 1957).

[9] Since early March the Administration had been defending itself against critics who had likened its policies to those of the New Deal (see no. 60). On March 9 Secretary of Commerce Sinclair Weeks had defended the Administration program against "critics who likened it to the New Deal and complained about its large budget" (*New York Times*, Mar. 10, 1957). Later, Vice-President Nixon complained to the American Iron and Steel Institute that the Administration's leaders found themselves "in the incongruous position of being subjected to attacks from groups holding completely opposing points of view" (*New York Times*, May 24, 1957).

170 — *EM, AWF, DDE Diaries Series*

To John Hay Whitney — *May 24, 1957*

Dear Jock: I am sending along with this note a formal letter to advise you that I would be very happy to accept the proposed gift of a Canteen of Silver from The Company of Cutlers. I thought that possibly something of an official nature might be desired in that case.[1]

Your letter was interesting and amusing. The amusing part was the recitation of your initiation into being the busiest person in London, but experiencing the feeling each evening that you have accomplished no work. I have had such a day today. In fact it is sort of a red letter occurrence when I have a different kind.[2]

Right now I have an engagement coming up with Al Gruenther, but within a few days possibly I shall get a chance to write you at greater length.[3]

Love to Betsey and all the best to yourself. *As ever*

[1] On May 9 British Ambassador Whitney had recommended that Eisenhower accept the gift from the Company of Cutlers of Hallamshire, Sheffield, England (AWF/A; see also Dulles to Eisenhower, May 22, 1957, AWF/A). The President's official letter

to Whitney (this same date) is in AWF/D. The presentation would take place on July 16 at the White House (see *New York Times*, June 22, 1957).

[2] Whitney had written on May 18 about the rapid pace of his life in London (AWF/A). "I can't say I am over-worked, but I certainly am over-busy."

[3] The engagement with General Gruenther may have been connected with Chancellor Adenauer's visit to the United States (see no. 186 and *New York Times*, May 29, 1957). Eisenhower would write to Whitney again on May 27 (see no. 173).

171

EM, AWF, DDE Diaries Series

TO WILLIAM STERLING COLE — *May 27, 1957*

Personal

Dear Stub:[1] Let me first thank you for your thoughtful letter of May twenty-second.[2] The whole question of testing of atomic weapons has engaged my concern from the time I took office. I have often talked with Lewis Strauss about it and, knowing my views and sharing them fully, he has held testing to the absolute minimum, ruling out shots which he felt could not be justified on the basis of the results sought. As you know, the fall-out of the last series in the Pacific was only a fraction of that from the 1954 tests.[3]

On the other hand, as you also know far better than almost any other person I can think of, there has been a great enhancement of our defensive strength through the developments which have come from the test program to date. We have increased the numbers, the deliverability, the efficiency and versatility of our weapons. Most recently, we have learned that certain of them can be made in such a manner that radioactive fall-out is very greatly minimized. The tactical usefulness of this latter development is known to you.

You are correct in your observation that I feel our large weapons (incidentally, now susceptible of being relatively the cleanest in the sense of fission product yield) are large enough and that we know we can make them larger on the same principles if ever there were strategic need for them, but I do not believe you are correctly informed that there is any approved plan to test larger weapons than were tested in 1954.[4] The Atomic Energy Commission at any rate has informed me that it has no such plans. If there is ever to be a test of larger weapons, this would have to be submitted to me, evaluated, and cleared by me. Chairman Strauss is opposed to any larger shot than we have had.

Some form of limitation either in numbers, explosive yield, fission product output, or even a temporary test suspension might well be the result of the current disarmament negotiations in London.[5]

To announce the concession unilaterally would deprive our negotiators of whatever trading advantage it might embody and that could be substantial. You have recommended registration with the United Nations in advance of tests and, in effect, we do this because we announce our tests in advance to the whole world. It was with this end in view, viz., to re-emphasize this fact that in the Bermuda Declaration in March we stated that we would register our intention to conduct tests with the United Nations in advance.[6]

I do want to assure you that my position is far from being inflexible—has indeed been a constant effort to find a way out of what has for so many years seemed an impasse. Meanwhile, our tests continue to develop very valuable information, not so much in the enhancement of the destructive power of atomic weapons as in civil effects tests to improve our protective measures in event of attack—in the development of warheads for missiles to be employed in defense against an airborne attack—and in the further development of the feature of cleanliness which, as of now at any rate, does not yet apply to weapons of small size and yield.[7]

It is a pleasure to find that our views are running concurrently and I hope that you will always feel free to let me know what is in your mind on this subject on which you are an authority.

With warm regard, *Sincerely*

[1] Lewis Strauss, Chairman of the Atomic Energy Commission and Special Assistant to the President, drafted this letter (Correspondence, Herbert L. Pankratz, Dwight D. Eisenhower Library, May 31, 1996, EP). For background on Cole, Congressman from New York and a leading Republican spokesman on atomic energy issues, see Galambos and van Ee, *The Middle Way*, no. 298.

[2] Cole had written of his "grave concern" over the "continuance of unlimited, unrestrained, uncontrolled, and even unreasonable testing of nuclear weapons." The tests already conducted by the United States had fulfilled security requirements, he wrote, and would only give the Soviets justification to continue their tests (WHCF/OF 108-A).

[3] For background on the 1954 castle tests see Galambos and van Ee, *The Middle Way*, no. 646, and Richard G. Hewlett and Jack M. Holl, *Atoms for Peace and War, 1953–1961* (Berkeley, 1989), pp. 168–82. Beginning in May 1956 the United States had conducted the redwing series of twelve nuclear tests at the Pacific Proving Ground. The first American airdrop of a multimegaton hydrogen bomb, which was part of the test series, had resulted in relatively minimum fallout over uninhabited areas (Galambos and van Ee, *The Middle Way*, no. 1968; and State, *Foreign Relations, 1955–1957*, vol. XX, *Regulation of Armaments; Atomic Energy*, pp. 292–93).

[4] Cole had told Eisenhower that the current plans of those government officials responsible for the testing program did not support the President's previously announced policy against testing weapons with yields greater than those already tested. He proposed that the United States record with the United Nations the time and place of all nuclear tests in advance of their occurrence and impose an annual limit on the total number and the megaton yield of all tests.

[5] On the London disarmament talks see no. 153.

[6] The declaration made at the conclusion of the Bermuda Conference is in State,

Foreign Relations, 1955–1957, vol. XXVII, *Western Europe and Canada,* pp. 740–42, 767.
[7] On U.S. policy regarding the testing of atomic weapons see Hewlett and Holl, *Atoms for Peace and War.*

172 — *EM, AWF, Administration Series*

To George Magoffin Humphrey — *May 27, 1957*

Dear George: Dr. Henry Wriston, ex-President of Brown University, is now head of The American Assembly, a project which I helped initiate while I was at Columbia University. The idea has developed splendidly since I left Columbia, and The American Assembly now enjoys in the United States a reputation in university, as well as thoughtful business circles, that is almost unique.[1]

Its fundamental concept is the selection every six months of one great problem of national interest to the United States. This subject is thoroughly and completely studied by university faculties (representing numbers of universities) and then a selected group of businessmen meet, in a three-day session, with the representatives of these faculties to go over the prepared studies and to reach conclusions which are published to other universities and in books. In addition, the results are always given to the members of the United States Government.[2]

Henry Wriston asked me to use whatever influence I might have with you to induce you—after resignation from your post, of which he has heard rumors—to become a member of The American Assembly Board.[3]

I think you know that I would not ask you to engage your time and interest in anything that I did not believe had great present and even greater potential value to the United States. The American Assembly is the only place in the country where any subject can be objectively studied, completely free of political bias, and where the findings are so representative of thoughtful opinion as to become authoritative in their field. The practical businessman and the professor are here given the chance to combine their experience and talents for the good of the whole country.

I do hope that when President Wriston approaches you on this matter, you will give it the most sympathetic consideration and accept his invitation if your other commitments will permit.[4]

I am writing to two other men with the identical request.[5]

With warm regard, *As ever*

[1] For background on the American Assembly, which Eisenhower had established in 1950, see Galambos and van Ee, *The Middle Way*, nos. 34 and 340; and Galambos, *Columbia University*, nos. 844, 953, and 987; on its influence and structure see *New York Times*, June 29, 1957, and April 6, 1958; for background on Wriston, who had been its executive director since August 1955, see Galambos and van Ee, *The Middle Way*, no. 674; Galambos, *Columbia University*, no. 254; and *New York Times*, August 29, 1955.
[2] The topics then under study encompassed a broad range of national and international issues: "International Stability and Progress: United States Interests and Instruments" (June 1957); "Atoms for Power: United States Policy in Atomic Energy Development" (Dec. 1957); "The United States and Africa" (June 1958); "United States Monetary Policy: Its Contribution to Prosperity without Inflation" (Dec. 1958). See also *New York Times*, April 6, 1958.
[3] Wriston had discussed potential trustees with the President during a White House visit on May 27, 1957 (Ann Whitman memorandum, May 27, 1957, AWF/AWD). On May 29 news of Humphrey's resignation would be made public (see no. 175, and *New York Times*, May 30, July 30, 1957).
[4] Humphrey would become a member of the Assembly's Board of Trustees in 1957.
[5] Eisenhower wrote similar letters to prospective Assembly board members Reuben B. Robertson, Jr., former Deputy Secretary of Defense (May 27, 1957, AWF/A); and Robert Winship Woodruff, chairman of the executive committee and director of the Coca-Cola Company (May 27, 1957, AWF/N).

173

EM, AWF, DDE Diaries Series

TO JOHN HAY WHITNEY
Personal

May 27, 1957

Dear Jock: In a six furlong race with, I think, a $5,000 purse, Banned ran first today, paying $13.40 and $6.40. As you well realize, I know nothing about race horses and have never made more than three or four bets in my life. But I felt that out of loyalty and respect for George and the Greentree Stables I should risk a small sum.[1] As a result I am $158 better off than I was before the race. That will pay a few caddy fees.

Incidentally, you ought to drop a note to George telling him that a great mistake was made and that the deal is no dice. You could provoke a scream that could be heard across the Atlantic.

Love to Betsey. *As ever*

[1] For background on Allen's purchase of the racehorse, "Banned," from Whitney see nos. 130 and 159.

174 *EM, WHCF, Official File 116-B*

TO LYNDON BAINES JOHNSON *May 28, 1957*

Dear Lyndon: I welcome your personal assurance of support of the International Atomic Energy Agency and the Mutual Security Program, as well as your forthright expression on their behalf on the Senate Floor. Both issues need every possible additional support—and I well know how essential yours is.[1]

As for the USIA—basically related, as it is, in many ways to the purpose of both MSA and IAEA—I am very disappointed that in this instance you found it desirable to reduce rather than to increase the pressure of our effort. You told me of the dissatisfaction with the USIA presentation before the Senate Committee on Appropriations; yet, it is still difficult for me to understand why this vital weapon in our arsenal would be blunted at this critical juncture in world affairs.[2]

Thanks again for your help on the other two important programs.[3] *Sincerely*

[1] For background on the International Atomic Energy Agency (IAEA) see Galambos and van Ee, *The Middle Way*, no. 667; State, *American Foreign Policy; Current Documents, 1957* (Washington, D.C., 1961), pp. 1371–78; and Hewlett and Holl, *Atoms for Peace and War*, pp. 308–10, 370–71. Eighty-one nations had signed the statute of the IAEA in October 1956, and Eisenhower had stressed its importance in his State of the Union message in January 1957. Conservative Republican senators, however, had mounted a campaign to oppose the agency, fearing the possibility of Chinese Communist participation, the shipment of nuclear material to the Soviet Union, and the development of atomic weapons in third-world countries. Senate Majority Leader Johnson had included in his May 23 letter to Eisenhower an excerpt from the *Congressional Record*, documenting his support for the Mutual Security Program and the IAEA, which he described as "one of the most imaginative but sound proposals in recent years." Johnson told Eisenhower that he had pledged to his constituents and to himself that he would support him "without hesitation" when he thought the President was right (same file as document; see also State, *Foreign Relations, 1955–1957*, vol. XX, *Regulation of Armaments; Atomic Energy*, pp. 497–98; *Public Papers of the Presidents: Eisenhower, 1957*, pp. 17–30; *Congressional Quarterly Almanac*, vol. XIII, *1957*, pp. 580–81; and Hewlett and Holl, *Atoms for Peace and War*, pp. 428–29; 432–35).

For background on the 1957 mutual security legislation see nos. 76 and 137; see also NSC meeting minutes, April 19, 1957, AWF/NSC and on previous foreign aid legislation, Galambos and van Ee, *The Middle Way*, nos. 1893 and 1901. Eisenhower had outlined his $3.9 billion foreign aid program on May 9 at a bipartisan meeting of congressional leaders and in a May 21 message to Congress. Johnson had told the Senate Foreign Relations Committee that the President's program was an important part of U.S. foreign policy, and he particularly supported the shift from direct grants to loan programs that would help other nations help themselves (Johnson to Eisenhower, May 23, 1957, same file as document; see also Memorandum of Discussion, May 9, 1958, AWF/D; *Public Papers of the Presidents: Eisenhower, 1957*, pp. 372–96; *Congressional Quarterly Almanac*, vol. XIII, *1957*, pp. 601–10; and Kaufman, *Trade and Aid*, pp. 108–12).

[2] The final version of the bill appropriating funds for the United States Information Agency had reduced Eisenhower's request by $31 million. On May 8 Arthur Larson, director of the USIA, had told the committee that the agency's "'awesome responsibilities' to offset Communist propaganda justified his request of more funds for additional personnel." At that time Johnson had told Larson that the USIA "wasted 'more money . . . than any agency I know of'" (*Congressional Quarterly Almanac*, vol. XIII, *1957*, pp. 697–99). At a meeting held as the Senate hearings concluded, Republican congressional leaders had told Eisenhower that Larson's inability to give the senators specific information regarding USIA programs was hurting the Administration's efforts. Johnson subsequently agreed to support restoration of the original USIA budget if the President and Secretary Dulles would agree to place the agency within the Department of State. Although Eisenhower had at first voiced some support for that proposal, he later accepted Dulles's stand against the merger (State, *Foreign Relations, 1955–1957*, vol. IX, *Foreign Economic Policy; Foreign Information Program*, pp. 587–89).

[3] The Senate would approve the atomic agency treaty on June 18, and Eisenhower would sign the bill on August 28. Although the foreign aid bill (signed on August 14) would authorize $625 million for the new Development Loan Fund, neither the authorization nor the appropriation would match Eisenhower's original requests (see no. 273).

Johnson would tell Eisenhower that he agreed that a strong information agency was vital and he was eager to increase the pressure. Nevertheless, he did not understand how increasing the allocation would change the way the USIA operated. "As the agency stands now," he said, "not only was it unable to justify the increase it asked for but it was unable to justify the money that it is currently using." The appropriation was as large as it was because of the hope that the agency would become part of the State Department "where Secretary Dulles could take a personal hand in its direction." Johnson told the President that the issue was not whether Congress supported the USIA but whether it supported the agency as it was being conducted. "And when some of our most internationally minded and responsible Senators tell me that even the Senate figure was too high for this agency, it is time for all of us to stop, look and listen" (Johnson to Eisenhower, June 3, 1957, same file as document). In his response, Eisenhower would tell Johnson that they "and perhaps one or two others should have a quiet visit to tie down whatever deficiencies exist that have persuaded Congress to keep this essential effort on short rations" (Eisenhower to Johnson, June 5, 1957, *ibid.*; see also Johnson to Eisenhower, June 6, 1957; and Harlow to Martin, July 8, 1957, *ibid.*). Eisenhower would discuss foreign aid appropriations with Johnson and other congressional leaders on August 12 and at a private breakfast meeting with the senator on August 26. In neither meeting, however, did they specifically discuss the USIA (see Ann Whitman memorandums, Aug. 12, 26, 1957, AWF/AWD; Memorandum for the Record, Aug. 14, 1957; and Memorandum of Appointment, Aug. 26, 1957, both in AWF/D). For more on the USIA controversy see no. 178).

To George Magoffin Humphrey *May 29, 1957*

Dear George: Although I have known for more than two years that your retirement from government service could not be indefinitely postponed, the actual receipt of your letter of resignation fills me with profound regret. Yet because of your personal situation, which I fully understand, I of course accept your decision.[1]

It would be idle to attempt expression of my feelings of gratitude for the extraordinary talents that, more than four years ago, you brought to the Treasury Department and for the loyal and tireless way in which you have, ever since, applied them to problems of the greatest import. It has been of real satisfaction to me that in working on these problems we have invariably found our conclusions and convictions to be practically identical.

I thank you further for allowing me to designate the actual date of your separation from the Federal service, with the commitment that such date will be no later than the close of the current Congressional session. There are a number of critical problems to be considered during this session and, until the bulk of these have been satisfactorily solved, I deeply believe that your experience and the confidence that you enjoy everywhere in government will be great assets in reaching the best answers. Consequently, the date you turn over your duties to your successor will, within the limits indicated, be dictated somewhat by circumstances.[2]

I share your satisfaction that Robert Anderson has been able to accept my nomination as the individual to take over your duties in the Treasury Department. I am sending his name to the Senate today. I agree with you that he will continue to follow the general path that you have so clearly marked out. So long as you must leave the post, I can think of no other to whom I would rather entrust the responsibilities of that office.[3]

Finally, I am grateful to you for your offer of future assistance to the Administration. From time to time I know we shall want to call upon you for advice and counsel, and have no doubt that such occasions will be of considerable frequency.

On the personal side, I cannot tell you what a sense of loss it is to Mamie and to me to know that you and Pam will shortly leave the intimate Cabinet family. But a friendship of the strength and depth of ours cannot suffer merely because of your departure from Washington.

With affectionate regard to you both, *As ever*

[1] Humphrey had written on May 28 (AWF/A) to tender his resignation as Secretary of the Treasury, "to be effective at the time which you determine will be best suited to the transfer of this office to my successor." The retirement of a former business

partner, Humphrey wrote, now made it imperative for him to resume the "responsibilities" he had left upon becoming Treasury Secretary.

[2] Humphrey had written that he would "be glad to continue to assist with Congressional consideration of the various items of the budget with particular reference to the Defense and Mutual Assistance programs which so vitally affect the security of our country, and with such other matters as are now pending in which I can be helpful." (For background see nos. 27, 90, 146, and 147.)

[3] Humphrey had endorsed Robert Bernerd Anderson (LL.B. University of Texas 1932) as his successor. Anderson, who had served as Secretary of the Navy (1953–1954), and Deputy Secretary of Defense (1954–1955), would be sworn in as Treasury Secretary on July 29, 1957 (see *New York Times*, May 30 and July 30, 1957; see also Galambos and van Ee, *The Middle Way*, no. 188).

176

EM, AWF, Administration Series, Summerfield Corr.

TO R. W. SUCHNER
Personal and confidential

May 31, 1957

Dear Mr. Suchner: Your letter is intensely interesting.[1] Before mentioning its substance, may I remark that I do not share your doubts about your own ability to express yourself. Consequently I shall put your name down on my list to invite, some day, to an evening at the White House. I should like to hear your views expressed to a group.[2]

You have discussed a factor affecting the Post Office Department which is at the very foundation of efficiency in any organization, large or small. That factor is morale. Without it an Army, for example, is worthless. With it an Army will unhesitatingly challenge a foe of far greater strength.

You do not say so in your letter, but you imply that morale is purely a function of pay.[3] If this is your assumption, I should like to make two observations. This does not agree with my experience in organizational work, extending back over the past half century. I do not minimize the importance of pay rates, but I do think that leadership throughout an organization, from its highest to its lowest echelon, is far more important.

My second observation is that in the statistical analyses dealing with the pay of government workers, including most of the postal groups, it appears that the over-all remuneration of these groups is higher than that received for comparable work in civil life. In making this statement I do include, of course, the continuity of employment, the rate of pay upon retirement from active service, ordinary and sick leave privileges, and such perquisites as opportunity for cheap insurance, as well as allowances for uniforms.[4]

In spite of these two observations, I by no means doubt the sincerity or even the accuracy of your conclusions. The only point I want to make is that possibly we must look elsewhere than merely to pay rates if we want to restore that great morale that you say declined rapidly in the Postal Service after 1937.

You are talking about a twenty-year period during which great and startling changes have come to the world. I have had businessmen come into my office and in describing their operations—some of them very large and some modest in size—they have made almost exactly the same statements about their companies that you make about the Postal Service. Possibly there has been a change coming over all of us—not merely those in the Postal Service. Maybe we are not sufficiently interested in doing "more than our share."

I agree with your further implication that if a man does not take pride and find joy in his work, then that work is mere drudgery. My question is—have we allowed this to happen to ourselves on almost a universal scale?

We have rules saying that if an individual works one minute beyond a fixed weekly schedule he must be on an over-time basis; other rules prohibit one individual from touching the type of work that belongs under the rules to another. We have possibly become more highly organized into pressure groups in the United States than ever before. As a consequence the farmer watches the city worker; the city worker resents the man in government service; and the man in government service resents the fact that his influence does not seem to be as great with the powers-that-be as that of some groups that he considers of far less importance. We watch each other with a suspicious eye rather than devoting ourselves completely to our own tasks in the confidence that all other Americans will do the same and thus as a single, united nation advance the interests of all of us, both at home and abroad.

These observations, even if true, have not necessarily any applicability to the specific situation you describe which, no matter what its cause, is serious. I shall give your letter to the Postmaster General in order that he may have both your account and your suggestions. I shall ask him eventually to give me his own impressions on the same subject.[5]

As you can imagine, I rarely have time to answer a letter at this length; but I have made the time to do so today because of my appreciation of the trouble you took to explain for me a matter in which of course, as President, I must be and I am deeply interested.

I do hope that we shall get to meet one day and I can hear more of your convictions.

With best wishes, *Sincerely*

[1] Suchner, a postal supervisor from Livonia, Michigan, had written Eisenhower on May 22 (AWF/D) to discuss low morale among postal workers. "The mail moves on a conveyor belt of human spirits," Suchner had written. Due to low morale, however, the "willingness to put forth the extra effort, the effort and spirit that is the oil of a good operating machine, is almost totally absent."

[2] Suchner said he had read that Eisenhower intended to invite ordinary citizens to one of his "stag" dinners. "I am not seeking an invitation because I am sure I would find it difficult to express myself in such company," Suchner had written. "However, if I was invited I would certainly try to tell you how I feel about one of your departments, the post office."

[3] The "only way" postal efficiency would be improved, Suchner believed, was "by creating a morale and spirit in the employees themselves so that once again they feel the desire to put forth that extra effort." "This feeling," he wrote, "can only be corrected by raising the level of the jobs back to where it was before the Second World War. That will cost money. But I sincerely feel it is costing more not to raise the level."

[4] Eisenhower may have been referring to a January 20, 1957, article in *The Washington Post and Times Herald* entitled "U.S. Workers Never Had It So Good," which Postmaster General Arthur E. Summerfield had sent him (Summerfield to Eisenhower, Jan. 24, 1957, AWF/A). The article stated that federal employees, after four years of the Eisenhower Administration, now had greater job security, higher salaries, more fringe benefits and greater future financial security than in any time in the past. Moreover, employee advances were not a "partisan political matter" but were supported by "Republicans and Democrats alike."

[5] The President would send Suchner's "highly interesting and intelligent" letter along with his reply to Summerfield on May 31 (Eisenhower to Summerfield, May 31, 1957, AWF/D). Summerfield would respond on June 10 (AWF/A), saying that he would be "delighted to write you my views and observations on this, one of the most troublesome and challenging problems of our Post Office Department." For developments see no. 248.

Civil Rights

JUNE 1957 TO SEPTEMBER 1957

3

“I am astonished and chagrined”

177

EM, AWF, DDE Diaries Series

To Christian Archibald Herter
Secret

June 1, 1957

Memorandum for the Under Secretary of State:[1] I send you herewith two documents. The first is a letter from our Ambassador in Britain giving some details of a conversation he had with the Prime Minister.[2]

The other is a copy of a draft of a letter that the Prime Minister is about to send to Bulganin.[3] I presume that this was sent with the thought that we might wish to send some comment, although as you see from Ambassador Caccia's note we would have very little time in which to do it.[4] On the other hand, Mr. Macmillan's draft does not seem to me to be of a character to call for any long analysis on our part, at least at this time. Do you not think that on Monday I might just send him a cable saying that I have received it, read it with great interest, agree with its general content, and believe that the whole thing is well presented.[5]

Please return the documents for my file.

[1] Secretary Dulles was vacationing on Duck Island in Lake Ontario.

[2] According to Ambassador Whitney, Macmillan had received the impression from Eisenhower's letter of May 10 (see no. 153) that the Soviet leaders might be ready to talk seriously about disarmament. If this were true, Macmillan told Whitney, discussions would not be successful at the conference level. They might succeed at the level of the heads of state, however, and the Prime Minister, who was interested in organizing such a meeting, wanted Eisenhower's opinion. According to Whitney, British leaders felt that since the Soviet economy was not doing well, the *de facto* Russian leader, Nikita Khrushchev, needed to increase his own prestige to the point where he would become "a figure of worshipful size. A meeting at the top level on this most dramatic of all issues would, of course, be a fine piece of personal promotion for him." Whitney concluded: "I guess that this is discussed with me because it is so tentative, and so fraught with wild hopes and bottomless traps that it is not the time to put anything on paper" (Whitney to Eisenhower, May 24, 1957, AWF/A). Whitney sent a copy of this letter to Secretary Dulles, who replied on June 5 that much preparatory work was necessary before such a meeting would be appropriate (State, *Foreign Relations, 1955–1957*, vol. XX, *Regulation of Armaments; Atomic Energy*, pp. 544–45). For Eisenhower's response to Whitney see no. 191.

[3] For background see no. 153.

[4] The British ambassador's note is not in AWF.

[5] Herter would agree and on this same day would send the President a suggested response (see no. 180).

178

EM, AWF, Dulles-Herter Series

To John Foster Dulles

Personal

June 3, 1957

Dear Foster: As you know, I have been emphasizing for some years my belief that the Voice of America is destroying a great deal of its own usefulness when it engages in the field of propaganda.[1] This is a function that I believe should be performed by other agencies, with the governmental connection concealed as often as may be possible.

I am firmly of the belief that the Voice of America ought to be known as a completely accurate dispenser of certain information. Emphasis should be placed on:

(*a*). Policies, pronouncements and purposes of the United States government;

(*b*). News of a character that has world interest and the dissemination of which can assist other peoples to understand better the aims and objectives of America and the progress of the world's ideological struggle.

I have heard it argued that some items of entertainment must be on the Voice of America in order to get people to listen. The Hungarian record shows that those people listen to the BBC rather than to the Voice of America because "the BBC provides us with more worldwide news."[2]

Because one of your responsibilities is to provide policy direction to the USIA, I should like for you to ponder this matter and issue such broad directives as may seem appropriate to you. Of course I have no objection to listening to contrary views. But I have been listening to them since 1950 and I am not yet convinced.[3] *As ever*

[1] For Eisenhower's previous statements regarding the role of the Voice of America, a division of the United States Information Agency, see Galambos and van Ee, *The Middle Way*, nos. 112 and 169. This letter was probably prompted by the conclusion of congressional debate on the 1958 budget for the USIA, resulting in a bill that cut Eisenhower's request for the agency by $48 million (*Congressional Quarterly Almanac*, vol. XIII, *1957*, pp. 697–700; see also Memorandum of Conversation, May 17, 1957, Dulles Papers, White House Memoranda Series).

[2] On April 24 the House Foreign Affairs Committee, Subcommittee on Europe, had compared the effectiveness of the Voice of America and the BBC during the Hungarian uprising of October 1956 (U.S. Congress, House Committee on Foreign Affairs, Subcommittee on Europe, *Hearings on Poland Aid Program and Eastern Europe*, 85th Cong., 1st sess., 1957, microfiche HFo-T.28).

[3] On June 27 Dulles would include this letter in one of his own to USIA Director Arthur Larson. The State Department had studied the President's letter, Dulles told Larson, and agreed that his suggestions would "achieve ever greater audience and credibility" for the Voice of America. He asked Larson how he could comply with the President's wishes. Larson replied that the problem was to suffuse a large orga-

nization such as the VOA "with a unified set of working ideas, particularly in view of the wide variety of backgrounds and convictions among the operating officials." Larson agreed to centralize the news desk and concentrate on output of news and policy rather than features and commentary.

Dulles would tell Eisenhower on August 9 that Larson had taken steps to provide the kind of credible broadcasting the President wanted. "Mr. Larson has provided for more emphasis on objective news broadcasts with particular attention to believability," Dulles wrote. "Features and music are dealt with as a means of retaining audiences so that our objectives can be achieved, not as ends in themselves" (State, *Foreign Relations, 1955–1957,* vol. IX, *Foreign Economic Policy; Foreign Information Program,* pp. 590–93).

179

EM, WHCF, President's Personal File 20-D

To Frank Owen Haywood Williams — *June 3, 1957*
Personal

Dear Mr. Williams: Of course I remember your visit to Paris in 1952, and again let me thank you for all you have done in the intervening years to support the policies for which this Administration stands.[1]

Your letter arrived on my desk coincidentally with a report from a former staff member who is now in Ohio. He is convinced, as you are, that the vast majority of the people of our country are solidly in favor of maintaining our defensive strength, despite the admittedly high costs.[2]

Incidentally, I feel that many of those who claim that they are following in the footsteps of the late Senator Taft are either unaware of his deepest convictions or are quite careless in their interpretation of his beliefs. During the last few weeks of his life he became one of my closest associates and collaborators in government, and I not only learned to respect him but found to my amazement that on many major issues he was far more of the so-called "liberal" than I was. I refer here particularly to an expansion of the public housing program and his advocacy of a general system of Federal aid to education.[3]

Thank you very much for the more than kind sentiments contained in your final paragraph.[4]

With best wishes, *Sincerely*

[1] Williams, a manager of Connecticut General Life Insurance Company, had been Eisenhower's Connecticut campaign finance chairman in 1952. Williams had visited Eisenhower in Paris in March of that year (for background see Galambos, *NATO and the Campaign of 1952,* no. 755). In a letter dated May 27, 1957, Williams had remi-

nisced about the meeting, which he termed "the most rewarding experience of my life" (same file as document). Williams said that he was "gr[i]eviously concerned over the apparent trend in the Republican party to a return to let us say, Taftism." He cautioned that if the conservatives who had opposed Eisenhower's nomination in 1952 should prevail, the Republican party would "go down to a defeat from which it will never recover. The security of this great nation," he wrote, "is far more important to those millions of citizens than what must be an insignificant cut in the budget or reduced taxes."

[2] For background see nos. 94 and 138.

[3] Republican Senator Robert Alphonso Taft had died in 1953; see Galambos and van Ee, *The Middle Way*, nos. 2 and 222. On Taft's support for federal aid to education see no. 196.

[4] Williams had written, "My prayers are with you and also an always increasing feeling of gratitude for the great sacrifices that you have made and are continuing to make as a citizen of our country."

180

EM, AWF, International Series: Macmillan

TO HAROLD MACMILLAN *June 3, 1957*

Cable. Confidential

Dear Harold:[1] Harold Caccia has been kind enough to pass to me the text of the reply you proposed to send to Bulganin's letter of April 20th.[2] I have read the text with great interest and find myself in general agreement with its content. I assume, as Harold suggests, that since Bulganin's references to the Middle East will be answered by our replies to the Soviet notes of April 19 to the three governments, you will not be able to send the letter until tripartite agreement on the replies has been reached.[3] I think you have presented matters very skillfully in the present draft.

I note that you have made your statement of policy on the China trade affair. While there was some unfavorable comment here in the States, both political and editorial, I am relieved to note that it has not caused the furor that could have taken place.[4] I have heard nothing yet of the reaction in the South East Asian countries.

With warm regard, *As ever*

[1] Eisenhower had approved Under Secretary of State Herter's draft of the first paragraph of this message and asked that the message be sent by cable (Herter to Eisenhower, June 1, 1957, AWF/D-H; see also no. 177).

[2] For background see no. 153.

[3] Noting his concern that "certain circles in Great Britain and in some other countries" were not considering the sovereign rights of the Arab states, Bulganin had asked that the great powers "strictly adhere to the principles of peaceful settlement" of all controversies in the area (AWF/I: Macmillan). On February 11 the Soviet

Union, in notes to the United States, Great Britain, and France, had proposed that those countries in cooperation with the Soviet Union renounce force in settling disputes in the Middle East, close all foreign bases in the area, and refuse to give arms to Middle Eastern countries. The U.S. reply, delivered on March 11, questioned the seriousness of purpose behind the proposals and stated that the United States would continue to work through the United Nations and would take measures at the request of the countries themselves, thus ensuring their sovereignty.

On April 19 the Soviet Union had repeated its request for a statement by the three governments condemning the use of force. In an answer delivered to the Soviets on June 11, the United States would maintain that the charter of the United Nations and the principles of U.S. foreign policy made such a statement unnecessary. The British and French governments would deliver replies on the same day. Macmillan would make an additional reply to Bulganin two days later (*U.S. Department of State Bulletin* 36, no. 927 [April 1, 1957] 523–26; *ibid.*, 37, no. 940 [July 1, 1957] 20–21; *New York Times*, Apr. 20, 21, June 16, 1957; and Macmillan, *Riding the Storm*, pp. 305–6).

[4] For background on the controversy over the China trade differential see nos. 161 and 168. In a May 29 statement Macmillan had explained the British decision, announced at the CHINCOM meeting in Paris, to eliminate some of the restrictions on trade with China in order to make them the same as those imposed on the Soviet Union. "As you realize, the commercial interests of our two countries in this area are not at all alike," Macmillan would write Eisenhower. "We live by exports—and by exports alone. So I feel that we cannot any longer maintain the existing differential between Russian and Chinese trade . . . " (State, *Foreign Relations, 1955–1957*, vol. X, *Foreign Aid and Economic Defense Policy*, pp. 467–68; and Macmillan, *Riding the Storm*, pp. 317–18).

181

EM, AWF, Name Series

To Wilton Burton Persons

June 3, 1957

Dear Jerry: I promised you a quotation from the Bible. This is the St. James' version of the 14th verse, Chapter 5, of Thessalonians:[1]

> "Now we exhort you, brethren, warn them that are unruly, comfort the feebleminded, support the weak, be patient toward all men."

You can see how I think it has a fine application to some of our problems.[2] *As ever*

[1] Wilton "Jerry" Persons, Deputy Presidential Assistant and Eisenhower's congressional liaison since 1953, had met several times with the President on the morning of that day. Eisenhower was using the King James version of the Bible.

[2] Eisenhower may have been referring to his conflict with Congress over the budget and foreign aid (see no. 183).

182 *EM, AWF, Dulles-Herter Series*

TO JOHN FOSTER DULLES *June 4, 1957*

Secret

Memorandum for the Secretary of State: Subject to such editing or minor change as you may deem desirable, please send the following cable to Harold Macmillan:

Dear Harold: I have just received your cable of June third and to say the least I am astonished and chagrined to learn of the developments you describe.[1] I have not even seen the final edited paper to which you refer, but I can assure you that there is no agreed-upon American position which is to be interpreted as a basis of negotiation with the Soviets.[2]

When Governor Stassen was here a number of meetings were held to fix upon clauses in a possible future agreement that would be acceptable to us provided they were satisfactory to our Allies and provided also that the entire negotiations took place in the certainty that adequate inspectional systems would be devised and established.[3]

I am particularly distressed to hear that the Russians saw even such a tentative sort of paper prior to full consultation with you and the French Government. The practice of the Western Powers has been, as you undoubtedly know, to discuss such views among themselves before presenting them to the Soviets.[4] I assure you that the cooperative spirit so obviously present at the Bermuda Conference is something that I regard as of the greatest value between our two countries and I shall do my best to preserve it and to live by it.[5] I might add that everybody here deplores this occurrence as deeply as I do.[6]

Foster will take steps to make certain that the correct status of the paper is understood by all and to insure that in the future our coordination with you will be as complete as we can make it. Unquestionably your Foreign Office will be hearing from Foster very soon in greater detail than I can employ in this cable.[7]

With warm regard,

If you think it better not to send even a tentative reply, please hold this up until evening when I will talk to you, but I am anxious that Harold know as quickly as possible that we did try to act in the spirit of our agreements at Bermuda.[8]

[1] On May 31 Harold Stassen, Special Assistant to the President and U.S. representative at the London disarmament negotiations, had given the Soviet delegation an informal thirty-five point memorandum that outlined a new U.S. disarmament proposal. The proposal, which had been developed at a White House meeting six days

earlier, was given to the Soviets without informing the British that this would be done. In his June 3 cable Macmillan, who complained that he had not been consulted in advance, called Stassen's "singularly inept" action one that allowed "the disarmament committee to develop a kind of life of its own without sufficient control from the Governments concerned." Describing disarmament as the greatest issue facing the world, he told Eisenhower that the matter was "one on which the freedom and survival of our island may depend: and, as we correspond on so many questions very freely, I would have hoped that we could have examined together the possible consequences of these proposals before they were put forward. I would not be straight with you," he added, "if I tried to disguise a certain feeling of distress that we were not told in advance that this document was to be given to the Russians" (PREM 11/[2186]; State, *Foreign Relations, 1955–1957*, vol. XX, *Regulation of Armaments; Atomic Energy*, pp. 572–90; and Macmillan, *Riding the Storm*, pp. 301–2; for background on the disarmament negotiations see no. 153).

The final version of this message to the British Prime Minister (see AWF/I: Macmillan) bears significant changes from Eisenhower's original draft as printed above. Later this same day it was cabled to U.S. Ambassador Whitney for delivery to Macmillan, but Whitney suggested in a telephone conversation with Dulles on the following day that the words "astonished" and "chagrined" should be changed. Eisenhower said that he did not mind "toning it down" by using the word "disappointed" as long as Macmillan knew "we can't forget what was said in Bermuda" (Memorandum of Conversation, June 4, 1957, Dulles Papers, White House Memoranda Series; and Telephone conversation, Eisenhower and Dulles, June 5, 1957, Dulles Papers, Telephone Conversations). See n. 8 for Eisenhower's discussion with Dulles regarding additional changes to the original draft.

[2] Dulles eliminated this sentence from the final outgoing cable and substituted a new sentence: "They took place without the knowledge or authorization of any of us here in Washington."

[3] Stassen had presented his proposals for a limited disarmament agreement to Administration officials on May 17. After a meeting with Eisenhower on the twenty-fifth, Dulles and Stassen had agreed that the latter would consult with the Western powers in an effort to reach a consensus on procedures before presenting the proposals to the Soviet delegation. Five days later Under Secretary of State Herter had cabled Stassen in London, asking him to submit promptly to the State Department the proposal incorporating the revisions agreed upon at the May 25 White House meeting. "[The] President expects this to be agreed by interested agencies here," Herter said, "and then submitted to him before you undertake detailed negotiations based on the revised policy." Stassen had sent the revised proposal to Secretary Dulles on May 31; Eisenhower would not see it, however, until June 8. Stassen would later tell Herter that the British, French, and Canadians had been "thoroughly consulted on the outlines of the new U.S. position" (State, *Foreign Relations, 1955–1957*, vol. XX, *Regulation of Armaments; Atomic Energy*, pp. 504–58, 565–85, 611–15, 620–26; see also NSC meeting minutes, May 24, 1957, AWF/NSC).

At this point in the final version of this message the following new sentences were added: "We had assumed that these positions would not be conveyed to the Russians as a statement of the United States position before they had been fully discussed with you and the French Government and with NATO. Also of course the Federal Republic of Germany is deeply interested in some of the possible implications of this disarmament matter" (For West German concerns see no. 186.).

[4] A single sentence replaced the preceding two sentences in this paragraph: "I am particularly distressed that matters have not gone ahead along this line and if the Russians have been informed on at least an 'informal memorandum' basis prior to the allied consultations which we have envisaged."

[5] On the Bermuda Conference see no. 78.

[6] This sentence was deleted from the final cable. (See Telephone conversations, Dulles and Quarles, June 4, 1957, Dulles Papers, Telephone Conversations).
[7] The preceding paragraph was modified slightly, and a new one was added: "I realize that once the Soviets have a piece of paper in their hands from the Head of the United States Delegation, it puts you and our other allies in an awkward position, one that is not easy to redress, but we shall do the best that we can."

In the first of two cables to Stassen later on this same day, Dulles would tell the negotiator that he had exceeded his authority "both as to substance and procedure." Dulles's second cable, drafted by Eisenhower, read: "You will notify Mr. Zorin [Valerian A. Zorin, head of the Soviet delegation] at the earliest possible moment that the memorandum you submitted to him was not only informal and unofficial, but had no approval in its submitted form either by the President or the State Department, and that there are some aspects of the memorandum to which this government cannot agree at this moment. Therefore, you will request that Mr. Zorin return the memorandum." Admitting that Stassen's "indiscretion" had taken the Administration "by surprise," Dulles would inform Macmillan of his reprimand by telephone on the same day (Dulles to Stassen, June 4, 1957, AWF/D-H; State, *Foreign Relations, 1955–1957,* vol. XX, *Regulation of Armaments; Atomic Energy,* pp. 595–97; see also Telephone conversation, Eisenhower and Dulles, June 5, 1957, Dulles Papers, Telephone Conversations and AWF/D).
[8] After receiving Macmillan's cable, Eisenhower had asked Ann Whitman to contact Under Secretary Herter with the message: "Again we seem to be working at cross purposes with our British friends. I am getting completely frustrated with these things" (Note for Files, June 4, 1957, AWF/A). Dulles would tell Eisenhower that he did not think they "could go quite as far in disavowing Stassen as the President's draft suggested." Such a repudiation could weaken Stassen's authority, Dulles said, and the Soviets "conceivably might use the disavowal as an excuse for breaking up the [disarmament] talks." Eisenhower approved Dulles's draft, which was sent to Macmillan through the American embassy (Memorandum of Conversation, June 4, 1957, Dulles Papers, White House Memoranda Series).

For developments see nos. 191 and 205.

183

EM, WHCF, President's Personal File 109

To Fred M. Manning, Sr.

Personal

June 5, 1957

Dear Fred:[1] Just a few minutes ago I had a call from your friend and physician, Dr. Smart. I found him very interesting, and I was particularly intrigued by his account of all he has been able to accomplish in the research laboratory you and some of your friends established there in Southern California.[2] I cannot help believing that its future possibilities are very great and I have no doubt that he will get the kind of support he needs. I congratulate you on playing such a prominent part in establishing the institution.

Of course he gave me the news of you and Hazel.[3] Incidentally

I want to tell you that the album you had prepared a few years ago of pictures of your home is a most intriguing thing. I have gone through it dozens of times. I often wish that I could see it—and the both of you.[4]

These are crowded days here in Washington. With a Congress where the opposition has a majority of votes and with so many members never for one single moment forgetting partisan politics, it is difficult indeed to get enacted into law even the simplest and most necessary proposals. So far as the domestic field is concerned, it is almost futile to attempt any logical reduction in the amounts of money spent by the Federal Government.[5] This is because some group or section either profits, or believes it profits, from these expenditures. Consequently, you will find on every domestic proposal certain groups almost violently in favor—and a certain predisposition on the part of other Congressmen not to disagree because they know too well that eventually they will want reciprocal votes.[6]

And the difficulties on the foreign aid programs you know about. There is little I can add to my many public statements on the subject. To me the issue is so clear that I find it hard to have to repeat, over and over again, the arguments that are so vital and compelling.[7]

All in all I find at the end of most days I have nothing but a feeling of great frustration. Incidentally tomorrow morning I leave early for a 36-hour change of pace. I know I shall enjoy the visit to the SARATOGA; it does me particular good to meet the young men who serve on the frontline of our country's defense.[8]

Again let me tell you how much I appreciated the opportunity to talk to Dr. Smart.

With affectionate regard to you and Hazel, *As ever*

[1] Manning was a wealthy oil man who founded an oil-drilling company in Fort Worth, Texas, in the 1920s. He suffered from emphysema and had moved to Rancho Santa Fe, California, to regain his health (for background see *Eisenhower Papers*, vols. X–XVII).

[2] Reginald H. Smart, whose visit with the President had been arranged by Ann Whitman, headed the medical research laboratory (see Whitman to Manning, May 25, 1957, and Manning to Whitman, June 10, 1957, same file as document; and Ann Whitman memorandum, June 5, 1957, AWF/AWD). Smart had discussed Manning's health with Eisenhower and he would write Whitman on June 20 that his account of their meeting had "given Fred a tremendous boost" (same file as document).

[3] Hazel was Manning's wife.

[4] In a letter of June 27, addressed to Whitman, Manning would invite Eisenhower and his staff to Rancho Santa Fe. He would also send, under separate cover, a photograph album, and maps of the area (*ibid.*).

[5] On Eisenhower's political concerns see no. 169; on the budget debate see no. 138.

[6] For Eisenhower's assessment of special interest groups see no. 248.

[7] See, for example, no. 163.

[8] On the aircraft carrier *Saratoga*, Eisenhower would observe demonstrations of naval weapons systems (see no. 188).

To Virginia Stuart Waller Davis *June 5, 1957*
Personal

Dear Mrs. Davis: I have kept your letter to one side since its receipt, in the hope that I could answer at leisure your comments.[1] But the time I had hoped for did not materialize and, since I am leaving early tomorrow morning on a two-day visit to the aircraft carrier SARATOGA, the least I can do is to send you this note of acknowledgement.[2]

However, let me assure you that no conversation of mine—in spite of piecemeal remarks obviously overheard by reporters—was ever meant to disparage the reputation of General Stuart for gallantry, courage and resourcefulness. The most I meant was that for the critical days of late June '63 the Confederate Army necessarily operated at a disadvantage because of lack of information.

Thank you for reminding me of our meeting at the home of Dr. Douglas Freeman some years ago. (Incidentally, that picture taken with Admiral Nimitz has occasionally plagued me, as you suspected.)[3] I am particularly grateful to you for enclosing in your letter the excerpts from letters sent to General Stuart just prior to the Battle of Gettysburg.[4]

With best wishes, *Sincerely*

[1] Mrs. Davis, of Alexandria, Virginia, was the granddaughter of Confederate cavalry leader James Ewell Brown ("Jeb") Stuart, a Major General in the Army of Northern Virginia. She had written to the President on May 15 about his alleged statements regarding Stuart's role in the Gettysburg campaign (WHCF/PPF 1-CC-2). On May 12 Eisenhower and Field Marshal Montgomery had inspected the Gettysburg battlefield (see no. 145). Throughout the tour, Montgomery criticized the commanding generals, and Eisenhower reportedly said that Stuart's forays had kept him out of touch with the Army of Northern Virginia and thus had deprived Confederate General Robert E. Lee of knowledge of the enemy's movements. Newspapers around the country had commented on these remarks (see LaFantasie, "Monty and Ike," p. 71, and *New York Times*, May 8, 11, 12, 13, 1957).

[2] On the President's first-hand observation of naval power see no. 188.

[3] In 1946 Eisenhower received an honorary degree from the University of Richmond. Mrs. Davis had attended a luncheon for Eisenhower hosted by Douglas Southall Freeman, Civil War historian and president of the board of trustees of the university. Admiral Chester William Nimitz—the World War II Pacific commander who was then serving as special assistant to the Secretary of the Navy and chairman of the presidential commission on internal security and individual rights—also received an honorary degree that day (see Galambos, *Chief of Staff*, no. 736). "You may recall," Mrs. Davis had written, "I suggested that the Mint Julep which you held might best be placed behind your back while being photographed . . . just in case some day you might be President!"

[4] The four letters, dated June 22, 23, 24, 1863, contained orders to seek and communicate information about the Union Army (WHCF/PPF 1-CC-2).

185

EM, AWF, Gettysburg Series

To Daniel Charles Gainey

June 5, 1957

Dear Mr. Gainey: For a month or so I have wanted to write you about Galila. We have completed the facilities at the farm for housing and pasturing her, and we could take care of her any time that it would be convenient for you to send her along.[1] On the other hand, it may be that she is at some particularly critical stage in her training, and if you think it would be better to keep her for a few weeks I would, of course, defer to your judgment. But I did want to tell you that we are ready at any time to take her over.

I would be delighted to arrange with some trucking company to call at your farm to accomplish the transfer. Or it would be even more convenient for me if you would make the arrangements you deem best and tell the trucker (or the railway) to send the bill directly to me.[2]

At the same time, I am wondering if there are any special details to observe in the handling of Arabs. I have found that different breeds of horses require different types of handling and I would, of course, be most appreciative if you could tell me any special procedures we should follow with regard to Galila.[3] Incidentally, I have observed closely the men who stay at the farm. They handle the stock quietly and very efficiently. They do not, however, have as much opportunity for exercising the animals as one would wish.

If you will give me your thinking on all these things, I will of course conform.[4]

With warm regard, *Sincerely*

[1] Gainey, a business executive from Owatonna, Minnesota, was vice-president of the Arabian Horse Club Registry. He had offered the Arabian filly to Eisenhower in August 1955. At that time Gainey agreed to keep the horse until Eisenhower's farm was ready to receive her (see Galambos and van Ee, *The Middle Way*, no. 1749).

[2] In his June 10 reply Gainey would suggest that one of his men accompany the filly in order to acquaint her with Eisenhower's personnel. He said that he would send typewritten feeding instructions.

[3] "There is really nothing about an Arabian that differs much from just a good mustang," Gainey wrote (June 10). "They are rugged, adaptable, and, particularly fillies, very lovable."

[4] Within a few days of this letter, the filly would suffer injuries in an accident (Whitman to Nevins, June 13, 1957, and Nevins to Whitman, June 17, 1957). On June 13 Gainey would tell the President of the mishap and would offer to train another filly in the coming year (see Eisenhower to Gainey, June 15, 1957). All correspondence is in AWF/Gettysburg.

186 *EM, AWF, International Series: Adenauer*

To Konrad Adenauer *June 6, 1957*
Cable. Confidential

My dear Mr. Chancellor: I much appreciate your thoughtful message of May 30. It gave me great personal pleasure to have you here.[1]

I think it was a particularly useful time for our discussions. I fully share your conviction that our work together has served to emphasize again the closeness of our aims and to advance our common purpose of establishing peace and freedom in the world.[2]

Permit me to take this opportunity of repeating my assurance given to you in Washington that it is our purpose not repeat not to make to other countries governmental proposals involving Germany on which we have not first consulted your government.

We shall seek better assurances of coordination, which will avoid the risk of unintentional lapses.[3] *Sincerely*

[1] After Adenauer had visited Washington, D.C., and Eisenhower's Gettysburg farm (May 24–29), he had sent the President a telegram expressing his appreciation. Secretary of State Dulles forwarded a translation of the German leader's message, adding that "While there is no requirement of protocol that a routine message of thanks following a visit demands a response, I think it would be appropriate and desirable to reply in this case." State Department officials drafted this response (Dulles to Eisenhower, June 5, 1957, AWF/I: Adenauer).

[2] Among the issues officials of both governments discussed were the reunification of Germany and its relation to disarmament decisions; the nuclear and conventional capabilities of NATO; the buildup of West German defense forces; the status of German assets in the United States; European integration; and support costs for U.S. troops in Germany (State, *Foreign Relations, 1955–1957*, vol. XXVI, *Central and Southeastern Europe*, pp. 249–95; see also nos. 114 and 134 for background).

[3] Eisenhower added in handwriting the substance of this paragraph at the bottom of the State Department draft. The West German leader had expressed concern that the United States, without consulting Germany, would initiate disarmament agreements that would adversely affect German reunification. Eisenhower had told Adenauer that the United States did not intend to take action involving one of its allies without that country's consent. "It would not only be discourteous to do so; it would be foolish" (State, *Foreign Relations, 1955–1957*, vol. XXVI, *Central and Southeastern Europe*, pp. 247, 250, 267, 282).

187 *EM, AWF, Name Series*

To Henry Agard Wallace *June 8, 1957*
Personal

Dear Mr. Wallace: Thank you very much for your letter of June first. The point of view you express is one in which I have had a longstanding interest. I need hardly tell you, I am sure, that the major energies of myself and my associates are being directed to attaining the goal you point out as so necessary—a stopping of the useless and futile race involving the continuing stockpiling of nuclear weapons which, in the hands of China as well as some other nations, are hardly conducive to continuing peace.[1]

Likewise the purpose of creating divisive rather than unifying influences between China and the Soviets is obviously a correct one. The problem is to discover ways of doing this without weakening our own ties with numerous allies—particularly in the Far East.[2]

With warm regard, *Sincerely*

[1] Former Vice-President Wallace had written Eisenhower on June 1, 1957 (AWF/N). Enclosing a *New York Times* editorial in which C. L. Sulzberger argued that the United States should be prepared to explore a Russian suggestion for halting the spread of atomic weapons, Wallace observed that "the thought of China equipped with hydrogen bombs is so frightening that I cannot forebear writing to you" (see C. L. Sulzberger, "Logic, Love and American Understanding of China," *New York Times*, May 29, 1957). For more on Eisenhower's position on nuclear non-proliferation and efforts to reduce nuclear arsenals see Galambos and van Ee, *The Middle Way*, nos. 395, 598, 1765, 1937, and 1968. See also Hewlett and Holl, *Atoms for Peace and War*, pp. 326–402. White House Chief of Staff Sherman Adams helped draft the first paragraph of this letter for Eisenhower.

[2] Wallace had also enclosed an article from *Harper's Magazine* which argued that in light of "potential grounds of disunity between Russia and China," the United States should change its China policy (George Steiner, "A Better Way To Deal with China," *Harper's*, June 1957, pp. 34–40). "Thinking realistically and not emotionally," Wallace wrote, the United States "should not try indefinitely to push Russia and China together when there are so many natural geographic and historical forces tending to drive them apart." Wallace added: "It will take China many years to reach her potential and when she does she will probably be more frightening to Russia even than to us." As early as 1953, Eisenhower and Secretary of State Dulles had already raised the possibility of promoting a split between China and the Soviet Union (U.S. Department of State, *Foreign Relations of the United States, 1952–1954*, 16 vols., Washington, D.C., 1979–89, vol. XIV, *China and Japan*, pt. 1 [1985], pp. 278–306; see also U.S. Department of State, *Foreign Relations of the United States, 1955–1957*, vol. III, *China* [1986], pp. 245–48, 502–3; and vol. XIX, *National Security Policy*, pp. 517–19; and Gordon H. Chang, *Friends and Enemies: The United States, China, and the Soviet Union, 1948–1972* [Stanford, 1990], pp. 81–202).

188

EM, AWF, International Series: Macmillan

To Harold Macmillan
Cable. Secret

June 8, 1957

Dear Harold: I have just returned to my desk after a brief sea voyage and I find your message in regard to the visit of Queen Elizabeth to this country.[1] I am so pleased to learn that she will be able to come, and I need hardly tell you how much we are looking forward to welcoming her here.

As you suggested, I am sending the formal invitation by telegram for delivery at the Palace by Ambassador Whitney. It should reach the Queen shortly after you receive this message.[2]

The dates you propose for the visit (October 16–21) are entirely satisfactory but I can not hide my disappointment over its shortness. All of us had sincerely hoped that Her Majesty could stay for as long as ten days. With a visit of such duration it might have been possible for Her Majesty to make a tour of the West, which I think would give her as much pleasure as it would Americans in that part of the country. Nevertheless, I appreciate the heavy demands upon the Queen's time and will not press you any further on this score.

Regarding the public announcement of the visit, our releases usually take the following form:

> "The President of the United States announced today that Her Majesty, Queen Elizabeth II, has accepted the President's invitation to visit the United States. Her Majesty, accompanied by the Prince Philip, Duke of Edinburgh, will begin her visit at Jamestown, Virginia, on October 16, followed by a three-day visit to Washington."[3]

I look upon the visit of Queen Elizabeth and Prince Philip as a very significant event in Anglo-American relations and realize that it affords an excellent opportunity to demonstrate to all peoples the close and natural ties which exist between our two countries.[4] *Sincerely*

[1] The President had been aboard the aircraft carrier *Saratoga* for a two-day cruise to observe demonstrations of naval weapons (*New York Times,* June 7, 8, 1957). We have been unable to find Macmillan's message in AWF.

[2] The formal invitation of this same date is in AWF/D. On June 12 the Queen would thank the President and add: "We keenly look forward to visiting . . . and to renewing our acquaintance with your great country" (AWF/I: Queen Elizabeth II).

[3] On the public announcements in Great Britain and the United States see *New York Times,* June 2, 10, 1957, respectively. The Queen and Prince Philip would also visit New York City (see AWF/I: Queen Elizabeth II; and *New York Times,* June 2, 10, Aug. 7, 11, 1957).

[4] For developments see no. 395.

TO CHARLES DOUGLAS JACKSON *June 8, 1957*

Dear C. D.: Before I ever had a chance to acknowledge the draft speech you sent me, I incorporated, as you know, the idea about the Party Platform in the talk I made yesterday to the members of the Republican National Committee. From all I can detect, it made sense to the listeners and even to the newspaper men. I am grateful to you and to Bill for stressing the point for me.[1]

I am not so sure I can incorporate anything about being a "lame duck" President in a speech (actually I quarrel with the term as applied to a President in his second term). But I do think I can get in a few licks sometime or other during a press conference.[2]

I shall mull over your suggestions further when I have a little time; meantime, warm thanks and, as always, personal regard. *Sincerely*

[1] On May 31, 1957, Jackson had forwarded a draft of a speech he thought Eisenhower might use (AWF/A). Saying that he had "picked up the germ of an idea" in a conversation with Eisenhower's friend, and Coca-Cola Company President William Robinson, Jackson had drafted a speech entitled "Platforms, Programs and Politics." Eisenhower had used Jackson's suggestion that he demonstrate a "linkage between the platform promise and Executive action" in his June 7 address to the Republican National Conference (see *Public Papers of the Presidents: Eisenhower, 1957*, pp. 447–58 and *New York Times*, June 8, 1957). The President had enumerated Republican party principles in areas such as agriculture, education, and foreign policy and had outlined the federal actions that were in accordance with these principles.

[2] Jackson had suggested that Eisenhower state that the Twenty-second amendment to the Constitution had not been passed in order to create a "lame duck" presidency: "To my mind, it is inconceivable that either the voters, or the legislators, would have deliberately created a political situation in which automatically the second term of every President of the United States, from now on and forevermore, should become a political nullity, that the delicate balance between the Executive and the Legislative should be deliberately thrown out of balance every other four years, that the effective relationship between the leader of either of our great political parties and his Party should be emasculated as part of the ordered nature of things political." In an August 7 news conference the President would respond to a question about the effect the "lame-duck" presidency was having on the Administration's record in Congress. Eisenhower would reply that he had "not noticed any effect of the so-called 'lame duck.' Maybe later in the term that might be noticeable. To me it is not now," he said (*ibid.*, p. 591).

To Milton Stover Eisenhower *June 8, 1957*

Dear Milton: Even were it possible for me tentatively to accept the invitation to throw out the football at the opening game of the professional football season, my attendance at the game would violate one unbreakable rule I have set for myself during my term in office. That rule is that I go to no athletic events of any kind on Sunday. The reason for this is simple and it does not involve any attitude of disapproval towards such contests on that particular day. It is merely that so many people in this country believe that this kind of activity on the Sabbath Day is a violation of the practices prescribed by religion; I avoid a lot of additional correspondence and laborious explanation by sticking to the limitation I have imposed upon myself in this regard.[1]

I realize that you cannot explain all of this to your friends in Baltimore. I suggest that you merely say that Mrs. Eisenhower and I have plans for that period that will undoubtedly prevent our attendance.

I am glad you told me about your September seventh engagement because, so far as I can remember, Mamie has not mentioned it to me. If Congress does not leave the city before the middle of August, Mamie and I would normally be at *some* vacation spot in early September. However, since Mamie does not want to go to Denver and every other site we consider has definite drawbacks, we may end up spending the summer between here and Gettysburg. If that is the case, it should be easy enough to come over to visit you on that day.[2]

New Subject. I have just signed a letter to the President of Mexico, to accompany the gift that you are taking him from me.[3] Do your best to squelch any thought that President Cortines should send a present to *me*. Apparently the State Department felt the value of your visit would be enhanced by some small personal gift to him, but I would merely be embarrassed if he should attempt to return it.

On the other hand, if he should decide to give you something—I would hope of sentimental rather than intrinsic value, like a decoration or something of that sort—I would consider that a nice gesture.[4] *As ever*

[1] Milton had explained in a letter of June 6 that the president of the Baltimore Colts had called on Milton to invite the President to throw out the football at the Baltimore Colt-Detroit Lion game on September 29. Anticipating the President's reasons for declining, Milton had offered to compromise by inviting the President to attend the game as his guest (AWF/N).

[2] Milton had asked the President and Mrs. Eisenhower to a September 7 reception at his home to mark the opening event of his daughter Ruth's debut. As it turned out, the President and Mrs. Eisenhower would vacation in Newport, Rhode Island,

from September 4 to 30. The President would, however, return to Washington on September 7 in order to attend Ruth's reception in Baltimore (see *New York Times*, Sept. 8, 1957).

[3] The President's letter to President Adolfo Ruiz Cortines is in AWF/I: Mexico. Milton would make the goodwill trip in early August (the 4th through the 11th; for background see Galambos and van Ee, *The Middle Way*, no. 1129). Ruiz Cortines would reply on August 6 (AWF/I: Cortines), thanking the President for the letter and gift. For developments see no. 239.

[4] On the exchange of gifts see no. 284.

191

EM, AWF, DDE Diaries Series

To John Hay Whitney
Secret

June 11, 1957

Dear Jock:[1] I have not had an opportunity to answer your fine letter of May twenty-fourth, even though several of us have studied it carefully in our consideration of the whole business of disarmament.[2] I was particularly glad that Macmillan called you in to talk the thing over on a preliminary basis. Such a practice is exactly in line with the hope both sides expressed in Bermuda that such matters would be discussed between us before being exposed to the world.[3]

About a week after you wrote your letter, I had one from Harold Macmillan, who was protesting very bitterly an action of Stassen in presenting a tentative paper of his own to the Russian representative on disarmament before coordinating it fully with the British, the French and the Germans.

So far as I was concerned, I was wholly on Harold Macmillan's side—in fact, I was more than angry. I dictated a telegram to Harold Macmillan which expressed my feelings in no uncertain terms. Foster toned it down and later called me to say that you had telephoned upon receipt of the message urging that it not be delivered to Harold Macmillan until further softening because of the lessening of the furor about the incident itself.[4]

My last few days have been terribly full, complicated by a day of illness yesterday, and I have not had time to catch up with all the loose ends attached to the incident.[5] Stassen is here for conversations and I assume has had some serious ones at the State Department. Nevertheless, it is going to be hard for me to forgive a man for what I believe to be, at this moment, one of the most stupid things that anyone on a diplomatic mission could possibly commit. I shall, of course, not close my mind completely, because I have not heard the other side of the story, but on the face of things it looks like he was more than clumsy.[6]

So far as the meeting at the top level is concerned, such a proposition always presents to me a very special and difficult problem.[7] As President, I have Constitutional duties which cannot be delegated. I must perform them or there would be varying degrees of chaos in a number of activities. I personally believe that any so-called "Summit" meeting should be preceded by one between the Foreign Secretaries, who would prepare the way for some success at the later one. To have a meeting of the Heads of Government (in my case also the Head of State), and to go back to the world with no more specific accomplishment than followed the Geneva meeting, would in my opinion sound the death knell of much of the stirring hope that is discernible in the world.[8]

The trouble with a Foreign Ministers' meeting is that none of the other three has the same confidence of his Government as does Foster Dulles. Selwyn Lloyd, Pineau and Gromyko are not in his class.[9] Consequently, there would be grave doubt that this group would have adequate authority to settle such questions as the agenda for the Summit meeting and to work out certain international arrangements that would later be agreed upon, with every confidence on all sides that such arrangements would be honored.

Of course this letter is not to be used as a special basis for any further discussion between yourself and Harold or Selwyn Lloyd. However, in the event such a conversation does occur with Harold, you might ask, for your own information, a few questions that would tend to bring out his thinking about the questions I have raised.

Give my love to Betsey—and warm regard to yourself, *As ever*

P.S. I delivered your letter to George, who looked puzzled and bewildered for a few moments and then said, "Oh, he's just kidding me because I told him all the horse needed was a change of ownership." Incidentally, Banned ran way out of the money yesterday, something like sixth I believe. Apropos of this, George Allen just this minute called Mrs. Whitman from New York, saying, "I recommend the President recall that fellow Whitney."[10]

1 Eisenhower sent a draft of this letter to Secretary Dulles, who suggested only minor changes to this final version (Eisenhower to Dulles, June 11, 1957, AWF/D-H; and State, *Foreign Relations, 1955–1957*, vol. XX, *Regulation of Armaments; Atomic Energy*, p. 616).

2 For the substance of Ambassador Whitney's letter, in which he had recounted British Prime Minister Macmillan's views regarding disarmament negotiations, see no. 177.

3 On the March conference between Eisenhower and Macmillan see no. 78.

4 On the Stassen incident, Eisenhower's cable to Macmillan, and the reactions of Dulles and Whitney see no. 182.

5 Eisenhower had suffered an attack of indigestion that had confined him to bed (see no. 198 and Ann Whitman memorandum, June 10, 1957, AWF/AWD).

6 Arriving from London on June 8, Stassen had told Under Secretary Herter that the United Kingdom and the other Western delegations "had been consulted on all

points in the informal talking memorandum before it was read to the Soviet delegation" (State, *Foreign Relations, 1955–1957*, vol. XX, *Regulation of Armaments; Atomic Energy*, pp. 613–15).

Before meeting with Stassen later this same day, Dulles would tell Eisenhower that they should have Stassen "surrounded by some dependable person" who would make sure that he would not "go off on his own in the future" (Memorandum of Telephone Conversation, June 11, 1957, Dulles Papers, White House Memoranda Series).

Stassen had "appeared very humble and contrite," Dulles would tell Eisenhower. The President suggested that Dulles tell "interested people" that the impulsive Stassen had reformed his ways (State, *Foreign Relations, 1955–1957*, vol. XX, *Regulation of Armaments; Atomic Energy*, p. 618).

[7] Eisenhower is referring to Macmillan's interest in a summit meeting on disarmament, a subject Whitney had discussed in his May 24 letter to the President.

[8] On the July 1955 summit in Geneva see Galambos and van Ee, *The Middle Way*, no. 1523. In many countries, the head of state (the Queen of England, for example) is different from the head of government (the prime minister in that case). In the United States, as Eisenhower noted, these two roles are combined.

[9] Christian Pineau had been French Minister of Foreign Affairs since 1955. Andrei Andreevich Gromyko had been Soviet Minister of Foreign Affairs since 1953.

[10] See no. 173 for background on Whitney's sale of a race horse to George Allen.

192

EM, AWF, Administration Series

To Bernard Mannes Baruch — *June 11, 1957*

Personal

Dear Bernie: Thank you for your letter. Only the other day I mentioned to a friend that it had been far too long since I had heard from you.[1]

I agree with you that an opportunity should be sought to point out that the Soviet Union had a wonderful chance in 1947 (or was it '46?) to banish forever the danger of fall-out and atomic war.

I think the plan that you presented at that time was a model of decency and generosity on the part of a great nation, and their refusal to accept was nothing more or less than their great fear of strangers inside their country.[2] The Soviets fear strangers both because of what they will learn and what the Russian people will learn from them.

In the same way, we are now hearing a so-called "new" plan for breaking down the Iron Curtain by an exchange of broadcasts and increase of "contacts." This suggestion has received a great deal of favorable editorial comment.[3]

Possibly we are just a forgetful people, but only in 1955 I went to Geneva and, aside from the so-called "open skies" proposal, the biggest point I tried to put over was an exchange of broadcasts and an increase of two-way tourism. Foster, in October of the same year, specifically recommended that we have weekly half-hour radio broadcasts, one by an American to the Russian people, the other by a Russian to the American people. The proposal was turned down by the Soviets.[4]

Many people fail to see the difference between a society subject to the dictatorial orders of a centralized government and one in which a commercial broadcasting company has the right without hindrance to put on the air any individual that it might select. Such a company has no responsibility to determine whether such action is to the national advantage or not.

So we have the curious spectacle that our government, having offered to exchange opportunities for broadcasts, is now in a position where it cannot prevent Russian appearances on our networks, but we are without any privilege of appearing on theirs.

So it goes.

With warm regard and with the hope that you are enjoying the best of health, *As ever*

[1] Baruch had written to congratulate Eisenhower on his news conference statement that he was unwilling to ban further nuclear tests except as part of a general system of controlled and inspected disarmament: "I am glad to see you maintaining the position that inspection and control are the first imperatives of any disarmament plan" (June 6, 1957, AWF/A; Eisenhower's statement on June 5 is in *Public Papers of the Presidents: Eisenhower, 1957,* pp. 429–30).

[2] On the Baruch Plan, rejected by the Soviet Union in 1946, see Galambos, *Chief of Staff,* nos. 902 and 946.

[3] In a speech delivered on June 8, Democratic Senator Lyndon B. Johnson had proposed an "open curtain" that would provide Soviet representatives radio and television time in the United States in return for reciprocal Soviet privileges (*New York Times,* June 9, 1957).

[4] On Eisenhower's exchange proposal and the recommendation that Dulles presented at the Foreign Ministers meeting in November 1955, see State, *Foreign Relations, 1955–1957,* vol. V, *Austrian State Treaty; Summit and Foreign Ministers Meetings, 1955,* pp. 475–76, 761–62, 776, 783–86.

On June 15 Dulles would discuss with Eisenhower Senator Johnson's proposal for a joint congressional resolution that would urge the President to make every effort to increase international exchanges of information. Eisenhower said that such proposals had been on their minds for nearly two years and that the Administration did not require congressional "urging." A "Congressional commendation" would, he thought, be more appropriate than Johnson's resolution (Memorandum of Conversation, June 15, 1957, Dulles Papers, White House Memoranda Series; see also *U.S. Department of State Bulletin* 37, no. 940 [July 1, 1957] 13).

193 *EM, AWF, Administration Series: Army*

TO WILBER MARION BRUCKER *June 11, 1957*

Dear Secretary Brucker: Nothing could have pleased me more than the unusual distinction you gave to General Heaton yesterday. He is, of course, not only an outstanding military surgeon, but is recognized throughout his profession as one of our finest performers in the field of general surgery.[1]

It occurs to me that he is in the ideal position for a man of his talents. Because of this, when the most recent vacancy occurred in the office of the Surgeon General, I was particularly happy that he declined to be considered for the post, believing that his greatest service could be rendered in the Army's great general hospital and where he would be able constantly to practice his specialty in his profession.[2] I feel so strongly about this that I think it would be a great error to consider his transfer from his present post—either for promotion or any other duty—as long as he is at the very peak of his capabilities. I hope that you fully share these views, but I do request that if the Army should ever consider such a transfer—as long as I hold my present office—you confer with me before any decision is made.[3]

With warm personal regard, *Sincerely*

[1] Commanding General of Walter Reed Army Hospital since 1952, Major General Leonard Dudley Heaton had recently been awarded the Army's Distinguished Service Medal for his skill in performing the ileitis operation on Eisenhower in June 1956 (see *New York Times,* June 11, 1957, and Galambos and van Ee, *The Middle Way,* no. 1316).

[2] In 1955 Heaton had been offered, and had declined, the position of Surgeon General of the Army (Galambos and van Ee, *The Middle Way,* no. 1316).

[3] Secretary of the Army Brucker would respond on June 17, 1957 (AWF/A: Army), saying that he "thoroughly" shared Eisenhower's views on Heaton. "Your message is most timely," he wrote. "No reassignment of General Heaton will be considered or undertaken without first conferring with you." Heaton would remain in his position until 1959 when he would accept appointment as Army Surgeon General (*New York Times,* Sept. 12, 1983).

194 *EM, AWF, Administration Series*

TO HERBERT BROWNELL, JR. *June 12, 1957*
Personal

Dear Herb: Whether or not you have seen the enclosed item from the Herald Tribune I do not know.[1] However, there are certain charges here made that disturb me—not because I am ever upset by charges made by extremists as long as they are directed to a matter of policy. But when they attack motive and fact I take a different view.

This particular item says that the Kefauvers, the O'Mahoneys and the Cellers are far less dangerous to business than is the Republican-dominated Justice Department.[2]

Additionally, I call your special attention to the last two paragraphs of this article.[3]

The real charge in this article is that we are not content with enforcing laws; that through threats which are actually blackmail, we force consent decrees that really go far beyond the requirements of the law.[4]

I am wondering how much personal attention you are able to give to the Anti-Trust Division. Assuming, as I do, that the whole article is based upon misapprehension and misunderstanding, if not downright prejudice, I wonder whether it would not be a good idea to seek a chance for a comprehensive speech on this matter to be made before a general business group. In fact, I should think that several articles might be needed to set before the business community the true attitude of this Administration. This attitude is that we believe there can be continued prosperity and growth of the economy only through the cooperation of labor, management and government, and that such cooperation requires a readiness of all parties to observe the law (or to seek legislative changes in it) but the avoidance on the part of government of all kinds of petty annoyances brought about merely by personal bias.[5]

I should like to talk to you about this some time. *As ever*

[1] Eisenhower was referring to the first of a series of newspaper articles by Donald I. Rogers (*New York Herald-Tribune*, June 12, 1957). Accusing the Administration of being "anti-big business," Rogers said that the Justice Department was preparing to launch an antitrust campaign that would target "any company that has piled up an 'undue' amount of concentration."

[2] Rogers had written: "The business men who keep wary eyes on the Democrats in Congress, expecting them to hand up the big problems, are being distracted by an obvious diversionary movement. The publicized Democratic antagonists—Sen. Estes Kefauver, Sen. Joseph O'Mahoney and Rep. Emanuel Celler—are not likely to come up with any specific harm for the business community, or any special contamination of the benevolent business atmosphere during this session of Congress. The important assault will come from the Justice Department—that arm of government embraced by the White House itself." At issue was antitrust legislation endorsed by Senators Estes Kefauver (Dem., Tenn.), Joseph O'Mahoney (Dem., Wyo.), and Representative Emanuel Celler (Dem., N.Y.). In 1950 Celler and Kefauver had sponsored a successful amendment strengthening the Clayton Antitrust Act. Five years later Celler had been active in passing measures to increase penalties for antitrust violations and to give the government the right to recover for actual damages sustained as a result of antitrust infractions. Senator O'Mahoney chaired the Senate Judiciary

Antitrust and Monopoly Subcommittee (see Theodore Philip Kovaleff, *Business and Government During the Eisenhower Administration* [Athens, Ohio, 1980], pp. 49–90; Neil Fligstein, *The Transformation of Corporate Control* [Cambridge, Mass., 1990], pp. 191–225; *Congressional Quarterly Almanac*, vol. XI, *1955*, pp. 466–68; *Congressional Quarterly Almanac*, vol. XII, *1956*, pp. 523–27.

[3] Rogers had written, "This is the Administration which will, before it is through, try to put a ceiling on bigness, a definite limit to size. I think the Republican business men ought to know it—that they ought to stop kidding themselves."

[4] The article had charged that "The big pusher against big business is the Republican-dominated Justice Department." Rogers alleged that the RCA, AT&T and IBM corporations had each been forced to sign consent decrees after "facing virtual blackmail at the hands of anti-trust attorneys. By blackmail, I mean that if A.T. & T. had not signed a consent decree to make public some of its most valuable patents, the Justice Department would have instituted an action against Western Electric, a subsidiary, seeking to have A.T. & T. divest itself of the property." A consent decree was a negotiated settlement between the government and the defendant which carried the essential force of a litigated judgment; see Kovaleff, *Business and Government During the Eisenhower Administration*, pp. 52–53.

[5] Brownell would respond to the President on June 21 (AWF/A). Noting Eisenhower's suggestion that "we present publicly to the business community our antitrust policies and philosophy," Brownell forwarded a speech by Assistant Attorney General Victor Russell Hansen on "What Antitrust Means to the American Businessman." Hansen had delivered the speech on June 3 to the American Management Association in New York. Brownell would write again on June 25 (AWF/A), listing specific statistics from the Justice Department's Antitrust Division. The Division had reviewed 2,128 corporate mergers and acquisitions since 1953, Brownell reported, and had filed only eleven suits to set aside the combinations. During the same period, sixty-one additional requests on proposed mergers were voluntarily submitted for advisory opinions; in twenty-nine cases the Justice Department approved; seven proposed mergers were abandoned; three withdrawn; in four instances, the Justice Department lacked jurisdiction; sixteen mergers were disapproved; and two requests were still pending. In the sixteen cases that were denied permission, half of the proposed mergers were abandoned. The Justice Department had filed suit to block one of the remaining eight; in the others, "our evidence, while strong enough to raise some doubts as to the legality of the transaction, was not strong enough to justify suit" (see also Brownell, *Advising Ike*, pp. 153–55).

195

EM, AWF, DDE Diaries Series

To Graeme Keith Howard
Personal

June 12, 1957

Dear Mr. Howard:[1] The chief premise of your letter, with which I completely agree, is that Republicans must *unite* in support of logical policies or disappear as a major influence in our national life.[2]

With this statement, subject to the realization that the degree of unity necessary is not an absolute, I think there can be little quarrel. If we are to break up into Moderate, Extreme, Rightist, Radical, or some other brand of Republican, then our future is nothing but futility.[3]

The real question centers around methods by which this is attained. Washington is a peculiar place and an individual in Congress is apt to think it more his duty to sustain the autonomy of the legislative process, vis-a-vis the executive, even though he may be of the same Party as the President, than it is to remember Party responsibility and general solidarity.

Having given some thought to this problem during recent weeks, I met with the national and many of the state leaders of the Republican Party on last Friday evening. I made a talk which dealt mainly with this particular subject. In the thought that you probably have not seen it—at least in its entirety—I venture to send you a copy.[4]

Incidentally, I am now in the process of meeting with individual members of the Congress in the hope of achieving some of the things that you so correctly see to be necessary.[5]

With best wishes, *Sincerely*

[1] Howard (A.B. Stanford 1917), a former General Motors corporate executive, had been vice-president and director of the international division of the Ford Motor Company at the time of his retirement in 1950 (see Galambos, *Columbia University*, no. 269). Active in civic planning in Hartford, Connecticut, he had also been an advocate of closer economic and political ties within the free world, a goal he had promoted in his book on *America and a New World Order* (1940).

[2] Writing on June 7 (WHCF/OF 138-C Republican Party), Howard urged the President to address his "*true* Republican supporters in Congress—those members of the House and Senate who genuinely believe in their party platform and who are 'modern' Republicans." He said that Eisenhower should tell them that "either the Senate and House Republican Leadership including Committee Chairmen, must support the Republican platform, or the Republican party will deservably and inevitably suffer an eclipse." Howard also suggested that Eisenhower advise modern Republicans that it was now "up to *them* to take resolute action in presenting a flat ultimatum to their Republican leaders and committee chairmen, either to support the President or to be displaced." Howard offered a "modern parable" to make his point: "If Casey Stengel during a close pennant race called for a double-play at second base and Senator Knowland insisted on throwing the ball over first base," he wrote, "the owners of the Yankees (the Republicans in Congress) would face the choice either to reduce Casey Stengel to impotency or support him. Otherwise, how can Stengel win the pennant (vital domestic programs) or the World Series (peace with justice)."

[3] On Eisenhower's philosophy of moderate republicanism see no. 101; on Eisenhower's difficulties with Congress see nos. 53, 80, and 123. See also David W. Reinhard, *The Republican Right Since 1945* [Lexington, Ky., 1983], pp. 138–58.

[4] The President was referring to his June 7, 1957, address to the Republican National Conference. Responding to congressional opposition to the President's budget proposal and to Administration efforts to pass a long-term foreign aid bill, Eisenhower had asked his audience how the party could take the decisive and unified action necessary for its survival while accepting the existence of some disagreement as "normal and natural" (see *Public Papers of the Presidents: Eisenhower, 1957*, pp. 447–58; and *New York Times*, June 8, 1957). "Unless a representative political party in Washington

can in its legislative and executive parts effectively enact the program for which it stands and which it is pledged," Eisenhower said, "then in the long run it will not deserve, nor will it get the support of the American people." He called upon Republican leaders to carry out their pledges to support the party's platform. "It's this simple," Eisenhower said. "We've got a good team. Let's look like one."

[5] Howard would respond on June 24 (WHCF/OF 138-C Republican Party). Noting that the chief premise of his June 7 letter "was *not* that the Republicans must unite in support of logical policy, but rather to suggest one *method* for obtaining such unity among the Republican members of Congress," Howard reiterated his suggestion that Eisenhower put pressure on the moderate Republicans in Congress to control Senators Knowland and H. Styles Bridges (Rep., N.H.). Ann Whitman would respond for the President on June 29, saying that "Since you specifically asked the President not to take the time to answer your letter of the twenty-fourth, I merely want to report that it arrived safely and that he read it with great interest."

196

EM, AWF, DDE Diaries Series

To Clarence J. Brown

June 12, 1957

Dear Clarence:[1] This morning you said that you could not go home if you stood for a school program.[2] Here is what Bob Taft said on the radio in Ohio on June 2, 1949:

> "One of the most important jobs the Senate did in the month of May was the passage of this Aid to Education Bill. This Bill provides 270 million dollars *a year* (meaning a continuous, never-ending program—DE) to the 48 States to enable them to improve their grade schools and high schools so that at least 55 dollars per child will be available to every school in the United States, including colored schools where there are separate schools. The purpose is to make available to every child minimum educational opportunities, no matter how poor the State or the district in which he may live. I was one of the sponsors of the Bill, and I believe that it is *absolutely necessary* if there is to be anything like equality of opportunity for children in many of the poorer States. No boy can possibly have equality of opportunity if he does not have enough education to understand at least what his opportunities are."[3]

The next year he was elected by the largest majority he ever got in his State. *Sincerely*

P.S. I supplied the underlining, but I just want to point out that the Bill that Senator Taft advocated was far more "liberal and radical" than anything to which I could ever agree.

[1] Brown, Republican Congressman from Ohio since 1939, had written the legislation creating the first and second Hoover Commissions on the Organization of the Ex-

ecutive Branch of the Government. He had later served on both commissions (see Galambos and van Ee, *The Middle Way*, no. 52).

[2] Brown appears to have made his remark at a breakfast meeting that Eisenhower hosted for forty members of Congress on that day (*New York Times*, June 13, 1957, and President's daily appointments).

[3] On the 1949 Federal Aid to Education bill see *Congressional Quarterly Almanac*, vol. V, *1949*, pp. 266–72; on Senator Taft's sponsorship and support see James T. Patterson, *Mr. Republican: A Biography of Robert A. Taft* (Boston, 1972), pp. 432–33. For background on Eisenhower's unsuccessful efforts during his first Administration to pass a school construction bill see Galambos and van Ee, *The Middle Way*, nos. 1483 and 1910.

In January 1957 Eisenhower had sent to Congress a Special Message on Federal Aid to Education, proposing a comprehensive program of federal assistance for school construction (see *Public Papers of the Presidents: Eisenhower, 1957*, pp. 89–95). Urging Congress to consider federal school aid as an "emergency measure" designed only to "stimulate" state and local efforts, the President asked for a bill that would be "enacted on its own merits, uncomplicated by provisions dealing with the complex problems of integration" (see also Barbara Barksdale Clowse, *Brainpower for the Cold War: The Sputnik Crisis and National Defense Education Act of 1958* [Westport, Conn., 1981], pp. 40–49). For developments see no. 324; see also Eisenhower, *Waging Peace*, pp. 139–40.

197

EM, AWF, Administration Series: AEC

To Lewis Lichtenstein Strauss

June 12, 1957

Dear Lewis: I sent off an interim reply to Charlie Wilson, along the lines you suggested. A copy is enclosed.[1]

As to the relative value of the kind of conference we are thinking of sponsoring by the government as against one sponsored by private citizens, I would much prefer the latter, provided always that the latter is capable of bringing together the right kind of people both because of its prestige and because it has adequate financial support.[2] *As ever*

[1] Eisenhower had written Atomic Energy Commission Chairman Strauss on June 11, 1957, to ask his comments on a letter he had received from former General Electric President Charles Edward Wilson (Eisenhower to Strauss, June 11, 1957, and Wilson to Eisenhower, June 6, 1957; all documents are in AWF/A: AEC). Wilson, who was now president of the People-to-People exchange program (see below), had proposed that his group sponsor a forum "for the purpose of exchanging views and recommendations freely and fully, that will result in understandings which would seek to guarantee to mankind safe conduct into the new and unexplored world which has been opened by the unlocking of the atom" (for background on Wilson see Galambos and van Ee, *The Middle Way*, no. 4). He had also alluded to an earlier proposal by Strauss that the government sponsor a conference of top men in the social sciences and humanities to discuss the peaceful uses of atomic energy (see Galambos and van

Ee, *The Middle Way*, no. 2168). Wilson believed that non-governmental sponsorship would allow the free "advance and exchange [of] ideas, plans, and recommendations, unencumbered by the stiff formalities of protocol requisite for the meetings of the representatives of governments when nations meet formally with other nations."

The People-to-People program was a response to Eisenhower's call in a May 25, 1956, speech at Baylor University for a "voluntary effort in people-to-people partnership" (see *ibid.*, no. 1891 and *Public Papers of the Presidents: Eisenhower, 1956*, pp. 526–37). On May 31, 1956, the White House had announced that Eisenhower had invited a group of Americans from a broad spectrum of professions to "explore the possibilities of a program for better people-to-people contacts throughout the world." Eisenhower's invitation would result in a People-to-People Conference in Washington, D.C., on September 11, 1956 (*Public Papers of the Presidents: Eisenhower, 1956*, pp. 749–52).

[2] Strauss had replied to the President on June 11, 1957. Admitting that he had not previously heard of the People-to-People program, he asked Eisenhower to provide further background information to enable him to "see if it is sufficiently endowed so that it would not be making a bid for funds on the strength of sponsoring the proposed conference." Strauss also wanted "to consider whether the fullest measure of benefit will accrue to the United States if the conference is called by a body which is independent of the Administration." Eisenhower would use most of Strauss's draft letter to Wilson in his June 12 response to Wilson. Saying that he had already given Strauss the go-ahead for a conference, Eisenhower noted that he did "not know how far along he is and whether or not it is committed beyond the point where your very interesting suggestion would be timely. However, since I understand that you have been friends for years, I am asking Lewis to get in touch with you about it." For developments see no. 283.

198

EM, AWF, Name Series

To Clifford Roberts

June 12, 1957

Dear Cliff: The only trouble with your suggestion is that it was not wienies and sauerkraut that hit me. It was rich foods, eaten *too rapidly*. Unfortunately I have never learned to dine—I just bolt.[1]

However, I will be careful.

I am glad that you found some of the Stouffer things that you liked.[2] *As ever*

[1] On June 10 Eisenhower had suffered an upset stomach that confined him to bed. Later that day Roberts advised the President to eat items he could handle "without having them backfire on you" (AWF/N). "Maybe you don't mind a bellyache but both my peace of mind and the Stock Market fall completely out of bed!" Following news of Eisenhower's illness, the stock market had declined sharply (*New York Times*, June 11, 12, 1957).

[2] Roberts had thanked the President for suggesting the use of frozen Stouffer products at the Augusta National Golf Club "—especially during the periods when there are only a few people at the Club." Eisenhower had sampled some of these items in April (see no. 33).

To Arthur Ellsworth Summerfield, Jr. *June 13, 1957*
Personal

Dear Bud: You use the expression "time-tested tradition" in referring to the practice of including a national chairman as a member of the Cabinet.[1] I think this is somewhat inaccurate and I believe if you will go back through the history of our country for the past seventy-five years, you will find that both parties have at times done otherwise.[2]

Nevertheless, your feeling that the national chairman's position is rendered less important by reason of his exclusion from the Cabinet deserves a little consideration on its own merits. The purpose in separating the two offices was exactly the opposite. My own belief is that if the chairman's job and any Cabinet post put so little demands on a person's time that one individual can discharge them both satisfactorily, then one or the other ought to be abolished. Moreover, I believe it lays any Administration open to the charge that it is being run mainly to perpetuate itself rather than to serve the country and to rest its chance of continuation on the character of service it renders.

On the other hand, I admit that in some of the so-called "patronage problems" the system may have some advantages. In this way all Cabinet officers would be more often reminded that political considerations should not be entirely forgotten—other things being equal—when appointments to political office are made. This could not, of course, include, in this Administration, any member of my own Cabinet or any Federal judgeship. These are kept within my own hands, with relative merit the sole criterion so far as we can determine.

In essence I believe that the solution lies in getting the right man for the post—one whom the entire party understands has the confidence of the President and the Administration. I believe that such an individual's success in action does not come from title or from extra pay—it comes from merit, personality, leadership.

You will understand that I am far from claiming that my views are sacrosanct. My ideas of organization are based on long experience, but in a different field from politics. Moreover, when I say the right man in the right place, I don't mean merely the Chairman of the National Committee (and here I think we have a truly good one),[3] but I mean state chairmen, national committeemen and national committeewomen, county chairmen and so on. If we get the right people—young, vigorous and real "believers"—then I think it will make very little difference if we are organized as you suggest or as we are at present.[4]

In any event, thanks for writing. It was fine to have you at the dinner.

With warm regard, *As ever*

[1] Summerfield, an automobile dealer and son of the Postmaster General, had written the President on May 29 (AWF/A). After thanking Eisenhower for hosting the previous evening's stag dinner, Summerfield said he hoped the President had not misunderstood the regret he had expressed at dinner over the fact that the national chairman of the GOP was no longer a member of the President's Cabinet. Summerfield felt that the lack of Cabinet status not only lessened the party chairman's "influence in the eyes of the party organization across the country," but also diminished "the importance of the National Chairman's position in the eyes of some Cabinet members and other executive department heads." "In the eyes of some people," Summerfield wrote, "the National Chairmanship has become a position of errand boy for the White House staff." Too many people had "not been frank on this matter," he told Eisenhower, "because of their personal love for you."

[2] During the first half of the twentieth century it was common for the national chairman of the party occupying the White House to hold cabinet rank—frequently as postmaster general—unless he also held elective office. Summerfield may have been thinking of his father, who in 1952 had been asked to choose between the position of postmaster general and Republican National Committee chairman (see Galambos and van Ee, *The Middle Way*, no. 3, and Eisenhower, *Mandate for Change*, pp. 91–92; see also James W. Davis, *The President as Party Leader* [New York, 1992], pp. 103–6, and Harold F. Bass, "The President and the National Party Organization," in *Presidents and Their Parties*, ed. Robert Harmel [New York, 1984], pp. 59–89).

[3] Meade Alcorn had assumed the party chairmanship on January 22, 1957 (see no. 20).

[4] See also no. 195.

200

EM, AWF, DDE Diaries Series

To Dorothy Girard

June 13, 1957

Dear Mrs. Girard: For nearly half a century it has been part of my duty to see that American fighting men, serving under my command, have had, under all circumstances, fair and just treatment. So, your letter touches me very deeply. I am glad you have so written to me.[1]

For your Government I pledge that, in your son's present difficulty, his every right will be fully protected. His defense counsel will be furnished all the evidence in your Government's possession essential to his defense, and throughout the trial your Government's representatives will remain in alert attendance to see that the trial proceeds fairly and that justice is rendered.[2]

Your letter implies that your goal in this distressing incident is, rightly, justice for your boy. You are, I feel, directing your concern soundly, for I have regretted, as perhaps you have, the impression on the part of some that assertion of national prerogative in this situation is of more significance than is justice itself.[3] I want, therefore, to assure you of my confidence that justice will be as surely rendered your son as would have been the case in court martial proceedings by our own armed forces.[4]

With best wishes to you, *Sincerely*

[1] Army specialist 3/c William S. Girard had been charged in January 1957 with "inflicting bodily injury causing the death" of a forty-six-year-old Japanese woman. The governments of Japan and the United States had agreed on the facts of the case: that while on routine exercises on the afternoon of January 30, Sergeant Girard had fired a blank cartridge case with a grenade launcher at two Japanese citizens as they were scavenging expended brass. The case struck a woman in the back and killed her (Eisenhower, *Waging Peace*, pp. 140–41; U.S. Department of State, *Foreign Relations of the United States, 1955–1957*, vol. XXIII, 2 vols., pt. 1, *Japan* [1991], pp. 293–96). The matter at issue, criminal jurisdiction over American forces in Japan, was governed by a treaty that gave the United States the primary right to exercise jurisdiction in "offenses arising out of any act or mission done in the performance of official duty."

The United States held that the shooting incident arose during Girard's proper efforts to guard a machine gun; the Japanese government argued that the shooting had no connection to the guarding of the gun. Girard's mother had written the President (n.d., WHCF/OF 328) asking him to use his "power to stop this injustice that is being done to my boy." Apologizing for not really knowing "just what to say," Mrs. Girard begged Eisenhower to "treat my boy like you would treat your boy." See also *New York Times*, February 7, 1957.

[2] As a consequence of the considerable public indignation the Girard case had aroused in Japan, American and Japanese authorities had reached a compromise on the jurisdiction issue. The United States government agreed not to exercise jurisdiction, without prejudicing its position that Girard's alleged offense arose in the performance of an official duty. For its part, the Japanese government agreed to indict Girard on no greater charge than "wounding resulting in death." See *ibid.*, May 18, 24, and June 5, 1957.

[3] The Department of the Army had made the decision to allow Girard to be tried by the Japanese without consulting the Department of State. Although unhappy with this decision, Dulles would ultimately decide that having agreed to accept Japanese jurisdiction, "an attempt now abruptly and unilaterally to reverse our position would be understandably judged by the Japanese to be a repudiation of our international agreement with them. The consequences of this could profoundly and adversely affect our position in Japan, our relations with Japan and our whole position in the Far East" (Dulles to Brucker, May 21, 1957, AWF/D-H; see also extensive telephone and written correspondence in State, *Foreign Relations, 1955–1957*, vol. XXIII, pt. 1, *Japan*, pp. 261–345; and Telephone conversations, Dulles and Brucker, May 21, 1957, and Dulles and Robertson, May 25, 1957, Dulles Papers, Telephone Conversations).

[4] During his June 6 news conference the President had stated that "merely because you let another nation try your man does not relieve the defense forces or, indeed, the Commander in Chief for the need for following that case and seeing that justice, fair justice is done." Eisenhower added, "We pay for the lawyer to defend him; we watch it through our lawyers all the way through; and if any possible injustice

happened to that man, it would be a case that would be taken up diplomatically, of course" (*Public Papers of the Presidents: Eisenhower, 1957*, p. 437). For developments see no. 248.

201

EM, AWF, International Series: Queen Elizabeth Visit

To Mary Jane McCaffree

June 13, 1957

Memorandum for Mrs. McCaffree: I would accept the Fair Lady thing because for the evening the visiting couple would find it probably more enjoyable. However, I admire and respect Kate Smith so in answering her, I would express gratitude for her offer and state that we hope, in the entertainment for the affair, to have some British personnel in the entertaining cast.[1]

[1] McCaffree, Mrs. Eisenhower's personal secretary, was assisting with the plans for the entertainment at a state dinner honoring Queen Elizabeth II during her visit to the United States (for background see no. 188). As it turned out, neither the cast of the New York production of "My Fair Lady" nor the radio singer and actress Kathryn Elizabeth ("Kate") Smith would perform at the state dinner (see related correspondence in AWF/I: Queen Elizabeth Visit).

202

EM, WHCF, Official File 104-N-7

To Thomas Jefferson Murray

June 14, 1957

Dear Mr. Chairman:[1] Your June seventh letter has reached me in the midst of strenuous Legislative and Executive efforts to create a budgetary position that will allow not only additional payments on the public debt but also, with continuing progress along this line, an eventual tax reduction for everyone.[2]

The success of this effort requires a continued healthy growth of the Nation's economy, as well as developments permitting a sharp reduction of Federal expenditures. General pay increases at this time would seriously impede our progress toward these goals.

Recent actions of the Congress and the Executive Branch have demonstrated the Government's continuing concern for proper and just compensation for its workers and have benefitted those workers in a number of ways. These include low-cost group life insurance, more liberal retirement and survivorship provisions, uniform allowances and unemployment compensation. Administration-sponsored legislation is now pending to establish a voluntary health and medical insurance program and to authorize the training of Government employees outside as well as within the employing agencies. As all of us know, the present difficulty in harnessing the Federal budget is attributable in part to increased personnel costs. Incidentally, it was only two years ago that general pay increases were approved.[3]

In view of the tax, budgetary and economic implications, and in view of my several appeals this year to private citizens to observe restraint in everything that could add to the inflationary pressures on our economy, I cannot at this time, in keeping with the national interest, recommend enactment of legislation for pay increases for postal workers which, as you point out, would lead to a pay increase throughout the Federal Government.[4] *Sincerely*

[1] Murray (B.A. Union University 1914; LL.B. Cumberland University 1917) had been Democratic Congressman from Tennessee since 1943, and Chairman of the House Committee on the Post Office and Civil Service since 1955.

[2] Murray had written the President on June 7, 1957 (same file as document) expressing his strong disapproval of the twenty-nine bills before his committee promoting salary increases for postal employees. He warned that the proposed raises would increase postal service payroll costs by over a billion dollars a year. He also cautioned that if similar salary increases were granted to other federal employees, the federal civilian payroll expenditures would be $2.75 billion higher. Murray expressed concern that the cumulative cost of congressional action could run well over $5 billion a year if military personnel were granted comparable increases in compensation, as they had been in the past. "Salary increases of such magnitude obviously would affect the entire economy," he said, "let alone completely disrupt the Federal Budget." On Eisenhower's efforts to hold down federal expenditures and concerns about congressional spending see Eisenhower, *Waging Peace*, p. 132; on his veto of postal employee pay raise bills during his first Administration see Galambos and van Ee, *The Middle Way*, no. 1054. See also *Congressional Quarterly Almanac*, vol. XIII, *1957*, pp. 632–34.

[3] In 1955 Congress had raised the pay of most classified government workers by 7.5 percent, at a cost of $325 million (see *Congressional Quarterly Almanac*, vol. XI, *1956*, pp. 364–66). On government measures to provide low-cost group life insurance, more liberal retirement, uniform allowances and unemployment compensation see Committee on Post Office and Civil Service, House of Representatives, "Major Legislative Problems Facing the Committee in the 85th Congress," February 7, 1957, AWF/A: Summerfield Corr. On Administration-sponsored legislation to establish a voluntary health and medical insurance program see *Congressional Quarterly Almanac*, vol. XIII, *1957*, pp. 419–21.

[4] Murray had appealed in his letter for a "personal message" from Eisenhower to the Congress "setting forth your views on this important matter." Eisenhower would underscore his opposition to the postal pay raise bill in a June 27 meeting with Murray, who would oppose—unsuccessfully—the bill in committee (see *New York Times*, June 28, 1957). For developments see no. 248.

203 *EM, AWF, Dulles-Herter Series*

To John Foster Dulles *June 15, 1957*

Dear Foster:[1] I am told that today marks the fiftieth year since you first began your service in the field of foreign affairs, when you served as secretary on the Chinese delegation to the second Peace Conference at The Hague. Apparently, your associates of that early date clearly recognized your ability to carry heavy responsibilities, for heavy they must have been for a young man of nineteen.[2]

In any event, through that experience you were committed to the waging of peace, and your name has been prominently associated with many of the International Conferences, since that date, which have had as their purpose the development of world stability and peace based on justice. In those years of enriching experience, you have gone on to ever increasing responsibility in the field of public service to which you have dedicated yourself, and have established a reputation for meeting every new assignment and challenge with wisdom, imagination and vigor.[3]

My personal appreciation of your extraordinary ability in the field of international relations has constantly grown since you became Secretary of State in 1953.[4]

Your statesmanship has been demonstrated in countless negotiations and conferences of international import. The beneficial results of your labors can never be accurately measured, but such accomplishments as the conclusion of the Austrian Peace Treaty, the formulation and adoption of the Caracas Resolution against Communist infiltration into this Hemisphere, the development of the Southeast Asia Treaty Organization, the Formosa Declaration of 1955, and the Doctrine for the Middle East which the Congress recently approved, bear witness to your competence as our country's chief representative in global relations.[5]

Recitation of these few instances serves at least to give some hint of the broad basis on which rests my personal and official gratitude to you. I am quite certain that as this Administration joins those which are viewed from long historical perspective, your accomplishments will establish you as one of the greatest of our Secretaries of State.

Nevertheless, at this moment, the future must occupy both you and me more than can the past. In extending to you my felicitations on a half century of fruitful service to your country, I also express my profound hope that the nation shall have the benefit of your experience and wisdom for many years to come.

With warm personal regard, *As ever*

[1] At the suggestion of the State Department, Eisenhower had drafted this tribute to Secretary Dulles on the preceding day. After hearing a report of the letter on the radio on June 15, Dulles thanked the President in advance, causing him to sign the letter hurriedly, even though it was still "in draft form." Press Secretary Hagerty apologized to Dulles about the leak, stating that "it was intended to be a 'surprise'" (Ann Whitman memorandums, June 14, 15, 1957, AWF/AWD; Dulles, Memorandum of Conversation, June 15, 1957, Dulles Papers, White House Memoranda Series).
[2] While a junior at Princeton University in 1907, Dulles received permission to postpone his final examinations in order to serve as personal secretary to his grandfather, former Secretary of State John Watson Foster, at the second Peace Conference at The Hague. Foster had attended the conference on the protocol and laws of war as a paid representative of the Imperial Government of China (*New York Times*, June 16, 1957).
[3] On Dulles's career in law and diplomacy see Galambos, *Columbia University*, no. 12; Galambos, *NATO and the Campaign of 1952*, no. 218; and Eisenhower, *Waging Peace*, pp. 361–62. See also Richard R. Immerman, *John Foster Dulles: Piety, Pragmatism, and Power in U.S. Foreign Policy* (Wilmington, Del., 1999).
[4] See, for example, Galambos and van Ee, *The Middle Way*, nos. 188 and 794; and Eisenhower, *Waging Peace*, pp. 361–73.
[5] For background on the Austrian Peace Treaty see Galambos and van Ee, *The Middle Way*, no. 1432; on the Caracas Resolution, see *ibid.*, no. 568; on SEATO, see *ibid.*, no. 974; on the Formosa Declaration, see *ibid.*, no. 1379; and on the Middle East Doctrine, see *ibid.*, nos. 1773 and 2155.

204 — *EM, AWF, DDE Diaries Series*

To Arthur Frank Burns — *June 15, 1957*

Dear Arthur: You aren't accusing me of a deliberate indisposition last Monday, are you? I assure you that for a few hours at least I was entirely too uncomfortable to consider even the existence of the stock market.[1]

I was so intrigued in the balance of your letter that I had it sent around to various Cabinet and other officials who would, I knew, be particularly interested.[2]

With warm regard, *As ever*

[1] Burns, former Chairman of the President's Council of Economic Advisors, had served as president of the National Bureau of Economic Research since 1956. He had written Eisenhower on June 12, 1957 (WHCF/OF 114), saying that there were "better ways of quieting the stock market than your getting ill." The President had suffered from a "mild stomach upset" that had briefly confined him to bed on June 10. News reports about the President's health had caused prices on the New York Stock Exchange initially to fall sharply in heavy trading. See no. 198 and *New York Times*, June 11, 1957; see also Ann Whitman memorandum, June 10, 1957, AWF/AWD. Eisenhower also wrote financier Bernard Baruch concerning his "indisposition" (AWF/A).
[2] Burns had included in his letter a report claiming that Soviet industrial output had

multiplied 5.6 times between 1913 and 1955. Burns compared this figure to comparable 40-year periods in U.S. history when, he said, industrial output had multiplied six or more times. Burns concluded that the report strengthened "the impression of our earlier studies that many prominent people have been greatly exaggerating the achievements of the Russians." Eisenhower had sent copies of Burns's report to Treasury Secretary George Humphrey, Secretary of Defense Charles Wilson, and Chairman of the Council of Economic Advisors, Raymond Saulnier.

205

EM, AWF, DDE Diaries Series

To Harold Macmillan

Secret

June 16, 1957

Dear Harold: I think now that we have removed the possibility that any more "flaps" can occur in disarmament negotiations, we can look forward to a bit smoother sailing in this particular business.[1]

We have worked very hard to find a position in the disarmament area that is as liberal and broad-gauged as elementary considerations of security would permit. Frankly, many of our people are getting exceedingly weary of carrying the national and international costs of some of the programs in which we are now engaged. Any real progress toward a disarmament plan—one which could be accepted with confidence by the free world—would probably be of greater relative relief to us than to any of our friends. This is because in so many cases we are not only meeting our own costs but trying to help others.[2]

I mention this only to show that we fully agree with your observation that "the real test is disarmament."[3]

Of course I can understand your disappointment about the restrictions that we finally had to put on the import of wool textiles.[4] I must explain, however, one phase of the problem that our friends should clearly understand.

This Administration stands firmly and squarely for liberalized and greater flow of trade among the nations of the free world. We have fought long and earnestly for acceptance of this doctrine in this country and, in executing the law, have time and again declined to listen to the special pleas of specialized industries in this country in order to promote the general concept of reciprocity and freer trade.

But while doing this we can never forget that the Congress has granted authority to the Executive for making reciprocal trade treaties only on a temporary basis. Once in a while there arises a case that has such great popular appeal that to decline flatly to give any of the relief contemplated by the law could easily result in a return of this country to its former high protection policy.

It is the task of deciding between these immediate and long-term damages to our friends—and to ourselves—that is difficult.[5] I and some of my trusted associates spend many hours of hard study on such questions. If I should approve every recommendation made to me by the Federal Tariff Commission—a body whose responsibility it is to see that justice is done to American industry—the total effect over the past four and a half years would have been almost catastrophic, and we would be totally defeated in the effort to promote trade.

So I beg of you that you try to understand the situation. I shall continue to fight as hard as I know how for the concept of freer and greater trade. But sometimes I am impelled, on such a wide front as that on which I operate, to beat a local and—I hope—temporary retreat.

I read with interest your letter to the Chancellor.[6] In spite of the German staff's decision that our M-48 had some characteristics that they preferred over your Centurion, I still think they made a mistake in their failure to adopt your tank for their forces. Actually I understand the number is not large—it could be possible that they are buying a relatively small number merely in order to have prototypes for their own later production.

I thoroughly enjoy and appreciate your letters.

With warm regard, *As ever*

[1] Eisenhower had told Secretary Dulles that he would personally prepare this reply to Macmillan's June 12 letter about the "flap" (Eisenhower to Dulles, June 13, 1957, AWF/I: Macmillan).

[2] For background see nos. 182 and 191. On June 11 Secretary Dulles, after consultation with Eisenhower, had asked Julius Holmes, former Assistant Secretary of State for NATO Affairs, to monitor the disarmament talks in London. All differences over procedures between Holmes and Stassen were to be referred back to Washington for a decision (Dulles to Stassen, June 12, 1957, AWF/D-H; see also Memorandum of Conversation, June 11, 1957, Dulles Papers, White House Memoranda Series).

[3] Macmillan had told Eisenhower that he thought the Russians were "very conscious of the harm which their brutality in Poland and Hungary" had done and were "anxious to find some kind of cover of respectability. . . ." The disarmament question needed "a lot of careful thought," Macmillan said. "The Russians will try to play us off one against the other and we must not allow this to happen" (June 12, 1957, AWF/I: Macmillan).

[4] For background on the wool tariff issue see Galambos and van Ee, *The Middle Way*, nos. 391 and 1307. On May 24 Eisenhower had announced a quota on most imported woolen and worsted fabrics and increased duty rates on all imports over the quota. On May 23 Assistant to the President Sherman Adams had told Secretary Dulles, who opposed the decision, that it was based on domestic wool industry statistics "which look pretty bad" (*U.S. Department of State Bulletin* 37, no. 941 [July 8, 1957], 84–85; and Telephone conversation, Adams and Dulles, May 23, 1957, Dulles Papers, Telephone Conversations).

[5] Macmillan had told Eisenhower that he was "terribly disappointed" at the decision. "Of course," he said, "I realize the pressures of some of your industrial interests. But

we have to fight very hard for our exports, because we cannot live without them, and when one of our trades really makes a good show it is pretty disheartening to be cut down in this rough way." "It makes me feel very pessimistic about the growth of liberal concepts in the world," the Prime Minister continued. "If countries with enormous surpluses and vast wealth resort to protection how can we expect countries in difficulties like Britain and France to move towards the freeing of trade."

[6] Macmillan's letter to West German Chancellor Adenauer is not in AWF. On June 10 Dulles had told Eisenhower that the Germans had decided to buy American tanks in preference to British Centurions, ending almost a year of indecision (for background see no. 162; see also Dulles to Eisenhower, June 10, 1957, AWF/D-H; Telephone conversation, Dulles and Wilson, June 11, 1957, Dulles Papers, Telephone Conversations; Staff notes, June 22, 1957, AWF/D; and *New York Times*, July 18, 1957).

206

EM, AWF, Dulles-Herter Series

TO JOHN FOSTER DULLES

Top secret

June 17, 1957

Memorandum for the Secretary of State: I have studied the draft of the attached letter that you propose to send to the Canadian government regarding a consultation on alert measures.[1]

Believing that it represents a feasible plan for joint observance by both our governments, I approve of the letter.[2]

[1] In May 1956 the Canadian government had proposed consultation between the United States and Canada whenever measures to be taken against foreign attack were considered necessary and desirable by either country. "The Canadian Government is looking ahead to the time when air defenses of both countries may be integrated under a single command," Dulles told Eisenhower. "Its proposal was made with a view to ensuring that consultation leading to national-type alerts would be carried out at the highest level of government, both through diplomatic and military channels, and not relegated to the command level (Dulles to Eisenhower, June 12, 1957, AWF/D-H). Dulles's suggested reply, which is not in AWF, accepted the Canadian proposal with the understanding that "the 'alert measures' under discussion should relate only to the national type affecting both countries at large as opposed to limited readiness measures of a purely military nature" and that military consultations should be conducted at the respective chiefs of staff level (*ibid.*).

[2] On August 1 the United States and Canada would announce an integration of their air defense operations for the North American continent with headquarters in Colorado Springs. The chiefs of staff of both countries would approve all plans and procedures (*U.S. Department of State Bulletin* 37, no. 947 [August 19, 1957], 306).

207

EM, AWF, Name Series

To Aksel Nielsen

June 19, 1957

Dear Aks: In a day filled with Senator Humphrey, a press conference, and—mainly—the Japanese, I find your note of the seventeenth completely distracting. And I don't think the resulting homesickness for fishing at Fraser helped the international negotiations one bit![1]

But many thanks. There are no definite plans yet and I can always hope.[2]

With warm regard, *As ever*

[1] Long-time friend Nielsen had written urging the President to visit his ranch in Fraser, Colorado (AWF/N). Nielsen had reported on the fishing at some of the President's favorite lakes and streams around Fraser. For background on Eisenhower's vacations with Nielsen see *Eisenhower Papers,* vols. X–XVII. Senator Hubert Horatio Humphrey, Jr. (Dem., Minn.) had reported on his trip to the Middle East. On the news conference see *Public Papers of the Presidents: Eisenhower, 1957,* pp. 468–80. The President had met with the Japanese prime minister and his official party at 11 A.M. Following a luncheon in honor of the prime minister, the delegation played golf at Burning Tree Country Club. Eisenhower returned to the White House at 6:44 P.M.

[2] In September the Eisenhowers would vacation in Newport, Rhode Island (see no. 243).

208

EM, AWF, DDE Diaries Series

To John Sherman Cooper

June 20, 1957

Dear John: I thank you for giving me your opinion with respect to Congressman Baker.[1]

I am usually, however, embarrassed by receiving a recommendation as to the filling of any particular Federal position when the recommendation is confined to a single name. We not only subject each individual to a searching investigation, but we have certain rules of thumb that we try never to violate. One of these—an understanding with the Republican leadership of the House—is that no sitting member of the Congress can be appointed to public office during the term for which he was elected. In other words, we have never even entertained the suggestion that we would appoint a man after he resigns. In adherence to this policy, we have declined to appoint applicants to the Federal bench and to positions in the Executive Department of government.[2]

While I do not maintain that the Republic would necessarily suffer a calamity if only a single exception were made to this rule, I do believe that anyone who has been elected to responsible office in the Federal government should faithfully serve out his term. In fact, I would think that any individual would feel a moral compunction to do so.

While I have no reason whatsoever to question your judgment as to the fitness of Mr. Baker for the post you want him to have, I certainly feel that the considerations I have just enumerated are very important.[3]

With warm regard, *Sincerely*

[1] Cooper, who had served as U.S. Ambassador to India from March 1955 until August 1956, had been Republican Senator from Kentucky since November 1956. He had written Eisenhower on June 18 (AWF/D) to recommend the appointment of Howard Henry Baker (A.B. University of Tennessee 1922; LL.B. 1924), Republican Congressman from Tennessee since 1951, as a director of the Tennessee Valley Authority. Calling Baker a "man of great ability and integrity," with "the experience and strength to carry out the duties of the office fairly and objectively," Cooper wrote that he hoped the difficulties inherent in appointing a member of Congress could be overcome because of Baker's "outstanding qualifications." This draft is marked "Letter not sent but indicative of Pres.' thinking."

[2] For an expression of Eisenhower's view on patronage see *ibid.*, no. 530. See also no. 85.

[3] On June 28 Eisenhower would appoint Arnold R. Jones of Kansas, Deputy Director of the Bureau of the Budget, to be a director of the TVA (see *New York Times*, June 29, 1957). Asked at his July 3 news conference why he had not chosen Baker, Eisenhower would respond, "I don't know that Mr. Baker is not qualified, but certainly, except in the most exceptional circumstances, I would not take a sitting Member of either House and appoint him to an appointive job. He was elected for a particular time, and from my viewpoint—maybe it's a simple and naive one—I think he ought to serve out his term" (*Public Papers of the Presidents: Eisenhower, 1957*, p. 520).

209

EM, AWF, Administration Series

To John Hay Whitney
Personal

June 20, 1957

Dear Jock: Herewith a file of correspondence which consists of:

Letter dated May 24, 1957 from Spyros Skouras to Archbishop Makarios;[1]

Letter dated May 24, 1957 from George V. Allen to Spyros Skouras;[2]

Letter dated June 14, 1957 from Spyros Skouras to me;

My letter of today to Mr. Skouras.

Frankly, I think that in this case Spyros Skouras, whom I like and whose opinions I normally respect, is shooting wide of the mark when he thinks there is anything you could properly do to "facilitate" the Archbishop's reception in London.[3]

I send you this file more as an indication of the thinking of certain individuals about the matter in general, rather than to imply any thought that you should take any action in the situation.[4]

Give my love to Betsey. *As ever*

[1] For background on Skouras, president of Twentieth Century-Fox Film Corporation, see Galambos and van Ee, *The Middle Way*, no. 1614; on the Cyprus situation see nos. 78 and 91. After the British had released Archbishop Makarios from detention in the Seychelles in March, Skouras had written the Greek Prime Minister to suggest that Makarios visit Britain "in order to win British public opinion to a greater understanding of the Cyprian situation" (Skouras to Eisenhower, June 14, 1957, AWF/A, Whitney Corr.). Skouras also urged Makarios to give more attention to British public opinion.

[2] According to Allen, U.S. Ambassador to Greece, Makarios believed that a visit to London could "help bring about a more favorable atmosphere, provided the way can be paved for him to do so effectively" (*ibid.*).

[3] Responding to Skouras, the President said that he saw no way that "any American—even our Ambassador" could facilitate Makarios's reception in London (Eisenhower to Skouras, June 20, 1957, AWF/D; see also Skouras to Eisenhower, July 2, 1957, WHCF/PPF 164).

[4] For developments see no. 236.

210

EM, AWF, Name Series

TO NORMAN COUSINS

Personal and confidential

June 21, 1957

Dear Mr. Cousins: I read with interest your letter of June seventh.[1] It seems to me that you have made a very personal interpretation of press conference statements which, even if fuzzy—as you imply—in the first uttering, were certainly amplified later in the same conference to say exactly what I meant.[2]

Of course I do not have the scientific competence to argue one side or the other of the question of the ultimate effects of radioactive fallout from bomb testings. What I had to say with respect to the composition of the signers of the so-called "Pauling petition" was based on information similar to that given in the attached tear sheet from the "U.S. News and World Report."[3]

With respect to America's intentions and good will in this matter, I call your attention to the fact that as long ago as 1947, this country, then enjoying a monopoly in the field, earnestly tried to put the whole development in the hands of an international organization and to insure that the atomic science would be forever devoted to man's betterment.[4]

You may examine my own public statements over the past five years and find no wavering from this position. I ask—as I believe any reasonable American should ask—only some assurances that we are not exposing ourselves unnecessarily to unacceptable risks in the military field.[5] *Sincerely*

[1] Because Cousins's letter had arrived while Eisenhower was recuperating from an intestinal upset, Ann Whitman had sent the message to Atomic Energy Commission Chairman Lewis Strauss. She later told the President that Cousins had asked that the letter be held until Eisenhower felt better since "he did not want any one 'down the line' to answer it." Although Strauss drafted a five-page reply, he told the President that his "strong feeling" was that Eisenhower should send Cousins "a simple note of acknowledgment and thanks." Defending news conference statements would establish an unwanted precedent, Strauss said. He was also "concerned by the question of the fate of an exchange of correspondence with the publisher of a magazine" (Strauss to Eisenhower, June 18, 1957, AWF/N; the magazine was the *Saturday Review of Literature*).

[2] At his June 5 news conference Eisenhower had been asked to comment on the testimony of top geneticists and scientists that fallout radiation could dangerously affect the lives and well-being of hundreds of thousands of people in present and future generations. The President cited an October 1956 report on radiation dangers of the National Academy of Sciences as "the authoritative document" that governed his actions. He continued by saying that in many instances "scientists that seem to be out of their own field of competence are getting into this argument, and it looks like almost an organized affair." When questioned further, Eisenhower said that although there did seem to be "some organization" behind the campaign, he did not mean "a wicked organization." Although many scientists were undeniably honest, Eisenhower stated, "when they begin to talk a little bit out of their fields, well then I would rather go myself to the Academy of Sciences, which has no axe to grind . . ." (*Congressional Quarterly Almanac*, vol. XIII, *1957*, pp. 795–96; and *Public Papers of the Presidents: Eisenhower, 1957*, pp. 429–30, 431, 434–35).

Cousins told Eisenhower that his statements had created the impression that the critics of nuclear testing were ill-informed and "that there was some suggestion of 'organization' in this opposition." "Various signers of that [National Academy] report," Cousins wrote, "have revised their opinion and have so stated publicly." He asked that Eisenhower reassess his reference to the academy's position (Cousins to Eisenhower, June 7, 1957, AWF/N).

[3] On June 3 Dr. Linus Carl Pauling, head of the chemistry department at the California Institute of Technology, had reported that 2,000 scientists had signed his petition asking for an international agreement to stop nuclear testing. According to *U.S. News & World Report*, only 1,351 names actually appeared on the petition and only half of those were listed among the 90,000 prominent scientists in *American Men of Science*. A number of the signers were graduate students, research assistants, and fellowship holders; others were prominent in such fields as astronomy, mathematics, and engineering (*U.S. News & World Report*, June 21, 1957).

[4] On the Baruch Plan for international control of atomic energy, which was presented to the Security Council of the United Nations in December 1946, see Galambos, *Chief of Staff*, nos. 556, 902, 1668, and in these volumes no. 192.

[5] For developments see no. 223.

211 *EM, AWF, DDE Diaries Series*

To Earl Warren *June 21, 1957*

Dear Mr. Chief Justice: As I have told you, I rarely read beyond the headlines on the front page of my newspaper. However, I was told this morning that some enterprising reporter has a story that at a private party I severely criticized the Supreme Court, expressing anger.[1] I have no doubt that in private conversation someone did hear me express amazement about one decision, but I have never even hinted at a feeling such as anger. To do so would imply not only that I knew the law but questioned motives. Neither of these things is true.

So while resolving that even in private conversations I shall be more careful of my language, I do want you to know that if any such story appeared, it was a distortion.[2]

With warm regard, *As ever*

[1] The President was referring to Ruth Shick Montgomery, special Washington correspondent for the International News Service since 1956. Montgomery had reported that Eisenhower had told friends at his June 18 stag dinner that he had "'never been as mad'" in his life as he was at the recent Supreme Court decision that opened secret FBI files to accused subversives and other defendants (Leo Katcher, *Earl Warren: A Political Biography,* [New York, 1967], pp. 363–66). Eisenhower's remarks were made in the midst of criticism involving a group of decisions handed down by the Supreme Court on June 17, 1957. These rulings limited broad interpretations of the term "sedition" under the Smith Act, which forbade conspiracies to teach or advocate the violent overthrow of the government. The Court had also moved to restrict both congressional and state rights to investigate private citizens (*New York Times,* June 18, 1957, and Jack Harrison Pollack, *Earl Warren: The Judge Who Changed America,* [Englewood Cliffs, N.J., 1979], pp. 187–92). The particular case that had aroused Eisenhower's interest was *Jencks* v. *U.S.* (353 U.S. 657), in which a decision had been announced two weeks earlier. In *Jencks* the Supreme Court had thrown out the conviction of a suspected Communist because the federal government had refused to turn over relevant FBI files to the presiding judge and defense counsel (see Paul L. Murphy, *The Constitution in Crisis Times, 1918–1969* [New York, 1972], pp. 326–29).

[2] Warren would write the President on July 15 (AWF/A). Apologizing for his delayed response, Warren said that while it was "considerate" of Eisenhower to write, it was "in no sense necessary." "Those of us who have long been in the public service know," he wrote, "that some columns are written in ignorance and others to deceive. Whatever the reason, if unfounded, they should be ignored." Noting that while in "other positions" he "could and did speak out to counteract such statements," at the Supreme Court "we do not respond regardless of what is said. We must live with what we write and are contented to do so."

212

EM, AWF, Administration Series

To Nelson Aldrich Rockefeller

June 21, 1957

Dear Nelson:[1] As Fred Dearborn has told you, the overseas public opinion reports that you helped to develop will be carried on, although on a reduced scale.[2] It is now anticipated that this will permit two surveys during the fiscal year in each of four major European countries, one in each of two Latin American countries, and two in one Far Eastern country.

Many thanks for staying alert to such developments even though you are not immediately on the spot.[3] Of course, it is no surprise to me that you have the willingness to do so.

With warm regard, *As ever*

[1] For background on Rockefeller, who had been both Under Secretary of Health, Education and Welfare (1953–1954) and Special Assistant to the President (1955), see Galambos, *NATO and the Campaign of 1952,* no. 218.

[2] Rockefeller had recently learned that budget cuts had forced the USIA to discontinue the public opinion reports, which, he said, were "a unique development of the socio-psychological aspects of our international relations." This research program involved only "a small amount of money," Rockefeller said, "and to lose this program and the highly specialized staff at key points around the world which have been so carefully trained would, I think, be a serious loss" (Rockefeller to Eisenhower, June 13, 1957, AWF/A; on appropriations for the USIA and the President's Special International Program see *Congressional Quarterly Almanac,* vol. XIII, *1957,* pp. 697–700).

Frederick M. Dearborn, Jr. (LL.B. Harvard 1936), former legal counsel to Massachusetts Governor Christian Herter (currently Under Secretary of State), had become Special Assistant to the President for Security Operations Coordination on May 27, 1957.

[3] After leaving the White House, Rockefeller had returned to private business in New York. He had, however, continued as chairman of the President's Advisory Committee on Government Reorganization.

213

EM, AWF, International Series: Saudi Arabia

To ibn Abd al-Aziz Saud

June 21, 1957

Your Majesty: I am taking this opportunity to convey my warm personal greetings to you through the pastor of my church, Dr. Edward L. R. Elson. I appreciate Your Majesty's willingness to receive this distinguished clergyman and interested student of the Middle East.[1]

When Dr. Elson suggested that he might seek an audience with you, we did not hesitate to recommend that he do so. Aware of the common bond of faith in God which has always been important to the relationship between Saudi Arabia and the United States, we were certain Your Majesty would find it of interest to receive one so closely associated with the spiritual life of our nation. He will, I know, discuss with you the important role of religion in the life of our nation and the deep respect in the United States for those who walk parallel paths to God.[2] *Your Good Friend*

[1] Elson, who was planning a six-week tour of the Middle East, had suggested to Secretary Dulles that he take a message from Eisenhower "dealing with the religious nature of American society." Dulles drafted this letter although, he said, the procedure was "somewhat unusual" (Dulles to Eisenhower, June 19, 1957, AWF/D-H).

[2] Although King Saud was away for "rest and recuperation" during Elson's visit, he told Eisenhower that he had made sure that leaders of his government would give the clergyman "all the assistance needed during his visit to this part of the world" (Saud to Eisenhower, July 28, 1957, AWF/I: Saudi Arabia).

214 — *EM, AWF, DDE Diaries Series*

To Howard Young — *June 21, 1957*

Dear Howard: Mamie and I are both profoundly grateful for your thoughtful invitation. Actually it would seem to me there is somewhat more chance that we could accept this year than has normally been the case. However, as you will surely understand, there are so many conditions to be fulfilled that I cannot talk with any great certainty about plans.[1]

First of all, we must stay here until Congress adjourns. I hope this will be no later than August tenth, but because of the civil rights argument they could run much longer than that.[2] If, however, a terminal date of early August should be achieved, then I think Mamie and I would want to go away from here for two or three weeks at the very least.[3]

We know that you normally ask a series of guests to visit you during the summer and we certainly do not want the possibility of our being able to come at some particular time to interfere with your entertainment of other guests. I will make a special point of keeping you informed of what goes on so that if and when the time arrives that we might leave, and you are completely free of all other "guest encumbrances," we could make the necessary arrangements.

I repeat that our movements for the summer are still in the lap of the gods. Nevertheless I shall have all of the airfield, communications, and other possibilities in the region examined at once so that if there should be a chance for us to come later, we could do so without having to be held up by administrative details.[4]

Again I assure you of our profound gratitude for your continued thoughtfulness to two old friends. *As ever*

[1] Young, who owned Young Galleries in New York City, had invited the Eisenhowers to vacation at Cedargates, his home in Minaqua, Wisconsin (June 18, 1957, WHCF/PPF 1-EE). The Eisenhowers had visited Cedargates several times since they first met Young in the summer of 1946. For background see *Eisenhower Papers*, vols. VI–XVII, especially Galambos, *Chief of Staff*, no. 1536; and no. 235 in these volumes.

[2] The Eighty-fifth Congress would not recess until August 30. The House would pass a modified version of the Administration's civil rights legislation in early August, but the Senate debated the measure for 24 days and made significant changes. Congress would pass the Civil Rights Act on August 29 and Eisenhower would sign it into law on September 9. For developments see nos. 248, 266, and 273; see also *Congressional Quarterly Almanac*, vol. XIII, *1957*, pp. 553–69.

[3] The Eisenhowers would vacation in Newport, Rhode Island, from September 4 until September 30. The President had considered visiting Newport earlier if the Senate had remained in session after the House recessed. He had finally decided to postpone his trip until the official end of the congressional session (*Public Papers of the Presidents: Eisenhower, 1957*, p. 557; *New York Times*, July 9, 10, 18, Sept. 1, Oct. 1, 1957). See also no. 291.

[4] In a July 9 letter to Young, Eisenhower said they would not be able to vacation in Minaqua due to "vast problems of administration and communications." He expressed hope that Young would "extend that rain check for a few years" (WHCF/PPF 1-EE).

215

EM, AWF, Name Series

To Edward Everett Hazlett, Jr.

June 24, 1957

Dear Swede: At this moment you are one of the mysteries of my office. We had clandestine information to the effect that you were entering Bethesda Hospital tomorrow. Inquiry at the hospital brings a report "We know nothing about it," so I will send this note to Chapel Hill in the hope that it will run you down somewhere along the line.[1]

I am just about to take off for Williamsburg where I am to address the Conference of Governors. I have a very banal and colorless talk to deliver. While it expresses an obvious truth—that governors ought to concern themselves more with retaining states' responsibilities if they are to attain states' rights—this subject has been so often discussed that I feel like I am giving a lecture on the virtues of sunlight. Some of these speaking engagements become mere ordeals.[2]

Of course if you are on the way here to the hospital, my office will know it before I get back and will probably have there a word of welcome to you.

I suppose it is those damnable headaches that are your present difficulty because you told me that your blood pressure situation was much improved.

These days find my riding the governmental merry-go-round at a dizzy pace. Abroad there are several problems that are immensely acute; for example, Jordan, disarmament efforts, Russian propaganda, and the Korean situation.[3]

At home, particularly here in Washington, the Budget governs the thinking, talking and action of almost every individual. Demagogues are having a field day with their particular venom being directed at "tight" money. This of course is one of the prices of prosperity. There is seemingly a much greater demand for money with which to expand than there is money.[4]

Some people doubt that it is possible for a free government to live too long with continued prosperity. It looks as if we are having a chance to prove or disprove the charge. Possibly nations have some of the characteristics of the individual, and we know many individuals who stand poverty with good grace grow insufferable, and degenerate in character, the moment they experience any good fortune.

Enough of all this—one of these days I will try to write a letter characterized by a bit more coherence and good sense.

Give my love to Ibby, and all the best to yourself. *As ever*

6/25/57. P.S. Immediately after I left for Williamsburg, my secretary discovered that you had indeed been admitted to Bethesda. Following my previous instructions, she sent you a few flowers and this note, of course, I shall now have delivered there. Captain Crittenberger will keep in touch with your doctors and report to me. I do hope this time the doctors will find the cause of your difficulty.[5]

[1] For background on Hazlett's health see no. 41. Eisenhower's good friend Swede Hazlett had written on June 6 (AWF/N) to say that for the first time since his return from the hospital two months earlier he felt well enough to type a letter. Complimenting Eisenhower on his "superb handling of the budget fight and the Old Guard," Hazlett wrote that it was time for the "Neanderthal Republicans" to realize that "the people of our country are devoted to Modernism and, if elections are to be won, the clock can't be turned back to 1920." For background see no. 138.

[2] For Eisenhower's June 24 address to the Conference of Governors see *Public Papers of the Presidents: Eisenhower, 1957*, pp. 486–97. Eisenhower would say that it was "idle to champion States' rights without upholding States' responsibilities as well. I believe that an objective reappraisal and reallocation of those responsibilities can lighten the hand of the central authority, reinforce our States and local governments, and in the process strengthen all America."

[3] On Jordan see no. 124; on disarmament efforts see nos. 182 and 205; on Russian propaganda see no. 153; on Korea see no. 244.

[4] See the following document.

[5] Dale Jackson Crittenberger (USMA 1950) was Assistant to the Military Aide to the President. For developments see no. 248.

216

EM, AWF, Administration Series

To Arthur Frank Burns

June 24, 1957

Dear Arthur: Thank you a lot for writing me the note that you did on the twenty-second.[1] The information in your sub-paragraphs one and two had been given me at various times and in varying degrees of urgency by George Humphrey and others.[2] The thoughts expressed in sub-paragraphs three and four, especially four, were new to me.[3] Because George is still testifying before the Senate Sub-Committee on Finances, I instantly called him up so that he would have these ideas in mind.[4] In addition, I am sending him a copy of your note to study at his leisure.

With respect to your sentence "my theme would be that inflation cannot be fought successfully by nineteenth century techniques in a twentieth-century world," I think that I could, even with my woefully limited knowledge of the subject, agree instantly with the generality. However, you have to spell it out a little bit more for the idea to be really meaningful to me. I would have to know just what is the twentieth century and what belongs to the nineteenth.[5]

I hope you have a good time at the farm; don't do too much writing because you should get a bit acquainted with the sun.

Remember me kindly to Mrs. Burns, and with warm regard, *As ever*

[1] Burns, former Chairman of the Council of Economic Advisors, had written Eisenhower on June 22 (AWF/A) with "a few quick observations" on the economy.

[2] Burns had termed the recent fall in bond prices "huge" and warned of "serious repercussions on the nation's economy" if the fall were to continue. In his second subparagraph, Burns had commented on "signs of disorganization" in the bond market. "The large and growing spread in yields between new and seasoned issues reflects," he wrote, "at least in part, uncertainty of people and a tendency to hold back on financial trading and decisions."

[3] Burns had commented that he did not believe "that the recent degree of tightness in the money market is serving any useful purpose." However, he continued, if the Federal Reserve deemed tight money a necessity, "it would at least be helpful to raise the discount rate—which is now way out of line with market interest rates. This would remove or reduce uncertainty concerning what the F.R. is up to. The business and financial world," he wrote, "has enough of uncertainty surrounding it, without the government following a course that adds to it." See Saulnier, *Constructive Years*, pp. 97–109.

[4] Treasury Secretary Humphrey had begun fourteen days of testimony before the Senate Committee on Finance on June 18. The committee had been prompted to examine the Administration's fiscal and monetary policies by the Treasury Secretary's resignation and by a recent rise in prices, interest rates, and government spending levels. See Humphrey, *Basic Papers*, pp. 296–98, and 330–52; on Humphrey's resignation see no. 175.

[5] Burns had told Eisenhower that during the summer he planned to "do some writing" on the problem of controlling inflation. In October 1957 Burns would present

to Fordham University a series of lectures on the economy. Fordham would publish Burns's lectures under the title *Prosperity Without Inflation* in the fall of that year.

217

EM, AWF, International Series: Macmillan

To Harold Macmillan *June 26, 1957*
Secret

Dear Harold:[1] I am delighted that you are prepared to join with us in putting forward in the Disarmament Subcommittee the proposals which Harold Stassen has been discussing with you and our French and Canadian colleagues in London.[2] We hope that this will pave the way for rapid progress in the Subcommittee.

Your concern about the possible effect on your nuclear position of the putting into effect of a program such as we propose is fully understood. I am, of course, happy to reaffirm the agreement which was reached in the exchange of letters between Harold Stassen and Commander Noble last February and March.[3] Your willingness to go along with our proposals in this respect will, I hope, be a significant step looking to increasing world security. Certainly, it will show the world our good intentions. Whether or not the Soviets will respond by accepting either the basic concept, or an adequate inspection system to support it, is, I fear, quite problematic. But we shall see.[4] *As ever*

[1] Eisenhower made no changes to the State Department draft of this message (see Dulles to Eisenhower, June 26, 1957, AWF/I: Macmillan).

[2] For background on the London disarmament meetings and the U.S. proposals see no. 205; see also State, *Foreign Relations, 1955–1957*, vol. XX, *Regulation of Armaments; Atomic Energy*, pp. 591–93, 620–26. On June 3 Macmillan had written Eisenhower questioning the provision that forbade the production of fissionable material for military purposes after a certain date, tentatively set as July 1959. This would prevent the United Kingdom "from developing the nuclear strength which she is just beginning to acquire," he said. "I am sure this cannot be your intention. It would involve a tremendous sacrifice for us, after we have put so much effort into our researches and, having made a success with our experiments, are ready to go forward with production" (PREM 11/2186). On June 21 Macmillan had reminded Eisenhower that the United Kingdom was "in a particularly difficult position" because they were "late starters" in the nuclear arms race (AWF/I: Macmillan). Writing three days later, the Prime Minister repeated his concerns: "As I have explained to you already, this must involve great risks for us. It might well prejudice not only our military nuclear programme, but the whole basis of our new defence policy. An early suspension of tests, and the cut off of the production of fissile material for military purposes, would prejudice both the development of our know-how and the accumulation of the supplies of material we need" (*ibid.*).

[3] Secretary Dulles had assured Macmillan that the United States would abide by the commitment it made in the exchange of letters between Stassen and Allan Herbert Percy Noble, British representative to the disarmament subcommittee. In this exchange the United States had agreed to talks with the British that would ensure that the adoption of the U.S. proposals would not preclude the development of nuclear weapons adequate to British needs (Whitney to Macmillan, June 19, 1957, PREM 11/2186; see also Whitney to Macmillan, June 24, 1957, *ibid.*; State, *Foreign Relations, 1955–1957*, vol. XX, *Regulation of Armaments; Atomic Energy*, pp. 463, 621, 637–38; and Telephone conversation, Eisenhower and Dulles, June 23, 1957, Dulles Papers, Telephone Conversations).

[4] For developments see no. 354.

218

EM, AWF, Dulles-Herter Series

To John Foster Dulles

June 26, 1957

Dear Foster: I have no comments—but I do have one question on your draft. The question applies to the statement on page three: "There is, of course, a distinction between formal diplomatic recognition and acceptance of the fact that a regime has power."[1]

Isn't this a rather recent development? In other words, did not diplomatic recognition mean, in the original sense, mere recognition of the fact that a regime had effective control over a given portion of the earth's surface and population? I recall vividly that when Mr. Wilson began to make distinctions among the several governments of Mexico that succeeded each other during the years from '13 to '17, the propriety of so doing was discussed at great length in some of our periodicals.[2]

I certainly do not question your statement as it applies to the present, but when I discussed this matter with Anthony Eden a couple of years ago, and with Winston before him, I remember that they answered me very simply, "We look on recognition as a mere acknowledgment of fact."[3]

It occurred to me that you might like to change your sentence simply by putting in an introductory phrase, "In these days . . .".[4] *As ever*

[1] Dulles had sent the final draft of a speech on communism in China to Eisenhower on June 25. The President had seen a previous draft of the speech, which he called "excellent," and had pencilled in "one or two slight questions." The new draft was "substantially what you saw before," Dulles said, "except that I have . . . somewhat developed the test for recognition which, as originally drafted, I based simply and solely upon national interest" (Dulles to Eisenhower, June 25, 1957; and Eisenhower, Note, June 20, 1957, both in AWF/D-H; see also Telephone conversation, Dulles and Hagerty, June 27, 1957, Dulles Papers, Telephone Conversations).

[2] On Woodrow Wilson, President of the United States from 1913 to 1921, and the difficulties arising from the Mexican Revolution, see John S. D. Eisenhower, *Intervention! The United States and the Mexican Revolution 1913–1917* (New York, 1993).
[3] On the British recognition of Communist China in 1950 see Galambos and van Ee, *The Middle Way*, no. 589; and Eisenhower, *Mandate for Change*, p. 249.
[4] Dulles would remove the entire sentence before delivering the speech to the international convention of the Lions International in San Francisco on June 28 (see John Foster Dulles, "Our Policies Toward Communism in China," *U.S. Department of State Bulletin* 37, no. 942 [July 15, 1957], 91–95).

219 — *EM, AWF, Name Series*

To Edgar Newton Eisenhower — *June 26, 1957*

Dear Ed: I made inquiry about your friend Mr. George Smith.[1]

Apparently there is general agreement that he is most competent in the field of communications law. The difficulty is that because of this competence, he has represented, before governmental bodies, so many of the communications firms that in most cases that come before the FCC he would have to disqualify himself from making decisions.

Whether or not this is completely correct, I am not sure—and I shall have made a thorough investigation.[2] *As ever*

[1] Eisenhower's brother, Edgar, had written on June 24 (AWF/N) in support of the appointment of attorney George Smith to the Federal Communications Commission. The planned retirement of Chairman George Carlton McConnaughey and his probable replacement by Commission member John Charles Doerfer would create an opening on the seven-man Commission (see *New York Times*, June 5, 27, 1957). Edgar reported that he had had "some business transactions" with Smith and had known him "personally" for some time. "He is an expert in the problems involved in communications, either by radio or television. He is a man of excellent character and is presently the President of the Bar Association of the Federal Communications Lawyers. He is regarded as one of the finest attorneys in this field." Despite Edgar's support, the President would not appoint Smith.
[2] On Edgar's previous suggestions for appointments see Galambos and van Ee, *The Middle Way*, nos. 75 and 415.

220

Dulles Papers, White House Memoranda Series

To John Foster Dulles

June 27, 1957

Dear Foster: I am truly getting a bit uneasy about the increasing stiffness of King Saud's attitude with respect to the Gulf of Aqaba.[1] It begins to look as if it would be easier to get unlimited use of the Canal for Israeli shipping than to make good on our efforts to have the Gulf of Aqaba considered as an international waterway.

The seriousness of the matter in my mind arises from the fact that he seems to have been making so much progress to lead most of the Arab world toward the Western camp.

I think we better do some very hard thinking on this matter.[2] *As ever*

[1] For background on the correspondence between Eisenhower and King Saud on the issue of free passage through the Straits of Tiran and the Gulf of Aqaba see no. 156. On June 25 the Saudi Arabian ambassador had delivered a note to the Department of State, protesting a June 5 circular that referred to the October 1955 "Notice to Mariners No. 44," with regulations for U.S. ships bound for the Gulf of Aqaba. Reminding ship owners and masters that the United States considered the gulf an international waterway, the memorandum stated that a denial of "free and innocent passage" through the waters to any ship of U.S. registry should be reported to the nearest available U.S. diplomatic or consular officer (AWF/I: Saudi Arabia; *U.S. Department of State Bulletin* 37, no. 942 [July 15, 1957], 112–13; and State, *Foreign Relations, 1955–1957*, vol. XVII, *Arab-Israeli Dispute 1957*, pp. 659–60, 682). In an accompanying message to Eisenhower, King Saud repeated his contention that the gulf and the straits were closed Arabian waterways and asked that the President personally intervene "in consonance with the principles of justice and equity, and in cognizance of our legitimate rights" (Saud to Eisenhower, June 25, 1957, AWF/I: Saudi Arabia).

[2] After receiving this letter, Secretary Dulles would tell Eisenhower that he thought they were "in a bad way. . . . Saud is acting as the head of the Moslem religion and not as head of state," Dulles said. "The route through the Gulf of Aqaba does not go through Saudi water. It is Egyptian and they are not kicking." Eisenhower suggested to Dulles that he tell King Saud that this was "one place where we don't see eye-to-eye and this is with great regret but we have looked at the thing and the entrance of the Gulf of Aqaba seems to be on the Egyptian side." The President also told Dulles that he would like to get on a plane and see Saud "if it would not create a storm" (Telephone conversation, Eisenhower and Dulles, June 27, 1957, Dulles Papers, Telephone Conversations; see also *ibid.*, pp. 660–61). For developments see no. 232.

To Edgar Newton Eisenhower *June 27, 1957*

Dear Ed: With respect to your letter of the twenty-fifth, there is a vast difference between Federal domination and Federal performance of a job that needs to be done.[1]

The point I tried to make in my speech was that inadequate education of our youth could, and would unless greater facilities were provided, become a *national* calamity. Consequently, the Federal government, without trying to take any control of education or to assume any dominant position with respect to it, still has to view with the deepest concern the failure of the states to move promptly and adequately in this regard.[2]

If we could only see our way out of this without Federal help I would be tremendously pleased. The same goes for urban renewal and rehabilitation, as well as for concerting highway rules and regulations. A good proportion of our forty thousand deaths a year on the roads can be attributed to lack of action among the states in coordinating standards and rules of the road.[3]

Give my love to Lucy. *As ever*

[1] Edgar Eisenhower had written on June 25 (AWF/N) to compliment the President on his speech to the Governors' Conference at Williamsburg (see no. 215). Noting that he agreed "wholeheartedly" with Eisenhower's theme, Edgar said that the federal government had "taken on certain functions which concededly belong to the states." "It is my concept of our form of government," he argued, "that the Federal Government does not have any functions except those particularly delegated to it by the Constitution. If my conception were followed, there are many things the Federal Government is doing today which would be prohibited."

[2] Eisenhower had stated that while he was opposed to "needless Federal expansion," he had found it necessary at times to urge Federal action in some areas traditionally reserved to the States. "In each instance State inaction, or inadequate action, coupled with undeniable national need," he stated, had "forced emergency Federal intervention." Eisenhower cited the education of youth as a prime example (see no. 196). Because classroom shortages were "potentially so dangerous to the entire nation" and local remedial action had been delayed, a temporary federal assistance plan had become a necessity. "Now, some have feared the sincerity of that word 'temporary,' Eisenhower had stated. "I at once concede that, in government as with individuals, there is an instinctive inclination to persist in any activity once begun. But if it be the people's will, and I believe it is, I have no doubt at all that we can defeat that inclination in respect to Federal help in school construction, once the emergency need has been satisfied" (*Public Papers of the Presidents: Eisenhower, 1957*, pp. 486–97).

[3] Eisenhower had stated in his speech to the governors that "day by day the American people are paying an increasingly fearful price for the failure of the States to agree on such safety essentials as standards for licensing of drivers and vehicles and basic rules of the road."

222

EM, AWF, International Series: Churchill

To Winston Spencer Churchill *June 28, 1957*

Dear Winston: Thank you so much for your note of the twenty-fourth. I am tremendously pleased that you have agreed to the idea of an exhibition of your paintings in the United States.[1] Without question the showing will be a great success, and will help to strengthen the close ties of friendship that exist between the peoples of our two countries.

Quite selfishly, I am even more delighted by your offer to give me one of your works.[2] I have long cherished a desire to own an original Churchill—and I have never quite found the courage to ask you.

I understand that you invited me to write a bit of a foreword to the brochure that will be used in connection with the paintings.[3] While I am probably little qualified for the task, it will be a great honor to make an attempt. *As ever*

[1] For background on the project, proposed to the former British prime minister in a hand-delivered letter from Eisenhower, see no. 86. In his note Churchill had agreed to make thirty paintings available for the exhibit (AWF/I: Churchill).

[2] Churchill had offered Eisenhower any painting in the selection as "a token of my continuing respect and affection." See also Telephone conversation, June 27, 1957, AWF/I: Churchill; and [Bernau] memorandum, July 1, 1957, Dulles Papers, Telephone Conversations.

[3] Eisenhower had learned of Churchill's request in a telephone conversation the preceding day (Ann Whitman memorandum, June 27, 1957, AWF/I: Churchill; see also *New York Times*, Mar. 7, 1958). For developments see no. 414.

4

“Logic and reason must operate gradually”

223 EM, AWF, Administration Series: AEC

To Lewis Lichtenstein Strauss *July 2, 1957*

Dear Lewis: I should like you to read the attached letter and examine the list of names of various scientists, suggested by Mr. Cousins.[1]

Because I did have in Dr. Lawrence, Dr. Teller and Dr. Mills, I rather think it might be a good idea for me to pick two or three scientists who represent a contrary view and ask them in for a visit. I see no need for asking Norman Cousins to accompany them.[2]

Might I have your comments?[3] *As ever*

[1] Magazine editor Norman Cousins had asked Eisenhower to meet with a small group of scientists who had no affiliation with the Atomic Energy Commission in order to discuss the dangers of radioactive fallout from atomic testing (for background see no. 210). "The impression has been created that only scientists connected with the A.E.C. have had a chance to present their evidence to you," Cousins had written. "I believe it would be only fair for a small group to be given the privilege of an audience with you in order to lay before you such facts as seem pertinent to the issue." Cousins had included a list of nine men and had offered to arrange a meeting with Eisenhower and any of the scientists (Cousins to Eisenhower, June 27, 1957, AWF/N).

[2] On June 24 Edward Teller (Ph.D. University of Leipzig 1930), Ernest Orlando Lawrence (Ph.D. Yale 1925), and Mark Muir Mills (Ph.D. California Institute of Technology 1948), all from the University of California Radiation Laboratory, had met with Eisenhower to discuss the progress that they and their colleagues had made in developing weapons that would limit radioactive fallout to the area of the initial blast. According to Secretary Dulles, the meeting had made "a deep impression" on Eisenhower and caused him to question the advisability of test suspension (State, *Foreign Relations, 1955–1957,* vol. XX, *Regulation of Armaments; Atomic Energy,* pp. 638–42, 649–50; Robert A. Divine, *Blowing on the Wind: The Nuclear Test Ban Debate 1954–1960* [New York, 1978], pp. 148–50; and Hewlett and Holl, *Atoms for Peace and War,* pp. 400–01; see also Telephone conversations, Dulles and Strauss, June 24 and 27, 1957, Dulles Papers, Telephone Conversations).

[3] Cousins did not understand the purpose of the meeting with the three physicists, Strauss would reply. "You did not invite them and they did not ask for the appointment." The scientists were in Washington to testify regarding nuclear weapons before the Joint Congressional Committee on Atomic Energy, Strauss said, and a committee member had requested the presidential meeting. "Since none of the persons suggested by Mr. Cousins have access to the national weapons program, it appears that Mr. Cousins has assumed that Drs. Lawrence, Teller, and Mills had come to see you to discuss the controversial issues that have been raised by Mr. Cousins and others on the biological effects of fall-out from weapons tests. Of course, this was not the case." If the President agreed to such a meeting, Strauss cautioned, the public could doubt "your confidence in the competence of the very eminent men who are devoting their talents and reputations to a vital, though presently unpopular, service to the Government" (Strauss to Eisenhower, July 3, 1957, AWF/A: AEC; see also *Congressional Quarterly Almanac,* vol. XIII, *1957,* pp. 795–96; and Lewis L. Strauss, *Men and Decisions* [New York, 1962], pp. 418–19. For Eisenhower's reply to Cousins see no. 231.

To Sinclair Weeks *July 2, 1957*

Dear Sinny: This afternoon I was visited by an old friend of mine, Albert Redpath, a lawyer of New York. He is a director of Northwest Airlines.[1]

He is very violently opposed, as you would guess, to the granting of any certificate to Pan American to operate on the Pacific Great Circle route to Tokyo. He opposes this even if Pan American's right to pick up passengers and mail is limited to San Francisco and points to the south.[2]

He gave me a number of statistics and arguments to support his view.

The purpose of this note is to ask that when the CAB acts on this case, you make the best analysis of the whole affair that you can possibly develop. I am anxious that when we have to make a decision on this situation, no matter which way it goes, we do it with all the available facts before us.[3]

Thanks very much.

With warm regard, *As ever*

[1] Columbia University Trustee Albert Gordon Redpath was also an investment banker and partner in the New York City brokerage firm of Auchincloss, Parker and Redpath (see Galambos, *NATO and the Campaign of 1952*, no. 374).

[2] In 1946 the Civil Aeronautics Board had concluded that there should be two competing U.S. flag routes across the Pacific. The CAB awarded to Pan American World Airways the route across the Central Pacific via Hawaii, while the Great Circle Route via Alaska had been given to Northwest Orient Airlines. In 1952 Pan American had applied for authority to use the Great Circle route between Los Angeles, San Francisco, Portland, Seattle and Japan. Although that petition was denied, the case was reopened in 1956 at Eisenhower's request. For background see Galambos and van Ee, *The Middle Way*, nos. 1080 and 1447, and the case files in WHCF/OF 62: West Coast—Hawaii. See also Marylin Bender and Selig Altschul, *The Chosen Instrument* (New York, 1981), pp. 408–9.

[3] On August 2, 1957, Eisenhower would write James R. Durfee, Chairman of the Civil Aeronautics Board, that he had approved the Board's decision granting Pan American World Airways the right to use the Great Circle route between Los Angeles, San Francisco, and Tokyo. "It is this Administration's objective," he would say, "wherever traffic justifies it, to provide competitive United States service on all international and overseas routes from all gateways" (see Eisenhower to Durfee and additional correspondence in WHCF/CF: CAB). Despite the President's remaining doubts about the wisdom of such action, Northwest Airlines would receive permanent certification to fly the Great Circle route between Seattle and Tokyo (see Ann Whitman memorandum, Aug. 21, 1957, AWF/AWD). For developments see no. 315.

225

EM, AWF, Administration Series

To Sherman Adams

July 2, 1957

Memorandum for Governor Adams: I should like to make a quiet check, possibly by telephone, on the qualifications of Walker Cisler, President of Detroit Edison.[1] I think your two best leads would be Lewis Strauss and Joe Dodge.[2]

Aside from his character and his standing in his community—and his background of training and experience—I am particularly interested in his organizational ability and his self-confidence.

If you could do this by tomorrow noon, I would appreciate it.[3]

[1] Walker Lee Cisler (M.E. Cornell University 1922), president and director of the Detroit Edison Company since 1951, had served as an adviser for the U.S. delegation to the International Conference on Peaceful Uses of Atomic Energy (1955). Treasury Secretary Humphrey had recommended Cisler as a possible replacement for Secretary of Defense Wilson, who had recently informed Eisenhower of his desire to retire (see Eisenhower, *Waging Peace*, p. 244; Telephone Call Chronology, July 2, 1957, AWF/D; see also Ambrose, *Eisenhower*, vol. II, *The President*, pp. 440–41).

[2] Eisenhower was referring to Chairman of the Atomic Energy Commission and Special Assistant to the President on Atomic Energy Matters Lewis L. Strauss, and Joseph M. Dodge, consultant to the President on foreign economic policies.

[3] There is no further correspondence on this subject in AWF. For developments see no. 369.

226

EM, WHCF, Official File 3-R

To Albert Pratt

July 3, 1957

Dear Mr. Pratt:[1] In acting on the Cordiner Report, the Administration has, it is correct, concentrated its immediate efforts on steps proposed by the Department of Defense as best suited to relieve the most critical situation—the loss of highly skilled and highly trained enlisted men and junior officers. This action was taken without prejudice to the deliberate consideration of the Report as a whole.[2]

Those who bear overall responsibility must obviously weigh the Report from many points of view, including its effects on numerous other phases of governmental activity and responsibility. For this reason, implementation of the entire Report will not be recommended at this time.[3]

I appreciate your thinking on this matter. With much of it I am in entire accord. *Sincerely*

P.S. I have several times stated publicly that I thought it would be a great saving to pay technicians enough to keep them in the service, thus obviating the necessity for excessive turnover and a vast school system.

[1] Pratt (A.B. Harvard 1933, LL.B. 1936), a partner with the investment firm of Paine, Webber, Jackson & Curtis, had served as Assistant Secretary of the Navy for Personnel and Reserve Forces between 1954 and 1956, and as a member of the Defense Advisory Committee on Professional and Technical Compensation, also known as the Cordiner Committee (for background see no. 73).

[2] Pratt had written the President on June 27, 1957 (same file as document) to express concern that Eisenhower's June nineteenth news conference remarks indicated a "misconception" about some of the Cordiner report's most important findings. During the news conference Eisenhower had reiterated his support for pay raises for skilled enlisted men and certain groups of young officers. However, the need for certain pay raises should not, Eisenhower stated, "be used as an excuse for a general overall pay raise to include all the generals and everybody else in the Army, Navy, and Air Force. I think that is wrong at this time" (see *Public Papers of the Presidents: Eisenhower, 1957*, pp. 474–75). Pratt reminded Eisenhower that the Cordiner Committee had found military pay rates at the lower levels to be reasonably comparable to civilian pay. It was at the higher levels, both officer and enlisted, where the disparity was the greatest. "Your statements to your press conference," Pratt wrote, "indicated that the need for pay raises existed primarily amongst young enlisted technicians and 'certain of the very young officers'. Actually, our philosophy was exactly the reverse."

[3] Eisenhower was concerned about reducing federal expenditures; on his efforts see no. 202. Although legislation to implement the Cordiner Committee's recommendations would be introduced in the Senate, no action would be taken in 1957 (see *Congressional Quarterly Almanac*, vol. XIII, *1957*, p. 636). For developments see no. 564.

227 *EM, AWF, DDE Diaries Series*

To John Sheldon Doud Eisenhower *July 3, 1957*

Dear Johnny: You may have seen in the paper a story to the effect that, at a social gathering, I mentioned the opportunity you had had to leave the service and part of your reasons for deciding not to do so. I hope that the story does not disturb you—even though its publication irritates me intensely.[1] I thought that I was talking to a group of gentlemen and I forgot that they are primarily politicians. Consequently, any opportunity to repeat a story told by the President gave them a chance to appear as a big wheel.

In any event I will in the future be more of a clam.

I hope you had a fine time on your trip. You must come up soon and tell me about it.[2] *Devotedly*

[1] During an off-the-record White House breakfast for Republican members of the House of Representatives, the President had mentioned that Major Eisenhower had rejected a teaching position at a large university (*New York Times,* July 3, 1957; see also Ann Whitman memorandum, July 3, 1957, AWF/AWD).
[2] On July 8 John would visit his father at the Gettysburg farm.

228

EM, AWF, DDE Diaries Series

To Leif John Sverdrup *July 3, 1957*

Dear General Sverdrup: We talked last evening about the possibility that a young bull I have from Scotland, Black Brutus of E. F., may develop into a fine herd sire. If and when he proves himself to be such, I would be glad to have him service a couple of heifers of your own choosing.[1]

Since Black Brutus is not yet eight months old, I should think it would be something like fifteen months from now before his first calves are on the ground. I will then give you a report on him, including—if I am able to get them—the opinions of some real experts in this field.

The dinner was over and the guests leaving before I learned that Mr. John Hanes, who sat next to you, was half owner of Eileenmere 1032. Possibly for some of the others we kept the conversation too much on "Angus" breeding. However, I thoroughly enjoyed it myself.[2]

With best wishes, *Sincerely*

[1] Sverdrup (B.S. in C.E. University of Minnesota 1921), president of the St. Louis, Missouri, engineering consulting firm Sverdrup and Parcel, had attended a stag dinner at the White House. During World War II Sverdrup had served with the U.S. Army Corps of Engineers. For developments on Black Brutus see nos. 15 and 250; for background see Heckett to Eisenhower, May 28, 1957, and Eisenhower to Heckett, May 30, 1957, AWF/Gettysburg. There is no further correspondence on this matter in AWF.

[2] John Wesley Hanes, Sr. (A.B. Yale 1915), a corporate executive at Olin Mathieson Chemical Corporation and at Ecusta Paper Corporation, also attended the stag dinner. On Eileenmere 1032 see no. 55, and Galambos and van Ee, *The Middle Way,* nos. 1297, 1746, and 1881.

229 *EM, AWF, Name Series: Guided Missiles*

TO CHARLES ERWIN WILSON *July 8, 1957*
Top secret

Dear Charlie: I want you to express to the Defense Department, and especially to Mr. Quarles, Mr. Holaday, Admiral Sides, and their associates, my appreciation of the comprehensive presentation which they made to the National Security Council on July 3 of the Defense Department's ballistic and aerodynamic missile programs.[1] It was superior and most informative. I understand that the full text, with charts, will be available about mid-July.

The presentation showed that the Department of Defense has already determined to phase out in the future these missile programs: CORPORAL, HONEST JOHN, MATADOR A and C, REGULUS I, and NIKE-AJAX.[2]

The presentation also seemed to indicate a number of overlapping programs,—for example: JUPITER-THOR, NAVAHO-SNARK, ATLAS-TITAN, TERRIER/TARTAR, NIKE/land-based TALOS, POLARIS-TRITON. However desirable it might be to provide to the Services a family of missiles that would cover all ranges and capabilities, it is necessary to consider the financial feasibility of each program in the light of competing Defense and other national security demands upon appropriated funds. I know that you realize the necessity for, and appreciate the need for accelerating, such decisions.[3]

Before I make any further decisions in this field beyond those reflected in 1957 NSC Actions 1653, 1690, and 1733, I wish you to give me your recommendations not later than August 15 as to any additional missile programs which can be eliminated before October 1, 1957.[4] Your recommendations should include an estimate of the effect of such eliminations on projected annual expenditure estimates shown in the presentation for the period through FY 1962.[5] *Sincerely*

[1] Eisenhower was referring to Donald Aubrey Quarles (B.A. Yale University 1916), who had served as Secretary of the Air Force from August 1955 through April 30, 1957. Quarles had been appointed Deputy Secretary of Defense on May 1, 1957. Accompanying Quarles were William M. Holaday, Special Assistant to the Secretary of Defense; Rear Admiral John H. Sides, Deputy to Holaday; Colonel Douglas E. Williams, USAF; Colonel Austin W. Betts, USA; and Commander L. A. Kurtz, USN (see NSC meeting minutes, July 5, 1957, AWF/NSC).

[2] Eisenhower was concerned about interservice rivalries and duplication in the missile program; see no. 127, and Galambos and van Ee, *The Middle Way*, nos. 1663 and 1750; for background see Alan J. Levine, *The Missile and Space Race*, (Westport, Conn., 1994), pp. 33–46, and David Milobsky, *Leadership and Competition: Technological Innovation and Organizational Change at the U.S. Department of Defense, 1955–1968*, Ph.D. diss. (Ann Arbor, Mich., 1996).

[3] Secretary Quarles had told the NSC meeting that the United States had spent $11.8 billion on its missiles program through FY 1957. "The cost of continuing these programs from FY 1957 through FY 1963," he said, "would amount to approximately $36.1 billion, for a grand total of some $47 billion." When Eisenhower received no response to his inquiry as to whether there were any questions on the presentation, he concluded that "everybody was thunderstruck at what he had heard on the subject of our missile programs and their costs."

[4] NSC Action No. 1653 noted the progress of research and development programs for the ICBM and the IRBM. It also observed that the President had not approved any specific numbers for force units and missile inventories; NSC Action No. 1690 had authorized the Department of Defense to achieve initial operational capability for the IRBM and ICBM programs (Thor, Atlas, and Titan) at the "earliest practicable date;" NSC Action No. 1733 said that the total cost of each weapon system, relative to its effectiveness, "must always be taken into account, in view of the fact that the maintenance of a sound U.S. economy sets limits to U.S. defense expenditures" (see State, *Foreign Relations, 1955–1957*, vol. XIX, *National Security Policy*, pp. 405, 455–56, 530).

[5] Wilson would respond to Eisenhower on August 9 saying that he still believed that the guided missile program "can and must be reduced to meet budget limitations." The Secretary stated that he had canceled the Navaho missile system, at a saving of $1,948 million for the FY 1958–FY 1963 time period. The "complex inter-relationship between projected missile force structures and those of other weapons system" led Wilson to decline to specify where other reductions might be made. "Certain programs will be phased out during the development cycle; others will not be carried into operational use; and in other programs there will be a general scaling down of force requirements" he said. "I assure you, Mr. President," he concluded, "that your aims are fully appreciated and that the effort to attain them will be prosecuted on an urgent basis. I shall report significant progress to you as appropriate" (same file as document). For developments see no. 389.

230

EM, AWF, Name Series

To Helen Rogers Reid

Personal

July 9, 1957

Dear Helen:[1] Some things are best done quietly. This unfortunately gives the impression that we are doing nothing. In a period such as the present, we must remember that respect for the national pride of the various nations requires that most of the specific plans and projects that promise to increase friendship and mutual cooperation must be kept secret, sometimes even after consummation. To acknowledge the existence, in some cases, of a friendly relationship could easily destroy that relationship.[2]

There was a most vigorous—and most secret—follow-up of Foster's speech of August 1955 to which you refer. Not only he but I myself personally participated actively in directing it. It came to naught as Soviet Communist influence became stronger in Egypt which at that time was a key factor because of the strong influence it exerted over Jordan.[3]

Now that events have weakened Nasser's influence in Jordan, it seems that another effort might be made.[4] This is being actively studied in the State Department, and I happen to know that Foster has spent a good deal of time over the last two or three weeks going over voluminous reports and data supplied by Eric Johnston, by officials of the United Nations, and his own staff.[5]

I know that he feels that it would probably again be necessary at least initially to feel out the situation on a quiet, inconspicuous basis, but you can know that we are constantly looking for any opening favorable to proceeding along the lines of our 1955 plan, either all at once or bit by bit. As Foster said in his July 2nd press conference, conditions seem to be ameliorating and we would hope that constructive developments could take place.[6]

With warm personal regard, *Sincerely*

[1] For background on Reid, former president and chairman of the board of the *New York Herald Tribune*, see Galambos and van Ee, *The Middle Way*, nos. 56 and 1351.

[2] A continuing interest in the problem of refugees displaced by the 1948–1949 Arab-Israeli conflict and a visit to the refugee camps in Jordan had prompted Reid to write Eisenhower. She had urged the President to increase American efforts on behalf of the Jordan River reclamation project, the resettlement of some of the refugees in Iraq, and a plan to persuade Israel of "the necessity of taking back a certain number of refugees and compensating others." "Please do something," she requested (June 28, 1957, AWF/N; for background see Galambos and van Ee, *The Middle Way*, nos. 457, 1575, and 1784).

Eisenhower had sent Reid's letter to Secretary Dulles, asking him to "allow no one else to see it" and to comment informally. Dulles drafted this reply, and Eisenhower added the last two sentences in the first paragraph (Eisenhower to Dulles, July 8; Dulles to Eisenhower, July 9, 1957, Dulles Papers, White House Memoranda Series; see also Telephone conversation, Eisenhower and Dulles, July 8, 1957, Dulles Papers, Telephone Conversations).

[3] In August 1955 Secretary Dulles had discussed the resettlement and repatriation of Palestinian refugees in a speech on U.S. policy in the Middle East. The United States would aid in the development of the Jordan River Valley, he said, which would create the arable land necessary to provide permanent homes for the 900,000 Arab refugees displaced by the creation of Israel. If Israel were unable to make adequate compensation to the refugees, the United States would help in securing an international loan to facilitate the process (John Foster Dulles, "The Middle East," *U.S. Department of State Bulletin* 33, no. 845 [September 5, 1955], 378–79; see also Alteras, *Eisenhower and Israel*, pp. 131–33). "Dulles' speech . . . was most heartening," Reid had written, "and I thought he intended to follow up on it."

Early attempts at negotiating an agreement for the reclamation of the Jordan River Valley had begun in October 1953 with talks in Israel, Egypt, Jordan, Syria, and Lebanon. However, Arab fears that the plan, devised by U.S. engineers and promoted by Eisenhower's special representative Eric A. Johnston, favored Israel and had prevented meaningful discussions. In March 1956 the United States and Lebanon had formulated a revised version of this plan, one that would incorporate many of the elements of the Johnston proposal but would be presented to the Arab states as the

Arab or "Lahoud" Plan (after Lebanese Foreign Minister Salim Lahoud, who helped negotiate the agreement). The United States would agree to carry out the provisions of the proposal if Lebanon could secure Arab support (State, *Foreign Relations, 1955–1957*, vol. XIV, *Arab-Israeli Dispute 1955* (1989), pp. 20–23, 109–12, 197–98; vol. XV, *Arab-Israeli Dispute January 1–July 26, 1956* (1989), pp. 286–87, 360–61, 429–30, 710–14; see also Alteras, *Eisenhower and Israel*, pp. 117–25; and Eisenhower, *Waging Peace*, p. 23; for background on Johnston see Galambos and van Ee, *The Middle Way*, no. 161).

[4] For background on the political situation in Jordan and Nasser's influence in that country see no. 124.

[5] On May 14, 1957, Under Secretary of State Herter had asked that State Department officials "promptly and diligently" investigate the issue of Palestinian refugees and present a proposal "that would move us ahead on this whole problem which is serious and could cause increasing difficulty." In a report dated July 2 State Department officials had recommended that the United States adopt Eric A. Johnston's idea of offering financial assistance to Iraq for the resettlement of refugees and to Jordan for the cost of developing the Jordan River in that country (on Johnston see n. 3 above). In September, however, the State Department would report that pro-Soviet trends in Syria, the deteriorating security situation in Lebanon, and political uncertainty in Jordan had produced conditions that were no longer favorable for a solution to the problem (State, *Foreign Relations, 1955–1957*, vol. XVII, *Arab-Israeli Dispute 1957*, pp. 618, 661–76, 698–701, 741–43, 749–51, 807–19, 821–26, 833–37, 859–63).

[6] On Dulles's news conference see *U.S. Department of State Bulletin* 37, no. 943 (July 22, 1957), 141–42. For subsequent developments see no. 233.

231

EM, AWF, Name Series

TO NORMAN COUSINS
Personal and confidential

July 9, 1957

Dear Mr. Cousins: Your letter of June twenty-seventh apparently assumes that I made an appointment with Doctors Lawrence, Teller and Mills to discuss the lively argument that seems to be occupying the attention of so many in the United States concerning the effects of radio-active fallout. This was not the case at all.[1]

These gentlemen were in the city to testify before a Committee of Congress. A member of that Committee, Congressman Cole, requested that I see them in order that I would be apprised of certain information which he thought was new in the general subject of weapon production. Their specific conference with me dealt with the work of these scientists in the weapons area.

By no means am I trying to act as the sole judge in a controversy which, by its very nature, must be more or less scientific in character.

As to my opinions and purposes in this whole great field of armaments, particularly atomic weapons, I refer you again to all the public statements and speeches I have made on the subject, beginning April 16, 1953.[2]

While I appreciate your offer to be helpful in bringing certain individuals to see me, I assure you that I have frequently heard scientific dissertations dealing with every phase of the atomic question, and from diverse viewpoints. So, while I carry on energetically the program I believe we must pursue at this moment to provide for the security of our country, I am working unceasingly for the time when war itself will be eliminated and the atomic danger will be a thing of the past. *Sincerely*

[1] For the contents of Cousins's letter and the details of Eisenhower's meeting with the three physicists see no. 223. Cousins had written in response to Eisenhower's letter of June 21 (no. 210). General Goodpaster had prepared a draft reply, which the President did not use (July 1, 1957, AWF/N).

[2] On the President's speech before the American Society of Newspaper Editors see Galambos and van Ee, *The Middle Way*, no. 132. In his reply (July 9, 1957, WHCF/OF 108-A), Cousins would praise Eisenhower's 1953 address and ask the President "for another major speech" on disarmament, one that would be "directed to all peoples in their status as fellow human beings rather than as members of this or that nation." For developments see no. 463.

232 — *EM, AWF, Dulles-Herter Series*

To John Foster Dulles — *July 10, 1957*

Dear Foster: In view of corrections I suggest at the bottom of page two, I return for your further consideration the draft of my reply to King Saud.[1] For your convenience and because my writing is not too legible, I am having the entire paragraph at the bottom of page two retyped so that you may consider it.

With respect to the Aide Memoire, I have no suggestions except for one word found on page four. You use the term "a recognized international pathway." Would it not be better to say "a recognized international right of use"? The term "pathway" seems to me could be interpreted by the King as meaning a special and restricted route, whereas I assume we mean that pilgrims could cross the Gulf of Aqaba at any point of their own choosing.[2] *As ever*

[1] For background on King Saud's June 25 letter to Eisenhower regarding passage through the Gulf of Aqaba see no. 220. For Eisenhower's letter, with his corrections to the State Department draft, see the following document (see also Dulles to Eisenhower, July 9, 1957, AWF/D-H).

[2] As a result of meetings between State Department officials and King Saud's special representative on June 12 and 17, the department had prepared an aide-memoire with four suggestions for courses of action for King Saud's consideration: Saudi Arabia could ask the International Court of Justice to rule on the legal status of the waterway; the United States could seek restrictions on the movements of Israeli warships in the Gulf; the United States could, if requested, ask its own vessels to avoid Saudi Arabian waters when passing through the Gulf; and Saudi Arabia could ask the Security Council to consider a resolution establishing "a recognized international pathway for pilgrims," a pathway on which their safe passage to the Holy Places of Islam would be guaranteed. The aide-memoire is in AWF/I: Saudi Arabia; see also Telephone conversation, Eisenhower and Dulles, July 1, 1957, Dulles Papers, Telephone Conversations; and State, *Foreign Relations, 1955–1957,* vol. XVII, *Arab-Israeli Dispute 1957,* pp. 693–94).

William Rountree, Assistant Secretary of State for Near Eastern Affairs, objected to the change in language, however, and suggested to Secretary Dulles that the department "omit all references to a 'pathway' or 'right of use' and instead to refer to 'the special character of the traditional pilgrim routes', which would, according to Rountree, leave the concept somewhat vague." After Dulles had presented the alternative language to Eisenhower later this same day, "the President said he would prefer not to use any language such as 'pathway' or 'traditional pilgrim' routes which might imply assigning a special character to west-east routes as well as north-south routes in the Gulf of Aqaba, pointing out that there were traditional pilgrim routes from North Africa across the Gulf. He said he was concerned that any recognition of these pathways might have the effect of blocking the passage of vessels to the northern portion of the Gulf" (*ibid.*, pp. 688–89).

The final wording, approved by Eisenhower, guaranteed U.S. support for a resolution "which would put the authority of the United Nations behind the rights of the pilgrims to undisturbed passage through the Gulf of Aqaba and give United Nations affirmation to His Majesty's rightful concern for the safe passage of pilgrims as Keeper of the Holy Places of Islam."

233

EM, AWF, International Series: Saudi Arabia

To ibn Abd al-Aziz Saud — *July 10, 1957*

Cable. Secret

Your Majesty: Since the receipt of your message on March 31, we have been giving the situation in the Gulf of Aqaba our most earnest consideration. We have appreciated the opportunity afforded by Your Majesty's acceptance of our suggestion of May 15 that the various aspects of this question be discussed with your representative. At all times in these discussions, we have been particularly aware of Your Majesty's position as the Keeper of the Holy Places of Islam, as well as the leader of an important Arab state on the Gulf.[1]

Secretary of State Dulles has kept me informed of the course of his discussions and those of other Departmental officers with Azzam

Pasha. I believe the talks have been useful in developing possible ways to ease the situation in the Gulf.[2] The Secretary of State has prepared an Aide-Memoire containing certain suggested avenues of approach, which is being provided to Azzam Pasha who will, I presume, arrange for its appropriate consideration by Your Majesty and your counselors.[3]

The memorandum seeks to be responsive to the principal points of concern which have emerged from your message and our further conversations with Azzam Pasha, namely: the presence of Israeli warships in the Gulf, the serious question of the safety of Moslem pilgrims transiting the Gulf, the responsibilities of United States vessels toward the coastal sovereigns on the Gulf, and the legal status of the Gulf of Aqaba and the straits leading into it.

In our consideration of this problem, we are mindful of the special responsibilities which Your Majesty bears during the current pilgrimage season. I can assure you, as I have in the past, that we would view most gravely any action by any nation which would interfere with the safe transit of pilgrims. If, in your deliberation with the representatives of other Moslem nations during the present pilgrimage, it would assist Your Majesty's position to make mention of our assurances on this matter, you may feel at liberty to do so.

I was grateful that Your Majesty brought to my attention in your letter of June 15 your special concern over a circular to shipowners regarding the Gulf.[4] The routine character of this circular, and the fact that it was not intended to forbid compliance with requirements of prior notification issued by a coastal state in accordance with the principles of international law, have been fully explained by the Department of State to Ambassador al-Khayyal and to Azzam Pasha.[5]

Our declaration on the legal status of the Gulf of Aqaba was motivated by the same reliance on principle and international law which governed our actions during the events of last October and November.[6] Even then we did not insist that our individual views were fixed and inflexible; to the contrary we expressed the hope that if there should develop differing views on the matter, the whole affair might be decided by the International Court at The Hague, which decision we stand ready, in advance, to accept. That our attitude then announced, should have created differences with Saudi Arabia at a time when the parallel nature of our objectives in the area are becoming increasingly apparent is a matter of particular regret. I am hopeful that what we are proposing will offer a way to reduce these differences and to maintain the peace and tranquility in the area which we both so earnestly seek.[7]

May God grant you His safekeeping. *Your sincere friend*

[1] On King Saud's March 31 letter see no. 154; Eisenhower's May 15 letter is no. 156. Although the monarch had agreed to the discussions, he had repeated the Saudi

Arabian position "that the Gulf of Aqaba was a closed Gulf" (State, *Foreign Relations, 1955–1957*, vol. XVII, *Arab-Israeli Dispute 1957*, p. 636).

[2] Abdul Rahman Azzam Pasha had met with William Rountree, Assistant Secretary of State for Near Eastern Affairs, on June 12 and 17 and with Secretary Dulles on July 3. At the conclusion of the June meetings, Rountree had told Dulles that the discussions were far from satisfactory and that the ensuing difficulties could threaten the effective relations that the United States had held with Saudi Arabia, as well as its general position in the area (*ibid.*, pp. 636–41, 648, 656–59, 681–87; see also Telephone conversation, Eisenhower and Dulles, July 1, 1957, Dulles Papers, Telephone Conversations).

[3] See the preceding document.

[4] On the State Department circular and Saud's June 25 protest see no. 220; see also Greene to Goodpaster, June 27, 1957, AWF/I: Saudi Arabia.

[5] At a June 27 meeting with Assistant Secretary Rountree, Azzam Pasha had emphasized how much the statement had upset King Saud (State, *Foreign Relations, 1955–1957*, vol. XVII, *Arab-Israeli Dispute 1957*, p. 660).

[6] For background on the crisis surrounding Egypt's nationalization of the Suez Canal and the resulting invasion by British, French, and Israeli forces, see Galambos and van Ee, *The Middle Way*.

Eisenhower had changed the State Department draft of this paragraph, adding the next sentence and changing the next sentence slightly, but he used this, except for substituting "our attitude" for "this" (AWF/I: Saudi Arabia; see also the preceding document).

[7] At the July 18 meeting of the National Security Council Secretary Dulles would report that King Saud had been "reasonably well satisfied" with the aide memoire and that relations with the Saudi monarch "appeared to be better than ever before" (NSC meeting minutes, July 19, 1957, AWF/NSC). For developments see no. 332.

234

EM, WHCF, Official File 100-A

To Edward F. Hutton
Personal

July 10, 1957

Dear Mr. Hutton:[1] Thank you for sending me your column bearing a release date of July fifteenth. I can well understand your feelings concerning some recent Supreme Court decisions.[2]

However, you reach one conclusion which seems to me a bit illogical. You say that the Constitution does not say the Court's "judgments are the supreme law of the land, binding on everybody."[3] I think one cannot quarrel with this specific statement, but I think he can properly question its application to our everyday affairs. The judgments of the Supreme Court constitute guide lines by which all our Appellate and District courts render their judgments. This means that the legal interpretation of Constitutional language is that given to that language by the decisions of the Supreme Court.

If this were not so, it seems to me the Constitution could mean different things for every citizen in the land. That would be chaos.

Putting all this in another way I should say this. Agreeing with you that it is not the function of the Court to legislate, yet what Constitutional body other than the Supreme Court is empowered to determine what is legislation and what is judicial decision?

I have always thought one of the great functions of the Supreme Court was to provide needed stability in a form of government where political expediency might at times carry parties and political leaders to extremes. I become fearful when I find the Court, within the space of one year, rendering two opposing decisions on the same set of facts, on the same individuals, on the same circumstances.

Turning to the personal, it was nice to hear from you again.[4]

With warm regard, *Sincerely*

[1] Hutton, founder of the New York Stock Exchange firm of E. F. Hutton & Co., and a director of the Chrysler and General Foods corporations, had also established the Freedoms Foundation in an attempt to promote patriotic ideals (see Galambos, *NATO and the Campaign of 1952*, no. 207).

[2] Hutton was the author of a column titled "Think it Through," which was syndicated in the *New York Herald-Tribune* and approximately sixty other newspapers. He had written the President on July 1, 1957 (same file as document) to complain that the Supreme Court was endangering the country by "writing and rewriting the laws and the Constitution according to its own caprice." This could lead, he said, to "government by *men*, instead of a government by *law*." Hutton's July 15 column, entitled "Judge-Made Chaos," added: "When the Court acts as judges only; upholds settled law and stays within its proper bounds, its decisions deserve respect and are generally followed. But the Court is hurting itself when eager beavers overrule long-settled law and become a super Congress, or a super Constitutional Convention." For background on the recent and controversial Supreme Court decisions limiting federal power to combat seditious activities see no. 211.

[3] Hutton had written that, as a practical matter, the judgment of the Supreme Court was final "*as to the parties to the case.*" The Constitution did not say, however, that the Court's judgments were "the supreme law of the land, binding on everybody."

[4] Hutton would respond on July 31 (same file as document). He agreed that in our everyday affairs, "the need for uniformity in the application of the Constitution, and the interpretation of statutes is so great that other Federal and State judges, as well as all public officials, civilian and military, *generally*—in fact, nearly always—*should* follow the Supreme Court's interpretations even if considered wrong." He noted, however, that the decisions of the Supreme Court were not "sacrosanct," and that in extraordinary cases, it was the right and duty of other public officials, or the people, to take steps to keep the Court from stating, *as law*, what is only their personal opinions or prejudices."

235 — *EM, AWF, Name Series*

To Milton Stover Eisenhower — *July 10, 1957*

Dear Milton: To give you a current example of my failing memory—and possibly mind—I just this minute called you on the phone at Baltimore.[1] Momentarily I am at least slightly recovered.

When I spoke to you about your rehabilitated plan for visiting Mexico, I think I failed to ask you what particular time of the month of August you intend to leave here. You did tell me you plan to stay only a week instead of the originally projected two. I ask you these questions only because my plans for the summer are as yet uncertain, and I was merely wondering whether I would be here as you got ready to depart.[2]

Assuming that we will be in Washington, we would be glad to have you spend the night with us if it would be a convenience to you in meeting the departure time. Moreover, I hope you will let me know of any way in which I can be helpful in order to facilitate your preparations.[3]

This noon I am having the Prime Minister of Pakistan to lunch with the regularly assembled governmental officials as my other guests.[4] I should use these ceremonies to compliment also a few of my personal friends here or around the country, but I never seem to think about it until it is too late.[5]

I am curious to know how the fishing is going. Friends who have been fishing in Northeastern Canada and in New England tell me that they are having an unusually good season in those areas. I would like to know whether you are catching a lot of bass and whether you are doing any fishing for trout and muskies.[6]

I am not sure that Ruth is with you, but if she is give her my love.[7] Remember me to Mr. Eakin and any of my other friends that are in the vicinity such as Mickey Lambert, Howard Young and Willard Cox.[8] *As ever*

[1] Milton was vacationing in Land O' Lakes, Wisconsin.

[2] Due to a kidney infection, Milton had delayed his departure from June until August 4 (see *New York Times*, June 12, 14, 1957; and Ruiz Cortines to Eisenhower, June 15, 1957, AWF/I: Cortines). For background on the goodwill mission see no. 190.

[3] As it turned out, the Eisenhowers would be in Washington the evening before Milton's departure (see no. 252). On July 13 (AWF/N) Milton would write to ask if "it would be appropriate and free of all possible criticism" for the President to send an airplane to pick him up. For developments see no. 239.

[4] Pakistani Prime Minister Huseyn Shaheed Suhrawardy was visiting the United States to discuss U.S.-Pakistan relations (see State, *Foreign Relations, 1955–1957*, vol. VIII, *South Asia*, pp. 481–84; and *New York Times*, July 14, 1957).

[5] Occasionally, the President would invite personal friends to state dinners (see, for example, no. 152).

[6] On July 13 Milton would describe the fishing as "fairly good" (AWF/N). "My best catch so far is a 19-pound Tiger Muskie."

[7] Milton's daughter, Ruth Eakin Eisenhower, was attending summer school and had not accompanied him to Wisconsin (*ibid.*).

[8] LeRoy Eakin was Milton's father-in-law. Marion "Mickey" L. J. Lambert, president of AMP Corporation in St. Louis, Missouri, owned Lambert Deer Farm in Minocqua, Wisconsin. Willard Cox, president and treasurer of Coca-Cola Bottling Company of St. Louis, owned a ranch at Boulder Junction, Wisconsin. For background on Eakin

see *Eisenhower Papers*, vols. I–XVII; on the others see Galambos, *Chief of Staff*, nos. 1019 and 1536.

236

EM, WHCF, President's Personal File 164

To Spyros Panagiotes Skouras *Personal*

July 10, 1957

Dear Spyros: This refers again to your suggestion that the American Ambassador in London might be useful in assuring "acceptance" of Archbishop Makarios there, if that dignitary should make a visit to Great Britain.[1] Through personal correspondence with the Ambassador I have learned a bit more of the situation. So far as I can tell, the existing prospects for an early composition of the whole difficulty are not too bright. Those who are friends of Britain, Greece and Turkey will continue to strive for an equitable solution acceptable to all, but I fear that the release of Makarios did not have the really important effect that many of us had hoped for it.[2]

Ambassador Whitney suggests that if you should be going through London any time, he would be glad to give you a briefing as he understands the situation.

With warm regard, *As ever*

[1] For background see no. 209.

[2] Ambassador Whitney had told Eisenhower that a recent attempt by Makarios to deal directly with the British government about the Cyprus issue had been rebuffed. This development had "blocked off any early visit of the Archbishop to London, postponed a renewal of even indirect discussions and dissipated the British hopes for cooperation from Makarios which had induced his release from detention." Public opinion was less sympathetic to the archbishop, Whitney added, and official opinion "has tended to support the Turks, who view Makarios with deep suspicion . . ." (Whitney to Eisenhower, July 2, 1957, AWF/A).

Skouras would reply that it was "regrettable that the prospects are not good for solution of the Cyprian problem or for rebuilding the good relationship which existed between Greece and Turkey and which the people of the United States did so much to bring about" (July 18, 1957, same file as document). For developments see no. 488.

237 *EM, AWF, Administration Series*

To Lauris Norstad *July 15, 1957*

Top secret

Dear Larry:[1] I have been very much concerned with the adverse economic situation existing in Turkey—a situation that is aggravated by the amount of military force being maintained in that country.[2]

Turkey has, of course, been extremely anxious to maintain and even increase her military strength and has insistently urged the United States to give her more, rather than less, financial help toward this end.

When negotiating with us she always pleads "NATO force goals." At the same time, our bilateral aid program for Turkey in effect sets the level of the Turkish contribution to NATO defense.

I have studied your letter dealing with this general subject and I am quite sympathetic with your views.[3] In fact, even if you should find yourself in complete agreement with my own feelings in the matter, hereinafter expressed, it would be improper for you to make any official or public statement to that effect, or, as NATO Commander, to make any official recommendation to your superiors that directly concerns the internal affairs of one of NATO's members.

However, there are certain facts of life that must be recognized if we are to carry on a collective security program effectively and continuously.

1. One of these facts is that the nuclear power of the United States is the indispensable element of Western collective security, although it must be supported by those other elements of political and military strength and unity needed to deter the Communists from attempting to take over western lands by political action or limited military power.
2. We must insure that military organization and force programs within each allied nation are properly related to the impact of advance[d] weapon systems and to the contribution of the whole security apparatus to the security of the individual member nation.
3. We must make certain that each recipient country is technically capable of absorbing, maintaining and exploiting advanced material and new weapons systems, as well as such conventional forces as may be required for the joint strategy, and that it carries its fair share of the economic burden of collective defense. I repeat that such force levels must take into account the first two facts I have stated above.
4. We must likewise always remember that the resources of the United States are not unlimited; moreover, the sustained eco-

nomic health and vigor of the United States is important to each one of the NATO nations.

Review of Turkish force levels for the past ten years reveals that in 1947 the Turkish armed services consisted of some 41 divisions of widely varying active strength and effectiveness, seven fortress commands, small armored and other supporting formations, an air arm totalling roughly 300 operational aircraft and a small navy.

Total mobilization strength was about 600,000 men. By 1951 a reorganization led to 19 6/3 active divisions, 11 air regiments and 25 ships. Under NATO aegis, Turkish goals for active forces have since increased to 20 8/3 divisions, 41 air squadrons and 64 ships.[4] Divisional strengths are roughly comparable to those obtaining in the 1947 time period.

Now the significant feature of the Turkish force picture is found in the fact that although the job to be accomplished has remained essentially unchanged, and although Turkey has reaped significant benefits in terms of the overall security provided by NATO, modernization under our military assistance efforts and protection afforded by the growing United States nuclear retaliatory capability, her force goals have increased. This to me represents an illogical end result which requires careful reappraisal.

I am aware of the impact upon local sensibilities that can result from an attempt to reduce United States supported force levels. On the other hand, it is essential that our limited resources be applied in such fashion as to achieve the greatest possible security for least cost. In this connection, one of my principal responsibilities to the American people is to insure that hard-headed economies are observed in connection with these same security expenditures. Failure on my part to do this could easily result in the collapse of our entire aid program. Exercise of this responsibility leads me to question the need for conventional forces in Turkey of the size now maintained, and our wisdom in supporting these levels.

You will appreciate that while my discussion has focused on Turkey, the same general philosophy applies in varying degrees to the total range of our military assistance programs.

Greece provides an important example. We must search diligently for more effective application of our resources, recognizing once again that highly expensive and complex modern materiel cannot be injected into the replacement stream without positive indication that the recipient country is capable of its employment and maintenance and that it is, in fact, militarily required as against simpler, less expensive items.

We need to see if we cannot, consonant with security, reduce overseas indigenous forces supported by military assistance and persuade our allies to place more reliance on our flexible nuclear capability to protect them from attack. At the same time, we must not foster tendencies on the part of our allies to let down in their support of their appropriate share of the deterrent, weaken the political foundations on which our security is based, or jeopardize the ability of ourselves and our allies to apply limited force effectively and in ways best calculated to avoid local hostilities broadening into general war.

It will not, of course, be feasible to single out any one country and impose economies by precipitate unilateral action. Instead, we must point toward phased reductions attuned to careful assessment of collective requirements under the impact of modern weapons systems. The phasing of these reductions will undoubtedly have to vary in relation to the situation in each country concerned. There are different domestic political factors involved in each case. The economic capability of each country also varies, and no standard rule can be established which would cover all. We must make a major effort to persuade those allies whose economies will not support currently programmed military establishments to give greater weight to the nuclear deterrent and get them to try to develop smaller yet more powerful forces that will meet the requirements of collective security.

To give practical expression to these ideas a program of real education will be essential. The fact that we, in the United States, must be prepared to make do with less than we have had in the past is, of course, an essential aspect of this undertaking and should serve as one convincing argument to others. If we are to help increase the military ability of our allies to perform as members of the collective security team, we may well be faced with the choice between reducing our expenditures in support of conventional contingents among the allied forces in order to increase strength in modern weapons and techniques or of reducing our expenditures for advanced weapons for our allies.[5] The question is how we can best go about this without loss of political and military strength of our collective security arrangements. In such a choice, we believe the first alternative by far the better.[6]

This letter is for the purpose of giving you an appreciation of the thinking in the American Government and to elicit your comments as to the soundness, from your point of view, of the objectives I have so roughly outlined. I know you are now making a study for the North Atlantic Council on the balance of nuclear and conventional forces. If you find yourself in general agreement with the thoughts herein expressed, I should like your ideas as to how we could set about a gradual correction of the existing situation. If, on the other hand, you do not agree with the contents of this letter, I should like you to give me a memorandum of your approach to the same difficult problem, bearing in mind the same "facts of life" that I mentioned at the beginning of this letter.[7]

With warm regard, *As ever*

[1] JCS Chairman Arthur Radford had written the original draft of this letter. Secretary Dulles suggested changes to the final draft, which Eisenhower approved after making two additional modifications (see n. 5; and Radford to Cutler, July 5, 1957; Dulles to Cutler, July 11, 1957; and Cutler to Goodpaster, July 12, 1957, all in AWF/A, Norstad Corr.). Copies of this letter were sent to Dulles, Admiral Radford, and Brigadier Generals Robert Cutler and Andrew Goodpaster.

[2] For background on NATO force levels and Turkey's membership in the alliance see Galambos, *NATO and the Campaign of 1952*, no. 423; and Galambos and van Ee, *The Middle Way*, no. 1944; on economic and military aid to Turkey see *ibid.*, no. 913; and *Foreign Relations, 1955–1957*, vol. XXIV, *Soviet Union; Eastern Mediterranean*, pp. 708–9, 715–17, 720–27. After a discussion of the effects of Turkish force levels on conditions in that country and Turkey's unfulfilled promises to institute economic and financial reforms, Eisenhower had told the National Security Council on March 14 that if countries receiving U.S. assistance refused "to do anything whatever to put their own houses in order," assistance should be reassessed. "Help to such countries ought to be conditioned on their willingness to do a little something to help themselves if the United States is footing the bill." The President then requested that the Joint Chiefs of Staff ask General Norstad about reducing the current NATO-approved force levels in Turkey, considering the availability of advanced—presumably atomic—weapons to that country (NSC meeting minutes, Mar. 15, 1957, AWF/NSC).

On May 15 the Joint Chiefs of Staff had reported that Norstad believed that the proposal was "neither practicable nor desirable at this time from the military, political, or psychological point of view." "Existing and projected force goals have already taken into consideration estimated availabilities and effects of new weapons in the time periods involved and . . . we should not once again use these same factors as military justification for still further reducing the force goals" (Cutler to Eisenhower, July 8, 1957, AWF/A, Norstad Corr.).

On June 26, after the NSC had rejected Norstad's appraisal, Eisenhower had approved a program that would support existing Turkish force levels of 20 divisions, eight separate brigades, 64 combatant ships, and 21 air force squadrons. The total Turkish aid program would provide for appropriate advanced weapons (i.e., weapons capable of use with atomic warheads) and conventional equipment with provision for recurring maintenance costs. The NSC also agreed to review the force levels after assessing the potential capabilities of the advanced weapons. At that time Eisenhower asked for the background material necessary to write this personal note to Norstad (NSC meeting minutes, June 27, 1957, AWF/NSC).

[3] This is a reference to Norstad's reply to the JCS query (see n. 2 above).

[4] Turkey was actually seeking 21 air squadrons (see Cutler to Eisenhower, July 8, 1957, AWF/A, Norstad Corr.). Since there were normally three brigades to a division, the reference to 8/3 of a division is equivalent to eight separate brigades.

[5] Eisenhower added the words "in order to increase strength in modern weapons and techniques or of" after the words "allied forces."

[6] The President added the concluding sentence in this paragraph.

[7] Norstad requested a meeting with Eisenhower before replying with "a rather long official letter." On July 26 he would tell the President that the Turks believed the United States had assured them of a $1 billion aid package and a squadron of F-100 aircraft. "On occasion," Eisenhower responded, "people have given them hopes or even promises that shouldn't have been given." Congress did not intend to provide

funds of this magnitude, he said, and the result could "only be collapse and economic depression in Turkey." Norstad said that the Turks "had no prospect of being able to support substantial forces any time soon"; reductions in Turkish force levels, he noted, could be justified on the basis of that country's strong defense position and contemplated cuts in the foreign aid program (Goodpaster memorandum, July 26, 1957, AWF/D; and *Foreign Relations, 1955–1957*, vol. XXIV, *Soviet Union; Eastern Mediterranean*, pp. 731–32).

In his August 14 reply Norstad would offer several suggestions for effecting economies within NATO as a whole. He advocated emphasis on the principle of a balanced collective military in developing the force structure; planning military aid on a three-to-five year cycle to enable individual nations to obtain a better balance of forces; downgrading the priorities of selected second-echelon units; and lowering the requirements for air units as newer technologies and nuclear capabilities were introduced. Norstad added that Turkey's military forces during the previous six years had increased only slightly: "In the broad NATO view, the Turkish strength programmed for 1960/62 is a reasonable minimum military requirement for the defense of our southeastern flank. If, however, this requirement cannot be supported, the force goals will have to go down." Such reductions, Norstad said, would both "heighten the general risk" and would be subject to interpretation "as evidence of dwindling U.S. interest in and support for the Alliance." If no alternatives to force reductions existed, the United States should begin preparing the Turkish government for possible reductions while offering to increase the nuclear capability of the remaining forces. Although his responsibilities made it hard for him to even consider reducing NATO strength, Norstad recommended that the strength of Turkish forces be balanced with the level of support the United States could offer. This, he recognized, "may well result in a reduction of our goals as they now stand" (Norstad to Eisenhower, Aug. 14, 1957, AWF/A; see also Goodpaster to Cutler, Aug. 22, 1957, *ibid.*).

Eisenhower would discuss NATO's role in the Middle East with Turkish Prime Minister Adnan Menderes at the NATO Heads of Government Meeting in Paris (Dec. 16–18). At that time the Turkish Foreign Minister would tell Secretary Dulles that with increased U.S. aid, Turkey would be able to improve its economic situation in approximately three years (*Foreign Relations, 1955–1957*, vol. XXIV, *Soviet Union; Eastern Mediterranean*, pp. 747–49). For developments see no. 746.

238 — *EM, AWF, DDE Diaries Series*

To Bernard Law Montgomery — *July 15, 1957*

Secret. Personal

Dear Monty: I have your letter telling of your intention to write your memoirs.[1] I am sure your book will be a great success.

As to using copies of letters and communications I sent you during the war, I personally have no objection whatsoever. I send you herewith a simple statement to that effect. So far as these documents were *not* of the kind recorded with our respective War Offices, I think that no one else can possibly object to your use of them so long as I agree.

But it is my impression that the United States government and your government have certain wartime agreements respecting the release of documents that were then classed as top secret. When I left the military service in '48, that agreement still stood, and I recall that when I published my own record of happenings in World War II, I found that there were certain records I could not use.[2]

With respect to these, I think you could submit them item by item to your own War Office and they could give you either special clearance on each one, or possibly they could give you a general clearance on this type of communication.

As to what you propose to say about me, this is the first time that I have ever read an article about myself in its pre-publication form. I have always avoided this for the reason that I felt that I should not be a partner, even a silent one, to any public praise about myself, while, on the other hand, I certainly did not want to be tempted to protest criticism, whether or not I felt it to be justified.

Nevertheless I am bound to say that I am not only flattered by what you have to say about me in the excerpt you gave in your letter, but I am pleased that you would want to have my opinion of it.[3] My immediate reaction is that you are the one who is truly kind—I am more than touched by the expression of your personal feelings toward me.

Of course I sincerely hope that, as you allege, I am a kind and considerate person. It is my conviction that the higher one goes in an organization and the more it becomes necessary for him to make decisions that are sometimes disagreeable for his subordinates and even resented by them, the more necessary it is that he have a keen sense of fairness as well as a full measure of human consideration in his makeup. Only thus can he keep a great organization on its toes and moving forward with the will to win. Two-thirds of strategy is getting subordinates to do their work with lasting enthusiasm.

Too many people mistake meanness and irascibility for strength; they think that desk pounding symbolizes determination. It is my conviction that the opposite is the case.

Having said this on the most personal and secret basis, my only further word is that I will be anxious to read your book when it comes out.

With warm regard, *As ever*

[1] Montgomery's private and confidential letter of July 11 is in AWF/N. In order to tell his story "effectively," Montgomery explained, he wished to "quote extensively from the various letters and orders" he had received from Eisenhower. "Can I take it," he asked, "that you will not mind if I do this?"

[2] In February 1948 Eisenhower had left the U.S. Army to become the president of Columbia University. His own wartime memoir, *Crusade in Europe* (Garden City, N.Y.), was published in the fall of 1948 (see Galambos, *Chief of Staff*, no. 2056, and Galambos, *Columbia University*, no. 80).

[3] Montgomery said he had paid "tremendous tribute" to the President in the last chapter. "I hope you will not mind if I say this about you in my memoirs." *The Memoirs of Field-Marshal The Viscount Montgomery of Alamein, K.G.* (Cleveland and New York) would be published in 1958. Montgomery would write: Eisenhower was "a great Supreme Commander—a military statesman. I know of no other person who could have welded the Allied forces into such a fine fighting machine in the way he did, and kept a balance among the many conflicting and disturbing elements which threatened at times to wreck the ship. . . . Ike reached his greatest heights as President of the U.S.A. . . . But his real strength lies in his human qualities. . . . He merely has to smile at you, and you trust him at once. He is the very incarnation of sincerity. He has great common sense. People and nations give him their confidence. . . ." After reading the manuscript, Eisenhower said that Montgomery was "'pretty clever . . . he doesn't want to say I was responsible for winning [the war]'" (Ann Whitman memorandum, July 15, 1957, AWF/AWD).

239

EM, AWF, Name Series

TO MILTON STOVER EISENHOWER

July 15, 1957

Dear Milton: As Ann already told you, I immediately made arrangements for a plane to pick you up when you are ready to come back East.[1]

The more I think of it, I wonder if you are not making a mistake in leaving Ruth at home—that is, if she herself is not particularly concerned about missing the final week of summer school. I think she would enjoy the trip immensely, and there is a lot to be gained for her by seeing Mexico under the best possible auspices.[2] Then, too, if she is with you perhaps you will reconsider and take time out for a little rest and fishing while you are there.[3] At any rate, those are my thoughts of the moment, for whatever they are worth.

I now discover that August third is Saturday night; of course you are welcome at the White House—but Mamie and I might possibly be in Gettysburg. I don't really know our plans for that weekend yet, but I shall be in touch with you.[4] *As ever*

[1] For background see no. 235. Milton had suggested that Presidential Secretary Ann C. Whitman telephone him regarding these arrangements (Milton Eisenhower to Eisenhower, July 13, 1957, AWF/N).

[2] This same day the President would ask Ann Whitman to write Milton "urging that he take Ruth to Mexico with him" (Telephone conversations, AWF/D). As it turned out, Milton's daughter would accompany him to Mexico and act as his official hostess (see Milton Eisenhower to Eisenhower, July 18, 1957, AWF/N; Milton S. Eisenhower, *The Wine Is Bitter* [New York, 1963], p. 208; and *New York Times*, Sept. 8, 1957).

[3] On Milton's description of the fishing in Mexico see his memoir, *The Wine is Bitter*, p. 208.

[4] For developments see no. 252.

240

EM, AWF,
Administration Series

TO GEORGE MAGOFFIN HUMPHREY *July 16, 1957*

Dear George: Attached hereto is part of a letter that I just had from Bill Robinson. It came about because, in a conversation, he stated that there are too many people who viewed inflation favorably. In other words they welcomed it. This piece of his letter gives some of his reasons.[1]

Please don't bother to return this; just tear it up.[2] *As ever*

[1] Eisenhower's close friend, Coca-Cola Company President William Robinson had written the President on July 13 (AWF/N). Referring to a July 11 stag dinner discussion on inflation, Robinson explained that when he had asked "who was really against inflation," he "had in mind the fact that, while most businessmen and a few labor leaders decry the effects of inflation, the very nature of their functions consciously or unconsciously impels them to support the elements that make for it." Among the examples cited by Robinson were corporate activities where "inflation tends to increase stock values which constitute at least an indirect testimony of the success of the management—and again, like insurance company and bank loans, tends to obscure the mistakes." For background see no. 216.

[2] Humphrey would respond on July 19 (AWF/A). Noting that he agreed with Robinson that there were many citizens "who would like just a little inflation for themselves, but none for anyone else," Humphrey disagreed sharply with Robinson's thesis that Eisenhower was the only political leader in his lifetime who had acted to combat the dangers of inflation. "You are in good company," Humphrey wrote. "In Germany, it has been a great subject of high policy debate, and I think because of their recent sad experience there is a strong and widespread opposition to trying it again." Similarly, in England, Japan, and a number of other places, anti-inflationists were taking strong positions. "I think this is going to be a continuing fight in this country," wrote Humphrey, "and will require constant education under your strong leadership to be effective." For developments see no. 245.

241

EM, AWF, Name Series: Guns

TO JOHN MERRILL OLIN *July 16, 1957*

Dear John:[1] Thank you for your letter of the eleventh. Please don't give another thought to my mix-up. I told you about the matter only as a joke on myself.[2]

Your note arrived just as I was giving Colonel Schulz[3] instructions to turn over my 28 inch Model 21 to Mr. Weaver. I fully agree with your suggestions as to what should be done about it.[4]

Incidentally, three of us went to the skeet range on Saturday afternoon and I did a little better than I did a week ago. I missed one bird on the doubles on #1 station, I missed two on #4, one on #5, and one on #7. My total score was 20 out of 25, which is the best I have done yet.[5]

We then went over to the trap shooting range, where the stations are sixteen yards behind the trap house. I simply could not get on the trick of the thing. I suppose I averaged about one hit out of six. I never felt so helpless, even though we kept the birds flying out always in exactly the same direction. I tried quick shooting, deliberate shooting, and everything else I could think of, but nothing improved my performance.[6]

Of course I repeat once again my profound thanks for your many kindnesses and courtesies to me. *As ever*

[1] Olin (B.S. Cornell University 1913) was chairman of the board and director of Olin Mathieson Chemical Corporation, which among other things manufactured ammunition and firearms. For background see *Eisenhower Papers,* vols. X–XIII.

[2] Olin had thanked the President for inviting him to a July 9 White House stag dinner (AWF/N; see also Olin to Eisenhower, July 2, 1957, AWF/N). After dinner Eisenhower and Olin had discussed the President's difficulties with skeet and trap shooting. In his letter of the eleventh Olin had repeated his offer to assist Eisenhower; he also suggested that Eisenhower "swing a little faster and not stop your gun, . . . [and] have a follow through just as you have in a golf swing. . . ."

[3] Colonel Robert Ludwig Schulz had served as Military Aide to the President since 1953; for background see *Eisenhower Papers,* vols. VI–XIV.

[4] Olin had given the Model 21 Winchester double-barrel shotgun to Eisenhower in July 1950 (see Galambos, *Columbia University,* no. 885). In the conversation following the stag dinner, Olin had advised the President to ship the gun to Olin employee Dick Weaver. On the eleventh he suggested that the gun be restocked and that the boring be changed to skeet boring, if necessary.

[5] Over the July 13 weekend Eisenhower had gone to his farm in Gettysburg and retrieved the gun (see Eisenhower to Olin, July 13, 1957, AWF/N). Olin would reply that he was "delighted to learn of the improvement" in Eisenhower's shooting (Olin to Eisenhower, July 22, 1957, AWF/N: Guns). For background on the shooting facilities at Eisenhower's Gettysburg farm see Galambos and van Ee, *The Middle Way,* no. 1899.

[6] Olin would say that Eisenhower's gun probably did not fit him. He said for standard trap shooting he used a gun with a "much straighter" stock. He went on to explain that since the target rises in trap shooting, it is best to get a line of sight along the top of the barrels, and then pick up the target from behind with a continuous swing (Olin to Eisenhower, July 22, 1957, AWF/N: Guns). On July 25 Eisenhower would thank Olin for his advice and add that his "education in skeet and trap shooting progresses, even if slowly." See also Nevins to Whitman, July 22, and Eisenhower to Jones, July 25, 1957, all in AWF/N: Guns. For developments see no. 287.

TO OWEN ROBERTSON CHEATHAM[1] *July 18, 1957*

Dear Owen: I am not enough of an artist either to approve of or to criticize the design of your bronze plaque.[2] To me it looks most attractive and suitable.

As for the text, my feeling is that that part referring to me should be somewhat simplified. As it stands I believe it emphasizes me, as an individual, too much—something that I find embarrassing in view of the heading, "The Redemption Window, Dedicated to the Glory of God," after which the next six lines have to do with me personally rather than with the prayer which I used and of which we spoke during our conversation.[3]

I suggest that starting with the third line the text read:

"And to record the Inauguration Prayer
on January 20, 1953
of the Thirty-third President of the United States
Dwight David Eisenhower
a frequent worshiper in this sanctuary."[4]

Language such as this would point the dedication to the prayer rather than to the individual. This seems to me to be much more fitting.

Of course I hold no brief for my exact wording, but I give you my reaction to the text of the plaque as it is written.

With warm regard, *As ever*

P.S. I think that technically I am listed as the 34th President.[5]

[1] Cheatham was founder, president, and chairman of Georgia-Pacific Plywood and Lumber Company. For background see Galambos and van Ee, *The Middle Way,* nos. 106, 582, and 596.

[2] Cheatham planned to dedicate a window to Eisenhower at Reid Memorial Presbyterian Church in Augusta, Georgia. On Cheatham's earlier effort to memorialize the President see Galambos and van Ee, *The Middle Way,* nos. 582 and 596. We have been unable to find any further correspondence on this matter in AWF.

[3] On May 16, 1957, the President met briefly with Cheatham and gave approval for a dedication of the inaugural prayer (Ann Whitman memorandum, May 16, 1957, AWF/AWD).

[4] Eisenhower had, at the last moment, composed his first inaugural prayer on the morning of the Inauguration (Galambos and van Ee, *The Middle Way,* no. 1027; Ann Whitman memorandum, May 16, 1957, AWF/AWD). For the text of the prayer see *New York Times,* January 9, 1957.

[5] Cheatham probably counted Stephen Grover Cleveland's two non-consecutive presidential terms (1885–89; 1893–97) as one. They are, however, officially counted as two separate presidencies.

243

EM, AWF, Administration Series

To John Hay Whitney

July 18, 1957

Dear Jock: It seems that I have had two or three notes from you since I last sent you a reply.[1]

First, Mamie talked to Betsey last evening—I got into the conversation for a few minutes through interruption by practically physical force. Mamie had such a laugh over some story that I insisted Betsey tell it to me. It was your remark about having sacrificed the ultimate for your country when you felt compelled to give a cocktail party for Adlai.[2] I told her to remind you that there was such a thing as diplomatic sickness.

Our plans for a summer vacation are crystallized, at least to the extent that if we are able to leave Washington at all for a stay of two or more weeks, we shall go to the Naval Base at Newport, Rhode Island.[3] That spot offered to us all the necessary communications, protection, privacy and, we hope, improved climate.

I have just glanced at the map and see that Newport is a little less than forty miles from Fishers Island. If landing fields are handy, we should be able to play a daily golf game by commuting by airplane. It seems to me that a boat trip, even a fairly fast one, would be a rather laborious business, unless, of course, there was good fishing both ways. In any event we will look forward to seeing you both.

I just recall that you spoke of the Fishers Island course as a "real" golf course.[4] If you mean one of these tough ones with a dozen sand traps on every hole, water, ditches, wind, and all sorts of natural and unnatural hazards, you will have to find another playmate. My idea of a good golf course is 290 yard par 4s, the par 3s with no traps, and everything over 400 yards in the par 5 bracket.

I am more than pleased that you find it possible to come home rather than go to Culzean this summer. You can do that later, either through Jimmy Gault or through Mr. Gray (who is always on the job in Ayrshire).[5] Incidentally, I know that you have met Jimmy Gault, but when we knew him through the war years and later, we always thought of him in connection with his wife, named Peggy.[6] She is a delightful person, truly a charming Scotch lady.

What happened between them I do not know, but I understand that he is very anxious to get a divorce from her. I have always thought that this was practically impossible in Britain, but it sounds as if he wanted to marry someone else. I thought I should tell you this inasmuch as I asked him to act for me in making the arrangements at Culzean.

With warm personal regard, *As ever*

P.S. My hope is that we can go to Newport not later than August tenth.

[1] Whitney's letters (July 2 and 15) are in AWF/A. In his letter of the fifteenth Whitney reported that U.S. relations with the British were "in pretty good shape." There were, however, some Britons who might not agree: "The main line of those who are dissatisfied with our relationship is that it is not 'special' enough. This is the reasoning that wants everyone to know that we are working out an Anglo-American answer to all our problems because even if other countries are concerned they will clearly be benefited by our solutions because our solutions will be right." Eisenhower's most recent letter to Whitney is no. 209.

[2] In May Adlai Ewing Stevenson, former Democratic governor of Illinois and Eisenhower's opponent in the 1952 and 1956 presidential elections, had received an honorary degree from Oxford University (*New York Times*, May 22, 23, 25, 1957). For background on Stevenson see *Eisenhower Papers*, vols. XII–XVII.

[3] Whitney had written that he and his wife would vacation at Fishers Island in August. "We hear that you may be using Newport as a cool weather retreat during August," he said, "and it would be great if we could meet there." As it turned out, the Eisenhowers would only be able to vacation in Newport, Rhode Island, September 4 to 30.

[4] In his July 15 letter Whitney had suggested that Eisenhower visit the course at Fishers Island.

[5] On the Whitneys' plans to visit Scotland see nos. 158 and 159.

[6] Mrs. Gault was the former Margaret Ella Campbell.

244 — *EM, AWF, International Series: Rhee*

To Syngman Rhee — *July 19, 1957*

Confidential

Dear Mr. President:[1] You have written me two letters on June 19, 1957, and June 24, 1957, counseling us to restore the military balance which Communist violations of the Armistice Agreement had upset and thanking us for our recent decision to redress that balance by the introduction of more modern weapons.[2]

I thank you for sending both these letters. I share your confidence that our decision is the right one. You can rest assured, Mr. President, that the security of the Republic of Korea is of deep concern to the United States, as it is to yourself.

It has become imperative for our own budget, Mr. President, that the costs of maintaining the forces of the Republic of Korea at their present combat power be reduced. The modernization of United States forces and the addition of improved equipment for your own, buttressed by the retaliatory power of this country, the Mutual Defense Treaty between our two countries and the Joint Policy Declaration signed by sixteen nations on July 27, 1953, should more than compensate for your reductions.[3] I know that you will welcome the increasing effectiveness of our aid program and the expansion to your own economy and over all strength which will be consequent on these military reductions.

These considerations, Mr. President, prompted my decision to instruct Ambassador Dowling and General Lemnitzer to lay before you a plan which jointly includes reduction in your armed forces and the improved equipment of the remainder. This plan, in all its aspects, has my wholehearted personal support and must, in my judgment, be accomplished soon for the attainment of our commonly held objectives.[4]

The unification of your country of which you spoke remains an important objective of the United States; the plan we have presented will in no way adversely affect its attainment. We shall lose no feasible opportunity to bring about the peaceful unification of a democratic and independent Korea.[5]

With my sincerest personal good wishes

[1] The State Department drafted this letter (see Dulles to Eisenhower, July 18, 1957, AWF/I: Rhee; and State, *Foreign Relations, 1955–1957*, vol. XXIII, pt. 2, *Korea* [1993], p. 468). For background on Rhee, President of the Republic of Korea, see Galambos, *NATO and the Campaign of 1952*, no. 976.

[2] On South Korean military forces and the plans to supply U.S. troops in Korea with more modern weapons see Galambos and van Ee, *The Middle Way*, no. 823; and State, *Foreign Relations, 1955–1957*, vol. XXIII, pt. 2, *Korea*, pp. 281–82, 292–97, 300–301, 303–34, 351–54, 375–84, 404–18; see also NSC meeting minutes, February 1 and April 5, 1957, AWF/NSC. Opinions differed among Administration officials regarding the type of weapons to be introduced and the fact that this modernization could be interpreted as an abrogation of the Korean Armistice Agreement. In May Secretary Dulles had announced that the United States was considering new weapons, and Secretary of Defense Wilson had indicated that these weapons could have both conventional and nuclear capabilities (*U.S. Department of State Bulletin* 36, no. 936 [June 3, 1957], 898; and *New York Times*, May 15 and 18, 1957).

At the June 13 meeting of the National Security Council Eisenhower suggested that instead of continuing "to talk about this problem for weeks on end" they make the decision to introduce the new weapons. At the same time, he said, the Secretaries of State and Defense should direct Walter C. Dowling (A.B. Mercer University 1925), U.S. Ambassador to Korea since May 1956, and General Lyman L. Lemnitzer, Commander in Chief, United Nations Command, to negotiate with President Rhee for a substantial reduction in Korean forces (NSC meeting minutes, June 14, 1957, AWF/NSC; for background on Lemnitzer see Galambos, *Chief of Staff*, no. 2010).

Before learning of the U.S. proposal, Rhee, who feared a renewal of hostilities by the Communists, had asked Eisenhower to strengthen his forces to meet the "perilously acute" situation. "Not only are many American officials supporting the need for modernization," Rhee wrote, ". . . but also leading newspaper writers in America are decrying the lack of modern weapon[s] for troops entrusted with the heavy responsibility of guarding the defenses of the free world in Korea" (June 19, 1957, AWF/I: Rhee).

[3] On the Mutual Defense Treaty see Galambos and van Ee, *The Middle Way*, no. 515; on the Joint Policy Declaration see *ibid.*, no. 788.

[4] Secretary Dulles had told Dowling and Lemnitzer that Eisenhower understood that the negotiations would be "delicate and difficult," and did not want them to deliver Rhee an ultimatum. At their meeting on June 21 the negotiators had told Rhee that some dual-capacity weapons would be provided to U.S. forces; the Korean air force would receive jet aircraft; and ground forces would receive better transportation and communication equipment. The U.S. commitment, they said, was dependent on the reduction of Korean ground forces (State, *Foreign Relations, 1955–1957*, vol. XXIII, pt. 2, *Korea*, pp. 457–62; see also Goodpaster memorandum, July 23, 1957, AWF/D).

Although gratified with the U.S. decision, Rhee told Eisenhower in his letter on June 24 that "it would have been a bold stroke for freedom if you had declared the entire Armistice Agreement invalid in view of the repeated violations of the Communist side and we hope that this further step will follow" (AWF/I: Rhee).

[5] Rhee had told Eisenhower that his country would "be more than willing" to consider a reduction in armed forces "if this can be accomplished without weakening our ability to achieve the establishment of a unified, independent and democratic government in Korea . . . the goal for which we have all made great sacrifice" (*ibid.*). For developments see no. 303.

245 — *EM, AWF, Name Series*

To William Edward Robinson — *July 19, 1957*

Dear Bill: By no means did I think of your question, at the stag dinner the other evening, as brash, cynical or inappropriate. On the contrary I thought it really pointed up in this whole confusing problem of inflation one of the factors that is frequently ignored.[1]

On the other hand, I think that most businesses have one real interest in a stable dollar; this involves the ability to make plans extending a long distance in the future.[2]

For your information I am enclosing a copy of a talk the Chancellor of the Exchequer of Great Britain, Mr. Peter Thornycroft, recently made on this general subject. I am sure you will find it interesting to note also that he argues that government alone cannot preserve the sound currency.[3]

With warm regard, *As ever*

[1] Robinson had written the President on July 13, 1957 (AWF/N) regarding the July 11 stag dinner discussion of inflation; see no. 240.

[2] For Eisenhower's frequently expressed views on inflation see no. 216; see also Galambos and van Ee, *The Middle Way*, no. 2060.

[3] George Edward Peter Thorneycroft, Chancellor of the Exchequer since January 1957, had served as president of the Board of Trade from 1951 until 1957. Eisenhower may have been referring to Thorneycroft's April 9, 1957, speech to Parliament presenting the Budget. The Chancellor had said: "If we are to find a solution to this problem [inflation], we all have a part to play—perhaps some sacrifice to make—management and workers and the spending departments of the Government—I am sure that no one wants to see our money steadily losing its value or sterling going the way of so many currencies in the past" (*The Times*, Apr. 10, 1957).

246

EM, AWF, Dulles-Herter Series

To John Foster Dulles

July 19, 1957

Dear Foster: I am assuming that when we are called upon in the future to send personal representatives to the Inauguration of a new Head of State, that the delegation will be made up of at least two members. It strikes me that this would be a nice way to give some recognition to individuals who have been longtime friends of mine, so I give you a list—arranged in couples and in somewhat the order that I would like to see them selected for future invitations to this kind of affair.[1]

Of course there is a second priority to be observed, namely an arrangement according to the importance of the capital to which the individuals are to be sent, but I suspect that as definite occasions become known we can work that out.[2]

With warm regard, *As ever*

[1] The State Department had asked Eisenhower to submit names for his representatives to the inauguration of Hector Bienvenido Trujillo for a second term as President of the Dominican Republic. In addition to the U.S. ambassador and other State Department officials, Eisenhower's friend Joyce Hall would attend the ceremonies. In a telephone conversation the preceding day Dulles had discussed Hall's trip, and the Secretary of State had assured the President that "he would have a good time" (Telephone conversation, July 18, 1957, Dulles Papers, Telephone Conversations; see also *New York Times*, Aug. 11, 15, 17, 1957). Eisenhower had added five names to his original list of twenty (AWF/D-H).

[2] For developments see no. 250.

247

EM, AWF, International Series: Macmillan

To Harold Macmillan

Cable. Top secret

July 20, 1957

Dear Harold: I have your letter which was delivered to me this morning July 20, 1957 regarding the location of the future West Indian capital. Of course, as you say, the United States Government and its people are vitally interested in furthering the legitimate aspirations of the people of the West Indies with whom we have a particularly neighborly interest.[1]

As you are fully aware it is basic policy with us never to force ourselves into a place where we are not wanted or to remain when we are not welcome. Accordingly, if your government or the British

West Indies Federation after careful consideration finally conclude that you definitely wish us to leave Chaguaramas, we would of course do so. However, such a move in my opinion would be most unwise in view of our continuing common defense requirements for a major naval operating base in the Gulf of Parla.[2] Let me make these points clear:

Chaguaramas Station is the only facility in that part of the Caribbean adequately equipped to safeguard our common defense interests. I assume Mountbatten has let you know of the strategic considerations.[3]

The base represents a replacement cost of some one hundred million dollars. Our large investment was predicated on a ninety-nine year lease. I would doubt that the Federation could finance relocation or that we could meet the cost of relocating this facility at a time when we have to curtail our defense expenditures generally. Also the fact that this problem was forced upon us by the British West Indies Federation would undoubtedly affect the attitude of the Congress toward it.

We also have to keep in mind the recommendations of the Inter-American Defense Board which includes the nineteen Latin-American nations. That Board has expressed its concern lest the United States deactivate the base.[4]

We realize that from the domestic standpoint within the West Indies itself, a statement such as you propose would be most helpful to the West Indies Federation and the present representatives in London but, in our opinion, it goes much too far.[5]

We are prepared to join in a commission composed of technical experts of the British West Indies, the United Kingdom and the United States to investigate all aspects of the British West Indies requests for assistance in making Chaguaramas available taking into full account military and economic considerations. We would not, however, want to do so under terms of reference which virtually commit us to make the move. We would hope to be able to satisfy your government and that of the Federation that such a move is inadvisable from the standpoint of each of us.

I hope that your government will do its best to obtain acceptance by the representatives of the British West Indies of a commission whose range of exploration will be wide but which will not start out committed to one or another solution.[6] *As ever*

[1] The Federation of the British West Indies—a union of the British colonies of Trinidad, Barbados, Jamaica, and the Windward and Leeward Islands—had been established in January 1957 and was scheduled to become part of the British Commonwealth early in 1958. Representatives of the fledgling federation, Great Britain, and the United States had been meeting in London since July 16. Having chosen Trinidad as the site of the new capital, the West Indian delegation had asked the

British government to petition the United States to release the eighteen square mile Chaguaramas Peninsula, in the northwest part of the island of Trinidad, which had been leased from Great Britain in 1941 for the construction of a naval base. Macmillan had told Eisenhower that the development of the federation was "going pretty well" and would be successful if the problem of a capital site could be resolved. The [West Indian] politicians dealing with the problem were "not very easy to handle," Macmillan wrote, "and I think it would be very embarrassing to us both if they insisted on visiting Washington and trying to discuss the question personally with you" (Macmillan to Eisenhower, July 19, 1957, AWF/I: Macmillan; see also David Lowenthal, "The Social Background of West Indian Federation," in *The West Indies Federation*, ed. David Lowenthal [New York, 1961], p. 69; Telephone conversations, Dulles and Radford, Eisenhower and Dulles, Dulles and Elbrick, July 20, 1957, Dulles Papers, Telephone Conversations; and *New York Times*, Jan. 30, Feb. 12, May 11, 1957).

[2] The Gulf of Parla lies between Trinidad and Venezuela.

[3] For background on First Sea Lord Louis Francis Albert Mountbatten see Galambos, *NATO and the Campaign of 1952*, no. 20.

[4] For background on the Inter-American Defense Board, established in 1942, see Galambos, *Chief of Staff*, no. 694.

[5] Macmillan had proposed the establishment of a joint commission to examine alternative sites for the naval base and to determine what nonessential part of the Chaguaramas base could be released immediately (Macmillan to Eisenhower, July 19, 1957, AWF/I: Macmillan; see also *New York Times*, Aug. 8, 1957).

[6] Earlier this same day Dulles had told Eisenhower that State Department officials studying the problem thought that a commission could be established to "stall it along for a while." According to Dulles, Eisenhower believed that the United States did not "have much of a choice" and was "going to be driven out" (Telephone conversations, Dulles and Eisenhower, and Dulles and Elbrick, July 20, 1957, Dulles Papers, Telephone Conversations). As a result of a decision at the London meetings to establish a technical commission to study the problem, the United States would send a three-man naval delegation to Port-of-Spain, Trinidad, in January 1958. The commission's findings, which were published in May of that year, would favor the retention of the naval base (*New York Times*, Nov. 10, Dec. 22, 1957, and Jan. 10, Mar. 30, May 5 and 15, 1958).

Discussing the issue during the President's visit to London in August 1959, Eisenhower and Macmillan would decide to defer their decision until a later date (U.S. Department of State, *Foreign Relations of the United States, 1958–1960*, 19 vols., vol. VII, 2 pts., pt. 2, *Western Europe* [1993], p. 851; see also Eisenhower, *Waging Peace*, p. 421).

248

EM, AWF, Name Series

To Edward Everett Hazlett, Jr.
Personal

July 22, 1957

Dear Swede: The fact that you had to remain in the hospital such a short time encourages me to believe that your condition must have improved definitely and rapidly. While I had hoped to get out to Bethesda some time when Ibby would be present, I am still delighted that you are not compelled to spend most of the summer in a hospital room.[1]

Concerning my present situation, I think it is best described by merely saying "the grind goes on." I am repeatedly astonished, even astounded, by the apparent ignorance of members of Congress in the general subject of our foreign affairs and relationships. I realize that by this time I should accept, as a matter of course, Congressional reaction that seemingly reflects either this abysmal ignorance or a far greater concern for local political sentiment than for the welfare of the United States.

I am sure that this second possibility is *not* correct so far as the conscious attitude of the average Congressman is concerned. In the general case each of them thinks of himself as intensely patriotic; but it does not take the average member long to conclude that his first duty to his country is to get himself re-elected. This subconscious conviction leads to a capacity for rationalization that is almost unbelievable.

In any event, right at this moment lack of understanding of America's international position and obligation accounts for the fact that we seem to be trying to make a national hero out of a man who shot a woman—in the back at something like ten to fifteen yards distance.[2]

As quickly as this incident became a popular one in some parts of the isolationist press, it was taken up by dozens of Congressmen who "viewed with alarm" and were "shocked and distressed" at the injustice done to this great soldier and citizen.

We have even had a serious attempt made to force me to denounce our Status of Forces treaties.[3] These treaties, as you know, are fair and just to Americans serving abroad and are the only means by which we retain jurisdiction in most offenses committed. Because they establish a reasonable jurisdictional balance between ourselves and the host country, they are at the very foundation of our defensive alliances. To denounce them would make us completely isolationist and force us to abandon practically every base we have abroad.

Of course there are people who believe that the United States would not only be secure but would greatly prosper by withdrawing into a fanciful "Fortress America." I say fanciful for the reason that any sensible man knows that there can be no such thing as security in isolation, no matter if our armed forces were multiplied threefold.

This same unreasoning attitude is reflected in the constantly repeated effort in Congress to slash mutual security funds. Again and again I have explained to individuals and to the public that, as of this moment, our mutual security operations represent America's best investment. Through them we are able to keep down the direct costs of our own military establishment. More than this, we are increasing the consuming power of many friendly nations and helping to build up future markets for our rapidly expanding productive capacity.[4]

Last year our excess of exported goods over imported was something on the order of nine billion dollars. Subtract from this all of the funds that we currently send out to aid the military establishments and economies of our friends and we still have a comfortable surplus. It is quite clear that except for the funds we have spent in the past in order to give help to economies in Europe and in Asia, there would not be the purchasing power in a number of countries to buy from us.

Some people worry that the long range competitive position of the United States will be damaged if we help now to build up the productive capacity of others. Some day this might be a problem. But there are two main points to remember.

(*a*). If other countries improve industrially their standards of living will usually go up. This means that in the normal case their wage scales will begin to rise and eventually will come closer and closer to our own. Consequently we will still have the competitive advantage of our deeper experience in management, production and, we like to think, in inventiveness and imagination. In the meantime we will have expanding markets. While you may argue that, in the case of Japan, increasing industrialization has raised living standards very slowly indeed, I think that as of today labor would be in a far better position in that country if their society had been a free one rather than a dictatorship.[5]

(*b*). Before any of the underdeveloped countries can reach a position where they can export to others, on a competitive basis with the United States, many years must elapse and during that period their purchasing power will multiply rapidly. We, if we are wise, will share prominently in that increasing market. This applies to all of South America, Africa, and to portions of Asia, particularly in the Mid East.

All this, of course, is nothing but a by-product of a process which has as its principal purpose the strengthening of freedom and the gradual exhaustion of Communism in the world. I merely refer to it to express my belief that both in the short term and in the long term our mutual security program will advance our country's best interests.

Undoubtedly I have written to you a number of times on the subject of "Civil Rights." I think that no other single event has so disturbed the domestic scene in many years as did the Supreme Court's decision of 1954 in the school segregation case. That decision and similar ones earlier and later in point of time have interpreted the Constitution in such a fashion as to put heavier responsibilities than before on the Federal government in the matter of assuring to each citizen his guaranteed Constitutional rights.[6] My approach to the many problems has been dictated by several obvious truths:

(*a*). Laws are rarely effective unless they represent the will of the majority. In our prohibition experiment, we even saw local opinion openly and successfully defy Federal authority even though national public opinion then seemed to support the whole theory of prohibition.

(*b*). When emotions are deeply stirred, logic and reason must operate gradually and with consideration for human feelings or we will have a resultant disaster rather than human advancement.

(*c*). School segregation itself was, according to the Supreme Court decision of 1896, completely Constitutional until the reversal of that decision was accomplished in 1954. The decision of 1896 gave a cloak of legality to segregation in all its forms. As a result, the social, economic and political patterns of the South were considered by most whites, especially by those in that region, as not only respectable but completely legal and ethical.

(*d*). After three score years of living under these patterns, it was impossible to expect complete and instant reversal of conduct by mere decision of the Supreme Court. The Court itself recognized this and provided a plan for the desegregation of schools which it believed to be moderate but effective.

The plan of the Supreme Court to accomplish integration gradually and sensibly seems to me to provide the only possible answer if we are to consider on the one hand the customs and fears of a great section of our population, and on the other the binding effect that Supreme Court decisions must have on all of us if our form of government is to survive and prosper. Consequently the plan that I have advanced for Congressional consideration on this touchy matter was conceived in the thought that only moderation in legal compulsions, accompanied by a stepped-up program of education, could bring about the result that every loyal American should seek.[7]

I think that some of the language used in the attempt to translate my basic purposes into legislative provisions has probably been too broad. Certainly it has been subject to varying interpretations. This I think can be corrected in the Congress.

But I hold to the basic purpose. There must be respect for the Constitution—which means the Supreme Court's interpretation of the Constitution—or we shall have chaos. We cannot possibly imagine a successful form of government in which every individual citizen would have the right to interpret the Constitution according to his own convictions, beliefs and prejudices. Chaos would develop. This I believe with all my heart—and shall always act accordingly.[8]

This particular quarrel is not completely devoid of some amusing aspects. For example, a violent exponent of the segregation doctrine was in my office one day. During the course of his visit he delivered an impassioned talk on the sanctity of the 1896 decision by the Supreme Court. At a pause in his oration I merely asked, "Then why is the 1954 decision not equally sacrosanct?" He stuttered and said, "There were then wise men on the Court. Now we have politicians." I replied, "Can you name one man on the 1896 Court who made the decision?" He just looked at me in consternation and the subject was dropped.

I suppose at the moment a problem of possibly even greater importance to us is the threat of inflation. Indeed it has passed the point of mere threat, as evidenced by the fact that in the last year we have had about a four percent rise in living costs. Since we had in the first three and a half years of this Administration succeeded in holding this rise to under one percent, the present situation shows that accumulated pressures are at last forcing prices up—or if you want to put it another way, the dollar down.[9]

There are so many contributory causes to inflation that it seems to be idle to pick out any one as the real culprit. Nevertheless many people try to do this. One man will wail about the wage-price spiral. Another lays everything to government spending. Still another will blame unlimited consumer credit, while others find banking policies to be wholly to blame.

Actually all these factors and even more enter into the problem. Even worse, not everybody acts consistently. Again consider the Congress. Suddenly convinced that governmental expenditures were too high—which they are—Congress entered upon a great economy drive. This it did under the belief that this subject would remain popular for so long that no better record could be taken to the voter in the fall of 1958 than one of consistent voting against expenditures.

This drive was underway long enough to provide opportunity for speeches by almost every individual member of the Congress, but by the time the first round was over, some of the boys began to wake up to the fact that a good many pressure groups wanted to dig a little deeper into the federal treasury. As a result, in the field of housing Congress insisted upon putting a billion dollars more in the authorization bill than the Administration had requested.[10] On top of that, Congress is in the process of passing a pay raise for mailmen that will give them a twelve percent increase even though Congress is well aware of the fact that this will practically compel raises for the entire classified civil service.[11] This vastly increases Federal expenditures. Worse than this, there can be little doubt that the industrial wage-price spiral would get a terrific upward jolt from any such action on the part of the Federal government. But in voting as he does the Congressman feels that he is winning votes for himself. So out the window goes his concern about the effect of governmental expenditures on inflation.

In the same way, I doubt that there is any Congressman who fails to realize that so-called cheap money likewise has a stimulating effect on inflation. Yet he is willing to expose the country to the ravages of inflation so long as he can make a showing that he is for "cheap money for the little fellow."

I know that you will understand I am not criticizing all Congressmen. I am talking mainly about those who strive for the headlines by reckless and impulsive statements. Indeed in the normal case the average Congressman, when met individually, seems to be a perfectly logical and high-minded individual. It is usually when he gets to operating in the mass with opportunities for making rash and unwise statements that we gain such a bad impression of his capabilities.

* * * * *

This letter is far too long—you will be worn out with its reading. In any event, when I started my chief purpose was merely to express the great hope that you were improving as rapidly as your short stay in the hospital seemed to indicate you would. Everything between this paragraph and the beginning represents only the meandering reflections of an individual who has daily to use up more than a normal ration of his sense of humor in order to keep right side up. Possibly I am something like a ship which, buffeted and pounded by wind and wave, is still afloat and manages in spite of frequent tacks and turnings to stay generally along its plotted course and continues to make some, even if slow and painful, headway.

Give my love to Ibby and, as always, the best to yourself. *As ever*

[1] Hazlett would respond to the President on September 4, 1957 (AWF/N). Apologizing for his long silence, Hazlett would thank Eisenhower for his hour-long visit to Bethesda Naval Medical Center on June 27 (*ibid.*): "I'm just not up to writing as frequently or as well as I used to. The pressure on my ears, and hence my unsteadiness continues unabated." For background see no. 215; for developments see no. 457.

[2] Eisenhower was referring to William S. Girard, a U.S. Army soldier who had been accused of killing a Japanese woman while on duty in Japan (see no. 200).

[3] On July 1, 1957, the Foreign Affairs Committee of the House of Representatives had reported a joint resolution to add a provision to the mutual security bill revising the Status of Forces Agreements so that foreign countries would no longer have criminal jurisdiction over United States servicemen stationed within their borders (see *Congressional Quarterly Almanac*, vol. XIII, *1957*, pp. 671–72; see also Eisenhower, *Waging Peace*, pp. 142–44). Expressing strong opposition to the bill at his July 17 news conference, the President had called the Status of Forces Treaties "absolutely essential to the system of alliances we have now." Without the treaties the alliances would "fall to pieces, because we would be compelled to bring our soldiers home" (*Public Papers of the Presidents: Eisenhower, 1957*, p. 549).

[4] See, for example, nos. 60, 137, and 138.

[5] On the complex relationship between government and big business in pre- and postwar Japan, see for example, Chalmers A. Johnson, *MITI and the Japanese Miracle: The Growth of Industrial Policy, 1925–1975* (Stanford, Calif., 1982); Arthur E. Tiedemann, "Big Business and Politics in Prewar Japan," in *Dilemmas of Growth in Prewar Japan,* ed., James William Morley (Princeton, 1971), pp. 267–316; and Ryōshin Minami, *The Economic Development of Japan: A Quantitative Study* (New York, 1994), pp. 315–19.

[6] For background see Galambos and van Ee, *The Middle Way,* nos. 341, 574, and 1121.

[7] In his 1957 State of the Union Address, Eisenhower had reiterated his 1956 call for a program to reinforce civil rights. Eisenhower had asked for the creation of a bipartisan commission to investigate civil rights violations; the establishment of a civil rights division in the Department of Justice; and the enactment of new laws to aid in the enforcement of voting rights and to permit the federal government to seek preventive relief in civil rights cases. On June 18 the House had passed the Administration's version of the bill virtually intact (see *Public Papers of the Presidents: Eisenhower, 1957,* p. 23; *Congressional Quarterly Almanac,* vol. XIII, *1957,* pp. 553–69). See also Eisenhower, *Waging Peace,* pp. 148–62; Robert Fredrick Burk, *The Eisenhower Administration and Black Civil Rights* (Knoxville, Tenn., 1984), pp. 204–26; Sherman Adams, *Firsthand Report: The Story of the Eisenhower Administration* (New York, 1961), pp. 335–43; and Brownell, *Advising Ike,* pp. 202–5. For developments see nos. 253 and 266.

[8] See no. 234.

[9] Inflation indices, which had begun to rise in 1956, had continued their upward spiral throughout the spring of 1957 (see Saulnier, *Constructive Years,* pp. 79–97). On Eisenhower's concern over inflation see nos. 216, 240, and 245. See also Sloan, *Eisenhower and the Management of Prosperity,* pp. 119–32.

[10] Eisenhower had signed P.L. 104, the Housing Act of 1957, into law on July 12. Despite the fact that it largely carried out the legislative proposals for housing programs submitted to Congress in his February budget message, Eisenhower had expressed his displeasure with "a number of very serious defects" in the act. Eisenhower said that he was "most concerned that the Act provides new budgetary authority greatly in excess of the amounts which have been requested" and that it threatened the "painstaking efforts" that had been made to "balance the needs of the various Federal programs while keeping overall Federal expenditures to the minimum" (*Public Papers of the Presidents: Eisenhower, 1957,* pp. 532–34; see also *Congressional Quarterly Almanac,* vol. XIII, *1957,* pp. 594–600).

[11] See no. 202.

249

Dulles Papers, White House Memoranda Series

To John Foster Dulles

July 22, 1957

Dear Foster: I notice that recently I seem to be signing a number of nominations for political figures to serve as Ambassadors. Are we running out of qualified career men? As you know, I much prefer the career men to others for most posts. I think this is particularly important in the newer countries where routines have not yet been firmly fixed.

Don't bother to answer this in writing; we can talk about it when I next see you.[1] *As ever*

[1] Later this same day Dulles would tell Eisenhower that except for the wartime and early postwar periods the United States had a higher percentage of career diplomats serving as ambassadors than ever before. He reviewed the new positions and pointed out that of sixteen appointments, only two could be considered non-career. In addition, Dulles said, the State Department considered anyone who was not technically in the Foreign Service as non-career, which would include men who "had had considerable prior diplomatic experience" (Memorandum of Conversation, July 22, 1957, Dulles Papers, White House Memoranda Series).

250 *EM, AWF, DDE Diaries Series*

To Allan A. Ryan *July 22, 1957*

Dear Allan: If, in the course of the next year or so, I am requested to send personal representatives to the inauguration of a foreign head of state—this can occur in Central and South America, in Africa and in Asia—I should like to know whether you would be willing to go as one of my representatives. Usually we ask two or three individuals to serve, and it is common practice for them to take their wives with them.

The reason for making the request in these indefinite terms is that I am making up a list of friends who are willing so to serve, and thus eliminating the necessity of making a hurried search when the occasion actually arises.[1]

Our young Scotch bull continues to develop well. He weighed 676 pounds on the day he was eight months old. At the moment he does not seem to be broadening out as much as he is growing in height and length. We hope that he will be balanced off in this regard by the time he has his first anniversary.[2]

Please remember me warmly to Mrs. Ryan and to Mr. Leachman, and, of course, all the best to yourself. *Sincerely*

[1] For background on the list see no. 246; a draft of the list is in AWF/D. On Eisenhower's invitations to friends see, for example, no. 167, and Eisenhower to Ewing, July 22, 1957, WHCF/OF 101-G. The President had planned to invite the Ryans to the May 1958 presidential inauguration in Argentina. For developments see no. 276.
[2] On Black Brutus, the Scottish bull, see nos. 15 and 228. For background on Eisenhower's interest in importing and breeding Scottish bulls see *Eisenhower Papers*, vols. XIV–XVII.

251

EM, AWF, DDE Diaries Series

To Peter Walgreen Dart

July 22, 1957

Dear Lieutenant Dart: I have heard from your father of the serious misfortune that struck you a few weeks ago.[1] I know just how difficult these weeks are for you, especially because you had just about completed your training as a jet pilot—and I know, too, that the contrast between your hopes for today and your present condition is an especially difficult burden to bear.

But when you consider, as I am sure you have, the great strides that have been made in preventing and treatment of polio, I pray that you will share my own conviction that you will in the not too distant future be able to resume your career. And I dare hope, too, that the weeks of inactivity that are forced upon you will bring to you a maturity and consciousness of the meaning of life that perhaps you had not found before. And lest you think that I am being overly optimistic, I might tell you that my own personal experience in the hospital in Denver a couple of years ago was, far from being a total loss, actually of great value to me.[2] So many of us have so little time to think, and when we do, we gain immeasurably.

You have my very best wishes for your complete and speedy recovery.[3] *Sincerely*

[1] Air Force Second Lieutenant Dart was the son of Justin Whitlock Dart, president of Rexall Drugs, Inc., and an active Republican party fundraiser. On July 16 the elder Dart wrote that his son, recently stricken with polio, was in an iron lung at Sheppard Air Force Base Hospital in Wichita Falls, Texas. Dart requested a get-well note for his son, stating that, "it would mean a lot to me and even more to him" (WHCF/PPF 1834; see also Whitman to Dart, July 25, 1957, *ibid.*).

[2] Eisenhower was hospitalized at Fitzsimons Army Hospital from September 24 to November 10, 1955, while recovering from a coronary thrombosis (see Galambos and van Ee, *The Middle Way*, no. 1595).

[3] Justin Dart would thank the President on August 20. On July 22, 1958, Lieutenant Dart would thank the President for his "inspiring letter of encouragement" and report that although he had since retired from the Air Force, "remarkable progress has been made" toward realizing "many other cherished dreams and ambitions." Three days later Eisenhower would write to the elder Dart of his admiration for his son's "maturity and understanding" (all papers are in WHCF/PPF 1834).

252

EM, AWF, Name Series

To Milton Stover Eisenhower

July 22, 1957

Dear Milton: As of now Mamie and I expect to be in Washington on the third and, of course, would be delighted for you and Ruth to spend the night with us.[1] The third is also John's birthday; it is possible the children will want us to come to their house for dinner that evening. I am sure you would not mind if we should be absent for two or three hours.

I doubt that John and Barbie would want to come to our house for dinner that evening for the simple reason that they would probably want all four children present at the celebration. This would represent quite a chore for Barbie in view of the fact that the youngest is only a year and a half old. However, if by any chance they should come in to the White House for dinner, we would expect you and Ruth, of course, to join in the celebration.[2]

Incidentally, it seems difficult to believe that John is to be thirty-five years old. Had our older youngster lived he would have been forty next September.[3]

I trust that the fishing remains good—and that you have more rain than we have been having here.[4] We are burning up.

Love to Ruth, and please remember me kindly to Mr. Eakin. *As ever*

[1] For background on Milton and his daughter's goodwill trip to Mexico see nos. 235 and 239. On July 18 Milton had written, "I think it would be pleasant and good public relations for us to stay at the White House and so begin the good-will trip from there" (AWF/N). See also *New York Times,* August 5, 1957; and Ann Whitman memorandum, August 3, 1957, AWF/AWD.

[2] As it turned out, the birthday celebration would be held at the White House with Milton and Ruth in attendance (see *New York Times,* Aug. 5, 1957).

[3] On Doud Dwight ("Icky") Eisenhower see Eisenhower, *At Ease,* pp. 180–82.

[4] Milton was vacationing in Land O' Lakes, Wisconsin (see no. 235).

253 *EM, WHCF, Official File 102-B-3*

To James Francis Byrnes *July 23, 1957*

Dear Governor Byrnes:[1] Your letter, just received, expresses sentiments shared by others who have written about the Civil Rights legislation.[2] Time and again in press conferences I have pointed out that the practice of segregating educational facilities was authorized by the law of the land, under Supreme Court ruling, from 1896 to 1954. Under that ruling, I have also explained, customs were established in certain sections of our country which were repudiated and declared illegal by the Supreme Court ruling of 1954, a ruling concerning which I had no more advance notice than did you or any other individual citizen.[3]

It was my purpose, thereafter, in considering the responsibilities of the Executive Department, to provide a moderate approach to a difficult problem and to make haste slowly in seeking to meet it. Certainly there has been no intent on my part to recommend punitive legislation.[4] Both of us know full well that in a government such as ours, primary reliance for law enforcement has to be upon general acceptance of legislation and voluntary compliance with it. I believe that in the question under discussion there are moral values as well as legal requirements to be considered; moreover, I am aware that emotions are deeply stirred on both sides.

The specific point you wrote me about—the jury trial—is essentially a legal matter. But as I read your letter, it seems to me that what you are really objecting to is the giving of authority to the Attorney General to institute civil actions.[5] The pending legislation, however, was conceived under the theory that the whole public has an interest in protection of the right, for example, to vote—that the Attorney General should be given authority to enforce this public right by civil action, just as he now has authority to enforce it by criminal prosecution.

It seems to me that the public interest in the protection of voting rights is at least as great as the public interest in the maintenance of minimum wages, or in the truthfulness of financial and other statements in connection with securities sales, or in the shipment in interstate commerce of contraband oil. In all of these instances—and there are many more that could be cited—the Attorney General is authorized to bring suits to enjoin violations of the law (for which criminal penalties are also provided), and violations of such injunctions are tried without a jury. It seems to me that the right to vote is more important in our way of life than are the regulations cited above.

Certainly I never said—and I have no recollection of the Attorney General ever having said—that "juries in the South will not convict."[6] But I don't see how we can provide for a jury trial in this legislation and leave the rest of the great body of Federal law covered by the rule of no jury trial.

With regard to a press conference statement of mine that I "did not fully understand some of the language of the bill," I was referring to conflicting legal opinions that had been given me regarding Section III. One of these opinions was that the authority sought would be clearly circumscribed and limited by other existing laws; the other opinion was that the authority could, in ambitious hands, be expanded to constitute a virtual police state procedure.[7] As I stated at the beginning of this letter, the last thing I desire is to persecute anyone.

I note you expressed hope that I should show confidence in the people of the South.[8] I am compelled to wonder why you have to express such a thought as nothing more than a hope. Many of my dearest friends are in that region, I spent a not inconsiderable part of my life in the South or in border states, and, moreover, this question of assuring the civil rights of all citizens does *not* apply exclusively to the southern areas.

I do not feel that I need to yield to anyone in my respect for the sentiments, convictions, and character of the average American, no matter where he may happen to dwell.

I would appreciate it if you would convey my warm greetings to Mrs. Byrnes and, of course, best wishes to yourself. *Sincerely*

[1] Byrnes, a former U.S. Senator and Associate Justice of the United States Supreme Court, had been Democratic governor of South Carolina from 1951 until 1955. For background see Galambos and van Ee, *The Middle Way*, nos. 220 and 976.

[2] Byrnes had written on July 17 (same file as document). He expressed his concern over a section of the Civil Rights Bill that would allow a judge to decide whether a defendant in a criminal contempt case involving voting rights should be tried with or without a jury. This provision, argued Byrnes, would allow the Department of Justice to "circumvent the laws of the United States." For background on the Civil Rights Act see no. 248.

[3] See Galambos and van Ee, *The Middle Way*, nos. 341, 574, and 1121.

[4] Eisenhower may have been referring to Senator Richard B. Russell's charge that the civil rights bill was not "a moderate bill to assure and protect the voting rights of American citizens," but a "force law designed to compel the intermingling of the races." The legislation, Russell stated, had been "cunningly designed to vest in the Attorney General unprecedented power to bring to bear the whole might of the Federal Government, including the armed forces if necessary, to force a commingling of white and Negro children in the state-supported public schools of the South" (*New York Times*, July 3, 1957). Russell, as well as many Southerners, had expressed concern over Part III of the pending civil rights legislation; this section permitted injunctions in areas other than voting rights, and allowed the President to use federal troops to uphold court orders (*Congressional Quarterly Almanac*, vol. XIII, *1957*, pp. 553–69; Burk, *The Eisenhower Administration and Black Civil Rights*, pp. 204–26; and Brownell, *Advising Ike*, pp. 216–29).

[5] Although the House on June 17 had defeated an amendment that sought to provide jury trials in cases of contempt arising under the Civil Rights Act, efforts in the Senate to guarantee jury trials in all civil rights contempt proceedings had continued. The assumption of those supporting jury trials in these proceedings was in most cases that the juries would not support the action of the federal government. Eisenhower had spoken out repeatedly against the amendment, saying at one point that "if we tried to put a jury trial between a court order and the enforcement of that order," the United States would be "welcoming anarchy" (*Public Papers of the Presidents: Eisenhower, 1957*, p. 433).

[6] Byrnes had written that, "The only excuse offered by the Attorney General for refusing a citizen the constitutional right of trial by a jury, is that 'juries in the South would not convict.'" Byrnes had termed this "an insult to the men and women of the South."

[7] In his July 3 news conference, Eisenhower had responded to a question concerning Part III of the Civil Rights legislation (see above) by saying that there were "certain phrases" in the legislation that he did not "completely understand," and that he would need to discuss the issue further with the Attorney General (*ibid.*, p. 521). The

Senate on July 24 would amend Part III so as to limit enforcement to the area of voting rights. For developments see no. 266.

[8] Byrnes had written that Eisenhower had submitted his "political fortunes to the people of the Southern States" who had shown "great confidence" in him. "I hope," he wrote, "you will show some confidence in them."

254

EM, WHCF, Official File 137-A

To Norman Mattoon Thomas

July 23, 1957

Dear Mr. Thomas:[1] I should like first of all to express appreciation of your public-spirited offer to come here to convey to me the disarmament views of a selected group of prominent citizens. I have had the interesting suggestion contained in your letter of July twelfth studied by several of my staff.[2]

As you are, of course, aware, the subject of disarmament is a most complex and demanding one. Basic United States policy has evolved over a long period of time and stems from many sources. Because of this complexity and the great range of subject matter, I do not believe that a relatively brief discussion, the only kind that is practicable for me on a normal office day, would be sufficient for a worthwhile exchange and analysis of views.

Therefore I make an alternative suggestion which appeals to me as being somewhat more feasible. It is that your group first prepare a written memorandum, accompanied by whatever you may consider to be suitable recommendations. My second suggestion would be that either upon the completion of that memorandum or as a possibly helpful step in its development, you meet with Mr. Gerard Smith, Special Assistant to Secretary of State Dulles, who has special duties in the field of disarmament.[3] He would be prepared to give you a full briefing on existing governmental policy and objectives in the disarmament field.[4]

With best wishes, *Sincerely*

[1] For background on Norman Thomas, leader of the Socialist party in the United States, see Galambos and van Ee, *The Middle Way*, no. 490.

[2] Thomas had suggested that he, together with several churchmen and members of the American Friends Service Committee, meet with Eisenhower to evaluate a plan for the "monitored suspension of nuclear tests with whatever else firm and wise negotiation may bring us" (Dulles Papers, White House Memoranda Series).

[3] Gerard Coad Smith (LL.B. Yale 1938), former Special Assistant to the Atomic Energy Commission, had been Special Assistant for Atomic Affairs since 1954.

[4] The State Department officials who drafted this message recommended that Eisenhower reject the offer of a meeting. The group itself was "in a rather amorphous state," the message stated, and such a meeting could generate adverse publicity dur-

ing the disarmament meetings in London (Howe to Bernau, July 19, 1957, Dulles Papers, White House Memoranda Series). Eisenhower's secretary Ann Whitman sent a revised draft to Secretary Dulles and asked if there was "anything wrong" with it. The Secretary indicated that he believed the group was pacifistic and had limited standing. Dulles also warned that once Eisenhower began seeing such groups there would be no end. He recommended elimination of the final sentence, which had read: "After such a meeting I could meet with you to get the highlights of your impressions" (Whitman to Bernau, July 23, 1957, Dulles Papers, White House Memoranda Series).

Thomas's response, accepting Eisenhower's suggestion and pleading for a "monitored moratorium on nuclear tests," is in the same file as this document. (See also Adams to Thomas, Aug. 12, 1957; and Thomas to Adams, Aug. 14, 1957, *ibid.*)

255 *EM, AWF, International Series: Macmillan*

TO HAROLD MACMILLAN *July 24, 1957*
Cable. Top secret

Dear Harold: I share your satisfaction in knowing that the Trinidad discussions have been put into channels that should bring out all the important factors applying to the case.[1]

We are, of course, sympathetic with your efforts to bring about a better understanding in the Mid East, particularly between King Saud and the Sultan of Muscat and Oman. I assume that this is just the latest incident of the old Buraimi trouble and I hope that however the matter is settled, you will achieve a better and firmer relationship with King Saud himself. I cannot help but believe that if we handle things correctly, he will be our best counterbalance to Nasser's influence in the region.[2]

In this connection we have heard that disturbing rumors are current in London to the effect that the present troubles in the Sultan's area have been brought about by the efforts of our major oil companies to damage the British oil possessions in that region.[3] Certainly I do not have to assure you that such rumors are completely false. If we were willing to tolerate this kind of thing we would never have been so ready to do our best to help solve the oil problems that were generated for you by the Suez crisis of last fall.[4] The reason that such rumors are disturbing, however, is that too great a readiness on our part to criticize each other for whatever troubles we may encounter in our dealings with other nations cannot possibly have anything but a harmful effect on our common problems in the world.

I do not suggest that there is anything you can do about this matter, but I call it to your attention merely as something that should be in my opinion of continued concern to us on both sides of the Atlantic.

I am quite certain that if you should address DePauw University next spring you and I can find a chance for an informal chat. I certainly would consider it a great privilege to have such an opportunity.[5]

With warm regard, *As ever*

[1] On discussions regarding the location of the capital of the West Indian Federation see no. 247. Macmillan had told Eisenhower that British officials were working "towards an arrangement which would allow this difficult question to be examined as dispassionately as possible." The West Indians, he said, had approved the U.S. terms "subject only to a few minor drafting changes, which I hope will be acceptable in Washington" (Macmillan to Eisenhower, July 22, 1957, PREM 11/1944).

[2] For background on the controversy between Great Britain and Saudi Arabia over the oil-rich oasis at Buraimi, located in the southeastern section of the Arabian peninsula, see Galambos and van Ee, *The Middle Way,* nos. 245 and 1744. In 1955 the Sultan of Muscat, in a military offensive backed by the British government, had expelled the Imam of Oman from the desert kingdom after an attempt by the Imam to establish an independent state. A July 1957 rebellion of tribesmen loyal to the Imam, and purportedly armed by Saudi Arabia, had inspired the Sultan to ask for British aid under the terms of a preexistent treaty between the two countries. Macmillan had told Eisenhower that the Sultan's forces were weak "and the obligations of friendship seem to us to demand that we should not desert him in times of trouble." Britain would provide limited air support, Macmillan wrote, that would deal "a speedy blow at the confidence and prestige of the rebel leaders" (Macmillan to Eisenhower, July 22, 1957, PREM 11/1944; State, *Foreign Relations, 1955–1957,* vol. XIII, *Near East: Jordan-Yemen,* pp. 222–30; Eisenhower, *Waging Peace,* pp. 195–96; Macmillan, *Riding the Storm,* pp. 270–75; and *New York Times,* July 20, 21, 22, 1957). On Eisenhower's attempts to strengthen King Saud's influence in the Middle East see Galambos and van Ee, *The Middle Way,* no. 1811.

[3] Secretary Dulles had enclosed excerpts from five London newspapers in a memorandum to Eisenhower on the preceding day. "The fact that so many papers expressed themselves at about the same time in interpreting the Oman and Muscat trouble as being due to oil rivalries and US-UK competition . . . suggests that this point of view is not alien to some at least of those in the Foreign Office," Dulles said. "I do not attribute it to Macmillan personally" (Dulles to Eisenhower, July 23, 1957; and Cumming to Dulles, n.d., AWF/D-H; see also Telephone conversations, Dulles and Eisenhower, July 23, 1957; Dulles and Cumming, July 24, 1957; and Dulles and Allen Dulles, July 25, 1957, Dulles Papers, Telephone Conversations).

[4] On this issue see Galambos and van Ee, *The Middle Way,* no. 2106. For developments in Muscat and Oman see no. 296.

[5] Macmillan, whose grandfather was the first graduate of the De Pauw Medical School, had been asked to give the commencement address to that university's graduating class in June 1958. In an earlier letter Eisenhower had told the Prime Minister that he "would be a most welcome visitor to America" if he decided to accept the invitation (June 24, 1957, AWF/I: Macmillan; see also Macmillan to Eisenhower, June 28, and July 18, 1957, *ibid.*; and Ann Whitman memorandum, June 20, 1957, AWF/AWD). Macmillan would deliver the De Pauw commencement address on June

8, 1958, and would meet informally with Eisenhower and other government officials in Washington during the following week (State, *Foreign Relations, 1958–1960*, vol. VII, pt. 2, *Western Europe*, pp. 810–18).

256 — *EM, AWF, Name Series*

To Clifford Roberts — *July 25, 1957*

Dear Cliff: Last evening I had a farewell stag dinner for George Humphrey.[1] Those present were members of the Cabinet and a few of my very senior staff officers. In addition, we had George's successor, Bob Anderson.[2]

During the evening there was only one man who felt impelled to "rise to his feet" to make a talk. That was George. And his effort took a strange turn. He described at some length his visit to the Augusta National. The incident or occasion that had impressed him most was a Sunday morning visit we had sitting in the golf shop. I do not recall the identity of those present, but George and I were sitting with three or four others scattered around the shop, one of whom was Pete.[3]

The informality of the occasion, the free exchange of views among good fellows, with no pressures or exhortations marring the quality of a pleasant conversation left an indelible imprint on George's mind. As we left that morning, I remember him remarking, "The greatest deliberative body this country has ever known was the old country store. This morning's experience was almost a replica of the thousands of such meetings that took place only a few years back, sitting around a round-bellied stove, and with a cracker barrel always handy from which a man could extract a soda cracker to nibble on while he listened."

George recited this whole experience at some length and said that from that moment on he had determined to provide a cracker barrel for the Augusta National Golf Shop. This he did, and he brought the result to the dinner and told the party about it.

The barrel has been made on special order (it is a keg that would hold, I should judge, about eight to ten gallons). The wood used was taken from timbers of the White House—timbers that were placed there in the rebuilding of 1817 and were removed about 1949.[4] The keg is beautifully bound with brass hoops and has a lid which is fastened to the keg itself by a chain. On the side is a little brass plate which reads "The Eisenhower Cracker Barrel, presented to the Augusta National Golf Club by G. M. Humphrey, in 1957." George of course intends that the cracker barrel shall be actually installed in the golf shop and he says that it is *your* responsibility to keep it properly supplied with crackers. (Personally I suggest a false bottom about ten inches from the top so that you don't have to fill a rather large cavity in order for men to pick out a cracker at the top. Incidentally, I might add there ought to be another smaller keg with floating dill pickles.)

Of course you would know nothing about these things. I understand you were raised as a city boy. But the glee that at least two-thirds of the dinner guests expressed upon hearing George's description of the cracker barrel, the sand box and the hot stove, provided ample evidence that the majority of Americans are well acquainted with the old grocery store SENATE.

Incidentally, George had kept the whole thing a complete secret. There was no one at the dinner who had the slightest idea what he was going to unveil when he began to unwrap the large package sitting on a chair. Now George and I expect you to make way for the cracker barrel, which I will bring or send down to Augusta as soon as the Club opens. I suggest also that on the basis of this letter you write to George, now in Cleveland, and tell him that you are looking forward to seeing his gift to the Augusta National.[5] *As ever*

P.S. I tried to call you on the phone but found you were golfing, so decided to write this letter.

[1] On Treasury Secretary Humphrey's resignation see nos. 175 and 260; on the stag dinner see *New York Times,* July 25, 1957, and the Chronology.

[2] Robert B. Anderson would become Secretary of the Treasury on July 29 (see nos. 175 and 260).

[3] This was long-time friend William Alton Jones.

[4] During the War of 1812 the British had burned the White House. Restoration of the building took three years. In 1949 the White House underwent another three-year renovation in which the interior walls (those used in the 1814–1817 restoration of the mansion) were demolished to allow for a new foundation. The scrap material was made into items for gifts to museums (see Frank Freidel and William Pencak, eds., *The White House: The First Two Hundred Years* [Boston, 1994], pp. 23, 26, 119–21, and *New York Times,* Sept. 28, Dec. 1, 5, 1949, Feb. 7, 19, 1950, and Mar. 28, 1952).

[5] For developments see no. 265. The White House would later release a modified version of this letter; see the press release in AWF/A, Humphrey Corr.

257 — *EM, AWF, Dulles-Herter Series*

To John Foster Dulles or Christian Archibald Herter — *July 26, 1957*

Memorandum for the Secretary of State—or Under Secretary of State: This morning I had breakfast with Senator Knowland. He told me that

Senator Lyndon Johnson had expressed some concern over the list of individuals submitted for appointment to the UN Delegation.[1] Apparently he was disturbed by the facts that:

(*a*). There are four Republicans to one Democrat on the Delegation.

(*b*). He, as Democratic leader in the Senate, had not been consulted as to the suitability of the Democrat selected for appointment.

Since it had been a considerable time since I had seen this list, I could not talk very intelligently to Senator Knowland. I could tell him only that we had always earnestly tried to preserve the bipartisan character of the Delegation and to get good people to serve on it. I did promise that the State Department would get in touch with him (Knowland) to explain the situation. I would appreciate it if you would do this as soon as possible.[2]

[1] Eisenhower was referring to Senate Minority Leader William Knowland. In regard to Majority Leader Johnson's influence on other presidential appointments see no. 52.

[2] On August 23, 1957, the Senate would confirm the following men as Delegates to the Twelfth United Nations General Assembly: Henry Cabot Lodge, Jr., permanent Ambassador to the United Nations, Republican; Representative A. S. J. Carnahan of Missouri, Democrat; Representative Walter H. Judd of Minnesota, Republican; George Meany, president of the American Federation of Labor and Congress of Industrial Organizations (AFL-CIO), Democrat; and Herman B. Wells, president of Indiana University, Republican. As alternates, the Senate would approve Republicans James J. Wadsworth; Irene Dunne; Mrs. Oswald B. Lord; and Genoa S. Washington; and Democrat Philip M. Klutznick. Although Johnson would complain that he "thought more of the alternates should have been Democrats," he did not oppose the confirmations (*New York Times,* Aug. 23, 1957; *Congressional Quarterly Weekly Reports* 36, Sept. 6, 1957, p. 1076). There is no further correspondence regarding these appointments in AWF.

258

EM, AWF, International Series: Macmillan

To Harold Macmillan — *July 27, 1957*

Cable. Top secret

Dear Harold:[1] I am sorry if our hurriedly formed arrangements for Foster to come to London to make sure of coordinated thinking between ourselves and the American Delegation should have caused you the slightest embarrassment. Foster is now in Canada so it was not easy to develop a feasible plan for the purpose we had in mind. But as quickly as we could make the decision by telephoning between here and Ottawa, I sent you what I thought to be an appropriate cable.[2]

I feel confident that the press guidance which you so promptly gave in London, and such statements as Foster may make upon leaving Ottawa or arriving in London will help to keep the reasons for Foster's trip in proper perspective without embarrassment to you.[3]

With warm regard, *As ever*

[1] Eisenhower had handwritten the original draft of this message, which Ann Whitman sent to Under Secretary Herter for transmission to Macmillan (see Whitman to Herter, and Eisenhower to Macmillan, July 27, 1957, AWF/A, Herter Corr.).

[2] Five days earlier Eisenhower had discussed with Dulles the possibility of an informal trip to London to demonstrate to the Disarmament Committee that he had "command of the situation." Dulles was reluctant at the time and had told the President that he thought his "going would probably be built up into a crisis or overoptimism." Eisenhower did not decide that Dulles should make the London trip until after the Secretary had left for a two-day informal visit to Ottawa, Canada. On July 26 Eisenhower had cabled Macmillan through the American embassy that Dulles would be coming to London "in order to renew our contacts with our delegation . . . and to make certain that in the highest echelons our thinking along disarmament is well coordinated." After receiving the message, Macmillan asked U.S. Ambassador Whitney to change the press release to include mention of a fictitious consultation between the Americans and the British. Macmillan had also written to Eisenhower that he felt "some concern lest the ill-disposed here might wrongly interpret Foster's visit, particularly in view of present events in the Middle East. I should therefore have liked, had there been time, to have agreed with you on a joint statement about Foster's visit which would have made it clear that we had consulted together about it" (Memorandum of Conversation, July 22, 1957, Dulles Papers, White House Memoranda Series; State, *Foreign Relations, 1955–1957*, vol. XX, *Regulation of Armaments; Atomic Energy*, pp. 664–65; Eisenhower to Macmillan, and Macmillan to Eisenhower, July 26, 1957, AWF/I: Macmillan; Macmillan, *Riding the Storm*, p. 272. On "events in the Middle East"—that is, the situation in Muscat and Oman see no. 255).

[3] In Eisenhower's original draft this paragraph had read: "I have now sent a message to Foster suggesting that upon leaving Ottawa for London he informally announce that his trip is in accordance with the wishes of the Prime Minister and the President because, in addition to its basic purpose, it will provide an opportunity for an appointment with the Prime Minister and others of our friends in England, and perhaps the Continent." Because he believed that Macmillan "was trying to duck seeing the Secretary of State" in order to avoid a discussion of the Middle East, Herter suggested changing the message to the form in which it appears above. Both Dulles and the President approved (Eisenhower to Macmillan, and Whitman to Herter, July 27, 1957, AWF/A; Telephone conversation, Herter and Dulles, July 27, 1957, Dulles Papers, Telephone Conversations; and Ann Whitman memorandum, n.d., AWF/A). On Dulles's statements regarding the trip see *U.S. Department of State Bulletin* 37, no. 946 (August 12, 1957), 272; and no. 947 (August 19, 1957), 304.

259

EM, AWF, Administration Series

To Christian Archibald Herter

July 29, 1957

Memorandum for the Acting Secretary of State:[1]

1. I assume that there is no question of "recognition" involved in the succession of President Gonzales Lopez in the Presidency of Guatemala.[2] This seems to be a succession that follows constitutional form so I suppose nothing is necessary. However, I do think it would be advisable to get together an early message from me to him which might emphasize the satisfaction we had in the friendship of his predecessor and the hope that the same type of feeling and the same type of government policies would continue.

At your convenience, let me know what you think about this.[3]

2. Last evening a friend came to see me with an account of Ambassador Gluck's appearance before the Foreign Relations Committee of the Senate.[4] The story given to me was that he exhibited an abysmal ignorance about the country to which he is accredited and about the entire region of Southeast Asia. Is it not possible, before sending one of these political appointees before a Congressional Committee for examination, to give them sufficient briefing so that they can make a better showing? The making of a political appointment always puts us a bit on the defensive, but to appoint one who has to undergo public examination with only meager knowledge of the history, geography and prominent personages of the country to which he is appointed increases the embarrassment immeasurably.[5]

[1] Secretary Dulles was in London, participating in disarmament discussions (see no. 258).

[2] On July 26 Guatemalan President Carlos Enrique Castillo Armas was assassinated by a palace guard, and Luis Arturo Gonzalez Lopez had assumed office immediately (State, *Foreign Relations, 1955–1957,* vol. VII, *American Republics: Central and South America,* pp. 142–43). For background on U.S.-Guatemalan relations see Galambos and van Ee, *The Middle Way,* no. 965).

[3] Gonzalez Lopez had been chosen the previous March by the Guatemalan Congress as First Presidential Delegate, Herter replied, "and as such succeeded constitutionally. We are merely continuing without interruption the relations we maintained with the [previous] administration . . ." (Herter to Eisenhower, July 30, 1957, AWF/A). Eisenhower's letter wishing the new president success and his condolence letter to Odilia Paloma de Castillo are in AWF/I: Guatemala.

[4] On June 26 Eisenhower had nominated from private life Maxwell Henry Gluck, board chairman of the Darlington Stores Corporation and a breeder of thoroughbred horses, to be U.S. Ambassador to Ceylon. Although testimony before the committee revealed that Gluck had contributed heavily to the Republican party and seemed to know little about Ceylon, the Senate had confirmed the appointment on July 3 (U.S. Congress, Senate, Committee on Foreign Relations, "The Nomination

of Maxwell Henry Gluck to be Ambassador to Ceylon," *Committee Hearings,* vol. 1275.2, 85th Cong., 1st sess. [1957], 1–6).

[5] Herter would send a summary of Gluck's background and a list of congressional endorsements to Eisenhower on the following day. The nominee, Herter said, had not had the benefit of substantial briefings prior to his appearance before the committee. "It has not been the custom in the past for the members of the Committee to cross-examine a person appointed from private life as an ambassador for the purpose of ascertaining his knowledge of the country to which he has been named or to determine his knowledge of international affairs." Prior briefings were not mandatory, he told Eisenhower, but considering the "tactics which certain members of the Committee are now employing, we shall, in the future, insist upon a thorough briefing by the Department in advance of their appearance before the Committee." "It would seem that the manner in which Ambassador Gluck was interrogated and the manner in which a portion of the transcripts was released must have been prompted by a desire to embarrass the Administration" (Herter to Eisenhower, July 30, 1957, AWF/A).

In testimony before the committee (Aug. 1) Herter would explain Administration policy on ambassadorial appointments (U.S. Congress, Senate, Committee on Foreign Relations, "Ambassadorial Appointments," *Committee Hearings,* vol. 1275.2, 85th Cong., 1st sess. [1957], 1–43). For Dulles's defense of Gluck and his comments to newsmen on ambassadorial appointments for campaign contributors see *U.S. Department of State Bulletin* 37, no. 948 (August 26, 1957) 345; see also Telephone conversation, Eisenhower and Dulles, August 7, 1957, Dulles Papers, Telephone Conversations and AWF/D.

260 *EM, AWF, DDE Diaries Series*

To George Magoffin Humphrey *July 29, 1957*

Dear George: Although we had, long ago, gone through all the preliminary events leading up to your separation this morning from governmental service, I must confess that the actual ceremony of turning over your duties brought to me a sense of loss and renewed regret.[1]

As you so well know, the prospect of a political career for myself, ever since it was first suggested back in the middle forties, was one that I could contemplate only with the utmost reluctance, even repugnance. Nevertheless the beginning of my life in political office brought me one great privilege and opportunity that I have valued highly. It was that of working day by day with people of stature who from the very first inspired in me feelings of respect, trust and confidence. Among these, as I think you realize, you have always stood in the front rank and I have been especially honored that, in addition, you and Pam have given to Mamie and me so unstintedly of your friendship.[2]

Of course I know that you stand ready constantly to help me in every appropriate way to carry the burdens that I must continue to bear for the next few years if the Lord spares me to do so. It is a great satisfaction to know that our official parting this morning was in no sense a farewell to all our intimate associations. Nevertheless I shall miss the opportunities that have been mine to reach for the phone to call you for a few minutes conversation on subjects where your counsel and advice have been so valuable.[3]

I shall regret your absence from our weekly Cabinet and National Security meetings and, of course, at those informal conferences where I have been accustomed not only to see you, but to lean upon your wisdom and experience and integrity.

Some weeks ago when I first received your letter of resignation I tried to tell you, in writing, of my feelings with respect to your impending departure. However, this afternoon I feel impelled to attempt once again to say that your going has left a truly permanent gap in my personal and official life. *As ever*

[1] For background on Humphrey's resignation as treasury secretary see no. 175. On the White House ceremony for his successor, Robert B. Anderson, see *New York Times*, July 30, 1957.

[2] For background on the Eisenhowers' relationship with the Humphreys see no. 7. For developments see, for example, no. 578.

[3] Humphrey would continue to advise the President about the federal budget (see no. 469).

261 — *EM, AWF, DDE Diaries Series*

To Dillon Anderson — *July 30, 1957*

Dear Dillon:[1] Your exposition of the national security effects of unrestricted crude oil imports strikes me as excellent.[2] In the main I agree; I think I disagree only with one point which I find in the first paragraph on page six:

> "At the same time our object should be to ensure that our economic and military strength do not become so dependent on the continued flow of Middle East oil that in time of crisis we would face the unacceptable alternatives of (a) resort to force to hold the source, or (b) suffer the crippling effect of its loss."

I think that you have, in the analysis presented in the letter, proved that should a crisis arise threatening to cut the western world off from the Mid East oil, we would *have* to use force. You specifically point out that an adequate supply of oil to Western Europe ranks almost equal in priority with an adequate supply for ourselves.[3] You argue that while the Western Hemisphere can on an emergency basis meet the short term requirements of the entire free world, the implication is included that we cannot do this on the long term. Hence my disagreement with the statement to which I call your attention.

By this I mean that you prove the facts of the petroleum world are such that the West must, for self-preservation, retain access to Mid-East oil.

In general, however, I merely express the hope that our long term national objectives in this field can be spelled out and formalized so that they will mean something—in other words, that they will encourage maximum exploration in our country and use of imports as a supplemental, not a ruinous substitute, for our own production.[4]

I was pleased that you were able to devote some of your time to the work of the Cabinet Committee. I know that you were a great help.

With warm regard, *Sincerely*

[1] Anderson, former Special Assistant to the President for National Security Affairs, had served as Eisenhower's consultant since October 1956. He was also a consultant to the Cabinet Special Committee to Investigate Crude Oil Imports, which Eisenhower had established on June 26, 1957, in response to reports from the Office of Defense Mobilization that the high level of oil imports threatened to impair national security. The committee had been charged with balancing factors such as the long-term requirements for crude oil, and the military, economic and diplomatic considerations involved in obtaining foreign crude oil with "the maintenance of a dynamic domestic industry that will meet national needs in peace or war" (*U.S. Department of State Bulletin* 37, no. 944 [July 29, 1957], 209–10, and State, *Foreign Relations, 1955–1957*, vol. X, *Foreign Aid and Economic Defense Policy*, pp. 693–94).

[2] Anderson had written the President on July 24 to present his views on the impact of crude oil imports. Convinced that U.S. security was closely related to the availability of oil, Anderson had said that "the complex problem of maintaining an appropriate balance between imports and domestic production" would be "with us in more or less acute form for a long time" (State, *Foreign Relations, 1955–1957*, vol. X, *Foreign Aid and Economic Defense Policy*, pp. 717–20).

[3] Anderson had based his analysis on two general assumptions. First, "the United States must have an assured source of energy (including oil in the measurable future) for continued sound economic growth and development as well as the strengthening of our military capabilities." Second, "an assured supply of energy—including oil—to our Western Allies is essential to the survival of the Free World." See also Edward W. Chester, *United States Oil Policy and Diplomacy: A Twentieth-Century Overview* (Westport, Conn., 1983), pp. 30–36, and Gerald D. Nash, *United States Oil Policy 1890–1964* (Westport, Conn., 1968), pp. 201–8.

[4] The Special Cabinet Committee would send its report and recommendations to Eisenhower on July 29 (AWF/A; Weeks Corr.). Noting that the increased volume of crude oil imports threatened to impair national security, the Committee recommended the establishment of a plan of voluntary import limitations. Eisenhower would order Secretary of Commerce Sinclair Weeks and Director of the Office of

Defense Mobilization Gordon Gray to enact the Committee's recommendations as "rapidly as possible." For developments see no. 302.

262 *EM, AWF, DDE Diaries Series*

To Henry Robinson Luce *July 30, 1957*

Dear Harry: I will, of course, have a record made of the statistics applying to the San Francisco Conference, with the thought that it may unexpectedly become possible for me to attend.[1] However, as of now, the number of invitations I have to important conventions, coupled with the involvement of the Queen's visit and my anxiety that her stay here will be perfectly arranged, make the chance of my acceptance remote, to say the least.[2]

For mid-October I have invitations to address several thousand members of the College of Surgeons, including a considerable number of foreign guests.[3] Another would take me to New York to address the supporters of the National Fund for Medical Education, and still another would take me to Miami for a talk before a great religious group.[4] Such a prospect, when placed over against the regularity of schedule that I attempt to maintain for reasons of health and vigor, creates for me a very considerable problem.

As all these conflicting considerations gradually clarify into what seems to me to be a reasonable solution, I shall, of course, communicate with you further.[5]

With warm regard, *As ever*

[1] The International Industrial Development Conference, jointly sponsored by Time, Inc., and the Stanford Research Institute, would take place October 14–18. The industrialists, financiers, and statesmen assembled there would address "the ways and means of business statesmanship for the future of the Free World" (Luce to Eisenhower, Sept. 6, 1957, C. D. Jackson Papers).

[2] Queen Elizabeth II and Prince Philip would visit the United States October 16–21 (see no. 395).

[3] See no. 160.

[4] As it turned out, Eisenhower would speak at the medical education dinner on October 22 at the Waldorf-Astoria (*New York Times*, Oct. 22, 23, 1957).

[5] For developments see no. 338.

President Eisenhower meets President Ngo Dinh Diem of the Republic of Vietnam in Washington, D.C., May 8, 1957.

President Eisenhower and Field Marshal Viscount Bernard Law Montgomery inspect the Gettysburg battlefield, May 12, 1957.

President Eisenhower visits with General and Mrs. George C. Marshall at Blair House, Washington, D.C., June 5, 1957.

The President and German Chancellor Konrad Adenauer tour the Eisenhowers' farm in Gettysburg, Pennsylvania, May 26, 1957.

President Eisenhower watches as Assistant to the President Sherman Adams swears in Dr. James R. Killian, Jr., as Special Assistant to the President for Science and Technology. Killian's wife looks on, November 15, 1957.

Vice-President Richard M. Nixon reports to newsmen outside the White House on November 26, 1957, on President Eisenhower's condition following a cerebral occlusion.

While vacationing in Newport, Rhode Island, President Eisenhower meets with Arkansas Governor Orval Faubus to discuss the desegregation crisis in Little Rock public schools, September 14, 1957.

The President, the First Lady, Queen Elizabeth II, and Prince Philip at the White House, October 17, 1957.

President Eisenhower and British Prime Minister Harold Macmillan talk with British Foreign Secretary Selwyn Lloyd (*left*) and Secretary of State John Foster Dulles (*right*) before an informal dinner at the White House, October 23, 1957.

President Eisenhower leads the U.S. delegation to the fifteen-nation NATO summit meeting in Paris, December 1957. Secretary of State John Foster Dulles, Treasury Secretary Robert B. Anderson, and Secretary of Defense Neil H. McElroy are seated behind the President.

The Eisenhower family poses for a Christmas picture in the East Room of the White House in December 1957. *L to R:* Susan Elaine, Colonel John S. D. Eisenhower, Dwight David II, the First Lady, Mary Jean, the President, Barbara Anne, and Barbara.

263

EM, AWF, *Administration Series*

TO CHRISTIAN ARCHIBALD HERTER

July 31, 1957

Memorandum for the Acting Secretary of State: A man named Henry A. Kissinger has just written a very provocative book entitled "Nuclear Weapons and Foreign Policy." The book was brought to my notice by Cabot Lodge, who spoke of it in terms of great admiration.[1]

I have not read the complete book, but I am sending you herewith a copy of a fairly extensive brief made by General Goodpaster of my office.[2] This at least I think you will want to read, and I believe that when Foster returns he will have some interest in it also.

I do not mean that you will agree with everything the man says. I think there are flaws in his arguments and, at the very least, if we were to organize and maintain military forces along the lines he suggests, we would have what George Humphrey always calls "both the old and the new." This would undoubtedly be a more expensive operation than we are carrying on at this time.[3]

However, the author directs his arguments to some general or popular conceptions and misconceptions, and, as I say, I think you will find interesting and worth reading at least this much of the book.

[1] German-born Henry Alfred Kissinger (A.B. Harvard 1950, Ph.D. 1954), a lecturer in the Harvard Department of Government, had been Executive Director of the Harvard International Seminar since 1951, and had become Associate Director of the Harvard Center for International Affairs in 1957. That year the Council on Foreign Relations published *Nuclear Weapons and Foreign Policy* [New York]. United Nations Ambassador Lodge had written the President on July 25 (AWF/A, Kissinger Corr.), regarding Kissinger's book, which he had recommended as "clear-headed, profound and constructive."

[2] Goodpaster's extended brief, as well as a shorter brief by John Eisenhower, can be found in AWF/A, Kissinger Corr.

[3] Kissinger had argued that the central dilemma of the atomic age lay in the fact that the development of more powerful nuclear weapons was accompanied by a greater reluctance to use them. This reluctance tended to give the Soviet Union a greater freedom to act on the international front. Because, Kissinger argued, American strategic doctrine recognized few intermediate points between total war and total peace, American policy makers had difficulty during periods of Soviet belligerency in relating the risks of resistance to with the issues actually at stake. American strategists, he thought, needed to create alternatives less cataclysmic than a thermonuclear holocaust. This could be done by formulating a military policy that avoided the assumption that war, if it came, would inevitably be total, and that gave our diplomacy the greatest freedom of action.

Kissinger envisioned a strategy of "limited nuclear war," to be fought for specific political objectives rather than complete annihilation. In limited war the effort was to affect the opponent's will rather than to crush it, and to make the conditions to be imposed seem more attractive than continued resistance. A successful policy of limited war could exist only behind the shield of a capability for all-out war. The United States would, therefore, need to maintain a retaliatory force sufficiently powerful and well-protected that by no calculation could an aggressor discern any benefit in resorting to all-out war. Kissinger proposed reorganizing American armed forces into two basic commands: a Strategic Force (the units required for all-out war), and a Tactical Force (the units required for limited war). These commands would be headed by a reorganized Joint Chiefs of Staff organization, consisting of a Chairman, a Chief of Tactical Force, a Chief of Strategic Force, and a Chief of Naval Operations (to represent operations such as anti-submarine warfare which did not fit into the other categories). Kissinger also suggested the establishment of a "Strategic Advisory Council" to help in the formation of national policy in the difficult areas where political, economic, psychological and military factors overlapped. See also Russell F. Weigley, *The American Way of War: A History of United States Military Strategy and Policy* (Bloomington, Ind., and London, 1977), pp. 413–17.

For developments see no. 275.

264 — *EM, AWF, DDE Diaries Series*

To Louis Hadley Evans — *July 31, 1957*

Dear Dr. Evans: I was disturbed by the implication, contained in the pamphlet you handed to me concerning the Presbyterian Convention in Miami, that I had agreed either personally or through a member of my staff to address that Convention.[1]

I have examined all the correspondence in my files and find that there is nothing that could possibly be interpreted as an acceptance. To the contrary, Mr. Shanley wrote to the Reverend Billy Graham as early as April 26th of this year to tell him that examination of my fall schedule compelled me to decline the invitation.

Because of an erroneous account in a Miami paper of early April and on the assumption that I would be in Florida in October, a number of other individuals sent invitations from political groups, church and veterans organizations and others. In each case these individuals were told that the invitation to the Convention had been declined.[2]

As a consequence I think a correction should go out now to all individuals to whom the pamphlet, referred to above, was sent. To wait until the Convention itself to make any explanation is to place me in a false, not to say embarrassing position. Consequently I would be most appreciative if you would do what you can to see that this correction is accomplished.[3]

With best wishes, *Sincerely*

[1] Evans (A.B. Occidental College 1918; B.D. McCormick Theological Seminary), associate general secretary and minister of the United Presbyterian Church of the United States of America, was serving as temporary pastor of the National Presbyterian Church in Washington, D.C. During his July 30 visit to the White House, Evans

had asked the President to attend the Miami convention and had presented a pamphlet containing an announcement of a presidential address (see signatures list, July 30, 1957, AWF/D, and Ann Whitman memorandum, July 31, 1957, AWF/AWD). Evans and the President had first spoken following Sunday morning services on July 28 (*New York Times*, July 29, 1957).

[2] See, for example, no. 126. In his April 3 news conference the President had announced that he had no plans to visit Florida (*Public Papers of the Presidents: Eisenhower, 1957*, p. 251; and *New York Times*, Apr. 4, 1957).

[3] Ann Whitman would note that the correspondence regarding this matter "has been very guarded and discouraging" (Ann Whitman memorandum, July 30, 1957, AWF/AWD). There is no reply in AWF.

265 *EM, AWF, Name Series*

To Clifford Roberts *July 31, 1957*

Dear Cliff: I have a sense of astonishment that in spite of some years of intimate association and friendship with you, I have never truly appreciated your ability to mix humor, exposition and a bit of philosophy into a "thank you" note in such fashion as to make it a piece of literature.[1]

By this I mean to say that your letter to George is a masterpiece. I sincerely hope that the Cracker Barrel ceremony can come off as planned, and that you, George and I, together with a substantial portion of the "gang" can all attend.[2]

One piece of incidental news. Yesterday I played nine holes and hit the ball straighter and farther than I have since I was ill last year.[3] At least I was good enough so I am planning to go out tomorrow to try again. *As ever*

[1] For background on George Humphrey's gift of the Eisenhower Cracker Barrel to the Augusta National Golf Club, see no. 256. Roberts, chairman of the Augusta National's executive committee, had written Humphrey on July 29 (AWF/A, George Humphrey Corr.). Although the club declined to accept several items, Roberts wrote, "a Cracker Barrel is something we can enthusiastically embrace because we understand it and like it and everything it implies. May its sturdy staves and strong bindings long offer the munching material for companionable gatherings and salty observations." He went on to say that he accepted his role "in humble gratefulness." He would, he added, dedicate his "personal fortune" and his "best efforts" to keeping the barrel full.

[2] Eisenhower and Humphrey would attend the dedication on November 17 (*New York Times*, Nov. 18, 1957). The President would again stress the meaning of the cracker barrel in no. 461.

[3] The President had played at the Burning Tree Country Club. On his ileotransverse colostomy in June 1956 see Galambos and van Ee, *The Middle Way*, no. 1894.

266

EM, WHCF, Official File 99-V

To William Fife Knowland — *August 2, 1957*

Dear Bill: I deeply believe that, when governmental affairs of these days become history, your courage, energy and idealism in leading our defeated forces in the Senate battle for civil rights will be remembered gratefully by the American people long after the names of the opponents of the measure have been lost to memory. You were fighting for a basic concept written into our Constitution; you were trying to make universally effective one of the rights for which the Republican Party has stood since the days of its founding.[1]

My great respect for your deep sense of responsibility, your integrity and your forcefulness in upholding your clear convictions, was never higher than it is at this moment. I felicitate you on a gallant effort and express the hope that time will yet give us an opportunity again to fight and, in our next effort, to win this battle.[2]

With warm personal regard, *Sincerely*

[1] For background see no. 253. On August 2, 1957, the Senate had voted to accept an amendment weakening the Administration's civil rights legislation. The amendment guaranteed jury trials in all cases of criminal contempt. Senator Knowland had led the opposition to the amendment, saying that acceptance, which would send the bill to conference, would effectively kill the chances for a civil rights act for the current session of Congress (see *Congressional Quarterly Almanac*, vol. XIII, *1957*, pp. 567–68; and *New York Times*, Aug. 2, 1957). Eisenhower called the vote "bitterly disappointing" to the many Americans who realized that the bill as amended would leave many Americans disenfranchised (*Public Papers of the Presidents: Eisenhower, 1957*, pp. 587–88).

[2] Knowland would respond on August 12 (same file as document). Thanking Eisenhower for his words of encouragement, Knowland added that civil rights was "an issue that will not be settled until it is settled right. We have made some progress this year," he said, "and ultimately, in the not too distant future, fully effective legislation will be enacted into law." For developments see no. 307.

267

EM, AWF, Name Series

To Ellis Dwinnell Slater — *August 3, 1957*

Dear Slats: Your report on your trip to Puerto Rico is far more interesting and valuable to me than many of the documents, written in government-ese, that file across my desk.[1] And your suggestion about the land the Defense Department controls on the island is one that I shall have studied seriously.[2]

Thanks once again for undertaking the trip on such brief notice—and for being an able and articulate and observant representative.[3]

I hope I shall see you soon, and shall look forward to hearing some of the details you did not incorporate in your letter.[4]

With warm personal regard, *As ever*

[1] On July 25 Slater, as Eisenhower's personal representative, had attended celebrations of Puerto Rico's fifth anniversary as a commonwealth. His five-page letter, dated July 31, is in AWF/N. Slater had written of the reception he received, the parade ceremonies he attended, and his impression of the Puerto Rican government officials. He described the leaders he had met as "capable, dedicated, thoroughly honest, and . . . the right men in the right place." See also Slater, *The Ike I Knew*, pp. 157–60; and *New York Times*, July 25, 26, 1957.

[2] Slater had suggested that any excess land held by the Defense Department should be leased or sold to the Commonwealth in order to ease the shortage of land available for use by a growing population. For developments see no. 289.

[3] Slater had accepted the assignment on July 23 (see Slater, *The Ike I Knew*, p. 157, and *New York Times*, July 24, 1957).

[4] On September 20–22 Slater would visit the Eisenhowers while they were vacationing in Newport, Rhode Island (see Slater, *The Ike I Knew*, pp. 160–63; on the Eisenhowers' vacation see no. 190).

268

EM, AWF, DDE Diaries Series

Diary

Top secret

August 5, 1957

1. This morning I made two telephone calls to the Defense Department, the first to the Chief of Staff of the Army, General Taylor.

Last week Mr. Wilson had a press conference in which he spoke very facetiously about an alleged Army intention of building an 800 mile ballistic missile. He spoke about it in terms implying strong disapproval, and he also implied that the Army had undoubtedly acted without any authority from the Secretary of Defense.[1]

A memorandum to me from the Army states that the proposition that was mentioned was incorrectly described in the question addressed to Mr. Wilson. On top of this, the Army has done nothing whatsoever in extending the range of the particular missile in question (I believe it is the REDPATH[2]) but requested authority to introduce a solid propellant which it is alleged would give the missile an effective range of 400 to 500 miles (not 800 as alleged in the question directed to Mr. Wilson). The Army also states that its plan would be to use this weapon to get greater flexibility, but dependent completely upon the Air Force for reconnaissance necessary to report targets and results of findings.

Actually the whole proposition seems sensible to me, particularly in that development costs would be limited to modification for the change in fuel.

I suggested that the Chief of Staff seek an appointment at once with the Secretary of Defense, telling the Secretary that he was doing so at my instruction.[3]

I am disturbed by the implication left in the newspaper stories that the Departments are operating in defiance of the Secretary of Defense's orders when, as a matter of fact, it appears to me that the Army did everything possible to keep this matter strictly within the limits of regular and proper procedure.

A copy of the Army memorandum is filed with this account.

2. My second call was to General White of the Air Force.[4] A newspaper story states that in a recent public speech, he made comparisons between the Air Force and its sister services in the matter of their readiness to appreciate modern conditions and adapt their methods and equipment to those conditions.[5]

I told him that I had no objection to his praising his own service as much as he pleased, but I did object to any representative of one of the services comparing himself or his own service with the others to their disadvantage and his own advantage. This in my opinion is destructive in terms of the whole general service morale.[6]

It is the old question of whether service men are working first of all for their own service or for the good of the United States.[7]

General White agreed that this had been an error, but stated that the document had been submitted to the Secretary of Defense before delivery as a public speech. He said also that he called specific attention to the paragraph that aroused my concern, and that the speech was approved by the Defense Department without comment. I suggested to him that hereafter if he had any doubt about any feelings that might be hurt, he consult with the Chiefs of Staff rather than with the Defense Department staff whose concern for such remarks might not be so acute.

[1] The *New York Times* had reported on August 5 that the Army was building six 800-mile range missiles, despite the fact that there had been no budget authorization for such a program. Secretary of Defense Wilson had told reporters that the Army would not be permitted to use the missiles operationally under any circumstances. Asked whether he had "absolutely rejected" the missiles, Wilson was said to have answered that they were "99.85 percent out." The *Times* had stated that Army officials were "crushed" by Wilson's comments since they viewed the weapons as filling "an important gap in missile development." In 1954 the Defense Department and the JCS had agreed to permit the Army to develop and use surface-to-surface guided missile systems with "no arbitrary limit" placed upon their ranges as long as the missiles were to be used to hit "tactical targets within the zone of Army combat operations that are the responsibility of the ground force commander, as differentiated from strategic targets" (Historical Section, JCS, "Chronology of Changes in Key West Agreements, April 1948–January 1958," Feb. 7, 1958, CCS 337 [4-2-49], B.P.).

[2] Eisenhower was referring to Redstone, the first large ballistic missile, and the progenitor of Jupiter, the nation's first intermediate range ballistic missile (see Wernher von Braun, "The Redstone, Jupiter, and Juno" in Eugene M. Emme, ed., *The History of Rocket Technology* [Detroit, 1964], pp. 107–21). On the struggle among the services over missile development see Milobsky, *Leadership and Competition*.
[3] Eisenhower had called Taylor to say that Secretary Wilson "did not know what he was saying" when he referred to the six test missiles. The President instructed Taylor to see the Secretary of Defense and "put Wilson straight" (AWF/D, Telephone Calls, Aug. 5, 1957). The President would meet with Secretary of Defense Wilson, JCS Chairman Arthur Radford and the chiefs of the various services in an August 12 conference to discuss intermediate-range ballistic missiles and the Redstone program. After discussions regarding the weight, and practicality, improvement costs, and accuracy of the Redstone, Eisenhower would conclude that the detailed planning and evaluation of all missile programs fell within the responsibilities of the Department of Defense; that no service should be restricted within a rigid range limit; and that "the Army should not be denied a 500-mile missile on the *mere* basis" that the missile had a range of over 200 miles (John S. D. Eisenhower, Summary of Conference on Army Missile Program, Aug. 14, 1957, AWF/D; and State, *Foreign Relations, 1955–1957*, vol. XIX, *National Security Policy*, pp. 572–86). For John S. D. Eisenhower's account of this meeting and the events leading up to it see his memoir, *Strictly Personal*, pp. 190–93.
[4] General Thomas Dresser White (USMA, 1920) had become Air Force Chief of Staff on July 1, 1957.
[5] White had made his remarks at the Air Force Association convention on August 2, 1957. The General had stated that the other services had not made "an over-all adjustment to the present era, equivalent to the Air Force adjustment." White added that he saw the major air power deterrent forces as the "survival forces." "Other forces must continue to exist," he said, "but on an austere basis, tailored to their contribution to the survival force" (*New York Times*, Aug. 3, 1957).
[6] Eisenhower had also told the General that his comments were destructive to unity among the Joint Chiefs of Staff. The President suggested that White tell the other Chiefs that he had "made a blunder" but "didn't mean it." White had thanked the President, saying "I appreciate your telling me—appreciate it very much" (Telephone Calls, Aug. 5, 1957, AWF/D).
[7] On Eisenhower's past struggles with interservice rivalry over guided missiles see, for example, Galambos and van Ee, *The Middle Way*, no. 1663.

269

EM, AWF,
Administration Series

TO ARTHUR ELLSWORTH SUMMERFIELD, SR. *August 5, 1957*

Dear Arthur: Attached is a letter from Arthur Hays Sulzberger of the New York Times.[1] Would you let me have a memorandum on which I could base a reply?

I like Mr. Sulzberger; he was one of the Columbia Trustees when I was at that University. We have remained friends through the years. I do not mean to be "pressuring" but I note his statement that the

Post Office Department did issue a memorial stamp to commemorate Pulitzer's hundredth birthday.[2] *As ever*

[1] *New York Times* publisher Sulzberger had written the President on August 1 (WHCF/OF 7-J) to request a stamp to honor the hundredth anniversary of the birth of his father-in-law, newspaper publisher Adolph Shelby Ochs. Sulzberger called the President's attention to *The Papers of Thomas Jefferson,* "presently being issued by Princeton University and which will consist when finished of some fifty-six volumes." The publication was dedicated to Mr. Ochs. Eisenhower had previously appealed to Summerfield on Sulzberger's behalf for a commemorative stamp to honor the Bicentennial of Columbia University; he had also interceded on behalf of a series of wildlife stamps (see Galambos and van Ee, *The Middle Way,* nos. 67 and 1587).

[2] The U.S. Postal Service had issued the three-cent Joseph Pulitzer Commemorative Stamp in 1947 (United States Postal Service, *Postage Stamps of the United States* [Washington, D.C., 1970], pp. 115–16).

Eisenhower would respond to Sulzberger on August 6 (WHCF/OF 7-J). Noting that Sulzberger was scheduled to meet with the Postmaster General on the following day, he assured him that the issue of an Adolph Ochs commemorative would be "given the utmost consideration by the Stamp Advisory Committee at its next meeting. I, of course, hope that their action will be favorable." A stamp honoring Ochs would, however, not be issued.

270

EM, WHCF, President's Personal File 771

To Norman Loyall McLaren — *August 5, 1957*

Personal and confidential

Dear Blackie: For some reason no one had told me that the Prime Minister of Pakistan was going to be a guest of Stowaway. I can well understand the feeling of exasperation—not to say frustration—that must have attacked you when you found your guest so indifferent to the requests and desires of the whole Bohemian Grove assemblage.[1]

When in Washington he apparently made a magnificent address before the Houses of Congress.[2] On all sides I heard him receiving compliments both on the content of his talk and its delivery. Perhaps for this reason he thought he was doing all of you a very great favor by giving you an hour and ten minutes!!! In any event, you were good sports to go through with the whole thing as you did. Let us hope it will have some good effect in promoting international good will.

For the weekend of High Jinks, three of my immediate associates decided that they could go out to the Grove.[3] This pleased me immensely and I asked all of them to remember me warmly to any old friends they met. They were Secretaries Humphrey and Wilson, along with Admiral Radford. I explained to each of them that they were missing the best part of the Encampment by reason of the fact that they were not guests of Stowaway, but suggested that they visit that Camp just to see how one should properly be run at the Grove. Incidentally, I did my best to get one of the Administration's most valuable men, Sherman Adams, to go along. He wanted to very badly, but it happened that the date coincided with his wedding anniversary and quite a family celebration had been planned. Next year I hope he can come out because it would do him good to live for a few days in that atmosphere of completely unselfish comradeship, and I think he would add something to the Encampment by his great knowledge of the government and his complete integrity and efficiency in serving the nation.[4]

With warm regard, and again my thanks for being so patient with a difficult guest, *As ever*

[1] McLaren (A.B. University of California 1914) was a certified public accountant and partner in the San Francisco firm of Haskins & Sells since 1952. A former president of the Bohemian Club, he had written Eisenhower (Aug. 2, same file as document) that Pakistani Prime Minister Huseyn Shaheed Suhrawardy, after arriving late at the Bohemian Grove encampment, had refused to shorten his planned speech, resulting in the elimination of some of the scheduled entertainment. Later, however, the Prime Minister and other guests at Stowaway, one of several Spartan camps at the Grove, had lunch and played bridge. "In summary," McLaren wrote, "we were happy to entertain him but he was not the most attractive nor appreciative guest we have ever had at Stowaway!" For background on Suhrawardy's visit to the United States see no. 235.

Bohemian Grove, near San Francisco, California, is the site of the annual sixteen-day retreat for members of the Bohemian Club (see Galambos, *Columbia University*, nos. 388, 804, 873, 887, 991; see also *Eisenhower Papers*, vols. XII–XVII). In July 1950 Eisenhower had accepted honorary membership in the club, and had been a guest at Stowaway.

[2] See *New York Times*, July 13, 14, 1957.

[3] On the final weekend of the Bohemian Grove encampment, known as High Jinks, the members wrote, produced, and acted in musical presentations (see *Fortune*, v. 112 [August 5, 1985], and *New York Times*, July 22, 1995).

[4] McLaren would reply on August 7 that if Adams could get away and "would prefer to be at Stowaway, we will be delighted to have him there." See also Eisenhower's August 9 memorandum to Adams (both are in the same file as the document).

271 *EM, WHCF, President's Personal File 339*

To Edward Bishop Dudley, Jr. *August 5, 1957*

Personal

Dear Ed: The status of my golf, which is not good, is of no importance whatsoever compared to the news contained in your letter that you are soon to leave the Augusta Club. I cannot tell you how deeply I regret the change, but I most emphatically agree that you must look out for your future financial security.[1] Of course there is no risk in the matter as long as you can lift a golf club even from a wheel chair; I am sure that most people who have had the benefit of your instruction agree that you are one of the master teachers.

But I repeat that I thoroughly endorse your decision, particularly if the new club has given you a long term guarantee. I believe it is true that Puerto Rico is becoming more and more popular as a resort and this, if accurate, could make a great success out of the new club. Certainly they will not be able to complain for any deficiency in the instruction department.

Wherever you go my good wishes—and my gratitude for the great patience you have shown toward my always erratic game—will be yours.[2]

Please remember me warmly to Ruth and, of course, all the best to yourself.[3] In these sentiments Mrs. Eisenhower sincerely joins. *As ever*

P.S. I don't know that I shall ever be able to come to Puerto Rico, but I can assure you that your being there vastly increases my desire to do so.

[1] Dudley had been the winter golf professional at the Augusta National Golf Club in Augusta, Georgia, since 1932 (for background see *Eisenhower Papers,* vols. X–XVII). On August 1 Dudley had written that he took a "personal interest" in Eisenhower's golf. He went on to say that he had accepted a position as the winter golf pro at the Dorado Club, a new resort, in Dorado, Puerto Rico. He would also continue his summer position at the Broadmoor Golf Club in Colorado Springs, Colorado (see also the *Denver Post,* Sept. 22, 1957). With his letter to the President, Dudley had enclosed a copy of a July 19 letter to Eisenhower's old friend and chairman of the Augusta National's executive committee, Cliff Roberts. In it he explained that the position in Dorado would benefit him and his family financially.

[2] On September 12 Dudley would thank the President for his letter. "It will be awfully difficult to have to leave such wonderful friends," he said. He also gave the President advice on his golf swing. For developments see the following document. All correspondence is in the same file as the document.

[3] Ruth was Dudley's wife.

272 *EM, AWF, Name Series*

To Clifford Roberts *August 5, 1957*

Dear Cliff: Not long ago Bill told me of Ed Dudley's transfer to a Puerto Rico golf club, and this morning I received a short note from Ed himself.[1] Of course I am sure you know how deeply I regret his going—a feeling that is unquestionably shared by the vast majority of Augusta's members.

What follows is not a recommendation and is *not* a suggestion. It is nothing more than information to you and requires no answer whatsoever.

You will unquestionably be looking for a new professional. My feeling is that Augusta does not need a "name" man. But I am quite sure that you will be looking for a man who is mature, settled, and a thorough gentleman. Unless you have already reached a decision in the matter, you might like to look up the professional at the Gettysburg Country Club. His name is Dick Sleichter and he is a man who was beaten by Finsterwald in the PGA only after his ball, in hitting the green, buried itself and he had to putt from that situation.[2] His integrity and sportsmanship are indicated by the fact that he called a penalty stroke on himself that no one else could possibly have detected.

I have met his wife and son, both quite attractive people.[3] He himself must be about thirty-six or thirty-seven and to the best of my knowledge is a thorough gentleman.

Beyond the above I know nothing at all about him, but I do know a few people in Gettysburg, including the newspaper editor, the hotel owner and the most prominent lawyer, who could provide any information you would want if you are at all interested. I have played golf with him a number of times and find him very companionable, as well as helpful.

That's about all there is to say; quite naturally I have no idea whether he would be in a position to accept, even if offered, the winter job at Augusta.

I really assume that you have already put out your lines and maybe have offered someone a contract. But as I said before, all this is completely gratuitous—so this letter can be burned without hurting my feelings in the slightest.[4]

With warm regard, *As ever*

[1] William E. Robinson had visited the White House on July 26. Eisenhower's letter to Dudley is the preceding document.

[2] T. Richard Sleichter (B.S. Tampa University 1941) was the golf professional, superintendent and manager of the Gettysburg Country Club from 1954–1962. He began his career as a golf professional at the U.S. Naval Academy. In addition to hold-

ing golf course records, he won PGA sectional tournaments in Pennsylvania and the mid-Atlantic areas. Dow Finsterwald, a competitor on the pro golf tour, would win the Professional Golfers' Association championship tournament in 1958. He had been runner-up in the 1957 tournament, the last match-play championship held by the PGA (see *New York Times,* July 21, 22, 1957).

[3] Mary Louise Griffin Schleichter and Charles H. Sleichter.

[4] As it turned out, Gene Stout would get the post (Telephone conversation, B. Spencer, Augusta National Golf Club, Sept. 27, 1996; see also the following document and Eisenhower to Woodruff, Aug. 12, 1957, AWF/D).

273 — *EM, AWF, Name Series*

To Robert Winship Woodruff — *August 6, 1957*

Personal

Dear Bob:[1] The occasion for this note is merely the fact that I have not seen you for so long I am beginning to wonder whether you are concealing something from me regarding your own physical condition. I learned—I think from Mrs. Whitman—that you had to have some teeth out, but that alone should not keep you out of circulation for a number of weeks. Do let me know how you are getting along.[2]

The week has been a depressing one. I think the country took an awful beating in the second defeat that the civil rights bill took in the Senate.[3] In the interests of gradual education and progress, I had no objection to the elimination of Section III from the bill. Moreover, the deletion of that Section seemed to me to make a stronger case for the enactment of Section I, which was directed exclusively to the right to vote. The distorted pictures that were presented concerning jury trials in actions rising out of injunctions to prevent interference with voting right—particularly distortions by some of the so-called liberals—were such as to confuse both the people and some members of the Congress. Add to this a lot of political log rolling, and it is no wonder that confusion and misunderstanding resulted.

No one has been more anxious than I to avoid the imposition of unfair legal requirements upon the people in any section of the country, particularly where such legal requirements would occasion dislocations in existing social systems. But in this day and time to assert that the entire area of judicial practices in cases of contempt where the United States is a party to the suit should have to be altered in order to avoid injustice to some possible offender is utterly absurd. A picture was painted of wholesale arrests and punishments. But no one stopped to think that there could be no arrest or punishment whatsoever unless some one did, without justification or wrongly, interfere with the voting rights of a citizen after the orders of a Federal judge had been issued to the contrary.

I am told that the list of laws in which no jury trial is required numbers about forty. These include laws in the antitrust field, labor disputes and so on. In this case, I am sure that you, for example, did not find in the proposed legislation regarding interference with the voting right, any cause for alarm with respect to your personal security in your own rights. Yet it would be made to appear that the whole country would have to stand in fear and trembling of an intemperate and prejudiced judiciary.

On top of all this, I am told that the Appropriation Committees, especially the one in the House of Representatives, are determined to slash our mutual security funds and that they will probably not allow us the requested authority for development loans on a three year basis.[4] Here again it is the country that will suffer. If this were nothing more than what some of the papers try to make it—a quarrel between the Executive and the Congress—I could take whatever defeats come my way with a very great deal of equanimity. But the present struggle is not that at all, except in the minds of some unthinking Congressmen—far from all of them. This is a struggle between enlightened self-interest and sheer ignorance, or possibly one should say between good sense and blind prejudice. Some people are still stupid enough to believe in the concept of "Fortress America."

Then comes the news of the death of Senator George. For some days I have understood that recovery was not to be expected—that his case was really hopeless. Yet it is too bad that a man who exhibited such a high average of understanding in the whole field of foreign relations should have to leave the Senate and pass from the scene of this world's struggles while all around us are these people whose actions, if they should succeed in influencing the majority of our people, would certainly lead us closer and closer to the destruction of all that we hold most dear in this world.[5]

I find that much as I have always loved a fight, it is difficult for me to keep my temper when I find that upon the outcome of this kind of struggle depends the future of the country itself, and those that I should have a right to think of as understanding allies are, on the contrary, prejudiced antagonists.

At least you can be sure of this: on this issue I shall never cease striving. If the result is bad this year, it will be because my most earnest efforts have not succeeded. Moreover, in that event I shall again begin the battle as quickly as the voting is over and continue it as long as I am in this office.

Coming now to a great anti-climax, but still a matter of interest to you and me, I learn that Ed Dudley is leaving us to go to a permanent job in Puerto Rico.[6] I am delighted for him, because he assures me that this will give him financial security for his old age. But for people like us who love to go to the Augusta National—one of the reasons for which is the opportunity to discuss our so-called golf with Ed—his departure will leave a definite void. I am already trying to figure out an excuse to make a winter trip to Puerto Rico, but I doubt if I shall be able to pull it off as long as I am in this job.

Let me say again that I am concerned about your health and I do pray that you are well on the road to recovery of your normal strength and vigor.

Give my love to your charming Nell and, of course, all the best to yourself.[7] *As ever*

[1] Woodruff, chairman of the board of the Coca-Cola Company until 1955, had continued to serve as a director (see Galambos and van Ee, *The Middle Way*, no. 1264).

[2] In his August 8 response (AWF/N), Woodruff would report that he was "quite all right—physically," except for a bout with the "Asiatic or Oriental flu" and continued problems with his teeth.

[3] For background see nos. 248 and 266.

[4] For background see nos. 146 and 147. Although the Senate on June 14 had passed the Mutual Security Act of 1957 (S. 2130), which set up a Development Loan Fund with three-year funding authorization as requested by the Administration, the House on July 19 had cut $5.5 million from the Senate version of the bill. The House had also limited authorization for the Development Loan Fund to one year. On August 8 the Senate and House would compromise by splitting the funding difference and agreeing to authorize the Development Loan Fund for two years. Congress would also reject the Administration's attempt to put military assistance programs in the Defense Department budget; instead of funding the programs on a continuing basis, Congress would decline to authorize such aid beyond fiscal 1958. Although Eisenhower would sign the bill on August 14, he would appeal, in the name of national security, to the Congressional Appropriations Committees to restore some of the cuts (see *Congressional Quarterly Almanac*, vol. XIII, *1957*, pp. 601–10; *New York Times*, Aug. 13, 14, 15, 16, 17 and 18; *Public Papers of the Presidents: Eisenhower, 1957*, pp. 604–9). For developments see no. 319.

[5] Senator Walter Franklin George, 79, had died on August 4 after a six-week struggle against a heart ailment (see *New York Times*, Aug. 5, 1957). On the President's tribute to George, see *Public Papers of the Presidents: Eisenhower, 1957*, p. 588. On Eisenhower's cooperation with George on foreign policy, see, for example, Galambos and van Ee, *The Middle Way*, nos. 1806 and 1872.

[6] The President had written on August 5 to congratulate Dudley, golf pro at the Augusta National Golf Club, on his decision to accept a position in Puerto Rico (see no. 271).

[7] For developments see no. 298. Eisenhower had added this postscript in longhand: (This thing grew—another Topsy).

274 *EM, WHCF, President's Personal File 1705*

To Dan Hendrickson *August 6, 1957*
Personal

Dear Mr. Hendrickson: From time to time and from various places in the world you have sent to Mrs. Eisenhower and me different mementos and gifts which have evidenced your thoughtful kindness and continued consideration. We have accepted them as such, and no more.[1]

Only today there arrived for Mrs. Eisenhower and me several robes of obvious quality and beauty. However, at the same time I learned that your brother visited Governor Adams recently with the suggestion that he again enter governmental employment. In these circumstances I cannot possibly accept the gifts, because I make it an invariable practice never to accept even a token gift from anyone who has a direct or indirect interest in any official act of the Executive Department. I know, of course, that you do not mean these presents as anything to influence my decision, but I have followed the inflexible policy described above, so that there can never be the slightest question in such a delicate matter.[2]

In this instance I am uncertain as to whether you or a number of commercial firms are actually the donors of the gifts, but I return the items to you with the request that they reach the proper individual.

I of course continue to appreciate your thoughtfulness and many courtesies to my wife and to me.[3] *Sincerely*

[1] Hendrickson worked for the National Cash Register Company of Cincinnati, Ohio. Although Eisenhower had accepted a selection of ties from Hendrickson in November 1954, he had asked Hendrickson at that time to discontinue sending gifts (see Galambos and van Ee, *The Middle Way*, no. 1150).

[2] In January 1955 Eisenhower had appointed Robert Clymer Hendrickson, former Republican senator from New Jersey, as U.S. Ambassador to New Zealand. The following year he had resigned the post to return to private life (see *ibid.*, no. 1242, and *New York Times*, Mar. 23, 1957).

[3] Hendrickson would reply on August 11 (same file as document). "In the future," he wrote, "I most certainly will convey my expressions of friendship and appreciation by letters and cards. I did not intend to cause you . . . any embarrassment." Hendrickson added that he regretted that "the critics, the press and yes reporters" should "indicate publically [*sic*] that an act of kindness, thoughtfulness and appreciation must carry behind it an ulterior motive for personal selfish gain."

275

EM, AWF, Administration Series

To Christian Archibald Herter — *August 6, 1957*

Dear Chris: I have no objection whatsoever to your telling Professor Kissinger of my interest in the thesis he propounds in his book, provided it is done on a confidential basis.[1] I would prefer, however, to avoid any publicity. I make this last statement simply because I have frequently been embarrassed by press reports as to my "reading habits."[2]

With warm regard, *As ever*

[1] For background see no. 263. Eisenhower was responding to Herter's August 3, 1957 (AWF/A), letter regarding *Nuclear Weapons and Foreign Policy* by Henry Kissinger. Herter had said that he was familiar with Kissinger's work, which he called "an extremely challenging book and one which I shall surely call to Foster's attention." Herter added that he had known Kissinger for many years and had asked Eisenhower's permission to tell Kissinger that the President was interested in his work.

[2] Robert J. Donovan, for example, in *Eisenhower: The Inside Story* [New York, 1956], pp. 206–8, had commented on the President's taste for adventure novels set in the Old West.

276

EM, AWF, DDE Diaries Series

To Allan A. Ryan — *August 6, 1957*

Dear Allan: I must write a little further word of explanation about my request that you represent me personally at some future inauguration in South America or elsewhere.[1]

Because in many cases wives accompany my appointees, I had assumed that the United States government took care of all expenses for the couple. My face is a bit red to discover that appropriations are so limited as to make it possible for us to pay the expenses only of the representative himself (or herself when the appointee happens to be a female). Of course the distaff side of the house is welcome to go, and we are delighted when she can accompany her husband—but in such cases the cost for her must be privately paid. The only exception to this rule is in those very few cases when an American military delegation is also invited, and special military aircraft is used for the party. In this event, of course, no travel expenses of any kind are involved.

I make this explanation to you immediately upon learning of it myself—not because I think it will make any great difference to you but in order that there could be no later misunderstanding.[2]

I hope you will tell Mrs. Ryan that so far as I am concerned, this rule would be inexplicable except for the sad state of State Department finances. Personally, if I were a private citizen, I wouldn't dream of going off on one of these jaunts unless Mamie accompanied me.[3]

With warm regard, *Sincerely*

[1] For background see no. 250.

[2] On August 5 Eisenhower had discussed the matter of personal representatives with the Secretary of State. Eisenhower then drafted this letter and asked for Dulles's comments (see Draft, [Aug. 5, 1957], and Whitman to Bernau, Aug. 5, 1957, both in Dulles Papers, White House Memoranda Series; see also Eisenhower to Ewing, Aug. 6, 1957, and other papers in WHCF/OF 101-G).

[3] On April 25, 1958, Ryan would fly aboard an Air Force plane to Argentina to attend the inauguration of President Arturo Frondizi (see *New York Times*, Apr. 26, 1958).

277

EM, AWF, Dulles-Herter Series

To John Foster Dulles

Personal

August 7, 1957

Dear Foster: I notice in the Department of State's summary of August sixth a statement to the effect that we have a reluctance to allow the Jordan government so-called "offensive weapons."[1]

I have little faith in distinctions of this kind. A weapon can probably not be classed as defensive or offensive except upon the basis of the identification of the original aggressor. I have a feeling that we can frequently destroy some of the value of our aid by being too restrictive as to quality and type.

Of course I do most heartily approve our restriction that weapons provided by us may be used only for defensive purposes; so if the receiving nation becomes identified as an aggressor, we will support the other side.

In any event, to be specific, I certainly do not blame King Hussein for wanting some modern tanks.

I tried to call you on the phone but they reported you had gone out to Walter Reed. We can talk about the matter at your convenience.[2]

[1] On May 15 the Jordanian government had formally requested from the United States an aid package that would include a large quantity of weapons. State Department officials, however, believed that military assistance could best be supplied by other friendly Arab states and Great Britain, Jordan's traditional supplier, combined

with an additional $10 million in military aid from the United States. On August 2 a joint State-Defense Department message had informed the U.S. ambassador to Jordan that the United States was unable to furnish the "heavy offensive weaponry" Jordan had requested. Supplying the tanks and guns requested, the message stated, "would produce 'seriously unfavorable' Israeli reaction; generate demand for a continuous supply for spare parts and other new U.S. equipment; and would be extravagant in view of Jordan's present financial condition." The Ambassador had taken exception to this position. If Jordanian forces were "left begging while everyone around is getting new and better weapons," the Ambassador had replied, serious morale problems would result. "We must be most careful not to trigger a change in political line-up of the Arab states by restrictions on [a] particular kind of hardware" (State, *Foreign Relations, 1955–1957,* vol. XIII, *Near East: Jordan-Yemen,* pp. 134–49, 155).

[2] Later this same day, after a physical examination at Walter Reed Army Hospital, Dulles would tell Eisenhower by telephone that the cable summary was "a little misleading. What we don't want to do," he said, "is to give heavy tanks to Jordan. If we do that it will raise complete hell with Israel and we will have to send a lot of heavy equipment that in turn will make more trouble with the Arab States." Although Eisenhower agreed that the policy "made sense," he replied that he did not want to put King Hussein, a courageous friend, "in a hole" (Telephone conversation, Aug. 7, 1957, Dulles Papers, Telephone Conversations, and AWF/D).

On August 24 Dulles would inform King Hussein that the United States would furnish Jordan with thirty-six M-47 tanks, including a one-year's supply of spare parts and ammunition (State, *Foreign Relations, 1955–1957,* vol. XIII, *Near East: Jordan-Yemen,* p. 158).

278 *EM, AWF, DDE Diaries Series*

To Ruth Baker and Robert G. Baker *August 7, 1957*

Dear Ruth and Bob: Since Mamie is temporarily unable to handle her mail, I am taking the liberty of acknowledging both your letter of July twenty-fifth to her and the one dated July tenth that you enclosed for me.[1]

Of course I am particularly interested in your comments about the individuals who comprised the Citizens for Eisenhower movement. I agree that they possessed a high degree of loyalty and dedication.[2] As a matter of fact I have had many conferences both with political associates and personal friends concerning how their potential could be directed in '58 and in '60.

The difficulty is, of course, that to be a strong and effective organization, such a movement almost of necessity must be of grass roots origin. It cannot possibly be inspired "from the top," so to speak. But we do have plans to do what we can to revitalize the movement, at the proper time. Incidentally, all the experts around here tell me that it is impossible to sustain political interest by amateurs throughout the period from election to election—that it is far more profitable to try to rekindle the flame than to keep it burning! As to the truth of this I am not sure, but possibly the use of "Citizens stationery" for mailing out prejudiced propaganda furnishes another reason for organizing such groupments for a specific campaign of temporary duration only.[3]

You have probably heard of Mamie's operation of yesterday. You will be relieved to know that the doctors report she came through it beautifully. She will be uncomfortable, of course, for a few days, but I am sure she will be fine again shortly.

With warm regard, *Sincerely*

[1] Robert Baker's July 10, 1957, letter to Eisenhower is in WHCF/GF 109-A-7. Ruth Baker's July 25 letter to Mamie is not in EM. The Bakers were long-time friends of the Eisenhowers. Robert Baker, who had practiced law in San Francisco, had apparently lived next door to Mamie Eisenhower in Denver, Colorado. See correspondence in EM; see also letter from Herbert L. Pankratz, February 18, 1997, EP. On Mamie's recent surgery see no. 291.

[2] For background on the Citizens for Eisenhower Committee, formed during the 1952 campaign, see Galambos, *NATO and the Campaign of 1952*, nos. 740 and 789. Baker had written that "There has never been a more selfless group of Citizens than Citizens for Eisenhower. Their standards of sincerity and integrity were the same as yours. Wealthy or poor, they hav'nt [*sic*] changed, they are loyal to you and your principles and only you could betray them and I know you never will."

[3] Baker, who had suggested putting together a new group of "Citizens for our Country," noted that someone was making improper use of the old California Citizens for Eisenhower roster. He enclosed copies of press releases he had received from the "Non-Partisan Voters Committee for Eisenhower"; the releases were supportive of the Egyptian position in the Mideast conflict.

279

EM, AWF, DDE Diaries Series

To F. J. Laher
Personal

August 7, 1957

Dear Mr. Laher: As I believe Senator Kuchel told you, I was most appreciative of your generous offer to give me a golf cart, to be delivered to my farm in Gettysburg.[1] However, only a few days ago I unexpectedly fell heir to a cart that a friend of mine had had for some time and for which he had no further use.[2] An additional one at Gettysburg would therefore be completely superfluous.

Because of this I suggest that you do not ship the one that you intended to present to me through Senator Kuchel. This does not imply any lack of gratitude for your kindly thoughtfulness; in fact I am deeply touched by your courtesy and I promise that if, in the future, I find a renewed need for a golf cart I shall go in the market and purchase one of yours.

I am providing a copy of this letter to Senator Kuchel, in order that he may be informed about this change in my situation.[3]

With best wishes, *Sincerely*

[1] Laher was president of Laher Spring and Tire Corporation in Oakland, California. California Republican Thomas Henry Kuchel had served in the U.S. Senate since 1953; for background see Galambos and van Ee, *The Middle Way*, no. 1221. In a letter to Ann Whitman (July 10), Kuchel explained that a local representative of Laher Spring and Tire Corporation had requested "the proper procedure to give President Eisenhower an electric golf car. . . ." On July 15 Eisenhower had accepted the offer in a letter to Senator Kuchel. On the arrangements for delivery see Whitman to Nevins, July 18, 1957, and Crawford to Whitman, July 26, 1957.

[2] See Nevins, *Five-Star Farmer*, p. 112.

[3] On August 22 Laher would express disappointment over the cancellation and would say he would be "honored to receive instructions at any time . . . to ship a car to Gettysburg." All correspondence is in WHCF/PPF 1-JJ.

280

EM, AWF, Dulles-Herter Series

To John Foster Dulles

August 9, 1957

Memorandum for the Secretary of State: Herewith a letter left with me this morning by the Greek Ambassador. It emphasizes that *they* believe that reduction in our foreign aid would be catastrophic, at least as far as they are concerned.[1]

Before you leave could you have some of your staff start work on the draft of a reply from me to the Prime Minister.[2]

Hope you have a good time on your vacation.

[1] Following a ceremony at the White House commemorating the presentation of four Black Angus cattle to the American Farm School at Salonika, Greece, U.S. Ambassador George V. Melas had given Eisenhower an August 3 letter from Prime Minister Constantine Karamanlis. Concerned that U.S. aid to Greece would be reduced in 1958, Karamanlis had asked for an amount at least equal to the 1957 level and an additional $13 million to meet increased military expenditures. He also requested a two-year loan of $25 to $35 million from the Economic Development Fund to build a nitrogen fertilizer factory and an inter-city highway (*Foreign Relations, 1955–1957*, vol. XXIV, *Soviet Union; Eastern Mediterranean*, pp. 593–94).

[2] Dulles would leave later this same day for a ten-day vacation at Duck Island in Lake Ontario. Although Eisenhower would not discuss the Prime Minister's specific requests in his reply, he would tell Karamanlis that the Administration would study the points he had raised and carefully consider them after Congress had enacted the necessary legislation (Eisenhower to Karamanlis, Aug. 14, 1957, AWF/I: Greece).

On January 4, 1958, State Department officials would inform the Greek government that Greece would receive $15 million in defense assistance in 1958, $10 million less than in 1957 (State, *Foreign Relations, 1958–1960,* vol. X, 2 pts., pt. 1, *Eastern Europe Region; Soviet Union; Cyprus* [1993], pp. 601–2).

281 — *EM, AWF, DDE Diaries Series*

To Henry Robinson Luce — *August 9, 1957*

Dear Harry:[1] This morning I was talking to Dr. Elson, the pastor of my church.[2] He gave me the news about the loss of the tract near American University, but expressed the hope that you would soon find a better one. He remarked that you feel that the time had come for you to have a preliminary talk with Sid Richardson.

I am sure that this can easily be arranged, and I shall ask George Allen to handle this part of it because it is just possible that later on you might want a word from me as an additional reinforcement.[3]

I shall try to get in touch with George this afternoon and ask him to telephone Sid in the next day or two—and then to call you to see whether a definite date cannot be set up between you.

With warm regard, *As ever*

P.S. I just talked to George and he says that Sid seems to be in a particularly difficult mood these days. But George will follow through and will let you know in the early part of next week.[4]

[1] Luce was leading the fund-raising campaign to provide facilities for the National Presbyterian Church (see no. 12).

[2] The Eisenhowers had joined the National Presbyterian Church in 1953. On Eisenhower's conversation with Elson see Memorandum for Files, August 9, 1957, AWF/D.

[3] Eisenhower had expressed interest in this project to Richardson earlier this year (see no. 12).

[4] The President would talk to Allen again on August 11. For developments see no. 1247.

282 — *EM, AWF, DDE Diaries Series*

To William Franklin Graham — *August 9, 1957*

Personal

Dear Billy:[1] The pressures toward the end of a Congressional session are such that I really don't feel that I should try to make a trip to New York.[2] I cannot yet tell when Congress will adjourn and currently I am attempting to spend parts of each evening at the hospital with Mrs. Eisenhower, who has had an operation.[3]

Immediately following adjournment, I shall have quite a hectic period either here or at Newport in clearing up the signing of bills and all the other administrative work that follows upon the closing of a Congressional session.[4]

So unless some unexpected relief should come from some corner, I have regretfully to decline your nice invitation to be with you on one of your evenings at Madison Square Garden. Of course I am highly delighted that you have experienced such a successful crusade. I have always agreed with you that human beings—especially Americans—do have an underlying spiritual hunger which from time to time manifests itself markedly. I believe that we are now experiencing such a period. This and your own inspirational qualities have, in my opinion, brought about the remarkable results you have achieved in this series of meetings.[5]

With warm regard, *Sincerely*

[1] Graham was an evangelist who had developed a wide following through his "Hour of Decision" radio and television programs and, more recently, through his revival campaigns (see Galambos, *NATO and the Campaign of 1952,* no. 475, and Galambos and van Ee, *The Middle Way,* no. 1802). Graham's latest evangelical revival had begun on May 15. Meetings were held in Madison Square Garden, in Yankee Stadium, and on Wall Street in New York City. The rally was expected to last through September 1 (*New York Times,* May 16, Aug. 9, 1957).

[2] See no. 302 for Eisenhower's description of the legislative and governmental pressures at that time. On August 2 Graham had written to urge the President to spend an evening at Madison Square Garden (WHCF/PPF 1-EE). "I am asking you to come," he wrote, "because of what it would symbolize to a confused, bewildered and perplexed world."

[3] The first session of the Eighty-fifth Congress would adjourn on August 30. The First Lady had undergone gynecological surgery on August 6 (see no. 291).

[4] The Eisenhowers would vacation in Newport, Rhode Island, September 4–30.

[5] Graham had told the President that his "evangelistic crusade" had broken attendance records at Madison Square Garden and Yankee Stadium: "I am convinced that there is a spirit of religious revival in every borough of New York. It has been beyond all our expectations." See also *New York Times,* May 16–September 2, 1957; and John Pollock, *Billy Graham, Evangelist to the World: An Authorized Biography of the Decisive Years* (New York, 1979), p. 28.

283 — *EM, AWF, DDE Diaries Series*

To Sherman Adams — *August 12, 1957*

Memorandum for Governor Adams: Attached is a supplement to the material Charlie Wilson left with me recently about the People-to-People program.[1]

I believe we should direct Arthur Larson to get someone on the job to follow up this matter energetically to see what we can possibly do to get this whole program off the ground.[2]

As I understand the matter, Mr. Wilson has no doubt of the eventual success of the program, if he can first get the necessary money to organize and advertise the effort, including that part of the effort that involves raising money for local committees throughout the United States. He estimates he needs something like $350,000 a year for three years.[3]

USIA should make a complete and thorough study of the attached memorandum, after which they should promptly hold a conference with Mr. Wilson and decide on what is to be done.[4]

I still earnestly believe that this would be a great and useful effort in getting ahead in the cold war; but if we cannot get private interest developed in the country we had better stop worrying our friends with it.[5]

[1] On August 1, at a White House meeting, Eisenhower and Charles Edward Wilson, president of the People-to-People Program, had discussed the financing of the project designed to promote international understanding through exchange of ideas (for background see no. 197). Wilson had given Eisenhower a "Summary of a Report to the President of the United States" (AWF/D). We have been unable to find the supplemental material in EM.

Wilson had reported that "certain unforeseen obstacles have appeared . . . that were not clear when [the program] was first announced." He went on to list as obstacles: insufficient funding for staff support in "so vast a voluntary program"; failure by chairmen to raise funds for individual committees; resistance by participating organizations whose members felt they were being ignored; reluctance of organizations to support the program until it is more clearly defined; and a suspicion of government, not private, control of the organization. Wilson recommended that the President assist the foundation in securing private funds; designate a week in January as People-to-People Week; and address a meeting of members over a nationwide broadcast during People-to-People Week to assure governmental help only at the "initial period of organization." The organization, Wilson wrote, needed strong financial leaders on its board of directors, "including well-known Democrats" and a finance committee appointed for fund raising. In addition to routine meetings, Wilson suggested that individual organizations represented in the Congress of European American Associations be contacted, as well as the Young Industrialists of Europe and labor organizations. He also thought radio and television sponsors could support the project. See also *New York Times*, June 10 and July 24, 1957.

[2] The program currently was operating under the Office of Private Cooperation of the United States Information Agency. Wilson had recommended that USIA Director Larson work out details of transferring leadership to the foundation once it became private and define lines of communication for the "most effective operation" of the program. He also thought the term "Foundation" should be dropped "to eliminate confusion with established financial foundations." The new name, he said, should be People-to-People, Inc.

[3] Wilson had recommended that the President assist the Foundation to secure from private sources $250,000 a year for three years.

[4] On August 28 the President would meet with Wilson, Adams, and Larson to discuss some governmental support of the program. Afraid that committeemen could not raise sufficient private funding, Wilson would request government support amount-

ing to $100,000 per year for three years (Ann Whitman memorandum, AWF/AWD, Aug. 22, 28, 1957).

[5] As it turned out, the People-to-People Program would begin operating as a private organization in September (see *New York Times*, Sept. 26, Oct. 5, 22, 1957). For developments see no. 350.

284

EM, AWF, International Series: Cortines

TO ADOLFO RUIZ CORTINES *August 12, 1957*

Dear Mr. President: When my brother returned to Washington last night, he came immediately to the White House to tell me in most enthusiastic terms of his visit to your country. He had a highly enjoyable and interesting experience, and feels that he learned a great deal that will be valuable to this government concerning our common problems. On my part, I am delighted that his trip was apparently so successful, and once again I want to thank you, the members of your staff, and the people of Mexico for the many evidences of friendship and cordial hospitality shown to him and to his daughter.[1]

Milton brought with him the gifts that you and Senora Ruiz Cortines so kindly sent to my wife and to me. As you know, Mrs. Eisenhower at the moment is in the hospital, but as soon as possible she will want personally to write to you.[2] Meantime, I add her appreciation of your thoughtfulness to my own indebtedness for the fine cigars and the handsome woolen robe of Mexican craftsmanship. I am more than proud of the beautifully carved case in which the latter arrived.

Mrs. Eisenhower asked me to tell you that she was deeply touched by your kindly inquiry as to her health. Both she and the doctors agree that she is progressing splendidly. Additionally, when she learned that your wife had suffered a sudden illness, she asked that she might join with me in expressing to you both our most sincere wishes for her early recovery.

Again, I express the gratitude of my brother and myself for the welcome accorded to him.[3]

With warm personal regard, *Sincerely*

[1] For background on Milton Eisenhower's trip to Mexico see no. 190. His thoughts on the "highly rewarding" visit are in his memoir, *The Wine is Bitter*, pp. 207–8.

[2] The First Lady had undergone gynecological surgery on August 6 (see no. 291).

[3] In his reply (Aug. 26) Ruiz Cortines thanked Eisenhower for "repeated acts of

friendship" and said that the two countries "must always take advantage of any propitious occasion to exchange ideas and opinions" (AWF/I: Cortines).

285

EM, WHCF, President's Personal File 1476

To Margaret M. Williams

August 12, 1957

Dear Captain Williams: Mrs. Whitman shared with me your letter of the seventh.[1] I must confess that I was somewhat startled to find that you are returning to the States in the fall to become a civilian. I am sorry, as I always am when the Army loses a fine and dedicated person like yourself.

This has seemingly been a long summer, aggravated by the fact that the Congress has been so torn internally that their adjournment is particularly late.[2] Mrs. Eisenhower and I have planned to go to Newport—and still hope to do so—but a combination of circumstances have kept us from counting too heavily upon it. As perhaps you know, Mrs. Eisenhower underwent an operation about ten days ago out at Walter Reed. She has made remarkable progress since then, but the necessary period of convalescence still makes uncertain our vacation plans. If all goes well, we hope to get away about the end of this month (which may, of course, be topcoat weather in Newport).[3]

I hope you will let us know of your plans and address. While I may frequently neglect my correspondence I do like to keep track of the people that helped me through my difficulties of a couple of years ago.[4]

With warm regard, *Sincerely*

[1] Williams, a nurse in the Army Nurse Corps, had cared for the President at Fitzsimons Army Hospital in Denver, Colorado, following his heart attack in September 1955 (for background see Galambos and van Ee, *The Middle Way*, no. 1704). Stationed in Germany, she had written Ann Whitman that she expected to return to the United States by early November to become a civilian (see also Whitman to Williams, June 20, 1957).

[2] For Eisenhower's difficulties with the first session of the Eighty-fifth Congress see no. 302. Congress would adjourn on August 30.

[3] On August 6 the First Lady had undergone gynecological surgery (see no. 291). The Eisenhowers would vacation in Newport, Rhode Island, September 4–30.

[4] Williams would thank the President for his letter on October 30. "I am sorry that I have to become again a civilian, but I know everything will work out for the best," she wrote. Eisenhower underlined this sentence and wrote "What in the world?" at the bottom of the letter. An investigation revealed that Army regulations dictated the mandatory separation because Williams would not complete twenty years' ser-

vice before reaching her fifty-fifth birthday. Although an exception could have been made, Eisenhower decided not to "interfere" (see related correspondence between Whitman and Schulz). All correspondence is in the same file as the document. See also no. 290.

286

EM, AWF, Administration Series

To Allen Welsh Dulles

August 13, 1957

Dear Allen: In a recent communication to me, a student of the oil industry referred to the Sumatra fields as a "vast lode." Do you believe this to be correct?[1]

With warm regard, *As ever*

[1] Eisenhower's correspondent may have been Sid Williams Richardson, who often wrote the President regarding affairs in the oil industry (see no. 302).

In Allen Dulles's absence Lieutenant General Charles Pearre Cabell, Acting Director of the Central Intelligence Agency, would tell Eisenhower that oil reserves in the Indonesian island of Sumatra were currently estimated to be approximately 1.2 billion barrels. "The geological features of the island, however, are such that prospects for eventual major additional discoveries are considered good," Cabell stated. "One competent oil executive thinks it is safe to estimate that reserves of over 20 billion barrels could be established." Reliable figures were difficult to obtain, he added, since the Indonesian government had prohibited foreign exploration and development (Cabell to Eisenhower, Aug. 14, 1957, AWF/A, Dulles Corr.; see also State, *Foreign Relations, 1955–1957,* vol. XXII, *Southeast Asia* [1989], pp. 178–79). On September 23 Allen Dulles would tell the National Security Council that three major oil companies—two American and one British—were operating in Sumatra. The assessment of oil resources had been increased recently, he stated: "A 20-billion barrel reserve is estimated, and this is only the beginning" (NSC meeting minutes, Sept. 24, 1957, AWF/NSC). On the Sumatran revolt in 1958 see no. 662.

287

EM, AWF, Name Series

To John Merrill Olin

August 13, 1957

Dear John: I was tremendously interested in your letter. I shall try the full choke barrel in my trapshooting. Moreover, I shall see if I get on to the birds before they get so far away. Of course with that set of barrels I can also use the three inch shells.[1]

The trouble with me making an arrangement with someone to come to the farm to help me out is that I never know when I am going to be there. Usually our trips are arranged on the spur of the moment and I have only Saturday afternoons for shooting. However, if I should be able to set up a trip in more orderly fashion, I shall certainly take you up on your offer to send one of your agents to the farm for an afternoon.[2]

In view of the difference between the two sports—as you have outlined—I think I shall probably stick pretty close to skeet shooting, because I shall certainly never have time to become even reasonably proficient in more than one of them.[3]

It seems that almost every day I have a new reason for being grateful to you. I am sure you know how much I appreciate your kindness.[4]

With warm regard, *As ever*

[1] Olin had written on August 8 about the President's interest in trap and skeet shooting. In trap shooting the clay birds are thrown from a single machine or trap; in skeet shooting, they are thrown from two traps and provide the shooter with a greater variety of angles and trajectories. Olin said he doubted that Eisenhower would become "very proficient at regular trap shooting using a 20-gauge gun. If you do use a 20 gauge gun," he wrote, "you should use the 28" barrels and shoot the single targets with the full choke barrel." He reasoned that standing sixteen yards from the trap with the targets flying about seventy miles per hour, "the targets are about forty yards distant when broken and therefore you need a concentrated pattern in order to break targets regularly at this distance."

[2] The President would make a last minute visit to his Gettysburg farm August 24–25. He would not return to the farm until October 4. It would be late December before he would practice skeet shooting (see Eisenhower to Olin, Aug. 28, 1957, WHCF/PPF 597, and President's daily appointments; see also Eisenhower to Olin, Feb. 6, 1958, AWF/D).

[3] Olin had explained that "the open barrels or the short barrels upon the 20 gauge Model 21 are appropriate" for skeet shooting because "the targets are broken usually within a twenty-five yard distance."

[4] In July, at Olin's suggestion, Eisenhower had agreed to have his Model 21 Winchester double-barrel shotgun restocked and the boring changed for skeet shooting (for background see no. 241). The shotgun would be returned to Eisenhower on November 1 (see Eisenhower to Olin, Nov. 5, Schulz to Whitman, Nov. 1, and Goodwin to Eisenhower, Nov. 12, 1957, all in WHCF/PPF 597).

288 — *EM, AWF, DDE Diaries Series*

MEMORANDUM FOR THE RECORD — *August 14, 1957*

This morning I had Senator Holland in to talk to me about the project for establishing a new airport in Fairfax County, commonly known as the Burke Airport. I had heard that Senator Holland was particularly hostile to the carrying out of the Burke project.[1]

The attitude of the Commerce Department (and the CAA in that

Department) is reported fairly accurately in the short summary of facts attached hereto.

Senator Holland has several emphatic objections, all of which appear to him, of course, to be valid.[2] He summarized them somewhat as follows:

(*a*). The area around Washington is being settled up rapidly as population grows and Fairfax County is one of the regions included in this rapid residential development. Only the eastern half of that country is available for the reason that drainage from the eastern half flows into the Potomac below Washington. In the western half of the county, the drainage is into the Potomac above Washington. By law no more storm or city sewerage can be dumped into the Potomac above Washington. Yet he points out that the Burke Airport development is in the heart of the eastern section of the county on ground that is especially valuable from a residential viewpoint. Since the airport will require a total of 4,400 acres held in fee simple, and 2,000 additional acres which will be released to prevent building in the areas used for approaches, he feels that condemnation of that amount of ground would be grossly unfair to the citizens of the area. Incidentally, he stated that the population of this particular region had more than doubled within very recent years, going from eighty thousand to about two hundred thousand.

(*b*). The Senator says that the one million dollars invested by the government in this project back in 1951 would not be wasted even if it should now be abandoned. The value of property has so increased in that area that he says the government could make a profit out of the deal.[3]

(*c*). Their Committee has testimony that with an airport located at Burke, there would be interference between the stacking areas needed by the National Airport and Burke Airport. As a consequence the full value of neither port could be realized.

(*d*). He maintains that construction at Chantilly—some distance to the northwestward—would be much less than at Burke. Commerce denies this, saying that the difference in construction costs would not be more than a million dollars out of a total budget of some 50 million.

(*e*). He is very much concerned with the bitter opposition to the Burke project of the four area Senators. These are Byrd and Robertson of Virginia, and Beall and Butler from Maryland. The opposition of the Virginia Senators is based on different reasons from that of the Maryland Senators. The latter want to compel part of the Washington traffic to use the Friendship Airport near Baltimore and thus share in the cost of maintenance of that facility. The Virginia Senators do not want the Burke Airport merely because the residents object and they of course are concerned politically.[4]

(*f*). He believes that when the new super highway running westward from Washington is completed (it will run directly along the border of the Chantilly airport), that the travel time from Chantilly to Washington or the Washington Airport will compare favorably with the travel time from the Burke Airport. In this connection he says that six major airports in the United States lie further from the cities they serve than does the Chantilly area from Washington.

(*g*). Finally he argues that Congress has never approved the Burke site. He says that authorization for a second airport was given by Congress in 1950, but the site was picked out by CAA. They got one million dollars from Congress on the representation that they could buy all the ground they needed. Actually they got only one-fifth and that is all the government owns in this region.

In view of all these things, Senator Holland believes that the project should be re-studied and he particularly suggests that the new Aeronautics Advisory Committee, under the direction of General Quesada, re-study the whole matter.[5]

In this situation, the Secretary of Commerce says that we have studied all of the possible solutions to the Washington traffic problem over the period of the past four years. Always the answer of the individuals making the study has been that the Burke Airport was the best site and the Commerce Department has adopted this as their official solution.

The House of Representatives has already passed an appropriation bill to acquire the remainder of the ground necessary and to get started on construction. He says therefore that the Commerce Department cannot back off from the proposition and will simply recite again to the Senate Committee all of the various steps through which this study has gone through the past years. They will then say in effect "The bill is now in your hands and with our recommendations, based on our best information and professional advice. You, of course, will have to do as you please with it."[6]

[1] Spessard Holland, Governor of Florida from 1941 to 1945, had been Democratic Senator from Florida since 1946 (see Galambos and van Ee, *The Middle Way*, no. 1192). Efforts to create a second airport to relieve congestion at Washington National Airport had begun in 1950, when Congress appropriated sufficient funds to purchase about one-quarter of the site for a new airport. The selection of Burke, Virginia, as the site had aroused opposition from area residents, as well as from officials and business leaders in Baltimore. The latter group felt that Baltimore's underutilized Friendship Airport should serve as Washington's second air terminal (*New York Times*, Dec. 25, 1955).

[2] On Holland's opposition to the construction of a new airport at Burke, Virginia, see also *Congressional Quarterly Almanac*, vol. XIII, *1957*, pp. 719–20.

[3] By the end of 1951 the federal government had purchased 1,046 of the 4,520 acres needed at the Burke site. See *New York Times,* January 2, 1952.
[4] Eisenhower was referring to Virginia Democratic Senators Harry Flood Byrd and A. Willis Robertson, and Maryland Republican Senators James Glenn Beall and John Marshall Butler (for background on Byrd, Robertson, and Butler see Galambos and van Ee, *The Middle Way,* no. 1192). Beall had been a businessman in real estate and insurance prior to his election to the Maryland State Senate in 1930. He had served as congressman from Maryland from 1944 to 1952, when he was elected to the U.S. Senate.
[5] Elwood Richard ("Pete") Quesada was Chairman of the Board of Topp Industries and a vice-president of Lockheed Aircraft and of Olin Industries. A retired Lieutenant General of the U.S. Army, Quesada had been appointed Special Assistant to the President for Aviation on June 25, 1957 (*New York Times,* June 15, 1957).
[6] The Senate and House had disagreed on funding for the new airport. On August 15 the Senate had voted to cut $12.5 million for the proposed Burke airport, and directed the new Airways Modernization Board to recommend (by January 15, 1958) a site for the airport or an existing field to be remodeled. In a subsequent conference with the House, it was agreed to restore the funds for the Washington, D.C., airport without specifying a site. Instead, the President was required to study alternate sites and make a recommendation to Congress by January 15.

The airport would be built at the Chantilly site. Renamed Dulles International Airport to honor John Foster Dulles, it would open on November 19, 1962, with a terminal designed by renowned architect Eero Saarinen. The total cost would be $108.3 million (*New York Times,* Jan. 19, Apr. 22, Sept. 28, Nov. 18, 1962).

289 *EM, AWF, Administration Series*

To Charles Erwin Wilson *August 14, 1957*

Memorandum for the Secretary of Defense: I have been disturbed to learn from friends of mine travelling in Puerto Rico that there is some feeling in that territory that the Armed Forces of the United States are occupying an excess amount of land, much of it unused at the present time.[1]

I do understand, however, that some action is being taken to return the unneeded land to civil control.

I would appreciate your checking into the matter and informing me of the progress made in transferring to civilian control whatever land is excess to our Armed Forces' needs.[2]

[1] For background see no. 267. The friend, Ellis D. Slater, had identified a shortage of land as one of Puerto Rico's most pressing problems (Slater to Eisenhower, July 31, 1957, AWF/N). With land selling at $500 or more an acre, Slater had suggested that some of the land held by the Army, Navy, and Air Force be freed for food production. "It might be proven, upon investigation," Slater had written, "that every acre is absolutely essential to present and future defense, but as I have observed elsewhere, there is a tendency to hold on and not let anything go."
[2] The United States government regularly exchanged land with the Commonwealth

of Puerto Rico in order to improve relationships between the military bases and the civilian population (see for example, U.S. Congress, Senate, Committee on Armed Services, *Providing for Exchange Between the United States and the Commonwealth of Puerto Rico of Certain Lands and Interest*, 83d Cong., 1st sess., 1953, S. Rept. 163, pp. 1–2; U.S. Congress, House of Representatives, Committee on Armed Services, *Authorizing the Exchange of Land Between the United States and Puerto Rico*, 83d Cong., 2d sess., 1954, H. Rept. 1335, pp. 1–4; and U.S. Congress, Senate, Committee on Armed Services, *Providing for the Exchange of Certain Lands in Puerto Rico*, 87th Cong., 2d sess., 1962, S. Rept. 1913, pp. 1–3). Eisenhower would discuss this subject with Puerto Rican Governor Luis Muñoz Marin during his visit to the United States on October 14. The President told Muñoz Marin that he was especially sympathetic in cases concerning land that could be used for agriculture, and he directed his staff to prepare an additional report on a particular army barracks forty miles from the capital, San Juan (Rabb memorandum, Oct. 16, 1957, AWF/D).

290

EM, AWF, Administration Series

To Lorraine P. Knox

August 14, 1957

Dear Lorraine: Almost daily I am reminded that it has been much too long since last I heard from you and of your doings at Fitzsimons.[1]

I had high hopes of getting to Colorado this summer, but a combination of circumstances made me put that pleasant possibility completely out of my mind. The deciding factor was the consensus of the doctors that if I did go to Denver and immediately indulged in exercise (which of course I would want to do) there might be cause for worry, as against a similar amount of exercise at sea level. So Mrs. Eisenhower and I decided we would try to spend whatever vacation time we can manage at the Naval Base in Newport.[2]

As you probably know, Mrs. Eisenhower, when she recently returned from Denver, was operated on—and has responded beautifully.[3] However, we don't yet know when she will be able to travel; so as of now our plans are still fairly tenuous. Since I know you are a great advocate of New England, I assume you look with favor on our decision.

I had a letter from Captain Williams just the other day; somewhat to my surprise she tells me that she is returning in the fall and will become a civilian.[4] I have had one brief note from Colonel Turner, I think, since she went to Hawaii, but I gathered that she was finding that experience just about perfect.[5]

Are you to have a vacation this summer? Also, I am wondering how you have liked the responsibilities of your new duties. Do bring me up to date.[6]

Please remember me kindly to Captain Koger, to Sergeant Vaughn, and to any others of the group that you chance to meet.[7]

I can never close a letter to you without once again thanking you for all you did for me when I was a rebellious and, I suppose, irritable patient.

With warm regard, *As ever*

[1] In 1955 Knox, a member of the Army Nurse Corps, had cared for the President while he recovered from a heart attack at Fitzsimons Army Hospital in Denver, Colorado. She had been promoted to a position supervising the hospital's Centralized Material Section in 1956 (for background see Galambos and van Ee, *The Middle Way*, nos. 1625 and 1767). Eisenhower had last written to her on April 8 (AWF/A: Fitzsimons).

[2] The Eisenhowers would vacation in Newport, Rhode Island, September 4–30.

[3] On August 6 Mrs. Eisenhower had undergone gynecological surgery (see no. 291).

[4] See no. 285.

[5] See nos. 111 and 854.

[6] Apologizing for being "such a poor correspondent," Knox would reply, "I worry about you constantly. . . . Many times a day I send up a prayer for you—for you, that is, not us—although we do need you. Please try to get as much rest and recreation as you can." She added that she was still going to school seeking her degree (Dec. 22, 1957, AWF/A).

[7] Army nurse Carline E. Koger also had cared for Eisenhower following his heart attack (for background see Eisenhower and van Ee, *The Middle Way*, no. 1626. Eisenhower would write to her on September 8, 1958 (see no. 847). Joseph B. Vaughn, of Birmingham, Alabama, was a medical corpsman at Fitzsimons Army Hospital.

291

EM, AWF, Name Series

To Earl Dewey Eisenhower

August 14, 1957

Dear Earl: Since writing to you on the third of August, you have probably noticed in the newspapers that Mamie had to have an operation.[1] As of this moment she is progressing remarkably well and may get out of the hospital by a week from next Saturday.[2]

Thereafter she will have a necessary period of convalescence, and I think the doctors would like for her to go away—probably to Newport—as soon as possible after leaving Walter Reed.[3]

So right now it would appear that we will not get to spend any time at the farm before the autumn. However, that is a very nice season and perhaps you can come on for a visit with us there on some weekend.

I'll be in touch with you about all of this later, since as of now all our plans are necessarily tenuous.[4]

With warm regard, *As ever*

[1] The President's brother Earl was an electrical engineer and general manager of the Suburban Life Newspaper Syndicate in LaGrange Park, Illinois (see *Eisenhower Pa-*

pers, vols. I–XVII). Earl had written on July 30 that he and his wife Catherine would like to visit the President in Washington, D.C., and see the Eisenhower farm in Gettysburg. Eisenhower had replied on August 3 that he and Mrs. Eisenhower would vacation in late August or September, but Earl and his wife were "always welcome" in Washington. "Keep in touch with me . . . and give me as much advance notice as possible" (both in AWF/N).

[2] The First Lady had had gynecological surgery on August 6. She would leave Walter Reed Army Hospital on August 30 (see *Public Papers of the Presidents: Eisenhower, 1957*, pp. 599, 618, 657, and *New York Times*, Aug. 7, 31, 1957).

[3] The Eisenhowers would vacation in Newport, Rhode Island, September 4–30.

[4] As it turned out, Eisenhower would go to Gettysburg August 24 and 25. The President and his brother would meet in Chicago on October 22, 1958.

292

EM, WHCF, Official File 102-B-3

To Chapman Revercomb

August 15, 1957

Dear Senator Revercomb:[1] Thank you very much for what you have to say about your desire to work with the Administration in the development and implementation of programs necessary to our country. Moreover, I appreciate the trouble you took to communicate with me to that effect.[2]

While I cannot agree with your stated position with respect to the jury system—since I am told we have a total of thirty-nine different laws in which this system has no application—I respect of course your right to your own beliefs. Certainly I hope that no other important question will arise where we will be forced into different sides of the argument.

With best wishes,[3] *Sincerely*

[1] Revercomb (LL.B. University of Virginia 1919) was Republican Senator from West Virginia. For background see Galambos, *Chief of Staff*, no. 669.

[2] The Senator had written Eisenhower on August 12, 1957 (WHCF/OF 102-B-3) to explain his vote for the jury amendment to the Civil Rights Bill (for background see no. 266). Revercomb stated that he acted without "any thought of opposition" to the President, but rather out of his "earnest belief in the use of the jury system whenever the liberty of anyone is at issue in our civil trial courts." Revercomb praised Eisenhower's leadership and added: "Be assured of my desire to work with you in the great service you are giving the country."

[3] In an undated note (same file as document) Ann Whitman asked White House congressional liaison Wilton B. Persons if he had any objection to sending this letter, which she said the President had dictated.

293

EM, AWF, Administration Series

To Sinclair Weeks

August 15, 1957

Dear Sinny: I called you on the phone to find that, like so many others of the Cabinet these days, you were spending your morning on the Hill.

The purpose of my call was to tell you about a suggestion brought to my office by a friend. It involves the naming of the new atomic merchant ship. Because the first steamship to cross the ocean was the SAVANNAH, he proposes that the new atomic ship have the same name. I confess the idea has some appeal for me.[1]

I assume that no name has as yet been chosen for it. Sometime when you have a chance, let's talk it over—on the telephone would be quite satisfactory.[2]

Attached hereto are some papers given to me by my friend. *As ever*

[1] In an August 15 meeting with the President, Major General Henry Benton Sayler had suggested this name for the new ship (Ann Whitman memorandum, Aug. 15, 1957, AWF/AWD). The original *Savannah,* a conventional sailing packet adapted to use an auxiliary steam-driven paddle wheel, had sailed from America to Europe in the summer of 1819. The vessel's owners, who were unable to secure either passengers or cargo, failed to sell her abroad. Upon return to the United States, she was sold to pay her debts (see Cedric Ridgely-Nevitt, *American Steamships on the Atlantic* [Newark, Del., London and Toronto, 1981], pp. 57–67).

[2] Commerce Secretary Weeks would reply on August 15 (AWF/A), explaining that no action would be taken prior to the laying of the keel in May 1958. The Nuclear Ship (N.S.) *Savannah,* the world's first commercial vessel powered by an atomic reactor, would be launched in July 1961. The ship, which would cost $45,000,000, could carry 10,000 tons of cargo and sixty passengers. Loading of atomic fuel would take place in December 1961 (*New York Times,* Nov. 25, 1961, and Michael W. Marshall, *Ocean Traders* [New York, 1990], p. 162).

294

EM, AWF, DDE Diaries Series

To Christian Archibald Herter

August 16, 1957

Confidential

Dear Chris: This morning I had breakfast with Senator Knowland. In the course of an extensive conversation he mentioned that he was still concerned about the present and probable future character of our relationships with Yugoslavia. His concern is directed toward any military help we might give Tito. I informed him that the airplane deal (which I thought we had already fulfilled) with Tito involved obsolete F-86s.[1]

Beyond this, I carefully explained to him that the central influence in all our foreign relations was the polarization of world power in Washington and in Moscow, with a whole group of free nations, loosely attached to each other by a common desire for independence and a religious basis, opposed to a monolithic and atheistic dictatorship. Everything has to be gauged and measured against this background and the problems created by this basic antagonism and struggle. I pointed out that consequently deals were made with Tito that were not in any sense to be interpreted as an approval of his regime. Their main purposes were two: (*a*) to make certain that he does not drift back again to the place where he would permit Soviet dictation of his policies, and (*b*) to induce him to conduct his affairs so as to conform more closely to Western standards of civilization. He merely asked at the close of this part of our conversation that State and Defense (to which might be added ICA) review our policies of the moment to see whether or not any changes would seem to us to be necessary or desirable.

I told him I would mention this to you. Actually I am under the impression that recently we have reviewed the Yugoslav National Security paper.[2] In any event, if you think there is anything valuable or significant that I could provide Senator Knowland, who seems very desirous these days of lining up solidly with the Administration, I would be delighted to have you pass it to him directly—or let me know so that I would have the necessary information when I see him some time in the future.[3]

With warm regard, *As ever*

[1] For background on military aid to Yugoslavia see Galambos and van Ee, *The Middle Way*, no. 2088. For background on Marshal Josip Broz Tito, President of the Federal People's Republic of Yugoslavia, see *Eisenhower Papers*, vols. I–XVII. In October 1956 Eisenhower, in spite of congressional opposition, had authorized the resumption of U.S. economic aid to Yugoslavia based on his determination that that country remained independent of the Soviet Union. He continued to block, however, the delivery of jet planes and other items of heavy equipment. On May 14, 1957, the State Department, with Eisenhower's approval, had announced the resumption of military aid to Yugoslavia, including jet aircraft at the rate of ten per month through November (State, *Foreign Relations, 1955–1957*, vol. XXVI, *Central and Southeastern Europe*, pp. 740–46, 765–78; see also Ann Whitman memorandum, Aug. 16, 1957, AWF/AWD; and *Congressional Quarterly Almanac*, vol. XIII, *1957*, p. 602).

[2] At its June 13 meeting the National Security Council had noted the Progress Report prepared by the Operations Coordinating Board on NSC 5601—U.S. Policy Toward Yugoslavia (see NSC meeting minutes, June 14, 1957, AWF/NSC; and *Congressional Quarterly Almanac*, vol. XIII, *1957*, pp. 707–14).

[3] There is no reply from Under Secretary Herter in AWF.

295 *EM, AWF, International Series: Macmillan*

To Harold Macmillan *August 17, 1957*
Cable. Secret

Dear Harold: I have your message regarding Oman and it is receiving my urgent study. As you no doubt know through Harold Caccia and Crosthwaite the view of my staff here is that abstention on the vote to inscribe would best serve our common interest and achieve the practical result you wish.[1]

After his return to Washington I will discuss this with Foster, to whom Selwyn has sent a note on the same subject and then communicate with you further.[2]

I appreciate not only the time factor involved but of course the larger consideration you mentioned. *Warm regards*

[1] For background on the rebellion in Muscat and Oman and the resulting British intervention see no. 255; see also State, *Foreign Relations, 1955–1957*, vol. XIII, *Near East: Jordan-Yemen*, pp. 231–35; NSC meeting minutes, Aug. 2, 1957, AWF/NSC; and Eisenhower, *Waging Peace*, pp. 195–96. On August 3 Eisenhower and Dulles had discussed their fear that the United States would be caught between its desire to maintain influence in Saudi Arabia and its desire to preserve a good relationship with Great Britain. The two agreed that "a small scale Suez might be in the making" (Memorandum of Conversation, Aug. 3, 1957, Dulles Papers, White House Memoranda Series). Anticipating a request by Saudi Arabia, which was supporting the rebels, and other Arab nations to inscribe the Oman situation on the United Nations Security Council agenda, Under Secretary of State Herter had advised U.N. Ambassador Lodge that no constructive purpose would be served by having the Security Council consider the issue. The "probable result," he said "would be [an] acrimonious and fruitless debate" that would benefit the Soviet Union and Arab extremists. Both British Ambassador Caccia and Ponsonby Moore Crosthwaite, Minister of the British Mission at the United Nations, had strongly objected to the U.S. decision to abstain, which the British believed had been made prematurely. On August 15 Caccia had told Deputy Under Secretary of State Robert Daniel Murphy that the British people would interpret a U.S. abstention as evidence that the United States was governed by selfish oil interests. Caccia asked Murphy if Dulles, vacationing on Duck Island, had been informed of the U.S. position. The Secretary had not, Murphy answered, but the question had received "thoughtful consideration" by State Department officials during his absence.

On August 16 British Foreign Secretary Selwyn Lloyd had urged Dulles to instruct the U.S. delegation to vote against inscription and to urge other friendly nations to do so also. On that same day Eisenhower had forwarded to Herter the draft of a friendly letter to Macmillan, supporting British actions in Oman. In the draft the President said that he understood the difficulties involved in the British decision to attack the rebels since Macmillan's "motives were bound to be deliberately misinterpreted in every corner of the earth where unfriendly people would have an interest in so doing. . . . I must say," Eisenhower added, "that under the circumstances I do not see that you could have acted in any way other than you did." The President then told Herter, in a memorandum accompanying the draft, that he had seen "in some staff notes that we were going to 'abstain' if this matter were brought up in the Security Council. I am not so sure that that is the attitude we should take," Eisenhower said, "and if this is really our intention, I should like to hear the reasons therefore." Unwilling to pass judgment on the letter to Macmillan, Herter had sent the draft on to the vacationing Dulles. According to Ann Whitman, Eisenhower "was deeply concerned" that the delay in giving him an answer had upset the timing and "the opportunity for the friendly gesture to Macmillan was now lost" (Briefing Items, Aug. 16, 1957; and Ann Whitman memorandum, Aug. 17, 1957, both in AWF/AWD).

Fearing that Dulles's absence had affected the U.S. position, Macmillan asked Eisenhower to look at the message Lloyd had sent the Secretary. "I would not worry you except for this one reason," he said. "We have done such a lot together during the past few months to get things right between us that it would really be tragic if they go wrong again." After unsuccessfully trying to reach Dulles in Ontario and Herter in Massachusetts, Eisenhower sent this interim reply through Murphy (Macmillan to Eisenhower, Aug. 17, 1957, AWF/I: Macmillan; and State, *Foreign Relations, 1955–1957*, vol. XIII, *Near East: Jordan-Yemen*, pp. 237–41).

[2] Dulles would return to Washington on the following day. For developments see the following document.

296

EM, AWF, International Series: Macmillan

To Harold Macmillan
Cable. Secret

August 19, 1957

Dear Harold:[1] This supplements my message to you of the 17th.[2] Foster is now back and although both of us are deeply engaged today in relation to the Mutual Security legislation we did have lunch together and he had a talk with Harold Caccia. It looks as though if you want quick action which will result in the non-inscription of the matter the best we can do, consistently with our prior practice and lack of knowledge of the complicated local facts here, would be to abstain. This is as good as a negative vote from the standpoint of keeping the matter off the agenda and I do not think you need to worry about the outcome.[3]

If you want to have the matter discussed and deal with the "Treaty of Sib" and such matters sufficiently to make a clear public case against there being an inscribable issue, then we might feel that we could vote positively against inscription.[4] This would of course depend somewhat upon the character of the presentation that was made. But we assume that you have a good case in this respect.

You may well decide that it is better not to have the argument and to get the matter quickly behind us so that we can work together on some constructive developments.

I know you would rather have us vote from the outset and immediately against inscription. However, I think that we can recognize that the common goals which we have cannot always be best achieved by our necessarily always taking a uniform public position.[5]

As you know, both personally and officially, Foster and I want always to be on the same slot with you but we think that all things considered the above is the best solution we can figure out at the moment.[6] *Sincerely*

[1] Secretary Dulles had read a draft of this message over the telephone to Eisenhower, who suggested an addition at the end (Aug. 19, 1957, Dulles Papers, Telephone Conversations).

[2] See the preceding document.

[3] Dulles had told British Ambassador Caccia earlier this same day that although he had not had much opportunity to study the question, he felt, after discussions with his staff, "that the conclusions seemed pretty well jelled." Dulles admitted that abstention was a weak position, but confessed himself unable to arrive at a better result (State, *Foreign Relations, 1955–1957*, vol. XIII, *Near East: Jordan-Yemen*, pp. 243–46; on the Mutual Security Act see *Congressional Quarterly Almanac*, vol. XIII, *1957*, pp. 601–12).

[4] The Agreement of Al-Sib, negotiated by Britain in 1920 between the tribal leaders and the Sultan of Muscat, recognized the autonomy but not the sovereignty of Oman.

[5] Macmillan had thanked Eisenhower for his prompt reply but had warned that "anything which may make the Sultan of Muscat feel that doubts are being cast on the essential unity of Muscat and Oman will make it almost impossible to get him to accept the idea of a meeting with King Saud. Both of us, I think, believe that direct negotiations between them is the thing to work for" (Macmillan to Eisenhower, Aug. 18, 1957, AWF/I: Macmillan). Macmillan would record in his memoirs that the Americans had behaved "outrageously" about Oman. Eisenhower answered his telegrams "agreeably enough," Macmillan wrote, "but does nothing" (Macmillan, *Riding the Storm*, p. 276).

[6] On the following day the Security Council would vote five to four against inscription. The United States abstained (see Telephone conversations, Dulles and Lodge, Aug. 20, 1957, Dulles Papers, Telephone Conversations).

297

EM, AWF, DDE Diaries Series

To Robert Bernerd Anderson

August 19, 1957

Personal and confidential

Dear Bob:[1] I do not know whether or not you have found the man you want for your Undersecretary for Monetary Affairs.

I have a recommendation from Bob Woodruff, who says that Robert Rouse, Vice President of the New York Federal Reserve Bank is a top-notch man in this field and a splendid citizen in every respect. He says that Sloan Colt and Bob Fleming both think very highly of Mr. Rouse.[2]

I pass this on to you for whatever use you may care to make of it.[3]

As I assume you know, Mr. Woodruff is, in my opinion, a man of excellent judgment and certainly he is a fine character.[4] *As ever*

[1] Anderson had been Secretary of the Treasury since May 29.
[2] Although Robert G. Rouse would not be appointed as Under Secretary for Monetary Affairs, he would become System Open Market Account manager at the Federal Reserve. Eisenhower was referring to Samuel Sloan Colt, chairman of the board of Bankers Trust, and to Robert Vedder Fleming, chairman of the board of the Riggs National Bank in Washington, D.C., and former vice-president of the federal advisory council to the board of governors of the Federal Reserve System, Fifth Federal Reserve District. Eisenhower would also discuss Rouse with former Treasury Secretary George Humphrey. Describing Rouse a "fine man," Humphrey would suggest that it would be better if they could find an "outsider," as Rouse was already working for the Federal Reserve System (Telephone Conversations, Aug. 20, 1957, AWF/D).
[3] Julian B. Baird would receive the appointment and be confirmed on January 23, 1958.
[4] See the following document.

298

EM, AWF, DDE Diaries Series

To Robert Winship Woodruff

August 19, 1957

Dear Bob: Thanks for calling back to give me the name of Mr. Rouse. I have sent it down to the Treasury Department so that Bob Anderson will have it as soon as he returns.[1]

I was truly delighted to see you the other day—particularly to find you looking so well.[2]

It seems to me that we must really organize an educational movement in this country to teach our people some of the facts of international life and especially what it means to us to keep the free world solidly behind a program of anti-Communistic expansion.[3] In such an effort I see a tremendous job for one Honorable Robert W. Woodruff. *As ever*

[1] See the preceding document.
[2] Eisenhower had met with Woodruff for a half-hour on August 15. On Eisenhower's concern for Woodruff's health see no. 273.
[3] On Eisenhower's efforts to inform the American public about the mutual security program see Eisenhower, *Waging Peace*, pp. 132–36 and 144–46.

299

EM, AWF, Administration Series, Adams Corr.

To William Pierce Rogers

August 19, 1957

Memorandum for the Acting Attorney General:[1] Attached is a letter I have just received reporting that there will soon exist a Kansas Federal Judgeship vacancy.[2]

Ed Arn and Emmett Graham are both good friends of mine. I would like to have Governor Arn seriously considered for this particular spot.[3] I am assuming, of course, that his appointment would have the approval of the American Bar Association.

[1] Deputy Attorney General Rogers would replace Herbert Brownell, Jr., as Attorney General on November 8, 1957. See no. 476.

[2] Eisenhower was referring to a letter from his Abilene friend Emmett S. Graham urging the appointment of former Kansas governor Edward F. Arn to replace Art Mellott as Federal District Judge (Graham to Eisenhower, Aug. 14, 1957, and other correspondence in WHCF/OF 100-B-10). For background see no. 85.

[3] Eisenhower would not appoint Arn to the federal bench; he would instead select Arthur J. Stanley, Jr., to be United States District Judge for the District of Kansas. After Arn complained (May 16, 1958) that he had been rejected unfairly because he was "too politically controversial," Eisenhower would reply six days later, expressing deep regret "that it turned out as it did." While both he and the Attorney General held Arn in the "highest regard," the decision, in Eisenhower's opinion, was in Arn's "own interest" (see the voluminous correspondence from Eisenhower's Abilene friends in WHCF/OF 100-B-10).

300

EM, AWF, DDE Diaries Series

To William Alton Jones

August 20, 1957

Dear Pete: Last evening I called you on the phone for a most inconsequential reason. Because of this, when I heard later in the night that you were then at home in Lake Placid, I did not bother you.

The reason was to tell you of an effort of mine to paint your portrait. You will remember that, under the overhang of the barn at the Brandon place, I took a snapshot of you.[1] I had this snapshot enlarged and from the enlargement I painted what I call your "portrait." It now represents the full limit of my feeble abilities in this line, and my purpose was merely to suggest that the next time you are this way, you be sure to give me a ring. I want to show the thing to you and if it meets with your complete disapproval—which I suspect it will—I shall immediately burn it up. Otherwise you may have it, for I doubt that Mamie would allow me to keep it in the house very long.[2]

Mamie continues to improve; in fact the doctors are quite pleased with her progress. I think, though, that she will be in the hospital for another week at least.[3]

As you will know from your newspaper, the Congress is in a state of confusion.[4] While this may not be news, it is very inconvenient to have it so evident in what should be the latter days of the session. As it is now, no one knows when Congress will adjourn, and of course this means that I am fastened down here as long as this situation persists.[5]

Love to Nettie and, of course, all the best to yourself. *As ever*

[1] For background on the Brandon farm see Galambos and van Ee, *The Middle Way*, no. 1155.

[2] In his reply (Aug. 22, 1957, AWF/N) Jones would call Eisenhower "courageous" to paint "a portrait of such an unworthy subject." He went on to say that he hoped the likeness would not be good so he could "appreciate it for the thoughtfulness that went into its making." On August 3 the President would tell Jones not to "belittle your handsome 'mug' just because I am no great shakes as an artist!" (AWF/N).

[3] The First Lady had undergone gynecological surgery on August 6 (see no. 291).

[4] Jones would reply that Eisenhower's assessment of Congress was "conservative . . . indeed." "As I think you wisely observed one time," he went on, "congressmen individually, for the most part, are nice fellows, but collectively they do a lot of queer things." See also no. 302.

[5] Congress would adjourn on August 30. The Eisenhowers would vacation in Newport, Rhode Island, September 4–30.

301

EM, AWF, International Series: Saudi Arabia

To IBN ABD AL-AZIZ SAUD — *August 21, 1957*

Cable. Top secret

Your Majesty:[1] I wish to share with you the concern which I feel regarding recent developments in Syria. It seems that by a series of steps, first seemingly innocent and now reaching a rapid pace, the Communists are taking over and effectively driving out the duly constituted authorities. There seems to be serious danger that Syria will become a Soviet Communist satellite.[2]

We are in receipt of messages of concern from the neighboring Arab countries—Jordan, Lebanon and Iraq. Turkey, too, feels that it is in danger of being caught within a Soviet vice.[3]

No doubt Your Majesty has also heard similar voices of fear and concern.

The United States has no purpose or desire to intervene. The recent extravagant stories put out from Damascus alleging United States plots and intervention are part of a slanderous campaign to distract attention from the actual Communist intervention that was going on. Of course, under the doctrine which Ambassador Richards explained to you, we would sympathetically consider a request to assist any country that was attacked by a Syria which itself was dominated by International Communism.[4] We believe, however, that it is highly preferable that Syria's neighbors should be able to deal with this problem without the necessity for any outside intervention.

In view of the special position of Your Majesty as Keeper of the Holy Places of Islam, I trust that you will exert your great influence to the end that the atheistic creed of Communism will not become entrenched at a key position in the Moslem world.[5]

May God have you in His safekeeping. *Your sincere friend*

[1] Secretary Dulles drafted this message to King Saud (see State, *Foreign Relations, 1955–1957,* vol. XIII, *Near East: Jordan-Yemen,* p. 645; and Telephone conversation, Dulles and Rountree, Aug. 21, 1957, Dulles Papers, Telephone Conversations).

[2] For background on the Communist influence in Syria see no. 132. After national elections in May had increased the number of Communist sympathizers in the Syrian Chamber of Deputies, the U.S. ambassador had characterized the country as a base for anti-American propaganda and Communist activity throughout the area. On August 12 Syrian officials had accused the United States of plotting to overthrow the government, and thirty members of the Syrian security forces had surrounded the U.S. embassy in Damascus. The following day the Syrian government had expelled three U.S. embassy officials.

After discussing the Syrian situation with Acting Secretary Herter on August 14, Eisenhower decided to protest the Syrian actions and to declare the Syrian ambassador, then in Damascus, as persona non grata. The President also instructed the U.S. ambassador, then in Washington for consultations, not to return to Syria and suspended visits to that country by groups and persons under the Cultural Exchange Program (State, *Foreign Relations, 1955–1957,* vol. XIII, *Near East: Jordan-Yemen,* pp. 618–36; see also Eisenhower, *Waging Peace,* pp. 196–98).

Dulles had advised Eisenhower on August 20 to avoid making any public announcement that stated or implied that Syria was or was not controlled by international communism. "Our Embassy is virtually blockaded," he said, "and we cannot yet make a clear political judgment as to the actual extent of Communist penetration." Dulles did not want to encourage Israel "to stimulate an incident with Syria on the theory that we have judged Syria to be Communist controlled. On the other hand," he said, "we would want to keep freedom of action to make such a decision under certain contingencies. We would like to keep the Syrian Government uncertain as to our intentions" (AWF/AWD).

In a meeting earlier on this same day Eisenhower and Dulles had agreed that the crisis could be an opportunity to mobilize feelings of concern among Syria's neighbors. According to Dulles, Eisenhower "threw out the suggestion that we might give arms and money rather freely to Syria's neighbors as part of some program" (Memorandum of Conversation, Aug. 21, 1957, Dulles Papers, White House Memoranda

Series; see also Telephone conversations, Dulles and Twining, and Dulles and Anderson, Aug. 21, 1957, Dulles Papers, Telephone Conversations).
[3] Jordan's King Hussein had suggested a meeting of the Arab countries bordering Syria; the Lebanese government had asked the United States for additional arms and equipment to withstand overt aggression from Syria; and the Iraqi Legation in Damascus had reported that those sympathetic to Iraq in the Syrian government were completely powerless (State, *Foreign Relations, 1955–1957*, vol. XIII, *Near East: Jordan-Yemen*, pp. 638–39, 642–44).
[4] For background on Ambassador James Richards's mission and the Eisenhower Doctrine see no. 63; and Galambos and van Ee, *The Middle Way*, no. 2155. Richards had met with King Saud on April 9 and 10 (see State, *Foreign Relations, 1955–1957*, vol. XIII, *Near East: Jordan-Yemen*, pp. 489–94).
[5] In discussing this letter with Dulles, Eisenhower called this sentence "a masterpiece" (Telephone conversation, Aug. 21, 1957, Dulles Papers, Telephone Conversations). For developments see no. 332.

302

EM, AWF, Name Series

To Sidney Williams Richardson *August 21, 1957*
Personal

Dear Sid: I do not know whether Mamie has yet gotten around to signing letters, but I do know that she was enormously pleased to get the flowers you sent her a few days ago. They were indeed beautiful and she drew my particular attention to them. She has steadily improved ever since the operation—in fact the doctors say she is doing remarkably well. On the other hand, she has felt quite miserable, with aches, pains, indigestion and so on. So—at times her disposition suffers.[1]

This session of Congress has been a most difficult period. Politics rage throughout the city—a situation I assume is more or less normal when one party controls the Legislative and the other controls the Executive branch, at a time when both parties are looking forward to a national election in which the President cannot be a candidate to succeed himself. While the United States has not had this exact experience before—it has survived worse situations. Nevertheless, it is disappointing, not to say frustrating, to find people from whom we have the right to expect reasonably intelligent statements, conclusions and reactions, take positions that they know cannot fail to damage the long range welfare of our country. I am talking now principally of our mutual security program. This is the most important tool we have in keeping the free world countries operating voluntarily in a loose confederation against the expansion of Communism.[2]

The Communist threat has not diminished. In fact since it has abandoned the single line of using force and the threat of force to gain its ends, and has instead broadened its front to include economic, political and cultural attacks, I think that the cause of the Western world has suffered. This is largely because of our failure to comprehend the nature of this new type of cold war—particularly our failure to comprehend its possible consequences. So—while we can boast of the finest civilization the world has known, the Soviets are convincing many peoples that they are the true exponents of progress, peace and of freedom! What a tragedy![3]

I have done everything that I can think of to increase the understanding of our people, but clearly I have not succeeded sufficiently so that the Congress feels upon its neck the breath of an aroused citizenry.

There are other important matters in which far more heat than light has been generated in the Congress. In these cases, however, I think there is some chance for good sense prevailing, especially in those areas where there seems to be a determined attitude made to nibble away at socialization of our economy. For example, the effort of many in Congress to see that the *Federal government* builds atomic reactors to produce power for ordinary civilian consumption. Actually we have been having a great success in keeping the Federal government's part in all this confined to research and to technical advice. Private capital has already started to build many times the number of reactors in our country that are projected in the rest of the world combined. Yet the public power boys are never silent. The unfortunate part about it is that they seem to confuse individuals who should have more sense.[4]

From my reports I feel that we are making real progress on limiting oil imports. I suppose you keep in close touch with this movement. Bob Anderson remains my greatest and closest adviser in this field.[5]

I did not mean to get started in an account of all our legislative and governmental difficulties of the moment. Such things are far better left for conversations, which I hope will not be too long delayed.

I really meant only to thank you for your kindly thoughtfulness about Mamie.

With warm regard, *As ever*

[1] On Mamie Eisenhower's illness see no. 291.

[2] For background on the political struggle over foreign aid see no. 273.

[3] This had long been a concern to Eisenhower. See, for example, the preceding document.

[4] On this day Eisenhower had signed into law P.L. 162. This act, which authorized funds for government construction and assistance in the development of atomic energy for both civilian and military purposes, was a compromise between the Ad-

ministration's call for private construction of atomic power plants with a limited federal role and congressional concern for the rate of progress in the development of atomic power (*Congressional Quarterly Almanac*, vol. XIII, *1957*, pp. 583–86; *New York Times*, Aug. 22, 1957; Brian Balogh, *Chain Reaction: Expert Debate and Public Participation in American Commercial Nuclear Power, 1949–1975* [Cambridge and New York, 1991]; and Hewlett and Holl, *Atoms for Peace and War*, pp. 401–10). Eisenhower had applauded the congressional action, saying that it was "a great improvement indeed over the bills introduced early in the session . . ." (*Public Papers of the Presidents: Eisenhower, 1957*, p. 628).

[5] See no. 261. Robert B. Anderson had served as Secretary of the Treasury since July 29, 1957.

303

EM, AWF, International Series: Rhee

TO SYNGMAN RHEE
Confidential

August 23, 1957

Dear Mr. President:[1] Thank you for your letter of August 2, 1957, commenting further on the question of the level of Republic of Korea ground forces. As you know, I have always welcomed the frank exchange of views between us.[2]

My letter of July nineteenth outlined the position we have taken with respect to the necessity for bringing about a reduction in Republic of Korea ground forces. This matter was given careful and thoughtful consideration by our Government and all factors were taken into account. The plan which resulted, and which Ambassador Dowling and General Decker have been discussing with you and representatives of your Government, was developed by the Secretaries of State and Defense and the Joint Chiefs of Staff. It has my full support and will, in our opinion, enhance rather than weaken the future security of the Republic of Korea against renewal of Communist aggression.[3]

I sincerely trust that Ambassador Dowling and General Decker, acting within my instructions, will shortly succeed in working out with you and your military advisers an orderly and planned reduction in Republic of Korea ground forces. This will enable the remaining forces to take advantage of certain new equipment available within the fiscal year 1958 Military Assistance Program. I would be less than candid if I did not state to you frankly that it will be impossible, because of United States budgetary considerations, to maintain the Korean aid program at present levels. Accordingly, failure to reduce the level of Republic of Korea ground forces at this time would not only result in a serious weakening of their defensive capabilities because of equipment deficiencies, but would also throw an increasingly heavy burden on the Korean economy with attendant inflationary pressures.

With regard to the two specific questions you raise as to the nature and extent of modernization of the Republic of Korea and United States forces, Ambassador Dowling and General Decker are being instructed to discuss this in more detail with you.[4]

May I take this opportunity to reaffirm United States interest in and support of the Republic of Korea, its military security, economic development and eventual peaceful reunification.

With my sincere personal good wishes, *Sincerely*

[1] The State Department drafted this letter to the South Korean President.

[2] Rhee had responded to Eisenhower's letter of July 19 (see no. 244) regarding the introduction of new weapons for U.S. forces in Korea, to be followed by a reduction of South Korean forces. Reducing the size of his troops at this time was unwise, Rhee had written. He knew nothing about the number nor the type of weapons that the United States was planning to send, nor did he know whether the modernization program applied equally to Korean and U.S. forces. "We have been fighting shoulder to shoulder against a common enemy who is bent on our destruction," Rhee wrote, "and if the United States were now to discriminate in the matter of armaments, please think of the adverse effect it would have, both militarily and psychologically" (Rhee to Eisenhower, Aug. 2, 1957, AWF/I: Rhee).

[3] George Henry Decker (B.S. Lafayette College 1924) had become Commander in Chief, United Nations Command on July 1, replacing General Lyman Lemnitzer, who, with U.S. Ambassador Walter Dowling, had first presented the plan to Rhee.

[4] State and Defense Department officials would discuss the modernization process on September 9 and would authorize Ambassador Dowling and General Decker to inform Rhee that if the Koreans reduced their ground forces, the United States would reorganize two of its divisions into units more capable of withstanding an atomic attack, introduce two battalions equipped with atomic weapons, and rotate its Air Force squadrons between Japan and Korea. Planes of one U.S. fighter-bomber wing would be transferred to the South Korean Air Force, and equipment made excess by the modernization of U.S. forces would be transferred to the Koreans.

Although fearing that a reduction would severely weaken his defensive capabilities, Rhee would agree to reduce Korean forces by 60,000 men. In December the United States would tell Korean officials that it would support armed forces of no more than 620,000 in FY 1959, a reduction of 100,000 men. Rhee would reject this proposal. On January 22, 1958, Eisenhower would approve a "final U.S. concession," agreeing to let the Koreans have an additional 10,000 men. He modified the language of the proposal, however, "to make it explicit that the statement of the U.S. position should not be presented to President Rhee as an ultimatum." The South Korean President would accept these figures on March 3 (State, *Foreign Relations, 1955–1957,* vol. XXIII, pt. 2, *Korea,* pp. 491–502, 505–10, 519–36; and State, *Foreign Relations, 1958–1960,* vol. XVIII, *Japan; Korea* [1994], pp. 425–32, 438–39, 446–47, 449–55; see also NSC meeting minutes, Aug. 9, 1957, AWF/NSC; and Daun van Ee, "From the New Look to Flexible Response," in *Against All Enemies: Interpretations of American Military History From Colonial Times to the Present,* ed. Kenneth J. Hagan and William R. Roberts [Westport, Conn., 1986], pp. 321–40).

304

EM, AWF, International Series: Macmillan

To Harold Macmillan
Personal

August 26, 1957

Dear Harold:[1] For some days a continuing intention of mine to send you a note has been defeated by preoccupations of a legislative character, brought about by the fact that we approach the end of a Congressional session with a great many controversial questions under debate.

The most serious of these, from the free world viewpoint, involves our mutual aid program. Although I have brought every possible personal influence to bear, the Congress, motivated by a belief that our people are getting weary of very high taxes and convinced that most of our citizens do not understand the aims and purposes of mutual security, has consistently refused to allow the amounts needed. I hope the situation can be partially corrected in the Senate, but in any event we are going to be hard pushed this year to carry on all the activities which the Administration believes to be in the best interests of the free world, including ourselves.[2]

Meanwhile, as you will know from Foster's messages, we are preoccupied by what is happening in Syria. It is encouraging that all of Syria's neighbors, including all of the Moslem neighbors, seem fully aware of the dangers which growing Communist influence in Syria poses for them. I believe it important that this Moslem opposition be demonstrated in all appropriate forms. We expect to keep in touch with you and your people as this problem develops.[3]

Recently I saw in a dispatch a statement by Selwyn Lloyd that certain British agencies believed we had been responsible for inducing the Germans to buy American rather than British tanks. As I have assured you previously—indeed as I assured Anthony, when he was Prime Minister, and the German Chancellor—our government did *not* want this business.[4]

Frankly I dislike the prospect of the bulk of the free world being dependent, in the event of an emergency, upon the United States as their arsenal for materiel replacement, repair and maintenance. I would far rather that the free world could develop several dependable sources for this kind of supply. Indeed, I believe that each country should, at the very least, develop its own capacity for producing ammunition and spare parts. Otherwise such universal dependence among the non-industrial nations upon a single source will be bound to create serious, if not catastrophic difficulties, should we ever be faced with a general war. Consequently my advocacy of German purchase of Centurions was not entirely altruistic.

It merely conforms to my idea of common sense in the business of free world cooperation against emergency.

I am under the impression that you enjoyed a holiday. I hope so, and I assure you that I wish that I were able to be away from my desk during these days. I now have some belief that Congress may adjourn by the end of this week, after which I would hope to spend several weeks in Newport, only an hour and a half from Washington by air.[5]

I trust that you and your Lady thoroughly enjoyed your break from normal routine.[6]

With warm personal regard, *As ever*

P.S. Just this minute I am told that six beautiful grouse have arrived as a gift from the Duke of Devonshire, sent at your direction.[7] Not only do I thank you for thinking of me—it is a great satisfaction now to *know* that you have had an enjoyable holiday.

[1] This message, suggested by Secretary Dulles, is the redraft of an earlier letter Eisenhower had wanted to send to Macmillan. It omits a paragraph expressing sympathy for Macmillan's plight in regard to Oman (see no. 295; Eisenhower to Macmillan, and Eisenhower to Herter, Aug. 16, 1957; and Dulles to Eisenhower, Aug. 23, 1957, all in AWF/D-H).

[2] Debate on the Mutual Security Act had begun in the Senate on June 7. The final appropriation was for $244 million more than the original House version, $256.9 million less than the Senate version, and $618.1 million less than Eisenhower had requested. He would sign the measure on September 3 (*Congressional Quarterly Almanac*, vol. XIII, *1957*, pp. 71–73, 601–12; see also no. 137; and Eisenhower, *Waging Peace*, pp. 144–47).

[3] For background on the Syrian situation see no. 301. On August 21 Dulles had told British Foreign Minister Lloyd, in a message that was forwarded to Macmillan, that there was "now little hope of correction from within" and that the United States and Great Britain "must perhaps be prepared to take some serious risks to avoid even greater risks and dangers later on" (AWF/D-H). On the following day he told Macmillan that Deputy Under Secretary of State Loy Wesley Henderson would be meeting with Turkish government officials to learn firsthand the attitude of Syria's neighbors (*ibid.*; see also Macmillan, *Riding the Storm*, pp. 277–80).

[4] For Eisenhower's letters to Macmillan on the purchase of Centurion tanks see nos. 115 and 168. On his correspondence with Anthony Eden regarding the issue see Galambos and van Ee, *The Middle Way*, no. 1991.

[5] Macmillan had been vacationing in Scotland. Congress would adjourn on Friday, August 30, and Eisenhower would leave the following Wednesday for Newport, Rhode Island.

[6] Macmillan's wife was the former Lady Dorothy Evelyn Cavendish.

[7] Edward William Spencer, the 10th Duke of Devonshire, was Macmillan's brother-in-law.

305 *EM, AWF, DDE Diaries Series*

To Robert Winship Woodruff *August 26, 1957*

Dear Bob: I think that Mr. Sibley's letter to Congressman Lanham is a little masterpiece.[1] I should like to have your permission to show it to Foster and others around here so that they may know of the voluntary support that we are receiving from such a thoughtful citizen as Mr. Sibley. It was a pity that Congressman Lanham did not give him an answer more in keeping with his strong presentation of the case.[2]

Thank you for letting me see the correspondence. *As ever*

[1] Eisenhower's close friend Woodruff, a former Coca-Cola Company president, had written Ann Whitman on August 24 (WHCF/OF 133-L) to suggest that "the Boss" might be interested in an exchange of letters on mutual security between John Adams Sibley (LL.B. University of Georgia 1911), chairman of the Trust Company of Georgia, and Henderson Lovelace Lanham, Democratic Congressman from Georgia since 1948. Sibley, who had been vice-president of the American Bar Association since 1922, had written the Congressman on August 9 (WHCF/OF 133-L) to say that the "most pressing national problem has been to maintain peace with justice." Calling the American failure to support the League of Nations the most "tragic event" in our national history, Sibley stated that funding the mutual security program was "the cheapest military security that we buy." "I think," he wrote, "the present program which supplies economic and military assistance, and through the Development Loan Fund provides for the repayment of advancements for economic development, is a significant step in the right direction. I also like the feature that provides such funds over a period of several years so that there may be continuity in carrying out the program. I doubt if the program could have its maximum effectiveness in any other manner" (for background see no. 273).

[2] Lanham had replied to Sibley on August 13 (WHCF/OF 133-L). Noting that he had always supported foreign aid although he knew "much of it has been wasted," Lanham said that it was his duty, as a member of the Appropriations Subcommittee, to be sure that the money appropriated for foreign aid was "the very minimum consistent with our national security." "Our Subcommittee," he wrote, "has had the able assistance of Senator Russell in holding these funds to the minimum so that there will be as little waste and extravagance as possible in the expenditure of these funds." Ann Whitman would forward the correspondence to Secretary of State Dulles on August 30 (WHCF/OF 133-L).

306 *EM, AWF, Gettysburg Series*

To Herman R. Purdy *August 26, 1957*

Dear Dr. Purdy: Thank you very much for your nice invitation to put a few head in your Pennsylvania Livestock Exposition this fall.[1]

As you know, there are some cows in my tiny herd that are quite good. These include Mole's Hill Barbara, Duncraggan Eline Erica, and some others, but it is my impression you'd prefer to have animals we have produced. I am not sure that Bob Hartley would want to exhibit anything that has actually been calved on the place. I should think the only possibility would be some very young daughters of Akonian 3551. I would not want to send any unless Bob considered them truly representative of the kind of herd we are *trying to build.*[2] At any rate, I have asked Bob to get in touch with you and whatever he decides will be satisfactory to me.

Of course, I have not up to this time participated in any kind of Exposition, nor have I sold any animals under my name.[3] While the chances that I could come to the Show are most remote, I am, as I say, willing to leave the decision as to exhibition to Bob.

As to Mr. Falk's visiting the farm to present me with the first ticket, I cannot be sure at this time when I shall be up there again. If all goes well, I think Mrs. Eisenhower and I will go to Newport for a few weeks and it could easily be late in October before I see Gettysburg again.[4] However, if Mr. Falk would like to come down here some time this week to present the ticket I should, of course, be glad to accept it. (I shall be equally glad to see him here after my return from Newport, but as of now I do not know when that will be.)[5]

With warm regard, *Sincerely*

[1] Purdy's invitation, dated August 22, is in AWF/Gettysburg. The show, sponsored by the Commonwealth of Pennsylvania, would run November 12–16. As the exposition's superintendent of beef cattle, Purdy said he "would be highly honored" if the President could attend one of the events in which Aberdeen Angus cattle would be judged.

[2] For background on these cattle see Galambos and van Ee, *The Middle Way.* On the efforts to improve the herd see nos. 10 and 70 in these volumes.

[3] See no. 15.

[4] Purdy had suggested that Leon Falk, the chairman of the show, visit the President's farm and present him with the first ticket to the Exposition.

[5] The Eisenhowers would vacation in Newport, Rhode Island, September 4–30. Eisenhower would spend the weekend of October 4–6 at his farm in Gettysburg. As it turned out, the President would not attend the exposition and would vacation in Augusta, Georgia, during the week of November 15–21.

307 *EM, AWF, DDE Diaries Series*

To Sherman Adams *August 27, 1957*

Memorandum for Governor Adams: If and when the Civil Rights Bill becomes law, we will be called upon promptly to name a Commission that is to be set up under that legislation.[1] Here are some names that occur to me.

Democrats

Robert Woodruff
Allan Shivers
Judge William Hastie[2]

Republicans

Tom Dewey
Franklin Murphy
Clare Boothe Luce[3]

Additional suggestions

Arthur Hays Sulzberger
Sidney Weinberg
Edward H. Litchfield
John McCone
C. D. Jackson
Henry Ford[4]

[1] Eisenhower would sign the Civil Rights Act of 1957 into law on September 9, 1957. For background see no. 266. The act called for the establishment of a six-member bipartisan body with a two-year lifespan. The commission was authorized to issue subpoenas, call witnesses, and set up state advisory committees (Burk, *The Eisenhower Administration and Black Civil Rights*, pp. 228–50).

[2] Robert Woodruff, former president of Coca-Cola, was a close personal friend to the President. Allan Shivers, former governor of Texas (1949–1957), had served as chairman of the board of Western Pipe Line, Inc., since 1957 (see Galambos, *NATO and the Campaign of 1952*, no. 969). William Henry Hastie (LL.B. Harvard 1930, S.J.D. Harvard 1933), an African American, had served as Judge of the Third Circuit Court of Appeals since 1949 and was a director of the National Association for the Advancement of Colored People (NAACP). Hastie had also been dean of the Howard University School of Law from 1939 to 1946, and governor of the Virgin Islands from 1946 to 1949.

[3] For background on Thomas Edmund Dewey, former Republican governor of New York and presidential nominee, see Galambos and van Ee, *The Middle Way*, nos. 457 and 2029. Franklin David Murphy had been chancellor of the University of Kansas since 1951 (*ibid.*, nos. 696, 988). For background on former U.S. Ambassador to Italy Clare Boothe Luce, see *Eisenhower Papers*, vols. I–XVII.

[4] Arthur Hays Sulzberger was publisher, president and director of the *New York Times*. Sidney James Weinberg, an investment banker and partner in Goldman, Sachs, & Company since 1927, had been vice-chairman of the Business Advisory Council, U.S. Department of Commerce, since 1952 (for background see Galambos and van Ee, *The Middle Way*, no. 2079). Edward Harold Litchfield (Ph.D. University of Michigan 1940) was chancellor of the University of Pittsburgh and president of the Governmental Affairs Institute in Washington, D.C., and New York. California industrialist John Alex McCone was president and director of the Joshua Hendy Corporation. He had also served as Secretary of the Air Force from 1950 to 1951 (for background see *ibid.*, no. 1997). For background on long-term presidential advisor Charles Douglas ("C. D.") Jackson see *ibid.*, nos. 8 and 830. Jackson had left the White House to return to Time, Inc., in April 1954. Henry Ford II had been Ford Motor Company president since 1945. An advocate of free trade and reduced government involve-

ment in the economy, Ford had served as chairman of the board of the American Heritage Foundation since 1953 (for background see *ibid.*, no. 87). None of the people suggested by Eisenhower would serve on the Civil Rights Commission. See also Eisenhower, *Waging Peace*, pp. 148–62.

308

EM, AWF, Administration Series

To George Magoffin Humphrey *August 28, 1957*

Dear George: While I admire very much your grandson's brand of golf, I am not prepared to accept him as a "substitute" for the golf I know you can play—*if* you would only practice.[1] I am sad that I can no longer exercise any control over that particular department.[2]

Incidentally, you might tell young George that had I been in his shoes, I would have done as he did. I thought that the rule against grounding the club applied only to a sand trap. But then, when I get in a water hazard I've found it cheaper to lift out and take the penalty.[3]

At the same time, won't you also give your grandson my congratulations on a very fine achievement?

Give my love to Pam and, as always, the best to yourself. *As ever*

[1] On August 23 Humphrey had sent the President a news clipping about his grandson's defeat in a local junior golf tournament. In his cover letter Humphrey said he was preparing the boy "as a substitute golfer." The younger George Humphrey was a fifteen-year-old high school sophomore at the Hotchkiss School in Lakeville, Connecticut (AWF/A). On the President's attempts to get Humphrey to play golf see, for example, no. 136.

[2] On Humphrey's resignation as Secretary of the Treasury see nos. 175 and 260.

[3] On the nineteenth hole of a match-play competition, a penalty had been called on Humphrey for grounding his club when he was in a water hazard (that is, placing the head of his club in the water before he swung). The violation obliged him to concede the hole and the championship match.

309

EM, AWF, DDE Diaries Series

To Aksel Nielsen *August 28, 1957*

Dear Aks: Thanks a lot for the reports.[1] Mrs. Whitman has a fancy machine on which she quickly made an extra copy of the long one so that John and I could each have a copy.[2] I feel an obligation to him and to the children to keep these things fairly up to date.

From the reports it seems to me that everything is going along even better than we could reasonably have expected. While I know that Broomfield has not gone as speedily as you had hoped, still the prospects there seem to be quite bright.[3]

The only one that I might like to dispose of before maturity is the University Hills project. I am not considering anything precipitous, and someday I shall talk to you and discuss my reasons. Perhaps they are without validity.[4]

Thanks again for all your trouble. *As ever*

[1] We have been unable to find the reports in AWF. Nielsen had advised the President on financial investments for many years (for background see Galambos and van Ee, *The Middle Way*, no. 9). Nielsen and Eisenhower had met at the White House on July 18 to discuss Eisenhower's Denver real estate holdings (see Nielsen to Eisenhower, July 7, 1957, AWF/N, and Eisenhower to Nielsen, July 31, 1957, AWF/D).

[2] For background on John Eisenhower's real estate investments see Galambos and van Ee, *The Middle Way*, nos. 1201 and 1686).

[3] Broomfield was a real estate development project in Boulder, Colorado. For developments see no. 764.

[4] University Hills, a shopping and business center in Denver, Colorado, was "entirely finished," Nielsen had written (July 7, 1957). He assured the President that business was "very good," but he went on to say that "additional new stores, the cost of leasing and preparation for new tenants, ran considerably higher than we anticipated. . . ." For developments see no. 612.

310 *EM, WHCF, Official File 61*

To Lewis Lichtenstein Strauss *August 29, 1957*
Personal

Dear Lewis: Thank you for your note regarding the success of the current legislative program of the Atomic Energy Commission.[1] Quite naturally I am delighted with the outcome. Congratulations!

The only thing I don't understand is why we should have had defections on our side such as Senators Aiken, Wiley and Cooper—but then I have decided I shall never fully understand the workings of the Congressional mind.[2] *As ever*

[1] Strauss had written on August 27 (same file as document) to report the success of the Atomic Energy Commission's legislative agenda in Congress (for background see no. 302).

[2] The Commission's major legislative objectives had included the defeat of bills that

would have required the AEC to build and operate additional nuclear reactors at a cost of $400 million. Strauss had praised those senators and congressmen who had supported the Administration. He named Senators William Langer (Rep., N.D.), George Aiken (Rep., Vt.), Henry Clarence Dworshak (Rep., Id.), Alexander Wiley (Rep., Wis.), and John Sherman Cooper (Rep., Ky.), as being among the "few defections" on the Republican side of the Senate; Democratic Senators Harry Flood Byrd (Dem., Va.), A. Willis Robertson (Dem., Va.), and Frank John Lausche (Dem., Oh.) had voted with the Administration. For more on Aiken, Cooper, and Wiley see Galambos and van Ee, *The Middle Way*, nos. 236, 244, 354, and 1183. Cooper had been reelected to the Senate in 1956 after having served as U.S. Ambassador to India between March 1955 and August 1956.

311 — *EM, AWF, Administration Series*

To Hugh Meade Alcorn — *August 30, 1957*

Personal and confidential

Dear Meade: It would appear that some new kind of approach is necessary to convince all Republicans that we are essentially of the same general group in political thinking. I think that we have succumbed too readily to the columnists' efforts to divide us into two "wings." I talked to Senator Knowland about this subject yesterday morning. He agrees generally with me.[1]

Take an example: The Senate Republican leader, Senator Knowland, is popularly depicted as a representative of the conservative wing, while I am placed in the so-called liberal wing. Here are a few facts.

(*a*). Senator Knowland stands among the first four or five of the Republican Senators in his record of voting for measures which I have proposed. With one or two exceptions over the five year period, his differing vote has been based upon some detail or technical feature. We have, at times, differed on applicable policy in foreign affairs—but in important Administrative projects, he has led the fights for approval.[2]

(*b*). He and I agree that we are conservatives. While I have recognized the necessity of the Federal government undertaking functions and responsibilities that far exceed those in which it was engaged forty years ago, yet I have consistently fought against the needless and useless expansion of these functions and responsibilities. Senate members of the so-called "right wing" have acted similarly. Among them are such men as Bridges, Ed Martin, Capehart, Dirksen and Hickenlooper, each of whom I suppose would be categorized by most observers as representatives of the conservative side of the Party.[3] Particularly we have fought against the theory that more and more of the financing of public services of all kinds should be undertaken by the Federal government.

On election night in 1956, over a television circuit, I used the expression "Modern Republicanism," meaning only, of course, Republicanism adapted to the problems of today.[4] Unfortunately that phrase has been used, by those who seek to divide the Republican Party, to indicate the existence of a deep and wide schism in the political thinking of two non-existent "wings" of the Party.

I would be perfectly happy to see some substitute phrase used for what I had in mind. In a press conference I once described a "Modern Republican" as anyone who supports the 1956 Platform. This seems wide enough to me to suit everybody except a few malcontents—but, as I say, I would be delighted to see the phrase dropped in favor of "Republicanism of the 20th Century" or "20th Century Republicanism," or any other appropriate designation.

In any event, I believe it should be possible, along with all the literature you send out to the faithful, to devise and hammer away continuously at the subject of unity. Such unity should be based upon adherence to a *few* common doctrines and beliefs.

For example:

(*a*). We believe that we should oppose the trend toward centralization of responsibility in the Federal government, with its consequent increasing dependence of every citizen upon the Federal government.

(*b*). We believe that agricultural programs should depend more upon increased research, enlargement of markets, increased use of agricultural products, and the setting aside of land to provide for its own enrichment and preservation, rather than upon rigid laws fixing certain monetary prices for given products.

(*c*). We believe that organizations borrowing money from the government should be required to pay interest rates no lower than the cost to the Federal government. In other words, we do not believe that through the guise of artificially low interest rates, we should require the American public to serve the selfish interests of any special group.

(*d*). We believe that private enterprise should be encouraged, but that the leadership of government should be devoted toward insuring a just and wide distribution of the profits from such enterprise.

(*e*). We believe (with McKinley) that isolation is not possible for the United States, and that our best ways of binding other free nations to us are:[5]

(1). By emphasizing our unity in spiritual values.

(2). By opposing Communism and other forms of dictatorship

with our whole might, achieving here at home a unified bipartisan foreign policy, to be developed and exploited by the State Department, supported by Defense, Mutual Aid, and Intelligence organizations.

(3). Through investments, by private capital wherever possible, in those countries whose future development is dependent upon the acquisition of outside investment capital.

(4). Through mutually beneficial, multi-lateral aid.

(*f*). We believe in the equality of all citizens before the law—meaning that the political and economic right of no citizen should be jeopardized because of his race or religion.

(*g*). We believe in sound fiscal policies for the government, thereby helping to combat inflation and to preserve the purchasing power of the working man's savings.

I have not attempted to give above a "Bible for Republicans." I am merely showing that if we agree on such things as these, there are a thousand details and technicalities on which we can disagree and still not destroy the *essential unity of the Republican Party.* In the things to which I have adverted there are plenty of good speeches for anybody seeking office in the United States, whether it be municipal or a national post.

If Republicans do *not want* to have a unity based on these essentially conservative principles applied to 20th century conditions, but instead would rather indulge their personal animosities by passive or active opposition in general elections against an individual who won a primary, then we are going to have a succession of Wisconsins, rather than the kind of sweep that was achieved by the national ticket in 1956.[6]

As a final notation, I have asked Governor Adams to arrange for a reasonably early meeting with you, possibly during the next six weeks, at which he will also invite Senator Knowland and Joe Martin, or their representatives, to discuss further the subject that was brought up at the legislative meeting the other morning when you were there.[7]

All this is for your private study and contemplation, but in your discussions and communications with others you are at liberty to use all, any or none of it as representative *of your own personal thinking.*

With warm regard, *Sincerely*

P.S. The mention of Wisconsin above recalls to my mind the coming election in New Jersey. It seems clear that in Wisconsin the organization did not work together—in fact it seems doubtful that there was any work whatsoever at the level where it counts most, namely the precinct level. I wonder if we are doing all we can to help the Jersey Republicans organize fully and effectively on the precinct, county, district and State levels. I believe that hard work now will save a lot of grief later. For example, I believe that the State organization should know the name of every precinct captain and his address. There should be available lists of all the block and apartment house workers that serve under the precinct captain. In fact, I believe that every precinct captain—maybe every precinct *worker* in the State—should get a letter signed by you telling that individual how important he or she is to the whole Republican Party and thanking them for the work that they do.[8]

We cannot leave these things to chance. Experience and common sense alike dictate a thorough and full organization of all the strength we can bring to bear.

P.S. II. I suggest consultation with Dick Nixon whenever you get a chance. He has a remarkably clear conception of what is necessary if we are to avoid future Wisconsins.[9]

[1] At their breakfast meeting on August 29, Senate Republican leader Knowland and the President had agreed that "despite the schism that newspaper columnists try to create between conservative and liberal Republicans," they were "in accord on much of their thinking" (Ann Whitman memorandum, Aug. 29, 1957, AWF/AWD).

[2] On Knowland's cooperation with Eisenhower during the second Administration see, for example, no. 266; on collaboration during the President's first term see Galambos and van Ee, *The Middle Way*, nos. 1221 and 1552.

[3] Eisenhower was referring to Republican Senators Styles Bridges (N.H.), Edward Martin (Pa.), Homer E. Capehart (Ind.), Everett McKinley Dirksen (Ill.), and Bourke B. Hickenlooper (Iowa). On Eisenhower's relations with Congress see Eisenhower, *Mandate for Change*, pp. 278–307; Eisenhower, *Waging Peace*, pp. 127–47; and Gary W. Reichard, *The Reaffirmation of Republicanism: Eisenhower and the Eighty-Third Congress* (Knoxville, Tenn., 1975), pp. 181–217.

[4] See Galambos and van Ee, *The Middle Way*, no. 2095.

[5] During his address to the Republican National Conference on June 7, 1957, Eisenhower had also quoted former President William McKinley's statement that isolation was no longer possible or desirable (see no. 195). See Lewis L. Gould, *The Presidency of William McKinley*, (Lawrence, Kans., 1980), pp. 32–36, 231–53.

[6] On the 1956 election see Galambos and van Ee, *The Middle Way*, no. 2064, and *Congressional Quarterly Almanac*, vol. XII, *1956*, pp. 751–60. Eisenhower was referring to the results of the August 27 special election in Wisconsin to fill the seat of the late Senator Joseph R. McCarthy. Democrat William Proxmire's victory over former Republican Governor Walter J. Kohler, Jr., was seen by many as a repudiation of Eisenhower and a major defeat for the state Republican party. Analysts blamed Kohler's defeat, in part, on a split within the state GOP between "modern" and "conservative" Republicans (*New York Times*, Aug. 28, 29, 1957).

[7] At an August 27 meeting of legislative leaders, Senator Dirksen had criticized the White House's failure to consult Congress on appointments. Sherman Adams explained the practical problems faced by the Administration in nominating qualified people, and strategies for improving the dialogue between the legislative and executive branches were discussed (see Goodpaster memorandum, Aug. 27, 1957, AWF/LM).

[8] In 1958 the Democrats would defeat incumbent Republicans in New Jersey in elections for one Senate and one House seat (see *Congressional Quarterly Almanac*, vol. XIV, *1958*, pp. 716–17).

[9] See Ambrose, *Nixon*, pp. 438–39.

312

EM, AWF, DDE Diaries Series

TO PERCIVAL FLACK BRUNDAGE *August 30, 1957*

Memorandum for the Director of the Bureau of the Budget: Although I have approved the general policy of holding expenditures to the 1957 level, it is necessary to make an exception in the case of mutual aid.[1] Plans in that area should push ahead as required by the world situation.[2]

[1] For background on Eisenhower's concerns regarding the tensions between balancing the budget and maintaining his foreign aid program see nos. 27, 94, and 137. Eisenhower's note followed weeks of congressional fighting over funding for the mutual security bill. On August 27 the Senate had voted to restore $500,900,000 of the funds cut from the bill by the House of Representatives. See no. 273; for developments see no. 319.

[2] On aid as an instrument of American foreign policy with Greece see no. 280; with Yugoslavia, see no. 294; and in the Middle East, see no. 301.

313

EM, WHCF, Official File 3-A

TO CHARLES W. SEIFERT *August 31, 1957*
Personal

Dear Captain Seifert: Thank you for your letter of August twenty-sixth. I have asked the Chief of Staff of the Army to send one or two representatives of fairly junior grade down to Fort Polk for a visit and to investigate more precisely the problems you present.[1]

Of course there are many matters to be considered in viewing our defense establishment as a whole. I might point out, however, that if we succeed in stabilizing our Army at anything like the levels now foreseen, we will have a force very much greater than we have ever before maintained in peacetime. On top of this, we have spent billions of dollars to give the Army the latest type of equipment and firepower, and we constantly strive to maintain and improve its high degree of effectiveness.[2]

Far from being indifferent to Army requirements and the needs of Army people, during this Administration the Army has benefitted by the passage of the following bills and others as well:

a. Substantial raise in pay in 1955[3]
b. Medical care for dependents[4]
c. Capehart Housing Act[5]
d. Survivorship benefits[6]

One thing the Army cannot promise is that every individual who has served for a period as a Reserve Officer can find in the Army a permanent career.[7]

In any event, I repeat that I shall ask the Chief of Staff to send someone down to your area. These visitors will probably contact you and get full details of your story.[8] *Sincerely*

[1] Seifert, a Captain in the United States Army Reserve serving with the 1st Armored Division at Fort Polk, Louisiana, had written to inform the President of the "considerable discontent, harassment, and low morale" that he claimed had resulted from cuts in the army budget (same file as document). "Every day," he said, "we read that Congress is concerned over the large number of resignations of Regular officers. If someone were interested in this problem to the extent of talking with these officers they would be able to learn why. In essence, most of us feel that we are being unduly criticized, that we are given missions to perform while our hands are tied behind our backs, and above all, that we are not receiving the support of our National leaders." On the 1955 Reserve Forces legislation see Galambos and van Ee, *The Middle Way*, no. 1488.

[2] For background see *ibid.*, nos. 471 and 1233. See also State, *Foreign Relations, 1955–1957*, vol. XIX, *National Security Policy*, pp. 384–94, 531–32, 542–46, and 553–65.

[3] See Galambos and van Ee, *The Middle Way*, no. 1275.

[4] See *ibid.*, no. 554.

[5] See *ibid.*, no. 1775.

[6] See *ibid.*, nos. 363, 1156, and 1478.

[7] Seifert had written that Army reserve officers no longer had the job security that had previously existed. "I am one of the many," he said, "who has been selected for release in order that our budget might be reduced." On the issue of retention of skilled military personnel see no. 226.

[8] We have been unable to locate any further correspondence concerning Seifert's complaints.

5
Little Rock

314

TO CHARLES FOUNTAIN WILLIS, JR.
Personal

September 2, 1957

Dear Charlie:[1] While it was nice to hear from you, there was no occasion for thanking me for signing the certification bill for the additional airlines leading into Alaska. There was nothing personal about my action.[2]

Actually, because this procedure violated my normal practice I was tempted to veto the bill and approved it only because the mass of the argument was that through permanent certification there would be greater chance for amalgamation of the four lines now running into Alaska. This would unquestionably reduce the amount of subsidy devolving upon the government. This has not only been a firm purpose of the Administration from its beginning, but frankly, I hope to get something into the law that will gradually eliminate payments as they become unnecessary.[3]

After I had approved the legislation, I was informed that both personally and by letter you gave your assurances to my Special Counsel that, with the legislation approved, within the year you would work out a merger between your company and one of the other States-Alaska carriers, and gave your further assurances that in any event, with the legislation approved, your company could be made self-sustaining within two years.[4] If this is the result of the legislation—and I hope it is—it will have produced great progress.

Please convey my greetings to your bride[5] and, of course, best wishes to yourself. *Sincerely*

[1] For background on Willis, president of Alaska Airlines, Inc., and assistant to Sherman Adams from 1953 to 1955, see Galambos and van Ee, *The Middle Way*, no. 1476.

[2] On August 26 the President had signed into law H.R. 4520, authorizing permanent certification of Northwest, Alaska, and Pacific Northern Airlines to operate routes between the United States and Alaska. The legislation did not affect the permanent certificate held by Pan American Airways on its United States-Alaska route (see *New York Times*, Aug. 27, 1957, and *Public Papers of the Presidents: Eisenhower, 1957*, pp. 632–33).

[3] Eisenhower had said that he signed the legislation with "some reluctance" due to the subsidies the government was paying the Alaska and Pacific Northern Airlines. The President was also concerned that the legislation had bypassed the normal certification procedure established by the Civil Aeronautics Act. Despite these reservations Eisenhower had approved the bill because the "complete dependency of Alaska upon air transportation presented unusual circumstances." Eisenhower was also persuaded by congressional belief that permanent certification would over the long run actually reduce the need for subsidy, since "the carriers will be in a better position to finance modern, economical equipment, and make long-range plans" (*ibid.*).

[4] No merger would take place. For developments see the following document.

[5] Willis had married the former Elizabeth Firestone in 1954.

315 *EM, WHCF, Official File 62*

To Gerald Demuth Morgan *September 2, 1957*
Memorandum

If at all possible, please let me have an answer to my question about the effect of the certificates as now granted for Northwest and Pan Am Airlines using the Great Circle route across the Pacific.[1]

A possibility presented to me is this. Northwest originates traffic in New York, Chicago and so forth for its trips across the Pacific. Since much of the trans-Pacific traffic originates in the East, it would be only natural for Northwest to send some of its flights direct from Chicago, via Anchorage, to Japan as the shortest and most economical route. But because Northwest can land only seven flights per week in Japan, this particular practice would deprive the northwest of direct Great Circle passage to the Orient.

If this is true, it would seem logical for us to recall our action on the Pan Am Great Circle route to allow the latter company to pick up mail and passengers in Seattle and in the northwest. I understand that, provided this seems a logical action under the circumstances now existing, I have until tomorrow, inclusive, to take such action. This belief is based on some information I have been given that for one month following approval of any CAB action involving foreign routes, I have authority for modification if I so desire.[2]

Any or all of the assumptions above indicated could, I realize, be incorrect, but the point is if they are correct and fair, then I think we had better take a good, hard and very quick look at the Pan Am certification over the Great Circle route.

[1] For background on Eisenhower's request to White House Special Counsel "Jerry" Morgan see no. 224; for background on Morgan see Galambos and van Ee, *The Middle Way*, no. 431. The President was responding to an application by Pan American Airways for permission to pick up passengers at Seattle and Portland on its "great circle" route flights to Asia. The Pan American request was opposed by Northwest Airlines, which currently possessed the exclusive rights to fly passengers on this route. Pan American had asked the Civil Aeronautics Board to reverse its August decision (which Eisenhower had approved) denying Pan American's certification because Northwest's claim that increased competition would cause it to lose eleven million dollars was exaggerated (see Pelly to Adams, Aug. 29, 1957, Milley to Thomas, Aug. 29, 1957, and other papers in same file as document; see also *Milwaukee Journal*, Sept. 5, 1957, and *New York Times*, Sept. 4, 1957).

[2] On September 3 Eisenhower would take action favorable to Pan American, as outlined in this memorandum. The President would tell the Chairman of the Civil Aeronautics Board that he had decided to hold "temporarily in abeyance final decision on the question whether Pan American World Airways should be granted authority to serve Seattle and Portland on the Great Circle route between California and Japan" (Eisenhower to Durfee, Sept. 3, 1957, same file as document). Eisenhower would also ask the CAB to send him the latest statistics on traffic between the United States and Tokyo and inform him of any changes that took place. In February, 1958, however,

the President would affirm the CAB's decision to deny Pan American the right to serve Seattle and Portland on its Great Circle route to Tokyo (see *New York Times*, Feb. 5, 1958); for developments see no. 573.

316 — *EM, WHCF, Official File 99*

To Samuel Taliaferro Rayburn — *September 2, 1957*

Dear Mr. Sam: I have made some informal inquiries into the allegations made to you by one of your associates that counterpart funds in various countries are provided to visiting Congressmen recklessly and immoderately, often at the insistence of local State Department officials.[1]

From reports made to me no authority for decision is left with the State Department, and that Department has no responsibility for determining the wisdom of expenditures made. I enclose a short report prepared by the Department.[2] It seems to me that whatever corrective action is taken must have a first requisite of action within the Congress.

If you should desire, I would be glad to go further into the matter and get as complete a report as possible, before the next session begins.

Incidentally, I could not look up the particular case reported to you for the simple reason that I had no identification as to individual or country from which to begin. However, I have asked the Secretary of State to inform all the Embassies that in no case are they to be in the position of "forcing" money upon anyone, no matter what the individual's authority for requisition may be.

Please let me know if there is anything more you want me to do at this time. Meantime, I hope that you will get the vacation and rest that you must badly need.[3]

With warm regard, *Sincerely*

[1] Counterpart funds, established by the Economic Cooperation Act of 1948 and succeeding Mutual Security Acts, were special local-currency accounts established in the countries where the United States had provided non-military assistance. A percentage of these funds, which were retained at many American embassies, was reserved for use by the United States, particularly by members of Congress to defray the costs of foreign travel. For background see Galambos, *NATO and the Campaign of 1952*, no. 68; see also Interviews with Raymond J. Saulnier, March 4 and 5, 1997, EP.

Eisenhower and Rayburn had discussed mutual security legislation at a breakfast meeting on August 19 (Diary, Aug. 19, 1957, AWF/AWD; see also McCabe to Persons, Sept. 4, 1957, same file as document).

[2] Under Secretary of State Herter had reported that controlling the use of counterpart funds by congressmen was "the primary responsibility of Congress." The De-

partment of State was only the "disbursing agent." After a congressional committee chairman had authorized the use of the reserves, the department instructed the embassies to provide the funds to the designated travelers (Becker to Herter, Aug. 21, 1957; and Herter to Adams, Aug. 22, 1957, same file as document).

[3] For further correspondence regarding the use of counterpart funds see no. 405.

317

EM, AWF, DDE Diaries Series

TO ANDREW JACKSON GOODPASTER, JR. *September 2, 1957*
Memorandum

In line with our discussion this morning, I suggest the following procedure for future handling of Congressional mail.[1]

As quickly as possible after the receipt of letters from Senators or Representatives, I should like to sign an answer, prepared by one of the liaison officers, along these lines:

a. A short letter indicating that sympathetic consideration will be given to the problem presented.

b. When applicable (relatively few) a statement that the matter is outside President's approved program and cannot be feasibly considered.

c. A statement that any further consideration or communication will, in the majority of cases, be between the Congressman and the liaison officer[2] (or Department to which matter is referred, etc.).

The only exception to this rule should be when the letter is obviously partisan in its criticism or complaint, in which case the staff officer may answer over his own signature.

[1] According to Ann Whitman, Eisenhower had discussed this issue "at length" with Goodpaster (Ann Whitman memorandum, Sept. 2, 1957, AWF/AWD).

[2] Wilton B. ("Jerry") Persons had been Eisenhower's congressional liaison since 1953.

318

EM, AWF, Administration Series

TO BERNARD MANNES BARUCH *September 3, 1957*
Personal

Dear Bernie: Thank you for your note, as well as for its enclosure written by Mr. Lubbell.[1]

There are some challenging thoughts in the document. One point on which he does not dwell is that Soviet economic aid can well be used as a vehicle for a political nomination that could make of a country a satellite. Turkey, in particular, is very alarmed that, facing the Soviet colossus on the north, she will wake up to find a Soviet power firmly planted directly in her rear. Iraq, Jordan and Lebanon are more than apprehensive.

With regard to the suggestion that "the issue could be handled to raise the question inside Egypt and Syria whether the rulers of these countries are wise in mortgaging so much of their resources for the purchase of arms instead of using those resources to build their countries economically." This was exactly the line we took when we were working with Egypt on the Aswan Dam and with Syria, Israel and others on the Johnston plan.[2] Specifically, the Aswan Dam project involved support by the British, by the World Bank and by ourselves—all to be given to Egypt on the basis that that country would avoid building up its fighting forces and would devote all possible economic resources to carrying out its portion of the project. You can see that there are a number of reasons for this—one being that only when the country itself had a big stake in the project would it be seriously prosecuted. Egypt demanded a number of concessions and we dropped the project.

Later, after Egypt had loaded up with arms from the Soviets and had recruited a much greater strength into their armed forces, she came back and suddenly stated she would accept the original proposals. But the conditions had changed, adversely so far as Egypt's capacity to support the project was concerned.

I recite this merely to show that we have tried to give a great deal of attention to the economic rather than military development in the Mid East.

As for your suggestion (and Mr. Lubbell's) that I make a major address, I rather think that between October first and January first I shall have to make at least three.[3] I think I shall have to deal with the question of our home economy and the threat of inflation, the world situation in general, including disarmament, and finally, with the question of mutual security pacts and aid, with special attention to the Mid East. However, my mind is not fully made up; as you probably suspect I despise giving "major speeches." But I have made up my mind that I am going to do it if for no other reason than to set an example to a lot of business, professional and governmental leaders, possibly encouraging them to go and do likewise.[4]

With warm personal regard, *As ever*

P.S. I thoroughly enjoyed your book, but in one respect I think I differ from the critics.[5] They find all its dramatic interest in the making of millions; I was more absorbed in those portions of your book that dealt with your family relationships. There are a number of lovely thoughts expressed, generally and very rightly indirectly, that touched me deeply.

[1] Samuel Lubell (B.S. Columbia 1933), a Polish-born newspaperman, author, and political analyst, often wrote Baruch on international matters. Lubell, prompted by Communist inroads into Syria (see no. 301), had suggested to Baruch that if Soviet aid to Syria were substantial enough to strain the Soviet economy, the Politbureau would split between those who favored "imperialistic adventures and those who want the domestic interests of Russia put first. In fact," he said, "it might even be worth an effort to try to stiffen Syria's bargaining power vis a vis the Soviets so the Syrians can extract more aid" (Lubell to Baruch, Aug. 25, 1957, AWF/A, Baruch Corr.). Lubell's point, "about our keeping our heads and not getting upset if the Soviets start giving things away is a good one," Baruch told Eisenhower. "Now is the time to sit steady in the boat" (Baruch to Eisenhower, Aug. 28, 1957, AWF/A).

[2] For background on the U.S. initial offer of aid to Egypt for construction of the Aswan Dam, and its subsequent withdrawal, see Galambos and van Ee, *The Middle Way*, nos. 1759 and 1946; on the plan developed by special Ambassador Eric Johnston to divert the waters of the Jordan River see no. 230.

[3] Both Baruch and Lubell had asked Eisenhower to consider a speech that would focus attention on the buildup of arms in the Middle East. Lubell believed that U.S. policy should focus on creating conditions that would enable Middle Eastern countries to concentrate their resources on peaceful economic development rather than armaments.

[4] Eisenhower would speak to the nation on science and national security on November 7 and on international communism and mutual defense on November 13 (*Public Papers of the Presidents: Eisenhower, 1957*, pp. 789–99, 807–16; see also Telephone conversation, Eisenhower and Dulles, Sept. 3, 1957, Dulles Papers, Telephone Conversations).

[5] The book was the first volume of Baruch's memoirs, *Baruch: My Own Story*.

319 — *EM, AWF, DDE Diaries Series*

To [Richard Milhous Nixon] — *September 3, 1957*

The subject that I wanted to talk about is so comprehensive, in fact so undefined in some of its aspects, that it scarcely makes a suitable topic for a letter. However, I am herein setting down something of what I had in mind, so that when we get a chance to talk you will have had some opportunity for advanced contemplation.[1]

My basic thought is that you might find it possible—and intriguing—to be of even more help in our whole governmental program dealing with affairs abroad than you have been in the past. By your extensive travel you have been of inestimable assistance to the Secretary of State and to me. In addition you have gained an understanding of our foreign problems that is both unusual and comprehensive. My belief is that this knowledge and comprehension, supplemented by your special position of having one foot in the Executive Branch and one foot in the Legislative Branch, can be advantageously used in helping to lay out advanced programs and schedules for obtaining favorable legislative action on Executive proposals dealing with these matters.[2]

I refer particularly to strictly State Department legislation, to Mutual Security Assistance, to the Reciprocal Trade Act, to Technical Assistance, to the Development Fund, and so on.[3]

I well realize that these subjects, vast as they are, cannot possibly be treated in isolation from all others that the Executive Department is compelled to put before the Congress. But because all foreign programs are—or should be—non-partisan in character, I believe that you could give special attention to them without compromising your necessary attitude of objectivity and non-partisanship in the performance of your Constitutional duties, (even if the knowledge that you are doing so should become public).

As an example of a problem: Foster suggests—and I tend to concur—that all military assistance, and perhaps defense support, should not only be carried in the Defense Budget, but the defense part of it should not even have a separate classification; possibly legislation could merely state that not to exceed "x" percentage of certain appropriations could be used at the President's direction for helping support troops of allied nations, where such action would provide the United States with necessary, as well as the most economical, security. So far I have not even had a chance to talk to the Budget Bureau about the possibility of submitting estimates on this basis, but the mere posing of the question illustrates how necessary it is that we get the earliest possible understanding and agreement between the Executive and Legislative officials.[4]

The timing of legislative proposals, beginning with the State of the Union speech and going right on through the session, is another matter that should be studied and, if possible, programmed in advance.

While dealing with such matters as these, it would be realized, of course, that there is an interrelationship between foreign programs and our expenditures and taxation—in fact, the domestic economy in general. Consequently, while the main mission I would see for you would be helping the State Department plan its legislative presentations, you would at the same time find it needful to maintain contact with Governor Adams and the liaison group here at the White House so that the entire legislative program could be presented in the most advantageous manner.

The above is dictated hurriedly and with no thought that the ideas expressed are complete or possibly even entirely clear. But you will see what I am getting at, and I assure you both Foster Dulles and

Sherman Adams would welcome your thinking and your help on such matters as these.[5]

[1] According to Eisenhower's handwritten notation at the top of this memorandum, copies were sent to Secretary Dulles and General Wilton B. Persons, who was in charge of legislative liaison in the White House. The proposals in this letter were to serve as the basis of a conversation Eisenhower would have with the three men at the Executive Mansion later on this same day.

[2] In February Nixon had told Dulles that he wanted to be more involved in substantive tasks for the Administration, particularly in international affairs. After the two men had discussed the possibilities again on September 2, Dulles and Eisenhower talked about a greater role for Nixon in guiding legislation through Congress. Although the President was concerned that Sherman Adams and Persons might react negatively to such a role for the Vice-President, he agreed to outline his ideas in this letter (Stephen E. Ambrose, *Nixon: The Education of a Politician 1913–1962* [New York, 1987], pp. 439–40).

[3] Eisenhower was undoubtedly eager for a way to facilitate passage of his legislative agenda in Congress. On this day he had signed the Mutual Security Act, which had cut more than one billion dollars from his original foreign aid requests. Frustrated by this and other actions of the Eighty-fifth Congress, the President would later characterize the 1957 session as "the low point in effective cooperation between the administration and the Congress" (Eisenhower, *Waging Peace*, pp. 144–47).

[4] On May 21 Eisenhower had requested that Congress appropriate funds for military assistance as part of the Department of Defense budget (see *Public Papers of the Presidents: Eisenhower, 1957*, p. 389; for background see nos. 119 and 312). For developments see no. 323.

[5] After his discussions with Eisenhower, Dulles telephoned Nixon, then vacationing in West Virginia, and read him parts of this message. Nixon expressed surprise that Eisenhower "seemed to accept the idea so quickly" and agreed to return to Washington later this same day to discuss the proposal (see DDE dictation, Sept. 1957, AWF/D; Telephone conversations, Dulles and Nixon, and Eisenhower and Dulles, Sept. 3, 1957, Dulles Papers, Telephone Conversations). At the meeting Eisenhower would propose that Nixon have primary responsibility for the preparation of that part of the legislative program that related to national security matters, including foreign aid. Nixon replied that he would be glad to undertake this function (Ambrose, *Nixon*, p. 440; and Ann Whitman memorandum, Sept. 3, 1957, AWF/AWD).

On the following day Secretary Dulles would relate the details of the meeting to Attorney General Brownell: "The Pres does recognize that this cannot be done in a vacuum," Dulles reported. "From a constitutional standpoint it is better to stick to an area where he has clear statutory authority." Dulles also told Brownell that Nixon was "very happy about it" (Telephone conversation, Sept. 4, 1957, Dulles Papers, Telephone Conversations). On the success of this expanded role for the Vice-President see Ambrose, *Nixon*, pp. 440–41.

320

EM, AWF, DDE Diaries Series

To Sherman Adams

September 3, 1957

Dear Sherm: For a variety of reasons I think that our plan for visiting Parmachenee Lake late in September should be most tentative and subject to almost instant cancellation.[1]

In the first place, I am told that with the advancing season many of the hotels, inns and so on are closed and that accommodations for secret service and press would be hard to get. On top of this, I also understand that it would be difficult to install the necessary communication lines.

Finally, Mrs. Ike is not returning to a feeling of health and vigor, even though her doctors say that medically she is doing splendidly, as rapidly as she had expected.[2] I would not want to be absent for two or three days at a time when she was feeling in the slightest bit apprehensive or uneasy—or, for that matter, just plain miserable.

I think in about a week we should take another good look at the whole proposition.[3] *As ever*

[1] Parmachenee Lake is a resort in western Maine on Rump Mountain. As it turned out, the Eisenhowers would vacation in Newport, Rhode Island, September 4–30.
[2] The First Lady had undergone gynecological surgery on August 6 (see no. 291).
[3] The President's Rhode Island vacation would be marred by the school desegregation crisis in Little Rock, Arkansas (see no. 330 and 355). He would not visit Lake Parmachenee.

321

EM, AWF, Name Series

To Aksel Nielsen

September 3, 1957

Dear Aks: Of first order of importance in your letter of the twenty-eighth is the fact that your bull won the grand championship at the Arapahoe Fair. I can't seem to remember which animal you might mean—and next time you write, I'd appreciate knowing a little more about him.[1]

I'm glad that Min is feeling well; I was in touch with her fairly frequently immediately after Mamie's operation, and Mamie has called her almost every day in the last week or so.[2] As far as the will is concerned, I think it is too bad that she wanted to make the change but I do understand the reason. The next time you are here I'll discuss it all with you.[3]

I am complimented to know that the new post office in Fraser has been built on "Eisenhower Drive" and it occurs to me that I would like to send some sort of memento to the people of Fraser, perhaps for the city hall if you think it would be appropriate. Do you have any suggestions?[4]

At any rate, you know how much I'd like to be there when the building is dedicated, and just how very much I'd like the opportunity for some time in Colorado this fall. I have resigned myself not to think in such terms, and as of the middle of next week Mamie and I are going up to Newport—she to continue her convalescence while I hope for at least a medium respite from official duties.[5]

I can't remember when you plan next to come East; I hope it will be soon. Meantime, my warm regard and thanks once again for all you do for all members of the Eisenhower family. *As ever*

[1] Eisenhower's marginal notes on Nielsen's letter (in AWF/N) indicate that he may have asked someone—possibly Ann Whitman—to draft this letter for him.

[2] Nielsen had reported on the health of the First Lady's mother, Elivera Carlson Doud. Mrs. Eisenhower had undergone gynecological surgery on August 6 (see no. 291).

[3] Nielsen said he had advised against a change in Mrs. Doud's will. "It was also Mamie's wish that it be changed," he added. "I just thought you ought to know." Nielsen would next visit the White House on January 13, 1958.

[4] The new post office building, Nielsen had written, would be dedicated on September 6. On October 4 he would send Eisenhower pictures of the dedication ceremony; the photographs would also show the exact location of Eisenhower Drive (AWF/N). Nielsen's reply is not in EM.

[5] The Eisenhowers would vacation in Newport, Rhode Island, September 4–30.

322

EM, AWF, International Series: Denmark

To Hans Christian Svane Hansen — *September 6, 1957*

Dear Mr. Prime Minister:[1] Your message of August 15, 1957 expressing the earnest hope that delay could be avoided in enactment of pending legislation to authorize settlement of the Danish shipping case, was very much in our minds during the final days of the recently closed session of the Congress. A similar hope impelled us to seek enactment of the enabling legislation, even through the last day of the session.[2]

The Congress, however, adjourned leaving the bill on the calendar of the House of Representatives. Accordingly, attempts to obtain passage of the bill can be resumed without the necessity of repeating any of the steps already taken toward the bill's enactment. I can assure you that I earnestly desire an early solution of the shipping case and every effort will be made to secure final legislative action early in the next session of the Congress.[3] *Sincerely*

[1] Hansen had been Minister of Finance and Minister of Trade before becoming Denmark's Minister of Foreign Affairs in 1953. He become Prime Minister in February 1955. The State Department drafted this letter.

[2] Denmark had long pressed the U.S. government to settle claims resulting from the requisition by the United States of forty Danish ships during World War II. The controversy had prompted the Danish government to withhold ratification of the Treaty of Friendship, Commerce and Navigation signed in 1951 and ratified by the United States in 1953. In December 1954 the former Prime Minister had asked Eisenhower to intervene personally in the case to avoid "further regrettable delays." At that time Secretary Dulles told Eisenhower that he believed that the Justice Department was handling the situation "on too much of a purely legalistic basis without regard to the attitude of Denmark during the war which, at great risk, gave us the facilities of Iceland and Greenland, and without regard to the present importance of Danish good will . . ." (Hedtoft to Eisenhower, Dec. 3, 1954; and Dulles to Eisenhower, Dec. 6, 1954, AWF/I: Denmark; see also Kauffmann to Dulles, Dec. 6, 1954).

Dulles had told Eisenhower in January 1955 that there was no progress to report to the Danish government and suggested that the President express to the Prime Minister his hopes that the problem could soon be resolved (Dulles to Eisenhower, Jan. 24, 1955; and Eisenhower to Hedtoft, Jan. 25, 1955, *ibid.*).

On April 4, 1957, a bill calling for the payment of $5.3 million to Denmark, a sum accepted by the Danes on the condition that the legislation be enacted by June 30, had been introduced in Congress. Failure to pass the bill had prompted Prime Minister Hansen's August 15 appeal to Eisenhower (AWF/I: Denmark). On August 23 Eisenhower had told Dulles that "he thought there was a strong moral case for the Danes" and that he wanted to push the legislation through Congress without using his special Mutual Security Fund to pay for the settlement (Memorandum of Conversation, Aug. 23, 1957, Dulles Papers, White House Memoranda Series). Later that same day Eisenhower would tell Dulles that General Persons was following the situation closely and would let the Secretary know of any new developments (AWF/D-H).

[3] Congress would pass the First Supplemental Appropriations Act of fiscal 1959, which would include a payment to the government of Denmark of $5.3 million, on August 21, 1958; Eisenhower would sign the bill on August 27 (*Congressional Quarterly Almanac*, vol. XIII, *1957*, p. 353; see also Hansen to Eisenhower, May 28, June 14, 1958, AWF/I: Denmark; and *U.S. Department of State Bulletin* 38, no. 991 [June 23, 1958], 1055).

323 — *EM, WHCF, Official File 101-Y*

To Cochran Bryant Supplee — *September 7, 1957*

Dear Mr. Supplee: I am glad to have your letter of August thirtieth recalling your visit with our late friend Thomas J. Watson. He was a great American and intensely concerned with the problems confronting our country.[1]

Some of the questions and comments in your letter dismay me as much as the situations provoking them apparently dismay you.[2]

With respect to civil rights let me say plainly that my position is simply that of being faithful to my oath to support and uphold the Constitution of the United States. A President of all the people must defend the rights of all citizens, most especially he must do all he rightfully can to make sure that the basic right to vote is not denied any citizen entitled to it.

You speak of the giving of billions to undeserving and unappreciative foreigners. I take it you are referring here to the Mutual Security program. I say to you quite frankly that in my opinion there are no more important dollars in our Federal budget than the dollars for Mutual Security. Of all the issues before the American people none approaches in significance the keeping of the peace and the preventing of the nuclear holocaust of World War III. Should that unspeakable disaster befall us, nothing else would matter much. Our Mutual Security program is not based on giving anything to those who are deserving or who are appreciative; it is based rather on the simple proposition that, in the event of an emergency, it is better to have the majority of the world's population and resources on our side rather than on the side of the Communists. That this program has been successful is evidenced by the fact that the Russians have turned away from trying to win their objectives by military aggression and have sought to imitate our own efforts in the field of economic assistance in various countries throughout the world.

Finally you speak of the problem of high prices. As I said in my most recent press conference, that is the central internal problem we face.[3] It has many causes. We must do all we can to alleviate these causes. We must continue to overbalance the Federal budget and hold down government spending to the minimum consistent with defense requirements. We must continue to pursue sound monetary policies so that undue credit expansion does not stoke the fires of inflation. We must, as consumers, exercise judgment in the prices we are willing to pay for postponable items in our personal budgets. We must impress upon the leaders of labor and management the significance of carrying out their wage negotiations with a mind toward the interest of the whole nation in price stability. We must work toward the day when we can reduce the high level of taxes which in many ways have contributed to inflation. All these avenues of action daily engage the energy and attention of this Administration.

I appreciate very much your expression of support of me and this Administration. I hope this letter will help to make clear the basis of some of the views I hold which have given rise to the questions you raise.

With best wishes. *Sincerely*

[1] Supplee (M.B.A. New York University 1952) was an account executive with Young and Rubicam. He had spent several hours discussing Administration policies with the former president and chairman of the board of International Business Machines Corporation, Thomas J. Watson, before his death in June. Although both men had agreed that Eisenhower was "the greatest President since Lincoln," Supplee was concerned that Americans had "much cause for worry" (same file as document). For background on Watson see Galambos, *Chief of Staff*, no. 789.

[2] "You have done your best to give the vote to the Negroes in the South," Supplee had written, "despite protestations of your white contemporaries. You have done your best to persuade Congress to give billions to undeserving and in many ways unappreciative foreigners. Do you not think it is time to devote all the energies of your great Administration to the subject of reducing prices?" (*ibid.*).

[3] See *Public Papers of the Presidents: Eisenhower, 1957*, pp. 643, 647–49.

324 — *EM, AWF, DDE Diaries Series*

To Clara Swinson — *September 7, 1957*

Dear Mrs. Swinson: Thank you for your letter. I sympathize fully with your desire to have better equipment in your classrooms.

Some of the difficulties have arisen out of conditions that were national in scope. By this I mean that two wars and the great depression of the early thirties interfered materially with the proper construction and equipping of our schools. I have urged the Congress to help correct these deficiencies—limiting Federal participation to what might be called emergency construction of the necessary buildings.[1]

But the problem is not one that lies exclusively with the Federal government, as you know. Indeed some states are stoutly opposed to any entry of the Federal government into school affairs, maintaining that the final result would be Federal control of education. At any rate, primary responsibility for the schools of our country has traditionally and properly devolved upon the local and state authorities. Only under unusual or special circumstances has the Federal government had any function in this field.[2]

However, I think you over-simplify the question when you imply that it is a matter of using funds for schools and equipment in our country versus schools that might be built with mutual aid funds in foreign countries. One of the paramount problems today is to insure the security of our country, and to have available the defense we must have against the great Communist threat that faces all free countries in the world today. We do not spend the money that is called "foreign aid" as charity; we spend it to provide one of the necessary insurances against war, the most costly action in which any nation could indulge. There is an important by-product, too. If we can help raise the standards of education and living of the people in the so-called under-developed countries and make of them staunch friends and defenders of the free way of life, then we have—cheaply—helped ourselves.[3]

I suggest that you constantly bring to the attention of your local school board, your local municipal officers, your State Congressmen and Senators, the situation that so much and so rightly troubles you.

With best wishes, *Sincerely*

[1] In January Eisenhower had sent to Congress a special message on federal aid to education (see *Public Papers of the Presidents: Eisenhower, 1957*, pp. 89–95). Repeating calls he had made in both 1955 and 1956 for federal aid for school construction, the President had argued that the lack of physical facilities, arising out of World War II civil construction bans, was a "temporary emergency situation" in which Federal assistance was appropriate. For background see Galambos and van Ee, *The Middle Way*, nos. 1483 and 1910. Swinson's letter is not in AWF.

[2] On July 25, 1957, the House of Representatives had defeated H.R. 1, a bill to provide federal aid for school construction (see *Congressional Quarterly Almanac*, vol. XIII, *1957*, pp. 588–93). State opposition to federal aid continued to be based upon fears of interference in the process of integration of schools, as well as concerns over control of curriculum. Some in Congress wondered why the government did not simply provide outright appropriations to the states. For developments see no. 333. See also Clowse, *Brainpower for the Cold War*, pp. 40–49.

[3] Eisenhower frequently reiterated his belief in the importance of the mutual security program; see nos. 60, 137, and 138.

325 — *EM, AWF, DDE Diaries Series*

To Carol Beane — *September 7, 1957*

Dear Carol: Thank you for your thoughtful letter. America will never tolerate the things you fear, though I admit that we do have many imperfections in our society. But the important thing to remember is that we are making progress toward their correction and that progress, to be lasting, must be steady and sometimes painfully slow.[1]

With best wishes, *Sincerely*

[1] Beane, a thirteen-year-old African-American girl, had written Eisenhower on August 29 (WHCF/PPF 24-B-3). She had commented that although she did not know all the details of the new Civil Rights Act (see nos. 266 and 307), she believed in the promise of the Declaration of Independence. "America has built a great nation with these words and others as its foundation," she wrote. "If we destroy the equality of men for a little thing such as color, and liberty for the same reason, You could well say the America that we know today has begun her downfall."

326

EM, WHCF, Official File 9

To George Magoffin Humphrey

September 7, 1957

Dear George: Many thanks for your note.[1] I am afraid it sounds immodest to admit it myself, but Mr. Baird wrote me a note the other day and said that I had completely "disarmed" him to the point where he accepted the appointment.[2] Now *why* can't I have the same success with members of the Congress?[3]

I agree that we must get down to earth in our thinking about some of our problems, but while this weather maintains I am going to push most of our worries to the back of my mind.[4]

Give my love to Pam and, as always, the best to yourself. *Sincerely*

P.S. I met your friend George Widener at the golf course yesterday.[5] While I am afraid (because Mamie is not yet completely strong) that we won't be able to see Mr. and Mrs. Widener socially during the time they are here, I hope in the future that we may do so.[6]

[1] Former Treasury Secretary Humphrey had congratulated the President on the appointment of Julian Braden Baird as Under Secretary of the Treasury for Monetary Affairs (Aug. 29, 1957, same file as document).

[2] Baird (Ph.B. Yale 1915) was chairman of the board of directors of the First National Bank of St. Paul, Minnesota. In his letter accepting the appointment (Sept. 2) Baird said he had expected to decline Eisenhower's offer, but "you were most disarming." Eisenhower had replied on September 4. Both Baird's letter and the President's reply are in the same file as the document.

[3] The first session of the Eighty-fifth Congress had adjourned on August 30 (see no. 302).

[4] The Eisenhowers were vacationing in Newport, Rhode Island.

[5] Widener, who resided in Philadelphia, Pennsylvania, had a vacation home in Newport.

[6] The First Lady had undergone gynecological surgery on August 6 (see no. 291). On September 9 the Eisenhowers would call to arrange a visit with the Wideners, but would discover that they had returned to Philadelphia (see Eisenhower to Widener, Sept. 10, 1957, AWF/D).

327

EM, AWF, DDE Diaries Series

To Robin and Terrill Scatena

September 9, 1957

Dear Robin and Terrill: I am complimented that you should write to me for an explanation of the things concerning our country and our government that are troubling your minds.[1] None of the questions you ask can be answered in any single or simple statement. Each is so difficult and so many factors are involved that all citizens, including those that have been elected to governmental office, are sometimes puzzled in the attempt to find a solution that seems completely logical.

In spite of this, there are one or two facts that could well serve as a starting point for our thinking in these matters. Every single generation of Americans has had its own individual problems. Frequently the future has looked dark and discouraging—even to those young people who, normally, have far more courage and optimism than do their elders. A second fact is that America has not only successfully surmounted every crisis and period of discouragement, but her people have invariably gone forward to enjoy a fuller and better life spiritually, intellectually and materially.

The first thing that I would say, therefore, is that just as courage, fortitude and faith carried our forebears through their trials and difficulties, so will the same characteristics today and tomorrow bring to us solutions that are just and fair.

You are fearful about the depreciating value of the dollar; you correctly observe that unless we are successful in halting this trend, the insurance policies for which we pay today will not, some years later, buy the things and services and conveniences that they would today. The same applies to our pensions, to our savings accounts and to our savings bonds.

Many things combine to cause this cheapening of the dollar—or, to put it another way, this constant rise in the cost of the things we need for daily living. In general the basic cause is that in recent years we have been trying to do too much too fast in terms of making and building things to sell. When too many Americans have too many plans in the economic field they want to carry out all at once, this creates pressures on resources—manpower, machines, material. In such a situation prices tend to rise.

The causes are of various kinds. One is the money spent by the government to provide all of the services that our population either needs or demands from the city, the state or the Federal government. Then, today, the Federal government has to spend an enormous amount—far more than half of all it collects—for the necessary defense of our country against the great Communist threat that faces all free countries today.[2] Incidentally, it is part of this process of providing for the common security that occasions our expenditures that you hear called "foreign aid." We do not spend this money as charity for others. We spend in the sense of a premium on insurance policies against war, the most costly action in which any nation could indulge. War's cost, moreover, is paid in the lives of our young people, as well as in staggering amounts of money.

Another expenditure that cannot be escaped is the enormous interest we pay on our public debt. This interest must be paid fully and exactly on time, otherwise all of the war bonds in the hands of all of our people would collapse in value.

The rest of the money spent by the Federal government goes in general for the services that our people demand: aid to the states for helping take care of disabled and unemployed; aid to farmers in an effort to help them in the transition from an expanded wartime economy to a more stable peace time condition in which they can share more equitably in the national income; pensions and aid for veterans (in the amount of some billions of dollars); aid to all kinds of medical and health research, and many other things. Some of these things *could* be done by peoples and families for themselves. Or, if not by themselves, then by cities and states, rather than the Federal government. But by action of the Congress, some of these services are pressed upon the Federal government and as long as the people seem to think this is the best way to do it, then the price must be paid. I have been carrying on an effort to get more people to understand that more things can be done locally and with more efficiency by private citizens groups themselves. To that end I have set up a Federal-State Commission, to consider problems such as these.[3]

Another cause of inflation is the rising cost of services. That is, if every workman gets higher wages for his services in excess of his increased efficiency, his employer is confronted with the need to raise the price of the things he sells. Consequently the dollar buys less and so we say it has been cheapened.

There are so many additional causes for rising prices or a cheapening dollar that eminent scholars and scientists have written whole books to describe them. More than this, some of these eminent scholars disagree with others, so that again we say that there just is no easy answer to the whole thing.

Nevertheless, there has been real progress made in recent years in slowing up this cheapening process. Usually the one or two decades immediately following the close of a great war have been an era in the effort of rising prices and cheapening money. In any event, right after World War II we had a very marked period of this kind and for some years, with only one or two brief interruptions, the cost of living went up at the rate of over seven percent a year. Beginning in 1952, this process was slowed up sharply, and in the past five years, the total rise has been something between five and six percent *for the entire period.* In the past year and a half, we have seen most of this increase.

But your parents are correct in saying that we should strive—all of us—to keep a sound dollar. By this I mean to stop the inflation as rapidly as possible, without bringing upon us serious consequences in other directions, and thereafter to keep it under watchful control.

Every agency of the Federal government is striving to do this. But all history shows that it is not easy. We want our workmen to earn more. But whenever they obtain a pay raise that is in excess of the increased efficiency of the workmen then, as I pointed out before, we have another inflationary force.

And so it goes throughout our entire industry.

This letter is admittedly rather rambling, and you will realize that I have little opportunity either to reduce its length or make it more exact in its explanation. But I put these things down so that you will realize also that I do have some understanding of and do deplore the things that are bothering your minds today. And I repeat that all of us must do our best to stop the process.

Now—having said all this, I believe that America will remain free and that she will remain great; that you will have an opportunity to go to school, to fit yourselves for any careers of your own choosing; and that when you grow up you will be able to obtain and pay for a farm out of your earnings.

Again I would call attention to our history and the number of people of no great means who have gone to school and later achieved the top of their professions. In the section of Kansas from which I came, there were very few boys and girls who ever went to college who did not have to work outside of hours, while in school, in order to help defray their own expenses. Parents in that region, in those days, simply could not entirely pay their children's way through school. Three of my own brothers earned almost every cent of the money it cost them to obtain college degrees and all three graduated high in their classes.

So don't be discouraged about America. We do not have perfection, but the great opportunity that lies in front of each of us is to help bring this great and good country a little nearer to the perfection that all humans seek.

With best wishes to you both and to your parents. *Sincerely*

[1] Robin and Terrill Scatena were two young sisters from Los Angeles, California. This is one of several letters Eisenhower wrote at this time to address the concerns young people had regarding government policies. See, for example, nos. 329 and 340. In their undated letter (WHCF/OF 114), handwritten perhaps by their mother or father, the sisters had told the President that they dreamed of owning a farm when they grew up but that the money they and their parents could save would not be enough if the dollar kept "being worth less and less. Maybe we can't go to college even," they said, "unless *you* pay for it from all those taxes you are collecting." Savings bonds, the proceeds from life insurance, and social security payments would not help their parents when they were old except to pay for a room "in some state housing home." The girls asked why individuals themselves could not decide to help foreign countries rather than having their tax money used without their consent.

"Mother and Daddy are teaching us about the Declaration of Independence and the Constitution and we don't think things are going the way they were meant to at all. What is happening?"

[2] See no. 27.

[3] Eisenhower was referring to the Joint Federal-State Action Committee, created at his recommendation and authorized by the annual Governors' Conference held in June (*Congressional Quarterly Almanac*, vol. XIII, *1957*, pp. 797–98; *Public Papers of the Presidents: Eisenhower, 1957*, pp. 486–97; see also Cabinet meeting minutes, May 23, 1958, AWF/Cabinet).

328 *EM, AWF, DDE Diaries Series*

To James L. Branch *September 9, 1957*

Dear Mr. Branch: I am always delighted to hear from a former comrade-in-arms, and your letter of August twenty-eighth particularly touched me. I remember, of course, that day in Rheims (although I had forgotten completely what I said at the time).[1]

By now, of course, you will know that I found it necessary to veto the postal pay raise bill.[2] I can only hope that you and your fellow workers who do such a splendid job in the Postal Service will understand that I had no choice but to take the action I did. (Since you may have missed the statement I issued, I am enclosing a copy).[3]

The Administration has made every effort, and will continue to do so, to curb rising prices. As a matter of interest, I might say that while the cost of living has risen about five percent in the last five years; by contrast it rose some six or seven percent *each year* in the years immediately after World War II (with one or two brief interruptions to this pattern). The increase in postal salaries voted by the Congress would inevitably have given impetus to that vicious and dangerous spiral.

There is one other side of the question that I would like to mention. The Postmaster General believes, as do I, that the Post Office Department should be operated in the main as a self-supporting business. We fought hard to get an increase in postal rates that would in large measure make this possible, and would give justification for a proper pay raise. That raise in rates the Congress denied; yet, because of political expediency, the Congress voted a raise in salaries. To me that was an illogical and foolhardy action, and consequently my only recourse—in the best interests of all our people—was to veto the bill.[4]

All this, of course, is difficult to understand when your home, your family, your conveniences and your comforts are concerned. But I pray that you will look at the problem from the broad viewpoint and realize what consequences to all of us might have resulted from approval of the bill.

Once again let me thank you for your fine letter.

With best wishes, *Sincerely*

[1] Branch, a post office clerk from North Little Rock, Arkansas, had recalled a day shortly after his liberation from a German prisoner-of-war camp when he and twenty other army air force troops were at an airfield outside Rheims awaiting transportation home. Eisenhower, who had been made aware of the hardships that the men had suffered, had spoken to them just before they departed. "You told us that we had carried the ball when the going was tough," Branch wrote. "You said that you and our country would never forget us or let us down in time of need." Now, he said, he and other veterans working for the postal department were "in dire need of a salary increase to meet the rising cost of living" (WHCF/OF 104-N-7; see also Chandler and Galambos, *Occupation, 1945*, no. 88).

[2] On September 7 Eisenhower had pocket vetoed the bill, which would have provided an average annual salary increase of 12.5 percent for postal workers (*Congressional Quarterly Almanac*, vol. XIII, *1957*, pp. 632–34; and Ann Whitman memorandum, Aug. 29, 1957, AWF/AWD; see no. 202 for background).

[3] The bill was inequitable, Eisenhower had said, and "would contribute unnecessarily to existing and incipient inflationary pressures in our national economy" (*Public Papers of the Presidents: Eisenhower, 1957*, pp. 669–70).

[4] Congress would pass a bill raising postal rates in May 1958 (see no. 784).

329 *EM, AWF, DDE Diaries Series*

To Jack F. Lane, Jr. *September 9, 1957*

Dear Jack: Thank you for the compliment you pay me in writing about some of the things that are troubling you.[1]

In the first place, I am sure you realize that I have, all my adult life, argued for an adequate defensive structure for our nation. The funds we spend for defense represent our insurance against another war—a war that would cost staggering amounts in lives and in money. Nevertheless, the money we spend for this purpose is more than half of our national budget. It is a burden for our people that must be carefully watched to insure maximum return for every dollar we use. To spend more than is necessary can have serious consequences for us all. As of this moment I believe our program is well suited to the world situation. This statement, of course, assumes the continuance of our aid in helping friendly nations maintain support bases and forces in other lands. If this were not so, we would have to spend many billions more in direct expenditures.

As you know by now, I vetoed the postal pay raise—though it is not quite accurate to imply, as you did, that money saved in that way could be used for additional defense forces.[2]

But I do congratulate you on the intelligent interest you take in the affairs of our nation; I hope you will always continue to do so.

With best wishes, *Sincerely*

[1] Lane, an Eagle Scout, had written Eisenhower from the Army Chemical Center in Maryland. He felt it his duty to tell the President that Congress was "making a grave mistake" in cutting the defense budget. Mentioning a visit he had made to Valley Forge for the Fourth National Boy Scout Jamboree, he recounted his admiration for the Revolutionary Army in their battle for freedom. He said "that many men lost their lives for freedom" during the world wars of the twentieth century, but now, to his alarm, the Soviet Union was "pushing at us from every side, planting Communism everywhere they can, and developing new and better weapons." Meanwhile congressional budget cuts were holding up "the progress of our military forces" (Sept. 2, 1957, WHCF/OF 133).

[2] Lane had criticized the proposal to raise the salaries of postal workers; he told the President that the country could not "fight Russia with postage stamps and air mail letters." On Eisenhower's veto of the measure see the preceding document.

330 *EM, AWF, Ann Whitman Diary Series*

To Orval Eugene Faubus *September 11, 1957*

I have your telegram in which you request a meeting with me. Would it suit your convenience to come to my office on the Naval Base at Newport, either Friday afternoon, September 13th, at 3:00, or Saturday morning, the 14th, at 9:00. If you would let my office know your method of transportation to the Newport area, my staff will arrange to have you met and brought to the Base.[1]

[1] For background see Galambos and van Ee, *The Middle Way*, nos. 341, 390, and 1802. Eisenhower was responding to a September 11 telegram from Governor Faubus requesting a meeting in an effort to defuse the mounting crisis over school desegregation in Little Rock, Arkansas. Faubus, who had been elected governor in 1954, was a southern populist who had for some years supported New Deal policies. Attacked during his 1956 reelection campaign as being "soft" on racial issues, Faubus had become a strong proponent of segregation in the South. In late August 1957, when the attempts to slow the pace of integration had failed, the Mothers' League of Little Rock had filed suit to block the federal court ordered desegregation at Central High School and had petitioned Faubus for his assistance. On September 2 the Governor had responded. He defied the court's desegregation orders and sent National Guardsmen to block the admission of nine African-American students to Central High School. When the local authorities continued to resist integration, the United States District Court had asked the Justice Department (Sept. 9) to file immediately both

a petition for an injunction and a supporting brief to restrain the Arkansas governor and the National Guard. Faubus was ordered to appear before the Court on September 20 to show cause why he should not be cited for contempt.

On September 11 Arkansas Congressman Brooks Hays (Dem.) offered his services as an intermediary in an effort to bring Faubus into compliance with the federal courts. He inquired whether Eisenhower would agree to a personal meeting with the Arkansas Governor if so requested. Acting against the advice of Attorney General Brownell, the President said he would meet with Faubus on the morning of September 14 in Newport, Rhode Island, where he was vacationing (see no. 290).

In his statement following the meeting, Eisenhower noted Faubus's intention "to respect the decision of the United States District Court" and his "inescapable responsibility . . . to preserve law and order in his state." "I am sure," Eisenhower added, "it is the desire of the Governor not only to observe the supreme law of the land but to use the influence of his office in orderly progress of the plans which are already the subject of the order of the Court." For Eisenhower's account of his meeting with Faubus see no. 374; see also *Public Papers of the Presidents: Eisenhower, 1957*, pp. 673–75; Eisenhower, *Waging Peace*, pp. 162–76; Brownell, *Advising Ike*, pp. 206–29; Adams, *Firsthand Report*, pp. 344–59; Telephone conversation, Eisenhower and Adams, Eisenhower and Brownell, September 11, 1957, AWF/D, and Ann Whitman memorandums, September 11, 14, 1957, AWF/AWD. For another view see E. Frederic Morrow, *Black Man in the White House* [New York, 1963], pp. 169–72. See also Burk, *The Eisenhower Administration and Black Civil Rights*, pp. 174–203. For developments see no. 357.

331 — *EM, AWF, DDE Diaries Series*

To J. H. Crawford — *September 11, 1957*
Personal

Dear Mr. Crawford: Thank you for your amusing letter about a very serious subject.[1] I am grateful to you for taking the trouble to write—and I particularly appreciate your kind comments about John and the members of his West Point Class.[2]

May I observe, however, that while you did a good "staff" job of posing the problem, you did not complete your work to the point of attaching "conclusions" and "recommendations." Without question the things you say are true, yet can you imagine what would be the result of trying to provide everywhere a generous supply of easy money? Inevitably there would be a very definite effect on the inflationary trends that are already at work.

I point this out merely to say that there are no easy answers. As one man put it, "It is sometimes as difficult to learn to live with prosperity as it is to live with adversity."[3]

In any event, I assure you of my appreciation of your letter.

With best wishes, *Sincerely*

[1] Crawford was president of Crawford and Company, insurance adjusters, in Atlanta, Georgia. Using a military analogy to underscore the dangers of a tight-money policy, he had told Eisenhower, whom he addressed as "General," that he hoped his quartermaster, the chairman of the Federal Reserve System, knew what he was doing about supplies [i.e., of money and credit]. On the platoon level, Crawford stated, people were becoming "jittery" even though they had saved some "'C' and 'K' rations from the last advance" (Sept. 4, 1957, WHCF/OF 115-L).

[2] In a postscript addressed to "Mr. President," Crawford had told Eisenhower that while he was an instructor at Fort Benning, he had taught John and other members of his West Point class. "They were a fine group of boys."

[3] Eisenhower may have been referring to Thomas Carlyle, who said: "Adversity is sometimes hard upon a man; but for one man who can stand prosperity, there are a hundred that will stand adversity."

332

EM, AWF, International Series: Saudi Arabia

To ibn Abd al-Aziz Saud *September 12, 1957*
Secret

Your Majesty: I have received Your Majesty's two messages of August twenty-fifth concerning the situation in Syria and the matter of the Gulf of Aqaba.[1] Your Majesty has spoken as one good friend should speak to another—in full frankness and sincerity. I am hopeful that out of such exchanges we can reach that measure of understanding which is so vital to all of us in this day of dangerous and conflicting currents.

I was gratified to learn that you will devote your wholehearted efforts to removing the danger which events in Syria have brought closer to the Middle East. There is no doubt that such action, as you say, is in the best interests of the Arabs.[2]

I appreciate, further, your frank report on the thoughts and feelings of the Arab people as they appear from your vantage point. I cannot but be concerned that concepts concerning the role and attitudes of the United States persist which are not only without foundation but which distort completely the strong desire of this nation to support the independence and integrity of the free nations of the Middle East.[3]

In this connection, we fully recognize the need of the nations of the area to possess adequate defense forces. We regret, however, that friendship should appear to be measured by the amount of arms one nation supplies to another. That is a Soviet Communist concept which coincides with the facts of their materialistic atheism and their ample stocks of surplus war material. We believe that Egypt benefitted far more from the steadfast adherence of the United States to the principles of the United Nations Charter than it did from the arms it had purchased from the Soviet Union.[4] To possess powerful friends who are loyal to protective principles such as those in the Charter is a very valuable asset.

The United States did not, furthermore, refuse to provide arms to Egypt and Syria. These governments declined to acquire arms in this country under procedures well known to Your Majesty and accepted by Your Majesty.[5]

We have, moreover, never been an important supplier of arms to Israel, nor are we now. You, of course, know that we are sending arms to Saudi Arabia, Iraq, Jordan, and Lebanon, and are aware of the special measures I have directed be taken to expedite the delivery of the arms Saudi Arabia is now obtaining in the United States.[6]

I am sure Your Majesty notes, with me, that those nations which have turned to the Communists for arms are a minority in the Arab world. It is my firm belief that the Egyptian and Syrian Governments turned to the Communists, not under the pressure of any action taken by the West, but because it suited their purpose to do so. They believed that they could undertake close relations with the Communists and obtain benefits from them without endangering their national independence and the security of the Middle East. I am sure you share with me the belief that they were wrong.

My purpose in repeating again what is, I know, familiar to you, arises out of my fear that these misconceptions about the role of the United States gain currency and divert attention from the danger of Communist imperialism. Your Majesty has mentioned the Arab fear of Israel. Should Israel attempt to conquer any Arab state the United States would, as it did last October, take action to prevent this. To do so would present far less difficulties than preventing the assumption of Communist control of the Middle East should one or more states of the area become captives of the Soviet system.

The United States stands fully prepared to meet aggression against the free states of the Middle East. The most dangerous form of aggression, however, is that which takes place through the quiet and masked subversion of independent nations. To meet this kind, any nation needs more than the force of arms. We all need the understanding and support of our friends.

I wish also to acknowledge the receipt of Your Majesty's letter on Aqaba. We received the Foreign Office note to which it refers on September ninth. You may be certain that the note will be given most careful study. I do wish to express initial regret, however, that, from your message, it would appear that you have found little basis for a closer understanding on this problem in the suggestions put forward by the United States in our Aide Memoire of July twelfth. This Aide Memoire was, as you know, drafted after extensive and fruitful discussions with your representative in the United States.[7] In it we sought to emphasize that the rights for which we stand are primarily rights for United States vessels and not those of Israel or, particularly, for any other nation. The United States, a maritime power since its earliest days, has always stood for the right of its vessels to use the seas outside of the three-mile limit and in waters involving access to multiple states. Only recently the United States felt impelled to protest proposed action with respect to certain international waters in the Far East, even though United States vessels in recent years have not often transited such waters.[8] Our Aide Memoire represented a sincere effort on the part of the United States, within the framework of its historic position in this respect, to assist in finding a meeting ground on this problem.

I have spoken frankly to Your Majesty because of the great value I place upon our friendship and because I know that you agree that good friends should not conceal from each other what is in their hearts. Even among the closest friends in the family of nations differences have existed and will continue to exist. This does not prevent mutually beneficial cooperation between these states. Though you and I may not always agree in all respects, I value our continuing fruitful collaboration. It is my hope and intention that the United States and Saudi Arabia will work together closely and harmoniously.[9]

I send Your Majesty my warmest regard and best wishes.

May God have you in His safekeeping. *Your sincere friend*

[1] In a meeting with Secretary Dulles and other State Department officials on August 28 Eisenhower had discussed the "extremely tough language" of King Saud's two messages. He later told Secretary Dulles that he thought the letters should be answered as quickly as possible and in a single communication. Dulles agreed but wanted to wait for the results of a meeting the following day between the U.S. Ambassador to Saudi Arabia and King Saud before finalizing the draft (see Eisenhower to Dulles, Aug. 28, 1957; and Dulles to Eisenhower, Aug. 29, 1957, both in AWF/D-H; and State, *Foreign Relations, 1955–1957,* vol. XIII, *Near East: Jordan-Yemen,* pp. 659–60). This message was sent to the U.S. embassy in Bonn for delivery to King Saud, then in Baden-Baden.

[2] For background on the political situation in Syria see no. 301. On September 2 Dulles had told Eisenhower that, without exception, the countries bordering Syria feared "that unless something were done to alter the course of events in Syria within the next 60 days, probably a communist directed regime would be so solidly installed that it could not be dislodged and that would have a grave impact upon the neighboring states" (Dulles, Memorandum of Conversation, Sept. 2, 1957, Dulles Papers, White House Memoranda Series). As a precautionary move Eisenhower had deployed U.S. aircraft from Western Europe to bases in Turkey, had ordered the Sixth Fleet to the Mediterranean, and had dispatched Deputy Under Secretary of State Loy Hen-

derson to the Middle East to meet with Turkish and Iraqi officials regarding the Syrian situation (see State, *Foreign Relations, 1955–1957,* vol. XIII, *Near East: Jordan-Yemen,* pp. 650–58; and Eisenhower, *Waging Peace,* pp. 196–202. On consultations with the British see Macmillan to Dulles, Aug. 30, 1957, AWF/D-H; Dulles to Macmillan, Sept. 5, 1957; and Dulles to Eisenhower, Sept. 6, 1957, both in AWF/I: Syria; Telephone conversations, Eisenhower and Dulles, Aug. 29 and Sept. 6, 1957; and Dulles and Caccia, Aug. 29, 1957, Dulles Papers, Telephone Conversations; and NSC meeting minutes, Sept. 13, 1957, AWF/NSC).

[3] King Saud had told Eisenhower that American failure to supply Syria with the arms it had requested had contributed to the strengthening of Communist influence in that country. The West had effectively prevented the sale of Arab goods, according to Saud, and had thus barred Arab countries from arming themselves at a time when the United States was supplying aid to Israel (Saud to Eisenhower, Aug. 25, 1957, AWF/I: Saudi Arabia; and State, *Foreign Relations, 1955–1957,* vol. XVII, *Arab-Israeli Dispute 1957,* p. 734).

[4] After receiving a draft of this letter (not located) while vacationing in Newport, Eisenhower suggested that Dulles emphasize the benefits Egypt had received as a result of U.S. adherence to the principles of the United Nations during the Suez Canal crisis. "By reliance on these arms alone," Eisenhower said, "[Egypt] would have been utterly defeated, but because of the United States' adherence to the principles of fairness and justice, it was saved from that fate" (Ann Whitman memorandum, Sept. 10, 1957, AWF/AWD; for background see Galambos and van Ee, *The Middle Way;* and no. 77 in these volumes).

[5] In December 1955 the United States had offered to negotiate a reimbursable military aid agreement with Syria to include equipment for internal security and self-defense. The Syrian government rejected the offer, saying the prices were too high, and subsequently negotiated an agreement with the Soviet Union. Eisenhower had asked Dulles to emphasize this fact in drafting a reply to King Saud (State, *Foreign Relations, 1955–1957,* vol. XIII, *Near East: Jordan-Yemen,* pp. 540–42, 546–47, 550–60, 660; see also no. 77).

The United States had also offered military aid to Egypt in August 1954. In January 1955, however, the Egyptian government rejected the conditions imposed by the agreement. In August 1955 the two governments were again close to an agreement, but the inability to reach a satisfactory settlement regarding the terms of payment prompted the Egyptian government to conclude an arms arrangement with the Soviet Union (State, *Foreign Relations, 1955–1957,* vol. XIV, *Arab-Israeli Dispute 1955,* pp. 238–39, 255–56, 271–74, 307–8, 332–34, 337–39, 353–54, 481–84; see also Galambos and van Ee, *The Middle Way,* no. 1611).

[6] On military aid to Saudi Arabia see no. 25.

[7] King Saud had told Eisenhower that he regretted the U.S. position expressed in the President's letter of July 10 and in the July 12 aide-memoire (see nos. 232 and 233). The President had promised not to reward an aggressor for his hostility, Saud wrote, and the two documents "were tantamount to a confirmation of rights which Israel did not possess prior to the conflict." In the Foreign Office note the Saudi government had rejected all of the U.S. suggestions contained in the aide-memoire. The International Court of Justice could not mediate the problem, the Saudis maintained; a country should not have to appeal to the court to establish sovereign rights over its own territory. U.S. willingness to support the restriction of Israeli shipping in the gulf did not go far enough; Saudi Arabia had often issued a "categorical protest" against all of Israel's attempts to exercise the right of passage through the gulf. The United States could not request masters of U.S. registered vessels to avoid Saudi territorial waters in the gulf; Aqaba was a closed gulf and only Arab countries could determine the rights of other countries to passage through these waters. The Saudi Arabian government also rejected the U.S. suggestion that the United Nations Se-

curity Council establish a safe pathway for pilgrims to the Holy Places of Islam; Saudi Arabia could not give an international body control over such a religious decision (see Saud to Eisenhower, Aug. 25, 1957, AWF/I: Saudi Arabia; and State, *Foreign Relations, 1955–1957*, vol. XVII, *Arab-Israeli Dispute 1957*, p. 722; see also Eisenhower, *Waging Peace*, p. 201).

[8] On July 20 the Soviet Union had closed the Peter the Great Bay, the sea approach to Vladivostok, to foreign ships and planes. On August 12 the U.S. embassy in Moscow had lodged an official protest with the Soviet Ministry of Foreign Affairs, calling the closing a violation of international law and the principle of freedom of the seas (*U.S. Department of State Bulletin* 37, no. 949 [Sept. 2, 1957], 388; and *New York Times*, July 21, 1957).

[9] In his September 14 reply King Saud would ask Eisenhower to remember that even though Arabs and Moslems had different outlooks, they were united in believing that international Zionism and Israel were their first enemies. "They consider that all who assist Israel financially, militarily, and politically and support their activities are antagonists and all those who assist them in all these fields of action against Israel are their friends" (Saud to Eisenhower, Sept. 14, 1957, AWF/I: Saudi Arabia). For developments see no. 483.

333

EM, WHCF, Official File 111-C-7

To George Landes

September 12, 1957

Dear Mr. Landes: Your recent letter is most interesting.[1] I completely agree with you in your argument that our greatest asset in providing for our national security is the inner security that comes to citizens through a comprehension of today's problems and a feeling of confidence in grappling with them. This means education.[2]

Nevertheless, your letter does not get to the heart of the problem involved in correction of the existing situation. Certainly no one in this country wants to "save money" at the expense of the education of our children, but your letter seems to imply that the matter lies exclusively with the Federal government.[3] The fact is that many states are stoutly opposed to any entry of the Federal government into school affairs, maintaining that the final result would be Federal control of education. This, of course, would be a calamity.

While I do not believe that such centralized control would accompany Federal aid that would be confined to emergency construction of the necessary school buildings, yet it is clear that primary responsibility for the schools in our country properly devolves upon local and state authorities.

This Administration will continue to stand for leadership and aid to the states in making good the great school room deficiencies that have resulted—partially at least—from national calamities such as two great wars and a great depression. The necessary conditions to such a Federal program are, I think, distribution of Federal funds on the basis of need and the certainty that the Federal government will withdraw from the field the instant critical construction needs have been met.[4]

But this is not enough. You should look in the first instance to your local school authorities and to your state officials to see that operation, maintenance and support of schools are adequate in every way to cope with the needs of our youngsters. The federal government's efforts in this line should be largely confined to the field I have suggested above. I believe that in this field the Congress should give generous and prompt authorization for funds.

I repeat that it is encouraging to read a letter from someone who realizes so fully that in the broader and better education of our young is to be found the source of the increasing greatness of our country.[5] *Sincerely*

[1] A high school teacher from New York State, Landes had written Eisenhower on August 31 (same file as document) to complain about the President's "lack of leadership and interest in the Federal Aid to Schools Bill" (for background see no. 324).
[2] Landes had written that the United States must "prevent the insidious seeds of insecurity, the horrible feelings of helplessness, the despair that comes with hopelessness from gaining a foothold in our youth." Defense was not to be found in "a deadly missile," but "in the inner security of our people." Without this security, Landes had said, "Americans were really defenseless, from ourselves and from others."
[3] "The schools are not the areas in which to save money," Landes had written. If the "top echelon" trusted to "luck, chance, or evolutionary tactics" in the area of education, America would "pay a price in human misery and suffering, unimaginable to our unimaginative Congressmen."
[4] For more on Eisenhower's views on education see his April 1957 address to the National Education Association in *Public Papers of the Presidents: Eisenhower, 1957*, pp. 263–69.
[5] See also Clowse, *Brainpower for the Cold War*, pp. 28–39.

334 — *EM, AWF, DDE Diaries Series*

To William L. Little — *September 12, 1957*

Dear Mr. Little: I am much interested in your letter of September fourth, but even after reading it carefully I am not quite clear as to your diagnosis of the reasons for the defeat of Governor Kohler and the ills of the Republican Party in general.[1]

I do firmly believe that certain columnists have built a feeling in this country that there is a wide chasm between "right-wing" and "left-wing" Republicans. They have exploited this to the maximum; to the point where they have many Republicans behaving as if other

Republicans are more to be distrusted than the opposite political party.[2]

Contrary to that artificial conception, I just as strongly believe that on basic doctrines, the majority of Republicans are in unity. Let me just mention briefly two areas. In my opinion all Republicans believe that we should oppose the trend toward centralization of responsibility in the Federal government, with its consequent increasing dependence of every citizen upon the Federal government. Likewise, I believe that all Republicans believe that isolation is not possible for the United States, and in the ways by which we must strive to bind other free nations to us.

To cite another instance in which the difference between Republicans and the controlling element of the Democratic Party is emphasized even more, I refer you to governmental fiscal policies. The Republicans believe that our national debt should not be further increased—in other words that we should not resort further to deficit financing. We feel that only the gravest kind of national emergency can justify such action.

This we believe because we are against every kind of inflationary pressure. In other words, Republicans are instinctively and by deliberate choice conservative in all fiscal policies.

I think I need not recite here the list of things that have been done under the influence of the controlling element in the Democratic Party to prove that their political philosophy is completely different from that of the Republicans.

In other questions, too, I believe there is great unity between *all* Republicans.

I cannot go into the other points in your letter as fully as I would like. But I do want to assure you that all Departments of the Administration are constantly aware of the danger of inflation, and our efforts are directed toward stopping inflation as rapidly as possible, without bringing upon us serious consequences in other directions.

I fully agree as to the need for statesmanship on the part of political leaders and business men, *and* labor leaders as well. Unfortunately such a characteristic seems to be increasingly rare, a fact that I deplore as much as you do.[3]

With best wishes, *Sincerely*

[1] Little was chairman of the board of the Bucyrus-Erie Company, manufacturers of surface-mining excavation equipment, in Milwaukee, Wisconsin. He had written Eisenhower about the defeat of the Republican governor of Wisconsin Walter J. Kohler, Jr., in a special election for the seat of the late Senator Joseph McCarthy (see no. 311). The *Milwaukee Journal* had reported that Eisenhower had blamed the defeat on exaggerated differences that divided the Republican party into right and left wings. "If this thinking is to be adopted as the party's analysis of the Wisconsin landslide," Little wrote, "then, in my judgment, the party is almost certain of defeat next

year and again in 1960." Little had implied that economic factors were behind the Republican defeat. High interest rates, which the Administration was using to retard inflation, could be "only partly effective, and they could lead to business recession" (WHCF/OF 114).

[2] One of the columnists may have been David Lawrence, whose magazine *U.S. News & World Report* had conducted a poll of Republican senators to determine their understanding of the term "modern republican" (see no. 101). Lawrence had also written an article "'Modern Republicans' and 'Modern Democrats,'" which had appeared in the magazine on April 5. For more on Eisenhower's conception of the term see *ibid.*; and nos. 311 and 363 in these volumes.

[3] Little lamented the lack of statesmanship: "Unless we in the Republican Party can provide it, the party itself may become a thing of the past." Writing further on September 18, Little expressed concerns that a "hair-curling" depression could result unless Eisenhower were successful in persuading both labor unions and management to exercise restraint in wage demands and pricing policies. "Even dyed-in-the-wool Republicans are concerned about the present situation" (WHCF/OF 114; see also Whitman to Little, Sept. 23, 1957, *ibid.*).

335 — *EM, WHCF, Official File 101-Y*

To Bion Rose East — *September 12, 1957*

Personal and confidential

Dear Mr. East: I remember well our pleasant association with you and Mrs. East at Columbia. Consequently, I read your letter with more than usual interest.[1]

While agreeing fully with some of the comments made in it, I am likewise of the opinion that in certain instances misunderstanding lies behind the criticisms you make.

First of all, you speak disparagingly of "modern Republicanism."[2] It seems to me that anyone who is willing to come face to face with the problems of today—rather than to lose himself in contemplation of those that beset the country a century ago—is a "modern," whether or not he calls himself Republican, Democrat or Independent. I personally have defined a "modern Republican" as anyone who supports the national platform of 1956. That platform was adopted unanimously by the Republican National Convention. If that Convention was not representative of the rank and file of Republicans, of which you speak, then I do not know how you would get a truly representative body of Republicans together.

I have time and again publicly pointed out that Republicans are conservative, citing as specific examples our adherence to sound fiscal policies, including a balanced budget, with payments on the national debt, and above all, opposition to the continuous trend toward centralization of power in Washington.

Deficit spending and centralization are the hallmarks of the New and Fair Deals.

On the other hand, government cannot refuse to grapple with the great problems that have been brought about by a high degree of industrialization in this country, the disappearance of the free lands that provided a reserve for unemployed workers in the last half of the 19th century, and the extraordinary financial burdens placed upon us these days by the existence of the Communist threat centered in Moscow. Clearly the programs of 1900 are not sufficient to meet the needs of this day.

We must stick to conservative principles, but we cannot be antediluvian.

With regard to your criticisms of Governor Stassen, I have nothing to say.[3] He has been a controversial figure; many people admire him while many dislike him intensely. Of course he is not actually what either his ardent friends or his ardent enemies picture him, but he is an assiduous worker and he is devoted to the whole purpose of disarmament. As an aside I might remark that some progress must be achieved along this line within the proximate future or there will be very bad effects upon our economy resulting from the amounts we will have to spend for "security."

As far as the Girard case is concerned, I feel sure you have not read the treaties to which you refer.[4] When I felt compelled—very sadly I might remark—to leave Columbia and my pleasant associations there to go back to Europe to lead the effort toward a combined military security for Western Europe, I was up against the problem of how to handle the question of offenses committed by our soldiers on foreign soil. In certain instances we believe that forward air bases in these areas are absolutely essential for our defense and we have sought for and obtained permission to keep our servicemen in those areas.

Here I might remark that both in peace and in war I have been responsible, in foreign countries, for seeing that the young Americans under my command receive fair and just treatment. I do not believe I should, by implication, be accused of failing to recognize and defend their rights as American soldiers.

When one of these soldiers commits an offense *which is not in line of duty,* the question becomes one as to what authority should take jurisdiction over him.

Let us reverse the circumstances for a moment. In this country we train numbers of foreign troops. Suppose one of these men while on leave in your community should burn your house. Would you be willing to send him back for trial to a group of officers of his own nationality at the base where he may be in training?

The only thing that made the Girard case particularly difficult was the determination of whether his act was committed in line of duty. Every country in which we have troops gives us a very great measure of leeway in these matters—far more than I think we would be willing to give in like circumstances.

It may be argued that we are helping to provide security for those nations, but in some cases at least they feel that we are making of them targets which they otherwise might not be. I am sure if you reflect more on this particular point you will come to understand that these treaties give our soldiers the maximum protection that we could possibly expect.

I have nothing to say about your criticism of Mr. Dulles, except to observe that some of the problems that we encounter in the foreign field change their complexion almost from day to day.[5] By and large he is by far the best qualified man in the nation to serve as our Secretary of State. He is courageous, steadfast and is the best informed and wisest man in the foreign field I have ever met, even though I am ready to admit that he and I may, and do, make mistakes in this field as well as in others.

As for foreign aid "getting completely out of the bounds of reason," may I point out that since I have been in the White House we have reduced this appropriation more than fifty per cent. Moreover, we have clearly defined its purpose and have placed it upon a much more business-like basis than ever before.

You say many of the voters believe that the late Senator McCarthy was unfairly treated by members of the Administration. So far as I am concerned, this statement is somewhat mystifying. Senator McCarthy, time and again, expressed very adverse views with respect to me. In spite of such provocations, never once in public did I mention his name. It would interest me to know just what you would suggest under the circumstances.

You mention another personality in Paul Hoffman.[6] You say he has a reputation as a "do-gooder" with other people's money. When he—a Republican—was called upon by the Truman Administration to administer the Marshall Plan (a plan which unquestionably saved all Western Europe from Communism) it was estimated that something like seventeen billion dollars would be required for the total project. He completed and *terminated* it at a total cost of something around thirteen billion, a fact for which he has never received any public credit of which I am aware. He often differs with others in the Republican Party, including me, but I personally believe he is honest in his convictions, and he does think that a little bit of self-criticism is sometimes as important as criticizing others.

I repeat that I value your letter as I do your friendship, but I do hope that you will reflect on some of the points I have raised. I should have liked, of course, to answer your letter fully, but this is impossible.

With best wishes to you and Mrs. East,[7] *Sincerely*

[1] East (D.D.S. University of Michigan 1908), director of the Veterans Administration Post-Graduate Training Center, had been educational administrator of dentistry and professor of dentistry at the School of Public Health at Columbia University during the years when Eisenhower was president of the university. East's September 2 letter (in the same file as this document) was prompted, he said, by the "debacle" in the recent Wisconsin election, when voters selected a Democrat to fill the unexpired term of the late Senator Joseph McCarthy (see no. 311).

[2] East believed that the majority of all voters longed "for a clear and definite split with [the] aims and policies that ruled the New and Fair deals. We are hungry," he wrote, "for the opportunity to be able to choose between the 'liberal' and conservative philosophies."

[3] Rank and file Republicans thought Stassen was "an opportunist," East said, ". . . loyal to no one or to anything except his own ambitions." They were "disgusted" with the Administration for retaining him.

[4] For background on the Girard case see no. 200. Although he had not referred to specific treaties, East generally had decried the agreements which allowed members of the U.S. armed forces to be tried and punished by foreign governments.

[5] "Many feel that Mr. Dulles should be muzzled until he can find time to reflect and to think a problem through before he speaks out," East wrote. "Many also feel that he should be grounded in Washington that he may better care for his administrative duties as the head of the State Department."

[6] For more on the Marshall Plan and Hoffman's involvement with that policy see Galambos, *Chief of Staff*, no. 1482; and no. 90 in these volumes.

[7] East's wife was the former Norma Schmidt.

336

EM, AWF, DDE Diaries Series

To Nancy Jewell Cross

September 12, 1957

Dear Dr. Cross: Thank you very much for your interesting letter concerning "equal rights for women." The statistics you give are enlightening and your arguments seem perfectly logical.[1]

As I have so often stated, I steadfastly favor the principle that women workers should have equal rights with men. I sincerely hope that this equality can be accomplished without unnecessary delay.[2]

With best wishes, *Sincerely*

[1] Cross, a consulting chemist from Stanford, California, had asked Eisenhower to make the Equal Rights Amendment (S.J.R. 80), which the Senate Judiciary Committee had reported favorably on August 27, "priority legislation" for the second session of Congress. She cited statistics showing that women received lower salaries than men and were restricted from entering medical schools and the faculties of colleges

and universities; she compared the U.S. situation in that regard with the Soviet Union, where women outnumbered men in some professions. "Is it any wonder when we struggle along with a masculinist theory in which science, medicine, and professorships at our universities are in effect reserved for one sex that we must lower our standards to meet the needs for humanpower in these fields?" (Sept. 2, 1957, WHCF/OF 158-A).

[2] Eisenhower had referred to his support of equal rights for women in his annual budget message in January and at his news conference on August 4 (*Public Papers of the Presidents: Eisenhower, 1957*, pp. 57, 594; see also *Public Papers of the Presidents: Eisenhower, 1956*, pp. 23, 710, 954, 1026). For more on the issue, unresolved during Eisenhower's presidency, see Jane L. Mansbridge, *Why We Lost the ERA* (Chicago, 1986); and Donald G. Mathews and Jane Sherron de Hart, *Sex, Gender, and the Politics of ERA: A State and the Nation* (New York, 1990).

337 *EM, AWF, DDE Diaries Series*

To Leon S. Hollingsworth *September 12, 1957*

Dear Mr. Hollingsworth: While I personally have no knowledge that any members of the Eisenhower family lived in Whitfield County in Georgia, I much appreciate your taking the trouble to tell me of the discovery you made during your research.[1]

It is entirely possible that the Isenhour family to which you refer is distantly related to my own branch.[2] When the family landed in Philadelphia along about 1740, English efforts to spell the German word resulted in immediate and glaring differences in the name by which different branches of the family became known. On the other hand, it is also possible that because the name itself means roughly "hewer of iron" that some completely independent group may have acquired it as their family name.

I shall take the liberty of sending your letter along to certain individuals who are making a study of my particular branch of the family.[3]

Again my thanks for your thoughtful kindness. *Sincerely*

[1] Hollingsworth had written the President of the results of his research at the Georgia Department of Archives and History in Atlanta, Georgia. His letter of August 31, 1957, is in WHCF/PPF 1-A-2.

[2] According to the 1870 census of Whitfield County, Georgia, a family by the name of Isenhour owned and operated a farm in northern Georgia near the Tennessee border.

[3] For background on the President's interest in Eisenhower genealogy see Galambos and van Ee, *The Middle Way*, nos. 184, 400, 770.

338

EM, AWF, DDE Diaries Series

TO HENRY ROBINSON LUCE

September 13, 1957

Dear Harry: I have reviewed my fall schedule, including the chores that are not yet actually on the calendar but which I feel I must perform. The load is formidable and I simply cannot add further to it.[1] While I think there is logic in your contention that the International Industrial Development Conference would provide a splendid audience for a particular type of talk, I am completely convinced that my principal job is to try to help Americans understand the international situation we face, rather than to couch a talk in such terms as to make it suitable for an international audience.[2] This conviction, coupled with the fact that the distance to San Francisco is such as to require more travel time than I will feel I can spare at the moment, compels me to adhere to my position that I cannot accept your invitation.

Of course, I do not have to tell you that I do not lightly send you this kind of an answer. Both because of the special friendship I feel for you and my admiration for the job you have done in getting together such a significant group, I truly regret my inability to be with you.[3]

With warm personal regard, *Sincerely*

[1] Luce had reiterated his invitation to the President to speak to the International Industrial Development Conference (Luce to Eisenhower, Sept. 6, 1957, C. D. Jackson Papers). Following receipt of Luce's "persuasive" letter, Eisenhower said he would "take the matter under advisement" (Eisenhower to Luce, Sept. 11, 1957, AWF/D). On Luce's previous invitation to the conference see no. 262.

[2] Luce had suggested a speech on sound economic behavior, the threat of inflation to U.S. prosperity, and "the principle of mutual aid" that "should be applied throughout the free world."

[3] Eisenhower had dictated an additional paragraph regarding his miscalculations as to the demands and "preoccupations" of a second term. On second thought, he decided not to include it, but planned to tell Luce in person (Memorandum, Sept. 13, 1957, AWF/AWD).

339

EM, AWF, DDE Diaries Series

TO JOAN M. LITCHFIELD

September 13, 1957

Dear Joan and Pat: I am more than grateful to you for your heartwarming letter.[1] All too frequently it seems to me that the only mail that comes to my desk either presents problems that defy solution or reflects great discontent on the part of the writer. It is refreshing and encouraging to read an understanding and, if I may say so, "fan" note such as the two of you wrote to me. I shall remember your words.

Mrs. Eisenhower joins me in warm appreciation of your generous comments, and in best wishes to you and Pat.[2] *Sincerely*

[1] Joan was a student at the Carnegie Institute of Technology in Pittsburgh, and Pat was a student at Rosemont College in Philadelphia. "We think you're great!" Joan had written on September 9 (WHCF/PPF 20-D-"L"). She went on to thank Eisenhower for "doing his best at a very difficult job" and added, "I have great faith in your judgment."

[2] The young women had written: "To us, you and Mamie are a wonderful example of a devoted couple doing your duty to your God and your country—and what more can you ask of a person?"

340 — *EM, AWF, DDE Diaries Series*

To Anne S. Hasley — *September 14, 1957*

Dear Mrs. Hasley: I am complimented that you should write to me about the problem of inflation which is troubling you so much, and I only wish I could write you as fully on the subject as I should like.[1]

But within the limits prescribed by a letter I can at least make one or two points. The first, and the most important is that I am convinced that the future for your children will present even greater opportunities than I had, or you and your husband had. Never forget that America has not only successfully surmounted every crisis and period of discouragement, but her people have invariably gone forward to enjoy a better and fuller life spiritually, intellectually and materially.

The problem of inflation troubles me just as it does you. I need not go into the causes that have brought it about. But I do want to mention that we had a very marked period of inflation immediately after World War II, with only one or two brief interruptions, when the cost of living went up at the rate of over seven per cent a year. Beginning in 1952, this process was slowed sharply, and in the past five years, the total rise has been something between *five and six per cent for the entire period.* (Most of this rise has been in the last year and a half). The present Administration is concerned about the situation and is doing everything possible to stop the trend, without bringing upon us serious consequences in other directions.[2]

Every agency of the Federal government is striving to bring the spiral to a halt and thereafter to keep it under watchful control. But all history shows that it is not easy. We want our workmen to earn more. But whenever they obtain a pay raise that is in excess of the increased efficiency of the workmen then we have another inflationary force.

The main point that I would like to leave with you is that every appointee of the Federal government, to the best of my knowledge, is intimately concerned with this problem; certainly it occupies a good part of my hours, even on what is called a "vacation" period.[3]

We in America do not have perfection, but all of us do have an opportunity to help bring this great country a little nearer to the perfection that all humans seek. I am, as I said before, firmly convinced that your children will find the world a better place in which to live.

Thank you again for writing. By this answer I hope, at the very least, that I have assured you that the problems which trouble you so much are matters constantly on my mind, and that I do understand how the rising cost of living troubles you.

With best wishes to you and your family. *Sincerely*

[1] "My husband and I are an educated, eager young couple struggling to maintain for our children the type of home life to which we ourselves have been accustomed," Hasley had written. "But, in rich America, inflation makes the task an impossible one. Won't someone please take an interest in us and others like us who enjoy neither the benefits of escalator clauses nor stock blocks" (Sept. 11, 1957, WHCF/OF 115-E).

[2] For more on the inflation problem see no. 323.

[3] Eisenhower was writing from Newport, Rhode Island.

341

EM, AWF, DDE Diaries Series

TO KATHERINE MURPHY HUGHES *September 14, 1957*

Dearest Kate: The other morning I experienced a feeling of dismay when Mamie told me you had heard nothing at all from me after Everett's death. Early on Friday morning a week ago I sat down and wrote a longhand telegram to you, which I of course assumed had been delivered.[1]

Because I have been myself fairly well run down with preoccupations of many sorts, I did not feel up to returning to Washington for the funeral itself.[2] In this circumstance I called Johnnie to ask him to serve as my personal representative, and having heard indirectly that you would like him to act as a pallbearer, I asked him to please accept that invitation.[3] In addition I informed him that if he needed any official orders to be excused from his office for the day, I would be glad to take care of the matter.

I am sure I do not need to tell you how truly saddened I am by the passing of one of my oldest and best Army friends. Although I did not know him well when he was my instructor at Leavenworth in 1925, from the time I met him, when we were both students at the War College in 1928, I developed for him not only a great admiration and respect, but a very deep affection. As you know, he served with me all through the European campaign of World War II and he did so with distinction and with complete dedication to his duty and to his country. So you can understand I feel exactly as if I had lost one of my own family.

In the same way I am sure you understand how deep is the sympathy Mamie and I feel for you in your great personal loss. Our prayers and our thoughts are with you constantly.

With much love, *Devotedly*

[1] Mrs. Hughes was the widow of Major General Everett Strait Hughes, who had died on September 5. During World War II Hughes had served on Eisenhower's staff in Europe and North Africa; he had also served as chief of the Army's Ordnance Department until retiring in 1950 (for background on the President's close friendship with him see *Eisenhower Papers*, vols. I–XVII; see also *New York Times*, Sept. 8, 1957). In his message of condolence (Sept. 6, AWF/D), Eisenhower said, "Everett's death is . . . like losing a member of our own family. He was one of the Army's finest. . . ."

[2] On the Little Rock school desegregation crisis see no. 330.

[3] This was John Sheldon Doud Eisenhower.

342 — *EM, AWF, Dulles-Herter Series*

To John Foster Dulles — *September 17, 1957*

Secret

Dear Foster: I have two comments to make on the passage of your speech which you sent to me last evening.[1]

First, until there is universal disarmament, the weight of arms maintained by those who know that they themselves will not be aggressors is presumably determined by their evaluation of the threat against their own safety.

The imminence and intensity of this threat dictates that the level of armaments does not fall below the danger point; the element of costs is an influence that keeps them from becoming unnecessarily large.

Second. The passage implies, I think, that through close cooperation of the free world, the minimum levels in the several countries might be further lowered, particularly if we concern ourselves as much with quality as with quantity. If this principle were carried to an extreme, then the safety of any country in the coalition would be directly dependent upon each of the others, because the *total* minimum would be maintained by a series of independent actions in the several countries. As a consequence, failure of one to carry out its commitments, or, worse, a defection to the other side, could very measurably upset the balance and expose all to great danger. The fact is that each nation feels it necessary to have some little margin of reserve over and above the minimum of its fixed contribution under any such collective arrangement, so that the element of risk is somewhat reduced.[2]

I concede that the purposes you are seeking are laudable ones. Entirely aside from the economy you would achieve, you would be serving notice on the Soviets that their refusal to bargain in good faith in the matter of disarmament will result in much closer military and political collaboration between the nations of the free world, and this, in turn, would bring about a more widespread deployment of nuclear weapons in order that security might be achieved at the lowest possible cost. I think that such warning or implication could be conveyed in not more than a sentence or two, whereas I rather feel your passage could possibly create some misunderstanding, even among our own people.[3]

[1] Secretary Dulles had transmitted by telephone four paragraphs from the speech he was to make before the United Nations General Assembly on September 19. The passage under discussion, Dulles said, was the only one that involved what "might be called new policy." It implied that if the Soviet Union rejected the disarmament proposals negotiated in London, the United States would be prepared to discuss with the free world nations a separate agreement on national arms limitation and the control of nuclear weapons. Although he did not specifically state these things, Dulles told Eisenhower, they were "perhaps implicit" in the language of his speech. "Therefore I did not want to say it without clearance with you." Dulles had approached the British, who, he said, seemed "to take to the idea," but he was not sure that the concept would appeal to the American Department of Defense (Whitman to Eisenhower, and Passage from Speech, Sept. 17, 1957, AWF/D-H). For Dulles's contact with U.N. Ambassador Lodge on the speech see Dulles to Lodge, August 28, 1957, Dulles Personal Papers; and Telephone conversation, Dulles and Lodge, August 29, 1957, Dulles Papers, Telephone Conversations; for background on the London disarmament negotiations see no. 217; and State, *Foreign Relations, 1955–1957*, vol. XX, *Regulation of Armaments; Atomic Energy*, pp. 707–20.

[2] Here Eisenhower wrote in instructions, which we deleted, to Ann Whitman.

[3] Dulles's speech briefly touched on the benefits of collective security: "Even if the Soviet Union now rejects the joint proposals, those proposals should not on that account be regarded as dead. Their principles are valid and will live on" (John Foster Dulles, "Major Issues Before the United Nations," *U.S. Department of State Bulletin* 37, no. 954 [October 7, 1957], 555–59).

343 *EM, AWF, DDE Diaries Series*

To Charles R. Sligh, Jr. *September 17, 1957*

Dear Mr. Sligh: It was thoughtful of you to send your telegram regarding my disapproval of the pay bills.[1]

As I stated in my message at the time, I did not feel that considerations of equity were sufficiently compelling to approve bills that by their very nature violated sound principles of employee compensation and that placed Government in the position of adding upward pressure to prices at a time when it is seeking responsible, long-range thinking from labor and management with respect to wage-cost-price matters.[2]

There is a great deal of adult education needed in America on these subjects if we are to keep our prosperity by keeping it healthy. *Sincerely*

[1] On September 7 Eisenhower had pocket vetoed H.R. 2474, a bill to authorize a 12½ percent pay increase for postal workers (for background see nos. 202 and 328). On the same day the President had also vetoed H.R. 2462, a bill to provide an 11 percent increase for federal classified workers and employees of the judicial and legislative branches (see *Congressional Quarterly Almanac*, vol. XIII, *1957*, pp. 632–36, and *New York Times*, Sept. 8, 1957). Sligh's telegram is not in AWF.

[2] Explaining his action to Congress, Eisenhower had said the bills would widen existing pay disparities within the federal establishment and put pressure on the public debt. Since federal salaries were not out of line with salaries in private industry, the raise was unnecessary (see *Public Papers of the Presidents: Eisenhower, 1957*, pp. 669–71). On Eisenhower's opposition to salary hikes that created inflationary pressures see nos. 73 and 248. See also Galambos and van Ee, *The Middle Way*, no. 1806.

344 *EM, AWF, DDE Diaries Series*

To William McChesney Martin, Jr. *September 19, 1957*

Secret

Dear Mr. Martin: The role of money, of credit, and of the entire financial system in the event of a massive attack on our country remains an unresolved question.

Reports of Operation Alert 1957 revealed two quite different views.[1] One view emphasized the enormous destruction that would result from such an attack; it suggested that functioning of the economic system as we know it—buying and selling through the use of money—would no longer be possible. According to this view major reliance for survival and victory would have to be placed on compulsory measures. The other view held that, though marginal areas would be badly shattered (in some target areas there would, of course, be complete destruction and disruption), the surest means for getting back on our knees and finally on our feet would be to patch together for productive activity the many surviving fragments of the economic system in the areas that escaped destruction. This view recognized the need for imposition of government controls but emphasized the contribution which our money and credit system could make in promoting private and individual efforts at salvage and recovery. It also emphasized the extent to which recovery efforts might be paralyzed if the financial system were prostrate.

The need for answers to the basic and related questions involved seems to me so compelling that I should like to have a small committee consider them and prepare a report designed to furnish a guide for future policy determination and action. I am happy to know of your willingness to take part in this work, and accordingly appoint you to the committee and designate you as chairman. In addition to yourself, I am appointing to the committee Mr. Anderson, Secretary of the Treasury; Mr. Brundage, Director of the Bureau of the Budget; Dr. Saulnier, Chairman of the Council of Economic Advisers; Mr. Gray, Director of the Office of Defense Mobilization; Mr. Hoegh, Administrator of the Federal Civil Defense Administration.

Among the specific questions the committee should consider are: What kind of advance plans can and should the Federal Government make for economic and financial postattack mobilization, including plans that would support effective local responses to the emergency? Which, if any, of these should be explained to the public in advance of an attack? More specifically, to what extent would assurances by the Federal Government for sharing of losses resulting from enemy action be necessary?

In the committee's consideration of the questions before it, I trust that full account will be taken of their many ramifications into other sectors of defense mobilization planning.

I am reluctant to ask for a report by a specific date, but I hope that the committee will submit its conclusions as promptly as possible.[2] *Sincerely*

[1] Operation Alert, a yearly civil defense exercise to test the nation's ability to meet the problems resulting from a nuclear attack, was held in three phases from July 8 to 15 (*New York Times*, July 7, 13, 16, 1957; see also Galambos and van Ee, *The Middle Way*, no. 1481). "Financial arrangements anything like normal in so vast an emergency situation" would be impossible, Eisenhower had told the Cabinet on July 19. Martial law would be a necessity, and "there would have to be other incentives than money for practically all in such a chaotic period" (Cabinet meeting minutes, AWF/Cabinet).

[2] A meeting with ODM Director Gray in April 1958 would prompt Eisenhower to tell Martin that he approved releasing the information that Martin's group, the Special Committee on Financial Policies for Post-attack Operations, was examining "the subject of tentative monetary and economic policy for use in a post-attack situation . . ." (Eisenhower to Martin, Apr. 25, 1958; and Martin to Eisenhower, Apr. 28, 1958, WHCF/OF 133-B-7-A). In an interim report of the committee, sent to the President on July 29, Martin would cite three possible approaches: authoritarian command; direct controls, such as rationing; and a monetary credit system. Any policy chosen, Martin said, "should be broad and flexible enough to be applicable in the areas of great damage, marginal areas, and areas that are relatively undamaged." The government should assure solvency and a "'fair' indemnification" for damages (AWF/A; see also Eisenhower to Martin, July 30, 1958, *ibid.*).

In evaluating Operation Alert the following year, Eisenhower would ask that the special committee complete its deliberations so that decisions could be made regarding the liquidity of financial institutions, a moratorium on debts, compensation for losses, and the use of cash or script (Approved Recommendations Growing Out of Operation Alert, Oct. 31, 1958, AWF/Cabinet; see also Cabinet meeting minutes, Oct. 9, 1958, *ibid.*). We have found no copy of a final report in AWF; see, however, National Plan for Civil Defense and Defense Mobilization, October 1958, *ibid.*).

345 — *EM, WHCF, Official File 101-Y*

To George E. Phelps — *September 19, 1957*

Personal

Dear Mr. Phelps: I read with interest your recent letter.[1] Completely agreeing with you that taxes are so high as frequently to be discouraging to individuals, especially the small businessman, I wonder whether you have ever stopped to think what causes the great bulk of these governmental costs.

In the first place, the government is spending a total of something over 45 billion dollars a year to provide for your security—the security of yourself, your family, your business and the people that work for you—against aggressions from without. This sum involves what we spend on our own direct defense, on the Atomic Energy Commission, on necessary stockpiling, and for the cost of our air bases abroad which, as you know, practically encircle the earth.[2] Assistance to the countries where those bases are located is therefore not a "give away" as you imply, but is definitely a part of our own defense arrangements. I feel sure you would not want to endanger our security by cutting down on these expenditures.[3]

The rest of the money that the government collects is spent for internal things of which the largest single item is for the interest we pay on our debt.[4] I assume you understand the reasons why that interest must be promptly and fully paid as it becomes due. Other huge items are for veterans[5] and for the farm program. Incidentally,

I note that you object to the farm program. The Republicans objected to the program they found when they were elected, in 1952, and are not satisfied with the corrections we have, so far, been able to make. We have tried to bring about a better and more economical program to achieve the results we seek—that is, an agricultural plant that receives its fair share of the returns from the functioning of the American economy.[6]

We must not forget that many of today's farm programs arose out of the rigid price guarantees by the government for food and fibre in time of war and which prices were continued thereafter, thus encouraging the building up of huge surpluses and a tremendous governmental cost. It takes time to work out of this kind of affair and to do so in such manner as not to wreck the farm economy, a tragedy which we know would have disastrous effects on the whole economy.

You imply that the social security laws should not be on the books.[7] With this I cannot agree. Hundreds of thousands of our aged would be in dire distress and a direct burden upon their communities except for the funds that have been collected from them and their employers during their earning years to provide for their sustenance in old age. I enclose with this reply excerpts from a letter I received just this morning from the widow of a veteran.[8] It will give you some idea of the other side of the picture. I could attach thousands of others from people who demand—sometimes with pitiful recitations of their personal difficulties—larger expenditures by the Federal government. Postal workers say that their wages are far too low to provide a decent living for themselves and their families; other federal workers say that they are in desperate circumstances because of the government's refusal to pay them adequately.[9]

This Administration has consistently urged that local and state governments take over more of the group responsibilities in this country and depend less on the Federal government for carrying out these functions. State and local governments are not anxious to do so because it would place upon them the burden of collecting the taxes for many things which now they seem to believe they get "free" because they get them from the Federal government.

This is the kind of thinking that must be combatted at every level—local, state and national.

Now just a moment to point up only one or two of the important differences between "Fair Deal-ism" and this Administration.[10]

(*a*). For the first time in a long time the budget has been balanced for two years in succession, with a planned balanced budget for the succeeding year. This means we have stopped deficit spending, with its consequent piling up of the national debt and greater charges for interest.

(*b*). We have fought against the centralization of power and authority in Washington.
(*c*). We have returned the tidelands to the seacoast states to which we believe they belong.[11]
(*d*). We have removed governmental controls from our economy.
(*e*). In 1954 we put over the biggest tax cut in history. It has saved to the American people over 25 billions in taxes, up to date.[12]
(*f*). We enormously reduced the spending plans we inherited upon coming to office.
(*g*). Finally, the Administration has worked constantly to find ways and means to help small business in numbers of ways that appeared applicable. I enclose a very short statement that was prepared only recently by a very knowledgeable man in this field.[13]

Having said all this, I realize that the subjects you bring up are far too lengthy to be completely covered in a single letter. But I did want you to know that the Administration is doing the very best it can to promote the best interests of all the American people.

With best wishes, *Sincerely*

[1] Phelps was the founder of the Phelps Manufacturing Company, designers and manufacturers of airline ground equipment. He had written the President on September 11, 1957 (same file as document). Phelps said he was a "*very* small businessman" struggling to meet his payroll, and pay taxes: "Federal old age taxes, Federal unemployment taxes, federal income taxes, Federal excise taxes, State unemployment taxes, State income taxes, State sales taxes, State and County personal property taxes and sundry other taxes"—Noting that Eisenhower had just signed the Civil Rights Bill (see no. 307), he asked when did his civil rights figure in the Administration's program.
[2] For background on the defense budget see no. 138.
[3] On mutual security see no. 60.
[4] See no. 27.
[5] See Galambos and van Ee, *The Middle Way*, no. 363.
[6] The Eisenhower Administration worked arduously but unsuccessfully to eliminate the agricultural subsidy programs inherited from the New Deal. See *ibid.*, nos. 652 and 1841.
[7] Phelps had written "Where is there concern in your philosophy for my right to enjoy the full fruits of my labor, without being forced by law to forfeit them to the farmers, many of whom have far more income than I; the unemployed laborers, who might be employed if they chose; the thousands of other recipients of government aid including the beneficiaries of all the grandiose Government schemes for improving the lot of the benighted peoples far and near, around the world."
[8] A woman had written to the President to complain about the amount provided by the government to widows of veterans who receive non-service connected pensions. For Eisenhower's response to the widow see no. 348.
[9] See nos. 328 and 343.
[10] Phelps had written that the Republicans had been elected with the hope that "the course of Government that had been pursued for the past twenty years was to be reversed." Now he wondered what had been changed. "Has one New-Deal law been repealed?" he asked. "Has one New-Deal principal [sic] been repudiated, either by law enacted or even recommended?"

[11] See Galambos and van Ee, *The Middle Way*, no. 26.
[12] See *ibid.*, nos. 783 and 784.
[13] For background see *ibid.*, no. 1957. The President had enclosed an eight-page paper on the actions favorable to small business taken by the Eisenhower Administration (same file as document). The paper was probably prepared for the President's Conference on Small Business, which would be held in Washington, D.C., September 23–25 (see *New York Times*, Sept. 23, 24, 25, and 26).

346

EM, AWF, DDE Diaries Series

To Joseph B. Ford, Jr.

September 19, 1957

Dear Mr. Ford: Many thanks for your letter regarding my action on the bill to expand the program of direct home loans for veterans.[1] I greatly appreciate your interest in writing on behalf of the veterans in Sheridan and other small cities in Arkansas.

In announcing my decision, I pointed out that approximately $700 million has already been disbursed in direct loans to veterans in rural areas and small towns. As your letter indicates, that program has been of material aid in providing an opportunity for veterans outside of urban centers to obtain home purchase financing.[2]

At the present time, however, the interest rate on guaranteed loans from private lenders is being held at the uneconomically low rate of 4½ percent because the Congress has declined to make the needed adjustment in the governing statutes. As a result, the large majority of veterans who live in metropolitan centers are precluded from obtaining assistance through the home financing programs of the Veterans Administration.[3] To make direct government loans available to some veterans while loans are not available to others through either public or private channels would be an obvious inequity. Furthermore, the program would have a serious inflationary effect at a time when government must use every means within its power to help prevent increases in the cost of things people buy.

The Housing Act of 1957, which I recently approved, now permits private lenders to make loans insured by the Federal Housing Administration to all citizens on downpayment and maturity terms that are close to those on which veterans' loans have previously been available. You will also be interested to know that the Federal Housing Administration is taking several steps designed to extend their activities into smaller communities, so that veterans and nonveterans alike may obtain insured loans on more favorable terms.[4]

Reaching decisions in matters such as these, affecting so intimately the lives of millions of our people, is not always easy. The issue is hardly ever cast in terms of black and white. I do earnestly believe, however, that the disapproval of the one bill and the approval of the other will prove to be in the best interests of my fellow veterans and of the country as a whole. It was in that spirit that I acted as I did.

With best wishes, *Sincerely*

[1] On September 2 Eisenhower had pocket vetoed H.R. 4602, a bill to encourage construction of veterans' housing in rural areas and small cities by providing funds for direct loans (see *Congressional Quarterly Almanac*, vol. XIII, *1957*, p. 600). Calling the bill discriminatory because it favored rural over urban areas, the President had said that Congress would do better to raise the interest rates on guaranteed and direct loans in order to attract private lenders into veterans' housing (see *Public Papers of the Presidents: Eisenhower, 1957*, pp. 653–55; and *New York Times*, Sept. 4, 1957). Ford's letter is not in AWF.

[2] The President was referring to the Housing Act of 1950 which had authorized direct loans to veterans who lived in rural areas and were unable to get regular GI mortgages.

[3] Eisenhower had already asked Congress to raise interest rates on VA guaranteed mortgages from four and one-half to five percent in order to stimulate private investment in VA mortgages.

[4] On July 12 Eisenhower had signed into law the Housing Act of 1957, which lowered the minimum downpayment required to buy a home with a Federal Housing Administration-insured mortgage. This measure also appropriated additional money to the Federal National Mortgage Association for buying home mortgages from banks and private lenders (see *Congressional Quarterly Almanac*, vol. XIII, *1957*, pp. 594–600).

347 — *EM, AWF, Administration Series*

To Robert Bernerd Anderson — *September 20, 1957*

Dear Bob: The best thing that I note about your experiment with the three issues of different time lengths at four percent is that all were so substantially oversubscribed.[1] It would appear that in our next offering we might shave our interest somewhat, particularly on the 12 year issues. It would be a wonderful thing if we could begin to do a little shaving instead of boosting.[2]

I am glad you sent me the memorandum about the workings of our monetary and credit system, and I shall study it carefully.[3]

With warm regard, *As ever*

[1] Treasury Secretary Anderson had asked Eisenhower's approval for a new public offering of $3 billion of government bonds and notes to raise money for the U.S. Treasury (Anderson to Eisenhower, Sept. 11, 1957, AWF/AWD; Telephone conversation, Eisenhower and Anderson, Sept. 11, 1957, AWF/D). He had told the President on September 19 that all of the offerings had been substantially oversubscribed—the

one-year certificates by 410 percent; the five-year notes by 350 percent; and the 12-year bonds by 930 percent. "While many interpretations will doubtlessly be placed on the offering," Anderson said, "I feel that it is indicative particularly of the establishment of a realistic market for some amount of longer securities that we have been offering which will give us very desirable debt extension and also of a developing confidence in the financial community that our efforts to curb inflation are taking effective hold" (Anderson to Eisenhower, Sept. 19, 1957, AWF/A).

[2] For developments see no. 961.

[3] Anderson's memorandum explained in brief some basic aspects of the money supply, inflation, and the manner in which the Federal Reserve determined the percentage of bank deposits to be held by the nation's banks (*ibid.*).

348 — *EM, AWF, DDE Diaries Series*

To Mrs. Harry Sugarman — *September 20, 1957*

Dear Mrs. Sugarman: I am more than sympathetic with your personal situation, and I would like to be able to hold out to you a promise of concrete help.

In the same mail with your letter I had a long and bitter complaint from a small businessman. He chiefly objected to high taxes and would, I gather, suspend all payments such as the pension you are receiving. The two letters presented directly contrasting points of view, each sincerely expressed.[1]

As I am sure you know, it is not an easy task to be fair to all segments of our society, but this Administration is, at the very least, trying exceedingly hard to do just that.

I shall ask someone in the government to reply to you more fully than I can at the moment, but I did want you to know of my understanding.[2]

With best wishes, *Sincerely*

[1] In mid-September, Eisenhower had received letters from Mrs. Sugarman and George E. Phelps (see no. 345). A large portion of Mrs. Sugarman's letter was included in Eisenhower's reply to Phelps (see papers in WHCF/OF 101-Y). Mrs. Sugarman had complained that widows of veterans received a pension of only $50.40 a month. "Can you for a moment realize," she wrote, "what this means or how one can live on such an amount? Half the time it barely covers your rent, gas and electricity." "At this late age," she added, "when all kinds of sicknesses come to one, and you cannot go out and avail yourself of a position that gives you a living wage it is very unfortunate, don't you think. I hope you and the Congress will see fit to give us at least something we can pay for the essentials of life without having to depend on charity."

[2] In his January 13, 1958, budget message to Congress, Eisenhower would say that he was planning a special message on veterans affairs, with an emphasis on improvements in veterans compensation and pensions. The President's Commission on Veterans Pensions (Bradley Commission) recommended, however, curtailing bene-

fits for uninjured veterans. Faced with a $12 billion deficit, the Administration would not send a message on improved veterans benefits to Capitol Hill (see *Congressional Quarterly Almanac,* vol. XIV, *1958,* pp. 584 and 626; and President's Commission on Veterans' Pensions, *Veterans' Benefits in the United States: Findings and Recommendations* [Washington, D.C., 1956]). There is no further correspondence on this subject in AWF.

349 *EM, AWF, Administration Series*

TO HOWARD PYLE *September 20, 1957*

Memorandum for Governor Pyle: I return herewith the preliminary report from the Council on Youth Fitness.[1] The only recommendation I find in it is for me to make a speech. I have no objection to making a television talk, providing a rough text is worked up that strikes me as making sense and carries real appeal to children and grownups alike. However, I am worried that this is the only recommendation in the paper. I find evidence that the Council is keeping up contacts with certain established organizations, but what I should like to know is "who else is making speeches." What are we doing to get thousands of people really stirred up about the subject and working on it every day?[2]

What I am getting at is that my talk should not be in a vacuum—sort of a one shot affair that people listen to more or less impatiently and then go back to their daily routines. I should like to be able to refer to school boards, city councils, mayors and governors and various associations that are really doing something about this serious matter.

When I return to Washington I should like to talk to you at your convenience about the whole thing.[3]

[1] The President's Council on Youth Fitness and the President's Citizens Advisory Committee on the Fitness of American Youth had held their first annual conference at the United States Military Academy on September 9 and 10. On the Council see its "Preliminary Report: Conclusions and Recommendations," AWF/A, Pyle Corr.; on the establishment of the citizens committee see *Public Papers of the Presidents: Eisenhower, 1957,* pp. 428–29.

[2] Although the preliminary report offered no concrete suggestions, it recommended that governors and mayors organize conferences to discuss fitness programs; that all schools develop physical fitness programs and offer their facilities for community use; and that the government require adequate recreation facilities in housing projects receiving federal funds (AWF/A, Pyle Corr.; *New York Times,* Sept. 11, 1957).

[3] Eisenhower would meet with Pyle several times in October (see President's daily appointments). Early in 1958 the council would publish its long-range goals as well as its immediate objectives. The plan stressed fitness in its broadest sense, including "the mental, emotional, social, spiritual, and physical attainment of the individual"

and encouraged organizations to reevaluate their own programs to meet the challenge (President's Council on Youth Fitness, "Action for Youth Fitness" [Washington, D.C., 1958]). In October 1958 Eisenhower would stress the importance of fitness in his remarks to those attending the first Football Hall of Fame dinner in New York (*Public Papers of the Presidents of the United States: Dwight D. Eisenhower, January 1, to December 31, 1958* [Washington, D.C., 1959], pp. 816–19; for more on the President's ideas about sharing "the speech platform" see Eisenhower to Milton Eisenhower, Sept. 20, 1957, AWF/D).

350

EM, AWF, DDE Diaries Series

To Henry Ford II

September 20, 1957

Dear Henry: I wonder whether it would be at all convenient for you to drop in here at the Naval base at Newport for a round of golf about the middle of next week. I should like to talk to you again about People to People, Inc., an organization in which I am vitally interested.[1] Since it is a conversation rather than a briefing that I have in mind, I think the golf course would be a good place to have the chat.

If this should not be convenient for you, please let me know and I shall try to talk to you on the telephone.[2] *With warm regard*

[1] Ford was president of the Ford Motor Company. The Eisenhowers were vacationing in Newport, Rhode Island. On April 4 the President and Ford had discussed the Ford Foundation's rejection of the People-to-People program's request for funds (Ann Whitman memorandum, Apr. 4, 1957, AWF/AWD). For background on the program see no. 283 (see also Memorandum for the Secretary of State, Sept. 21, 1957, AWF/D-H).

[2] On September 26 Eisenhower and Ford would play eighteen holes of golf at the Newport Country Club. For developments see no. 380.

351

Dulles Papers, White House Memoranda Series

To John Foster Dulles

September 21, 1957

Memorandum for the Secretary of State: Following is an item in my staff notes of today.

"*Sarasin Views on SEATO.* SEATO's first Secretary General, Pote Sarasin, has been struck with the intensity of the effort in the treaty area to set Asians against the US and the West.[1] He believes it cannot be countered merely by attacking Communist policies. People must be shown the tangible benefits of the free way of life and the advantages of cooperation in other than military fields. Sarasin feels that the Asian members individually and together must develop SEATO-labeled projects primarily with their own resources and then invite Western members to make supplementary contributions."

This is the kind of thing where the People-to-People program would be very helpful as a supplement to what the Secretary General recommends.[2]

I wonder how effective our USIA is in that region.

Presumably our Assistant Secretaries of State are the best informed individuals we have on this type of thing, each with respect to his own area. Does each of these men keep close contact with the USIA and does he influence that organization in the kind of effort it should undertake in the locality?[3]

[1] Sarasin, formerly Thailand's ambassador to the United States, became Secretary General of the Southeast Asia Treaty Organization in July 1957. Following a government reorganization in September he was named Prime Minister of Thailand. Although there were doubts about the extent of his political power, Sarasin was considered to be friendly toward the West (see State, *Foreign Relations, 1955–1957*, vol. XXII, *Southeast Asia*, pp. 930–34; and NSC meeting minutes, Sept. 24, 1957, AWF/NSC).

[2] For background on the People-to-People program see no. 197.

[3] Dulles would tell Eisenhower that programs under government sponsorship were better adapted to the particular problems found in the Far East than unofficial ones such as those sponsored by the People-to-People program. Cultural, technical, and military exchanges had been effective, Dulles said, as well as trade fairs and the tours of American performing artists. He would ask the Assistant Secretary of State for Public Affairs to explore the possibilities of using the People-to-People program more effectively in conjunction with the cultural and information officers in the various embassies. "Our Assistant Secretaries of State in charge of geographic areas do indeed exert a direct influence on U.S. Information Agency programs," Dulles added. "On the whole, I feel that this system works pretty effectively" (Dulles to Eisenhower, Sept. 26, 1957, AWF/D-H).

352 — *EM, AWF, DDE Diaries Series*

To Jill Robin Steinberg — *September 21, 1957*

Dear Jill: You have presented to me a different kind of problem—one that, I am afraid, would quite mistakenly place me in the middle of a family disagreement.[1]

If I may venture to advise you, I would suggest that you have a little conversation with yourself to discover the reasons why you are getting these spankings. Possibly you have your hand in the cookie jar too often or are careless about keeping your room neat. Whatever the reason, I believe that the best place to begin putting a stop to these unpleasant experiences is to avoid those things that little girls should not do. I am quite certain that in this way the spankings will be fewer and you will have just as much fun as you are having now.

With best wishes, *Sincerely*

[1] The child had written: "Dear Present; My name is Jill Robin Steinberg and I get to many spankings." The letter was postmarked September 6, 1957, and mailed from New York City (WHCF/PPF 33: Human Interest).

353 — *EM, AWF, Dulles-Herter Series*

To John Foster Dulles — *September 22, 1957*

Top secret

Dear Foster: I should like you to have this at once because Harold implies that the time element is important, from his viewpoint.[1] As you know, I have long been sympathetic to some such idea as this, but at the moment we have this long series of tests coming up and of course we cannot wreck AEC plans that are already far advanced.[2]

However, I am doubtful about the propaganda value of saying that we would limit our tests to the number that would create only a specified amount of radiation. On the other hand, any joint statement announcing the intention to register in advance, to fix a reasonable limit and, incidentally, to state that this would never exceed a certain level of radiation, might have real worth.

Possibly I can talk to you about it tomorrow morning at the Security Council.[3]

[1] Eisenhower is referring to a letter from British Prime Minister Macmillan regarding nuclear disarmament. This message was telephoned to Secretary Dulles from Newport, Rhode Island, where Eisenhower was vacationing (Ann Whitman dictation, Sept. 22, 1958, Dulles Papers, Telephone Conversations).

[2] Unwilling to enter a United Nations General Assembly debate on the disarmament question without "a definite and 'constructive' plan," Macmillan had offered a three-point proposal: First, all tests would be declared beforehand and registered with the United Nations, or some other international body. Second, explosions in the succeeding two years would be limited unilaterally, whether the Soviet Union agreed or not. Third, the radiation created by the explosions would not exceed a previously specified figure (Macmillan to Eisenhower, Sept. 18, 1957, PREM 11/2187; State, *Foreign Relations, 1955–1957*, vol. XX, *Regulation of Armaments; Atomic Energy*, pp. 721–22; and Macmillan, *Riding the Storm*, pp. 313–14).

The Atomic Energy Commission had scheduled Hardtack, a program of twenty-five thermonuclear experiments at the Bikini and Enewetok atolls beginning in May 1958. In August Eisenhower had discussed with AEC Chairman Strauss his concerns regarding the number of explosions and the duration of the testing period. Conducting these tests at the same time that the United States was professing a desire to suspend testing in a disarmament program, the President said, "may bring accusations of bad faith" from much of the world. Eisenhower had agreed, however, to proceed with the tests (John Eisenhower, Memorandum of Conference, Aug. 9, 1957, AWF/D; see also Divine, *Blowing on the Wind,* pp. 157–60; and Hewlett and Holl, *Atoms for Peace and War,* pp. 456–62).
[3] Dulles would meet with Eisenhower the following day. For the President's response to Macmillan see the following document.

354 *EM, AWF, International Series: Macmillan*

TO HAROLD MACMILLAN *September 23, 1957*
Cable. Secret

Dear Harold: I have your letter on disarmament—dated the 21st I think. I spoke briefly to Foster about it when I was in Washington this morning.[1] I am going back to Newport this afternoon and he in the meantime will speak to Lewis Strauss.

We have, together, already moved quite a distance in the direction you suggest and perhaps by putting it all together, and putting it in a fresh package with some little addition, it could be made into what would catch the popular imagination.

I shall be in touch with you later after I get a further report of the talk between Foster and Lewis Strauss.[2]

I share your happiness over our close working relations with reference to the Middle East.[3]

With warm personal regard, *As ever*

[1] Macmillan's letter was probably dated September 18; see the preceding document.
[2] In response to Dulles's request for an Eisenhower/Macmillan statement on nuclear testing, AEC Chairman Strauss submitted a draft stating that the security of the free world depended on the nuclear deterrent, a fact that made weapons testing inescapable. Without a satisfactory agreement on reliable inspection, Strauss wrote, testing would continue with prior announcements, international inspections, radiations controls, and the publication of test results (Strauss to Dulles, n.d., AWF/D-H). Dulles would send Strauss's statement to Eisenhower on September 29. "I must confess," Dulles said in an accompanying message, "I am somewhat disappointed that he does not seem to feel it is possible to go further with specific proposals to limit testing" (*ibid.*). For developments see no. 384.
[3] Macmillan's September 18 letter to Eisenhower (AWF/I: Macmillan) had briefly mentioned the Middle East; see also Dulles to Macmillan, September 19, 1957, AWF/D-H.

355 *EM, AWF, Administration Series*

To Alfred Maximillian Gruenther *September 24, 1957*

Dear Al: It is difficult but necessary to learn that anyone in public position must expect criticism, some of it based upon stupidity and ignorance, and even at times, deliberate misrepresentation.[1]

You and I know that I had *no* part whatsoever in having you appointed to the head of the Red Cross. In fact, so far as I can recall, no one even asked me for a recommendation. We know that the Status of Forces Treaties were *not* negotiated independently of the military; in fact you and I were serving in the military at the time and we know that the Army was desperately anxious to get them enacted. Such knowledge as this makes you want to strike back at the perpetrators of such falsehoods.

It is better, I think, to learn to ignore the Clarks and the Lewises, remembering that such people are trying to achieve headlines and have discovered that it is far easier to do it by the demagogic method of attacking something that is constructive and practical, and by appealing to emotion and prejudice.

So take a relaxed stance when in the batter's box and hit them as you see them! *As ever*

P.S. Thanks for your suggestion that I come back to Washington. From the beginning of the Arkansas trouble I have thought about the matter, but I feel about as follows:[2]

> The White House office is wherever the President may happen to be. To rush back to Washington every time an incident of a serious character arose would be a confession that a change of scenery is truly a "vacation" for the President and is not merely a change of his working locale. This is untrue. I have never been away from Washington when the important problems did not follow me and the necessity for making the decisions remain with me.
>
> Another portion of my thinking involves the idea that I do not want to exaggerate the significance of the admittedly serious situation in Arkansas. I do not want to give a picture of a Cabinet in constant session, of fretting and worrying about the actions of a misguided governor who, in my opinion, has been motivated entirely by what he believes to be political advantage in a particular locality.
>
> The Federal government has ample resources with which to cope with this kind of thing. The great need is to act calmly, deliberately, and giving every offender opportunity to cease his defiance of Federal law and to peaceably obey the proper or-

ders of the Federal court. In this way the actions of the Executive in enforcing the law—even if it becomes necessary to employ considerable force—are understood by all, and the individuals who have offended are not falsely transformed into martyrs.

On the other hand, for a number of reasons I wish I were back there. My work would be a lot easier to do.

[1] Gruenther had written Eisenhower in the wake of criticism generated by his message to the thirty-ninth national convention of the American Legion in Atlantic City. Gruenther, who was representing Eisenhower at the convention, had spoken in favor of the Status of Forces Agreements of 1953, which among other things gave foreign countries jurisdiction over offenses committed by U.S. forces stationed abroad. He called the agreements "an integral part" of the U.S. alliance system and asked the Legion not to pass a resolution denouncing them. General Mark Wayne Clark, however, had denounced the agreements before the Legionnaires, saying that they had been designed by the State Department without consulting the armed forces. In a broadcast on September 18, Fulton Lewis, Jr., national affairs commentator for the Mutual Broadcasting System, had praised Clark's speech and called the agreements "screwball and thoroughly un-American." The Legion, Lewis said, "was not much impressed" with Gruenther, who was "beholden to the Eisenhower administration, not only for the long series of promotions he was given up to the very top in military rank, but for the super-plush job of President of the American Red Cross" (Broadcast excerpt, Sept. 18, 1957, AWF/A, Gruenther Corr.; *New York Times*, Sept. 18, 1957). For background on the Status of Forces Treaties see Galambos and van Ee, *The Middle Way*, no. 316; on the Girard case, which had aroused public opinion against the agreements, see no. 200 in these volumes.

Gruenther told Eisenhower that he was upset at Lewis's "swing" at the Red Cross. "But what really pains me," he wrote, "is Wayne Clark's stand. He has hit the alliance system constantly in the fashion of a demagogue" (Gruenther to Eisenhower, Sept. 20, 1957, AWF/A). Assistant to the President Sherman Adams would teasingly add to the President's advice: "If you don't carry out orders better than you are doing I will see that you get another promotion" (Adams to Gruenther, Oct. 2, 1957, Gruenther Papers).

[2] On the situation in Little Rock see no. 330.

356 *EM, AWF, DDE Diaries Series*

To Marie Helene Sasselli *September 25, 1957*

Dear Miss Sasselli: Thank you for your letter of September 3, 1957, concerning proposed legislation to extend educational benefits to peacetime ex-servicemen.[1]

The administration has been making a thorough study of the needs of veterans and peacetime ex-servicemen, and legislative proposals will be submitted to the next session of the Congress.[2] We believe it is a sound premise that the benefits provided should be related to special needs which result directly from military service and which are not met by other means. Careful studies show that, except in those cases where actual disability is incurred, the handicaps resulting from peacetime service are less extensive than the problems associated with service in time of war and there is less need of special benefits.[3]

Sudden involvement in war produces serious disruption of educational and career plans for the young men who enter the Armed Forces. In contrast, peacetime military service can be anticipated and incorporated into personal plans well in advance. Selective service policies now promote reasonable integration of schooling with military service obligations. In addition, peacetime service offers wide opportunities for off-duty education and training while in uniform. The demand for skilled personnel in the Armed Forces has also increased the scope of on-duty training and many of the skills thus developed are useful in later civilian occupations. Because of all these factors we do not believe that peacetime military service creates educational problems and inequalities comparable with those which result from wartime service. The problems of securing education which peacetime ex-servicemen have are common to all young people.

The general problem of ensuring adequate post-high school education for our young people is one with which I am deeply concerned. In 1956, I appointed the Committee on Education Beyond the High School to study the problems of higher education and to develop proposals which our Nation could take in meeting them.[4] As you know, our federal system of government places primary responsibility for higher education on State, local, and private resources. Under this system great institutions of learning, both public and private, have been developed and the freedom of these institutions must be protected from centralized control.

The Committee on Education Beyond the High School recently submitted its second report containing, among other things, recommendations as to the appropriate role of the Federal government in post-high school education.[5] These recommendations will be carefully reviewed and evaluated. Until such time as this is done, I am, of course, not in a position to comment on them in detail.

I have written you as fully as possible on this subject in order that you may realize that sympathetic and careful consideration is given to all phases of the matter.

With best wishes, *Sincerely*

[1] Sasselli's letter is not in AWF.

[2] In January 1955 Eisenhower had established a Commission on Veterans' Pensions, chaired by General Omar N. Bradley, to "assess the structure, scope, philosophy, and

administration of pension, compensation, and related nonmedical benefits" furnished to veterans (see *Public Papers of the Presidents of the United States: Dwight D. Eisenhower, January 1 to December 31, 1955* [Washington, D.C., 1959], pp. 320–22). See also no. 348.

[3] Beginning with the Servicemen's Readjustment Act of 1944, the U.S. government had sought to address the special problems of veterans that resulted from the interruption of their normal lives by military service. The GI bill granted ex-servicemen readjustment allowances, money for education and training, guaranteed loans for purchase of homes, farms or businesses, mustering-out pay, reemployment rights, and preferential treatment in the civil service and public employment sectors (President's Commission on Veterans' Pensions, *Veterans' Benefits in the United States*, pp. 231–72). The central purpose of the 1944 act and subsequent Korean GI bill was to provide transitional benefits to be used during the period in which the veteran was adjusting to civilian life. The Bradley Commission had concluded, however, that military service during peacetime constituted a significantly smaller disruption to the veterans' civilian life than wartime service. Since selective service deferment policies allowed all young men who so desired to complete high school and college before induction, and since military service was reasonably well compensated and provided substantial opportunities for training and useful experience, the Commission decided that military service did not involve sufficient interruption to the educational progress of servicemen to warrant a special educational program (*ibid.*, p. 17).

[4] See Committee for the White House Conference on Education, *Report to the President* (Washington, D.C., 1956), and *Public Papers of the Presidents: Eisenhower, 1956*, pp. 1035–38.

[5] The Committee had urged the federal government to meet the challenges the postwar "baby boom" presented to higher education. Among its suggestions were income tax credits for college tuition and low-interest loans to students (*New York Times*, Aug. 11, Oct. 27, 1957). For developments see no. 416.

357 — *EM, AWF, DDE Diaries Series*

To Woodrow Wilson Mann — *September 26, 1957*

Dear Mr. Mayor: The events since your telegram of the twenty-fourth was sent to me in themselves, I am sure you will agree, serve as both reply and reaction to your request.[1] Your estimate of the situation as it existed at that time was helpful.[2]

With best wishes, *Sincerely*

[1] For background on Little Rock Mayor Mann's telegram describing the urgent need for federal troops see no. 330. "The mob is much larger in numbers at 8 AM than at any time yesterday," Mann had stated. Calling the situation "out of control," Mann pleaded with Eisenhower that "in the interest of humanity, law and order," he should send the necessary federal troops quickly (AWF/D). The Mayor's message came after several weeks of growing tensions surrounding the court-ordered integration of Central High School in Little Rock. Although Eisenhower initially believed that he had secured Arkansas Governor Faubus's pledge at their September 14 meeting to comply with the federal court order, the White House by September 19 realized that

Faubus was instead planning "to engage in some legal manoeuvering to try to block and frustrate the order of that Court" (Goodpaster memorandum, Sept. 19, 1957, AWF/D). Both Sherman Adams and Attorney General Brownell had advised the President to make no public statement at that time, but wait until Governor Faubus refused to comply with a court directive to admit the children at once. Since the federal government would then be obligated to require Faubus to comply by whatever means necessary, the President should then speak to the country.

On Friday, September 20, Faubus had removed the National Guard from Central High. He further advised the African-American students to remain away from the school until a "cooling off period" had elapsed. On Monday, September 23, after a violent mob threatened the African-American students and caused their removal from school, Eisenhower had issued a statement calling the events in Little Rock "disgraceful." Stating that federal law could not be "flouted with impunity by any individual or any mob of extremists," Eisenhower made clear that he would "use the full power of the United States including whatever force may be necessary to prevent any obstruction of the law and to carry out the orders of the Federal Court" (*Public Papers of the Presidents: Eisenhower, 1957,* p. 689). Eisenhower ordered units of the 101st Airborne Division into Little Rock the following day (see *New York Times,* Sept. 21, 24, 25, 26, 27; see also Eisenhower, *Waging Peace,* pp. 168–70). For another view see Melba Pattillo Beals, *Warriors Don't Cry* (New York, 1994); Elizabeth Huckaby, *Crisis at Central High, Little Rock, 1957–58* (Baton Rouge, 1980), pp. 1–50; and Daisy Bates, *The Long Shadow of Little Rock: A Memoir* (New York, 1962), pp. 59–112. For Faubus's view see Orval Eugene Faubus, *Down From the Hills* (Little Rock, Ark., 1980), pp. 205–328.

[2] For developments see no. 359.

358 *EM, AWF, DDE Diaries Series*

To J. E. Phillips, Sr. *September 26, 1957*

Dear Mr. Phillips: I read your letter with the greatest sympathy for the problems that you are experiencing on your Arizona farm.[1] While I cannot possibly answer it personally in the detail it deserves, I am asking the Secretary of Agriculture to give your suggestions his personal attention.

In regard to the problems of the farmer in general, I would like simply to say this. As you point out, the agricultural situation that the Republicans inherited in 1952 was far from satisfactory, as was the program then in force for solving the problems. We are not satisfied with the corrections we have, so far, been able to make. But we have tried to bring about a better and more economical program to achieve the results we seek—that is, an agricultural plant that receives its fair share of the returns from the functioning of the American economy. I assure you that we want to help, not complicate, the problems of the small farmer.[2]

As I say, I shall ask Mr. Benson to give you a fuller explanation of the actions that the government felt necessary; meantime, I do want to thank you for a fine presentation of a situation that I know is most distressing to you.[3] I am indebted to you for writing to me.

With best wishes, *Sincerely*

[1] Phillips had written on September 19 (AWF/D) regarding "the plight of the small farmer" in America. Phillips wrote that he was "a man 62 years old—far too old to compete with the requirements of younger men in industrial plants, or anywhere else. However, I can still drive a tractor and hoe a row." Since the initiation of the Eisenhower Administration's soil bank program (see Galambos and van Ee, *The Middle Way*, no. 1595), he had seen his cotton acreage reduced from seventy to twenty-one acres and his farm's profitability cut in half. Meanwhile, he said, the large-scale farmers in his area were continuing to plant thousands of acres of cotton.

[2] On the Eisenhower Administration's farm program see Galambos and van Ee, *The Middle Way*, nos. 1748 and 1841. See also Benson, *Cross Fire*, pp. 289–359; Willard W. Cochrane and Mary E. Ryan, *American Farm Policy, 1948–1973* (Minneapolis, 1976), pp. 30–35, 76–79, 145–50; and Don Paarlberg, *American Farm Policy: A Case Study of Centralized Decision-Making* (New York, 1964), pp. 237–46.

[3] Eisenhower would write to Secretary of Agriculture Ezra Taft Benson on September 27 (AWF/D) asking him to examine Phillips's letter. "I cannot understand," the President would write, "how a seventy-acre production was cut to twenty-one acres since I know that our overall cotton acreage has not been reduced by a similar seventy percent." The Agriculture Department would respond that Phillips lived in an area where large-scale cotton planting was a relatively recent phenomenon, and such areas had been hit relatively hard by the latest production quotas. Some large farmers had chosen to grow cotton in excess of the allotments, a practice the government permitted so long as a penalty was paid on each excess pound the farm marketed (McLain to Phillips, Oct. 16, 1957, and Benson to Eisenhower, Oct. 22, 1957, WHCF/OF 106).

359

EM, AWF, Administration Series: Little Rock

To Richard Brevard Russell — *September 27, 1957*

Telegram

Few times in my life have I felt as saddened as when the obligations of my office required me to order the use of force within a state to carry out the decisions of a Federal Court.[1] My conviction is that had the police powers of the State of Arkansas been utilized not to frustrate the orders of the Court but to support them, the ensuing violence and open disrespect for the law and the Federal Judiciary would never have occurred. The Arkansas National Guard could have handled the situation with ease had it been instructed to do so. As a matter of fact, had the integration of Central High School been permitted to take place without the intervention of the National Guard, there is little doubt that the process would have gone along quite as smoothly and quietly as it has in other Arkansas communities. When a State, by seeking to frustrate the orders of a Federal Court, encourages mobs of extremists to flout the orders of a Federal Court, and when a State refuses to utilize its police powers to protect against mobs persons who are peaceably exercising their right under the Constitution as defined in such Court orders, the oath of office of the President requires that he take action to give that protection. Failure to act in such a case would be tantamount to acquiescence in anarchy and the dissolution of the union.

I must say that I completely fail to comprehend your comparison of our troops to Hitler's storm troopers. In one case military power was used to further the ambitions and purposes of a ruthless dictator, in the other to preserve the institutions of free government.[2]

You allege certain wrong-doings on the part of individual soldiers at Little Rock. The Secretary of the Army will assemble the facts and report them directly to you.[3] *With warm regard*

[1] For background see nos. 330 and 357. On September 24, 1957, Eisenhower had ordered United States Army paratroopers to prevent interference with federal court orders directing the admission of nine African-American pupils to Central High School in Little Rock, Arkansas. The President had also ordered into federal service all 10,000 members of the Arkansas National Guard in order to prevent state-federal clashes or further obstruction. Speaking to the American people by radio and television that evening, Eisenhower explained his action. "Whenever normal agencies prove inadequate to the task and it becomes necessary for the Executive Branch of the Federal Government to use its powers and authority to uphold Federal Courts, the President's responsibility is inescapable." Eisenhower, who had returned to Washington from his holiday in Newport, Rhode Island, said that he had hoped that local authorities would have handled the disturbance. "But," he added, "when large gatherings of obstructionists made it impossible for the decrees of the Court to be carried out, both the law and the national interest demanded that the President take action." If the President and the Executive Branch of the Government did not insure the carrying out of the decisions of the Federal Courts, the basis of American individual rights and freedoms would be undermined. Mob rule could not be allowed to override the decisions of the courts or anarchy would prevail. Eisenhower emphasized that the troops were in Little Rock "solely for the purpose of preventing interference with the orders of the Court," and not to relieve state and local authorities of their duty to preserve peace in the community (see *Public Papers of the Presidents: Eisenhower, 1957*, pp. 689–94, and *New York Times*, Sept. 25, 1957).

[2] Georgia Senator and Chairman of the Senate Committee on Armed Services, Russell had sent a telegram to the President on September 26 (AWF/A: Little Rock). Russell protested the "highhanded and illegal methods" of the Army, which was "disregarding and overriding the elementary rights of American citizens by applying tactics which must have been copied from the manual issued the officers of Hitler's storm troopers."

[3] Russell had cited several instances where soldiers had supposedly struck or pushed unarmed civilians standing on private property. The Senator was also concerned about the alleged arrest of eight persons who reportedly had been held, incommunicado, in jail overnight and without formal charges. "There are a number of other

aspects of this case as reported in the press which do not reflect credit upon those in command of this army of troopers," Russell wrote. "Unless corrected this will bring the armed services into disrepute. I earnestly insist that orders be issued prohibiting these acts of violence," the Senator urged. He also demanded that the government "investigate these attacks and properly punish all of those who may have been guilty of unnecessary violence against inoffensive and peacable [*sic*] American citizens." For developments see no. 362.

360 *EM, AWF, Administration Series*

To Henry Cabot Lodge, Jr. *September 27, 1957*

Dear Cabot: Thank you for writing me, in characteristically understanding fashion, regarding the Little Rock situation.[1] I realize, with you, the harm that our prestige has suffered, and if you have any ideas as to how we might try to repair the damage, after the situation calms down, I would be most interested.[2]

I am, of course, gratified by your reaction to the Meany appointment. You can't imagine what a relief it is to hear something pleasant for a change![3]

With warm regard, *Sincerely*

[1] For background on the use of federal troops to enforce federal court integration orders in Little Rock, Arkansas, see no. 355. Lodge had praised Eisenhower's "magnificent decision" to intervene and had expressed sympathy for the "anguish" that it had caused the President (Lodge to Eisenhower, Sept. 25, 1957, AWF/A).

[2] "More than two-thirds of the world is non-white," Lodge had told Eisenhower, "and the reactions of the representatives of these people is easy to see."

Responding to the President's request, Lodge would suggest that diplomatic representatives in all countries "make a sustained effort to extend hospitality to distinguished colored people." He further recommended that the United States make a loan to India, "a key country with much of the non-white world," and support the concept of multilateral economic aid under the United Nations (Lodge to Eisenhower, Oct. 15, 1957, *ibid.*).

[3] Lodge had told Eisenhower that he had "made a ten strike" by appointing George Meany, president of the American Federation of Labor and the Congress of Industrial Organizations, to the United States delegation to the United Nations. "His appointment is not only good politics, but very useful to our foreign relations" (Sept. 25, 1957, *ibid.*).

361

EM, WHCF, Official File 142-A-5-A

To Robert Raymond Brown

September 27, 1957

Dear Bishop Brown: From Walter Robertson I have learned with gratitude of your offer, made on behalf of the church leaders in Little Rock, to be helpful in the present troublesome situation arising there out of court decisions affecting desegregation of the races in the public schools. I deeply believe that there is much that Little Rock's ministers, as the spiritual and moral leaders of the community, can do to help place the matter in proper perspective before all citizens.[1]

The founders of our nation clearly felt that free government is a political expression of religious faith, with basic human rights deriving directly from the individual's Creator. Religious leaders have an especial opportunity I think, to help keep such a government strong and vital and continuously devoted to the concepts that inspired the signers of our Declaration of Independence.

What is now at stake is whether we as citizens of this great nation will remain faithful to the institutions that have been provided for us to make effective the will of the majority as authorized and limited by our Constitution. The immediate question is not at all whether any particular individual agrees with a particular decision of the Supreme Court. The real question is whether we shall respect the institutions of free government or, by defying them, set up either a process of deterioration and disruption or compel the authorities to resort to force to obtain that respect which we all should willingly give.

Never has it been more important than now that we, as a united nation, give to our system and to our laws the unswerving loyalty and devotion which has always been the strength of free government.

Today the very concepts of freedom are under relentless attack by an atheistic ideology that denies any right or any dignity to the individual not accorded him by the state. The liberties we so much love, that we can practice among ourselves because of the basic belief that we constitute one brotherhood under the fatherhood of God, demand that we stand together steadfastly against the relentless assaults of international communism. If we ourselves defy the instruments by which our liberties have been and are being preserved, our vulnerability to the outside threat will be vastly, even terrifyingly, increased.

On the positive side to obey the law is one mark of our devotion to our country. It is one means open to every individual through which he may make that country stronger.

Consequently I hope that you and the ministers of Little Rock will be able not only to lead all the citizens of the city to disregard the incitements of agitators, but will join in support of the law and the preservation of our country and the institutions of government under which it lives. And I could hope that your prayers would seek the power for all of us to cast out rancor and prejudice in favor of understanding and compassion. In such a climate the distressing problem that has so stirred up the emotions of many citizens in our land can, in good time, be solved. All of us realize that not through legislation alone can prejudice and hatred be eliminated from the hearts of men. Leadership, including religious leadership, must play its part.[2]

Again my gratitude to you and your associates in the clergy for your offer to be helpful. I am convinced that if all of us work together in the spirit implicit in your suggestion, we should eventually be able to work out all our problems, including those of race, and as a consequence, our beloved country will be greater, stronger and more secure in all the years to come. *Sincerely*

[1] Brown (B.D. Virginia Theological Seminary 1937), the Episcopal Bishop of Arkansas, had telephoned Assistant Secretary of State for Far East Affairs Walter Spencer Robertson (LL.B. Davidson College 1912) to voice his and other Arkansas church leaders' support of the President's decision to use federal troops to enforce the court-ordered integration of Central High School in Little Rock (for background see nos. 330 and 357). On September 25 Robertson telephoned Attorney General Brownell, who in turn transmitted the message to Presidential Secretary Ann Whitman.

[2] The President would call upon religious leaders to advocate moral and spiritual values in an October 3 news conference (see no. 412). On October 4 Brown would reply that the President's call had been "received enthusiastically by clergy of all faiths" in Little Rock. Jewish, Roman Catholic, and Protestant leaders, Brown wrote, would hold services to "pray for the support and preservation of law and order." On October 9 Brown would report that on Saturday, October 12, approximately eighty-one churches "of all denominations will conduct services according to their own worship forms in line with the request contained" in Eisenhower's letter. Brown added that the National Council of Churches of Christ of America and the Union of American Hebrew Congregations were calling for similar services to be held on the same date. All correspondence is in the same file as the document.

362 *EM, AWF, DDE Diaries Series*

To Harold Engstrom *September 28, 1957*

Personal

Dear Mr. Engstrom: Thank you very much for your letter; it is heartening to have such tangible evidence that a citizen of Little Rock, a member of the School Board, is thinking so clearly and fearlessly about the problem in your city now occupying the attention of almost the whole country.[1] I was particularly encouraged by your forthright statement that you, the School Board, and other conscientious citizens, will continue your efforts to restore respect and support for the true ideals of America.[2] I believe that if all of us are patient and considerate in our dealings with others, but firm in support of principle, we shall proceed toward a solution to this problem much faster than if we allow emotion and ignorance and demagogic appeals to characterize our words and actions.[3]

With best wishes, *Sincerely*

[1] Engstrom, Chief Engineer at the Arkansas Foundry Company, had written the President on September 25 (AWF/D). He said that he and the other members of the Little Rock School Board could make no public statement without further agitating "the people here who are doing great harm to our community and nation. . . ." Nevertheless, Engstrom said, he thought all of Eisenhower's "statements and . . . actions have been most appropriate and accurately analyzed." Had Eisenhower not acted as he did, "education at Central High would have been warped." For background see nos. 330, 357, and 359.

[2] Engstom had apologized for "the petty politics which has brought this difficult problem to its present status" but assured the President that he, the school board, and all other conscientious citizens would "continue our efforts to restore the respect and support for the true ideals of America which you so ably stand for."

[3] As the mobs dispersed and integration proceeded at Central High, Eisenhower sought a speedy removal of federal troops from Little Rock. On September 25 he agreed to meet with the governors of Tennessee, Florida, North Carolina, and Maryland to discuss Southern compliance with the Supreme Court rulings on school integration, as well as the removal of troops from Little Rock. The President would meet with the governors on October 1 (see *New York Times*, Sept. 26, 27, 1957). For developments see no. 365.

363 — *EM, WHCF, Official File 101-MM*

To Charles Phelps Taft — *September 30, 1957*

Dear Charlie: Thank you for sending me a copy of the talk you made about the "modernism" of your father in public office.[1] It told me much of which I was unaware; I was delighted to read it.[2]

Frankly, the hatred of some people for the word "modern" seems to me to be very much forced—and certainly ridiculous. I am sure those Congressmen who pretend to fear the word do not drive to their offices behind a team of bays, nor refuse to eat any food that is not cooked on the coal stoves of Lincoln's time. Either we are modern, or we do not belong in the year 1957.

Again my gratitude to you for your thoughtfulness in sending me a copy of your most interesting talk.

With warm regard, *Sincerely*

[1] Taft, son of William Howard Taft (1857–1930; 27th President of the United States), was mayor of Cincinnati, Ohio. He had delivered the talk at the opening of the University of Cincinnati Law School on September 16. The younger Taft had referred to his father as a "'modern Republican.'" As examples, Mayor Taft cited the enactment of the corporate income tax and the establishment of the U.S. Postal Savings System. He added that his father appointed as the first director of the newly-created Children's Bureau "the first woman to hold a high post in the U.S. government." Taft's speech and September 23 cover letter are in WHCF/OF 101-MM.

[2] Eisenhower had outlined his concept of "modern Republicanism" in a speech following his election victory in November 1956 (see no. 101). See also *New York Times*, November 19, 1957.

The Space Age Begins

OCTOBER 1957 TO JANUARY 1958

6

Sputnik and "the fears of our own people"

364

EM, AWF, International Series: Japan

To Nobusuke Kishi
Cable

October 1, 1957

Dear Mr. Prime Minister:[1] I have for a long time given serious and thoughtful consideration to the issue you raise in your communication of September 24 regarding the continuation of nuclear testing, which has been the subject of discussion between us in the past.[2]

Unfortunately, I have been able to reach no other conclusion than that for the time being and in the present circumstances, the security of the United States, and, I believe, that of the free world, depends to a great degree upon what we learn from the testing of nuclear weapons. We are at a stage when testing is required for the development of important defensive uses of nuclear weapons, particularly against missiles, submarines, and aircraft, as well as to reduce further the fallout yield from nuclear weapons. To stop these tests in the absence of effective limitations on nuclear weapons production and on other elements of armed strength and without the opening up of all principal nations to a measure of inspection as a safeguard against surprise attack in which nuclear weapons could be used is a sacrifice which would be dangerous to accept.[3]

We are aware of the preoccupations with the question of health hazards connected with nuclear testing.[4] We believe that these are ill founded. However, we have pledged to conduct those tests which may be necessary only in such a manner as will keep world radiation from rising to more than a small fraction of the levels which might be hazardous. Also, as you know, the General Assembly has established a scientific committee to study this problem. This committee is due to report by July 1958, and its findings will no doubt be fully debated in the United Nations.[5]

We believe that nuclear tests can and should be suspended if other limitations of the type I have mentioned are agreed upon. Accordingly, the United States has joined with the Governments of the United Kingdom, France, and Canada in presenting proposals which provide for the suspension of testing in this context.[6] Of special importance, I think, is the proposal that further production of fissionable materials for weapons purposes be stopped and a beginning be made in the reduction of existing weapons stockpiles. We believe that if this proposal is widely supported in the General Assembly, it will be accepted by the Soviet Union. In this event, we would be assured that atomic energy in the future would be devoted to peaceful purposes everywhere in the world.[7] *Sincerely*

[1] Kishi, formerly Japan's Foreign Minister, had become Prime Minister in February 1957.

[2] Kishi had asked Eisenhower to support a proposal, submitted by the Japanese delegation to the United Nations General Assembly, to suspend all nuclear testing for one year. Such a decision, he said, would enable disarmament negotiations to proceed without countries "repeating their tests, creating a vicious cycle of the most regrettable kind, which does nothing to lessen the distrust among nations" (Kishi to Eisenhower, Sept. 24, 1957, AWF/D-H; see also State, *Foreign Relations, 1955–1957,* vol. XX, *Regulation of Armaments; Atomic Energy,* pp. 345–46; for background on the London disarmament negotiations see no. 217). Secretary Dulles had recommended that Eisenhower reply personally to Kishi, due to "the extreme Japanese sensitivity on this question and the importance of securing Japanese support for our armament position" (Dulles to Eisenhower, Sept. 28, 1957, AWF/D-H). The State Department drafted this response.

[3] Eisenhower made two "minor changes" in the preceding sentence, which, he told Dulles, "make clearer the intent" (*ibid.*).

[4] See, for example, nos. 223 and 231 on the dangers of radiation.

[5] On December 3, 1955, the United Nations General Assembly had unanimously adopted a resolution establishing the multinational committee. The governments of eleven nations, including Japan, had each appointed one scientist to the committee (State, *Foreign Relations, 1955–1957,* vol. XX, *Regulation of Armaments; Atomic Energy,* pp. 234–35, 236–39).

[6] The United States, Great Britain, France, and Canada had presented the Western proposals to the Soviet Union on August 29. The plan included a prohibition on the future production of fissionable materials for anything but peaceful purposes, the placement of some armaments under international supervision, the cessation of nuclear weapons testing for one year, a ban on the use of nuclear weapons except in self-defense against an aggressor, and the establishment of an inspection system to prevent surprise attacks (State, *Foreign Relations, 1955–1957,* vol. XX, *Regulation of Armaments; Atomic Energy,* pp. 620–26, 695–97, 703–5, 710–18; see also Dulles, Memorandum of Conversation, Oct. 1, 1957, Dulles Papers, White House Memoranda Series).

[7] For developments see no. 494.

365 *EM, AWF, Administration Series*

To Richard Milhous Nixon *October 2, 1957*

Dear Dick: I had been hoping to play golf this afternoon, but will probably not know before 12 or 1 o'clock whether it will be possible for me to be absent from the office.

In the event I do go, I wonder whether you would play with me. We could get Tom Belshe and anyone else you might suggest.[1]

If you already have a game, please don't think of changing your plans because mine are necessarily so uncertain because of the stupidity and duplicity of one called Faubus.[2] *As ever*

[1] Retired Air Force Colonel Belshe was greens chairman at Burning Tree Country Club, where he frequently golfed with Eisenhower.

[2] On the preceding day Eisenhower had met with the governors of Florida, North

Carolina, Maryland, and Tennessee, representing the Southern Governors Conference, in a continuing effort to resolve the problems in Little Rock (see no. 362). During the meeting the President stated that he would withdraw the federal troops from Little Rock and return control of the National Guard to Arkansas as soon as Governor Faubus gave satisfactory assurances that there would be no obstruction in carrying out the orders of the federal court and that he would maintain order. Contacted by telephone, Faubus agreed to pledge publicly that he would uphold the orders of the federal court. In his statement to the press, however, Faubus would only promise that "the orders of the Federal Court will not be obstructed by me." Later in the evening Eisenhower announced his refusal to remove federal troops. Because Faubus had added the words "by me," his statement, the President said, did not constitute "the assurance that he intends to use his full powers as Governor to prevent the obstruction of the orders of the United States District Court" (see Memorandum of Conversation, Oct. 1, 1957, and other papers in AWF/A: Little Rock; Ann Whitman memorandum, Oct. 1, 2, 1957, AWF/AWD). See also Eisenhower, *Waging Peace*, pp. 173–74; *Public Papers of the Presidents: Eisenhower, 1957*, pp. 701–2; Adams, *Firsthand Report*, pp. 356–59; and *New York Times*, Oct. 1, 2, 1957. For developments see no. 374.

As it turned out, the President would play a round of golf with Nixon and Belshe on this afternoon (see Ann Whitman memorandum, Oct. 2, 1957, AWF/AWD and Telephone conversation, Eisenhower and Nixon, Oct. 2, 1957, AWF/D).

366

EM, WHCF, President's Personal File 415

To Edwin Palmer Hoyt *October 2, 1957*

Dear Ep: Thanks very much for sending me the story about Ed Dudley. I agree with you that that Puerto Rico job sounds very attractive, and I only wish I had the slightest possibility of a trip down there. Augusta won't seem the same without Ed.[1]

Golf at Newport was enjoyable. I got to the point where I was hitting as long a ball as I ever did, but with that development came a corresponding slump in my putting. I liked the course (with the exception of the wind that often came in from the bay) and the pro there, named Norman Palmer, is a very nice man and an excellent instructor.[2]

Needless to say, I greatly appreciate your comments about the Little Rock situation.[3] At this writing I don't know what the outcome will be. I am unhappy not only because of the turmoil that has been aroused in our own country, but I confess the reaction in friendly countries has been a source of great distress.[4]

With warm regard, *Sincerely*

[1] Hoyt had enclosed the article, which appeared in *The Denver Post* on September 22, with his letter of September 27. He said he planned to visit Puerto Rico (same file

as document). Dudley, the former golf professional at the Augusta National Golf Club, had taken a position at the Dorado Golf Club in Puerto Rico (see nos. 271, 272, and 273).

[2] The Eisenhowers had vacationed in Newport, Rhode Island, September 4–30 (see nos. 243 and 373).

[3] Hoyt had commended Eisenhower's "courageous and efficient handling" of the crisis in Little Rock, Arkansas. On Eisenhower's decision to send federal troops into Little Rock, see no. 358.

[4] The foreign press had given a great deal of attention to the episode in Little Rock (see no. 360; see also *Public Papers of the Presidents: Eisenhower, 1957*, p. 709). On this same day Director of Central Intelligence Allen Dulles had described for Eisenhower the impact of Little Rock on world opinion (NSC meeting minutes, Oct. 3, 1957, AWF/NSC). For developments see no. 418.

367

EM, AWF, Administration Series: Little Rock

To William M. Shepherd *October 3, 1957*

[Telegram]

I have just seen a press notice of the petition sponsored by leading business and civic leaders of Little Rock, urging upon your neighbors calmness in the present situation and traditional respect for law and order.[1]

I think your action to be in the finest traditions of American citizenship. I cannot help but believe that under this kind of leadership, the City of Little Rock may rapidly return to normal patterns of peaceful living.

Would you please express, on my behalf, these sentiments to all who joined with you in signing the petition?[2]

[1] On October 1, 1957, the *New York Times* had reported that twenty-four business and civic leaders in Little Rock were seeking a solution to the integration crisis at Central High (for background see nos. 330, 357, and 359). After meeting twice in secret, the group held its first public meeting on October 1 at the Little Rock Chamber of Commerce. This group of local leaders pleaded for time on the integration issue and stated that it would be "unwise" for Governor Faubus to call the Arkansas legislature into session while emotions were "aroused" and the situation was "tense." Eisenhower may have meant to address Joshua K. Shepherd, principal spokesman for the group, who was a former president of the Little Rock Chamber of Commerce. William M. Shepherd, also a member of the group, was vice-president of the Arkansas Power and Light Company and former national president of the Junior Chamber of Commerce. The two men were not related.

[2] Eisenhower made handwritten corrections to the draft of this telegram (Oct. 3, AWF/A: Little Rock). For developments see no. 374.

368

EM, AWF, DDE Diaries Series

TO ROBERT BERNERD ANDERSON

October 3, 1957

Dear Bob: This morning I was visited by Mrs. Jessie Sayler, Collector of Customs at Savannah.[1] Her current appointment expires early next year and she came to see me to state that she was a candidate for reappointment. I informed her that changes of this kind were rarely made except for some evidence of inefficiency or other failure in office and that consequently, if her record of efficiency so justified, I felt sure she would be reappointed.

At your convenience, would you let me have some indication as to the Department's opinion of her competence in her post?[2] *As ever*

[1] Jessie Dale Dixon Sayler was the wife of Eisenhower's USMA classmate and longtime friend Major General Henry Benton Sayler (see *Eisenhower Papers*, vols. I–XVII; see also Memorandum, Oct. 3, 1957, AWF/AWD).

[2] We have been unable to find Anderson's reply in AWF. Sayler would serve as Savannah's Collector of Customs until March 1962.

369

EM, AWF, Administration Series

TO NEIL HOLSER MCELROY

October 4, 1957

Dear Neil: As I sign your commission as Secretary of Defense, I am reminded of the purport of a statement I made when you and I were first discussing the possibility of your acceptance of this assignment. I remarked that, while I was keenly appreciative of the sacrifices you would make in order to serve your country in this Administration, in view of the circumstances now existing and your generally recognized qualifications for this difficult position, I felt justified in requesting you to undertake the duties of the office.[1] Nevertheless, because of my understanding that too long an absence from your company would require a greater sacrifice on your part than seemed justified or necessary during what we hope will be normal years of peace, I also said that if you could serve approximately two years in the post, I could at that time find someone else to serve satisfactorily as Secretary of Defense.

There is, of course, no reason for writing this note except the realization that man and his memory are frail and weak, and a permanent record of this understanding would not be out of order.

Again my grateful thanks for joining us and my confidence that you will find your work challenging, interesting and—at times at least—enjoyable.[2]

With personal regard. *Sincerely*

[1] On August 7, 1957, Eisenhower had named McElroy, president of Procter and Gamble since 1948, to replace Charles E. Wilson as Secretary of Defense. Wilson had informed the President during the summer of his decision to retire (for background on McElroy see Galambos and van Ee, *The Middle Way,* no. 1180). The Senate had confirmed McElroy's appointment without debate on August 19 (see Eisenhower, *Waging Peace,* p. 244; *New York Times,* Aug. 6, 7, 8, Oct. 10, 1957). See also Ann Whitman memorandum, Oct. 9, 1957, AWF/AWD. For Eisenhower's opinion of the success of the McElroy appointment see no. 472.

[2] For developments see no. 389.

370

Dulles Papers,
White House Memoranda Series

To John Foster Dulles *October 4, 1957*

Dear Foster: I have written a few paragraphs which I think would be helpful in introducing the talk on mutual security. I send you a very rough draft herewith. Would you look it over and tell me whether you think that something like this would be helpful in making such a speech?[1] *As ever*

[1] Eisenhower had suggested introducing the speech by outlining three major objectives of American foreign policy: the first, "over-riding" aim was to gain a just and lasting peace, which would produce a better life for the citizens of all nations; the second, to maintain the military, political, and economic strength of the United States while searching for solutions to the disarmament dilemma; and the third, to capitalize on the strength inherent in the unity of Western nations in the search for security and peace (Draft of Speech on Foreign Policy, Oct. 3, 1957, same file as document).

Although he thought the paragraphs were "good," Dulles would tell Eisenhower that the second and third objectives were "perhaps better described as 'means' to secure the first objective. Perhaps this criticism," he added, "is met by the fact that you describe the first objective as 'overriding.'" He also suggested that Eisenhower's reference to "consultations with heads of friendly states" be broadened to include the foreign ministers of those governments (Dulles to Eisenhower, Oct. 5, 1957, *ibid.*).

Although Dulles would later agree that former speech writer Emmet Hughes should "work over" the manuscript, Eisenhower would not deliver another talk on mutual security in 1957 (see Telephone conversation, Dulles and Adams, Oct. 7, 1957, Dulles Papers, Telephone Conversations). For his special message to Congress in 1958 on the Mutual Security Program see *Public Papers of the Presidents: Eisenhower, 1958,* pp. 160–68. For more on presidential speeches see no. 386.

371

EM, WHCF, Official File 142-A-5-A

To Martin Luther King, Jr.
Personal

October 7, 1957

Dear Mr. King:[1] Thank you for sending me your comments regarding the necessity of the decision I had to make in the difficult Arkansas situation.[2] I appreciated your thoughtful expression of the basic and compelling factors involved.

I share your confidence that Americans everywhere remain devoted to our tradition of adherence to orderly processes of law.[3] *Sincerely*

[1] King (A.B. Morehouse College 1948; D.D. Chicago Theological Seminary 1957) was president of the Southern Christian Leadership Conference. In 1955–56 he had led a successful boycott to desegregate public buses in Montgomery, Alabama (see Galambos and van Ee, *The Middle Way*, no. 1802).

[2] On the desegregation crisis at Central High School in Little Rock, Arkansas, see no. 330; on Eisenhower's September 24 decision to send federal troops to enforce court orders see no. 357. King had sent a telegram (Sept. 25) expressing his "sincere support" for the President's efforts "to restore law and order in Little Rock." "Justice finally must spring from a new moral climate," he wrote, and not from "a situation of mob violence." In a telegram of September 9 King had told the President that "if the Federal Government" failed to take "a strong positive stand" it would "set the process of integration back fifty years" (see also Rabb to King, Sept. 30, 1957).

[3] An "overwhelming majority of Southerners, Negro and white," King wrote, were "firmly" behind Eisenhower's action. He went on to say that history would reveal that the "small and confused minority" who opposed integration will soon realize that it benefitted "our nation" and "the Christian traditions of fair play and brotherhood." All correspondence is in the same file as the document.

372

EM, AWF, DDE Diaries Series

To Clement Hale Wright
Personal

October 7, 1957

Dear General Wright: I appreciate greatly your note regarding the actions that were necessary in the Little Rock situation.[1] And, my thoughts turned, as did yours, many times during the last few weeks to the Bonus March of 1932.[2] It has always been something of a mystery to me that the actual facts of that day have never been exposed in public.

With warm regard, *Sincerely*

[1] Wright, who had been General Staff Secretary under General Douglas MacArthur in 1932, had written the President on October 2 to congratulate him on both his

"forbearance and patience" and his "decisive action to end an unbearable situation" in Little Rock (WHCF/OF 142-A-5-A). On Eisenhower's decision to use federal troops to ensure the integration of Little Rock's Central High School see nos. 357 and 359.
[2] Wright had said that the Little Rock situation had reminded him of the 1932 Bonus March, "another occasion when Federal troops were used in a civil disturbance." As a young officer Eisenhower had been involved in the actions that Army Chief of Staff MacArthur had taken to break up the so-called Bonus Expeditionary Force, a group of impoverished veterans who had come to Washington in order to request government assistance (on Wright's earlier correspondence with Eisenhower on this matter see Galambos and van Ee, *The Middle Way*, no. 1735; on the Bonus March see Eisenhower, *At Ease*, pp. 215–18, and D. Clayton James, *The Years of MacArthur*, 3 vols. [Boston, 1970–85], vol. 1, *1880–1941* [1970], pp. 384–405).

373 *EM, WHCF, President's Personal File 307*

To Gene Sarazen *October 7, 1957*

Dear Gene: Sorry as I am to confess it, the name of that Aberdeen Angus family that you so much admired at one of the Iowa sales keeps slipping from my memory. Would you be so kind as to write me a note with that name in it, so that I can make it a matter of record; hereafter I will not have to bother you with this particular question.[1]

I enjoyed my golf at Newport; it was entirely different from anything I had ever done before.[2] The only drawback was that I was pulled and hauled at by problems and demands in Washington, so that I never did seem to concentrate as I should.[3] Nevertheless, here and there I played better than I had any right to expect and I had lots of fun, in spite of the fact that there are 136 traps on the course, all situated to bother the duffer and never the pro. There are several really fine holes on the course.

Many thanks for the trouble I am causing you.

With warm regard, *Sincerely*

[1] Sarazen, winner of seven major golf championships, owned Mountain Range Farm in Germantown, New York (for background see Galambos, *Columbia University*, no. 838). Cattle of the Cherry Blossom line, Sarazen would reply on October 10, "are handsome, sturdy animals" with "all the earmarks of champions" (same file as document).
[2] The Eisenhowers had vacationed in Newport, Rhode Island, September 4–30. Sarazen said he was glad the President played golf because "your responsibilities are cruelly heavy and your mind and body need as much recreation as you can possibly manage" (Oct. 10, 1957, same file as document).
[3] On the desegregation crisis in Little Rock, Arkansas, see no. 330. "The Arkansas affair is shocking," Sarazen had written in a letter that crossed Eisenhower's desk (Oct. 5, 1957). "Your patience prior to your ultimate decision," Sarazen said, "was as

praiseworthy as the decision itself." Eisenhower would thank Sarazen for his comments on October 10 and add: "There was no alternative to the plain duty I had in the matter" (both in same file as document).

374

DIARY

EM, AWF, Ann Whitman Diary Series

October 8, 1957

What he had to say was pretty well represented in the press releases given out that day (attached). Governor Faubus protested again and again he was a law abiding citizen, that he was a veteran, fought in the war, and that everybody recognizes that the Federal law is supreme to State law.[1] So I suggested to him that he go home and not necessarily withdraw his National Guard troops, but just change their orders to say that having been assured that there was no attempt to do anything except to obey the Courts and that the Federal government was not trying to do anything that had not been already agreed to by the School Board and directed by the Courts; that he should tell the Guard to continue to preserve order but to allow the Negro children to attend Central High School. I pointed out at that time he was due to appear the following Friday, the 20th, before the Court to determine whether an injunction was to be issued. In any event, I urged him to take this action promptly whereupon the Justice Department would go to the Court and ask that the Governor not be brought into Court. I further said that I did not believe it was beneficial to anybody to have a trial of strength between the President and a Governor because in any area where the Federal government had assumed jurisdiction and this was upheld by the Supreme Court, there could be only one outcome—that is, the State would lose, and I did not want to see any Governor humiliated.

He seemed to be very appreciative of this attitude and I got definitely the understanding that he was going back to Arkansas to act within a matter of hours to revoke his orders to the Guard to prevent re-entry of the Negro children into the school.

He told me of his war experiences and vigorously asserted his deep feelings of loyalty and dedication to the Federal government, and repeated several times that he had shown respect for the law in all his actions.

After some 20 minutes of personal conference, we invited Governor Adams and Brooks Hays, and later, the Attorney General, to join us. The ensuing conversation was generally along the same lines as he had talked to me in private.[2]

[1] Governor Faubus had met with the President in September. Ann Whitman had titled her diary entry, *"Notes dictated by the President on October 8, 1957 concerning visit of Governor Orval Faubus of Arkansas to Little Rock* [i.e., Newport, Rhode Island] *on September 14, 1957."* For background see no. 330. Whitman also noted that the "Interview was held in the President's tiny office at the Naval Station at Newport. At the beginning of what was approximately a two-hour session, the President and the Governor were alone in the President's office for about twenty minutes. They then adjourned to acw's office, which was larger." For other accounts of the meeting see Adams, *Firsthand Report*, pp. 350–52, and Brownell, *Advising Ike*, pp. 209–10.
[2] For further background on the crisis in Little Rock see nos. 359, 362, and 365. With resistance to segregation at Central High lessening, Eisenhower would withdraw half of the army forces and defederalize four-fifths of the National Guardsmen, on October 14. The African-American students would enter Central High without escort for the first time on October 23 (see Burk, *The Eisenhower Administration and Black Civil Rights*, pp. 188–91).

375 — *EM, AWF, DDE Diaries Series*

TO WALTER T. FORBES — *October 8, 1957*
Personal

Dear Mr. Forbes: I have pondered carefully your letter of October first, since in it you state clearly and, I know, sincerely your personal convictions as to the problem now troubling so many of us.[1] May I ask you, in return, to concern yourself for a moment with the decision facing me when the National Guard of Arkansas was ordered by its Governor to block the execution of the orders of a Federal Court.[2] The question then became solely that of supporting or failing to support that branch of government which, in the last analysis, is the one that protects each of us against capricious action by government.[3]

As President of the United States, I have taken an oath to uphold the Constitution. That Constitution, due to the wisdom of our forebears, is subject to the interpretation of one of the three separate branches of our government, the Supreme Court.

A situation arose in Little Rock that distresses me as much as it does you. Many thoughtful Americans agree with you as to the unwisdom of the 1954 decision of the Supreme Court. But those Americans, and in this group I include the Governors of the four Southern States who, with me, have worked hard to try to find a solution to the Arkansas question, respect our laws and know they must be obeyed. Those Governors emphatically agreed that I, as President, had a *duty* of making certain that the Court's order was not obstructed.[4]

From the beginning, in 1789, there have been individuals in our nation who have publicly and emphatically disagreed with particular laws. Parenthetically I might say that America would not be the nation of freedom of thought and expression that it is, and of which we are so proud, were not such disagreements possible. But such disagreements must not be translated into open defiance of the Constitution, as interpreted by the Courts.[5] If we allow that, we have anarchy.

With portions of your letter I entirely agree, and I would most earnestly hope that you would understand the position of the Administration and would, in your area, do everything possible to further the good race relations that have been achieved in your own company. Time and again I have personally and publicly urged patience, education and understanding as the real cure to this problem and have pointed out the difficulties that arise from extremism on any question.

With best wishes, *Sincerely*

[1] Forbes, from Chattanooga, Tennessee, was president of the Walter T. Forbes Company, which made knitting and weaving yarns. He had written the President on October 1 (WHCF/OF 142-A-5-A) to decline a luncheon invitation with Sherman Adams and to demonstrate his displeasure with the "unsound advice" that Adams, Nixon, and Brownell had offered Eisenhower on integration: "Outside agitators, a biased press, NAACP lawsuits, and a lack of understanding on the part of your close associates—and particularly Attorney General Brownell—are bringing this situation rapidly to chaos, which will only lead to lasting hatred between the races." For background see nos. 330, 359, and 362.

[2] Eisenhower had made extensive handwritten changes to his dictated draft of this letter. In an earlier version of this sentence he had asked Forbes to "put yourself in my place when the decision was necessary to send the Federal troops to Little Rock to see that the orders of the Federal Court were carried out" (Eisenhower to Forbes, n.d., AWF/A: Little Rock).

[3] Eisenhower had originally said: "protects each of us against capricious and unconstitutional decisions of temporary majorities."

[4] On the President's conference with the Southern governors see no. 365. Eisenhower added the words "They emphatically agreed" to the earlier version of this sentence.

[5] This draft sentence had read, "But when a particular law is being openly flaunted, I as President, had no alternative to the decision I made."

376

EM, WHCF, Official File 142-A-5-A

To George A. Poole, Jr. *October 8, 1957*

Dear George: I don't quite know when anything has pleased me as much as your letter.[1] Incidentally, I might add that in addition to the good advice I get daily from the columnists, my mail concerns itself in large measure to two types of letters.[2] There are those who write to the President because of the headlines they read (and I assure you they rarely read further than the headlines). These letters follow with astonishing accuracy the "suggestions" of the so-called liberal press. The other, and more difficult to handle, is mail that comes from people who have real problems and who in desperation turn to the President. (And in so many cases the President or the government cannot do a single thing, even in cases of obvious injustice).[3]

At the very least I mean to imply by the above lengthy paragraph that I deeply appreciate the sentiments you express in your letter of the fourth. Thank you for taking the trouble to write me.

With warm regard, *Sincerely*

[1] Poole, a Chicago Republican and printing company executive, had been a member of the Active Citizens for Eisenhower in 1952 (for background see Galambos, *NATO and the Campaign of 1952*, no. 798). On October 4 Poole said he sympathized with Eisenhower's position as a world leader whose critics, especially the press, "could have long since solved many of the problems with which you are still wrestling" (same file as document).

[2] Poole also had complimented Eisenhower on the appropriateness of his answer to a reporter during his October 3 news conference. The columnist had asked the President if he thought the results of the current desegregation crisis in Little Rock, Arkansas, would have been different if the President had "acted sooner instead of, as your critics say, letting the thing drift?" The press corps laughed when Eisenhower replied that he was "astonished how many people know exactly what the President of the United States should do." Eisenhower went on to say that he "believed" he had "preached patience, tolerance [and] the purpose of understanding both sides before you move" (*Public Papers of the Presidents: Eisenhower, 1957*, p. 707). For background on the Little Rock crisis see no. 330; on Eisenhower's decision to use federal troops to enforce a federal court's integration of Central High School see no. 357. For further comments on the news conference see no. 414.

[3] See, for example, nos. 950 and 951.

377 — *EM, AWF, Administration Series*

To Gordon Gray — *October 9, 1957*

Confidential

Dear Gordon:[1] A year or so ago we had a Transportation Committee of Cabinet members, who concluded their work with a series of findings and recommendations.[2]

As I recall, the report showed that the railroads of the United States were operating under obsolete laws and regulations, and that for a number of other reasons our railway system was steadily deteriorating in quality, at least as compared to the improved types of transportation in other fields. At the same time, the report emphasized the vital need of keeping our network of railroads operating efficiently and effectively throughout the country. I am trusting entirely to memory in writing this note, but I believe that among other things the Committee suggested it should be made easy and legal for certain of our railways to merge.[3]

My interest was renewed this summer by a number of statements from personal friends to the effect that most of our railways were really getting in desperate shape. I think that in general they were referring to railways east of the Mississippi, although some of the others may be in a similar situation.

I wonder whether the Committee report should not be examined again by the ODM, from the standpoint of the responsibility of that office, with a view to preparing definite recommendations to be undertaken during this coming session of the Congress. While I realize that some of the regulations applying to railways are generated by the Interstate Commerce Commission, I imagine that any extensive authority for major reorganization would require new legislation.

In any event, let me have your *brief* comments on this suggestion.[4]

With warm regard, *As ever*

[1] Gray (LL.B. Yale University 1933), former Secretary of the Army, and president of the University of North Carolina, had also served as Assistant Secretary of Defense for International Security Affairs (1955–1957). Eisenhower had appointed Gray director of the Office of Defense Mobilization on March 14, 1957 (see *New York Times*, Mar. 15, 1957; Galambos, *NATO and the Campaign of 1952*, nos. 32, and Galambos and van Ee, *The Middle Way*, no. 8).

[2] In March 1954 Eisenhower had asked his brother Milton to propose steps that could be taken to improve the situation of the railroads in the United States (see Galambos and van Ee, *The Middle Way*, no. 790). As a result of Milton's report, Eisenhower had established (July 1954) a special Cabinet committee on transportation policy, headed by Commerce Secretary Weeks. The Weeks Committee sent a list of recommendations to Eisenhower in April 1955. The Eisenhower Administration sent proposed legislation based on these recommendations to Congress, but neither the House nor the Senate would pass the bill in 1955, 1956, or 1957 (*Congressional Quarterly Almanac*, vol. XIV, *1958*, pp. 244–45).

[3] On the deterioration of the railroads see, for example, John F. Stover, *American Railroads* (Chicago, 1961), pp. 210–45, and Dudley F. Pegram, *Transportation: Economics and Public Policy* (Homewood, Ill., 1968), pp. 395–421.

[4] Meeting with Gray on October 28, Eisenhower would give him authority to hire a special consultant to study the railroad issue. The two men would also discuss the need for mobilization planning for transportation, and Eisenhower would tell Gray to move forward in this area (Goodpaster memorandum, Oct. 28, 1957, AWF/D). The Senate would take action on the Weeks Committee proposals in 1958. For developments see no. 610.

378

EM, WHCF, Official File 142-A-5-A

To Ralph Emerson McGill *October 9, 1957*

Personal

Dear Ralph: I am always at a loss in trying to acknowledge any comment favorable to me that appears in the public print, but I cannot resist thanking you for your editorial of the fifth. You are highly sensitive to my emotions and convictions—and more articulate than I could possibly be about them; in addition, you understand fully the necessity for the decision I had to make in the troublesome Little Rock situation. About all I can say is that I am truly more than grateful to you.[1]

With warm regard, *Sincerely*

P.S. Some day, if I am so fortunate as to have the opportunity, I shall tell you the story of how I learned, the hard way, to practice patience and conciliation in human affairs. For a man of my disposition it was not easy.[2]

[1] McGill, editor of the *Atlanta Constitution,* had written that Eisenhower's "patience was never more in evidence" than in the desegregation crisis in Little Rock, Arkansas. Although charged by critics with "timidity" and "'naivete,'" Eisenhower had waited and asked Governor Faubus to observe the law before deciding to use federal troops to enforce integration (for background see nos. 330, 357, and 376). McGill went on to say that only Eisenhower could "provide leadership" and support for the "Southern people who, while opposing segregation, nonetheless believe in law," and only the President could "prevent the issue from falling into the hands of extremist mobs." McGill concluded by asking his readers to appreciate that the President had acted, not for political gain, but out of "good will and moderation."

[2] Eisenhower may have been referring to a childhood episode in which he lost his temper and was lectured by his mother on the importance of self-control (see Eisenhower, *At Ease,* pp. 51–52, and no. 387 in these volumes).

379

EM, WHCF, Official File 142-A-5-A

To Ted Dalton *October 10, 1957*

Dear Ted:[1] I deeply appreciate your telegram of September twenty-eighth. I believe the excerpt from the Republican platform contains some good logic. In fact, that language (after considerable consultation) had my personal approval, even after some of my consultants had made radically more drastic suggestions.[2]

However, in this particular situation the problem with which I was faced, while arising out of the integration plans of the Little Rock

School Board, did not directly concern that matter. To be faithful to my oath as President I am compelled to prevent obstruction of the orders of a Federal Court. The troops were used only after State authorities had shown that they would not do anything to prevent such obstruction in that locality.[3]

Our free institutions depend upon a respect of all citizens of our Courts and their decisions. Chaos and anarchy will prevail if their orders can be flouted by mobs.

I am most anxious that a solution be evolved which will assure obedience to the orders of the United States District Court, the protection of the Negro children involved, and the maintenance of law and order. When these conditions prevail there the necessity for Federal troops will exist no longer.[4]

With warm regard, *Sincerely*

[1] Dalton (LL.B. College of William and Mary 1926), a member of the state senate of Virginia since 1944, was a member of the Republican National Committee.

[2] Dalton said he had argued against forced integration before the platform committee at the Republican National Convention in 1956. The excerpted statement read: "We believe that true progress can be attained through intelligent study, understanding, education and good will. Use of force or violence by any group or agency will tend only to worsen the many problems inherent in the situation" (same file as document).

Eisenhower rewrote this first paragraph (see Ann Whitman to Jack [Anderson], n.d., same file as document).

[3] On the desegregation crisis at Central High School see no. 330; on Eisenhower's September 24 decision to send federal troops to Little Rock see no. 357. Dalton had urged withdrawal of the troops because, he said, Virginians and Southerners feel that this action is not "in keeping with that pledge." Not all Southerners reacted in the same manner (see, for example, nos. 371 and 378).

[4] On October 14 Eisenhower would begin withdrawing the army forces and would release most of the National Guardsmen from federal service. Nine days later the African-American students would enter Central High without escort (see no. 374, n. 2).

380

EM, AWF, Administration Series: People to People

To Henry Ford II

October 10, 1957

Dear Henry: Thank you very much for carrying my message to your Trustees.[1] I don't know exactly where I shall now turn, but I do not intend to give up on an idea which envisions an effort which I am quite sure is essential to the world today.[2]

The two Trustees visiting me both complimented you on the vigor of your representations on behalf of the project and I assure you of my gratitude.

What was a bit of a shock to me was their identification of the members of your Trustees group. Because so many of them have been my warm friends, I was a bit taken aback by the knowledge that not one of them seemed to be impressed by my personal conviction that the project is worthy of real support.[3]

Anyway, the golf game was fun. I am sorry you could not stay for the trip on the submarine. I think it was the most interesting visit I ever had to a military facility.[4]

With warm regard, *As ever*

[1] On September 26 Eisenhower and Ford had discussed the Ford Foundation's funding of the People-to-People program while playing golf at the Newport Country Club. For background see nos. 283 and 350.

[2] Earlier this day Eisenhower had met with the president and vice-president of the Ford Foundation, as well as with Director of Intelligence Allen Dulles and Under Secretary of State Christian Herter, to discuss the foundation's reasons for not supporting the People-to-People program. The Foundation had rejected four applications since March because it was unwilling to make any substantial addition to its foreign projects. Furthermore, when operating abroad, the Foundation made grants on a selective, case-by-case, basis: it did not fund general programs run by intermediaries. According to General Goodpaster, who had attended the meeting, the President said he was "astonished regarding these points." He could not see how selectivity was "connected with this particular request, inasmuch as the money asked for was to provide administrative support so that the central organization could go out and raise funds for particular efforts." The President restated his high opinion of the program and remarked that without private funding "to support this effort we as a nation are doomed to a very bad future" (Goodpaster, Memorandum of Conference, Oct. 11, 1957, AWF/D; People-to-People, Inc. Application, Oct. 7, 1957, AWF/A; see also Ann Whitman memorandum, Oct. 10, 1957, AWF/AWD).

[3] For developments see no. 385.

[4] Following the golf game with Ford, the President traveled to Naragansett Bay to board the U.S.S. *Seawolf*, the Navy's newest atomic-powered submarine. Eisenhower had lunch with the crew and as he made an inspection, the *Seawolf* dived sixty feet below the surface of the Atlantic Ocean (*New York Times*, Oct. 27, 1957).

381

EM, WHCF, President's Personal File 149

TO NELSON ALDRICH ROCKEFELLER *October 10, 1957*

Dear Nelson: There were a couple of other things I wanted to talk to you about today, but I just didn't find the proper opportunity.[1] Just now I tried to reach you by phone, only to learn that you were at the airport en route to New York.

I wanted to discuss the Tex McCrary telegram (and your telephone message about it);[2] and the New York School of Social worker dinner (but I am told Ann brought that subject up anyhow).[3]

At any rate, I seem to remember that you are coming down for The Queen's dinner. Perhaps we can arrange a few minutes in the office either the day before or the day after.[4] If this seems feasible, will you give Tom Stephens a ring and ask him to set up a convenient time?

As always, it was nice to see you.

With warm regard, *As ever*

[1] Rockefeller had met privately with Eisenhower before attending a luncheon meeting of the President's Advisory Committee on Government Organization (see Memorandum, Oct. 10, 1957, AWF/AWD; see also no. 385).

[2] John Reagan ("Tex") McCrary, a New York City radio commentator and Eisenhower's long-time political friend, had telegraphed the preceding day (same file as document). Learning of Eisenhower's meeting with Rockefeller, McCrary asked the President to urge Rockefeller to seek the New York Republican gubernatorial nomination in 1958. Rockefeller, McCrary said, was "the only repeat only candidate through whom you can put forever the imprint of your own character and ideals on our party at a taproot point that will reach the whole nation through the media of information nerve centered in New York." Comparing Rockefeller to Eisenhower before the 1952 election, McCrary described him as "the only candidate sure to win this psychologically most crucial contest next year. . . ." Rockefeller would make thousands of Spanish speaking New Yorkers feel welcome in the Republican party, McCrary concluded, and was "certainly the only candidate who can whistle hundreds of people like . . . me back to work for the party again as we have worked whenever you whistled." On McCrary's earlier attempt to persuade Rockefeller to seek the nomination see Cary Reich, *The Life of Nelson A. Rockefeller: Worlds to Conquer 1908–1958* [New York, 1996], pp. 537–39.

[3] Eisenhower was an honorary trustee of Columbia University's New York School of Social Work. On December 16 the school would present the first Social Welfare Award to the family of Nelson Rockefeller's father, John Davison Rockefeller, Jr. (see Galambos and van Ee, *The Middle Way*, no. 461, and *New York Times*, Nov. 11, Dec. 15, 1957).

[4] Rockefeller would attend the White House dinner for Queen Elizabeth on October 17. For background on the Queen's visit see no. 395.

On October 18 Eisenhower would encourage Rockefeller to enter the race for New York governor and suggest that he speak to Presidential Political Aide Tom Stephens for advice. The President later confided to Ann Whitman that he would like to see "some fresh faces in the political picture" (Gwen to Stephens, Oct. 11, 1957, same file as document; Ann Whitman Memorandum, Oct. 18, 1957, AWF/AWD; and Reich, *The Life of Nelson A. Rockefeller*, pp. 684–89, 705). Speculation regarding Rockefeller's political plans would continue. For developments see no. 830; see also *New York Times*, Nov. 7, Dec. 25, 1957.

382 *EM, WHCF, President's Personal File 275*

To Harry Amos Bullis *October 10, 1957*

Dear Harry: Thank you very much for your letter of the fourth. Although I have already expressed my thanks for the action of the Board of General Mills in releasing Nate Crabtree for 1958, I again want to assure you of my appreciation of your part in arranging the matter.[1]

I had not seen Dick Wilson's column concerning the press conference of a week ago, and I am grateful to you for bringing it to my attention. Certainly in the last few weeks some of the responsible people in America have demonstrated clearly the results of emotion and prejudice; but whether a moral or spiritual revival (which, incidentally, church leaders tell me we have seemed to be having) is the answer I do not know. Certainly it would be helpful if we would govern our actions more by the Golden Rule, and less by the color of our neighbor's skin.[2]

Again, my thanks for your support and help,[3] and warm regard, *Sincerely*

[1] Bullis was chairman of the board of General Mills, Inc., in Minneapolis, Minnesota (for background see *Eisenhower Papers*, vols. X-XVII). He had written to confirm that the General Mills executive committee had agreed to release Nate L. Crabtree (A.B. Illinois Wesleyan University 1929) from his duties as public relations director in order to head the National Citizens for Eisenhower-Nixon 1958 Committee. On October 2 the President had asked Bullis to assist with the arrangements for Crabtree, one of the founders of the Crusade for Freedom and the "Freedom Bell" program (for background on those programs see Galambos, *NATO and the Campaign of 1952*, no. 331; see also no. 278 in these volumes). Later that same day Bullis wired Eisenhower that General Mills would give Crabtree a leave of absence "for as long as necessary . . ." (Telephone conversation, Eisenhower and Bullis, Oct. 2, AWF/AWD, and Eisenhower to Bullis, Oct. 3; see also Bullis to Shanley, Oct. 4, and Shanley to Bullis, Oct. 7, 1957).

[2] Bullis had enclosed a copy of the article by Richard Lawson Wilson, chief of the Washington Bureau of the *Minneapolis Tribune* and winner of the 1954 Pulitzer Prize for distinguished reporting of national affairs. Wilson had written that during Eisenhower's October 3 news conference, the discussion had focused on the failure of religious principles in the school desegregation crisis in Little Rock, Arkansas. The President emphasized religious leaders' responsibility in support of free government, and he advocated a "strong reliance on the spiritual values of life" (see also *Public Papers of the Presidents: Eisenhower, 1957*, pp. 704–16, and Bullis to Eisenhower, Oct. 2, 1957; on the crisis in Little Rock see no. 330).

[3] As it turned out, poor health would force Crabtree to decline the assignment (see Ward to Bullis, Oct. 23, 1957; Bullis to Eisenhower, Oct. 24, 1957; and Eisenhower to Bullis, Oct. 28, 1957; see also *New York Times*, Apr. 27, 1958). All correspondence is in the same file as the document.

383 *EM, AWF, Gettysburg Series*

To Lester Goodson *October 10, 1957*

Dear Mr. Goodson: Since you were kind enough to send me a copy of your letter to General Nevins, I am taking the liberty of acknowledging it for him.[1] Needless to say, I am more than grateful for your advice on the quarter horses, and particularly appreciative of your suggestion that you would purchase the stallion colt or exchange him for a filly. Obviously, however, you have no great need for the colt, so I think that I shall keep him and have him gelded. My only thought in making the initial inquiry was that perhaps the stallion colt was too valuable for use for riding about the farm. However, in view of your comments, I shall proceed with that plan.[2]

I am not sure just how many horses I need or have facilities for at the farm, so I think we will let the matter of having the mares bred ride along until the spring.[3] At that time either General Nevins or I will be in touch with you again.[4]

With warm regard, *Sincerely*

[1] Goodson, former president of the American Quarter Horse Association, had presented Eisenhower with two quarter horse mares in June 1956 (see Galambos and van Ee, *The Middle Way*, no. 1890; see also Eisenhower to Goodson, June 12, and Goodson to Pick, June 20, 1957). On September 26 Nevins had written Goodson about Eisenhower's interest in locating suitable stallions for rebreeding the mares and the disposition of a colt that one of the mares had foaled earlier. The President had received, through Ann Whitman, a copy of Goodson's October 7 reply to Arthur Nevins.

[2] Goodson had reminded Nevins that he had suggested having the colts gelded for use as riding horses.

[3] Goodson had offered to make arrangements with a friend who had offered the services of his stallion.

[4] On October 15 Nevins would thank Goodson for his advice and would add that his veterinarian recommended that Eisenhower should wait to have the young stallion gelded until the following Spring. All correspondence is in AWF/Gettysburg.

384 *EM, AWF, International Series: Macmillan*

To Harold Macmillan *October 11, 1957*
Cable. Top secret

Dear Harold: I hasten to send this immediate reply to your challenging letter, pending the time we can give you a further answer as a result of pondering the many important questions you raise.[1]

As you know, I have long been an earnest advocate of closer ties between our two countries. I believe that the nations of the free world cannot possibly carry the burdens and sacrifices necessary in the preservation of free systems of government unless they can have the confidence that those to whom they look for world leadership are bound together by common convictions, purposes and principles. I believe that all countries that fear themselves threatened by Communism or any other form of dictatorship look primarily to your country and to ours for the leadership they need. I think, therefore, that it is necessary not only that the highest officials of our two countries are close together in these matters, but that this understanding and agreement should, to the greatest possible measure, extend to our two people and indeed to as many more as we can reach.

In one of the suggestions you make, we have already done some preliminary thinking. I refer to the Russian activities in pre-emptive buying.[2] Existing legislation gives us no scope in this field.[3] However, I hope that before long our staffs here will have some clear opinions on this matter, and certainly we will be more than happy to try to coordinate with your people these and other tentative conclusions.[4]

With warm personal regard, *As ever*

[1] In a message responding to Eisenhower's September 23 letter regarding disarmament (see no. 354), Macmillan had discussed the implications of the Soviet launching of the first man-made "Sputnik" satellite on October 4. The feat had emphasized to the British that the Russians were "formidable people" who threatened the free world on every front. Macmillan proposed that the United States and Great Britain pool their resources and lead other free countries toward a common goal. "Each of the countries of the free world has its contribution to make—it may be military or scientific or economic or political. Surely these resources if purposefully directed will succeed where unco-ordinated effort is bound to fail," Macmillan said (Macmillan to Eisenhower, Oct. 10, 1957, PREM 11/2329; see also Macmillan, *Riding the Storm*, pp. 314–16; on the satellite see no. 389).

[2] Macmillan had noted the Soviet penchant for using "their position as a Socialist State for buying commodities above market prices, for making barter deals, and so on. We had 'economic warfare' in the war. We may need it in the cold war." Under Secretary Herter had told Eisenhower that the State Department was working on a study of economic warfare and preemptive purchases of "seed, crops and materials" (Telephone conversation, Eisenhower and Herter, Oct. 11, 1957, AWF/D).

[3] This sentence was added, probably by Herter, to Eisenhower's original draft (see *ibid.*; and Whitman to Herter, Oct. 11, 1957, Dulles Papers, White House Memoranda Series).

[4] Macmillan would write again on October 16 suggesting that he and the President meet in Washington to "see whether we cannot together initiate some new approach to all these interconnected problems—military, economic, and political" (PREM 11/2329). He would meet with Eisenhower on October 23 and 25 (see no. 409; see also Memorandum of Conversation, Oct. 15, 1957, AWF/D-H; and Telephone conversations, Eisenhower and Dulles, Dulles and Lloyd, and Dulles and Hagerty, Oct. 16,

1957; and Dulles and Merchant and Dulles and Hagerty, Oct. 17, 1957, Dulles Papers, Telephone Conversations).

385

EM, AWF, Administration Series: People to People

NOTE FOR FILES

October 11, 1957

It was reported by Nelson Rockefeller privately that the real reason all foundations are against the People-to-People program is that the individuals heading it have expressed themselves in such a manner as to arouse feeling that they would barge into this field and take over everything that everybody else has been doing. Since many foundations are supporting particular phases of a People-to-People program, they naturally resent such statements. According to Mr. Rockefeller (and I emphatically agree) the only thing that can be done here is to organize enthusiasm and raise money with the promise to everybody that in no case will there be a competition with an existing organization, but that where suitable services exist the effort will be to expand them and to coordinate them.[1]

New projects will be initiated only in those cases where the field is not covered.

[1] Eisenhower had met with Rockefeller on October 10. For background on Eisenhower's efforts to raise funds for the People-to-People program see no. 380. On the President's continuing interest in the project see no. 546.

386

EM, AWF, Dulles-Herter Series

TO JOHN FOSTER DULLES

October 14, 1957

Dear Foster: Here is the most thoughtful document I have received from any volunteer adviser or group of advisers in the country.[1] (My opinion as to the soundness of it is in conformity with the old saw, "He is a great man, he agrees with me." I also say this in spite of two other comments: (1) I do not agree with the apparent appraisal of the extent of the deterioration in the relative situation of the free world vis-a-vis the Soviets; (2) there are members listed on the National Planning Association who command something less than my complete admiration.)[2]

With a truly effective speech covering the points (or at least most of them) that the attached document makes, I would be more than delighted to find the proper platform to make such a speech—a platform that would give to it the widest possible publicity.

If such a draft could be quickly prepared, I think it would be well to make a general speech even before I deliver the one on mutual aid which is now in the works.[3]

I would not, of course, agree to the implication in the attached letter—although it is not specifically stated—that we can continue to spend money at home for all the things that our hearts may desire and at the same time do the things that they recommend in the foreign field. I think that the kind of talk they are advocating should be a "guns *or* butter" proposition, and that this should be made very clear.

What is your reaction?[4] *As ever*

P.S. Another point that they don't happen to mention is that there is a limit to the amount of defense that money can buy.

[1] Disturbed by the growing power of the Soviet Union, sixteen members of the Committee on International Policy of the National Planning Association had expressed their findings and recommendations in a nine-page letter to Eisenhower on October 8. The balance of power, the writers said, was steadily shifting to the Soviet Union, strengthening its ability to dominate the world. They cited Soviet strength in scientific research, as evidenced by the launching of the Sputnik earth satellite on October 4, and pointed to aggressive Soviet actions in the Middle East, Asia, and Africa. Although some positive events had occurred during the previous year, they believed that the position of the free world had deteriorated—a fact unrecognized by the American public.

An informed public opinion was crucial to a sound foreign policy, the document stated, "otherwise the Congress remains responsive to the changing moods of an uninformed citizenry and it becomes increasingly difficult to hold the free world together." The writers pressed Eisenhower to assert his leadership and inform the American people about the policies he wished to pursue and the appropriations required to implement them. The letter, with Eisenhower's handwritten comments in the margins, is in AWF/D. See also Altschul to Eisenhower, October 15, 1957, Dulles Papers, White House Memoranda Series.

[2] Eisenhower may have been referring to Walter Reuther, president of the Congress of Industrial Organizations, and Leon Henderson, who had served in the New Deal and was currently a member of Americans for Democratic Action.

[3] On the mutual aid speech see no. 370. In a November 13 speech on national security, Eisenhower would include references to the strength of the Soviet Union and recommend ways that the United States could meet the challenges it faced (*Public Papers of the Presidents: Eisenhower, 1957*, pp. 807–17).

[4] In the draft of a reply, which he did not send, Dulles described the document as "a useful paper" but "unduly pessimistic." The Soviets had gained strength in missiles, and communism had gained strength in heavily populated Asian countries, he wrote, but "a good deal of progress has been made. Perhaps most encouraging of all is the fact that the leaven of freedom is perceptibly at work within the Soviet empire" (Draft, Dulles to Eisenhower, Oct. 17, 1957, Dulles Papers, White House Memoranda Series). Eisenhower would discuss his reply to the association with Dulles on October 18. "The active members of the group," Dulles said, seemed to him to be "quite strongly Democratic and actively partisan" (Memorandum of Conversation, Oct. 18, 1957, *ibid.*). For developments see no. 404.

387

EM, AWF, Administration Series

To Charles Douglas Jackson

October 14, 1957

Dear C. D.: I was slightly astonished, and highly complimented, to see you breaking into print this morning with a piece in the Herald Tribune. Despite the fact that I rather hate to see those inescapable figures given such prominence, I was more than pleased by all that you said.[1]

Sometime, if opportunity presents itself, I shall tell you the story of how I developed the characteristics of "patience and moderation" that some of our people find so objectionable. For a man of my temperament, as you can readily understand, it wasn't easy.[2]

At any rate, I do want you to know of my deep gratitude for your friendship and understanding.[3]

With warm regard, *As ever*

[1] In the introductory paragraph of his published birthday tribute, "An Appreciation of the President at 67," Jackson had said that there probably were few other birthdays in Eisenhower's life when he "found himself so beset and so in need of the fervent birthday wishes of his friends." Jackson wrote of his first meetings with Eisenhower in Algiers in 1943, when he had only "grasped dimly" the strength of the President's personality. After fourteen years those qualities of "patience, human insight, generosity, forthrightness, unsanctimonious morality, and unpompous authority" had remained unchanged (*New York Herald Tribune,* Oct. 14, 1957).

[2] In *At Ease: Stories I Tell to Friends,* Eisenhower described his youthful reaction to his parents' decision that he was too young to accompany his older brothers on a Halloween outing. Overwhelmed with anger and resentment, he punched a tree trunk until his fists bled. He was, he wrote, completely beside himself with rage. Counseling her son after the incident, his mother spoke of the futility of hatred and the need to control his temper: "He that conquereth his own soul is greater than he who taketh a city." Eisenhower wrote later, "I have always looked back on that conversation as one of the most valuable moments of my life" (pp. 51–53).

[3] Jackson would reply on October 18: "Although I was myself astonished at the unorthodoxy of the Herald Tribune asking me to write the birthday salutation, I jumped at the chance because it gave me an opportunity to say publicly something that I have felt quite deeply" (AWF/A).

388

EM, AWF, International Series: Macmillan

To Harold Macmillan

October 15, 1957

[Dear Harold:] I completely agree that birthday anniversaries are getting harder and harder to accept. But I confess that, perhaps as a direct result of my increasing years, I seem to derive even more plea-

sure than formerly in the good wishes of my friends. At any rate, I assure you of my deep appreciation of your kind note.[1]

Washington—and, indeed, all the United States—is working itself up to a great pitch of excitement in anticipation of the visit of The Queen and Prince Phillip.[2] I might add that the White House has not in the slightest escaped the prevalent mood!

With warm regard, [*As ever*]

P.S. I keep torturing my imagination to discover ways and means whereby we could occasionally meet together, without creating the necessity for a communique or embarrassment for either of us in other countries.[3]

[1] In his birthday message Macmillan had told Eisenhower how much he "valued the friendship between us" (Macmillan to Eisenhower, Oct. 8, 1957, AWF/I: Macmillan).
[2] For background on the visit see no. 188; see also no. 395. The Queen and Prince Philip would arrive in Washington on October 17 after staying in Williamsburg, Virginia. "I am sorry that The Queen will not have reached the United States on October 14," Macmillan wrote, "for I feel that if Her visit had coincided with your birthday it would have made the day especially memorable for you."
[3] Macmillan would meet with Eisenhower at the White House on October 23 and 25 (see no. 409).

389

EM, AWF, Name Series: Guided Missiles

To Neil Hosler McElroy *October 17, 1957*
Confidential

Memorandum for the Secretary of Defense: Some time ago your predecessor reported to me that there was a great deal of overtime work involved in the production of various types of weapons and vehicles for the Army, including all types of guided missiles. He stated that he believed that this practice, except for testing stations and certain production bottlenecks, was not only very expensive but, in his opinion, rather ineffective. Since overtime requires premium pay rather than employment of others for similar hours at regular rates, he felt it was entirely proper to eliminate the overtime as stated.[1]

As far as my memory goes, one, or perhaps two, missile projects were excepted from this program.[2]

Recently Mr. Wilson recommended that these restrictions be removed on certain missile items where he felt they might possibly cause some delay. I approved.[3]

The purpose of this note is to say that if the elimination of overtime is serving to slow up the testing and production of missiles, then I believe that if at all possible the prior order should be revoked, at least on a selective basis.

Would you look into the whole matter and give me a report? Since this is written from memory it is possible that there may be some slight error, but I am sure that the intent of the order will be found to be about as I have described.[4]

[1] Concerned about the rising defense budget, Eisenhower had ordered then-Secretary of Defense Wilson in July 1957 to look for ways to reduce duplication in the missile program and to develop other areas of defense savings (see no. 229). In his response (Aug. 9), Wilson had outlined cuts in missile programs, as well as a "general scaling down of force requirements" in an effort to reduce military expenditures (see State, *Foreign Relations of the United States, 1955–1957*, vol. XIX, *National Security Policy* [1990], pp. 580–83; see also Edmund Beard, *Developing the ICBM* [N.Y., 1976], pp. 207–8).

Eisenhower's concern for the pace of missile development was undoubtedly prompted by the successful launch on October 4 of the Soviet earth satellite, Sputnik (see *New York Times*, Oct. 5, 1957; see also NSC meeting minutes, October 11, 1957; and Eisenhower, *Waging Peace*, pp. 210–13). At his October 9 news conference the President had responded to numerous inquiries about the pace of American missile development. Questions had also arisen about "unnecessary delays" that might have allowed the Soviet Union to precede America into space (see *Public Papers of the Presidents: Eisenhower, 1957*, pp. 719–32; see also Eisenhower's October 9 public statement "Summarizing Facts in the Development of an Earth Satellite by the United States," *ibid.*, pp. 733–35; and Milobsky, *Leadership and Competition*).

[2] In addition to limiting overtime, Wilson had cut $170 million from Defense Department spending for research and development, given the Titan missile a lower priority than the Atlas, limited spending on Polaris to 95 percent of its 1958 budget, and halted all further production of Jupiter and Thor missiles pending a decision on which IRBM to build (see Robert A. Divine, *The Sputnik Challenge* [New York and Oxford, 1993], p. 30).

[3] In a meeting with the President on October 8, Wilson's last day in office, the Secretary of Defense had said that the success of Sputnik had necessitated an increased emphasis upon the American missile program. Wilson suggested that he remove the overtime restrictions which, although minor in influence and cost, could allow some people to "charge a slow-up in the program" (Goodpaster memorandum, Oct. 8, 1957, AWF/D).

[4] McElroy would respond to Eisenhower on October 21 (AWF/N: Guided Missiles). After reviewing the background on overtime restrictions in the ballistic missile and satellite programs, he reported that on October 18 he had approved all service requests for relief from these limits (McElroy memorandum, Oct. 18, 1957, AWF/A). McElroy had told the service chiefs that the missile development schedules represented "the best balance of technical knowledge, trained manpower and test installations that we can make at this time." He had also asked the Service Chiefs to provide him with weekly progress reports on missile development and assured Eisenhower that he planned to use "all means" at his disposal to insure that the programs remained on schedule. "If any major problems or delays are encountered, I will advise you promptly." For developments see the following document.

390

EM, AWF, Administration Series

To Neil Hosler McElroy

October 17, 1957

Personal and confidential

Dear Neil: From our talks in the last few days, I know you are giving consideration to a "Manhattan District" type of organization for the so-called anti-ICBM—one purpose being to overcome the problem of inter-service rivalries.[1] I understand that a somewhat similar problem may be in prospect with respect to a reconnaissance satellite, on which both the Army and the Air Force have study and development projects under way—the Army's based on the Jupiter and the Air Force's based on the Atlas, when available.[2] It occurred to me that you might want to give consideration to the same type of organizational approach in this case as in the other.[3] *Sincerely*

[1] Eisenhower was referring to the Manhattan Project, the name given to the scientific, strategic and governmental aspects involved in the building and eventual delivery of the atomic bomb. The Manhattan Engineer District, a special unit within the Army Corps of Engineers, had completed this task shortly before World War II ended. For background see Stephane Groueff, *Manhattan Project: The Untold Story of the Making of the Atomic Bomb* (Boston, 1967); Vincent C. Jones, *Manhattan: The Army and the Atomic Bomb*, Special Studies, U.S. Army in World War II (Washington, D.C., 1985); and Leslie M. Groves, *Now It Can Be Told: The Story of the Manhattan Project* (New York, 1983). On the President's continuing concern that interservice rivalries might slow the pace of missile development see no. 268, and Galambos and van Ee, *The Middle Way*, nos. 943, 1585, 1663, and 1750.

[2] Despite a 1956 decision not to make missile development a centralized research effort (Galambos and van Ee, *The Middle Way*, no. 1815), Eisenhower had continued to entertain the idea in discussions at the October 10 meeting of the National Security Council, and in an October 11 conference with Defense Secretary McElroy (see State, *Foreign Relations, 1955–1957*, vol. XIX, *National Security Policy*, pp. 601–4, and Goodpaster memorandum, Oct. 11, 1957, AWF/D). Remarking on the difficulties faced by various scientific groups engaged in defense work in keeping informed on what each was doing, Eisenhower had wondered whether there should be a fourth service established to handle all missile activity; he would also instruct the Department of Defense to continue studying the issue. On the Soviet earth satellite, Sputnik, see the preceding document.

[3] At a White House conference on October 8, Eisenhower had reaffirmed the decision of the Science Advisory Committee to separate the earth satellite program from the missile development program in order to stress its peaceful character. Eisenhower had said that a sudden shift in the American approach to satellite development would belie the attitude that the United States was working simply to develop and transmit scientific knowledge (see Goodpaster memorandum, Oct. 9, 1957, AWF/D; on the Science Advisory Committee see Galambos and van Ee, *The Middle Way*, no. 1644. The pressure to launch an American earth satellite would, however, remain intense; see John B. Medaris, *Countdown for Decision* [New York, 1960], pp. 151–79; and State, *Foreign Relations of the United States, 1955–1957*, vol. XI, *United Nations and General International Matters* [1988], pp. 754–67). For developments see no. 394.

391 *EM, AWF, DDE Diaries Series*

To Mary Jane McCaffree *October 17, 1957*

Memorandum for Mrs. McCaffree:[1] Since the beginning of my Administration the people named below have been accorded rank with, but immediately following, the Cabinet:

The Assistant to the President
The Chairman of the Atomic Energy Commission
The Director of the Bureau of the Budget
The Director of the Office of Defense Mobilization[2]

Normally when one of these is asked to any Washington function, all should be asked. The only exception would be when any individual is absent from the city, or where a series of social events are coming up and it is more convenient to ask them one at a time. In this case when the first one is asked to a function, the others should be asked to reserve a particular evening later in the season for a social event (describing its nature).

Another possible exception is when we give an intimate, formal dinner for the Cabinet alone, in which case it would be proper to ask only Governor Adams from among these four.

Next in line following the above are Under Secretary of State Herter and Deputy Secretary of Defense Quarles. Following in order are Chairman Saulnier of the Council of Economic Advisers, and Secretaries Brucker, Gates and Douglas, of the several Armed Services.[3] In the case of this second group, it is not necessary to ask all merely because one is invited to a function unless the function is a very large one such as a reception. However, rotation should be observed among them so that each is entertained in due course.

Here an exception could easily arise in the case of visiting foreign dignitaries, since it would be more logical to ask Under Secretary Herter than the others, especially if the Secretary of State should be absent on any particular occasion.[4]

[1] McCaffree was Mrs. Eisenhower's personal secretary and the White House social secretary (see no. 152).

[2] These were Sherman Adams, Lewis L. Strauss, Percival F. Brundage, and Gordon Gray.

[3] Former Under Secretary of the Navy Thomas Sovereign Gates, Jr. (A.B. University of Pennsylvania 1928) had been appointed Secretary of the Navy in March. Gates, a decorated veteran of World War II was a former vice-president and director of the Navy League of the United States. Eisenhower also appointed Under Secretary of the Air Force James Henderson Douglas, Jr. (A.B. Princeton 1920; LL.B. Harvard 1924) as Secretary of the Air Force in March. An officer in both World Wars, Douglas served on the boards of directors of several civic organizations, including the Boy Scouts of America and the Ford Foundation, respectively (see *New York Times*, Mar. 2, 27, 1957).

[4] Later this evening Adams, Strauss, Brundage, Gray, Herter and Secretary of State Dulles would attend a White House dinner honoring Queen Elizabeth and Prince Philip (for background see no. 395). On upcoming state functions see the President's daily appointments, especially October 23, 24, and November 25, 1957.

392 *EM, AWF, Name Series*

To Milton Stover Eisenhower *October 17, 1957*

Dear Milton: When you found yourself unable to attend the meeting of the Inter-American Press Association, we staged a frantic hunt around here to find an adequate substitute. This proved to be impossible, so I, buttressed by the dignity of my *official* position, volunteered to carry a message of greetings and welcome to the assembled editors and publishers.[1]

It seemed to me to be a fine meeting and my welcome was most cordial. In opening my little talk I gave the reasons why I felt particularly privileged to be present. Among these I pointed out that for once I was able to act as a representative of my brother, thus reversing the procedure that I suspected sometimes grew irksome for you. This observation got me my biggest laugh and the ensuing applause was obviously for you and their memory of you.

Another time, when they seemed to enjoy a chuckle was when I noted that among my numerous failings had to be listed my inability to express myself in the language that none of the delegates used. In connection with this point, I remarked that if they should read the press of our country they would find that this was not considered by any manner of means my most glaring fault.[2] *As ever*

[1] On the preceding day Eisenhower had addressed the general assembly attending the thirteenth annual meeting of the Inter-American Press Association at the Mayflower Hotel in Washington, D.C. The association, founded in 1942, represented more than 600 newspapers and magazines in the American republics (for background see Galambos and van Ee, *The Middle Way*, no. 1547). For background on Milton Eisenhower's good will visits to Latin America see nos. 190 and 235.

[2] The President said: "First, I offer my humble apologies for my inability to express myself in the language that most of you use" (see *Public Papers of the Presidents: Eisenhower, 1957*, pp. 746–48; and *New York Times*, Oct. 17, 1957). On Eisenhower's relationship with the press see, for example, no. 1.

Earlier this same day, Eisenhower had telephoned Milton only to learn that he was en route to Washington. The President then canceled the call and wrote this letter (see Telephone conversation, Oct. 17, 1957, AWF/D, and President's daily appointments).

393 *EM, WHCF, PPF 47: New Hampshire Historical Society*

To New Hampshire Historical Society *October 17, 1957*

To The New Hampshire Historical Society: I am complimented by your request to have a letter from me to add to your collection, and delighted to comply.[1]

The State of New Hampshire has a special place of honor in the Administration's roll call. Your former Governor, Sherman Adams, is serving with distinction in one of the most complex and difficult positions in the governmental service—as The Assistant to the President. As you know, he is sometimes called "The Rock," a name that seems eminently suitable for a native of New Hampshire, especially for one who typifies, as he does, sturdiness, forthrightness and integrity. I am personally deeply indebted to him and to his native State for his invaluable contribution to our country. *Sincerely*

[1] The New Hampshire Historical Society in Concord, New Hampshire, had requested a signed letter or an autograph from the President and Mrs. Eisenhower. The society's librarian had suggested a sentence or two about Sherman Adams. The First Lady would also send a letter to the society (Oct. 18) congratulating them for their work on preserving the state's past (Bass to Shanley, Oct. 7, Shanley to Bass, Oct. 15, Shanley to Whitman, Oct. 15, and Whitman to Bass, Oct. 18, 1957). All correspondence is in the same file as the document.

394 *EM, AWF, Administration Series*

To Neil Hosler McElroy *October 18, 1957*

Personal and confidential

Dear Neil: As you take up the reins in your new assignment, I suppose that it has occurred to you that there might be something to gain in getting a temporary outside body which could examine each of the major missile projects for you—to determine where management might be better coordinated or other ways in which the individual projects could be speeded up.[1]

If you were to do this, I assume you would want as chairman some outstanding man of broad experience, such as Jack McCloy or Bob Lovett, together with an eminent scientist and a top-flight production engineer.[2]

This is just a suggestion, and I am not asking for an answer. *Sincerely*

[1] McElroy had taken office as Secretary of Defense on October 9 (see no. 369). Although no outside committee would be established, Eisenhower would elevate William Marion Holaday (M.E. Ohio State University 1925) from his position as assistant to the Secretary of Defense for Guided Missiles to the newly established post of Guided Missiles Director (see *Public Papers of the Presidents: Eisenhower, 1957*, pp. 789–99, and *New York Times*, Nov. 16, 1957).
[2] John Jay McCloy (LL.B. Harvard 1921), an attorney and former assistant secretary of war from April 1941 to November 1945, had been chairman of the board of the Chase Manhattan Bank since 1953. Robert Abercrombie Lovett (B.A. Yale 1918), Secretary of Defense from 1951 to 1953, was a general partner with the investment firm Brown Brothers Harriman. Both men were serving on the Security Resources Panel of the ODM Science Advisory Committee, which would present the report of its chairman, H. Rowan Gaither, Jr., to the President on November 7 (see no. 463).

395

EM, AWF, International Series: Queen Elizabeth Visit

TO ELIZABETH II, QUEEN OF ENGLAND, AND PHILIP, THE PRINCE, DUKE OF EDINBURGH

October 20, 1957

Your Majesty and Your Royal Highness: Before you leave the United States I want to tell you of the great pleasure and honor it has been for Mrs. Eisenhower and me to have had you as our guests at the White House.[1] We greeted you as old friends and we see you leave, reluctantly, with that warm feeling of friendship intensified and renewed. On the more official side, Mrs. Eisenhower and I are more than fortunate we have been privileged to act as hosts to two such delightful representatives of the British Commonwealth.

I shall deeply treasure the map table that you gave to me.[2] It is a piece that will be a valued heirloom of the Eisenhower family for many generations to come.

If you have had a moment in your hectic schedules to read any of our newspapers, you know that you both have captivated the people of our country by your charm and graciousness. I earnestly believe that your visit to this country will not only strengthen the ties that exist between our two peoples, but that it will serve to give evidence to all the free world that our nations are firmly united in the search for a just and lasting peace.[3]

With expressions of my highest esteem and personal regard, *Sincerely*

[1] Queen Elizabeth and Prince Philip had visited Williamsburg, Virginia, before visiting Washington, D.C., and were currently in New York City. For background on the

visit see nos. 188, 201, and 388. See also Dulles, Memorandum of Conversation, August 30, 1957, Dulles Papers, White House Memorandum Series; Eisenhower to Douglas, October 18, 1957, AWF/D; Diefenbaker to Eisenhower, October 18, 1957; and Eisenhower to Diefenbaker, October 21, 1957, both in AWF/I: Canada. The President wrote this letter in longhand; a draft is in Dulles Papers, White House Memoranda Series.

[2] The mahogany coffee table, now in the Dwight D. Eisenhower Museum in Abilene, Kansas, features a map of the situation at H-Hour, June 6, 1944, and traces the routes taken by the invading armada at Normandy. The Special Order of the Day message is placed in the lower left corner, and the seals of Great Britain and the United States are in all four corners. A gold inscription on the leather border reads: "Given to President Eisenhower by Queen Elizabeth and the Duke of Edinburgh on the occasion of their state visit to the United States October Nineteen Fifty Seven." A glass top protects the border and the map (facsimile transmission from Dennis Medina, Feb. 3, 1997, EP, and accession sheet, Oct. 1957, Dwight D. Eisenhower Museum).

[3] On the day of her departure the Queen would thank the President "for the welcome which we have received in your great country." "I am proud," she wrote, "to be the bearer of so much goodwill" (Oct. 21, 1957). On November 7 the Queen would restate her appreciation: "No words can easily express what I feel about the welcome we received, and our deep gratitude for that welcome." Both letters are in AWF/I: Queen Elizabeth Visit.

396

EM, AWF, DDE Diaries Series

TO CHARLES EDWARD POTTER
Personal

October 21, 1957

Dear Senator Potter: The events of the past few days have delayed my replying to your thoughtful letter of October sixteenth.[1]

Your letter outlined questions to which we have long been giving earnest thought and quite naturally, since the orbiting of the Soviet satellite, with increased intensity.[2]

You suggest a new Federal Agency to be responsible for policy-making and planning in the scientific field, with particular reference to legal, diplomatic, scientific, technological, and all other aspects relating to outer space. You further suggest giving to this "Scientific Progress Agency" Cabinet rank and National Security Council participation.[3]

You are undoubtedly aware that for some years I have had the benefit of both individual and collective advice from scientific groups, some organized for specific aspects of the security problem, some serving on Advisory Boards of a permanent character. Through this means the government has been fortunate enough to have the recommendations of some of our most eminent and respected scientists.[4]

Two weeks ago I initiated discussion with the Science Advisory

Committee of the Office of Defense Mobilization with reference to the prospect of improving coordination in the responsibilities of the Federal Government in the wide and variegated field of scientific endeavor.[5] This standing group is currently under the Chairmanship of Professor Rabi—a Nobel Prize winner.[6] I particularly wished the views of this Committee on how better to utilize the competence of our United States scientists in differing fields of endeavor in furthering the work of agencies of the Federal government, and the overall functions of the Chief Executive.

While in the last few weeks attention has been focused on the large missile and rocket programs of the Department of Defense, being developed under policies recommended by scientific personnel and by the National Security Council and approved by me, it is necessary also to keep in mind the wide areas of scientific responsibility and achievement which pertain to the Atomic Energy Commission, the Department of Health, Education and Welfare, the National Science Foundation, and others.

I have asked the Science Advisory Committee to give me their views—not only in the field of outer space to which your letter refers, but in the fields of nuclear energy and radioisotopes, of the care of health and the cure of disease, the teaching of science, the awakening of more widespread scientific interest in our people, and so forth. The Science Advisory Committee agreed forthwith to consider the dimensions of the problem to be studied and soon to provide me with their outline.

Certainly, one part of such a study should deal with some mechanism to relate together, at a very high level, and keep under continuing surveillance, the manifold aspects of science relating to our governmental needs. Because of the very great ramifications of scientific endeavor in the national government, it is a sound course to await receipt of the highly qualified advice to which I have referred. You will agree that whatever may be done should point to constructive solutions of future problems and not, in an already scarce field, take top scientific ability from the requirements of the vital work now being done for our people.

Incidentally, it may interest you to know that in the conversation referred to above, my scientific friends identified as probably the most serious and difficult phase of our situation, not the proved current competence and advances of Soviet scientists, but rather the difficulties we in the United States face in strengthening, over the coming years, our personnel trained in science and attracting to this pursuit of science an increasing number of individuals of quality and promise. To this part of the problem, also mentioned in your letter, they feel we should devote efforts calculated to enlist nation-wide support. One expressed it, "I'm not frightened concerning the present, for we have the capacity to destroy any nation on earth; but I am frightened as to the prospect we would face ten years hence if present trends continue." We must start recruiting and educating scientists *now.*[7]

Possibly you will give some thoughts to this phase of the matter.

It is encouraging to me to know that you are approaching these questions so seriously and studiously. *Sincerely*

[1] Potter, Republican Senator from Michigan, had written on October 16 (WHCF/OF 133-Q) regarding questions raised by the October 4 launch of the Soviet earth satellite, Sputnik (see no. 389). Eisenhower dictated this reply based on a draft by his Special Assistant for National Security Affairs, General Robert Cutler (see Cutler to Hagerty, Oct. 19, 1957, and Hagerty to Harlow, n.d., both in WHCF/OF 133-Q).

[2] Potter had said that Sputnik had affected basic American policies on defense, disarmament and foreign affairs so much that it required a "revamping of national perspectives." He asked: "What, for example, are the legal implications of the baby 'moon?' Who owns outer space? Should we expand research in rocketry? What steps should be taken to stimulate development of scientific talent? Should we recast our entire educational system, gearing its emphasis to new scientific vistas?"

[3] Potter had suggested that Eisenhower create a new federal department "for the purpose of keeping United States policy and planning ahead of the swiftly-changing technological world." "An agency for scientific progress would constantly develop such new means of adjustment to a world where miracles follow miracles," he wrote.

[4] Eisenhower had added this paragraph to the Cutler draft. For background see Galambos and van Ee, *The Middle Way,* nos. 1474, 1644, 1653, and 1815.

[5] On October 15 Eisenhower had met with the Science Advisory Committee of the Office of Defense Mobilization (for background see Galambos and van Ee, *The Middle Way,* no. 1644), which had noted the lack of a scientific adviser for the President even though he encountered many policy matters that had a strong scientific component (see Goodpaster memorandum, Oct. 16, 1957, AWF/D; State, *Foreign Relations,* vol. XIX, *National Security Policy, 1955–1957,* pp. 607–10; and Divine, *The Sputnik Challenge,* pp. 47–52; for background see no. 389). Eisenhower supported the suggestion that a science adviser and a "back up" committee similar to the Council of Economic Advisors would be useful. He would appoint Dr. James Rhine Killian, Jr., president of MIT, to a newly created post of Special Assistant to the President for Science and Technology the following week. The Science Advisory Committee of the Office of Defense Management would be enlarged and reconstituted as the President's Science Advisory Committee (see Adams, *Firsthand Report,* pp. 415–16; *New York Times,* Nov. 8, 1957; *Public Papers of the Presidents: Eisenhower, 1957,* pp. 789–99). See also Eisenhower, *Waging Peace,* pp. 211, 223–25; James R. Killian, Jr., *Sputnik, Scientists, and Eisenhower: A Memoir of the First Special Assistant to the President for Science and Technology* (Cambridge, Mass., 1977), pp. 16–36, and I. I. Rabi, *My Life and Times as a Physicist* (Claremont, Calif., 1960), pp. 26–28. For developments see no. 408.

[6] On Columbia University physicist Isidor I. Rabi see Galambos and van Ee, *The Middle Way,* no. 1968; see also John S. Rigden, *Rabi: Scientist and Citizen* (New York, 1987).

[7] For developments see no. 422.

397 *Wyche Papers*

TO IRA THOMAS WYCHE *October 21, 1957*
Personal

Dear Bill: Thank you for your birthday greetings. I am delighted to have a chance to reciprocate by sending you my felicitations on your seventieth anniversary.[1]

I share your concern over the antagonisms created by racial problems.[2] It is the kind of thing that seems to preclude any easy and quick answer. For example, were there a Constitutional Amendment affecting the matter, it would certainly eliminate arguments as to what is the true meaning of the Constitution. But, assuming that such action would tend to uphold the 1954 decision of the Supreme Court, we would be little further along in the elimination of the emotions and arguments that have developed around the problem itself.

So far as I am concerned, I am still clear in my mind that, regardless of all corrections attempted by legal means of whatever character, we still have a great task of education and conciliation. While I had not previously seen the article that you attached, I am going to have it studied instantly by my legal experts to see what they think of it.[3]

In any event, it was nice to hear from you, and this note brings to you my best wishes for many more birthdays—all of them happy.

With warm regard, *Sincerely*

[1] Former Army Inspector General Wyche (for background see Galambos, *Chief of Staff*, no. 1141) had written Eisenhower on October 16 (same file as document) to celebrate the President's sixty-seventh birthday.

[2] Wyche thought that the school integration problems presented "a cloud darker than has faced this country since the Civil War." For background see nos. 330, 357, 367, and 375.

[3] Wyche had enclosed an article by David Lawrence, published in the October 4, 1957, *Charlotte Observer*, which he thought might offer a solution to the school integration dilemma. Lawrence had argued that the 1954 Supreme Court decision, which had overturned the "separate-but-equal" doctrine established in 1896, had confused many Americans who desired to respect the law of the land. The average citizen, Lawrence argued, had difficulty understanding that the fundamental law had not "changed overnight without any action by the people," and that nine men, appointed for life, could "dictate changes in the Constitution that the people must accept." He believed that the solution lay in a constitutional amendment that would declare that "the control of the whole educational system—with power to prohibit any discrimination on the basis of race or color or creed—shall be vested concurrently in the federal government and the states and that, in case of conflict, federal law will be considered to supersede any law of the states." Lawrence argued that the ratification process would give the people the right to decide on the meaning of the Constitution.

398

EM, AWF, DDE Diaries Series

To Herbert Brownell, Jr.

October 21, 1957

Memorandum for the Attorney General: Herewith the identification of a lawyer whom I have known since 1911. His name is Burton Mason, and his card shows that he is General Counsel for the Southern Pacific Company, San Francisco. He was sixty-three in September, 1957.[1]

In about 1914 he left West Point under a bit of a cloud, accused of getting unauthorized help in an examination but, as I remember it, the only evidence against him was circumstantial.

In any event, I should like to have a thorough FBI report made upon his possible qualifications as a United States Judge. I realize that he is about a year older than individuals should be in accordance with the policy on which we have agreed. But over the years I have thought of him and heard of him as a man of the highest character. Even if we should decide that his experience does not qualify him on a judgeship, I should like to know if the FBI examination would substantiate my opinion. I know that he has argued cases before the Supreme Court, and he is now in Washington representing all the Class I railroads in some controversy before the Interstate Commerce Commission. This being so, I should think there is no doubt as to his general competence in the legal field.

Since Mr. Mason is already sixty-three, will you kindly push the FBI investigation?[2]

[1] Eisenhower would not appoint Albert Burton Mason, a West Point classmate whom he had seen on this same day. Mason (J.D. University of California 1922) had served in the Canadian Expeditionary Force and the Royal Air Force in World War I. He practiced law in Oakland, California. We have been unable to locate any further correspondence regarding him in AWF.

[2] For more on the President's personal interest in the appointment of federal judges see nos. 593 and 638. See also no. 85; Whitman to Brownell, October 23, 1957, and Earl Eisenhower to Eisenhower, October 18, 1957, both in AWF/N.

399

C. D. Jackson Papers

To Charles Douglas Jackson

October 21, 1957

Dear C.D.: In my hurried letter of the other day, I neglected to tell you something that is strictly personal and that has still been on my mind a great deal of late.[1] That is simply how much I miss you—your imagination, your energy, and your refreshing point of view. In these days, when seemingly the problems have been multiplied a million-fold, I often wish that I had someone around, like yourself, who is willing to tackle a large problem, eager to think it through, and to come up with a concrete suggestion for a coordinated plan of attack (and not merely another speech by me!).[2]

At any rate, that's the way I feel.

With warm regard, *As ever*

[1] Eisenhower's letter to Jackson, in which he thanked him for his birthday wishes, is no. 387.

[2] A telephone call Jackson made to the White House on this same day may have prompted this letter. Ann Whitman would tell Eisenhower that Jackson had wanted to send him a memorandum about Prime Minister Macmillan's forthcoming visit but in the interest of time had dictated his thoughts to her. Jackson believed that the Macmillan meeting could enhance U.S. prestige abroad, "provided the end product . . . is not 'standard barley water.'" He recommended that the two men emphasize the military aspect of the Anglo-American alliance in "unmistakably clear and strong" terms. He urged joint support of the International Development Fund (see no. 831) as a "'benevolent weapon' which must be used to satisfy the pressing needs of people." He pushed for scientific cooperation between the two countries, particularly regarding atomic energy. The way to prevent the proliferation of atomic weapons, Jackson said, was "to get cracking with the only people we really trust" (Whitman to Eisenhower, Oct. 21, 1957, AWF/D-H). On the Eisenhower/Macmillan meetings of October 23 and 25 see no. 409.

400 — *EM, AWF, Administration Series*

To Robert Cutler — *October 23, 1957*

Memorandum for General Cutler: A friend of mine from California, Preston Hotchkis, dropped in to see me, leaving two suggestions.[1]

The first one was that we call in a selected group of citizens, at their expense, to give them a briefing on the United States defensive posture. His idea was that the briefing should be as thorough as possible consistent with security requirements. The type of person would be one who is respected in his community and who normally would probably be a member of local civic organizations such as the Chamber of Commerce, Kiwanis, and so on. Mr. Hotchkis believes that by this method a lot of hysteria and apprehension could be quieted in the country.[2]

His second suggestion was that we ask Dr. Wriston, who now runs Arden House, to conduct a seminar studying the question of the general size and character of our armed forces (avoiding technical considerations so far as possible), to see whether out of a study by scientists, educators, service people and others that might be called into the seminar, there might be developed a general concept that would take into consideration all the major morale, material and economic factors, and come up with something that would be useful. Since Arden House has a group of subsidiary seminars that now reach all over the country, I thought that this might have a very good long range effect in disseminating proper information.[3]

Would you take these matters up informally with the Secretary of State, the Secretary of Defense, the Director of ODM, and with your own staffs to see what they think of both ideas?[4]

[1] Hotchkis, an insurance executive and member of the Business Advisory Council of the Department of Commerce, had visited the President that morning (for background see Galambos, *Columbia University*, no. 938).

[2] On the American reaction to the launch of the Soviet earth satellite Sputnik see no. 389.

[3] For background on Wriston see no. 172. On Arden House, the home of the American Assembly, see Galambos, *Columbia University*, nos. 605 and 844.

[4] Cutler would respond to the President on November 4 (AWF/A). With regard to Hotchkis's suggestion that a select group of citizens be briefed on the American defense program, the Secretaries of State and Defense, the Director of ODM and Cutler's own staff agreed that Eisenhower's planned speeches on this subject would be the most effective means of reassuring Americans about the defense program (see *Public Papers of the Presidents: Eisenhower, 1957*, pp. 789–99, 807–17).

Regarding the suggestion that a special group be used to formulate policy, Cutler would tell the President that all the officials consulted "foresaw serious difficulties in asking a non-governmental group (like Arden House) to develop recommendations regarding the size and character of our armed forces." He recommended, instead, that the Arden House seminar technique be used to "*spread information* about the Administration's policies and determinations." For developments see no. 455.

401

EM, WHCF, Official File 3-R

To Donald S. McChesney
Personal

October 24, 1957

Dear Mr. McChesney: Thank you very much for your letter written, by coincidence, on my birthday.[1]

With many of the arguments you advance in favor of real unification of the Armed Services I am not only in agreement, but presented them to the Congress as forcefully as I could as far back as 1947. Indeed, when I returned briefly from Europe in June of 1945, I remember making one speech in which I proposed a single uniform for everybody who served in the Armed Forces of the United States. The reaction from the Services was what you would expect, but I must say that the passage of twelve years has only served to confirm my confidence in the soundness of the basic idea I then held and which you express in your letter.[2] That idea is that through the elimination of artificial and unnecessary divisions and barriers among the Services we could, without sacrificing specialized training, secure many advantages and make many economies that would work together toward greater efficiency for the same amount of expenditures.

The matter is again under earnest study by both civilian and military groups in the government.[3] As you point out, accomplishment will not be easy, but the anguished cries of special groups that you foresee would not be the important obstacles to achievement of unification. The problem will be to convince Congress, many of whose members are veterans and are naturally highly prejudiced in favor of the organizations with which they served.[4]

Finally, there is some limit to which amalgamation and integration can proceed with efficiency. For example, those who go to sea will naturally always have to have a different kind of training from those who serve on land or from those who man the land-based aircraft. These, however, are not overriding difficulties; I merely mean to say that there are real obstacles to be overcome if we are to produce greater efficiency and not merely a paper reorganization.

I assure you again of my appreciation of your writing. I have sent a copy of your letter to the governmental officials who are studying this problem daily.[5]

With best wishes, *Sincerely*

[1] McChesney had written on October 14 (same file as document) to recommend the reorganization of the Army, Navy and Air Force into a single unit to be known as the Armed Services of the United States. "Under this plan," he said, "separate service identity would be lost; complete freedom of movement and reassignment of personnel would be possible; tremendous savings of procurement, administration and services (medical and so on) could be effected and immeasurably greater efficiency would result."

[2] See Chandler and Galambos, *Occupation*, no. 206, and Galambos and van Ee, *The Middle Way*, nos. 207 and 1963.

[3] See, for example, John C. Ries, *The Management of Defense: Organization and Control of the U.S. Armed Services* (Baltimore, 1964), pp. 150–73; and Arnold, *Making the Managerial Presidency*, pp. 173–74, 214–18.

[4] In his 1958 State of the Union message, Eisenhower would place the reorganization of defense at the head of a list of items requiring action. For congressional reaction see *Congressional Quarterly Almanac*, vol. XIV, *1958*, pp. 133–35.

[5] For developments see no. 540.

402 *EM, WHCF, Official File 142*

To Kenneth Dale Wells *October 24, 1957*

Dear Ken: Of course I give serious consideration to any request from you, but in this particular instance I cannot set up the appointment with Mr. Carter that you requested.[1] The reason is simply this—so many individuals, all of whose opinions I value and whom I would like personally to talk to—have asked for meetings with me on this particular subject that I could not possibly find the time in a day or a week or a month to see them all.[2]

Max Rabb tells me that the proposal Mr. Carter submitted has been sent to the Secretary of Health, Education and Welfare, where I know it will receive Mr. Folsom's personal attention.[3]

Won't you please explain the situation to Mr. Carter—and to both of you, my regret that I cannot make this particular appointment. I shall hope to see Mr. Carter at a later, and hopefully less crowded, time.

With warm regard, *Sincerely*

P.S. If Mr. Carter would like an appointment with Governor Pyle, we will be happy to arrange it.[4]

[1] Wells, an economist, was a personal friend of Eisenhower. He had been associated with the Freedoms Foundation at Valley Forge since 1949, and had become president of the organization in 1951 (for background see Galambos, *NATO and the Campaign of 1952,* no. 207). Wells had written on October 18 to ask the President to meet with W. Beverly Carter, Jr., publisher of the *Pittsburgh Courier,* a widely-read African-American newspaper.

[2] The recent desegregation crisis at Central High School in Little Rock, Arkansas, and Eisenhower's subsequent decision to use federal troops to enforce the court order on integration had focused attention on racial issues (see nos. 330 and 357). The President had received many letters and telegrams on this subject (see, for example, nos. 361 and 371).

[3] Carter had proposed a youth conference in conjunction with the Freedoms Foundation; the conference would focus on the concept of responsibility. On October 21 Presidential Assistant Stephens had forwarded Wells's letter and Carter's proposal to Rabb. Rabb replied that it would "cause embarrassment" to grant Carter "the appointment in preference to the others who have requested audiences with the President" (Rabb to Folsom, Oct. 21, Rabb to Stephens, Oct. 23, 1957, and related correspondence).

[4] In his November 4 reply to Eisenhower Wells would say he understood the problems with making an appointment. He added that Carter would appreciate meeting with former governor of Arizona and Deputy Assistant to the President Howard Pyle. Carter and Pyle would meet on December 10 (Pyle to Wells, Dec. 11, 1957). All correspondence is in the same file as the document.

403 *EM, AWF, Name Series*

To William Alton Jones *October 24, 1957*

Dear Pete: I was disappointed that I had no chance to talk to you Tuesday evening—other than to say "I am glad you are back." Perhaps you will be coming down this way soon and can stop in to see me. I would be glad if you could spend an evening and stay overnight—or come down some time during the daytime.[1]

The main idea is that I just want to have a long, leisurely chat with you.

(On Tuesday afternoon, incidentally, a famed and competent economist talked me out of calling up Cliff to ask him to place what few pennies I had saved up into the market. My purpose was not that I thought I was a genius in stock market operations—but I had gotten so sick and tired of hearing people moan and wail about the dark outlook of the American economy that I just wanted to prove, at least to myself, that I was willing to bet a little on my own faith.)[2]

Give my love to Nettie, if she is home, and if you find it possible to get down here just give Mrs. Whitman a ring and she will fix up a date of some kind. We might even have a little golf. *As ever*

[1] Eisenhower had addressed the attendees of the National Fund for Medical Education in New York on October 22 (see *Public Papers of the Presidents: Eisenhower, 1957,* pp. 754–63; and *New York Times,* Oct. 23, 1957). For developments see no. 421.

[2] The President had met with Arthur Burns (see Ann Whitman memorandum, Oct. 22, 1957, AWF/AWD). Cliff Roberts was an unofficial adviser and close friend of the President. For Eisenhower's views of the 1957–1958 economic recession see his memoir, *Waging Peace,* pp. 305–11.

404 *EM, AWF, DDE Diaries Series*

To Frank Altschul *October 25, 1957*

Personal

Dear Mr. Altschul: I have acknowledged receipt of the letter you sent me as Chairman of the Committee on International Policy of the National Planning Association.[1] The following comments and observations are primarily for your eyes alone. However, with the assurance from you that you will not allow quotations from the letter and will not circulate it beyond showing it to Mr. Sonne, I am sending it along in the hope that you may find at least parts of it of interest.[2]

Though I find myself unable to share, without reservation, some of your conclusions and opinions, I do, in the main, agree with your analysis of the world situation and the trend of its mood. But, for example, it seems to me that there is in your paper the implication that the causes of the deterioration of which you speak have been of recent origin and growth. Yet most of the recent Soviet successes have been in the making for many years. I refer, for example, to the Soviet scientific development, which is a steady forty year growth, and to the increased Soviet influence in the Near East, which is a concomitant of the Arab identification of the West with Israel.[3]

I agree that the purposes and objectives of the Soviet society have remained unchanged for decades. In the recurring clashes, some on the record and some not, there have been incidents both favorable and unfavorable to the Western cause.

The greatest defeat, by all odds, that the Western world has taken in this long contest, if we exclude the subjugation of the satellite states immediately following World War II, has been the communization of China.[4] The years embracing the late forties and early fifties were filled with incidents which were examples of Soviet pressure designed to accelerate Communist conquest of every country where the Soviet government could make its influence felt. Thus we had the Korean invasion, the Huk activities in the Philippines, the determined effort to overrun all Viet Nam, the attempted subversion of Laos, Cambodia and Burma, the well-nigh successful attempt to take over Iran, the exploitation of the trouble spot of Trieste, and the penetration attempted in Guatemala.[5] In the past four years most of these have either been defeated or neutralized. In addition, the trend toward greater individual and national freedom is being manifest within the Soviet bloc.

This is not said in the attempt to deny that there are some somber conclusions to be drawn, but merely to point out that the struggle of which you speak is not a temporary one nor is the tension of recent origin.

It follows that whatever means the free world, and more particularly our Nation, take to combat and defeat the Soviet effort must be designed for indefinite use and endurance. Hasty and extraordinary effort under the impetus of sudden fear on the one hand, or unjustified complacency because of the lack, over a period, of overt aggressive action, cannot provide for the West an adequate answer to the threat. We must decide upon programs based upon all the pertinent factors in the problem; we must be prepared to sustain the programs for years, even decades.

Here is presented one of the most difficult of all problems in a free governmental system. It may be that in the coming session of Congress, because of certain recent successes by the Soviets, there may be obtainable some very large appropriations—some possibly unjustifiably large. On the other hand, in the recent session, before some of the incidents had occurred, and though there were presented to Congressional leaders in Committees many of the same arguments, almost in the same words, that are contained in your letter, proposed Defense, Mutual Aid, and Information Programs were cut drastically by the Congress. Many programs of these agencies have no pressure groups to support them.

I assume that I do not need to tell you that many times I have had Congressional leaders, often of both parties, into my office to lay before them:

(*a*) The bare facts of the world struggle in which we are engaged;

(*b*) The growing competence of Soviet militarists and technicians, and therefore the increased danger to ourselves;

(*c*) The broad character of their offensive around the world, including the employment of force, the threat of force, economic enticement and sheer propaganda; and

(*d*) The critical need for free governments, notwithstanding the limitations of the democratic processes, to adopt a long range, steadfast policy and program designed to meet the grave threat to our way of life.

I do not include here a list of or quotations from the public speeches and statements I have made upon this subject, but I do assure you that I have done far more behind closed doors than I have in public.

You mention the truism that security is more important than balanced budgets. The difficulty with this, as in most aphorisms, is that the problem is not so simple as the statement implies. I refer again to the fact that our plans must be based upon the probability of their lengthy prolongation. We face, not a temporary emergency, such as a war, but a long term responsibility.

Along with this fact we must remember that we are defending a way of life, not merely property, wealth and even our homes. That way of life, over the long term, requires the observance of sound fiscal policies, and wise distribution and use of the fruits of our productivity so that the system may continue to work primarily under the impulse of private effort rather than by the fiat of centralized government. Should we have to resort to anything resembling a garrison state, then all that we are striving to defend would be weakened and, if long subjected to this kind of control, could disappear.

While I do not believe that, in properly making sure that our security efforts match the seriousness of the threat, we shall need to turn our country into a garrison state, neither do I believe that given the existence of a major threat a country such as ours can *permanently* and by itself support abundance in both "guns *and* butter."

I emphatically agree with your statement that the public has not become sufficiently conscious of the gravity of the growing Soviet capabilities. There are other parts of your letter which express, in better words than I have at my command, many of my deepest convictions on the battle of ideologies.

I differ somewhat, however, from your implication that I, alone, can through a series of speeches, statements and pronouncements make certain of the public understanding we need. I believe that I have my part to do, and I intend to do this part as well as I can. But this is not a task for one individual. This is a case where all who believe as you do and as I do, must do their parts, each to the extent of his ability and to the limit of his endurance.

I note also that except for a suggestion that I undertake a renewed campaign to inform the American public—which I shall certainly try to do—your letter makes no specific suggestions for improving of basic policies, nor does it deal with the underlying causes of our difficulties today. For example, you point out that general war is unthinkable, yet you rightly say that we must be ready to make an exception to this when our priceless values are directly threatened.

I feel that the real difficulty is found in the fact that a group of diverse democracies are opposing a single despotism. If an immediate preventive war—even assuming military victory—is not advocated as a solution (and certainly neither of us suggests such a thing), then the free world survival depends upon its voluntary sticking together over a long period of time, with each one of the partners ready to carry its share of the burden. Here again great difficulties are presented because of the diverse interests represented in local conflicts in many parts of the so-called free world. In the Mid East, the Arab-Israeli conflict absorbs the entire populations even more than does the danger of Communist aggression. Kashmir is a symbol of deep-seated antagonisms in the Pakistan-India area.[6] The hatred in Korea for Japan is traditional.[7] These are merely examples of the things that governmental leaders must contend with as they strive to build up that unity in the free world in which lies our common security. That effort is waged continuously both in public and behind the scenes. Obviously we can do better if better supported by adequate appropriations, but it is equally true that the answer is not to be found in money alone.

In the area of administrative excellence, alertness in pursuing scientific research and advances, and in coordination of all parts of the government involved in this world struggle, we constantly find other opportunities for improvement. These improvements we try to make.

And bearing upon your observation with reference to world economic programs, I close by remarking that even so long ago as 1947, when I was writing a book later published under the title "Crusade in Europe," I devoted its last chapter to some reflections on the Soviets and to the menace of communism. In that I pointed out that the most dangerous communist program could well be economic, making an appeal to the destitute and the desperate, while the free nations, each too much occupied with its own local and selfish affairs, might allow the world to fall victim to the most ruthless despotism of the ages.[8]

Having said all this, I want again to thank you for your letter; it is helpful and interesting to me to have the benefit of your thinking on this most vital problem of our day.

With best wishes, *Sincerely*

[1] New York City business executive Frank Altschul (B.A. Yale University 1908) was chairman of the board of the General American Investors Company, Inc., and vice-president and secretary of the Council on Foreign Relations. On his October 15 letter to Eisenhower see no. 386. Secretary Dulles had advised against sending this reply. "It is difficult," he told Special Assistant for National Security Affairs Robert Cutler, "to avoid a 'defensive' note." He suggested that the President merely acknowledge receipt of the letter and tell Altschul that he had referred it to the State Department "where it would be a useful addition to a continuously operating process of evaluating foreign policy trends" (Telephone conversation, Dulles and Cutler, Oct. 21, 1957, Dulles Papers, Telephone Conversations; and Dulles to Cutler, Oct. 22, 1957, Dulles Papers, White House Memoranda Series).

In separate acknowledgment sent on this same date the President told Altschul that he had given his "provocative and thoughtful material" to the State Department "for further study and analysis" (*ibid.*; see also Whitman to Bernau, Oct. 28, 1957, *ibid.*).

[2] Hans Christian Sonne (University of Copenhagen 1912) was former chairman of Amisinck, Sonne & Company, merchant bankers in New York. He was chairman of the Board of Trustees of the National Planning Association.

[3] The Soviet Union had launched the first earth satellite (Sputnik) on October 4 (see no. 389). On growing Communist strength in the Middle East, particularly in Syria, see no. 301.

[4] See Galambos, *Columbia University*, no. 788; and Galambos and van Ee, *The Middle Way*, no. 951.

[5] On the Korean invasion see Galambos, *Columbia University*, no. 865; on the Huk Rebellion see *ibid.*, no. 788; on the Communist inroads in Vietnam see Galambos and van Ee, *The Middle Way*, nos. 718 and 841; on subversion in Laos, Cambodia, and Burma see *ibid.*, nos. 174, 434, 882, and 1966; on Iran, *ibid.*, nos. 174 and 281; on Trieste, *ibid.*, nos. 441 and 1060; and on Guatemala, *ibid.*, no. 965.

[6] On the Indo-Pakistan dispute over Kashmir see no. 113.

[7] Longstanding animosity between the two countries had been exacerbated by the inability to negotiate property settlements in the aftermath of World War II and the Korean decision to prevent the Japanese from fishing in extensive areas in the Sea of Japan (State, *Foreign Relations, 1952–1954*, vol. XIV, *China and Japan*, pp. 1251–52, 1255–56, 1259–61; State, *Foreign Relations, 1955–1957*, vol. XXIII, pt. 1, *Japan*, pp. 165, 482–83, 521; and *ibid.*, vol. XXIII, pt. 2, *Korea*, pp. 108, 370). South Korean President Syngman Rhee had expressed his fear of Japanese expansion in an August 2 letter to Eisenhower (AWF/I: Rhee).

[8] See Eisenhower, *Crusade in Europe*, pp. 457–78.

405

EM, AWF, Dulles-Herter Series

To John Foster Dulles

October 26, 1957

Dear Foster: Howard Cullman came to see me today. As you know, he is very pessimistic about his ability, with the funds he has, to put on a good show at the Brussels Fair next year. He insists he needs some two million dollars more than he has.[1]

He wanted me to authorize the use of this much money in counterpart funds for completing construction of the building; thus freeing the money he now has but which he is compelled to save for operations.[2]

I told him I was unsure whether counterpart funds could be used for a project in which Congress had fixed the limit of appropriations. On the other hand, I was equally uncertain whether there is any objection to the use of such funds as long as it was limited to operations only.

In any event, will you have some one reply either directly to Mr. Cullman or give me a short memorandum on which I can send him an answer.[3]

Incidentally, he told me that it would do him little good to get a supplemental as late as March, when his project must begin to operate in the middle of April.[4] *As ever*

[1] For background on Howard Stix Cullman, former chairman of the New York Port Authority, see Galambos, *Columbia University*, no. 858. In October 1956 Eisenhower had appointed Cullman U.S. Commissioner General of the Brussels Universal and International Exhibition, scheduled to open in April 1958 (see Galambos and van Ee, *The Middle Way*, no. 1699). On the meeting see Ann Whitman memorandum, October 25, 1957, AWF/AWD.

[2] For background on the establishment of local-currency counterpart funds see Galambos, *NATO and the Campaign of 1952*, no. 68, and no. 316 in these volumes.

[3] In his reply to Eisenhower Dulles would enclose a copy of a letter he had written to Cullman, explaining that the State Department was making "an exhaustive study of the possibility of providing such funds." He promised to inform Cullman of the results (Dulles to Eisenhower, Oct. 29, 1957, AWF/D-H).

On November 16 Eisenhower would send Dulles two more letters from Cullman. "One thing is sure," the President said, "if the Russians again outshine us—this time at Brussels—we will be the ones to get the blame" (AWF/D-H). Dulles would tell the President that there were "one or two possible devices that might be used to provide additional funds" and that he might have to call on Eisenhower for assistance (Dulles to Eisenhower, Nov. 19, 1957, *ibid.*; see also Telephone conversation, Dulles and Adams, Oct. 29, 1957, Dulles Papers, Telephone Conversations).

[4] In his January 1958 budget message to Congress Eisenhower would ask for a supplemental appropriation for the exhibition. Previous congressional action, he said, had left the United States "badly hampered" in comparison with the programs of other nations (*Public Papers of the Presidents: Eisenhower, 1958*, p. 41). In March Congress would authorize the transfer of $2.2 million from previously appropriated funds for the U.S. exhibit (*Congressional Quarterly Almanac*, vol. XIV, *1958*, p. 334). For reactions to the American exhibition see no. 756.

TO SHERMAN ADAMS *October 26, 1957*

Dear Sherm: When Harry Luce was here the other day he told me that Mrs. Luce was again completely recovered.[1] My impression is that she would like a job. You might think of her on one of these commissions.[2]

What have you heard from George Humphrey about Simpson?[3]

I'll see you next week about both these things, but I send you this note so that they do not slip my mind.[4] *As ever*

[1] On Eisenhower's meeting with Henry Luce see Ann Whitman memorandum, Oct. 25, 1957, AWF/AWD; and Memorandum for the Record, Oct. 27, 1957, AWF/D. Clare Boothe Luce had resigned her post as U.S. Ambassador to Italy in November 1956 because of ill health (see Galambos and van Ee, *The Middle Way*, no. 2008). The physician who had been treating her for chronic enteritis and anemia said that she had been the victim of lead and arsenic poisoning, caused by flaking paint from the ceiling of her bedroom in the U.S. embassy (*New York Times*, July 17, 20, 1956).

[2] Eisenhower would appoint Luce to be ambassador to Brazil in 1959, but she would withdraw her name during controversy in the Senate over her confirmation. One of the commissions was the Civil Rights Commission. For background on Adams's involvement see no. 307; for developments see no. 666.

[3] For background on Richard Murray Simpson, Republican Congressman from Pennsylvania and chairman of the Republican Congressional Campaign Committee, see Galambos and van Ee, *The Middle Way*, nos. 170 and 482. In a speech to state Republican leaders released on October 20, Simpson, a member of the party's conservative wing, had urged candidates running for seats in the House of Representatives in 1958 to inform voters of their disagreements with Administration policies (*New York Times*, Oct. 21, 1957). In this instance Eisenhower probably was referring to a report that Simpson was preparing to separate the congressional campaign group from the Republican National Committee. In a conversation with former Treasury Secretary Humphrey, the President had recommended withholding campaign funds from Simpson's group in order to "beat him to the draw" (Diary, Oct. 25, 1957, AWF/AWD).

[4] We have been unable to find a record of further discussion regarding these issues.

407 *EM, WHCF, Official File 3-G*

TO WILLIAM C. LUTZ *October 28, 1957*
Personal

Dear Mr. Lutz: Thank you for your letter of October eighteenth. The problem that you raise is constantly under review by both civilian and military groups in the government.[1]

I cannot, in the short space of a letter, go into all of the arguments that are raised for and against the suggested reappraisal of the concept and function of the Joint Chiefs of Staff.[2] One of the difficulties would of course be to convince the Congress of the necessity for changing the present setup; another is that should such a change be made, inevitably we would lose much time in "shaking down" the new organization—time that we cannot now afford to lose.

This note is merely to assure you that the suggestion has *not* been ignored and that it is, as I say, still under active consideration.[3]

With best wishes, *Sincerely*

[1] Lutz, supervisor of field operations for the New York Life Insurance Company, had written on October 18 (same file as document). Responding to an article in the October 21, 1957 issue of *Newsweek* on the recent launch of the Soviet earth satellite Sputnik, Lutz had asked about the fate of the Rockefeller Committee. This group, appointed in 1953, had been charged with reviewing "proposals for reforming the concept and function of the Joint Chiefs of Staff." On Sputnik see no. 389.

[2] *Newsweek* had interviewed Dr. Vannevar Bush, who had been the head of the Office of Scientific Research and Development during World War II. Bush had argued that the most serious problem faced by the United States in the aftermath of Sputnik was the lack of unified military planning. He suggested that Eisenhower follow the Rockefeller Committee recommendations and divest the Joint Chiefs of Staff of command-operational responsibility. Bush also proposed that the JCS should be restricted to planning functions and the review of war plans (for background see no. 401; see also E. Bruce Geelhoed, *Charles E. Wilson and Controversy at the Pentagon, 1953 to 1957* [Detroit, 1979], pp. 62–64).

[3] For developments see no. 540.

408

EM, AWF, DDE Diaries Series

DIARY
Top secret

October 29, 1957

I was visited by Professor Rabi, Admiral Strauss, Gordon Gray, and one or two others. The purpose was to bring to me certain conclusions reached by Professor Rabi's Committee, called the Scientific Advisory Committee to the Director of Defense Mobilization.[1]

Briefly, their conclusion was that we now enjoy certain advantages in the nuclear world over the Russians and that the most important of these gaps can be closed only by continuous testing on the part of the Russians. Professor Rabi's Committee has therefore reached the conclusion that we should, as a matter of self-interest, agree to a suspension of all tests subject only to the installation of inspectional systems that would almost surely reveal the occurrence of a test.[2] Scientists differ as to whether certain nuclear tests can be conducted without any knowledge reaching the outside world, but the

Rabi Committee believes that with a half dozen or so properly equipped inspectional posts inside of Russia, any significant explosion could be detected.[3]

While the Rabi Committee agreed that certain advantages in our weaponry could be realized by advancement of testing, they say that the expected advantage would be as nothing compared with maintaining the particular scientific gap that exists in the design of the Russian H-bomb as compared to ours.

The nature of this gap is that Russian bombs are unshielded against certain types of radio activity that could be placed around them as they approach. The effect of this would not be to destroy the bomb but to reduce its effect by something like 99%.

Admiral Strauss and his group of scientists do not believe some of the assumptions made by the Rabi Committee. They are keenly afraid that should we discontinue our tests, the Russians would, by stealing all of our secrets, equal and eventually surpass us. So Admiral Strauss and his associates believe we should continue all of our experiments and testing out in the open, refusing to be victimized by Russian duplicity. They are quite firm in their belief that we could not protect ourselves adequately against that duplicity.[4]

The outcome was that Gordon Gray, Admiral Strauss and General Cutler are going to try to get (if possible) an agreement of scientific opinion in this whole matter to see what we should do about it.

Incidentally, I learned that some of the mutual antagonisms among the scientists are so bitter as to make their working together almost an impossibility. I was told that Dr. Rabi and some of his group are so antagonistic to Drs. Lawrence and Teller that communication between them is practically nil.[5]

[1] Eisenhower was referring to Columbia University physicist Isidor Rabi and AEC Chairman Lewis Strauss. Gordon Gray, Assistant Secretary of Defense for International Security Affairs from July 1955 to February 1957, had been appointed Director of the Office of Defense Mobilization in March 1957. The group had met for an hour that morning to discuss the findings of the Scientific Advisory Committee regarding an emergency defense against the Soviet ICBM (see Goodpaster memorandum, Oct. 30, 1957; for background on the Scientific Advisory Committee see no. 396).

[2] Rabi had reported that the Soviet Union was close to developing an ICBM with an atomic warhead. Because this warhead was likely to have the same weakness as did early American warheads, however, the United States could build an effective antiballistic missile system. Rabi also recommended that the United States examine the option of stopping further weapons tests in order to retain the American advantage, since the Soviet Union was certain to discover the weaknesses in their weapons systems if they continued testing (Goodpaster Memorandum of Conversation, Oct. 30, 1957, AWF/D).

[3] For background see nos. 8 and 171.

[4] In a separate meeting with the President also held on the twenty-ninth, AEC Chair-

man Lewis Strauss had reiterated his concern over the recommendation that the United States cease weapons testing in order to "freeze" its lead. Strauss called Rabi a "friend of long standing" and a "brilliant scientist," but suggested that sometimes proposals of this sort had "not been thought through, and must be modified when mature, experienced judgment in these broader matters is applied to them" (Goodpaster Memorandum of Conversation, Oct. 30, 1957, AWF/D).

[5] Rabi had told Eisenhower that it had been a "great mistake" to accept the views of nuclear scientists Ernest Orlando Lawrence and Edward Teller of the University of California (Berkeley) Radiation Laboratory. When the President asked if "mutual respect" existed among the antagonists, Rabi had merely replied "that they had known each other for twenty years or more." Strauss would later tell Eisenhower that Rabi and Teller had "opposed each other very sharply over many years" with respect to the development of the hydrogen bomb as well as other issues.

409

EM, AWF, International Series: Macmillan

To Harold Macmillan

October 29, 1957

[Dear Harold:] The note you wrote to me just before you left Washington expressed in words far better than any I have at my command the feeling of gratification I have that our two countries are increasingly good partners—in the eyes of the world as well as in the reality that always existed despite our misunderstandings.[1] There never has been any doubt in my mind that in an emergency we would, as we have done before, find ourselves shoulder to shoulder. But it is reassuring to know that in the more difficult job of waging the peace we are, all of us, again working toward a common goal. I, too, am certain that our pledge of confidence in each other will be reflected in a lessening of tensions among all the nations of the free world.

It does seem as if that bugaboo of suspicion of bilateral talks has been at least diluted, and for that, too, I am delighted.[2]

I hope that you will keep in close touch with me. I value our correspondence, as I do our friendship.[3]

With warm regard

[1] Macmillan had written on October 25, at the conclusion of his meetings with Eisenhower (for background see no. 384; see also Telephone conversation, Eisenhower and Macmillan and Eisenhower and Dulles, Oct. 23, 1957, AWF/D). The Prime Minister had suggested the meetings to improve coordination of the effort by the United States and Great Britain to work toward, he said, a "marriage of heart as well as worldly goods" in meeting the Communist threat. The two men discussed ways the United States and Great Britain could achieve a closer union while maintaining full partnership with other Western nations. Macmillan was particularly interested in an amendment to the Atomic Energy Act of 1954, which had hampered American ef-

forts to share nuclear information and materials with the British. Eisenhower told Macmillan that he thought the United States had "made a great mistake" in establishing these guidelines and that he had worked hard to change the law (State, *Foreign Relations, 1955–1957*, vol. XXVII, *Western Europe and Canada*, pp. 788–839; Eisenhower, *Waging Peace*, p. 219; and Macmillan, *Riding the Storm*, pp. 315–26. On the Atomic Energy Act see Galambos and van Ee, *The Middle Way*, nos. 812 and 1640; and nos. 23 and 514 in these volumes).

The meetings had inspired him, Macmillan had written. "We have got a pretty difficult job, but it is fine to feel that we are setting about it with such confidence in each other" (Macmillan to Eisenhower, Oct. 25, 1957, AWF/I: Macmillan). In a letter to Secretary Dulles, Macmillan had written that he felt "quite a new spirit" and that they had found the right approach to the task (Macmillan to Dulles, Oct. 25, 1957, AWF/D-H; see also Dulles to Eisenhower, Oct. 28, 1957, *ibid.*). For the Declaration of Common Purpose released after the meetings see "President Eisenhower and Prime Minister Macmillan Agree on Closer U.S.-U.K. Cooperation," *U.S. Department of State Bulletin* 37, no. 959 (November 11, 1957), 739–41.

[2] On Eisenhower's concern that a meeting between the two might raise suspicions in other countries see no. 388; see also Macmillan to Eisenhower, October 16, 1957, PREM 11/2329.

[3] For developments see no. 501.

410 — *EM, AWF, DDE Diaries Series*

To George Magoffin Humphrey — *October 29, 1957*

Dear George: Thank you very much for sending me a copy of your talk at Columbus. It was not only timely—your ideas were clearly and succinctly stated.[1]

By chance I opened my paper to the market page and saw where General Motors 1958 prices were to be up.[2] I wonder whether this was such a smart move for the biggest automobile company we have in the United States. It appears to me that, at the very least, their timing is bad. Regardless of the reasons leading to the action, I am quite certain that its inflationary effect will be noticeable.

It was wonderful to have a talk with you, even if it was all too short.[3]

Give my affectionate regard to Pam and, of course, all the best to yourself. *As ever*

[1] Humphrey's speech is not in AWF.

[2] The October 29 *New York Times* reported that General Motors had announced it was raising factory-suggested prices for 1958 models by 2 to 5.7 percent in all five of its divisions. The divisions, which made their announcements separately, contended that increased production costs made the higher prices necessary. Chrysler and Ford were expected to follow General Motors in raising prices. The *Times* also stated that the automobile industry had indicated that the price rise was lower than expected and should be regarded as a move to stimulate sales, especially on mid-priced cars

where the smallest percentage increases had been made. On the effects of increased automobile prices on the economy see Saulnier, *Constructive Years*, pp. 97–98.
[3] Eisenhower had met with Humphrey for an hour on October 22.

411

EM, AWF, DDE Diaries Series

To Horace C. Flanigan

October 29, 1957

Dear Hap: Thank you for your letter. I am glad that Julian Baird called you on the phone to discuss the idea which you suggested to me when we visited at the Waldorf.[1]

I see that you reflect a slight misconception that has been going the rounds ever since I made my statement that I would make a few talks this fall on important subjects troubling our people. I had in mind two or three talks or, at maximum, four. The next day I saw it interpreted as four to six—now you have it six to eight.[2] Have a heart, Mister!

Give my love to Aimee,[3] and, of course, all the best to yourself. *As ever*

[1] Flanigan had been chairman of the board of Manufacturers Trust Company since 1956; see Galambos, *Columbia University*, no. 810. Eisenhower had met with him for twenty minutes in New York on October 22, prior to the President's speech to the supporters of the National Fund for Medical Education (see no. 416). They had discussed whether the recent change in Defense Department payment policies, which increased the demand on banks for credit, would necessitate a change in the Federal Reserve Board reserve requirements. Baird, who had been appointed Under Secretary of the Treasury for Monetary Affairs in September 1957 (see no. 297), had told Flanigan that the increased amount of credit was "so small as to not have any noticeable effect on the money market or present any great problem to the banking system" (Flanigan to Eisenhower, Oct. 25, 1957, WHCF/OF 115).
[2] In his October 22 speech, Eisenhower had said that he would "seek opportunities to talk with the American people . . ." (*Public Papers of the Presidents: Eisenhower, 1957*, pp. 754–63). On October 23, the *New York Times* reported that Eisenhower planned to make "four to six speeches" regarding American achievements in science and defense, on the economy, and on U.S. responsibilities abroad. For developments see no. 434.
[3] Eisenhower was referring to Flanigan's wife, the former Aimee Magnus.

412

EM, WHCF, Official File 101-JJ

To Stanley Hoflund High

October 29, 1957

Dear Stanley:[1] I think you, of all people, know that I have never neglected, in my thinking or in public pronouncements, any lack of appreciation of the value of moral and spiritual values.[2] But in this area I can speak only as a layman. I would hope that the spiritual leaders of our country would themselves be, perhaps unconsciously, the mechanism by which the "defeatism" you deplore could be overcome.[3] In other words, *I* can't do everything—and I think I have, perhaps more than most individuals in my position would have done, stressed constantly the strength that is inherent in such values.

With warm regard, *As ever*

P.S. Of course I hope I will never be remiss in doing my part in producing the appreciation that our whole country should have of moral values.

[1] High, *Reader's Digest* editor since 1952 and a Methodist lay leader, had served as one of Eisenhower's speechwriters during his first presidential campaign (for background see *Eisenhower Papers*, vols. X–XVII).

[2] Eisenhower had called upon religious leaders to advocate moral and spiritual values in an October 3 news conference (see no. 382; see also no. 282).

[3] High had written on October 24 (same file as document). He said he looked forward to Eisenhower's forthcoming speeches "regarding America's capacity to meet the current scientific and economic challenges." He also noted "the moral-spiritual" challenges that had arisen in the wake of the desegregation crisis in Little Rock, Arkansas. There was, he said, "a vast amount of unjustified defeatism abroad in the land." America, he concluded, needed "a heartening, inspiring word." For background on a similar letter to the President in early 1953 see Galambos and van Ee, *The Middle Way*, no. 99.

413

EM, AWF, Administration Series

To Sherman Adams

October 29, 1957

Dear Sherm: As you know, Spyros Skouras is trying to publicize a few of our younger Republicans by keeping them on the news reels whenever they attend some ceremony or function. In addition to those we now have on the list, would you please speak to Mr. Rogers and Mr. McElroy, asking each to give Mr. Skouras an appointment if he should ask for it. I suggested to Mr. Skouras that he add these two names to his list.[1] *As ever*

[1] The President had met with Twentieth-Century Fox President Skouras earlier this same day. Skouras's company made Movietone newsreel films, which were shown with feature motion pictures in theaters. On Eisenhower's desire to see younger, "'fresh faces'" in the Republican party see, for example, no. 381; see also Reich, *The Life of Nelson A. Rockefeller*, pp. 705–7. Although Deputy Attorney General William P. Rogers was born in 1913 and Defense Secretary Neil H. McElroy was born in 1904, Eisenhower doubtless considered their faces as "fresh."

414

EM, AWF, Name Series

To Joyce Clyde Hall

October 29, 1957

Dear Joyce: I am today writing a letter to Roland Redmond, with the prior assurance I have received that the Metropolitan will show Sir Winston's exhibit.[1]

The trip to Europe is still indefinite; I would like, of course, to attend the NATO conference.[2] There are, however, endless problems to be solved before I can give a definite and affirmative answer, and, as always, the trip itself cannot be undertaken unless conditions at home are fairly stable. But I am tremendously gratified, quite naturally, that you think my presence briefly in Europe would be of benefit in solving some of the problems that face us.[3]

With warm regard, *As ever*

[1] For background on the Churchill exhibition see nos. 86 and 222; see also Eisenhower to Murphy, August 12, 1957; Eisenhower to Hall, September 3, 1957; and other supporting material in WHCF/PPF 833. On Roland Livingston Redmond, president of the board of trustees of the Metropolitan Museum of Art, see Galambos and van Ee, *The Middle Way*, no. 761. Dr. Alfred Frankfurter, a well-known art critic and editor who had been working with Hall on the exhibition, had recommended that either Eisenhower or the State Department should ask the museum to show Churchill's paintings. After former Presidential Assistant Nelson Rockefeller had determined that the Metropolitan would show the paintings if requested, Hall then told Eisenhower that it was "most important" to take this action because of the disappointment Churchill would feel if the paintings were not exhibited in New York (Hall to Eisenhower, Oct. 26, 1957, AWF/N; see also Whitman to Eisenhower, n.d., AWF/N, Hall Corr.). For Eisenhower's letter to Redmond see the following document.

[2] During Eisenhower's conference with Macmillan, which had ended on October 25 (see no. 409) NATO Secretary General Paul-Henri Spaak had proposed that the Heads of Government be invited to the December NATO meeting to be held in Paris. Eisenhower and Macmillan had agreed, saying that such a meeting "might give a lift to NATO at an important juncture" (State, *Foreign Relations, 1955–1957*, vol. XXVII, *Western Europe and Canada*, pp. 813, 823, 835–36; see also Houghton to Dulles, Oct. 28, 1957; and Dulles to Houghton, Oct. 31, 1957, AWF/D-H; see also Paul-Henri Spaak, *The Continuing Battle: Memoirs of a European, 1936–1966* [Boston, 1971], pp. 263–66]).

[3] Hall had told Eisenhower that he was excited about the proposed trip. "I realize how tremendous your influence is [in Europe] and I know what a great deal would be accomplished by your presence even for an extremely short time" (Hall to Eisenhower, Oct. 26, 1957, AWF/N; and *New York Times*, Oct. 26, 1957). For developments see nos. 444 and 454.

415

Dulles Papers, White House Memoranda Series

To Roland Livingston Redmond *October 30, 1957*

Dear Mr. Redmond: I write this letter in a dual capacity. As an Honorary Fellow of the Metropolitan Museum of Art, I am hopeful that you will give favorable consideration to the request that the exhibition of Sir Winston's paintings be shown at the Museum on the forthcoming tour.[1] I realize that such an exhibition does not exactly fit in with the requirements that you have quite wisely laid down. On the other hand, I feel that an exception could well be made because of the unique place Sir Winston holds in the hearts of most Americans and the fact that he is not only a painter of interest but one of the greatest of living statesmen.

In a personal capacity, I might add that I initially urged Sir Winston to approve the tour of the exhibition because of the fact that I was convinced it would help better our relationships with Great Britain. At the time of my original letter to him, in April of this year, relations between our two countries were, as you know, not as cordial as they might have been.[2] Fortunately, since the visit of The Queen, followed by the trip to the United States of the Prime Minister, the ties between our two countries have been greatly strengthened.[3] I truly believe that Sir Winston's exhibition will add much to our firm bonds of friendship and will prove a source of pride to the British, in addition to being highly interesting to the American public.[4]

With warm regard, *Sincerely*

[1] For background see the preceding document.

[2] Eisenhower had written Churchill on April 16 (see no. 86). On tensions between the United States and Great Britain after the Suez crisis see Galambos and van Ee, *The Middle Way*, nos. 2118 and 2124A.

[3] The Queen and Prince Philip had visited the United States from October 16 to 21; Prime Minister Macmillan from October 23 to 25 (see nos. 395 and 409).

[4] Eisenhower had asked Secretary Dulles to approve this letter before sending it to Redmond. "Apparently Sir Winston would feel very badly," Ann Whitman would tell Dulles's secretary, "if the Metropolitan did not show his paintings in the New York

area" (Whitman to Bernau, Oct. 30, 1957, Dulles Papers, White House Memoranda Series).

After talking to the director of the museum and the board of trustees, Redmond would tell Eisenhower that the museum had agreed to host the exhibit. "I greatly appreciate your interest in the subject," he said, "and agree with you that there are moments in which an exception to almost any rule is justified" (Redmond to Eisenhower, Nov. 6, 1957, WHCF/PPF 833). Joyce Hall, one of the principal organizers of the project, would tell Eisenhower that museum officials considered Churchill's paintings important and were displaying them "with enthusiasm and not as a duty" (Hall to Eisenhower, Nov. 6, 1957, *ibid.*). Several museums, including the Carnegie Institute in Pittsburgh and the Cincinnati Art Museum, declined to show the paintings, stating that a museum should determine its exhibitions based on the quality of the art and not the stature of the artist. The exhibition would open at the Metropolitan on March 7, 1958. For developments see no. 568.

416

EM, AWF, DDE Diaries Series

To F. Douglas Lawrason

October 30, 1957

Personal

Dear Dr. Lawrason: I am grateful to you for taking the trouble to write me your impressions of the talk I made in New York last week.[1] There is no doubt in my mind that our business corporations will increasingly turn their attention to the support of higher education, including medical.

On the other hand, as I pointed out in my talk, I think there are very grave dangers that accompany any initiation of *general* Federal support for these institutions. In this statement I do not mean, of course, to be opposed to support that is provided in special areas to meet special and pressing needs of the government.[2]

Nevertheless, I believe that my objections to the concept of generalized and direct Federal help for all higher education are sound. Included in them are:

(*a*). The United States government can obtain no money for this purpose that is not already in the hands of its citizens, corporations, states and localities. Consequently, the process of taking the money away from citizens to return it to localities for special purposes implies a centralization of wisdom in Washington that certainly does not, necessarily, exist.

(*b*). The more that our institutions, in general practice, lean on the Federal government for this kind of help, the more they invite a kind of Federal influence and domination that could have very bad effects. These I do not need to elaborate.

(*c*). The more we lean upon the Federal government, the more we blur and erase the lines between Federal responsibility and authority on the one hand, and Federal, state and individual initiative and responsibility on the other. I am a firm believer that one of the reasons our nation has prospered above others is because of the degree of authority and responsibility that our founders so wisely preserved to the state and to the people.

Geographic as well as functional distribution of power has benefitted this nation enormously. I hope that this concept may always continue to rule our thinking.

Having said this, I do assure you that I frequently approve Federal aid for special educational purposes as indicated above. Moreover, I am heartily in favor of liberal support of public institutions by the states themselves, believing that there is no more necessary function in the country than the proper education of our youth.[3] This means that opportunity must be open to the poor as well as to those who can defray the costs of their own education. Institutions supported by the several states do much to make this possible.

I hope that I have not given the impression that I consider myself the final authority in such matters; I merely mean to give you my own convictions on a subject whose importance is fully as great as you intimate. In my opinion it could not be greater.

With best wishes, *Sincerely*

[1] Lawrason (M.D. University of Minnesota 1944) had served as Dean of the University of Arkansas School of Medicine since 1955. His letter is not in AWF. Eisenhower had addressed the National Fund for Medical Education in New York on October 22 (see *Public Papers of the Presidents: Eisenhower, 1957*, pp. 754–63). The President had recognized the increasing support that American corporations were providing higher education, with contributions rising from under twenty-five million dollars in 1948 to more than one hundred million dollars in 1956. "Industry," said Eisenhower, "is accepting the support of higher learning as the normal responsibility of a successful business, because it senses a fundamental truth, too long veiled: that, by contributing to the strengthening of our educational resources, each giving corporation makes a sound investment in its own as well as in our nation's future."

[2] Eisenhower had warned against the "disturbing disposition" for groups to "seek solutions to their problems from sources outside themselves." While some of the growth in the role of the federal government in the American economy was the unavoidable consequence of depressions, wars and the continuing world tensions, the President argued, it would be wrong to develop a "doctrinaire and expedient reliance upon government." Americans must be "critically insistent" that the necessity and value of governmental activities be clearly demonstrated, and that "these activities be conducted at a level as close as possible to the people."

[3] Recognizing national concern about Soviet scientific achievements in the wake of Sputnik, Eisenhower had said: "I shall seek opportunities to talk with the American people, telling them of my beliefs and my determinations in these matters." The President explained in his memoir, *Waging Peace*, that he had referred to "the methods of raising the level of our achievements in science, the character and power of our defense and economy, and our responsibilities abroad" (Eisenhower, *Waging Peace*, pp. 215–18). Eisenhower's plan to make four to six speeches, and his deter-

mination "to assume leadership in rallying the country to a resurgence of confidence in the nation's scientific, defense and economic programs" would receive headlines the following day (see *New York Times*, Oct. 23, 1957). On Sputnik see no. 389; for more on Eisenhower's views on education see Galambos and van Ee, *The Middle Way*, nos. 741 and 1188; for developments see no. 434.

417

EM, WHCF, Official File 154-N-2

TO IVAN SCHMUTZ
Personal

October 30, 1957

Dear Ivan: Thank you very much for your nice letter. I am delighted that you and your family are enjoying your life in America.[1]

I understand the desire of your father and uncle to have their own business, and I am sure that in due time it will become possible. While so far it has been impossible to secure legislation that regularizes the status of the Hungarian "parolees," I am quite sure that this country will never be so indifferent to them that it would require them to leave United States territory.

Meantime, I hope you will be patient and that you will realize that the laws under which we operate, which sometimes are hard to understand, are still for the protection of all of us.[2]

With best wishes, *Sincerely*

[1] Schmutz, a thirteen-year-old Hungarian refugee, had come to the United States with his family in December 1956 under the program developed for the resettlement of those Hungarians escaping Soviet domination (for background see Galambos and van Ee, *The Middle Way*, no. 2044; and no. 163 in these volumes). His father and his uncle, who worked in a scrap metal company, wanted to start their own business, Ivan wrote, and he feared they could not obtain a license to do so as so-called "parolees" (who were not regarded as permanent entrants). He was also concerned that his family would be sent back to Europe, which, he said, "would be the biggest catastrophe of our life" (Schmutz to Eisenhower, Oct. 23, 1957, same file as document).

[2] On December 28 Eisenhower would announce that the emergency program for Hungarian refugees would end at the end of the year; 38,000 refugees had entered the country under this policy. In July 1958 he would sign a bill enabling 32,000 refugees to gain both permanent entry and the accompanying right to naturalization (*Public Papers of the Presidents: Eisenhower, 1957*, pp. 850–52; and *Congressional Quarterly Almanac*, vol. XIV, *1958*, p. 60).

418 *EM, AWF, DDE Diaries Series*

To Vivian Carter Mason *October 31, 1957*

Personal

Dear Mrs. Mason: Thank you very much for your letter of October twenty-fifth.[1] I deplore, along with you, any damage to the prestige of our country that was a result of the Little Rock situation. And I can well understand the embarrassment you felt on your recent trip to Europe in an effort to find logical answers to the many questions that you say were put to you on the subject.[2]

I am interested in your suggestion that a conference of the leading women's organizations in the country be called both for the purpose of giving representatives of these organizations a better comprehension of the problems confronting us in the area of race relations and to try to formulate definite plans to avoid a repetition of incidents such as the recent one. Two questions occur to me. First, I wonder whether the Conference would not be more effective if it developed from within the organizations themselves, rather than upon call from me; secondly, there is always the delicate question of timing—and, frankly, I don't know whether the country, in all its parts, is calm enough now for the Conference to be fully representative and still be objective and productive.[3]

At any rate, I shall ask my associates here to give the most serious consideration to your suggestion, and as soon as Mr. Rabb returns to this country I am sure he will be in touch with you further.[4]

With renewed appreciation of your letter, and best wishes, *Sincerely*

[1] In mid-October Mrs. Mason, president of the National Council of Negro Women, Inc., had visited Radio Free Europe installations on a trip sponsored by the Crusade For Freedom (see Galambos, *Columbia University*, nos. 428 and 739). Her letter is in WHCF/OF 142-A-5-A: Little Rock School Integration.

[2] Mrs. Mason said she had experienced the Europeans' deep indignation and resentment over the events in Little Rock. "The injury to our prestige," she had written, "must be a tangible reminder for a long time of how far-reaching our misdeeds are in a world that is in mortal combat over conflicting ideas and ideals." On Eisenhower's decision to send federal troops to Little Rock to enforce federal court-ordered integration of Central High School see nos. 330, 357, and 365.

Eisenhower had been distressed over the reactions by foreign countries on both sides of the iron curtain (see nos. 360 and 366). During an October 3 news conference a reporter had asked the President what advice he would give to Americans traveling overseas when they were asked, "how this could happen in America?" In his response Eisenhower had stressed the importance of the courts as "our bulwarks, our shield against autocratic government." He said, "you can say with certainty . . . the mass of America believes in the sanctity of the court" (*Public Papers of the Presidents: Eisenhower, 1957*, pp. 709–10).

[3] Mrs. Mason had suggested that presidential sponsorship of such a conference would give "tremendous impetus" to women's organizations in "undergirding and bolster-

ing" their goals. In November 1960 Eisenhower would send a greeting to the National Council of Negro Women at its twenty-fifth anniversary meeting (*New York Times*, Nov. 13, 1960).

[4] On November 1 Presidential Assistant and Cabinet Secretary Maxwell Rabb would address the America-Japan Society in Tokyo, Japan (see *New York Times*, Nov. 2, 1957).

419

EM, AWF, Administration Series

To Nelson Aldrich Rockefeller

October 31, 1957

Dear Nelson: Thank you for your memorandum, written as a result of the story in the *New York Times* last Sunday. I am always glad to have the benefit of your thinking.[1]

I am sure you saw the statement I made yesterday on the size of the budget for next year.[2] Actually I can't possibly yet predict what it will be, and in another month I should have a much better idea where we can economize and where we *must* spend. I agree with most of the points you make in your memorandum, and I have no intention of allowing our security to be endangered—though at the same time there is a limit to the amount we can spend effectively.[3]

I wrote the letter to the Metropolitan Museum yesterday; I know Sir Winston will be pleased if they do agree to the exhibition and for his sake I appreciate your willingness to act as intermediary in the matter.[4]

With warm regard, *As ever*

[1] On October 26 the *New York Times* had reported that Eisenhower had set a preliminary ceiling of $70 billion on the 1958 budget. This budget, the *Times* had stated, was $2 billion lower than the latest estimate for the current fiscal year and would greatly increase the chances for a tax cut. Rockefeller had found the article "disturbing" because people reading the article would think it directly reflected Eisenhower's appraisal of the world situation, and conservatives would be encouraged to expect a cut in federal expenditures. Rockefeller also said that the general public would conclude, erroneously, that the world situation was less dangerous than it actually was and that the article would seriously undermine the public support essential to passing the Administration's program in Congress (*Notes on the New York Times Article*, Oct. 28, 1957, AWF/A: Rockefeller Corr.).

[2] Asked at his October 30 news conference whether the pressures to increase defense spending would require the Administration to raise the $70 billion budget ceiling, Eisenhower had said that he "would think it would require very serious retardations elsewhere if we are going to keep within the $70 billion budget" (*Public Papers of the Presidents: Eisenhower, 1957*, pp. 784–85).

[3] Rockefeller had argued that the *Times* story was misleading and "highly damaging" to measures the Administration might propose that were essential to national security. He believed that sources within the Administration had inspired the article, and

recommended that "a procedure of clearances on budgetary statements be instituted that will adequately safeguard the national security aspects of the budget." For developments see no. 469.
[4] For background see nos. 414 and 415.

420 *EM, AWF, Name Series*

To Clifford Roberts *October 31, 1957*

Dear Cliff: All four of the items in your note were of real interest.[1] Of course I shall not allow anything other than inescapable duty to interfere with my visits to Augusta.[2] But I have to tell you that at the moment the prospect of saving out a week to come down in the middle of November grows dimmer and dimmer.

I certainly think you are right about the "sweat and tears" suggestion.[3] *As ever*

[1] Roberts had written on October 30 (AWF/N). In addition to the points covered in nn. 2 and 3 below, Roberts told Eisenhower that the Augusta National Golf Club had invited former Secretary of the Treasury George Humphrey to become a member, and that Roberts hoped the President could "soon develop a plan that will at least indicate your desire to get those troops out of Arkansas." For background on the Little Rock desegregation crisis see no. 330.
[2] "Under no circumstances," Roberts had advised, should the Little Rock crisis prevent the President from following his "accustomed practice" of a November vacation in Augusta, Georgia. Roberts's contacts in Augusta had informed him that the worst they feared was that "some 'poor white trash' in a crowd might yell 'boo'" at the President. As it turned out, Eisenhower would vacation in Augusta November 16–21.
[3] "In your speeches," Roberts had suggested, "give them some 'blood, sweat and tears'—not all assurances."

421 *EM, AWF, Name Series*

To William Alton Jones *October 31, 1957*

Dear Pete: Since early Tuesday morning I have been seeking an opportunity to write you a note about a tempest in a teapot that you stirred up before you left here Sunday evening.[1]

To start at the end and work backward: On Monday evening Mamie and I were having dinner with David who, with his baby sister, has been spending a few days with us while Susie is recovering from the flu.[2] We were having a nice chat when a phone call came in from John, who called up to protest gifts to his children, particularly when they are of a size to defeat his efforts to get them to do a half hour of serious chores at a going rate of ten cents each. Mamie did a little prying to find the cause for this outburst and discovered that Monday afternoon David visited his home briefly and nonchalantly reached in a pocket, pulled out a sizeable bill with a request that it be put in his savings fund. He reported that he had been very careful and it had been held all day long by a security man for safekeeping. Nevertheless John did not seem to be overwhelmed by his son's display of good judgment. He rather seemed to want to voice his sense of frustration in teaching David the value of a dollar.

Most of this conversation being immediately reported to David, he said, "Yes, I was surprised when Mr. Jones gave me the money. He asked me if I had a bank account and I said I did. Then he gave me the bill and I said 'thank you.'" So far as he was concerned, this seemed to dismiss the subject, except that I asked him whether he sent you a little note to assure you of his appreciation. He remarked with the utmost seriousness, "Well, that was a big bill; it deserves a letter." Nevertheless, boylike I suspect he is likely to forget it.[3]

We talked a bit last Sunday about the abruptness of the American withdrawal from the Aswan Dam negotiations. As I am sure you remember, at the time of our withdrawal Congress had already announced its opposition to any loans for the Aswan Dam. This will explain the reference in the attached papers, which otherwise might be a bit obscure.[4]

It was great fun to have you come down here; I hope you will keep yourself flexible to come again soon, particularly when Al gets back.[5] I am sure we can avoid trespassing on my son's efforts to establish strict discipline for his children. After all, a fellow might remember that they are *my grand*children.[6]

Give my love to Nettie. *As ever*

[1] Jones had visited the President at the White House the weekend of October 28–29 (Ann Whitman memorandum, Oct. 26, 1957, AWF/AWD). For background see no. 403.

[2] The Eisenhower grandchildren were Dwight David II, born in 1948; Barbara Anne, born in 1949; Susan Elaine, born in 1951; and Mary Jean, born in 1955.

[3] In his thank-you letter of this same date (AWF/N), Jones would say that getting to know David was a "highlight" of the weekend. As the grandfather of two boys, he wrote, "I am an expert judge . . . and David measures up in every respect."

[4] Jones recently had spent two hours with Egyptian President Nasser (memorandum of telephone conversation, n.d., AWF/N, Jones Corr.). For background on the Suez crisis see Galambos and van Ee, *The Middle Way*, nos. 1932, and 1948. With this letter Eisenhower attached a news release of July 1956 and a copy of a note from Secretary Dulles to Nasser. "At the risk of being presumptuous," Jones would reply on November 9, "I am sorry that Mr. Dulles furnished President Nasser the *excuse* for

the Canal seizure. In retrospect, I am sure [Dulles] would agree that even though Nasser had designs on the Canal, he would not want to precipitate his action." Jones added that he did not see "much progress in trying to win over Egypt and Nasser to our side."

[5] Jones would say he looked forward to a "return engagement" when General Gruenther returned from the International Red Cross Conference in New Delhi, India (Nov. 9, 1957, AWF/N, and Gruenther Papers). For developments see no. 431.

[6] On November 9 (AWF/N) Jones would ask Eisenhower to "do what you can to help me out with John." He added: "Being a mere father, he would not appreciate how doting a grandfather can be. You will understand, and you can promise John that I will restrain myself so as not to undo his good training." The President would circle this paragraph and write: "To JSDE Please return to my file."

422 — *EM, AWF, DDE Diaries Series*

To James Van Gundia Neel — *November 1, 1957*

Personal

Dear Dr. Neel: I have read with the greatest interest your letter of October twenty-fifth.[1] As far as the basic problem presented in your letter is concerned, I might say that I have discussed the matter with many of the top scientists of our country. Their chief concern is, as is yours, with the scientific man-power that might be available to the United States in the next ten years, and they feel that the first step toward providing an adequate pool of trained scientists is to awaken the people of the United States to the necessity of increasing the scientific output of our colleges and universities, and where necessary, offering material help on the part of the Federal government. The Scientific Advisory Committee of the Office of Defense Mobilization is already at work on a report on the entire subject.[2]

There is one implication in your letter, however, with which I disagree. Certainly I am entirely in accord with the idea that the gifted child should receive the maximum amount of education he can assimilate. On the other hand, the great heart of America would be weakened if we neglect the handicapped. All children should receive, in my opinion, the type of education that will insure their being able to cope with their personal problems and to contribute, no matter how small that contribution may be, to the advancement of all. Parenthetically, I might add that Steinmetz immediately comes to mind as a physically handicapped person who achieved, despite his difficulties, the greatest heights.[3]

With renewed thanks for your letter, and best wishes, *Sincerely*

[1] Neel (Ph.D. University of Rochester 1939; M.D., 1944), a professor of human genetics and internal medicine at the University of Michigan Medical School, had been

a member of the Committee on Atomic Bomb Casualties since 1951. His letter concerning the consequences of "long-standing defects in *American educational philosophy*" is in WHCF/OF 133-Q.

[2] The launch of the Soviet earth satellite Sputnik on October 4 (see no. 389) had aroused concern that the United States had fallen behind the Soviet Union not only in technological developments but in the training of scientists as well (see nos. 396 and 416; see also Clowse, *Brainpower for the Cold War*, pp. 49–65). Eisenhower would address this issue in his November 7 speech to the nation on science in national security (see nos. 434 and no. 448; see also *Public Papers of the Presidents: Eisenhower, 1957*, pp. 794–99). On the recommendations of the Science Advisory Committee see no. 408. For developments see no. 447.

[3] Neel had said that it was essential to identify "brilliant minds" and to provide special educational facilities so that they could realize their potential, at the earliest possible time. "It is a sad fact," he said, "that in the American school system today, the term 'exceptional' child is usually a euphemism for the handicapped child. It is he for whom there are fund drives and special classes." Neel argued that the "inescapable fact," was that it was "not upon this group that our national survival depends, but upon our top 5 per cent." Eisenhower was referring to Charles Proteus Steinmetz (original name Karl August Rudolf Steinmetz, 1865–1923), the German-born American electrical engineer whose ideas on alternating current systems helped inaugurate the electrical era in the United States. Steinmetz was born with a deformed back.

423

Dulles Papers,
White House Memoranda Series

To Estelle K. Butler

November 1, 1957

Dear Mrs. Butler: I most deeply appreciate the sense of personal responsibility that impelled you to write to me as you did on October twenty-fourth.[1]

It goes without saying that your suggestion is founded in good sense and in recognition of the favorable responsiveness of humans to courtesy and politeness.

While it is difficult for anyone making a public address on the subject of our foreign relationships to avoid the classification of the Communist leaders as our bitter opponents, I think it is clear that nothing is to be gained by name calling and that just possibly there might be an easing of tensions if we could refer to them if not in friendly terms at least in impersonal ones.

In any event thank you for the trouble you took to write to me and please accept my assurance that I will ponder your words deeply.[2]

With best wishes, *Sincerely*

[1] Butler, a fellow member of the National Presbyterian Church, had written to Eisenhower in response to a recent sermon by their pastor, Dr. Edward Elson, calling peace

the responsibility of each individual. "I decry the public mention of Russia as our *Enemy*, or potential Enemy, by any public official," she stated, "for I feel that a Christian nation should not thus label any other nation." She suggested that a "love your enemies" approach might be more effective. "My feeling is that both the Soviet Government and the Russian people see themselves surrounded by our bases, realize that we are in a race to outstrip them in ballistic missiles, and must fear us to the point of wondering if their only chance of survival may not depend on striking at us while they have a possible superiority in atomic power. Could we allay some of that fear by a less belligerent attitude towards them?" she asked.

[2] Eisenhower sent Butler's letter and a copy of this reply to Secretary Dulles. "Don't bother to make any reply," he said, "but sometime you and I might have a little talk about the suggestion the lady makes" (Eisenhower to Dulles, Nov. 1, 1957, Dulles Papers, White House Memoranda Series).

424 *EM, WHCF, Official File 2-B*

TO HAROLD BOESCHENSTEIN *November 1, 1957*
Personal

Dear Mr. Boeschenstein: I have just finished signing several score letters to the individuals who helped you in your effort during the last session of the Congress to secure authorizations for the mutual aid programs in accordance with the Administration's proposals.[1] While all of us have frankly to admit that we were not nearly as successful as we hoped, nonetheless I know that the work of your informal "Committee" was invaluable.[2]

In view of the temper of the Congress at that particular period (which I trust will not be repeated this next year), I think your achievement was splendid, and thank you once again for your dedication to the program that I consider, as do you, to be vital to our national interest.

Quite naturally, I pray that next year the Congress may prove more alert to the problems we face in this ever changing world and that we may be able to persuade more of the members that the mutual security funds actually represent a bargain rate of defense for us and for the rest of the free world.[3]

With warm regard, *Sincerely*

[1] For background on Boeschenstein's appointment to head a citizens' group to work toward passage of the Administration's mutual security program see no. 137. Among those Eisenhower thanked were James F. Brownlee, former deputy director of the Office of Economic Stabilization and partner in the J. H. Whitney Company; Elliott V. Bell, chairman of the executive committee of McGraw-Hill Publishing Company; John Stuart, director of the executive committee of the Quaker Oats Company; and George Whitney, former chairman of the board of the J. P. Morgan Company (all letters are in the same file as this document).

[2] On the 1957 Mutual Security Act, which cut $618 million from Eisenhower's original request, see nos. 273 and 304.
[3] He and his committee were developing a plan to overcome "public confusion and inertia," Boeschenstein would tell Eisenhower, and they would begin earlier the following year in order to be more effective (Boeschenstein to Eisenhower, Nov. 4, 1957, same file as document). For developments see no. 762.

425

EM, AWF, Dulles-Herter Series

To John Foster Dulles

November 1, 1957

Dear Foster: I shall send to the Bureau of the Budget and to those helping me in preparing talks, a copy of your memorandum on the need for obtaining mutual aid appropriations. I shall also send a copy of this reply.[1]

I most heartily agree that the experiences of the past have shown the need not only for us to maintain an urgent pace in the production of scientific weapons of great destructiveness, but also to maintain a readiness and ability to help the nations of the free world so that they may cooperate with us effectively in the defense of freedom.[2]

With warm regard, *As ever*

[1] "My people are much concerned over the possibility that Sputnik will lead Congress to be liberal with military appropriations, perhaps even with the military aspects of mutual security," Dulles had told Eisenhower, "but will offset this by cutting down on the economic aid. This seems to us of at least equal importance" (Dulles to Eisenhower, Oct. 31, 1957, AWF/D-H). In addition to the Director of the Bureau of the Budget, Eisenhower would send the memorandum and his reply to Presidential Assistants Arthur Larson and Bryce Harlow.
[2] On this day Eisenhower would tell Dulles that mutual security expenditures for the first quarter of the fiscal year were $45 million less than in the corresponding period the previous year. Eisenhower emphasized "that with the need as great as it was he hoped that actual spending would not fall behind and thus put him in an awkward position *vis-a-vis* the next session of Congress" (Dulles, Memorandum of Conversation, Nov. 1, 1957, Dulles Papers, White House Memoranda Series). Eisenhower would stress the importance of economic aid to national security in his November 13 speech in Oklahoma City (*Public Papers of the Presidents: Eisenhower, 1957*, pp. 807–17).

426 *EM, AWF, Name Series*

To Edward John Bermingham *November 1, 1957*

Dear Ed: Bob Schulz tells me that you are not feeling at all well and worse, that you have been in the Harkness Pavillion for some time. This note is merely to say "I'm sorry" that you have again been laid low; Mamie and I pray that before long you will be your usual robust and cheerful self.[1]

Incidentally, your little elephant continues to stand guard over the papers that flow across my desk. My only complaint is that *he* doesn't attempt to solve any of my problems![2]

With affectionate regard to Kay and, as always, the best to yourself, *As ever*

[1] Bermingham would reply on November 5, "your thought of me has buoyed me beyond words to express." Eisenhower had first learned of Bermingham's illness on October 13, when Bermingham had written that an "unexplained accident" had kept him "up and down for some months." Bermingham would remain in Harkness Pavilion Hospital in New York City through the Christmas holidays (see Eisenhower to Bermingham, Dec. 23, 1957). He would die on July 13, 1958.

[2] Bermingham had attended a White House stag dinner on July 11 and probably had given the elephant to Eisenhower at that time. In his July 12 thank-you note Eisenhower had said he would display the elephant in his office because it is "frequently visited by good Republicans." In a letter of October 16 Eisenhower told Bermingham that he would "try to follow your suggestion" of letting the "elephant bear the brunt of the frustration and irritation that seem so characteristically a part of this job." See also Bermingham to Eisenhower, October 13, 1957. All correspondence in AWF/N.

427 *EM, AWF, DDE Diaries Series*

To Ralph Emerson McGill *November 4, 1957*
Personal

Dear Ralph: Thank you very much for sending me, through Jim Hagerty, a copy of the letter you wrote recently to the Chief Editorial Writer of the New York Herald Tribune.[1]

May I say that I have nothing but praise for your thoughtful, reasoned viewpoint. I particularly agree with your comments on the futility, at this time, of a conference comprising all Southern Governors. The outcome would almost certainly be that which you outline. There is no question that many political leaders in the South now realize that some beginning toward accommodation should be undertaken; but they are prisoners of their own prior statements and pronouncements.[2] (Incidentally, I have one or two problems in the foreign field where the same situation prevails.)[3]

I do hope that you will continue writing on this general subject in the tones that have been noticeable in the two or three editorials I have seen of yours. In the long run the pen is still mighty; the teaching and preaching of moderation cannot fail to be helpful.

With warm regard, *Sincerely*

[1] McGill, editor of *The Atlanta Constitution,* had written a guest editorial which appeared in the *New York Herald Tribune* on October 29. The letter, entitled "The True South Speaks," was in response to an October 15 editorial written by William Johnson Miller, a North Carolinian by birth and a former war correspondent and associate editor with *Newsweek, Time,* and *Life.* James Campbell Hagerty was Press Secretary to the President.

[2] McGill said he was in "complete agreement" with the general thesis of Miller's editorial: the need for a moderate and peaceful solution to the desegregation problem in the South and the "desperate need to sustain the moderate leadership which stands on law and order and which opposes any form of violence." McGill disagreed, however, with Miller's proposal that the Southern position would be helped by a conference of Southern governors called by Eisenhower.

McGill considered an attempt to assemble Southern leaders "futile and damaging" because as many as six Southern governors and as many attorneys general had pledged to defy the Supreme Court decision to desegregate public schools. Although these leaders privately realized the inevitability of integration, he wrote, they also know that it is political suicide to state publicly that segregation is doomed. McGill believed that the governors would "eagerly" accept an invitation to the conference and they would "thereafter be able, in effect, to be defiant from the White House itself."

Instead, McGill suggested an assembly of governors of the states where moderate integration efforts had begun. He also said that the President could "reach over the heads of politicians and sustain the moderates" in the deep South by delivering speeches on the subject and by maintaining his moderate leadership. For background on the desegregation crisis and Eisenhower's decision to send federal troops to Little Rock see nos. 330, 357, and 365.

[3] See, for example, nos. 408 and 423.

428

EM, AWF, DDE Diaries Series

TO HAMILTON D. SCHWARZ

Personal

November 4, 1957

Dear Mr. Schwarz: Thank you for your note. I am particularly appreciative of your understanding of and sympathy with the problems that seem of late to have been more complex than ever.[1]

I am afraid that there is more than a little truth in the assertions that we Americans have become too complacent, too fond of the good things of life, and too disinclined to make the sacrifices that are going to be necessary if we win the peace we so devoutly desire.[2] But I still have, as I am sure you do, enormous faith in the ability of the people of our country to meet every challenge, including those of the present day. I truly think I can sense, from every report that comes to me, an awakening to the situation and a rising tide of determination to prove ourselves again.[3]

With best wishes, *Sincerely*

[1] Schwarz, an investment banker with F. S. Smithers and Company in New York, had written on October 31 (WHCF/PPF 20-D). That morning he had read a *New York Times* story about Eisenhower's October 30 news conference. The article had called attention to the increasing and "unremitting crises" the President had been under for the last eighteen months. Schwarz said that after reading the article he had recalled the time when he had "ardently" hoped Eisenhower would become a presidential candidate. "At that time no one could have foreseen all the difficulties and trials which you were to face but believe me, Sir, my sympathies are with you." For background on Eisenhower's difficulties see nos. 330, 396, 469, and 480; on the news conference see *Public Papers of the Presidents: Eisenhower, 1957*, pp. 774–87.

[2] The "basic difficulty," Schwarz said, is a general unwillingness to "make real sacrifices" and a lack of understanding of the "true spirit of sacrifice."

[3] During Eisenhower's news conference a reporter had asked him if "all of these great problems sap your strength physically or mentally in any way." The President referred to the Suez crisis in July 1956 and said "if you can point out a day since then that there hasn't been some critical problem placed upon my desk, I can't remember when it was. . . . I find it a bit wearing, but," he added, "I find it endurable, if you have got the faith in America that I have" (*Public Papers of the Presidents: Eisenhower, 1957*, p. 786; on the Suez crisis see Galambos and van Ee, *The Middle Way*, no. 1946).

429 — *EM, AWF, DDE Diaries Series*

To Arthur Frank Burns — *November 4, 1957*

Dear Arthur: Thank you for your report of November first.[1] As I hope you realize, I consider you one of my most reliable "listening posts" and certainly one of my most valued advisers—despite your removal from the immediate scene.[2] I shall ponder carefully all you say and see that pertinent parts of your letter are distributed among my associates here who are working with me on the complex and difficult problems you touch upon.

For your information alone, the first speech will be on the subject of "Science and Security." I, too, feel that if we can allay some of the fears that seem to be prevalent on the subject of our scientific achievements, other problems will seem less overpowering.* [3]

And thank you, too, for your last paragraph. I still want to get some sort of a break before the beginning of the Congressional session, but at the moment I simply cannot see where it might come.[4]

With warm regard, *Sincerely*

[1] Burns had praised Eisenhower's decision to make a series of speeches on national problems and policies. New Soviet advances in weapons and space technology had "confused, troubled, mystified, and in a sense humiliated" the American people. Burns added that the issue of school integration, though less prominent in the newspapers, had not disappeared. "I find a sense of helplessness, at times of actual hopelessness, about this even among members of the clergy," he said. Regarding the economy, Burns expressed concern that inflation and unemployment in the United States were fueling fears among U.S. allies of a depression in the Western world. "The point about all this," he concluded, "is simply that the nation, and in fact the entire world, needs your factual, authoritative, and lucid voice at this time" (Burns to Eisenhower, Nov. 1, 1957, WHCF/OF 133-Q).

[2] Burns had resigned as Chairman of the Council of Economic Advisors in December 1956.

[3] A notation at the bottom of this letter indicates that at this point Eisenhower added the words: "At the same time, complacency would be worse." The President would deliver this speech on November 7 (see *Public Papers of the Presidents: Eisenhower, 1957*, pp. 789–99).

[4] Burns was "unhappy" to have read that Eisenhower might not be taking a vacation in November. "In view of the kind of summer you had, and the rough time that the Democrats are planning to give you in the next session of Congress, you really should regard a vacation as a must." The Eisenhowers would visit Augusta National Golf Club in mid-November (see no. 439).

430

EM, AWF, International Series: Macmillan

To Harold Macmillan
Top secret

November 4, 1957

Dear Harold: Please inform Her Majesty that I am most deeply appreciative of her gracious thought that, provided we might be able to accept, she would issue to Mrs. Eisenhower and me an invitation to visit the United Kingdom at the conclusion of the NATO meeting.[1] I must regretfully inform you of my belief that an invitation should not be issued for reasons that are largely personal, but nevertheless, I believe, very important.

The doctors deem it inadvisable for Mrs. Eisenhower now to undertake a trip that would be as arduous as would two trans-oceanic journeys within a period of five or six days. They believe that her present satisfactory rate of progress toward her accustomed health and vigor would receive a definite setback and one that could be very damaging to her general nervous system; whereas if she does nothing more than routine over the next several months, they are sure she will continue her rapid improvement.[2]

It seems to me a State visit would lose much of its appeal to the ordinary person and could not fail to lose in sentimental value unless I were accompanied by my wife in making a visit to The Queen. Consequently, I think that for me individually to stop for a day or two in London could not by any means be considered as adequately fulfilling the desirable objectives of a State visit.

Therefore I believe it would be better to defer the matter in the hope that before the end of this Administration Mrs. Eisenhower and I could find an opportunity to come to your country, even if it might require on our part a brief visit to other major countries in the NATO region.[3]

I realize that if I were able to accept your present suggestion, we could make the proposed visit without the implied need for going elsewhere and with the minimum of travel complications. Consequently I am doubly grateful to you for this consideration of our convenience and time. But in view of Mrs. Eisenhower's situation, I have given you my full thought on the matter.

And I should add not only a repetition of my gratitude for the Queen's hospitable gesture but my sincere hope that at some later date my wife and I can make the trip.

If possible, please convey our greetings and best wishes to Her Majesty and to Prince Philip.

With warm regard, *As ever*

[1] At the request of Prime Minister Macmillan, the British Ambassador had extended the Queen's invitation to the President and his wife (Caccia to Eisenhower, Oct. 31, 1957, AWF/I: Macmillan). On the upcoming NATO Conference see no. 444. A draft of this letter with Eisenhower's handwritten emendations is in AWF/D-H (see also Eisenhower to Dulles, Nov. 4, 1957, AWF/D-H).

[2] The First Lady had undergone gynecological surgery on August 6 (see no. 291). After discussing Macmillan's message with Secretary Dulles on November 1, Eisenhower had asked Dulles to request a delay until Mrs. Eisenhower received a follow-up examination on November 4. In a personal note to the President (Nov. 4, 1957, AWF/I: Macmillan), Macmillan expressed concern and said he hoped that Mrs. Eisenhower's examination "will show any misgivings to be quite unfounded, for I know that The Queen is much looking forward to seeing you both in December" (see Telephone conversation, Eisenhower and Dulles, Nov. 1, 1957, AWF/D; Telephone conversation, Dulles and Caccia, Nov. 1, 1957, Dulles Papers, Telephone Conversations; and Dulles, Memorandum of Conversation with the President, Nov. 1, 1957, Dulles Papers, White House Memoranda Series; see also Eisenhower to Macmillan, Nov. 4, 1957, AWF/I: Macmillan).

[3] The Eisenhowers would travel to Europe and Great Britain in December 1959. For developments see no. 1282.

431

EM, AWF,
Administration Series

TO ALFRED MAXIMILIAN GRUENTHER — November 4, 1957

Dear Al: To answer your specific inquiry: I have had, I think three bouts since you left and, if I may mix a metaphor, I haven't had anything remotely resembling a home run.[1] There is nothing spectacular about the report—about this phase of life—but Pete Jones is back in this country and I have warned him to be on the alert for a session after your return.[2]

As you probably know, Mamie and I spent Friday afternoon and Saturday at West Point.[3] It was nice to see Gar and Verone again, and I still manage to recharge my batteries when I have the opportunity to visit the Academy.[4]

Is your return still scheduled for the fourteenth?[5] *As ever*

[1] Gruenther had written on October 30 from New Delhi, India, where he was attending the International Red Cross Conference. He said he was "well informed of the state of health of the President" but he had "no information about his bridge, and that causes me some concern."

[2] William Alton Jones recently had returned from Egypt (see no. 421). For background on Eisenhower's bridge games with Gruenther and Jones see no. 106. For developments see no. 670.

[3] The President had attended a reunion with his Military Academy classmates from the class of 1915 (see no. 442, and *New York Times*, Nov. 2, 3, 1957).

[4] General Garrison Holt Davidson (USMA 1927) was superintendent of the United States Military Academy. His wife was Gruenther's sister, the former Verone M. Gruenther.

[5] Gruenther would return to Washington on November 15 (Gruenther Out-of-Washington Engagements—Sept. 8–Nov. 15, 1957, AWF/A; see also Gruenther to Beck, Nov. 21, and Eisenhower to Gruenther, Dec. 3, 1957, both in Gruenther Papers; and *New York Times*, Dec. 7, 1957).

432

EM, AWF, DDE Diaries Series

TO PERCY WALTER THOMPSON — November 4, 1957

Dear Perc: I am reminded that soon you will celebrate your birthday anniversary.[1] I hope the day will be a pleasant one and that the year to come will bring you nothing but happiness and satisfaction.

The grandchildren amaze me every time I see them, and, fortunately, we are able to see much more of all four now that they live comparatively close to the White House. Mary Jean is developing into a real personality, and the other three seem to grow an inch every week or so.[2] Again I congratulate both of us on having such youngsters to be proud of.

With affectionate regard to Bea, and, of course, my felicitations and best wishes on your anniversary.[3] *As ever*

[1] Thompson, born November 8, 1898, was John Eisenhower's father-in-law.

[2] The Eisenhower grandchildren were living with their parents at Fort Belvoir, Virginia. Mary Jean, the youngest, was born in December 1955.

[3] Thompson's wife, and Barbara Eisenhower's mother, was the former Beatrice ("Be*e*") Birchfield.

433 — *EM, AWF, DDE Diaries Series*

To Neil Hosler McElroy — *November 5, 1957*

Secret

Dear Neil:[1] As a result of my recent conversations with the British Prime Minister we agreed, in our concluding talk, on certain procedural measures to achieve the maximum political coordination of the policies of our two Governments in the political, economic, defense, scientific and psychological warfare fields.

Mr. Macmillan and I nominated our respective Secretaries of State for Foreign Affairs to consult together and to agree on particular areas of policy or on specific problems of a character which cannot be easily dealt with through normal channels. In such cases they were directed to establish working groups of American and British officials with the composition varied according to subject and including representation from all interested Departments and Agencies of the two Governments. The main objective of these working groups will be to facilitate the processing of problems where the main responsibilities are Anglo-American in character or where prior concert of Anglo-American policy would contribute to the more effective functioning of the multilateral organizations to which they both belong. Similarly, there will be occasions when it would be desirable, after preliminary Anglo-American discussions, to make an approach to particular friendly governments with a view to concerting action with them also.

The North Atlantic Council meeting in December, which is to be attended by heads of government, will offer the first opportunity for us to address ourselves to the implementation of the broader objectives enunciated in the communique issued at the end of Mr. Macmillan's visit.[2] Preparations for United States participation in this meeting and the formulation of programs and policies to be discussed with our allies there will be the responsibility of the Secretary of State who will coordinate the views of all Government agencies. I am asking General Robert Cutler of my staff to assist Secretary Dulles in this effort.

In informing you of these policy decisions and in requesting your full cooperation with the Secretary of State, I would add my personal interest in insuring that all who may participate in the working groups to be established by the Secretary of State carry out their tasks in the spirit as well as the letter of the Anglo-American Declaration of Common Purpose issued by Prime Minister Macmillan and myself at the end of our conference. I am attaching a copy of this Declaration which I hope you will keep close at hand in connection with whatever responsibilities your Department may have for United States activities abroad. Finally I would ask you to observe the confidential nature of the Anglo-American procedural arrangements described above and, to the extent possible, the existence of any Anglo-American working groups which may be established as a result.[3]

Sincerely

[1] In a handwritten note to Secretary Dulles, Eisenhower approved the State Department's draft of this letter. Dulles had suggested this "personal directive" to insure that the responsible departments and agencies would implement "in letter and in spirit" the Declaration of Common Purpose, signed by the President and Prime Minister Macmillan at the end of their October meetings (see Dulles to Eisenhower, Nov. 4, 1957, AWF/D-H; on the meetings see no. 409). Copies of this letter, which were sent to the three service secretaries, the Secretaries of the Treasury and Commerce, the Chairman of the Atomic Energy Commission, the Director of the Central Intelligence Agency, and the Acting Director of the United States Information Agency, are in AWF/A; see also Anderson to Eisenhower, Nov. 6, 1957, *ibid.*).

[2] On the communiqué see "President Eisenhower and Prime Minister Macmillan Agree on Closer U.S.-U.K. Cooperation," *U.S. Department of State Bulletin* 37, no. 959 (November 11, 1957), 739–41.

[3] For developments regarding the NATO meeting see no. 444.

434 — *EM, AWF, DDE Diaries Series*

To Arthur Larson — *November 5, 1957*

Memorandum for the Honorable Arthur Larson: Will you please consider the following as you work on the draft of your speech today?[1]

One reason I feel so strongly that the educational phases in your draft must be contracted is because there are so many parts of the defense problem that have *really* to be put before the American people.[2]

For example, our talk gives not even a sketchy recitation of our ballistic missile effort. It does not give the approximate time of starting the effort. It does not say anything about the initial scientific survey undertaken in connection with the "New Look" and which started us on the road.[3]

It does not give any idea of the magnitude of the present effort (something like a billion dollars a year devoted to part of this one project alone).

It gives no idea of the amount of money the Defense establishment is spending annually on total research and development (something over five billion a year). It does not sufficiently emphasize the fact (which should be handled in connection with the introduction of the Killian paragraph), that I have over these years been in informal but close contact with scientists and that what Dr. Killian is going to do is to regularize these connections and make them broader, permanent, and, in addition, be my adviser in the coordination of the connection between the Federal government and the scientific world. Similar advisers will be in subordinate places.

I think you should get the strongest possible statement that you can from Secretary McElroy.

Finally, it should be pointed out that money alone will not solve this problem.[4]

* * * * *

I think a sentence or two could emphasize the fact that a purely materialistic dictatorship has concentrated in particular areas and has accomplished a very significant scientific achievement. I think we have not stressed that we are not merely racing in the materialistic way; we are defending priceless spiritual values.

Finally, I think the paper should end on a note of determination and earnest purpose.

There should be no thought of complacency in the whole paper, but in every point brought up there should be the expression of complete conviction that the American people can meet every one of these problems and these threats if we turn our minds to it.

[1] Larson, Director of the United States Information Agency since 1956, had been appointed Special Assistant to the President for special projects in international affairs on October 28, 1957 (*New York Times*, Oct. 17, and Oct. 29, 1957). Eisenhower had announced on October 22 (see no. 416) that he planned to address the American people on matters of defense, the economy, and international affairs. The timing of his talks was probably affected by the announcement (Nov. 2) that the Soviet Union had launched a second satellite containing a dog (see *New York Times*, Nov. 3, 1957), and by news stories about the Gaither report's warning that the defenses of the United States were inadequate to deal with a Soviet attack (see no. 463 and Levine, *The Missile and Space Race*, pp. 65–68).

[2] Eisenhower would decide to give two speeches in November 1957. The first, delivered from the White House on the evening of November 7, would focus on the re-

lationship between science and defense (*Public Papers of the Presidents: Eisenhower, 1957*, pp. 789–99). The second, a radio and television address on "Our Future Security," would be delivered in Oklahoma City on November 13 (see no. 448, and *Public Papers of the Presidents: Eisenhower, 1957*, pp. 807–17).

[3] In his November 7 talk the President would review the achievements in ballistic missile development and declare that the American security posture was "one of great strength" as a result of the reorganization of the defense establishment under the "New Look" (see Galambos and van Ee, *The Middle Way*, nos. 168 and 727). Admitting for the first time since the launch of Sputnik (see no. 389) that the Soviet Union was "quite likely ahead in some missile and special areas," and was "obviously ahead of us in satellite development," Eisenhower told the American people that "the overall military strength of the free world is distinctly greater than that of the communist countries." Eisenhower would announce the appointments of James Rhine Killian, Jr. to the newly created position of Special Assistant to the President for Science and Technology (see no. 396) and William Marion Holaday to the new post of guided missiles director (see no. 394).

[4] Eisenhower would make this point in the November 13 Oklahoma City speech (see no. 448).

435 *EM, AWF, Administration Series*

To Sinclair Weeks *November 6, 1957*

Memorandum for the Secretary of Commerce: Thank you for your note of November fourth.[1]

I have looked up the records and find that yours was the only agency out of a total of some seven or eight reporting that recommended disapproval.[2]

Actually the Council of Economic Advisers believe that under the provisions of this bill the airlines subsidy of the affected companies can be cut about fifty percent of the passenger miles.

[1] Weeks had written the President (AWF/A) regarding the November 1 Cabinet meeting discussion of recent legislation supporting government subsidies of feeder airlines. S. 2229, introduced in the Senate on August 1 and signed into law as P.L. 307 on September 7, had authorized the Civil Aeronautics Board to guarantee ninety percent of each loan made to commercial short haul and feeder air and helicopter lines for equipment purchases. The goal of the legislation was to reduce the annual $30 million airline subsidy by stimulating the aircraft industry to develop a new plane more suited to the needs of the feeder airlines than the obsolete DC-3 (*Congressional Quarterly Almanac*, vol. XIII, *1957*, p. 680). The Department of Commerce had recommended a veto (see Williams to Brundage, Aug. 28, 1957, AWF/A: Weeks Corr.).

[2] In a handwritten note on the bottom of Weeks's letter, Eisenhower had instructed Presidential Aide Andrew Goodpaster to "Please see why (if we have records) the bill was not vetoed."

To Leslie W. Nelson *November 7, 1957*
Personal

Dear Professor Nelson: With your general thesis that a common language would be of the greatest boon to establishing friendship and understanding between peoples of the world I am in complete agreement (and one which I have long shared).[1] I have had many conversations with educators and others on the subject, many of these individuals from other countries. In general, (and I feel from your letter that you agree) the feeling has been that to invent a language would not be as effective as would an agreement among nations to pick one language as its "second" tongue, and that second tongue would be taught in every country in the world.[2]

Because the English language has within the past few years been so widely adopted, on this basis, most of the men with whom I have talked have argued for English as a logical second tongue. For example, ten million Russians are today studying our language. It is taught in a similar manner in almost every nation in Europe. France and Italy may be exceptions—of this I am not sure.

In any event, I shall pass your letter on to my associates in the Department of Health, Education, and Welfare where your letter may possibly be answered in more detail than I can devote here.[3]

I am grateful for your offer to be of service. *Sincerely*

[1] Nelson (Ph.D. Ohio State University 1944), a faculty member in the Division of Education at Los Angeles State College, had written on October 28 (WHCF/OF 111-E). While on sabbatical and traveling through Europe, Nelson had investigated the idea of a "common world language" which, he thought, would increase "the chances for a continued peace."

[2] According to Nelson's plan, the universal language could be developed by a committee of linguists from "a few key countries." The language would contain "common elements of various languages" and would be learned in addition to each country's "native tongue."

[3] Marjorie C. Johnston, a specialist in foreign languages from the Department of Health, Education and Welfare, would reply to Nelson on November 21 (see Johnston to Nelson and Route Slip, *ibid.*). Affirming the desirability of a common language, she would note some of the difficulties preventing the "acceptance of either a natural or a planned auxiliary language." Established languages lacked "simplicity and logic," while "constructed languages" functioned "largely as codes" because they inadequately expressed "the concepts of the cultures of all peoples."

437 *EM, AWF, Dulles-Herter Series*

TO JOHN FOSTER DULLES *November 7, 1957*
Eyes only

Dear Foster:[1] Will you please carefully read the enclosed documents, both of them directed to the subject of establishing good relationships with the Congress. One is by Cabot Lodge; the other by General Persons.[2] These are given to you for such value as you can derive from them. After you have studied them carefully, I request that you personally destroy them both. I am particularly anxious that no word of any concerted effort along this line ever reach the outside because a leak would tend to destroy the value of the effort.

Of course there is no objection to your repeating to your own staff, but as your own ideas, any of the thoughts contained in these documents.[3]

With warm regard, *As ever*

[1] Eisenhower sent this same letter to the Vice-President, to each Cabinet member, and to the directors of the International Cooperation Administration, the Office of Defense Mobilization, and the Bureau of the Budget (all letters are in AWF/A).

[2] Lodge had sent the President a memorandum containing advice for agency and department heads. After recommending that all legitimate congressional demands should "be responded to courteously, thoroughly, quickly, and accurately," Lodge had emphasized the importance of social contacts, the clear and positive presentation of a department's objectives, the need to separate congressional mail from public mail, and the reduction in the number of "free wheeling" news conferences. Members of Congress "expect leadership," Lodge stated. "They are very quick to spot a coward and take advantage of him" (Lodge to Eisenhower, Oct. 21, 1957, Lodge Papers).

Eisenhower had sent Lodge's memorandum to General Persons, who "generally endorsed" the recommendations. Persons stressed, however, the importance of working closely with eighty selected members rather than the entire Congress and the importance of establishing "mutual confidence more than merely friendly relations." He also recommended the creation of a central congressional relations office within each department (Eisenhower to Persons, Oct. 23, 1957; and Persons to Eisenhower, Oct. 29, 1957, AWF/N; see also no. 317; and Ken Collier, "Eisenhower and Congress: The Autopilot Presidency," *Presidential Studies Quarterly* 24, no. 2 [1994], 309–25).

[3] Although both papers contained "much good sense," Dulles would tell Eisenhower, he "could not possibly work with as many as eighty Members of Congress and have time left for anything else" (Dulles to Eisenhower, Nov. 21, 1957, AWF/D-H). For more on congressional relations see no. 616.

TO LYNDON BAINES JOHNSON *November 7, 1957*

Dear Lyndon: Thank you for your letter of October twenty-eighth setting forth your views with regard to Texas' claim to rights in the submerged lands lying off her Gulf shore.[1]

It is my view that the State of Texas should have the right to explore and exploit those submerged lands which extend seaward of the State into the Gulf of Mexico for a distance of three marine leagues. It is my earnest hope that the Submerged Lands Act establishes this as a matter of law.[2]

Whether the Act, as a matter of law, accomplished this purpose is of course a proper matter for the Supreme Court to consider and decide.

In any action which the Attorney General may have to take by reason of the order of the Supreme Court, the public statements which I have made bearing upon this controversy will of course be presented to the Court and the statements of the Attorney General which were in accord with mine, will also be presented.[3]

Needless to say, I appreciate having your comments on this important subject.

With warm regard, *Sincerely*

[1] For background on the Tidelands oil controversy see Galambos and van Ee, *The Middle Way*, no. 26. Senate Democratic leader Lyndon Johnson had written regarding the possibility that Texas might be drawn into a Justice Department suit before the Supreme Court involving submerged lands off the Louisiana coast (same file as document). Johnson had said that the overwhelming majority of Texans were convinced that "title to the submerged lands for a distance three marine leagues to seaward resides in the State." (A marine league is equal to 3.45 land miles [5.5 kilometers]). They believed that "this title is based upon history, recognized in treaty and confirmed by Act of Congress—the so-called Tidelands Act which was approved on May 22, 1953, and which you signed" (see Ernest R. Bartley, *The Tidelands Oil Controversy: A Legal and Historical Analysis* [Austin, 1953], pp. 53–58, 79–94). In April 1957 the Justice Department had brought suit against Louisiana in the Supreme Court, seeking ownership of the oil-rich lands beyond the three-mile limit. Texas had petitioned the Court in June to decide only the boundaries of Louisiana and not to involve Texas. In an amended complaint filed November 7, the U.S. Justice Department had claimed for the United States rights in all undersea land more than three miles from shore in the Gulf of Mexico. The territories involved included those of Texas, Louisiana, Mississippi, Alabama and Florida (see *New York Times*, Apr. 8, June 4, Nov. 19, 1957). On October 20 Johnson had wired Eisenhower expressing concern over the Justice Department's actions in this matter. Eisenhower would send a similar letter on November 7 to Texas Governor Price Daniel (same file as document).

[2] The Submerged Lands Act of 1953 had vested title to submerged lands and their natural resources in the states, within the states' historic boundaries (see *Congressional Quarterly Almanac*, vol. IX, *1953*, pp. 388–96).

[3] In his November 11 response to Eisenhower (same file as document), Johnson would note: "I only wish that your former Attorney General had been motivated by the philosophies which you have expressed and I hope that ways and means can be found to make that philosophy the official policy of this Government." For developments see no. 473.

439

EM, AWF,
DDE Diaries Series

To Arthur Bradford Eisenhower *November 8, 1957*

Dear Arthur: I am ashamed to realize how long it has been since I have been in touch with you, and that this note is primarily motivated by your approaching birthday.[1] At any rate, I do want you to know that you have my warmest felicitations, and best wishes for your happiness and health in the years to come.

This past year—actually the period since the beginning of the Suez crisis last July—seems to have been one of steadily mounting crises and pressures, culminating in the Little Rock situation at home and the blows to our prestige by that and by the Russian scientific achievements in the past few weeks.[2] When I wake up in the morning I sometimes wonder just what new problem can possibly be laid on my desk during the day to come; there always seems to be an even more complex one than I could have imagined.

As you probably know my vacation this year was hardly worthy of the name.[3] I practically commuted between Newport and Washington, and since Mamie was still recovering from her operation, neither one of us really got to enjoy ourselves too much.[4] I had hoped to go down to Augusta for ten days of golf the middle of this month, but that dream, too, seems to have gone a-glimmering.[5]

I hope you are taking care of yourself, and that you are feeling reasonably well.[6]

Have a happy birthday; give Louise my affectionate regard; and, as always, the very best to yourself. *As ever*

[1] Arthur, the eldest Eisenhower brother, was born on November 11, 1886. He and the President had last corresponded in August (see Dwight Eisenhower to Arthur Eisenhower, Aug. 6, 1957, and related correspondence in WHCF/OF 62).

[2] On the Suez crisis see Galambos and van Ee, *The Middle Way,* nos. 1932 and 1946; on the desegregation crisis in Little Rock, Arkansas, see no. 330; and on the two Soviet earth satellites, Sputnik I and Sputnik II, see nos. 394 and 434.

[3] The Eisenhowers had vacationed in Newport, Rhode Island, September 4–30 (see no. 190).

[4] Mrs. Eisenhower had undergone surgery on August 6 (see no. 291).

[5] As it turned out, the President would vacation in Augusta November 16–21 (see also no. 420).
[6] For developments see no. 558.

440

EM, AWF, International Series: Ghana

To Kwame Nkrumah

November 8, 1957

Dear Prime Minister:[1] Thank you very much for your letter of October seventeenth regarding the Volta River Project and enclosing the Report of the Preparatory Commission.[2]

As a result of the Vice President's trip to Ghana earlier this year and my subsequent talks with him and with Mr. Gbedemah, I feel that I have acquired a certain familiarity with your vital new nation.[3] I am sure you know that your country has our best wishes for success in its efforts to solve its problems and to realize its aspirations for a peaceful, stable and prosperous future.[4] *Sincerely*

[1] Nkrumah had been Prime Minister of the Gold Coast until March 1957 when it became the independent country of Ghana. State Department officials drafted this letter (see Howe to Goodpaster, Nov. 7, 1957, AWF/I: Ghana).

[2] For several years government officials in the Gold Coast had studied the feasibility of constructing a hydroelectric dam on the Volta River, primarily to take advantage of extensive bauxite deposits needed in the production of aluminum. Although the country had allocated funds for the project, it had solicited additional support from the British government and Aluminium, Limited, of Canada. Foreign interest in the project had waned with the approach of independence, however, and a number of Gold Coast officials had visited the United States seeking technical and financial assistance. In June 1957 the United States had signed a technical cooperation agreement with Ghana that had provided $700,000 toward community development and agricultural extension services (State, *Foreign Relations, 1955–1957,* vol. XVIII, *Africa,* pp. 49–50, 60, 376; see also Kwaku Obosu-Mensah, *Ghana's Volta Resettlement Scheme: The Long-term Consequences of Post-colonial State Planning* [San Francisco, 1996], pp. 4–5, 6–16; and Kwame Nkrumah, *Ghana: The Autobiography of Kwame Nkrumah* [New York, 1957], pp. 155, 165, 235).

After the Preparatory Commission had investigated all aspects of the project "with unusual thoroughness," Nkrumah had told Eisenhower that his country could begin construction immediately if financing were available. "I and my colleagues regard the Volta River project as being of supreme importance to the future of Ghana and we are determined to do all in our power to implement it" (Nkrumah to Eisenhower, Oct. 17, 1957, AWF/I: Ghana; the commission's report is in *ibid.*).

[3] On Vice-President Nixon's trip to the Ghanaian independence ceremony see no. 11. Komla Agbeli Gbedemah, Ghana's finance minister, had been in the United States to attend meetings of the International Monetary Fund (IMF) and to lead Ghana's delegation to the United Nations. Eisenhower had invited Gbedemah to breakfast on October 10, two days after a Dover, Delaware, Howard Johnson restaurant had refused to serve him (Ann Whitman memorandum, Oct. 10, 1957, AWF/AWD; see also State, *Foreign Relations, 1955–1957,* vol. XVIII, *Africa,* pp. 378–79).

[4] Citing a temporary reduction of demand for aluminum and a reluctance by Canada and Great Britain to begin this large project, Nkrumah would ask Eisenhower (Nov. 12) for help through the Development Loan Fund (*ibid.*, pp. 384–86). Eisenhower would assure Nkrumah that he would give "careful consideration" to his proposal (Nov. 21, 1957, AWF/I: Ghana; see also Howe to Goodpaster, Nov. 20, 1957, *ibid.*). For developments see no. 510.

441

EM, AWF, Name Series

To Evan Peter Aurand

November 8, 1957

Memorandum for Captain Aurand: My riding in the choppers has created a real tempest in a teapot.[1]

Actually, one of my responsibilities to the American people is to take no more chances with my physical well-being than normally falls to the lot of the American citizen.

When Colonel Draper got concerned about the safety of operation of the navy ships here on the White House lawn, I merely thanked him for his concern.[2] I am likewise grateful to you for the attention you have given the whole matter.

What I think I shall do is follow the advice of Mr. Rowley, who has the legal responsibility of looking after the safety of my poor old carcass.[3] His opinion is that I should use helicopters in emergencies, but normally stick to other kinds of transportation. I don't particularly agree with him, but as long as it causes me no real inconvenience, I shall go along with him.

Thanks again for your concern.

P.S. Above all, don't let such an insignificant matter create any difficulty among my Aides, all of whom are valuable to me.[4]

[1] Aurand (USNA 1938) was Eisenhower's Naval Aide. For background on the President's use of helicopters see no. 104. Apparently questions had been raised inside the White House about the safety of the Navy helicopters used to transport the President. See *New York Times*, July 6, 1957.

[2] Presidential Air Force Aide Colonel William Grafton Draper was commander of the presidential aircraft; for background see Galambos and van Ee, *The Middle Way*, no. 1036. On the helicopter testing see no. 446, and *New York Times*, July 24, 1957.

[3] This was Special Agent in Charge James Rowley, United States Secret Service, White House Detail (for background see Galambos and van Ee, *The Middle Way*, no. 1193).

[4] In a memorandum of this same day Aurand would say that he had ordered "a thorough check made on the record of various military helicopters" (AWF/N). The results of the research indicated that the Navy's H-34 was the best helicopter for the President's purposes. As a commercial vehicle, he wrote, the H-34 had a perfect accident record. The Secret Service received a written result of the study, he concluded, and had approved the operation of the H-34 for Eisenhower's use from the South Lawn of the White House.

To Earl Henry Blaik *November 8, 1957*

Dear Red: I was a bit astonished to read in your letter, "Certainly the internal recognition is far more casual than in years past." I found not only the Superintendent but his wife to be about as rabid and partisan football fans as I have ever met. While, of course, I was not consciously looking for any measure of West Point enthusiasm for the team, my feeling was, gained through visits to a number of spots, that morale was high and interest keen.[1]

Incidentally, I am very sorry I did not realize you were practicing in the Field House. I went down to see the end of the 150 pound game right next door to the Field House, and then went over to the Summer Camp to see the last part of the plebe game. I would have considered it a most enjoyable thing to have visited briefly with the squad and to have watched their workout.[2]

By the way, if I didn't get so darn excited at a football game when "my team" is playing, I would never miss an Army game. But I simply can't take it.[3] Even 53 to 6 was scarcely big enough for me![4]

Please convey my warm greetings to Mrs. Blaik and, of course, all the best to yourself—and once again good luck to the team.[5] *Sincerely*

[1] Blaik had been head football coach at West Point since 1941 (see Galambos and van Ee, *The Middle Way*, no. 801). In his letter of November 6 Blaik had commented on the team's success in spite of the lack of support given to the football program at the Military Academy. He added: "Perhaps this is in keeping with change, though. I must admit I am not impressed with the present trend of West Point affairs" (WHCF/PPF 1-F-86). Over the weekend of November 2–3, the Eisenhowers had attended a reunion with the President's West Point classmates (see no. 431). The Superintendent of the United States Military Academy and his wife were General Garrison Holt Davidson and Verone Gruenther Davidson.

[2] Blaik had apologized for not having thanked Eisenhower personally for visiting the cadet team. And, he added, he was "sorry that the varsity squad . . . did not have the inspiration and lasting memory of meeting the President." Eisenhower had made unscheduled visits of about four minutes each to the games between the 150-pound teams representing Army and the University of Pennsylvania, and the Army plebes and the Colgate University freshmen (*New York Times*, Nov. 2, 1957).

[3] Eisenhower had written a similar message to Blaik in October 1955. Following his September 1955 heart attack, the President's physicians had urged him to avoid situations that produced irritation, annoyance, frustration or tension (see Galambos and van Ee, *The Middle Way*, nos. 1598, 1703, and 1772, and nos. 1 and 97 in these volumes).

[4] Army had defeated Colgate 53 to 6 (see also Eisenhower to Case, Nov. 12, 1957, AWF/D).

[5] Mrs. Blaik was the former Merle McDowell. On November 9, the day of the Army-Navy football game, Eisenhower would send best wishes to Blaik and the team (AWF/D).

443 *EM, AWF, International Series: Pakistan*

To Ismail Ibrahim Chundrigar *November 9, 1957*
Cable. Secret

Dear Prime Minister:[1] Thank you for your message of October 29 dealing with the Kashmir issue in the Security Council.

The Secretary of State has kept me informed of the course of the discussions over the past several months and at present between our representatives. These discussions were fully taken into account in arriving at this Government's position as outlined in the United States representative's recent speech in the Security Council. Our entire position, however, has again been reviewed in the light of your message. In view of the report before the Security Council submitted by the Swedish representative on that body, our already announced position and the views of other members of the Security Council, it seems certain that the Council cannot avoid some reference in its resolution to the present status of the cease-fire order.[2]

However, I fully believe that, if the Council does adopt a position in accordance with that outlined by our representative, such action will constitute a definite step forward. I wish to assure you that I shall follow the developments on the Kashmir dispute in the Security Council with continuing deep interest and with trust that any progress toward ultimate solution of the problem cannot but be welcome to both Pakistan and India.

The basic objective of the Government of the United States remains, as always, a just and peaceful solution of a problem of such importance to the future of the Subcontinent. In the absence of a solution through direct negotiations, I believe that the only constructive course of action lies in the implementation of the Security Council's basic resolutions. This I feel certain is in accordance with your own Government's objectives.[3] *Sincerely*

[1] Chundrigar, drafter of the Pakistan constitution and former Minister for Law, had become Prime Minister of Pakistan on October 18. The State Department drafted this message for Eisenhower.

[2] For background on the Kashmir dispute and the United Nations Security Council resolutions calling for a plebiscite to determine the future of that area see Galambos and van Ee, *The Middle Way*, no. 2139; and no. 113 in these volumes. See also State, *Foreign Relations, 1955–1957*, vol. VIII, *South Asia*, pp. 127–28. In April 1957 Gunnar Valfrid Jarring, Swedish Representative to the United Nations and president of the council, had reported on his recent conferences with Indian and Pakistani officials. He found that negotiations had broken down over the status of the cease-fire provision of the resolutions: India had refused to proceed with the plebiscite until Pakistan had fully complied with the cease-fire order, and Pakistan had maintained that the order had been fully and faithfully implemented. Although Pakistan had

agreed in principle to submit the question to arbitration, India had rejected arbitration as inappropriate and inconsistent with its rights in the territory ("The India-Pakistan Question," in United Nations, *Yearbook of the United Nations*, 1957 [New York, 1958], pp. 80–85).

Addressing the Security Council on October 25, U.S. Deputy Representative James J. Wadsworth had reviewed the Jarring report, focusing on the need for a new resolution leading toward demilitarization of the area and the implementation of the U.N. cease-fire order. He recommended that the council ask Dr. Frank Porter Graham, United Nations Representative for India and Pakistan, to try to achieve a settlement between the two countries (United Nations, *Security Council Documents, 1957: Twelfth Year, Plenary Meetings, United Nations Security Council, Verbatim Record of the 797th Plenary Meeting, Oct. 27, 1957*, S/PV.797, Microfiche; State, *Foreign Relations, 1955–1957*, vol. VIII, *South Asia*, pp. 51, 112, 136–42, 144–52; *New York Times*, Mar. 23, May 1, Oct. 26, 1957).

In his message Chundrigar's had objected to some provisions of the proposed resolution, including its reference to the status of the cease-fire order. The resolution, he said, "would tend to prolong the agony" of the Kashmir people and would convince the Pakistanis that their allies were supporting India (Chundrigar to Eisenhower, Oct. 29, 1957, AWF/I: Pakistan). Acting Secretary Herter had reminded Eisenhower that the governments of Pakistan, the United States, and Great Britain had spent five months discussing the formulation of a new resolution that both India and Pakistan could accept. Because Chundrigar's message had not mentioned the discussions or the agreements the parties had reached, Herter had urged Eisenhower to approve this cable, which specified those aspects of the U.S. position (State, *Foreign Relations, 1955–1957*, vol. VIII, *South Asia*, p. 151; Herter to Eisenhower, Nov. 8, 1957, AWF/I: Pakistan).

[3] On November 22 the United States, the United Kingdom, Australia, Colombia, and the Philippines would introduce a resolution calling on Graham to discuss with India and Pakistan procedures necessary to implement the 1948 and 1949 resolutions, taking into consideration his previous reports, the text of the original resolutions, and the Jarring report. The resolution also called for Indian-Pakistani cooperation with Graham on the formulation of demilitarization procedures and the reduction of forces on each side of the cease-fire line. The Security Council would adopt an amended version of the resolution on December 2, and Graham would leave for the subcontinent in January 1958 (State, *Foreign Relations, 1955–1957*, vol. VIII, *South Asia*, pp. 151, 154–57, 159; *New York Times*, Nov. 14, 17, 29, 1957). For developments see no. 656.

444 *EM, AWF, Dulles-Herter Series*

To Wayne Levere Hays[1] *November 9, 1957*
Cable

It gives me great pleasure to extend best wishes to the NATO Parliamentary Conference. It appears particularly appropriate that your meeting should come at this time, just before the Heads of Government of the NATO countries will be meeting in Paris.[2] I am sure that the conclusions of your conference will be of interest and significance to the Heads of Government, and I, for one, will be looking forward with interest to the results of your deliberations.

I need hardly reiterate my own deep devotion to the cause of the Atlantic Alliance and the particularly close tie I have felt with NATO. Indeed, conditions in the world have combined to make the potential of NATO more essential today than ever before in maintaining world peace and stability.[3]

In closing, let me reiterate my best wishes for the success of your endeavors which are of interest to all who are concerned with the future and strength of the NATO Alliance.[4]

[1] Wayne Levere Hays (B.S. Ohio State University 1933), former chairman of the board of directors of the Citizens National Bank in Flushing, Ohio, had first been elected to Congress in 1948. He was president of the NATO Parliamentary Conference, which provided an unofficial link between NATO officials and the legislatures of the member countries.

[2] Secretary Dulles had suggested sending this greeting to the parliamentarians (meeting from November 11 to 16) because Eisenhower was scheduled to attend the NATO meeting in December (Dulles to Eisenhower, Nov. 7, 1957, AWF/D-H; for background see no. 414).

[3] At the bottom of the State Department draft of this message Eisenhower had penned a request to Acting Secretary Herter that he add the words "in maintaining world peace and stability" (AWF/D-H).

[4] For developments see no. 454.

445

EM, AWF, International Series: Churchill

To Winston Spencer Churchill *November 9, 1957*

[*Dear Winston:*] Today I find on my desk both your letter of November fourth, and the inscribed copy of your third volume of "A History of the English Speaking Peoples." It goes without saying that I shall read this book with the same great interest and enjoyment that I have found in all your works, and particularly in your most recent series.[1]

Of course you will be most welcome in Washington in April. I am delighted that you feel able to come.[2]

As a rule our Congress takes a short Easter vacation some time during the month, and I likewise try to seize a part of the period to get away for a few days in April.[3] As of now I am not sure of the exact dates I shall be away from Washington, but I do most earnestly hope to be here when you are.

As soon as I am able to determine my April schedule, I shall let you know so that we may coordinate our plans, if at all possible. Naturally if Mamie and I are here then, we invite you most warmly to stay with us. I think we could protect you fairly well from public engagements, although I suppose there would be emphatic demands that I stage something in your honor, to which people could come to pay their respects. If you think you could be more easily and better protected at the British Embassy, we would thoroughly understand—but we do want you to know what a warm welcome awaits you with us.[4]

As the weeks go by, we should be able to work everything out more exactly. In the meantime, please convey my warm greetings to Clemmie and, of course, all the best to yourself.[5] [*As ever*]

[1] The former British Prime Minister had replied to Eisenhower's October 14 letter regarding the possibility of visiting the United States. Eisenhower was referring to Churchill's newly published *The Age of Revolution* (see Winston S. Churchill, *A History of the English Speaking Peoples*, 4 vols. [London, 1956–1958]). For Eisenhower's comments regarding the first volume in the series see Galambos and van Ee, *The Middle Way*, no. 1853.

[2] Churchill said he would "value the opportunity of seeing [Eisenhower] and my other old friends." He also said that although it was difficult to make definite plans at his age, he hoped to come to Washington in April for the opening of the exhibition of his paintings (for background on the exhibition see no. 222).

[3] The second session of the Eighty-fifth Congress would adjourn for Easter recess April 4–14 (see *New York Times*, Mar. 28, Apr. 4, 14, 1958). Eisenhower would make two brief trips to Augusta, Georgia, April 11–13, and April 25–28.

[4] "For my own part," Churchill had written, "I should hope to avoid public engagements while in your country." On November 14 he would accept the President's invitation to stay at the White House. All correspondence is in AWF/I: Churchill. For developments see no. 668.

[5] Churchill's wife was the former Clementine Hozier.

446

EM, AWF,
DDE Diaries Series

To James Henderson Douglas, Jr.

November 11, 1957

Dear Mr. Secretary:[1] I am submitting a report on the performance of duties of Colonel William G. Draper, 12383A, as presidential Air Force Aide and Commander of the Presidential Aircraft, for the period from August 1, 1956 to July 31, 1957.[2]

During that period Colonel Draper has performed the same duties as outlined in previous reports, as follows:

1. He is my liaison officer on matters pertaining to the Air Force.

In line with this duty, he represents me in appropriate official ceremonies, in escorting distinguished visitors of foreign countries; and he performs special assignments of a classified and highly responsible nature.

2. Colonel Draper also handles personal inquiries from government departments, the Congress and the general public on Air Force matters; he also acts as liaison with the Air Force in matters of a personal nature.

3. During the year Colonel Draper supervised the purchase of two helicopters, and the training of the pilots who fly them. He is meticulous as far as considerations of my safety are concerned.[3]

4. He is responsible for my air transportation and for all the air transportation directed by me, in the Super-Constellation and the Aero-Commander (which aircraft he commands himself.) Additionally, he makes arrangements for the transportation of governmental officials and staff to any place where I may be, when necessary.

In such reports I normally make mention of special flights that require extraordinary preparation. Colonel Draper devotes special care to the details of such flights, to protocol and similar matters. He makes a splendid impression on dignitaries of other countries, and is in every way an able representative of the United States.

In addition, Colonel Draper performs normal Aide de Camp duties.

In all his duties, his performance is outstanding. In every respect he is a "superior" officer.

Colonel Draper has inculcated in the members of the crews of the ships he commands the same respect for the high standards that he himself observes; in addition, the crew is admirably disciplined, courteous and efficient.

I rate him an outstanding pilot and aircraft commander. I am acquainted personally with only a limited number of Air Force officers of Colonel Draper's grade and age, and it would not be fair for me to compare him with his contemporaries. But I do want to emphasize his technical competence, his fine personality, and his outstanding worth to the Air Force and to government service.

In view of the information provided in this letter, the attached copies of Air Force Form 77 are returned without completion. *Sincerely*

[1] Former Under Secretary of the Air Force Douglas (A.B. Princeton 1920; LL.B. Harvard 1924) had become Air Force Secretary on May 1. Eisenhower would appoint him as Deputy Secretary of Defense in 1959 (*New York Times*, Mar. 27, May 1, 1957, and Dec. 11, 1959).

[2] Draper had served as Eisenhower's personal pilot since 1950. He would remain in

this position until 1959. A similar performance report on Draper for the period from January 1 through July 31, 1955, as well as related correspondence, is in AWF/A: Air Force.

[3] See, for example, no. 441.

447 *EM, AWF, Administration Series*

To John Alex McCone *November 12, 1957*

Dear John: Many thanks for your letter about the speech of last Thursday night. I, too, am delighted that Dr. Killian has found it possible to come down here to undertake this vital and important assignment.[1]

Currently I am working on the speech I am to give in Oklahoma City tomorrow night which will present (at least as it stands at the present moment) some of the stark realities of the rate at which we are training scientists vis-a-vis the Russians.[2] I am touching on the sacrifices of what we call "the good things of life" that we must make, which I am afraid may not be too palatable to some people.[3] I can only hope that this particular talk will alert, but not unduly alarm, us to some of the dangers in our present way of thinking.

With affectionate regard to Rosemary[4] and all the best to yourself, *As ever*

[1] For background on Eisenhower's November 7 speech on science and defense see no. 434. California businessman McCone had served as Secretary of the Air Force from 1950 to 1951. His letter is not in AWF. On the appointment of MIT President James Rhine Killian, Jr., to the newly created post of Special Assistant to the President for Science and Technology see no. 396.

[2] On the President's November 13 Oklahoma City speech see no. 448. Eisenhower would say that he had been advised that America's most critical problem was the need to train scientists and engineers in order to remain competitive with the Soviet Union. "We need scientists in the ten years ahead," Eisenhower would say. "They say we need them by thousands more than we are now presently planning to have." The President would call for federal, state and local cooperation to implement nationwide testing of high school students; incentives for high-aptitude students to pursue scientific or professional studies; a program to improve teaching in mathematics and the sciences; more laboratory facilities; and "measures, including fellowships, to increase the output of qualified teachers" (see *Public Papers of the Presidents: Eisenhower, 1957*, pp. 807–17; and Clowse, *Brainpower for the Cold War*, pp. 40–65). For developments see no. 516.

[3] Eisenhower would say that the real strength of the self-governing democracies was to be found in the "quality of our life, and the vigor of our ideals" and in "the ever-astonishing capacity of free men for voluntary heroism, sacrifice and accomplishments when the chips are down." Thus, increased savings in other areas would pay for the accelerated American defense program whenever possible. This, said Eisen-

hower, would be "one of the hardest and most distasteful tasks that the coming session of Congress must face" (*Public Papers of the Presidents: Eisenhower, 1957*, pp. 808, 813).

[4] McCone's wife was the former Rosemary Cooper.

448

EM, AWF, Administration Series

To Arthur Larson
Memorandum

November 12, 1957

The present draft gives too much of an impression that we must spend a *lot* more money on our military defenses.[1] I think we should put in a disclaimer on this in the very first part.[2]

Although we mention in one paragraph mutual military assistance, I think something should be said as to the support we gain through economic assistance.[3]

[1] Recently appointed Special Assistant to the President, Larson was drafting the second of Eisenhower's talks to the nation regarding science and defense (for background see no. 434). Originally intended as a single speech, Eisenhower had divided the subject into a talk on science and national security, delivered on November 7, and an address on "Our Future Security," to be delivered in Oklahoma City on November 13 (see the preceding document and *Public Papers of the Presidents: Eisenhower, 1957*, pp. 789–99, 807–17). Larson had also sent a draft of the speech to Secretary of State Dulles for comments (Larson to Dulles, Nov. 11, 1957, AWF/D-H). In a memorandum to Eisenhower on November 12 (AWF/A), Larson had mapped out themes for two future speeches on overseas activity and security, and the economy and security.

[2] The President would say that the United States had averaged 42 billion dollars a year in defense expenditures during the last five fiscal years. While the development of the long-range ballistic missile could not be markedly accelerated by the expenditure of more money, the cost of missile production, deployment and installation, and the need to raise military salaries would add to this total. "We must," Eisenhower would say, "once more go over all other military expenditures with redoubled determination to save every possible dime. We must make sure that we have no needless duplication or obsolete programs or facilities."

[3] Eisenhower would say that the answer to the need for economy did not lie in "any misguided attempt to eliminate conventional forces and rely solely upon retaliation." "And, most emphatically," he would say, "the answer does not lie in cutting mutual defense funds overseas—another important part of our own assistance agreements." The President would reiterate the importance of economic aid in helping others to avoid dependence upon the Soviet Union. The foreign aid program also demonstrated "the free world's ability to develop its resources and to increase its living standards" and helped allied economies support essential military units (see also *New York Times*, Nov. 14, 1957).

449 *EM, AWF, Name Series*

To Harry Cecil Butcher *November 12, 1957*

Dear Butch: I would never have remembered—but for your telegram—the anniversary of the north African landing.[1] Alleged interservice rivalry, guided missiles, Sputnik II, Little Rock, Syria, and a variety of other problems seem to clog my memory these days.[2] At any rate, many thanks.

With warm regard, *As ever*

[1] Butcher, Eisenhower's naval aide between 1942 and 1945, had sent the wire (Nov. 7, 1957, AWF/N) through Ann Whitman with a directive to ask the President: "Does he expect to be shaving in cold salt water tomorrow morning?" For background on Butcher see *Eisenhower Papers*, vols. I–XVII. The first Allied combined offensive, Operation TORCH—the invasion of North Africa—began on November 8, 1942 (see Eisenhower, *Crusade in Europe*; *Eisenhower Papers*, vols. I–V; and Harry C. Butcher, *My Three Years with Eisenhower: The Personal Diary of Captain Harry C. Butcher, USNR* [New York, 1946]).

[2] See nos. 401, 394, 447, 330, and 332, respectively.

450 *Dulles Papers, White House Memoranda Series*

To John Foster Dulles *November 13, 1957*

Personal. Eyes only

Dear Foster: Do you think there would be any percentage in initiating a drive to attempt to bring back Nasser to our side? I do not have in mind anything spectacular or, indeed, anything that would get in the papers. My thought would be that either through the Ambassador or anybody else you can trust, you would start inquiring from him whether he saw any basis for rapprochement and [what] he would be prepared to do in the way of easing tensions in the Mid East if we on our part would resume efforts to help him over some of his difficulties.[1]

If we do this it will, of course, have to be skillfully done—certainly we don't want to be in the position of "bootlicking a dictator."

Please do not send me any written answer. This note is merely to suggest that we talk about the subject when we have a little time together.[2] *As ever*

[1] For background on U.S. relations with Nasser, the Egyptian leader's domestic problems, and his influence in the rest of the Arab world see nos. 78 and 142; see also

Nigel John Ashton, *Eisenhower, Macmillan and the Problem of Nasser: Anglo-American Relations and Arab Nationalism* (London, 1996). For background on Raymond A. Hare, U.S. Ambassador to Egypt since September 1956, see Galambos and van Ee, *The Middle Way*, no. 2141. During the preceding month Secretary Dulles and other State Department officials had discussed ways to improve U.S.-Egyptian relations. Nasser, they believed, was concerned by the close ties that Syria had developed with the Soviet Union and feared that Egypt's prestige in the area had weakened. Responding to an earlier Eisenhower question about the chances of reestablishing satisfactory relations with Nasser, Dulles had replied that he was restudying the matter "in the light of what Nasser might have learned from the Syrian experience" (State, *Foreign Relations, 1955–1957*, vol. XVII, *Arab-Israeli Dispute 1957*, pp. 752–59, 762–64, 775–78, 785–91; Memorandum of Conversation, Oct. 28, 1957, Dulles Papers, White House Memoranda Series; and Holland, *America and Egypt*, pp. 147–52; on Communist infiltration in Syria see no. 301).

[2] At the Cabinet meeting on November 15, Dulles would tell Eisenhower that he was giving the matter his "closest consideration." With the exception of Egypt and Syria the United States had maintained good relations with all the Arab states, Dulles said, and he did not want to jeopardize those relationships. "There was danger that Nasser would be satisfied with nothing less than our willingness to treat him as the leader of the Arab world; . . . the position he coveted." According him this recognition would antagonize King Saud and the other Arab countries that perceived Saud as their leader. Eisenhower agreed that the United States could not be disloyal to the Saudi Arabian monarch "or attempt to push Nasser into leadership ahead of Saud" (Memorandum for the Record, Nov. 15, 1957, Dulles Papers, White House Memoranda Series; see also Telephone conversation, Dulles and Rountree, Nov. 15, 1957, Dulles Papers, Telephone Conversations). For developments see no. 776.

451 — *EM, AWF, International Series: France*

To Félix Gaillard — *November 13, 1957*

Cable. Secret

My dear Mr. Prime Minister:[1] I received late yesterday your message with respect to the furnishing of arms to Tunisia for its defensive purposes.[2] I cannot at this time deal with all aspects of your message as I am leaving this noon for Oklahoma and the matter permits of no delay.[3]

Secretary Dulles in his message to foreign Minister Pineau of November 11 reviewed the history of this matter.[4] He recalled our position that Tunisia as an independent nation was entitled to arms for security and defensive purposes and that, in order that Tunisia might not have to turn to dangerous sources to fill its needs in this respect, the US had pledged itself last September to see to it that Tunisia obtained a limited supply of small arms for defensive purposes in the near future. We had hoped that the Tunisian Government would be able to get them from the French Government as a normal source of supply.[5]

About mid-October we had told President Bourgiba that if he could not get arms from France or elsewhere in Western Europe we would get him some by the first of November. The UK associated itself with this position. Your Government was informed accordingly.[6]

On October 18 the French Ambassador urged that we should delay until there should be established a new French government and indicated that he personally felt that a first act of any such government would be promptly to arrange to deliver arms to Tunisia.

As the result of subsequent effort we obtained the agreement of President Bourgiba further to postpone the date of our delivery from November 1 to November 12. Your Government was informed of this on November 4.

In reply to the Secretary of State's message of November 11 we received word that your Government would itself be prepared to deliver to the Government of Tunisia arms on November 12 if we did not do so.[7]

Accordingly on November 12 the Secretary of State informed your Government and the Government of Tunisia that it would suspend the delivery of arms on that day and understood that the Government of the UK would probably do likewise on the understanding so far as the US was concerned that the French Government would itself that day be delivering to Tunisia an equivalent in arms and ammunition to that which had been planned by the US and the UK with no conditions other than that the arms would be for defensive purposes and not transferred elsewhere. It would be further understood that this initial transaction would not of itself solve the basic problem but that Tunisia would remain entitled to get further arms, preferably from France but if not elsewhere from a Western country and that the US would supply them if need be.

Our Ambassador in Paris communicated this message to Foreign Minister Pineau and understood that the terms under which we would suspend delivery were acceptable and that the French Government would itself make the equivalent delivery yesterday November 12.[8]

I must point out that the Secretary's message above referred to was sent prior to my receipt of your message of November 12 and that there is a variance between the terms of your message to me and the Secretary's message to Foreign Minister Pineau which we understood to be acceptable to your Government. One notable difference is that you state that your delivery would be subject to the condition that the furnishing of arms by France will be exclusive of all other foreign arms deliveries. While we appreciate the traditional concern of France in the area of North Africa and while we hope that in fact France would continue to be a normal source of supply of Tunisia we could not agree that Tunisia, as an independent country, should feel constrained to accept any one country as a sole supplier of arms and thus in effect make its own defense and security requirements a subject for determination by another country and not of its own government. This, in our opinion, would be incompatible with genuine independence.

I do not at the time of writing this message to you, Mr. Prime Minister, know what may have transpired today but I greatly hope that arrangements have been concluded on the basis of what we thought was the understanding with Foreign Minister Pineau of yesterday. If unhappily this proves not to be the case then we feel in honor bound to carry out our engagement to the Government of Tunisia and will plan to make delivery to them tomorrow morning November 14, Tunisia time, of the token delivery of arms which had been planned.[9]

I have naturally taken most serious note of your suggestions with reference to the possible impact of this action upon the enactment of the *Loi-cadre* for Algeria and also upon the position of the French Government in relation to the projected meeting of the NATO Heads of Government.[10] I would assume that if the *Loi-cadre* is voted upon that vote will be determined by the judgment of the French Parliament upon the merits of the matter and upon whether or not it is judged that this law will in fact promote a just and peaceful settlement of the Algerian problem.[11] As far as the NATO meeting is concerned I most earnestly hope that there will prevail the atmosphere of friendly cooperation without which the meeting would indeed be of doubtful value. If there should unhappily subsist any differences between us that would be an occasion for you and me to talk them over in an atmosphere of friendship and of earnest search for that mutual understanding which has so long characterized the relations between our two countries.[12] *Sincerely*

[1] Félix Gaillard, former Minister of Finance and architect of France's austerity program, had been a member of the French Resistance and was a strong proponent of European integration. He had become the youngest prime minister in French history on November 6. Secretary Dulles drafted this cable, a copy of which was sent to the American embassies in London and Tunis (Telephone conversation, Eisenhower and Dulles, Nov. 13, 1957, AWF/D; and State, *Foreign Relations, 1955–1957*, vol. XVIII, *Africa*, pp. 750–51).

[2] We have been unable to locate Gaillard's letter in AWF. See, however, *ibid.*, pp. 746–47. For background on U.S. aid to Tunisia see Galambos and van Ee, *The Middle Way*, no. 2108; see also Eisenhower, *Waging Peace*, pp. 103–6.

[3] On Eisenhower's trip to Oklahoma City and the speech he would deliver later this same day see no. 448.

[4] Christian Pineau had been a member of the Resistance and a prisoner in Buchenwald during World War II. Formerly French minister of Public Works, Transport, and Tourism, he had been foreign minister since February 1956. Dulles's message is in State, *Foreign Relations, 1955–1957*, vol. XVIII, *Africa*, pp. 744–45.

[5] Fearing that the arms it might supply would be diverted to Algerian rebels, the

French government had suspended all aid to Tunisia the previous May. In spite of French attempts to thwart Tunisia's efforts to procure arms from sympathetic Western nations, the Tunisian government had asked Italy, Belgium, Spain, and Switzerland for help to meet its internal security needs. On September 22 Secretary Dulles had informed Tunisia that if negotiations with these governments were unsuccessful, the United States would find "other means" to meet its requirements (*ibid.*, pp. 671–95).

[6] The Tunisian Constituent Assembly had abolished the monarchy on July 25 and established a republic. M. Habib Bourguiba, former Tunisian prime minister and an influential negotiator for Tunisian independence, became Chief of State. On Britain's concurrence see *ibid.*, pp. 721–23; and Macmillan, *Riding the Storm*, pp. 330–31; on the meeting between State Department officials and French Ambassador Hervé Alphand see State, *Foreign Relations, 1955–1957*, vol. XVIII, *Africa*, pp. 723–26.

[7] On the October 18 meeting, the Bourguiba agreement, and the French decision to supply arms from its stocks then in Tunisia see *ibid.*, pp. 726–29, 732–35, and 746–48; see also Telephone conversation, Eisenhower and Dulles, Nov. 11, 1957, Dulles Papers, Telephone Conversations.

[8] The United States and Great Britain had agreed to a token shipment of 500 rifles and 50,000 rounds of ammunition. U.S. Ambassador Amory Houghton had delivered the message in the evening of November 12 (State, *Foreign Relations, 1955–1957*, vol. XVIII, *Africa*, pp. 748–49; see also Goodpaster memorandum, Nov. 16, 1957, AWF/D; and Telephone conversation, Eisenhower and Dulles, Nov. 12, 1957, Dulles Papers, Telephone Conversations).

[9] Dulles would inform Eisenhower by telephone in Oklahoma City later this same day that the French had yet to make a delivery. They were using the situation "as a useful domestic political tool," Dulles said, "to build up internal strength which will make it unpleasant [at the NATO conference] in December." "The thing to do is deliver [the] arms," Eisenhower replied, "and then we can talk" (Telephone conversation, Eisenhower and Dulles, Nov. 13, 1957; see also Telephone conversations, Dulles and Rountree, Dulles and Houghton, Dulles and Jones, Nov. 13, 1957, *ibid.*). Later on this same day Foreign Minister Pineau would request a further delay until the French Council of Ministries could meet at 8 P.M. Dulles would instruct Houghton to wait until 10 P.M. at which time the United States would inform Bourguiba that unless the French government immediately delivered arms, without the qualification that France would be Tunisia's only source of supply, the United States would fulfill its agreement the following morning (Telephone conversations, Dulles and Rountree, Dulles and Houghton, Nov. 13, 1957, *ibid.*).

[10] The Loi-Cadre, a bill designed to give Algeria some autonomy over their affairs, proclaimed that the country was an integral part of France composed of federated territories divided along ethnic lines, each administering its own affairs. Muslim local control would be subject to the approval of the French government. The French National Assembly had defeated the law on September 30, resulting in the collapse of the government. Pineau had told Ambassador Houghton that a U.S. decision to supply Tunisia with arms regardless of the action of the French government would have the "most deplorable and dangerous effect" and could result in a second defeat for Loi-Cadre. Gaillard had told Houghton that the delivery of U.S. arms to Tunisia on November 12 would be considered "an unfriendly act," and would, unfortunately, take place shortly before a NATO meeting designed to solidify the Atlantic alliance (State, *Foreign Relations, 1955–1957*, vol. XVIII, *Africa*, pp. 737, 746; see also nos. 414 and 454).

Immediately before leaving for Oklahoma City, Eisenhower had told Dulles that he was "unhappy about the French threats" and that he had thought the new prime minister was a "good guy." He suggested that Dulles tell Gaillard that Eisenhower appreciated his difficulties, but that the French position would tend to throw the Tunisians toward the Soviet Union. "That," the President warned, "we would not permit" (Telephone conversation, Eisenhower and Dulles Nov. 13, 1957, AWF/D).

[11] The French assembly would pass the Loi-Cadre for Algeria, with minor amendments to the previously defeated bill on November 30. For developments in the Algerian conflict see no. 600.

[12] Eisenhower and Gaillard would meet in Paris on December 15. For developments see the following document.

452

EM, AWF, DDE Diaries Series

DIARY

Top secret

November 14, 1957

For the past three days we have been in a terrible difficulty with France and Tunisia, based partially upon misunderstanding but mostly on what we believe to be French stupidity and refusal to face international facts as they exist.[1]

For a long time Prime Minister Bourguiba of Tunisia has been trying to obtain some arms from the West. His demands have seemed reasonable to us and he asked for the arms on the basis of purchase, not grant.

Our own hope was that because of the close ties of France with the North African area that the French would be the ones to deliver such arms and we urged them to do so. We conferred with the British who felt about the matter as we did.

While the French have nominally accorded Tunisia complete independence, they have so far retained in Tunisia five military bases (I believe all these are in addition to Bizerte which was to be retained by the French under the Independence Treaty). They have given to Tunisia no satisfactory answer as to when these bases are to be evacuated, if ever.[2]

Apparently a few weeks ago the French told Bourguiba that they would deliver arms, but they demanded certain conditions to be agreed to in advance. The most unacceptable of these conditions was an engagement on the part of the Tunisians that they would not accept arms from any other nation—that France would be the sole source of supply of such equipment.

We have felt this condition to be unjustified and so informed the French, again urging them to attach a single condition that the arms be used only for defensive purposes.

In view of the inconclusive character of their talks with the French, Bourguiba finally grew desperate. He is, I think, our most independent and enthusiastic friend in the Arab World. But in view of the demands of his people for some military equipment, it became more and more difficult for him to maintain his position. Some weeks ago, therefore, we told Bourguiba that in the event the French did not deliver arms for internal order and minimum defense purposes we would, in combination with the British, deliver him a token shipment by November first. The idea was that a small token shipment (only five hundred rifles) would establish his right as head of an independent government to purchase arms from the west, in whatever area he could get the best treatment.

Soon thereafter the French government fell and there was only a caretaker government in Paris for a number of weeks.[3] In view of this and on French request we postponed the delivery date of our token shipment to November twelfth.

Suddenly on November 11th or 12th the French protested that they had not heard that we had promised delivery on a specific date; that their new Premier Gaillard had not been in office long enough to pay attention to this problem and that they would regard our delivery of a token shipment to Tunisia as an unfriendly act. Their reaction was violent, so much so that they even held that they might have to withdraw from NATO, or at least not attend the December meeting of that body.

This put us in a dilemma. While NATO is the organization to which we attach a maximum importance in the attempt to maintain collective security against the Russian threat, we could not afford either to see Bourguiba begin to purchase arms from the Soviets nor could we be in the position of breaking our pledged word to Tunisia.

In early November the situation was complicated by a sudden move on the part of Nasser in Egypt to start a shipment of arms to Tunisia—as a gift.[4] Bourguiba could not possibly afford to turn this offer down, which was apparently widely publicized in that area, and he attached the most extraordinary importance to the delivery of some Western arms in Tunisia before the Egyptian shipment could reach there, somewhere between the 15th or 16th of this month.

In the situation that has developed within the last three days, we have had numerous trans-Atlantic telephone calls with some very stiff notes passing between ourselves and the French, to urge them to get busy and deliver a token shipment of arms and without conditions other than that of using the arms merely for defense.

In spite of promising such delivery on the 12th, they failed to carry it out and spent the 13th in arguing among themselves and apparently with Bourguiba and the British and us. In these cables and telephone calls they threatened the most dire things such as a complete breakup of the Western Alliance.

Finally, we felt that we simply could not be blackmailed by the French weakness, and in two notes I definitely notified Gaillard that having put off Bourguiba for two additional days, we are going to deliver the token shipment of arms to him on the morning of November fourteenth.

So far as we can find out, the French have made no move to satisfy the situation so presumably the British-American shipment of arms was delivered to Bourguiba this morning.[5]

So far as we can tell at this moment, the French reaction has not been as violent as they themselves said it would be, but it is certain that there will be trouble in the offing about the whole affair.[6]

Incidentally, the French objection was based on the argument that Bourguiba was trying to arm his country for far more than defensive purposes. They said he was trying to buy arms from Spain, from Italy and from every other country in the West and would play one off against the other in the threat to purchase them, otherwise, from Russia.

We hold that Bourguiba is a true Western friend and will not take arms from Russia unless he is forced to by our own attitude and his internal pressures. If he purchases arms from the West, he can never be armed very heavily for the simple reason that he has not the money to buy arms in quantity. The only way he could begin to build up a big military machine would be to have gift arms.

This is approximately where the situation stands this morning.[7]

[1] For background see the preceding document.

[2] In addition to Bizerte, the French retained control over: Gabes, Sfax, Remada, the El Aouina airbase, and Salammbo Headquarters (State, *Foreign Relations, 1955–1957*, vol. XVIII, *Africa*, pp. 703, 709).

[3] A defeat of the Algerian reform bill by the French National Assembly had caused the fall of the government headed by Maurice Bourgès-Maunoury. Félix Gaillard became prime minister on November 6, after thirty-six days and four previous attempts to end the government crisis (see the preceding document).

[4] For details of the Egyptian offer see State, *Foreign Relations, 1955–1957*, vol. XVIII, *Africa*, pp. 699, 710.

[5] The French had continued to insist that Tunisia should not accept arms from any other nation. After a brief delay, U.S. arms would arrive in Tunisia on the evening of November 15 (*ibid.*, pp. 757–63; see also Telephone conversation, Dulles and White, Nov. 14, 1957, Dulles Papers, Telephone Conversations).

[6] The French foreign minister had expressed his government's regret over the U.S.-British actions, which he called contrary to the principle of Atlantic solidarity. He would lodge a formal protest with State Department officials later this same day. In a later conversation, however, Pineau would tell Dulles that "there is more bitterness against the Br[itish] than us" (State, *Foreign Relations, 1955–1957*, vol. XVIII, *Africa*, pp. 761–63; Telephone conversations, Eisenhower and Dulles, Nov. 16, 20, 1957, Dulles Papers, Telephone Conversations and AWF/D; see also Dulles to Eisenhower, Nov. 18, 1957, AWF/D-H; *New York Times*, Nov. 15, 16, 1957; and Secretary Dulles's remarks at his news conference on November 19, Dulles Personal Papers).

[7] In a meeting on November 19 Dulles would tell French officials that the United States had no plans for further arms deliveries and agreed that the French and Tunisian governments should have the opportunity to begin negotiations which

would lead to future arms shipments from France (State, *Foreign Relations, 1955–1957,* vol. XVIII, *Africa,* pp. 764–70). For developments see no. 650.

453 *EM, AWF, Administration Series*

To William Pierce Rogers *November 14, 1957*

Memorandum for the Attorney General: In Oklahoma City last evening a group visited me who seemed to be largely interested in oil and gas production. Some of them, I think, were also interested in pipe lines.[1]

They wanted to ask that there be no anti-trust suit entered against oil companies who own interests in pipe lines. They had a long story to tell me about it, but of course I know nothing of the details. But it is quite clear that they think it would be terribly unjust to force complete divorcement between the oil producers and any pipe line interests because over the years they have developed their businesses, many of them, in this direction.[2]

I could not tell them whether there was even a thought of instituting such suits, but I did promise that if there was any such idea I would first have a talk with you about it.

I am sending a copy of this memorandum to the Secretary of the Treasury because he is so knowledgeable in this field and he may have something to add. At the very least he could tell you what individuals who are interested in the matter you could call in for a preliminary discussion to get their side of the story.[3]

[1] Eisenhower was in Oklahoma City to deliver his second speech on science and defense (see nos. 447 and 448). The President was referring to his brief meeting on October 13 with Donald Sipe Kennedy, Streeter Blanton Flynn, and William Kelly Warren (see Ann Whitman memorandum, Nov. 13, 1957, AWF/AWD). Kennedy had been president of the Oklahoma Gas and Electric Company since 1949 and was director of Oklahoma City's First National Bank and Trust Company (see Galambos and van Ee, *The Middle Way,* no. 1070). Flynn served as general counsel to the Oklahoma Gas and Electric Company, and was also vice-president of the Flynn Oil Company (see *ibid.,* no. 758; and Galambos, *Columbia University,* nos. 1022 and 1044). Warren was the chief executive officer and chairman of the Warren Petroleum Company.

Rogers, formerly Deputy Attorney General, had become Attorney General on November 8.

[2] Kennedy, Flynn, and Warren were probably responding to an October 21 announcement by the Department of Justice that it had begun a full-scale investigation of pipelines jointly owned by the major oil companies to search for anti-competitive aspects of joint ownership. The investigation had been revealed at congressional hearings on oil company practices that violated antitrust statutes (*New York Times,* Oct. 22, 23, 25, 1957). Among the companies being investigated was Service Pipe Line of Tulsa, Oklahoma, a subsidiary of Standard Oil Company of Indiana. For back-

ground see nos. 47, 169, and Galambos and van Ee, *The Middle Way*, nos. 1748 and 1754. See also Edward C. Gallick, *Competition in the Natural Gas Pipeline Industry: An Economic Policy Analysis* (Westport, Conn., 1993), pp. 12–15; and Sanders, *The Regulation of Natural Gas*, pp. 94–124.
[3] There is no further correspondence on this subject in AWF.

454

EM, AWF, Dulles-Herter Series

To Adlai Ewing Stevenson

November 14, 1957

Dear Governor:[1] I am delighted that you and Foster will be getting together on Monday to discuss our preparations for the NATO Meeting in December.[2] I have asked Foster to coordinate these preparations as they affect all Government agencies, and I share his view that you can be of real help to us in this work.

I regret that on Monday I shall be absent from Washington—at least I hope so—but I am sure that later there will be opportunity for conferences at which we can both be present.[3]

With best wishes, *Sincerely*

[1] In his handwritten emendations to the original draft of this letter, Eisenhower changed the salutation from "Dear Adlai" (AWF/D-H).
[2] For background on the NATO meeting see no. 414. In October the President had suggested that Dulles ask Stevenson to head a task force that would draw up guidelines for the conference, although, Eisenhower said, he doubted that Stevenson would accept the assignment (Memorandum of Conversation, Oct. 28, 1957, Dulles Papers, White House Memoranda Series). Dulles had discussed the proposal with Stevenson and had described the need to establish a program for the sharing of atomic information among the NATO countries (Telephone conversations, Dulles and Stevenson, Oct. 28, 29, 1957, Dulles Papers, Telephone Conversations; see also Telephone conversations, Dulles and Knowland, and Dulles and Johnson, Oct. 31, 1957, *ibid.*).

After having thought "long and anxiously" about the proposal, Stevenson told the Secretary of State that he could not "assume the responsibility for formulating United States policy and position." He did, however, offer to review the proposals and "do such 'missionary' work as I can and give such policies all the support, private, public and political, as I can, both here and abroad" (Stevenson to Dulles, Nov. 3, 1957, AWF/D-H; see also Telephone conversation, Dulles and Stevenson, Nov. 3, 1957, Dulles Papers, Telephone Conversations). Eisenhower had then told Dulles that he thought they should reject the offer because Stevenson's response was "indecisive" and that he had "looked this thing over so carefully to pick out the things he could do without adverse personal involvement" (Telephone conversation, Eisenhower and Dulles, Nov. 3, 1957, Dulles Papers, Telephone Conversations).

At a meeting on this same day to outline the structure of the NATO meeting, Eisenhower had told Dulles that if after his meeting with Stevenson, he thought the governor saw the job in a "true bipartisan sense of participation" and not to be used "as a sounding board for backbiting at the Administration," then he wanted him to be included in the delegation to Paris, in spite of "the difficulties having him along that would be involved" (Meeting of the President and Secretary of State, Nov. 14, 1957, AWF/D-H). The announcement of Stevenson's role would continue to generate controversy; see Telephone conversations, Dulles and Eisenhower, Dulles and Stevenson, and Dulles and Hagerty, November 12, 1957, *ibid.*; and *New York Times*, November 13, 1957.

[3] Eisenhower added this paragraph to the original draft and would leave on the following day for Augusta, Georgia. In his response, Stevenson would tell Eisenhower that he hoped his discussions with Dulles would be helpful. "Perhaps I should take this opportunity," he wrote, "to say what I am sure we all understand—that while I must be free to seek [advice] in my informal consultative capacity from persons outside the Department, including leaders of my Party, and also to express my views, whatever they may be, I shall strive to promote national unity in furtherance of the great tasks before us" (Stevenson to Eisenhower, n.d., AWF/D-H).

After meeting with Dulles on November 18, Stevenson would agree to help the State Department in any way possible to the extent that he could agree with Administration policy (*New York Times*, Nov. 19, 1957). He would meet briefly with Eisenhower on December 3 before attending a bipartisan congressional meeting (see Dulles to Eisenhower, Nov. 21, 1957, *ibid.*; see also Telephone conversations, Dulles and Hagerty, Dulles and Macomber, and Dulles and Stevenson, Dec. 1, 1957, Dulles Papers, Telephone Conversations). For developments see no. 481; see also John Bartlow Martin, *Adlai Stevenson and the World: The Life of Adlai E. Stevenson* (New York, 1977), pp. 418–25.

455 — *EM, AWF, DDE Diaries Series*

To Preston Hotchkis — *November 15, 1957*

Dear Preston:[1] Since we talked in my office last month, I have been turning over in my mind your suggestions in the light of views expressed by some of my associates.[2] Bobby Cutler tells me that you amplified to him your suggestion relative to my inviting to Washington a carefully screened group of sixty men of both political parties (selected from business, industry, labor, agriculture, and education) for a briefing on broad aspects of our national defense, with a view to their later spreading in their communities the information which they had received in Washington.[3]

Perhaps you may think that since we had our talk, the apprehension of the American people about our defense posture has been diminished. The additional speeches which I am scheduled to make will, I hope, further reassure our citizens that necessary steps for our defense are being taken.[4]

In view of the major effort which I have undertaken since we met, to get as much information as possible to all our citizens by means of nationwide TV and radio coverage, I am somewhat hesitant at this time to adopt the suggestion of a full briefing in Washington for a relatively small group of leaders. Such a project might detract from this major effort, which has the same informative purpose as your suggestion.[5]

Secretary McElroy tells me that the Defense Department carries on a broad program of Defense Orientation for leaders drawn from all over the United States.[6] He believes this program (which annually includes several hundred people) would probably include the same type of persons whom you suggested should be invited by me to come to Washington for a briefing.

I am asking Secretary McElroy to send you a full description of his briefing program. After hearing from him, will you let me know how well you think this Defense Orientation program meets the need which you expressed to me.

Similar programs to inform people as to our defense posture are carried on, as well, by the three Services. Also, through the frequent meetings of the Business Advisory Council and through the use of consultant groups with the National Security Council, substantial information concerning the national defense posture is provided to leading citizens.

If it is not too much trouble, I would like to have your opinion after I return from the NATO meeting in Paris, whether the efforts which by then will have been taken to disseminate information among our people need to be further expanded.[7]

In any event, I am most grateful for the stimulating views which you expressed when you were in my office. *Sincerely*

[1] Eisenhower asked Presidential Assistant Robert Cutler to draft this message (see Eisenhower to Cutler, Nov. 10, 1957, AWF/A; and Cutler to Eisenhower, Nov. 14, 1957, AWF/D).

[2] For background see no. 400.

[3] Cutler had described for Eisenhower Hotchkis's idea that the President's guests "would be briefed on the over-all national security posture of the United States—military strength, modern weapons, military and peaceful atomic uses, scientific break-throughs, domestic economy, full employment, budgetary problems, etc." (Cutler to Eisenhower, Nov. 4, 1957, AWF/A; and Extract from Hotchkis to Eisenhower, Nov. 5, 1957, AWF/A, Cutler Corr.).

[4] Eisenhower had made speeches about national defense on November 7 and on November 13. His speech on international cooperation, scheduled to be delivered in Cleveland on November 26, was canceled after he suffered a stroke (see *Public Papers of the Presidents: Eisenhower, 1957*, pp. 789–99, 807–17; see also nos. 470 and 477).

[5] "I could invite sixty men to come to the White House," Eisenhower had told Cutler, "but obviously any briefing would have to be done by others. I have enough on my plate as it is" (Eisenhower to Cutler, Nov. 10, 1957, AWF/A).

[6] See Cutler to Eisenhower, Nov. 4, 1957, AWF/A.

[7] Cutler would enclose a copy of this letter to Secretary McElroy (Cutler to McElroy, Nov. 19, 1957, AWF/A). For developments see no. 522.

456 EM, WHCF, *Official File 72-A-32*

TO RALPH EMERSON MCGILL *November 17, 1957*
Personal

Dear Ralph: First, I want to thank you very much for your telegram of welcome to Georgia. As always, I am delighted to be back here.[1]

I am grateful, too, for your thoughtfulness in sending me your column on Dr. Killian.[2] I agree that it is always interesting and sometimes revealing to have an insight into the manner of boy that grows over the years to the greatness of stature of a person such as Dr. Killian.[3]

If you will permit a personal anecdote, I am reminded that the Abilene High School Yearbook of 1909 predicted that my brother Edgar would be President of the United States and that I would be a professor of history at, I think, Yale. There are many times when I certainly wish *that* particular prophecy had come true.[4]

With warm regard, *Sincerely*

[1] McGill, editor of the *Atlanta Constitution*, had sent his telegram on November 15. Eisenhower was vacationing in Augusta, Georgia.

[2] James Rhine Killian, Jr., had taken the oath as the President's Special Assistant for Science and Technology on November 15 (see no. 396). McGill's editorial had appeared in the *Atlanta Constitution* on November 10.

[3] In his November 12 cover letter McGill had written that both he and Killian had attended McCallie Preparatory School in Chatanooga, Tennessee. Upon learning of Killian's appointment, McGill said he interviewed McCallie's former headmaster and one of Killian's former teachers. McGill's column praised Killian's academic success at McCallie which, together with Killian's accomplishments as a scientist and as president of Massachusetts Institute of Technology, meant that the organization of the nation's scientific program was in good hands.

[4] McGill had also enclosed a copy of the article about Killian by his McCallie classmates in the 1921 yearbook. The high-school seniors had written that Killian's "exceptional ability and his high seriousness of purpose coupled with his sense of honor and duty will surely make him a leader in whatever work he undertakes." McGill had noted, "sometimes these prep school yearbooks can be rather prophetic." All correspondence is in the same file as the document.

457 *EM, AWF, Name Series*

TO EDWARD EVERETT HAZLETT, JR. *November 18, 1957*
Personal

Dear Swede: It is too bad that your condition of weakness does not respond more readily to treatment. If the writing of a full letter seems to become too much of a burden, why don't you, from time to time, just jot down a note, in a few words, about anything that occurs to you. When you get a package of them, send them on to me. I do think you should not waste your strength trying to compose a coherent letter—much as I like your communications.[1]

Since July 25th of 1956, when Nasser announced the nationalization of the Suez, I cannot remember a day that has not brought its major or minor crisis. Some of these have been handled in secret; that is, no explanation or recitation of fact is possible for the simple reason that to bring some of them out in the open would cause as much trouble as the wrong answer. For example, had we published an account of the long, patient and hard work we did with the British and French, as well as the Israeli, in order to prevent the attack on Egypt and in making plain what would be our attitude in the event that such an attack was undertaken, there would have been the greatest political trouble in Britain, and probably in France. So we just had to let people think that we acted on the spur of the moment and astonished our friends by taking the action we did. Actually, they knew exactly what we'd do.[2]

In the matters that currently seem to be disturbing the country so much, namely our relative position with Russia in arms development, you can understand that there are many things that I don't dare to allude to publicly, yet some of them would do much to allay the fears of our own people.[3]

The most recent difficulty in the foreign field of which you have read involves our shipment of token arms to Tunisia. This we did in conjunction with the British after conversations with them demonstrated we were thinking in parallel lines.[4]

What happened was this. Somewhere along about early September the Tunisians came to us saying that they simply had to have arms for internal security and some protection against border raids. We knew that the French were maintaining close ties with Tunisia and we urged the French to make a satisfactory arms deal with Tunisia, in order that the latter country would not turn to the Soviets for help. The political leader in the country, Bourguiba, is a very fine friend of the West and the most intelligent man that I know of in the Arab world.

He became more and more insistent when he found that the French were using delaying and evasive tactics and he told us frankly that he would simply have to take the Soviet's offer which, financially, was far more favorable to him and his country than anything we could give him.

We and the British told the French that we would have to send a token shipment by November first because in our opinion we would otherwise risk the loss of that important area. You do not even have to glance at your map to know what the strategic value of the region is. The French then replied that they would make some delivery of the necessary arms to Tunisia and asked us to abstain. To this we gladly agreed, provided they would do it by November first.

When their government fell, they pointed out that there was no one there in power to take action and asked us to delay still further. This we did, much to the anguish of Bourguiba.

I have forgotten for the moment exactly how we fixed the date, but we then stated that we would wait until November twelfth, but we told both the French and the Tunisians that, on that date, we would deliver a token shipment of arms (from us only 500 rifles). When November twelfth came, the Gaillard government was in power but the matter had not been settled. Under our pressing, the French government finally said it intended to deliver the arms and had agreed in principle to do so, but before actual delivery could take place *the Tunisians would have to agree that their whole source of arms supply from then on would be France.*

In other words, even though Tunisia is ostensibly a free government, one with which we have exchanged Ambassadors, the French asked them to agree that for any military purposes they would be completely subservient to the French.

As you might expect, Bourguiba flatly rejected this condition and insisted that we deliver the token shipment of arms, as promised.

On our part, we felt it was a matter of good faith to deliver on November twelfth, but since the French seemed at last to be aware of the grim seriousness of the situation, we put off, with the British, actual delivery for another twenty-four to forty-eight hours, to give the French a renewed chance to settle the matter.

(I should have remarked that while all this was going on, Egypt suddenly decided to make Bourguiba a *present* of a certain amount of arms and shipped them from Cairo so as to assure their arrival in Tunisia by November fifteenth or sixteenth. Bourguiba considered it to be vitally important that some Western arms be received prior to the arrival of the Egyptian shipment. He said if this were not done his whole pro-Western policy would collapse around his ears and he would be forced into the arms of the Communist bloc.)

In spite of our actions, taken with the utmost caution and after long and exhaustive conferences, to postpone delivery after November twelfth, and so again breaking a promise we had given in good faith, the French went back to the Tunisians with the same old argument—namely that they, the French, had to be the sole source of supply of arms for Tunisia.

With the matter in this highly unsatisfactory state, we finally delivered the token shipment on November fourteenth, and France has since been acting like a spoiled child.

Of course we were well aware that France was seeking any kind of excuse to blame someone else for its own difficulties. That is a favorite trick of French politicians these days. But no matter how serious the consequences, we decided that if we were to hold on to the Mid East and have any kind of decent relations with the Arab world, we simply had to go ahead with an agreement that seemed to us to be based on Tunisian rights and on fairness in our dealings with other nations.

Just what the outcome will be I cannot say. The French are fully capable of the most senseless action just to express their disagreement with others.

Their basic trouble is that they are still trying to act as if they headed a great empire, all of it, as of old, completely dependent on them. If they would center their attention mainly on their European problems and work with others in their solution, they could be a happy and prosperous country.

Today their production per man is, I am told by the experts, even higher than that in Germany. Yet Germany is making money hand over fist, and France is on the verge of bankruptcy.

* * * * *

I am slated to make two or three more speeches this fall, or at least by the end of January. Subjects still to be covered are such things as "The function of mutual security assistance in our nation's defense," "The farm problem," and the "Economic situation." This last I will defer for some time because of the hope that a few of the uncertainties will be cleared up and I can make a more meaningful talk on the matter.[5]

You mention the Little Rock situation and your conviction that I had done the right thing.[6] My biggest problem has been to make people see, particularly in the south, that my main interest is not in the integration or segregation question. My opinion as to the wisdom of the decision or the timeliness of the Supreme Court's decision has nothing to do with the case.

The point is that specific orders of our Courts, taken in accordance with the terms of our Constitution as interpreted by the Supreme Court, must be upheld.

I said to a man the other day: "You disagree with the decision and tell me that I should show my disapproval by refusing to prevent violence from obstructing the carrying-out of the Court's orders.[”]

"Let us take a different example. Suppose you had been thrown into jail by an arbitrary sheriff or United States marshal. Your lawyer asked for a writ of habeas corpus and it is granted by the judge. But the feeling in the locality is such that the sheriff feels completely safe in telling you he will not obey the order, and you will remain in jail. Now comes my question: Would you consider I was doing my solemn duty as the President of the United States if I did not compel your release from jail?"

If the day comes when we can obey the orders of our Courts only when we personally approve of them, the end of the American system, as we know it, will not be far off.

Along with these speaking chores that I mentioned a while back, I have the State of the Union speech to make, a Budget in preparation to send to Congress, the Economic Report to approve and send on, and then the endless conferences with legislative leaders while Congress is in session.[7] The only hope I see for any real letup is some time around next July. Several things would have to happen to make that period any better than the present.

The Congress would have to adjourn early. There would have to be a general easing off of tensions in the free world. And fewer people must be struggling to see me with "very important messages and pieces of advice." If all three of these things happen, possibly my family, my associates, my secretary and I can give less attention to our blood pressure and the condition of our general nervous systems.

Having said all this, I must tell you that physically I seem to stand up under the burden remarkably well. Yesterday I think the doctor said my blood pressure was 130 over 80 and my pulse something on the order of 66.

The biggest worry of all is the constant question of "doing the right thing." Certain of the problems are so complex and so difficult that there is no really satisfactory answer. As Foster explained it the other day when we were talking about the French-Tunisian mess, "This is a matter of choosing whether you want your arm broken in two places—or your leg broken above the knee." But I have the satisfaction of knowing that I do my best, that I have with me a group of honest, dedicated, and in some cases very wise men to advise and help, and that, finally, the Almighty must have in mind some better fate for this poor old world of ours than to see it largely blown up in a holocaust of nuclear bombs.

So with this kind of support I manage to keep at least the shreds of a once fairly good disposition—a matter on which Mrs. Whitman may write you a minority report—and all in all feel that the job is being done about as well as it can be under the circumstances.

While I am often urged to be more assertive, to do a little more desk-pounding, to challenge Russia more specifically and harshly, I do not do these things for the simple reason that I think they are unwise. Possibly I do not always control my temper well, but I do succeed in controlling it in public. And I still believe that a frequent exhibition of a loss of temper is a sure sign of weakness.

I seem to have gotten into a spate of introspective thinking here and making you the victim of its expression. Actually I have nothing quite so important to do as to wish for you a reasonable and quick return to a state of good feeling, particularly in getting rid of those blankety-blankety headaches. Along with this, I want to send my love to Ibby and your family. *As ever*

[1] Hazlett had been suffering from high blood pressure and severe headaches (see no. 248). He had written Eisenhower on November 11 (AWF/N).
[2] On the Suez Canal crisis and U.S. relations with Britain, France, and Israel during the period see Galambos and van Ee, *The Middle Way*, volume XVII.
[3] Eisenhower may have been referring to information gathered by high-altitude reconnaissance flights over the Soviet Union by the U-2 airplane (see no. 82; on the Soviet launch of Sputnik see no. 394. Hazlett had lamented that Eisenhower's Newport vacation had been interrupted by "the Soviet ascendancy in missiles and satellites, and the ensuing criticism of our own programs in the scientific field."
[4] On the Tunisian arms situation see nos. 451 and 452.
[5] After his State of the Union message, Eisenhower's next speech would be on Administration policies at the Republican National Committee breakfast on January 31, 1958 (*Public Papers of the Presidents: Eisenhower, 1958*, pp. 135–40). For his special messages to Congress regarding agricultural policy, the economic situation, and the mutual security program see *ibid.*, pp. 100–107, 151–52, 160–68.
[6] "Personally, I feel that you played your cards exactly right in that situation," Hazlett had written. "I know how you must have felt about that double-dealing skunk from Arkansas, but none of it showed through your entirely legal veneer." For background on the Little Rock issue see no. 330.
[7] For the State of the Union Address, the budget message, and the economic report see *Public Papers of the Presidents: Eisenhower, 1958*, pp. 2–15, 17–74, 151–52.

458

EM, AWF, Dulles-Herter Series

TO JOHN FOSTER DULLES
Confidential

November 18, 1957

Memorandum for the Secretary of State: Attached is a file of papers dealing with a suggestion that I send to the head of every other state in the world a monograph dealing with America's hopes for peace and disarmament.[1] I have no objection to signing such a paper if, after thorough discussion between us, we decide the thing could be helpful. The question of possible embarrassment does not concern me in the least.

Speaking personally, the idea has some appeal and my general feeling is that if done in a dignified and effective manner it can hurt nothing and just possibly might help in making our position clear to the world.

In any event, I will be ready to talk to you about it at your convenience.[2]

[1] The papers mentioned by Eisenhower are not in AWF. On this same day, however, Eisenhower had replied to a letter from magazine editor Norman Cousins that included both a public statement on the uncertainties facing the world and specific recommendations to achieve international peace, justice, and disarmament. Cousins and a group associated with the statement agreed with Eisenhower that security did not depend "solely on bigger missiles or satellites or propulsion devises." It was, instead, dependent on "the big ideas and the big designs that are concerned with the making of a better and safer world" (Cousins to Eisenhower, Nov. 13, 1957, WHCF/OF 133-Q; see also Eisenhower to Cousins, Nov. 18, 1957, *ibid.*; and Telephone conversation, Eisenhower and Dulles, Nov. 18, 1957, Dulles Papers, White House Memoranda Series, and AWF/D).

[2] The topic would be part of the agenda of the NATO conference, Dulles would tell Eisenhower, and could be a fitting principal subject for a possible speech Eisenhower might give at the United Nations on his return from the Paris meetings. If Eisenhower did not speak at the United Nations, Dulles said that such a paper might be appropriate. The President agreed (Memorandum of Conversation, Nov. 25, 1957, Dulles Papers, White House Memoranda Series; for background on the NATO conference in December see no. 414; on the possibility of a United Nations speech see no. 470). For Eisenhower's remarks at the beginning of the NATO conference see *Public Papers of the Presidents: Eisenhower, 1957,* pp. 835–42; for his address to the nation at the conclusion of the meetings, *ibid.*, pp. 247–49; and for disarmament discussions at the NATO meeting see *Foreign Relations, 1955–1957,* vol. IV, *Western European Security and Integration,* pp. 244–51.

Eisenhower would write to Indian Prime Minister Nehru regarding disarmament on December 15 (see no. 494).

459 — *EM, AWF, Name Series*

To Wilton Burton Persons — *November 18, 1957*

Dear Jerry: When Senator Ellender was telling me the other day how well Russia was doing scientifically, he asserted that in America we did not build a single generator of more than 105 kw. capacity.[1]

Please note the attached letter from the President of the Westinghouse Corporation. I send it to you in the hope that you may get some casual opportunity to enlighten Senator Ellender.[2] *As ever*

[1] Louisiana Democrat Allen Joseph Ellender had met with Eisenhower and Persons on November 9 to report on his month-long tour of the Soviet Union (see Appointments, Nov. 9, 1957, AWF/AWD, and *New York Times,* Nov. 10, 1957). Eisenhower probably meant to say "105 megawatts" (mw).

[2] Westinghouse Electric Corporation Chairman and President Gwilym Alexander Price (LL.B. University of Pittsburgh 1917) had attended the Crusade For Freedom luncheon at the White House on November 12. At that time Eisenhower had asked Price about the size of electric turbine generator units in service in the United States. On November 14 Price had replied that an estimated twenty-nine steam turbine generator units of 250,000 kilowatts and larger—totaling approximately 8.7 million kilowatts—had been built by, or were on order with, American manufacturers. As of that

date, five units totaling approximately 1.5 million kilowatts were in service. Enclosed with Price's letter was a schedule listing the numbers of units, unit ratings in megawatts, customers, stations, shipping dates and dates of service (WHCF/OF 225 Soviet Union).

460

EM, WHCF/OF 3-Q

To George Patton Waters

November 18, 1957

Dear George: I was delighted to receive a letter from the grandson of General Patton, who was my intimate friend dating from World War I.[1]

As I think you will understand, I cannot recall all the technical details of the M-47, the Patton tank. However, I do know that when we received it, we knew we had a fast, reliable and powerful machine. It was a much finer weapon than any of its predecessors.[2]

For the purpose of writing a theme, I am sure you would want something more than this general comment. Of course you undoubtedly have the details of weight, speed, thickness of armor and ballistic quality of its armament, but I am asking one of my assistants, General Goodpaster, to give you any additional comments that he possibly can that apply to the history of the tank in both war and peace.[3]

Please convey my warm greetings to your father, and with best wishes to yourself,[4] *Sincerely*

[1] Waters, a student at Episcopal High School in Alexandria, Virginia, had written on November 12. For background on General George Smith Patton, Jr., see *Eisenhower Papers*, vols. I–XVII.

[2] Waters had asked Eisenhower for his personal comments on the tank for a school paper he planned to write.

[3] Goodpaster would write to Waters on November 23. In a November 25 thank-you note to the President, Waters would say that the information from Goodpaster would make his theme "a wonderful peace [sic] of interisting [sic] data." All correspondence is in the same file as the document.

[4] For background on General John Knight Waters see Chandler, *War Years*, no. 925.

TO RALPH EMERSON MCGILL *November 19, 1957*
Personal

Dear Ralph: This morning I read your piece about the cracker barrel. So far as I am concerned, and with this I think George Humphrey would agree, you have, to some extent, misinterpreted the thought that led George to have it made up.[1]

Anyone who has spent considerable time in an administrative position of government in Washington soon sadly learns one inescapable lesson. It is that everybody is always so busy with urgent things that he never has any time for the important. This is often true of business executives, as well. The important things require some thought and deliberation, and such thoughts develop and crystallize under the stimulus of conversations with others who have one's respect and liking.

In modern days our hectic civilization has produced, as an inadequate and wholly unsatisfactory substitute for the old cracker barrel discussions, cocktail lounges in the hotels and gin rummy tables in the bars of our clubs. Real conversation in such places is not only unlikely, it is impossible. And in the ordinary case, the effect of two or three martinis incites the loudest, rather than the wisest, man to hold the conversational lead.

One of the great virtues of the cracker barrel is that it offers nothing but the cracker barrel, a piece of cheese and an occasional peach (this last is a luxury, in my boyhood it was a dried prune.) The conversation itself had to be interesting enough to hold the individual's attention or the meeting broke up. George hopes to help revive the art of conversation.

To say that gathering around a cracker barrel is merely trying to live in the past or to apply 1900 thinking to the year 2000 that is galloping so rapidly upon us, is shooting wide of the mark that George had in mind.

As a final observation there were, after all, some awfully good things in the past to which you refer—crackers are still good food. I do not believe that a thing is necessarily bad because it is old, or necessarily good because it is new.[2]

Incidentally, you will be glad to know that the Governor of Vermont, seeing in the paper the story of the cracker barrel, has dispatched to the Augusta Club some special cheese and crackers from that State to make more enjoyable our Sunday morning conferences around our modern version of the cracker barrel.[3] I am sure that Cliff, Bob and others here would join me in saying that we would hope that some day you might be with us on some such occasion.[4]

With warm personal regard, *Sincerely*

[1] For background on the cracker barrel, presented to the Augusta National Golf Club by former Treasury Secretary Humphrey, see nos. 256 and 265. McGill was editor of the *Atlanta Constitution*; his piece had appeared in that paper on this same morning. The nostalgic aspects of the barrel led him to accuse "certain members" of Eisenhower's Cabinet of "looking back at the past and trying to recreate it, instead of realizing that the year 2,000 was being born while they thought about cracker barrels." McGill added that Humphrey and his associates had accelerated the course of the industrial revolution, which in turn had "doomed the country store, the cracker barrel and that way of life."

On this same date Eisenhower would send Humphrey McGill's editorial and a copy of this letter (AWF/A). See also Ann Whitman memorandum, November 15–21, 1957, AWF/AWD.

[2] McGill had written of his fond boyhood memories of the country store with its cheese, crackers, and "yellow peaches in heavy, sweet syrup which a boy savored. . . ." " As far as I am concerned," McGill had added, "it is too bad those days are gone. . . . It WAS a pleasant time."

[3] Joseph Blaine Johnson (B.S. University of Vermont 1915) was governor of Vermont from 1955 to 1959 (see also Signatures, Nov. 21, 1957, AWF/D).

[4] Cliff Roberts and Robert Woodruff were Eisenhower's friends and members of the Augusta National Golf Club.

462

EM, AWF, Administration Series

TO FREDERICK M. DEARBORN, JR. *November 19, 1957*

Dear Fred: By instinct I agree with what you had to say in your memorandum of the fifteenth.[1] Actually progress along the lines you mention can, of course, be achieved only by action of the Congress. The danger will be that again a majority will want to increase grants to agriculture and veterans, on the grounds that in this way they automatically achieve greater popularity in their own states and districts. We may be able to curtail rivers and harbors programs, reclamation, public building, subsidies and things of that nature.

While the prospects for really large savings are probably not bright, I do agree with you that it is worth while to make the effort.[2]

With warm regard, *Sincerely*

[1] Dearborn, Special Presidential Assistant for Security Operations, had told Eisenhower that he believed the American people had "recovered from their early unease about Sputnik" and would be willing to support new Administration proposals "to defer, reduce or cut out some of the hidebound policies and unnecessary expenses in our agriculture, reclamation, veterans, and rivers and harbors programs, if shown that unnecessary expense had been eliminated from defense programs and if the savings are applied to defense and education" (Dearborn to Eisenhower, Nov. 15, 1957, AWF/A).

[2] For more on budget negotiations see no. 497.

463 *EM, AWF, Dulles-Herter Series*

TO JOHN FOSTER DULLES *November 19, 1957*
Personal

Dear Foster: Here's an interesting idea from Mr. Sprague, who recently appeared before us in the Security Council.[1] It strikes me that it might possibly be an antidote to free-wheeling things such as Norman Cousins and his group will be doing.[2]

Don't bother to make any formal reply; I shall soon be seeing you.[3] *As ever*

[1] Robert Chapman Sprague (M.S. Massachusetts Institute of Technology 1924), was a former naval officer and at one time had been a candidate for the post of under secretary of the Air Force. He was chairman of the board and treasurer of the Sprague Electric Company in North Adams, Massachusetts, and since 1954 had been a consultant on continental defense for the National Security Council. He had become director of the Security Resources Panel of the Office of Defense Mobilization Science Advisory Committee after the former director, H. Rowan Gaither, Jr., chairman of the board of the Ford Foundation, had become ill. The panel, which the National Security Council had established on April 4, had studied the measures needed to protect the civil population in the event of a nuclear attack. Three days before presenting the panel's findings to the NSC, Gaither had told Eisenhower and other Administration officials that the active defenses of the United States were inadequate and that the passive defenses were almost insignificant. The planes of the Strategic Air Command could be destroyed on the ground, Gaither said, and by 1959 the population would be critically vulnerable (Goodpaster memorandum, Nov. 6, 1957, AWF/D; see also Cutler to Eisenhower, Nov. 4, 1957, AWF/A).

Among the recommendations the panel presented to the NSC on November 7 were measures to protect SAC bombers from surprise attack and to increase their offensive power; a nationwide fallout shelter program to protect the civil population; and organizational changes in the Department of Defense to improve control of performance and expenditures (NSC meeting minutes, Nov. 8, 1957, AWF/NSC; see also NSC meeting minutes, Nov. 1, 1957, and April 5, 1957, *ibid.*; Goodpaster memorandum, Nov. 7, 1957, AWF/D; Ann Whitman memorandum, Nov. 9, 1957, AWF/AWD; Cutler to Eisenhower, Nov. 6, 1957, AWF/A; *Congressional Quarterly Almanac*, vol. XIV, *1958*, pp. 672–73; Divine, *The Sputnik Challenge*, pp. 35–41; and Levine, *The Missile and Space Race*, pp. 65–66). The full report, often referred to as the Gaither Report (NSC 5724), is in State, *Foreign Relations, 1955–1957*, vol. XIX, *National Security Policy*, pp. 638–61.

In a letter on November 14 Sprague had told Eisenhower that the panel's recommendations, if adopted, would only buy time. "The time bought," he said, "will vary from a few years to possibly as many as twelve to twenty years, depending on our total effort and the relative success of this effort." Sprague suggested that Eisenhower name a group whose sole responsibility would be to make recommendations "to take the maximum advantage of the very modest time which we will be able to buy with our most effective efforts" (Sprague to Eisenhower, Nov. 14, 1957, AWF/D-H; see also Eisenhower to Sprague, Nov. 18, 1957, *ibid.*).

[2] Magazine editor Cousins was acting chairman of the recently-formed National Committee for a Sane Nuclear Policy. The group of writers, educators, and clergymen had urged Eisenhower to recommend to the United Nations that all nuclear test explosions be stopped. They also wanted all outer-space satellites under U.N. control

and all scientific information about space exploration shared (see no. 458; and *New York Times,* Nov. 15, 1957; on Cousins's correspondence with Eisenhower regarding nuclear issues see no. 231).

[3] Dulles would tell Eisenhower that having independent groups dealing with segments of an issue complicated the problem and demanded an amount of briefing time that offset the positive advantages. The matter, Eisenhower replied, deserved "further thought" (Memorandum of Conversation, Nov. 25, 1957, Dulles Papers, White House Memoranda Series).

The Administration would continue to discuss the issues covered by the Gaither Report in the early months of 1958. For developments on the reorganization of the Defense Department see no. 630. On August 8 Eisenhower would sign legislation giving the federal government and the states joint responsibility for civil defense programs (*Congressional Quarterly Almanac,* vol. XIV, *1958,* pp. 63, 205). For Eisenhower's assessment of the Gaither Report and its repercussions see Eisenhower, *Waging Peace,* pp. 219–23.

464

EM, WHCF, Confidential File: Defense Department

To Francis Higbee Case — *November 20, 1957*

Personal and confidential

Dear Francis: I appreciate your thoughts on Defense organization, a subject to which I have given a great deal of attention these past ten years.[1]

Secretary McElroy may come to the conclusion that some reorganization within the Defense Department is desirable. He will certainly base his recommendations on thorough study, possibly calling in some of the retired people from the services themselves. What actions he and I believe to be indicated will be promptly placed before the Congress.[2]

A drastic reorganization such as is suggested in your proposal would seem likely, at this time, to create such an upheaval as to make it inadvisable. It may well be, however, that the future will bring about the kind of line-up you suggest.[3]

It is well to remember that since World War II, the Defense establishment has been organized and reorganized a number of times; we must be careful to avoid disrupting efficiency by too frequent modifications.[4]

Nevertheless, it is gratifying to know that you are thinking so seriously about such matters. I am grateful to you for writing.

With warm regard, *Sincerely*

[1] Spurred by the growing demand for greater speed in the development of the U.S. missile program in the wake of the October 4 launch of Sputnik (see no. 389), South

Dakotan Republican Senator Case had written the President on November 12 (same file as document). Case had suggested a sweeping reorganization of the armed forces in order to free up funds for missile development. On Case see Galambos and van Ee, *The Middle Way*, no. 617.
[2] Case was not alone in calling for Defense reorganization. On November 15 Nelson Rockefeller, Chairman of the President's Advisory Committee on Government Organization, had suggested to Eisenhower that he "put forward an Administration proposal for reorganization of the Department of Defense early in the next session of Congress" (AWF/A, McElroy Corr.; see also Eisenhower, *Waging Peace*, pp. 244–53). For developments see no. 540.
[3] Case had suggested that the armed services be restructured around two main branches, a "land-based air," and a "sea-based air." This would, he wrote, "be putting the Army and Air Force back together as they were in the old War Department and letting the Army become an air-minded, airlifted, mobile force, providing for the Air Force something comparable to what the Marines provide for the Navy." Case suggested that Eisenhower appoint a presidential commission to study such an approach.
[4] See Galambos and van Ee, *The Middle Way*, nos. 291, 471, and 727; see also C. W. Borklund, *The Department of Defense* (New York, 1968), pp. 50–70.

465

EM, AWF, Administration Series

To Arthur Ellsworth Summerfield, Sr. *[November 20, 1957]*

Please show this to Bob Anderson.[1] If what this man says is typical—and from his description of the N.Y.U. Symposium it is clear that he is not reporting an isolated instance—then the matter needs correction.[2] Such correction should be accompanied by a statement that the abominable practices will stop at once.[3]

[1] Eisenhower had written this directive across the top of a three-page letter, dated November 20, from John Sorokin, a certified public accountant from Flint, Michigan, to Postmaster General Summerfield. Anderson was Secretary of the Treasury.
[2] Sorokin, who recently had attended a forum on income taxes sponsored by New York University, had reported on the informal "bull sessions" following the lectures. The attorneys and accountants in attendance were troubled, he said, by the deteriorating relationship between taxpayers and Internal Revenue Service (IRS) employees. IRS supervisors had been reopening so many compromise settlements that Sorokin's firm had been recommending that its clients engage in much costly litigation. According to Sorokin, IRS employees had changed from disinterested examining officers to witch-hunters. IRS audits had developed into "absurd examinations of travel expenses," resulting in extortionate settlements.
[3] Summerfield would report that there was "a lot of unhappiness in the country, occasioned by conviction or belief that the government is 'nagging.'" As a result, morale was low (see Ann Whitman memorandum, Nov. 15–21, 1957, and Diary notes, Nov. 22, 1957, both in AWF/AWD). Earlier in the fall the IRS had announced changes to the Individual Income Tax Return, Form 1040, designed to help auditors spot especially large deductions for non-existent or non-deductible expenses. As it turned

out, on November 25 the IRS would rescind its order for 1957 tax returns. The new order, however, would become effective on tax returns filed for 1958 (*New York Times*, Nov. 8, 11, 26, 1957; *Wall Street Journal*, Nov. 26, 1957; *Business Week*, Nov. 16, 1957, Feb. 8, 1958; *Newsweek*, Apr. 15, 1957; *U.S. News & World Report*, Nov. 22, 1957).

466

EM, AWF, Administration Series

To Arthur Ellsworth Summerfield, Sr. *[November 20, 1957]*

Arthur: Will you talk this over with Sec. Mitchell? Why do citizens have to stand for this type of racketeering?[1]

[1] Eisenhower had handwritten this note at the top of a letter that Woody Skaff, president of the Skaff Furniture Company in Flint, Michigan, had sent to Summerfield on November 20 (AWF/A, Summerfield Corr.). Skaff had described the coercive and often violent tactics that had been used against his company by officials of the Teamsters Union in attempting to force the company's employees to join the union. He asked for laws that would protect companies from having to become unionized without the consent of their employees, prevent picket lines when the majority of the employees were opposed to them, and prohibit unions from implementing secondary boycotts that would affect the business of a company having difficulty with the union.

A Skaff Company representative had testified before the Senate Select Committee on Improper Activities in the Labor and Management Fields on November 4 (see *Congressional Quarterly Almanac*, vol. XIII, *1957*, pp. 777–87; and *New York Times*, Nov. 5, 1957).

We have found no record of a reply by Summerfield or Labor Secretary Mitchell.

467

EM, AWF, DDE Diaries Series

To Sherman Adams

November 20, 1957

Memorandum for Governor Adams: Can't we get the members of the Civil War Commission and the Lincoln Sesqui-Centennial Commission appointed? We seem to be flooded with recommendations, and I'd like to see them both out of the way.[1]

[1] On September 7 Congress had established the Civil War Centennial Commission, P.L. 85-305, to commemorate the one-hundredth anniversary of the Civil War. The commission would include: the President; the President of the Senate; the Speaker of the House of Representatives (all of whom would serve *ex officio*); and twelve presidential appointees (two from the Defense Department). Five days earlier Congress had established the Lincoln Sesquicentennial Commission, P.L. 85-262, and had given the President the duty of appointing the group's twelve public members. The

commission would plan for a nationwide observance of the 150th anniversary of the birth of Abraham Lincoln on February 12, 1959. Appointments to both commissions were to be completed within ninety days from enactment of the resolutions (*U.S. Statutes at Large,* vol. 71, [1957], pp. 626–28, 587–89; see also *New York Times,* Apr. 6, 1958, Jan. 14, 1959).

Several senators and congressmen had recommended appointments for these two commissions; see lists of correspondence in Signatures, September, October, 1957, AWF/D.

On January 11, 1959, Eisenhower would address Washington officials and diplomats at a dinner in the Statler Hotel inaugurating the Lincoln sesquicentennial ceremonies (see *Public Papers of the Presidents of the United States: Dwight D. Eisenhower, January 1 to December 31, 1959* [Washington, D.C., 1960], pp. 183–84; see also *New York Times,* Feb. 12, 1959). For that commission's final report see U.S. Lincoln Sesquicentennial Commission, *Abraham Lincoln Sesquicentennial 1959–1960* (Washington, D.C., 1960).

468 — *EM, AWF, DDE Diaries Series*

To Howard D. Dawson — *November 21, 1957*

Dear Mr. Dawson: Thank you for your recent letter and its interesting suggestion that individual income taxpayers be allowed to pay their taxes by turning in United States Government bonds at par value.[1] I can see the attractions of your plan; but looking at it from the administrative side of the fence, the Treasury can see some serious problems.[2]

From a tax standpoint it would undoubtedly result in a windfall to some taxpayers at the expense of others. Those people with substantial funds to invest and considerable investment experience would be the ones in a favorable position to buy bonds when they were selling at a substantial discount and, by turning them in at par for taxes, receive a discount on their income taxes. Moreover, the value of the tax discount dollarwise would not be the same for all bondholders. It would be greater for those with large tax liabilities and large bond holdings and of little or no value to many others.

The Government has no authority under existing law to alter the terms in any way of its outstanding bond contracts. While the terms might be changed by legislation, it would appear highly questionable for the Government now to make the terms more favorable to the bondholders in view of the inequities it would create, including favoring current bondholders over previous ones.

Perhaps even more important, as I see it, is that the adoption of your suggestion would seriously complicate sound debt management planning since it would, in effect, turn what are now fixed bond maturities into demand debt at the option of the taxpayers holding these securities. This shortening of the maturity structure of the debt would materially increase our problems in managing the public debt to promote economic stability. When the Government's debt maturities are concentrated heavily into too brief a period, it means that the Treasury must be almost constantly in the market with new financings. This limits the effectiveness of action taken by the Federal Reserve in carrying out its statutory responsibilities to keep the supply of money and credit in line with the needs of the country.

Again, my sincere thanks for your letter and the active interest you are taking in our fiscal and monetary problems.[3] *Sincerely*

[1] Dawson, of Los Angeles, California, had written on October 31. Acknowledging the Administration's efforts to help various interest groups, Dawson said very little had been done to help "the largest single group to which we all belong . . . the taxpayer." He argued that since bonds were "essentially an obligation to pay on the part of the government," acceptance of bonds as payment of income tax would cancel both the taxpayer's debt and the government's debt at par value. Dawson maintained that under his plan taxpayers, and not the Federal Reserve Board, would help support the open market price of U.S. bonds.

[2] In an undated note to Special Assistant Gabriel Hauge, Ann Whitman said the President found Dawson's idea "intriguing" and wanted it studied. Hauge asked Under Secretary of the Treasury Scribner to draft this reply (see Hauge to Scribner, n.d., Scribner to Hauge, Nov. 20, and Hauge to Whitman, Nov. 21, 1957).

[3] All correspondence is in WHCF/OF 148-A.

469

EM, AWF,
Administration Series

TO GEORGE MAGOFFIN HUMPHREY — *November 22, 1957*

Personal and confidential

Dear George: This noon I took your letter home with me and read it thoroughly. My instant reaction is that if confidence in this country will be won only if we have a significant reduction in the budget, and damaged or even destroyed if the budget goes up, then there better be some looking for storm cellars.[1]

There has been at least a 6 percent rise in the cost of everything during the last two years, much of it in the last year.[2] This factor alone destroys hope of any substantial reduction, particularly when you remember that Charlie and I, working on the military budget a year and a half ago, battled our way down to the 38 billion mark only with the greatest difficulty.[3] Since 6 percent of 38 billion is more than 2 billion, you can see what a bloody fight I have been waging in the current sessions.

I am making copies of your letter, and on a confidential basis furnishing it to Neil McElroy, Dr. Saulnier, Percy Brundage and Sinny Weeks. I am likewise giving a copy to Ezra Benson, but I am not giving one to Bob Anderson.[4] Upon delivering your letter to me, he said he was thoroughly acquainted with its contents.

Over the past five years it seems to me that I have put in two-thirds of my time fighting increased expenditures in government, yet only this morning we had our mid-year review of the budget and we find that with the exception of one or two very unimportant agencies, the '57 expenditures for every single Department of government exceed comparable ones in the year '56. (I am talking calendar years here.) Every one of these increases has been brought about by law, except that of the Treasury Department where the extra amount is entirely for interest.[5]

With warm regard, *As ever*

[1] Humphrey, who had retired as Secretary of the Treasury on July 28 (see no. 175), had written on November 21 (AWF/A). He said that after conversations with Eisenhower and Treasury Secretary Anderson, he had come to the conclusion that the 1958 budget needed to be reduced below the amount of the 1957 budget by a "significant amount." "Adjustments between departments," he wrote, "can be made both throughout the Government and in the Pentagon itself. It is the total that is of first importance." "Unless this next Budget," he added, "begins to adequately control the expenditures in total and points out to the people how and why it should be done, our actions will increase the already prevalent fears that we are going the way of our predecessors. . . . If this happens, in my opinion it will so shock the confidence of the great mass of good sound Americans that they will curtail their own spending by many times the amount of any increase that can be made in Government expenditures, and deficits and difficulties will be multiplied."

[2] At that morning's Cabinet meeting, Budget Director Brundage had reported increased spending rates in the Departments of Agriculture (for price supports and the soil bank), Defense, Treasury (interest), AEC, and Veterans (increased compensation and direct housing loans) (Cabinet meeting minutes, Nov. 22, 1957, AWF/D). On the onset of the 1957–1958 recession see Saulnier, *Constructive Years,* pp. 106–15 and Iwan W. Morgan, *Eisenhower versus 'The Spenders': The Eisenhower Administration, the Democrats and the Budget, 1953–60* (London, 1990), pp. 74–98.

[3] For background see nos. 27 and 138. See also Galambos and van Ee, *The Middle Way,* no. 1963; and Sloan, *Eisenhower and the Management of Prosperity,* pp. 98–104, 119–25. The reference is to former Secretary of Defense Charles Wilson.

[4] Secretary of Defense Neil McElroy (see no. 369); Council of Economic Advisors Chairman Raymond J. Saulnier; Budget Bureau Director Percival F. Brundage; Secretary of Commerce Sinclair Weeks; Secretary of Agriculture Ezra Taft Benson; and Treasury Secretary Robert B. Anderson.

[5] Eisenhower would raise the issues mentioned in Humphrey's letter during a meeting that day with Defense Secretary McElroy, Assistant Defense Secretary Quarles, Dr. James R. Killian, Jr., and General Goodpaster (Goodpaster memorandum, Nov. 23, 1957, AWF/D). Concerned about growth in the military budget in connection with the public unease after Sputnik, Eisenhower said that he wanted to examine the budget on the basis of "should we do it," and not "can we do it in response to public outcry." The President stressed that money should not be spent "simply be-

cause of public pressure," but be "based on real need." Assuming that Soviet ICBMs would not overmatch American bomber power in the next few years, he suggested the United States go forward "simply as fast as our good sense and the probabilities of the situation seem to warrant." The President said he was agreeable to adding $700 million for pay increases to the $38 billion dollar military budget. He also agreed to an additional $573 million for acceleration of the missile program. For developments see no. 472.

470

Dulles Papers,
White House Memoranda Series

TO JOHN FOSTER DULLES
Personal

November 22, 1957

Dear Foster: In pondering the talk I am trying to get together for the American people next Tuesday night—on the general subject of "Waging the Peace"—I have the feeling that possibly I should speak again to the UN on the same subject.[1]

You will recall that Cabot thought I should speak to the UN on the way over to the NATO Conference. We decided, properly I think, that that was not good.[2]

On the other hand, suppose I should get together a talk to deliver to the UN Assembly after our return from NATO.[3] It seems that the world will be expecting a rather militant tone in whatever we have to say at NATO. There probably, therefore, would never be a better time to assert again in the strongest possible language that our purpose is peace and to discuss the manner in which it could be achieved.

The theme might be nothing more than a combination of my April 16, 1953 speech and the talk before the UN of December 8 of that same year, but we could add to that some of the suggestions we put before NATO such as a scientific brains alliance for combatting disease, poverty, squalor, privation and so on.[4]

What do you think of the idea—as the French would say—"in principle"?[5] *As ever*

[1] Eisenhower was to deliver a nationally televised speech on international cooperation in Cleveland on November 26 (see n. 5). He had previously spoken to the United Nations in December 1953 (see n. 4).

[2] On the NATO heads of government meeting see no. 454. Lodge had told Eisenhower that he would not have to "make a major speech with a sensational proposal." Instead, a short talk that stressed the relationship between NATO and the United Nations would "promote the solidarity of the non-communist world" (Lodge to Eisenhower, Nov. 7, 1957, Lodge Papers; see also Lodge to Dulles, Nov. 16, 1957,

ibid.). At Dulles's suggestion, Eisenhower had rejected the idea, believing that a pre-meeting speech "would give the impression either of propagandizing for the NATO meeting or apologizing for it" (Eisenhower to Lodge, Nov. 14, 1957, *ibid.*).

[3] Lodge had asked Eisenhower to consider a speech after the meetings. Because news of the meetings would be "of a military character," he said, the United States should again identify itself with peace (Lodge to Eisenhower, Nov. 20, 1957, *ibid.*). He would consider seriously the suggestion, Eisenhower answered, although "the trip, as tentatively outlined, sounds so crowded that I simply do not see how an appropriate speech could possibly be prepared" (Eisenhower to Lodge, Nov. 21, 1957, AWF/N).

[4] In his speech before the American Society of Newspaper Editors in April 1953 Eisenhower had offered a five-point program for world peace, disarmament, and reconstruction. In December he had expanded the theme to include a proposal for peaceful uses of atomic energy (see Galambos and van Ee, *The Middle Way,* nos. 132 and 598).

[5] A speech before the United Nations would be a good idea, Dulles answered; "it always is if you have something to say." He did not think, however, that time would allow for proper preparation (Telephone conversation, Dulles and Eisenhower, Nov. 23, 1957, Dulles Papers, Telephone Conversations; see also Telephone conversations, Dulles and Lodge, and Dulles and Eisenhower, Nov. 25, 1957, *ibid.*).

Two days after discussing the speech with Dulles, the President would suffer a stroke. Although he would attend the NATO meeting, Eisenhower would not speak before the United Nations or in Cleveland (see Telephone conversations, Dulles and Adams, Nov. 25, 1957; and Dulles and Larson, Nov. 26, 1957, Dulles Papers, Telephone Conversations; and Ann Whitman memorandums, Nov. 25, 1957, and Dec. 10, 1957, AWF/AWD). For his remarks at the opening of the Paris meetings and his televised report to the nation at the conclusion of the meetings see *Public Papers of the Presidents: Eisenhower, 1957,* pp. 835–45, 847–49.

471 — *EM, AWF, Administration Series*

To David Lawrence — *November 22, 1957*

Dear Mr. Lawrence: I, too, like your idea very much. While it does not fall into the pattern of ordinary diplomatic practice, I think that we simply must manage to find a way to communicate to all the peoples of the world what freedom can really mean.[1]

Your specific suggestion I shall have earnestly considered and I shall, of course, respect the anonymity of its originator.[2]

With warm regard, *Sincerely*

[1] At a recent dinner with Vice-President Nixon and Attorney General Rogers, syndicated columnist and editor Lawrence had read a memorandum proposing that the President, in "a dramatic and historic step," should address the Soviet people directly "in a crusade for peace." Such an appeal, featuring the idea that the key to peace was in the hands of the American and Soviet people together, would be like launching a "new 'Sputnik.'" His dinner companions had suggested that Lawrence send the memorandum to the President (Lawrence to Eisenhower, Nov. 22, 1957, AWF/A; see also "Memorandum on a New Kind of 'Sputnik,'" Nov. 20, 1957, AWF/A, Lawrence Corr.).

[2] Eisenhower would send a copy of Lawrence's memorandum, with the author's name withheld, to Secretary Dulles on the following day (see Whitman to Bernau, Nov. 23, 1957, AWF/D-H).

472

EM, AWF, Administration Series

To George Magoffin Humphrey *November 23, 1957*
Personal and confidential

Dear George: Right after writing you yesterday noon, I had another National Security meeting.[1] The fur flew, with Bob Anderson and I doing most of the currying. We really loosened up the hides of the animals.[2]

Neil McElroy is a jewel; it is a pity that he had to come into office at this particularly difficult time and before he has established for himself an independent understanding of our basic needs and a confidence in differentiating between the convenient and the desirable.[3]

However, in every meeting he makes some statement that establishes the basic common sense of his approach. While I think that the Generals and Admirals have made him overly sensitive to the harsh criticisms we have been getting for our failure to be first with Sputnik, it is clear that he is getting his feet on the ground and is going to be a tremendous help. He seems to have a natural sense of public relations.

I hope that my letter yesterday did not give you the impression that I have become completely pessimistic as to our ability to keep federal expenditures down, but I did mean to say that this year is more difficult than ever, not only because of Sputnik and the resultant reaction in this country, but because of the generally higher costs, particularly for all our hardware. I do still believe that if we could have appropriated directly to the Secretary of Defense an amount equal to our expenditures of this year, we would have an ample sum to meet all defense requirements.[4] But such is not possible under our system.

With warm regard, *As ever*

[1] For Eisenhower's letter to Humphrey see no. 469.

[2] At the November 22 NSC meeting Eisenhower had questioned the costs of the space program. While expressing satisfaction that the Department of Defense was to have $100 million for this program, the President was highly critical of an apparent attempt by the Air Force to budget funds for its own space efforts, saying that he did not believe that the Air Force should have "one cent" for this purpose (NSC meet-

ing minutes, Nov. 25, 1957, AWF/NSC). Eisenhower also cited former Treasury Secretary Humphrey's recent letter warning that the United States was "going to go to Hell as a result of our large Government expenditures."

[3] McElroy had assumed his position as Secretary of Defense on October 4, the same day as the Soviet launch of their Sputnik satellite (see nos. 369 and 389).

[4] See no. 76.

473

EM, AWF, DDE Diaries Series

To Dillon Anderson

November 23, 1957

Personal and confidential

Dear Dillon:[1] I sometimes wonder whether there are any so blind as those who will not see. I have placed myself on record times without number as to my belief that whatever claims or rights the United States has in the Gulf of Mexico belong, in the case of Texas, to the extent of three leagues from its shore line, to that State.[2]

You quote in your letter something from what the Solicitor General said.[3] I know nothing about court proceedings, but I do know that the Attorney General has not yet filed his brief and his brief is going to recite in detail the statement I made just above. I know nothing at all about the responsibilities resting with the Solicitor General in making a statement to this effect, but, as I say, when the Attorney General files his brief, it will state categorically what I have just said above.[4]

My predecessor in this office vetoed the Tidelands Bill.[5] I supported it and signed it. I tried to get a bill that did not mention the word "possessions" but only the right of exploitation, and tried to get a map attached to the bill so that there could never be any question as to exactly what was meant. My ideas were rejected by Senator Daniel, who said they wanted to use the title "historic boundaries" and would let the courts decide. In the meeting in my office he was supported by Governor Kennon of Louisiana.[6]

When a legal action was brought in the case of Louisiana, Texas, as I understand the matter, volunteered to get into the case. The Attorney General thought that unwise and when the matter was placed before the Court, that body directed that Texas be included as one of the parties.[7]

The Attorney General and I agreed that the statements that he and I had both made publicly regarding the rights of Texas would not only be repeated in a press release, but would be categorically stated before the Court.

I can do no more for Texas than I have done in this matter, and

I get weary of the constant nagging at me for "changing my mind." I have never done so, but it is obviously not possible for me to intervene in the actions and deliberations of the Supreme Court. It belongs to an entirely different branch of government and the Attorney General is an officer of that Court. The only thing I can do is to make certain that he does not misinterpret my views, but, on the contrary, states them exactly as I have repeated them time and again.

Recently Lyndon Johnson was in my office and I recited in detail exactly what is in this letter. He was very happy about the whole matter and stated that he was certain in view of the circumstances the Court would find in favor of Texas. So far as the pleadings are concerned, I am informed that the statement to which you refer had to be made in order to put the issue before the Court. But I repeat that the views of the Attorney General and of myself will be clearly expressed before that Court at the proper time.[8]

I am sending a copy of your letter to the Attorney General; you may possibly hear from him. *As ever*

[1] Anderson, former Special Assistant to the President for National Security Affairs, had served as a consultant to the White House since June 29, 1957. A draft of Eisenhower's letter with handwritten emendations is in AWF/A.

[2] For background see no. 438.

[3] Anderson had written on November 21, 1957 (AWF/A) regarding his concern over the Justice Department's suit seeking federal rights to Texas offshore lands beyond the three-mile limit. He quoted the Solicitor General as having said that when Texas became a member of the Union, "its boundary did not extend into the Gulf of Mexico more than three geographic miles from the ordinary low-water mark, or from the outer limit of inland waters. . . . ," and expressed his fear that Eisenhower was abandoning his support of the Texan position on submerged lands. While the action of the Justice Department could not "tarnish the image I hold of your great role in our history, the result of this recent action is a bruising one in this part of the country." He added: "The point that this is the Justice Department and not you is buried in the undeniable proposition that the heads of Justice are responsible, and presumably responsive to you and your policies." Anderson also described the actions he had taken to try to obtain assurance from the Justice Department that they would not act counter to the President's stated position on the tidelands issue, and he listed some of the legal precedents in support of Texas's claim to three leagues of submerged lands (see also Anderson to Adams, Oct. 24, 1957, and other correspondence in WHCF/CF: Tidelands Oil).

[4] Ann Whitman records that Anderson's letter had made the President "very angry." He called the new Attorney General, William Rogers, and told him that both he and former Attorney General Brownell had always "supported the Texas ownership up to three leagues." Rogers reassured Eisenhower that the technical requirements of federal procedure had forced him to claim in the pleadings presented in court that Texas should be "in the same position as Louisiana," but that the formal brief would "make the President's position clear" when the case was considered by the Court (Telephone conversation, Eisenhower and Rogers, Nov. 23, 1957, AWF/D).

[5] On Truman's veto of the tidelands bill of 1952 see *Congressional Quarterly Almanac*, vol. VIII, *1952*, pp. 334–37; and Galambos, *NATO and the Campaign of 1952*, nos. 773, 841, 871, and 892.

[6] Eisenhower was referring to Texas Senator Price Daniel (see Galambos and van Ee, *The Middle Way*, no. 1192). Robert Floyd Kennon (A.B. Louisiana State University 1923; LL.B. 1925), Democratic governor of Louisiana since 1952, had also served as a justice of the Louisiana supreme court between 1945 and 1946.
[7] See no. 438 and *New York Times*, November 19, 20, 1957.
[8] For developments see no. 705.

474

Dulles Papers,
White House Memoranda Series

To Jawaharlal Nehru

November 23, 1957

Dear Mr. Prime Minister: Thank you very much for your kind letter written upon the return to your country of your Finance Minister.[1]

I assure you that I always deem it a privilege when I have an opportunity to talk, even briefly, with one of your associates in the government of India. I think I need not again assure you of my abiding interest in the efforts you are making within that great Nation to bring about those developments and improvements which will mean for all Indians a better and fuller life.

Please accept my grateful acknowledgment of the complimentary things you had to say about me personally. I could, in addressing this note to you, repeat the words that are in your final paragraph. At the very least, I do want to say that I share fully your earnest desire that persons occupying such positions as yours and mine may find some way of leading the world, step by step, closer to a just peace.[2]

With the assurances of my kindest regard, *Sincerely*

[1] Indian Minister of Finance Tiruvallur Thattai Krishnamachari had discussed his country's economic potential and U.S. aid with the President on October 8 (State, *Foreign Relations, 1955–1957*, vol. VIII, *South Asia*, pp. 387–90; for background on economic aid to India see no. 42; see also Goodpaster memorandum, Nov. 16, 1957, AWF/D). Nehru had thanked Eisenhower for the "uniform courtesy and kindness" Krishnamachari had received and "the understanding that [Administration officials] showed to our problems and difficulties" (Nehru to Eisenhower, Nov. 12, 1957, same file as document).
[2] Nehru's final paragraph read: "I trust that you are keeping well. The world is full of difficult problems and a very heavy responsibility rests on the shoulders of a person occupying the high position that you hold. Large numbers of people in the world look to you to help them in coming out of this impasse and leading them toward peace."

475

EM, AWF, Gettysburg Series

TO BILLY G. BYARS

November 23, 1957

Dear Billy: I, too, enjoyed our all too brief visit in the office a week or so ago.[1] I tried to follow your instructions on my so-called Augusta "vacation," but I found that crises, large and small, and speech drafts managed to get in my way, as usual.[2]

Thanks for the tips on how to hang and cure steers, and for the procedure you follow in the preparation of hamburger meat.[3] I shall see that your instructions are sent to the various people who handle this business for me.[4]

With warm regard, *As ever*

[1] Byars had visited the White House the morning of November 12. His letter of November 19 is in AWF/Gettysburg.

[2] Byars had commented on Eisenhower's healthy appearance and "good constitution," and he had urged the President to "get in plenty of golf and rest" during the vacation (Nov. 16–21). Among the crises Eisenhower encountered were those involving Sputnik, Little Rock, and Syria (see nos. 401, 394, 447, 330, and 332, respectively). On the speech drafts see nos. 434, 457, and 470.

[3] Byars had followed up their November 12 discussion about steer meat with written instructions. First, he said, "a good fat steer two years old, or older, should be hung from two to three weeks at a temperature of 38 degrees." After two weeks, he advised, the steer should be checked daily. When it was completely molded over, curing was complete. "You know of course," he had added, "about wiping the mold off with a cheesecloth dipped in vinegar before cutting up and freezing." In order to avoid a rancid taste in the hamburger, Byars had suggested having the meat frozen as large cuts and then ground in the amounts needed.

[4] For developments see no. 486.

476

EM, AWF, Administration Series

TO THELMA CATHERINE PATRICIA RYAN NIXON

November 23, 1957

Dear Pat: That was a lovely party you gave the other evening for the Brownells.[1] I not only enjoyed the company and the hospitality, but I was amazed at the musical performance. In fact, I am not quite sure I understand it yet.

Thank you both very much for asking us and for giving us such a pleasant evening. *Sincerely*

[1] Vice-President and Mrs. Nixon had given a dinner party at the F Street Club in Washington, D.C., on November 21, honoring Herbert Brownell, who on October 23 had resigned his position as Attorney General to return to private law practice (*New York Times*, Oct. 24, 1957; see also no. 22).

477 — *EM, AWF, DDE Diaries Series*

To Lewis Lichtenstein Strauss — *November 25, 1957*

Dear Lewis: The purpose of this note is to invite you to ride on the Columbine with me when we go to Paris.[1] Possibly a trip like this will give us a chance to talk about one development, as I sense it from the papers, that troubles me greatly. This is the extent to which generals, admirals and laymen are talking on science, and conversely, the extent to which scientists have suddenly become military and political experts.[2] All of these seem to be obsessed with a consuming desire to "tell all."[3]

It reminds me of an old German folk song involving a quack doctor. A rough translation was: "I make the blind so they can hear; I make the deaf so they can see."[4]

With warm regard, *As ever*

P.S. By the general term "admirals" I do not, of course, mean one particular one who is an authority in the field to which I refer![5]

[1] On the upcoming NATO meeting see no. 444. Atomic Energy Commission Chairman Strauss would accompany the President to Paris on December 13.

[2] The launching of the Russian satellites Sputnik I and Sputnik II on October 4 and November 3 had produced increasing anxiety and disagreement among military, political, and scientific experts about the capabilities of the American satellite programs. As a result, Eisenhower had appointed a special assistant for science and technology to coordinate the nation's scientific efforts. For background see nos. 389, 394, 447, and *New York Times*, November 19, 21, 22, 24, 25, 1957; see also Medaris, *Countdown for Decision*, pp. 165–79.

During the October 5 news conference one reporter had asked about the military significance of satellites. To the amusement of the attendees Eisenhower had replied: "Suddenly all America seems to become scientists, and I am hearing many, many ideas" (see *Public Papers of the Presidents: Eisenhower, 1957*, p. 724).

[3] Eisenhower was referring to atomic scientist Edward H. Teller, who had appeared before a Senate investigating committee the preceding day. Teller, known for his work in developing the hydrogen bomb, had said that the Soviet launching of Sputnik I and Sputnik II "was a greater defeat for our country than Pearl Harbor" (see Telephone conversation, Eisenhower and Strauss, Nov. 25, 1957, AWF/D; see also *New York Times*, Nov. 19, 21, 22, 24, 25, 26, 1957; Ann Whitman memorandum, Nov. 15–21, 1957, AWF/AWD, and Maxwell D. Taylor, *Swords and Plowshares* [New York, 1972], pp. 164–77).

[4] Eisenhower was probably referring to the German-American folk song, "Doktor Eisenbart" (Correspondence, J. A. Gray, Library of Congress, Oct. 1, 1997, EP).

[5] Strauss had been a Rear Admiral in the United States Navy during World War II.
Later this afternoon the President would suffer a cerebral occlusion. For Eisenhower's account of the stroke see his memoir, *Waging Peace*, pp. 227–30; see also John S. D. Eisenhower, *Strictly Personal*, pp. 195–97, and Adams, *Firsthand Report*, pp. 195–97. For developments see no. 480.

7

NATO and the Cold War

478

EM, AWF, DDE Diaries Series

To John Foster Dulles

December 3, 1957

Memorandum for the Secretary of State: I should like a draft of a reply to King Saud's message of November twenty-eighth.[1]

It appears that the King now has one simple, even though completely unrealistic, solution to the Mid East problem. That solution is the destruction of Israel. Indeed, as I read the King's telegram, he would have the objectives and aims of the NATO Conference be humanity and world peace through the elimination of Israel as a nation.[2]

It looks as if it would be difficult to write a considered reply.

[1] King Saud had written Eisenhower on November 21; the State Department had received the translation on November 28. The Saudi Arabian monarch, writing in advance of the upcoming NATO conference, had told the President that the time had come to end the "tragedy" of the creation of the state of Israel and to return the Palestinians to their homes, with "compensation for their losses in wealth and properties" (AWF/I: Saudi Arabia; on the NATO conference discussions see no. 493).

[2] For Eisenhower's reply see no. 483.

479

EM, AWF, DDE Diaries Series

To Robert Luther Duffus

December 3, 1957

Personal

Dear Mr. Duffus: I was truly touched by your Saturday's editorial in the New York Times.[1] My feeling of personal compliment and gratification at what you had to say was indeed deep—but it is only plain honesty to say that my sense of humility was equally profound. Whatever sense of duty that has, through the years, helped to guide my thinking and actions, has been implanted, I suppose, by my parents, and possibly emphasized by my experiences in West Point and in the Army. I define it as a feeling of obligation to America and to her people. So, whatever my duty seems to me to be, I pray that I may do my best to perform it.

A simple thank you is totally inadequate, but it comes from the bottom of my heart.[2]

With best wishes, *Sincerely*

[1] Duffus (A.M. Stanford 1911) had been a member of the *New York Times* editorial staff since 1937. He had written several books including *The Sante Fe Trail* (London, 1930); *L. Emmett Holt: A Pioneer of A Children's Century* (New York, 1940); and *The In-*

nocents at Cedro: A Memoir of Thorstein Veblen and Some Others (New York, 1944). In his November 30 editorial Duffus had commented on Eisenhower's "amazing comeback" from the cerebral occlusion he had suffered on November 25 (on the illness see no. 477). Duffus attributed Eisenhower's speedy recovery to "the fortitude of a man who has all his life been bound by a selfless devotion to duty." He added: "With this devotion has evidently gone an inner serenity and it is this, we are sure, that has been a healing influence."

[2] In a letter to *New York Times* publisher Arthur Hays Sulzberger the President said that Duffus's editorial had renewed his determination "to get the better of this latest mishap" (Dec. 2, 1957, AWF/N).

480

EM, AWF, International Series: Macmillan

To Harold Macmillan — *December 4, 1957*

Eyes only. Personal

[*Dear Harold:*] My recovery from my sudden illness of ten days ago has apparently been steady and rapid.[1] The earliest symptoms of my indisposition were sufficiently slight that the doctors did not class the difficulty as a "stroke." However, I did suffer a marked "word confusion," with, also, some loss of memory of words alone.

In all other respects, I was not aware of any physical impairment, and within twenty-four hours I began to improve. While I still speak a bit more slowly and will occasionally mispronounce a word, I am sure that the doctors are most optimistic of my complete recovery.

All this means, as of this moment, that I am planning to be at the NATO meeting in mid-month. It is possible that I will try to avoid any lengthy public addresses, but otherwise I see no reason for curtailing my normal activity.[2]

All this I have told you in some detail so that you will not overstress whatever remaining difficulty that I may have when I see you.

We have been having a series of meetings preparing programs for the coming session of Congress, starting in early January. With these out of the way, Foster and I will be right busy in preparatory work for the NATO meeting.[3]

I believe that the first meeting is to be Monday noon. In order that I may have a reasonable period of rest after my transatlantic trip, I may plan on reaching Paris about Saturday noon. I might use this interval not only for some rest and additional briefing, but I should like also, if possible, to take a short visit to SHAPE just to see how my old headquarters has prospered. It would be fun to see the place once more.[4]

Looking forward to seeing you in Paris, and with my warm regard,
[*As ever*]

[1] Eisenhower had suffered a stroke on November 25. Upon hearing of the President's illness, Macmillan had cabled his wishes for a rapid recovery. "Pray take care of yourself," he said, "for you are very precious to us all" (Macmillan to Eisenhower, [Nov. 26, 1957], AWF/I: Macmillan; see also Eisenhower to Macmillan, Nov. 30, 1957, *ibid.*; and Eisenhower, *Waging Peace*, pp. 227–30).
[2] After a physical examination on December 10, Eisenhower's doctors would approve his attendance at the meeting, although, according to Ann Whitman, there was not "the slightest doubt for the last two weeks that he *was* going" (Ann Whitman memorandum, Dec. 10, 1957, AWF/AWD).
[3] On this day Eisenhower had attended meetings with the congressional legislative leaders. A bipartisan legislative leadership meeting had been held the preceding day (see the President's appointment calendar).
[4] Eisenhower would arrive in Paris on Saturday, December 14, and would spend approximately one hour at SHAPE headquarters three days later (see Eisenhower, *Waging Peace*, pp. 231–32). For developments see no. 493.

481 *EM, AWF, Name Series*

To Adlai Ewing Stevenson *December 4, 1957*
Confidential

Dear Governor Stevenson: I have just had an opportunity to read your memorandum of November twenty-ninth.[1] I, of course, agree with much of what you say, even though I doubt that advance publicity has noticeably depreciated the value of the meeting.[2] I am quite certain that the document will be useful to the government and some of its ideas should be helpful in stimulating the thinking of our Allies.[3]

With best wishes, *Sincerely*

[1] For background on Stevenson's consultations with the State Department regarding the upcoming NATO meeting see no. 454.
[2] In addition to his concerns that the meeting was being held too early for proper preparation and that publicity had somehow lessened its value, Stevenson believed that NATO should become a stronger political instrument with greater emphasis on humanitarian needs. The final communiqué, he said, "should stress: arms only for defense, aid for needy and underdeveloped nations, and cooperation with all states, including Communists, to promote peace and progress" (AWF/N).
[3] At Secretary Dulles's suggestion, Eisenhower would send another letter to Stevenson on this day regarding the latter's decision not to attend the Paris meeting (Telephone conversation, Eisenhower and Dulles, Dec. 4, 1957, Dulles Papers, Telephone Conversations and AWF/D; see also Memorandum of Conversation, Dec. 2, 1957, Dulles Papers, White House Memoranda Series). Although Stevenson had declined

Eisenhower's invitation to be part of the U.S. delegation, he had stated publicly that he agreed with most of the proposed positions, and he had thanked Eisenhower personally for the President's confidence in him (Stevenson to Eisenhower and Statement by Adlai E. Stevenson, Dec. 3, 1957; and Eisenhower to Stevenson, Dec. 4, 1957, AWF/N; see also Telephone conversations, Dulles and Eisenhower, Dulles and Nixon, Dulles and Goodpaster, and Dulles and Hagerty, Dec. 3, 1957, Dulles Papers, Telephone Conversations and AWF/D; and Eisenhower and Wiley, Dec. 12, 1957, AWF/D). For developments see no. 493.

482 — *EM, AWF, DDE Diaries Series*

To Several Yale Students — *December 4, 1957*

To "Several Yale Students": I am not at all sure that the Postoffice Department approves of a letter addressed in this fashion, but with a little luck it may reach its proper destination.[1]

I most deeply appreciate your interesting letter and, even more, the thought that prompted you to send to me a unique and sentimentally valuable gift. While I am not in the habit of accepting what I am told is known to your generation as "hot goods," I am reassured that a successful violation of rules during Harvard Week makes the whole proceeding legitimate. I have been intrigued by the process by which tradition has created a situation of extra legality, the result of which is a transformation of illegality to legality.[2]

Ultimately I shall send the Saybrook Banner of Arms to the Eisenhower Museum in Abilene, Kansas, where its safekeeping may be better assured than under the hazards of undergraduate venturesomeness.[3] I hope that some of you eventually will view it with pride in your successful exploit.

Again my thanks for the sentiments that prompted you to take risks in which the stakes were so high, and my best wishes. *Sincerely*

[1] The students had written to Eisenhower on November 24 (Eisenhower Museum, Abilene, Kansas). Eisenhower addressed his letter to the Yale University's Masters Office at Saybrook College in New Haven, Connecticut.

[2] The students had sent the Saybrook Banner of Arms in appreciation of the President's dedication, patience, and guidance in "an era of precipitate change in its mode of life coinciding with the greatest external threat to its traditions it has ever faced." The flag belonged to Yale and was obtained in "extra-legal fashion" at "considerable risk" over the Harvard weekend. Throughout the weekend of the Harvard-Yale football game, the young men wrote, all rules and regulations remain in effect and violations were punishable. Any successful violation, however, became completely legitimate.

[3] The Saybrook Banner, approximately five feet high and six feet wide, depicts the coats of arms of Lord Saye and Sele and Lord Brooke. The family names of these two seventeenth-century British land owners had been combined to name the town

of Saybrook, which was the site of the college before its removal to New Haven. The banner remains in the Eisenhower Museum (see correspondence with Dennis Medina, Apr. 7, 1997, EP).

483

EM, AWF, International Series: Saudi Arabia

To Saud ibn Abd al-Aziz
Secret

December 5, 1957

Your Majesty: I was happy to receive your message of November twenty-first and to have the opportunity once again to exchange views with my good friend on matters of importance and common concern.[1] We particularly appreciate your expression of interest in the forthcoming meeting of the North Atlantic Treaty Organization.

Your Majesty has expressed an understandable hope that the North Atlantic Treaty nations not make decisions regarding the problems of the Middle East, and particularly problems relating to the Arab states and Israel, without consultation with the states immediately concerned. Such consultation in matters of this nature is a fundamental principle of the United States, and I assure Your Majesty that the United States will not depart from this principle should the Middle East be discussed at the Paris meeting.

Your Majesty will, I am sure, understand that, in any discussion of current world problems, the general question of the interest and activities of international Communism in the Middle East is certain to be raised. The nations of the North Atlantic Treaty Organization are also fully aware of the opportunities afforded to international Communism by the continuing tension in the Middle East, particularly with respect to the repercussions of the dispute between the Arab states and Israel which Your Majesty has described. Your Majesty may rest assured, however, that the United States contemplates no decisions regarding Middle Eastern matters at Paris and that any participation by the United States in discussions of these questions will be on the basis of a full awareness of the views of the Saudi Arabian Government, of other interested governments in the area and of the role and responsibilities of the United Nations.

I thank Your Majesty for your good wishes and, on my part, send to you my hopes for your continued good health and for the continued success of Your Majesty's efforts in behalf of peace in the Middle East.[2]

May God grant you His safekeeping. *Your sincere friend*

[1] For King Saud's letter see no. 478. On the State Department draft of this letter Eisenhower had added the words "with my good friend" to this sentence (see no. 478; and Dulles to Eisenhower, Dec. 4, 1957, AWF/I: Saudi Arabia).
[2] Eisenhower had also received letters from Iraq's King Faisal and Camille Chamoun, President of Lebanon, regarding the Paris meetings. Both men had echoed King Saud's fear that the heads of the NATO governments would make decisions regarding the Middle East without consulting the governments involved (see Faisal to Eisenhower, Nov. 27, 1957, AWF/I: Iraq; and Chamoun to Eisenhower, Dec. 5, 1957, AWF/I: Lebanon). Eisenhower would tell both leaders that the U.S. government would take no such action (Eisenhower to Faisal, Dec. 12, 1957; and Dulles to Eisenhower, Dec. 11, 1957, AWF/I: Iraq; see also Eisenhower to Chamoun, Dec. 12, 1957; and Dulles to Eisenhower, Dec. 11, 1957, AWF/I: Lebanon).

For the portions of the NATO meetings that concerned the Middle East see State, *Foreign Relations, 1955–1957*, vol. IV, *Western European Security and Integration*, p. 241; and State, *Foreign Relations, 1955–1957*, vol. XXIV, *Soviet Union; Eastern Mediterranean*, pp. 747–48.

484 — To John Michael Budinger

EM, AWF, Name Series

December 7, 1957

Dear Jack: Thank you for your note of the fourth, and also for the letter from Paris that Mrs. Whitman showed me after I returned to the office early this week.[1] As I think she told you, I like your idea very much—but right now, of course, I am making no plans for resuming any social activities. It is not necessary to add that official duties necessarily have a priority on whatever time and strength I have.[2]

With warm regard, *As ever*

[1] Budinger, senior vice-president of Bankers Trust Company in New York City since 1951 and a member of the Augusta (Georgia) National Golf Club, had thanked Ann Whitman for acknowledging an earlier letter to the President (Budinger to Eisenhower, Nov. 21, 1957, and Whitman to Budinger, Nov. 28, 1957, WHCF/OF 101-B-1; Budinger to Whitman, Dec. 4, 1957, AWF/N, Budinger Corr.). Budinger had reminded the President that during their meeting of October 28 he had suggested that Eisenhower meet with U.S. business leaders from time to time. These should be men, "whose intellectual and business integrity you could depend upon—although some of their views might be colored by selfish interests, which is a perfectly natural instinct under the free enterprise system." They also, Budinger wrote, should come "prepared to express frankly their views to you." For background on Budinger see Galambos, *NATO and the Campaign of 1952*, no. 143; see also Ann Whitman memorandum, Oct. 28, 1957, AWF/AWD.
[2] On November 25 Eisenhower had suffered a mild stroke (see no. 477). Whitman had explained to Budinger that she would hold his letter until the President indicated that he wanted to resume stag dinners. On the White House stag dinners, Eisenhower's source for keeping in touch with the thinking of business and professional men, see Galambos and van Ee, *The Middle Way*, nos. 341 and 697.

485 *EM, AWF, DDE Diaries Series*

To Ward Murphey Canaday *December 10, 1957*

Dear Ward: Eighty scholarships does not by any means constitute a straw-in-the-wind; to me it is a highly encouraging sign of the responsibility that industry throughout the country will, I hope, increasingly assume. I sincerely congratulate you and those companies in your area who have far-sightedly and generously taken a concrete step toward providing our country with the trained engineers and scientists it so badly needs.[1] I know Dr. Killian will be pleased, too, if he does not already know of this particular development.[2]

With warm regard, *Sincerely*

P.S. I shall give the good news to Dr. Killian at once.

[1] For background on Canaday, president of the Overland Corporation and a trustee of Toledo University see *Eisenhower Papers,* vols. XII–XVII. He had written on December 7 that industries in the Toledo area were offering competitive scholarships in engineering to high school graduates. The University of Toledo was also "undertaking means of motivating" students to prepare for college and emphasizing studies in engineering and science (WHCF/OF 133-Q-2).

Since the launching of the two Sputnik earth satellites by the Soviet Union, the Administration had begun to stress the importance of science in national security. On November 13, in a nationally broadcast radio and television address, Eisenhower had called on industries and private organizations to share the cost of the government's expenditures in stepping up basic research programs (see *Public Papers of the Presidents: Eisenhower, 1957,* pp. 807–17).

[2] In October Eisenhower had appointed James R. Killian, Jr., as Special Assistant to the President for Science and Technology (see no. 396).

486 *EM, AWF, Gettysburg Series*

To Arthur Seymour Nevins *December 10, 1957*

Dear Art: In order that you may have a written memorandum of our plan for distributing the beef I give you the following.[1]

My first thought in this meat cutting business is that I asked for all of the really good steaks to be cut on the basis of 1¼ inch thick and the round steaks an inch thick. With this kind of good meat, however, I now think all these steaks should be ¼ inch more—or 1½ inch for the top quality and 1¼ inch for the round steaks.

Now as to disposition:

(*a*). George wants the carcass of his steer to be disposed of as follows.

He wants only the rib roasts as well as all of the steaks forward of what is called the chuck roast. George wants nothing else except the rib roasts and these particular steaks of his steer. He does not want round steaks.

Special note. I originally asked that all the rib sections be divided on the basis of 7 and 6-rib roasts. But so far as the rib sections of George's steer are concerned, Mr. Grim should cut each side into four roasts, one 4-rib and 3 each of 3-ribs.[2] This is because George does not have a power saw and it would be difficult for him to manage the cutting of frozen meat.

After George's rib roasts and steaks have been packaged, he would like to have half of these rib roasts and half of the steaks stored in the deep freeze at the farm. The other half will be sent to the deep freeze at the Sheraton Park Hotel.

(*b*). All other parts of George's steer will be marked for John. This will include the flanks, the eye roast, the chuck, round steaks, and so on. Mr. Grim will not bother putting the weight on the package but each one will be marked "For Major Eisenhower," and the description of the meat such as "meat for hamburger," "soup meat," "soup shank," "round steak," and so on.

(*c*). My steer will be cut up as I have already indicated to Mr. Grim, will be quickly frozen and will be brought here to the White House. As in George's and John's case, mine will be marked with my name and the description of the meat.

Incidentally, both my meat and John's will be put in one of the White House deep freeze[s]. It is possible that the cutting and the quick freezing will all be done about Saturday or even possibly Monday. In any event, I think that Chief West could take the truck and do the actual delivering.[3] Of course the meat may be delivered during my absence in Europe, but I think that with the aid of this letter and with my instructions given to the Usher, everything will go well.[4]

Of course I do think that you should notify Mary of when you expect to deliver her meat to the Gettysburg and Sheraton addresses.[5]

Sincerely

[1] For background on the President's interest in cutting and curing beef see no. 475. Eisenhower had spent the weekend of December 7–9 at his farm in Gettysburg. While there the President, Major John Eisenhower, partner George Allen and Nevins had visited the slaughterhouse and ordered the cuts of beef (see Eisenhower to Grim, Dec. 2, 1957; see also Memorandum, [Oct. 25, 1957], and Nevins to Eisenhower, Nov. 27, 1957).

[2] The slaughterhouse was operated by Clair M. Grim of Table Rock, Pennsylvania.

[3] This was Navy Petty Officer Walter A. West (for background see Galambos and van Ee, *The Middle Way*, no. 1573).

[4] Eisenhower would attend the NATO meeting in Paris December 16–19 (see no. 480).

[5] Allen and his wife resided at their Gettysburg farm and at the Sheraton Park Hotel in Washington, D.C.

Nevins would reply on December 11 that Presidential Secretary Ann Whitman had telephoned him regarding the changes desired in preparing the beef and that he had delivered the message to Grim. In a post script Nevins would add that he had just received the President's letter and that his instructions to Grim "seemed to comply in full" with Eisenhower's wishes. All correspondence is in AWF/Gettysburg.

487

EM, AWF, Name Series

To Clifford Roberts

December 10, 1957

Dear Cliff: Chief West has both shipments of the hedge shoots well in hand. I am sorry I caused you additional trouble by requesting them on the installment plan, but we needed more than I originally anticipated and I was told that the Club had them in abundance.[1] Many thanks.

Won't you please tell Luke, or whoever helped you with the project, of my appreciation of the work entailed?[2]

And thanks, too, for sending me the "Spectacle of Sport." It is a handsome and interesting volume. Of course I was especially intrigued by the account of the Masters (to say nothing of Mr. Roberts himself). I thought that the pictures and narrative of that particular piece made up the best presentation in the whole book. Of course I can be prejudiced—but so far as I am concerned there was no close second.[3]

With warm regard, *As ever*

[1] Walter A. West, a Navy Petty Officer stationed at Camp David, was a horticulturist. On December 2 Presidential Secretary Ann Whitman had asked Roberts, chairman of the executive committee of the Augusta National Golf Club, for an additional two hundred shoots of amur privet hedge (*ligustrum amurense*), a native of Northern China, for planting at the President's Gettysburg farm (Memorandum, Dec. 2, 1957, AWF/N, Roberts Corr.). Prior to its purchase and conversion to a golf course in 1931, the lawns of the Augusta National had been one of the South's leading commercial nurseries. The nursery had grown the privet from plants imported from France before 1860.

[2] Marion I. Luke had been the golf course superintendent at Augusta since 1945.

[3] Eisenhower was referring to *The Spectacle of Sport* from *Sports Illustrated*, edited by Norton Wood (Englewood Cliffs, N.J., 1957). The book had sections on annual sporting events within each season. The chapter on the Masters, written by Herbert Warren Wind, outlined the golf tournament's history and rise to prominence. Roberts, whom Wind described as "that one-man gang . . . 'the works,'" had been instrumental in organizing and establishing the tournament. He also had served as chairman of the Masters tournament committee since its inception in 1934.

488

EM, WHCF, Confidential File: State Department

To Bernard Law Montgomery
Secret

December 11, 1957

[*Dear Monty*]:[1] Your recent letter on Cyprus was very much appreciated here. Foster and I share your concern about the bad effect this controversy is having on the North Atlantic Alliance. I agree that some way has to be found to bring the Greeks and Turks closer together.[2]

I have already tried to persuade both the Greeks and the Turks to restrain themselves in the debates of the United Nations General Assembly because, as you say, bitter debate there would make a solution more difficult and could further interfere with the working of our Alliance. I also have urged the Greek Government to keep E.O.K.A. from further violence.[3]

You probably know that the United States is supporting Mr. Spaak's efforts to find some common ground between the Turkish and Greek positions in the hope that these efforts may contribute to some solution. During the NATO Meeting in Paris we will encourage the Greeks and the Turks to talk to each other directly.[4]

After the new Governor has had a chance to look over conditions on the Island and make his report to London, I think it might be worthwhile for us to go over with the British Government possible lines of action to see if there are ways in which we can further support Mr. Spaak's effort and encourage the Greeks and the Turks to make the sort of concessions of which you speak.[5]

As I am sure you know I am ready to do whatever is right to do to bring an end to this quarrel.

I look forward to seeing you in a few days.[6] *With warm regard*

[1] State Department officials drafted this letter (see Dulles to Eisenhower, Dec. 9, 1957, same file as document; see also Whitman to Bernau, Dec. 6, 1957, Dulles Papers, White House Memoranda Series; and State, *Foreign Relations, 1955–1957*, vol. XXIV, *Soviet Union; Eastern Mediterranean*, pp. 517–19).

[2] For background on the conflict among Great Britain, Greece, and Turkey over Cyprus see no. 92; see also State, *Foreign Relations, 1955–1957*, vol. XXIV, *Soviet Union; Eastern Mediterranean*, pp. 472–503. Montgomery had told Eisenhower that it was "high time we got the Cyprus problem settled." He recounted recent acts of terrorism by the National Organization of Cyprus Fighters (E.O.K.A.) and reminded the President that widespread terrorism would lead to renewed clashes between Greeks and Turks and weaken the anti-Communist front in the entire region. The United Nations debate on the Cyprus question "must be rendered harmless," Montgomery said, and the Greek government must control the E.O.K.A. to allow time for renewed efforts to reach a settlement. "We have got to break the log-jam *now* and avert another catastrophe. Somebody must bang together the heads of [the Greek and Turk-

ish leaders], and you are the man to do it" (Montgomery to Eisenhower, Nov. 1957, Dulles Papers, White House Memoranda Series).
[3] On July 12 Greece had asked for the inclusion of the Cyprus question on the agenda of the twelfth session of the General Assembly. Although the United States agreed to support any resolution agreeable to the three countries involved, it continued to emphasize that the only way to solve the problem was through quiet diplomacy. For more on this issue see State, *Foreign Relations, 1955–1957,* vol. XXIV, *Soviet Union; Eastern Mediterranean,* pp. 514–17, 519–20).
[4] During the previous two months NATO Secretary General Paul Henri Spaak had held discussions with both Great Britain and Greece. He proposed a settlement that guaranteed independence for Cyprus, a NATO base on the island manned by British forces, and international guarantees to preserve the rights of minorities (*ibid.,* p. 513).
Spaak would meet privately with the foreign ministers of Great Britain, Greece, and Turkey in Paris on December 18. Earlier on that day Greek Prime Minister Constantine Karamanlis would tell Eisenhower that the problem was having unfortunate repercussions in NATO and that Greece was prepared to support independence for Cyprus. He asked that the United States intervene in getting Turkey to accept what Karamanlis described as a simple solution—one that would benefit all parties involved. Although Eisenhower would confer with Turkish Prime Minister Menderes immediately after this meeting, the two men did not discuss Cyprus independence. Menderes would emphasize the importance of Cyprus to Turkish security and would tell the President that he supported efforts to find an early and just solution to the problem (State, *Foreign Relations, 1955–1957,* vol. XXIV, *Soviet Union; Eastern Mediterranean,* pp. 524–26, 747–48; State, *Foreign Relations, 1958–1960,* vol. X, pt. 1, *Eastern Europe Region; Soviet Union; Cyprus,* p. 577; and *New York Times,* Dec. 19, 1957).
[5] The British government had announced on October 22 that Sir Hugh Foot would succeed General John Harding as governor of Cyprus. For developments see no. 744.
[6] The two men would meet briefly at the airport when Eisenhower arrived in Paris on December 14. On the following day Montgomery would write Eisenhower, thanking him for his concurrence on the Cyprus problem. Obligations in England, Montgomery said, would prevent him from seeing the President again during his stay (State, *Foreign Relations, 1955–1957,* vol. XXIV, *Soviet Union; Eastern Mediterranean,* p. 521).

489 — *EM, AWF, Administration Series*

To Charles Douglas Jackson — *December 11, 1957*

Dear C. D.: I literally cannot possibly tell you how appreciative I am of your help on the Orly talk.[1] It's a wonderfully satisfying thing to know that you are always at the other end of the telephone, always perceptive to the thought I am trying to convey, and always capable of converting my somewhat scattered ideas into a coherent whole.

As you know, I wanted the original draft to be made a little more frankly sentimental. Now I think we have just about the document I wanted and while I shall probably tinker with it a little, I shall not make any major changes.[2]

Many thanks for your help. I include also a word of appreciation to Miss McCrum, since I understand she participated to a large extent in this long-distance transaction.[3]

With warm regard, *As ever*

[1] On December 4 Eisenhower had asked Jackson to "work up something frankly sentimental" that he could say upon arriving in Paris for the NATO meetings—something that expressed "his veneration for France, its greatness in times of crisis, its honor." Jackson had promised "to pull out all the stops" (Telephone conversation, Eisenhower and Jackson, [Dec. 4, 1957], AWF/D).

[2] Eisenhower had thought the original draft was too much of a technical discussion of NATO and had asked Jackson to rewrite it. The reference to NATO was included, Jackson said, "because of the character of the meeting and the presence of the Allies at Orly" (Jackson to Eisenhower, Dec. 6, 1957, AWF/A; see also Draft Remarks by the President, Dec. 6, 1957, AWF/A, C. D. Jackson Corr.). Although Eisenhower was satisfied with the revision, Secretary Dulles had thought that it was "too flowery and too long" (Telephone conversation, Eisenhower and Dulles, Dec. 10, 1957, Dulles Papers, Telephone Conversations). The President would deliver the speech—a tribute to the gallantry and honor that had "enriched and embellished France's success in war and peace"—on his arrival in Paris on December 14. He recalled the day Paris was liberated and told his audience that it was a day that lived brightest in his heart and would remain forever indelible in his life. "The record of France's accomplishment since the liberation of Paris is signalized by her visible progress in culture, in art and in productivity," Eisenhower said. "Above all else, it is signalized by her indestructible sense of destiny, and her readiness to meet the present and the future" (*Public Papers of the Presidents: Eisenhower, 1957,* pp. 830–32; and *U.S. Department of State Bulletin* 38, no. 967 [January 6, 1958], 15). For developments see no. 493.

[3] Marie McCrum was Jackson's secretary.

490 *EM, AWF, Name Series*

To Earl Dewey Eisenhower *December 11, 1957*

Dear Earl: Tom Stephens tells me that he had a satisfactory talk with you last evening. I am sure he ably represented my views on the subject on which you asked for my opinion. Needless to say, I think it would be well if when you talk to your friends, you say that you reached your decision *without* consultation with me.[1]

In answer to one of the points that Tom says you brought up—that of possible disagreement with my own views in the matter of voting, should the project have materialized, we both know that all the Eisenhower brothers have fought for nearly sixty years—and loved every minute of it!

With all the best to you and Kathryn for a happy holiday season, and warm personal regard,[2] *As ever*

[1] In an undated, longhand letter Earl Eisenhower had said that he had been asked to run for Congress in the tenth district in Illinois (AWF/N). He had declined be-

cause he believed "the situation in Washington would be intolerable" to the President and himself. His friends, however, did not agree. "Will you write me one line," Earl asked, "to show them exactly how you feel?"
[2] Earl's wife was the former Kathryn McIntyre.

491 — *Gruenther Papers*

To Alfred Maximilian Gruenther — *December 11, 1957*

Cher General: One of the greatest problems I have is to be sure of the quality of the advice I get. This is especially true when the adviser sets himself up as being so expert or so much a master in his field as to be able to coach me in what I should do.[1]

Before I could consider submitting myself to your "extra instruction" in French, I must make a test of your competence. To that end, I will have ready for you one or two passages of elementary English that I have rendered into French, to see with what facility you can re-translate them into the original text. So that you can sharpen up, I enclose a few practice paragraphs.[2]

Don't think that any assertion that the nuances are too finely drawn will have any weight with me—anyone who presumes to give advice must of course be held to realize that the finest shadings of philosophical thought are of extreme importance in the kind of activities I will be engaged in.[3]

I await four o'clock when I shall know whether, in these terms, you can really make good your offer.[4] *Sincerely*

[1] On December 10 former SACEUR Gruenther had written a witty letter suggesting that the President review his French before departing for the upcoming NATO meeting in Paris (see n. 3 below). Gruenther had enclosed "a few French phrases" and had asked Eisenhower to learn them "as a very very special favor." Gruenther also had anticipated Eisenhower's objections. "You will say: (a) 'I already know them,' (b) 'What business is it of yours?' and (c) 'What will be accomplished?'" Gruenther continued, "I respectfully submit that your French never was that good." Secondly, he said, he had "a vital interest in NATO," and he wanted Eisenhower to succeed. Finally, Gruenther acknowledged the President's hard work "to pull some tear jerkers" from his "bag of tricks." Sounding off with "'bon jour, mes amis'" at the first press conference at Orly Airport, Gruenther promised, would make all of France "swoon."
[2] Gruenther said he was prepared to give the President "individual instruction" at 4 o'clock this same day. We have been unable to find the paragraphs in AWF.
[3] The President would be engaged in meetings from early morning to late in the evening December 16–18. See no. 480; *New York Times*, December 11, 14, 17, 24, 29; and the Chronology.
[4] According to the President's daily appointments Gruenther would arrive at the White House at 4:04 P.M., and would leave at 4:10 P.M.

On the final day of the conference (Dec. 18) Eisenhower would cable Gruenther.

The message, written in French, said that although it would surprise Gruenther, "excellent" work had been accomplished without him. That same day Gruenther would reply that the French version of the message was garbled "indicating that the translation was made by an amateur." He gathered, however, that Eisenhower desired to thank him for his "great contribution" to the success of the conference. And he accepted "this credit," he said, "with usual modesty." All correspondence is in Gruenther Papers.

492 *EM, AWF, Name Series*

To Elivera Carlson Doud *December 11, 1957*

Dear Min: Do you know that it is a real job to find a Christmas gift for you, just as it is for your older daughter? I've struggled with the problem for days, and finally decided prayerfully that you might like a vase that appealed to me very much. It came to me as a gift from the people in a little town in Japan, as an expression of their appreciation for the friendly interest the American soldiers there had shown in the children of the community. It was such a nice thought—and such a lovely vase—that I wanted you to have both the vase and the thought. I hope you like it as much as I do.[1]

As you know by now, I have fortunately made such steady progress from my latest difficulty that the doctors have agreed that I can make the NATO trip.[2] Not only do I want to do whatever I can in this important project, but quite personally I want to see how the SHAPE establishment has improved since I was there.[3] I only wish that you and Mamie were going along with me, and—to make it absolutely ideal—that we would have freedom and time to enjoy ourselves as we used to do.[4]

I do hope you are feeling better. We shall be thinking of you constantly during the holidays and wishing above all that you could be with us.[5] *Devotedly*

[1] The people of Uenohara Town, Japan, had sent the vase in appreciation of the members of the armed services at the Yokohama Engineering Supply Center (signatures list, Dec. 9, 1957, AWF/D).

[2] On November 25 Eisenhower had suffered a mild stroke (see no. 477). On the upcoming NATO meeting (Dec. 15–18) see no. 480.

[3] Eisenhower had been designated the first Supreme Allied Commander, Europe (SACEUR) in December 1950. He had requested relief from the post in April 1952 in order to return to civilian status and actively campaign for the Republican nomination (see Galambos, *NATO and the Campaign of 1952*, nos. 1, 784, and 785). For Eisenhower's comments following his December 17 visit to the Supreme Headquarters of the NATO Forces see his memoir, *Waging Peace*, pp. 231–32.

[4] Mrs. Doud had visited her daughter and son-in-law in Paris on several occasions (see, for example, Galambos, *NATO and the Campaign of 1952,* nos. 235 and 240).
[5] For developments on Mrs. Doud's health see no. 612.

493

EM, AWF, Dulles-Herter Series

TO JOHN FOSTER DULLES
Cable

December 12, 1957

If you find it possible, I believe it would be well to obtain the texts, or at least the outlines, of the speeches to be made by Beck and Gaillard. The purpose of this would be to achieve some coordination in our talks and possibly eliminate repetition in the description of the nature of the challenge we face and the cataloguing of assets that we possess.[1]

You already have a copy of my Monday noon talk. I have done considerable rephrasing of Sections I and II in the interest of personalizing the beginning of the talk and to compress the text in this particular portion. Otherwise the text is largely unchanged.[2]

I probably will dispatch to you by cable the draft for the Orly talk so that Walters may put it into written French and will send to you for your further revision the Monday noon talk.[3]

My party and I are still counting on arrival at 3 P.M. Paris time Saturday.[4]

[1] Eisenhower had asked State Department officials to deliver this message to Secretary Dulles, who had left on this day for the NATO meetings in Paris. Félix Gaillard, France's Prime Minister, and Joseph Bec*h,* Premier and Foreign Minister of Luxembourg and president of the North Atlantic Council, would welcome the heads of government at the opening meeting on December 16. Both men would cite the interdependence of the Western nations and the need to reconcile political and economic differences, and both would stress the hope and confidence that Eisenhower's presence brought to the meeting. "None better than President Eisenhower," Bech said, "who is said to have a genius for conciliation, can ease the tension between the countries of the West" (Statements at the Opening Session of the NATO Council Meeting, Dec. 16, 1957, Dulles Personal Papers; see also State, *Foreign Relations, 1955–1957,* vol. IV, *Western European Security and Integration,* p. 220; and Eisenhower, *At Ease,* p. 375).
[2] Eisenhower and Dulles had reviewed the State Department draft of the speech before Dulles left for Paris. His only criticism, Eisenhower said, was that "it lacked punch and he thought it needed some hard-hitting paragraphs." He also thought that the focus should be on winning the peace; "the purpose was not to appear angry, but to appear enthusiastic." Dulles had suggested that Eisenhower rework the speech himself (Goodpaster, Memorandum of Conference, Dec. 12, 1957, AWF/D; see also NSC

meeting minutes, Dec. 13, 1957, AWF/NSC; Dulles, Memorandum of Conversation, Dec. 12, 1957, Dulles Papers, White House Memoranda Series; and Telephone conversations, Eisenhower and Dulles, Dec. 4, 1957; and Dulles and Cutler, Dec. 10, 1957, Dulles Papers, Telephone Conversations). After citing the progress European countries had made toward unity, Eisenhower would emphasize the vast resources of the NATO nations not only in material goods but "the political and moral assets that are national heritages." "The sense of sharing moments of crisis and decision is a moving and lasting one," he said. "Too often these moments come only in time of war. It would indeed be a tragedy if we could not, in waging peace, share the joy of common decision, common effort, and common sacrifice" (*U.S. Department of State Bulletin* 38, no. 967 [January 6, 1957], 3–6).

[3] For background on the speech Eisenhower would deliver upon his arrival in Paris see no. 489. For background on Vernon A. ("Dick") Walters, Eisenhower's long-time interpreter, see Galambos and van Ee, *The Middle Way*, no. 1220; and Vernon A. Walters, *Silent Missions* (New York, 1978), pp. 276–310.

[4] Among those traveling with Eisenhower were Presidential Science Adviser James R. Killian, Jr., AEC Chairman Lewis L. Strauss, Major John S. D. Eisenhower, General Howard McC. Snyder, General Andrew Goodpaster, and Ann Whitman.

494 — *EM, AWF, International Series: Nehru*

To Jawaharlal Nehru — *December 15, 1957*
Cable

Dear Prime Minister:[1] I have read with great sympathy your earnest and eloquent public appeal of November 28 on disarmament.[2] This is a matter which has also concerned me deeply for a very long time. In the days immediately following the end of World War II, the United States proposed that the dreadful power of the atomic bomb, which we alone then possessed, be forever denied all nations. We hope[d], instead, that the wonders of the nuclear age could be devoted wholly to the uses of peace. This plan was refused and we were left with no choice but to maintain our armed strength.[3] Since this time the United States has continued an unremitting effort to achieve a just system of disarmament and a secure peace for all nations. We have repeatedly stated our readiness, indeed our anxiety, to reduce the possibility of war through arms regulation and control, to stop tests of nuclear weapons, and to devote a part of our huge expenditures for armaments to the great causes of mankind's welfare. Our only concern is that these measures be accomplished in a way that will not increase the risk of war or threaten the security of any nation. We earnestly believe that the plan which we jointed with the United Kingdom, France and Canada in suggesting at the London disarmament talks on August 29 offers a meaningful opportunity for removing fear and gaining international trust.[4] It is a source of great personal regret to me that these proposals have not so far been found acceptable by the Soviet Union even as a basis for negotiations.

In these circumstances, I have been able to reach no other conclusion than that, for the time being, our security must continue to depend to a great degree on our making sure that the quality and quantity of our military weapons are such as to dissuade any other nation from the temptation of aggression. The United States, I can assure you unequivocally, will never use its armed might for any purpose other than defense.

I know that the subject of testing of nuclear weapons is of understandable concern to many. I have given this matter long and prayerful thought. I am convinced that a cessation of nuclear weapons tests, if it is to alleviate rather than merely to conceal the threat of nuclear war, should be undertaken as a part of a meaningful program to reduce that threat. We are prepared to stop nuclear tests immediately in this context. However, I do not believe that we can accept a proposal to stop nuclear experiments as an isolated step, unaccompanied by any assurances that other measures—which would go to the heart of the problem—would follow. We are at a stage when testing is required particularly for the development of important defensive uses of these weapons. To stop these tests at this time, in the absence of knowledge that we can go on and achieve effective limitations on nuclear weapons production and on other elements of armed strength as well as a measure of assurance against surprise attack, is a sacrifice which we could not in prudence accept. To do so could increase rather than diminish the threat of aggression and war. I believe that bolder and more far-reaching measures are required. Specifically, I believe that any government which declares its desire to agree not to use nuclear weapons should, if they are sincere, be prepared to agree to bring an end to their production. Agreement to devote all future production of fissionable material to peaceful uses is, as I see it, the most important step that can be taken. Together with this we have proposed that we begin to transfer to peaceful uses, on a fair and equitable basis, fissionable material presently tied up in stocks of nuclear weapons. We believe this is the way to a true reduction of the nuclear threat and to an increase in confidence among nations. We have not had a reasoned explanation from the Soviet Union of whatever objections it might have to this program.

I agree that it is in the power of my country along with those others who possess nuclear weapons to put an end to the fear and horror which the possibility of their use imposes. I want to assure you with all the sincerity of which I am capable that we stand ready, unbound by the past, to continue our efforts to seek a disarmament agreement, including the cessation of nuclear testing, that will promote trust, security and understanding among all people.[5] *Sincerely*

[1] The text of this message was sent to the White House from Paris where Eisenhower was attending the NATO meeting (see German to Whitman, Dec. 15, 1957, AWF/I: Nehru).
[2] Nehru's statement was an appeal to the leaders of both the United States and the Soviet Union to stop all nuclear test explosions and move toward effective disarmament in order to "save humanity from the ultimate disaster which faces it" (*U.S. Department of State Bulletin* 38, no. 967 [January 6, 1957], 18).
[3] On the Baruch Plan for international control of atomic energy, presented to the Security Council of the United Nations in December 1946, see no. 192.
[4] On the four-power disarmament plan see no. 364.
[5] For developments see no. 508.

495 — *Dulles Personal Papers*

To John Foster Dulles — *December 16, 1957*

The reason I'm trying to be good—because I'll play hookey tonight.[1]

[1] Eisenhower had written this note in longhand to Secretary Dulles toward the end of the opening session of the NATO meeting in Paris. The note appears below another note that Dulles had written saying: "I think that after [British Prime Minister Harold] Macmillan speaks, [NATO Secretary General Paul Henri] Spaak will 'sum up.' I should doubt you need to stay for that." Eisenhower had answered: "I would suppose Spaak would sum up tomorrow" (Dec. 16, 1957, all in the same file as document). Eisenhower would surprise the NATO delegates by announcing at the conclusion of the day's meetings that he would not attend dinner that evening with the other heads of government. When told of the resulting concerns for his health, an amused Eisenhower would suggest that Press Secretary James Hagerty: "Tell those gentlemen that I am a 9:30 or 10 o'clock boy tonight and I am going to bed at that time" (*New York Times*, Dec. 17, 1957). The President would dine at the American embassy with Dulles, John Eisenhower, and Ambassador and Mrs. Amory Houghton. For Macmillan's speech see State, *Foreign Relations, 1955–1957*, vol. IV, *Western European Security and Integration*, pp. 241–42; and Macmillan, *Riding the Storm*, p. 336. For developments see no. 493.

496 — *EM, AWF, International Series: Churchill*

To Winston Spencer Churchill — *December 18, 1957*

[*Dear Winston:*] Thank you so much for your personal note of welcome to Europe.[1] I have been feeling fine since I arrived here—and

I must confess that the many evidences of friendship shown me have been the best possible tonic. I do wish I could visit your country, but I want Mamie to be with me on such an occasion.

I know that the exhibition of your paintings will be outstandingly successful and an event that will excite and interest all Americans. Mamie and I look forward to having you as our guest some time the latter part of April.[2]

With warm regard, [*As ever*]

[1] In his welcoming message Churchill had told Eisenhower that if he had been able to include Great Britain in his tour, "we should not have been behindhand in showing you what we think and feel about you" (Churchill to Eisenhower, Dec. 16, 1957, AWF/I: Churchill).

[2] For background on the exhibit see no. 414. Churchill had chosen thirty-five paintings for the exhibition. He told Eisenhower of his hope that they would be "considered worthy of the honour you have done them." For developments see no. 568.

497 *EM, AWF, DDE Diaries Series*

To James Paul Mitchell *December 21, 1957*

Dear Jim: I have studied the memorandum that you sent me in response to the thoughts presented by Arthur Burns on the whole budgetary and economic situation.[1]

Your document reflects accurately my own general thinking on these problems.[2]

Almost everyone agrees with the basic thesis that balancing the budget is not so important as the performance of those governmental functions that are designed to sustain our security and promote economic development. The difficulties arise when each individual supports his own views as to the best way of observing this truth.

The thing that I particularly like about your memorandum is that it appeals to me as reasoned and logical. It avoids slavish adherence to slogans just as it refrains from impossible extremes.

I am sending a copy of your paper to the Secretary of the Treasury. I know that Sherman Adams has already read it and discussed it with Dr. Saulnier.[3]

With warm regard, *As ever*

[1] Former Council of Economic Advisors Chairman Burns had written the President on November 27 (Dulles Papers, White House Memoranda Series). Burns said that it was of "great importance" that the budget for FY 1959 "strengthen the confidence of people in their own and the nation's economic future." While a balanced budget

was desirable, it was not essential since the confidence of the American people would not be "impaired by a temporary budget deficit if they see an essential purpose (such as defense) or a conservative objective (such as tax cuts as a preliminary to closer control over expenditure) served by the deficit." The FY 1959 budget, Burns said, should bolster confidence by providing "for *dramatic* increases of expenditure for defense, scientific research, and education," while also conveying a need for austerity through "*dramatic* cuts of expenditure on agriculture, veterans' and welfare programs." Eisenhower had sent Burns's letter to various members of the Administration for comment (see Whitman to Dulles, Dec. 3, 1957, Dulles Papers, White House Memoranda Series).

[2] In his response to the President (n.d., AWF/A), Secretary of Labor Mitchell, said that a balanced budget, just for the sake of a balanced budget, was "not necessary at this time." He called for "prompt, definitive action by the Administration to bolster sagging business confidence and to prevent a further unduly rapid rise in unemployment." The budget, said Mitchell, "should be de-emphasized as a controlling factor in our economic policy." Mitchell suggested two major types of administrative steps which would not only strengthen the economy, but would "also permit businessmen to plan ahead." First, the government should accelerate expenditures for authorized and budgeted federal programs, including orders for missile and defense programs. The government should also, he said, stimulate construction by expanding the public roads program, by promoting the lease-purchase program for federal buildings, and by making mortgage loans more easily available to potential home buyers of modest means. See also Eisenhower, *Waging Peace*, pp. 217–19.

[3] Eisenhower had discussed Mitchell's letter with Sherman Adams in a telephone call on that same day (Telephone conversations, Eisenhower and Adams, Dec. 21, 1957, AWF/D).

498 *EM, AWF, DDE Diaries Series*

To Martin Withington Clement *December 21, 1957*

Dear Clem:[1] Thank you so much for your letter, which I found on my desk upon my return from the NATO Conference. I am more than grateful for your across-the-board support.[2]

Political problems—and by this I mean internal political problems—are the most wearing in this difficult job. I think perhaps I find them more frustrating than I should, but I am always upset when I know that a politician is putting selfish interest ahead of the interest of his country. So many of them do just that.

With best wishes for a happy holiday season, and much appreciation of your note,[3] *Sincerely*

[1] For background on Clement, former president of the Pennsylvania Railroad, see Galambos, *NATO and the Campaign of 1952*, no. 278.

[2] Clement was not writing a sympathy letter, he had told Eisenhower, because of the President's "recent little upset." It was more appropriate, he said, to sympathize with

Eisenhower's "problems from the vacillations of the splinter groups that once made up the Republican and Democratic Parties." Comparing American politics to French political factionalism, Clement wrote: "It has been interesting to me to see the de Gaullists on the right and the Communists on the left combine to upset the Government of France every few months. It is just as interesting here to see the 'de-Gaullists' on the right and the 'central state' boys on the left and some of the vagaries in the center gradually bringing an end to the representative form of government in the United States." Clement added that he supported Eisenhower "in whatever you are doing and am agreeing with your right to do it" (Clement to Eisenhower [Dec. 11, 1957], WHCF/PPF 610. On Eisenhower's stroke see no. 477; on the NATO conference, no. 501).

[3] Eisenhower added the handwritten postscript: "I am more than touched by your thoughtfulness in sending me such a message."

499 — *EM, AWF, DDE Diaries Series*

To Edward Bishop Dudley — *December 21, 1957*

Dear Ed: I enclose a clipping from the December issue of "The National Golfer." The author of the article, named Lester Rice, believes very much in the light club, particularly for people who do not have the opportunity to keep their hand and wrist muscles in good shape.[1]

In his description he does not mention "swing weight" but confines himself to talking of overall weight. In other words, he compares a 12½ ounce club to the heavier ones.[2]

I would like to have your comments on his article for the simple reason that I have believed, for a long time, that there are some advantages to using lighter clubs as one grows older and has fewer opportunities to exercise. In any event, I would like to have your opinion.[3]

I have just returned from Europe to find myself astonished with the speed with which the Christmas season is catching up with us.[4] I hope that you and Ruth will have a very splendid holiday season to climax your first months in Puerto Rico and that 1958 will be one of the best years for you.[5] Of course "Miss Mamie" joins me in best wishes for a Merry Christmas.

With warm regard, *As ever*

P.S. I am sending you a little gift that I hope you will like. Incidentally, I have an extra copy of a very handsome book called "The Spectacle of Sport" which, if you do not have one, I should like to send you as a New Years' present.[6]

[1] The article to which Eisenhower referred was entitled "Light Club Big Hitter." *The National Golfer* was published in San Mateo, California.

[2] For background on Eisenhower's interest in swing weight see Galambos and van

Ee, *The Middle Way*, no. 1492. Rice had explained to the "average player . . . how much easier he could swing a twelve ounce club rather than one of thirteen or fourteen ounces."

[3] Dudley would reply on January 2 that he agreed with Rice's observation. "The faster the club head the more distance anyone is to get," Dudley wrote. If Eisenhower could swing a lighter club faster, a reduction in swing weight might improve distance and accuracy. Dudley would offer to have a new set of lighter golf clubs made for the President. Eisenhower would accept Dudley's offer on January 7 and would say he was interested to see what difference the lighter golf clubs would make, especially regarding distance. On January 30 Eisenhower would tell Dudley he was "completely delighted" with the new set of clubs: "I have played so little golf of late that my wrist muscles are weak and I have no real basis for comparison of these swing weights with the old ones" (see also Tait to Eisenhower, Jan. 8, 1958).

[4] The President had attended the NATO conference of heads of government (see no. 480).

[5] On Dudley's move to Puerto Rico see no. 271.

[6] On January 2 Dudley would thank Eisenhower for his gift and would ask for the copy of the "Spectacle of Sport." For background see no. 487; see also Eisenhower to Dudley, January 7, 1958. All correspondence is in WHCF/PPF 1-A-7.

500

EM, WHCF, Official File 133-L

To Arthur Sherwood Flemming

December 24, 1957

Dear Arthur:[1] I cannot tell you how touched I am by your fine letter of the twentieth, or how grateful I am for the warmth and depth of your continuing friendship.[2]

The point you make—that we are helping other peoples because of our belief in spiritual values—has perhaps been neglected in some of the appeals for support for our mutual security programs. I don't want to take undue credit for an off-the-cuff thought, but perhaps we can use that approach more effectively than we have. Certainly I would like to enlist the confidence of the churchgoing people of the Middle and Far West in the programs that I believe to be so vitally important.[3]

Mamie joins me in best wishes to the Flemmings for a fine holiday season and a good New Year, and in warm personal regard. *Sincerely*

[1] For background on Flemming, former director of the Office of Defense Mobilization, see Galambos and van Ee, *The Middle Way*, nos. 52 and 1295. Flemming had resigned his ODM position in February to resume his duties as president of Ohio Wesleyan University; he would become Secretary of Health, Education and Welfare in August 1958.

[2] Programs that helped others to reach their highest potential, Flemming said, were

the most important to the nation. He noted that Eisenhower had told the Business Advisory Council that the belief in spiritual values and the desire to apply them to practical daily problems formed the basis of the country's foreign aid programs. Flemming had tried to express the same thoughts to groups of citizens, he said, and he had found that many church people, when challenged to view the aid programs in such a light, often respond positively. "When we are able to bring such people to the place where they see the relationship between the application of spiritual values and these programs we are tapping a source of real power as far as support for our program is concerned" (Flemming to Eisenhower, Dec. 20, 1957, same file as document; for background on the mutual security program see nos. 174 and 273).
[3] For more on mutual security legislation see no. 603.

501

EM, AWF, Dulles-Herter Series

To Harold Macmillan
Cable. Confidential

December 26, 1957

Dear Harold: One of the nicest Christmas presents I had yesterday was your warm message of greetings and good wishes. As you would know, I have been much preoccupied since my return from Paris, not only in preparing my part of Foster's and my joint report to the American people, but with public and private Christmas chores.[1]

I thoroughly agree with your appraisal that the NATO meeting was a definite plus for the free world. Added to that is my conviction that your stellar performance was one thing that accounted for such successes as we achieved.[2]

For a number of years I have had, in one capacity or another, occasions to confer seriously with individuals or governments other than American. Never have I experienced any greater degree of satisfaction in such conferences than in talks with you. Always your approach to any difficult task seems to be based upon fact, logic, readiness to consider opposing viewpoints, and what seems to be a never-failing friendliness.

I shall be very interested in your speech of the fourth, as well as in the message that you promise me before you start on your Commonwealth tour. Like you, I am concerned with what we should next do; by no means can we sit still. To do so would make certain of deterioration. Instead we must make certain that NATO becomes constantly a stronger, more confident and more peaceful organization—something that will come about only as all our partners, and most particularly as we two, everlastingly stay on the job.[3] Especially I was pleased to learn that we are getting additional task forces to keep after the business of concerting our viewpoints in particular situations, the latest one being Indonesia.[4]

With my warmest wishes for the holiday season and a successful New Year,

[1] For background on the NATO heads of government meeting see no. 493. In a radio and television address on December 23 Eisenhower and Dulles had said that the NATO countries had unanimously agreed to establish stocks of nuclear warheads that would be readily made available if the need arose and that intermediate-range ballistic missiles would be placed on the European continent. The NATO nations would work toward an effective disarmament agreement and had agreed to more sharing of scientific facilities and information. Dulles had cited the economic pressures exerted by the Soviet Union, particularly in underdeveloped countries, and said that NATO was committed to economic aid for "the capital-hungry free-world nations." The permanent representatives to NATO had pledged to keep each other informed of national policies that might impact the alliance (*U.S. Department of State Bulletin* 38, no. 968 [January 13, 1958], 47–52; see also Telephone conversations, Dulles and Hagerty, Dec. 22, 1957; Dulles and Stevenson, and Dulles and Knowland, Dec. 23, 1957, Dulles Papers, Telephone Conversations; for the communiqué issued at the close of the conference see *U.S. Department of State Bulletin* 38, no. 967 [January 6, 1958], 12–15; see also Eisenhower, *Waging Peace*, p. 232; Macmillan, *Riding the Storm*, pp. 338–39; and Spaak, *The Continuing Battle*, pp. 266–67).

[2] Although he was "brooding" over the next step, Macmillan had told Eisenhower that he thought their NATO colleagues were "thoughtful and anxious, but by no means lacking in courage or determination. In the new situation," he said, "the more active part we can make them play, the better it will be" (Macmillan to Eisenhower, [Dec. 25, 1957], AWF/I: Macmillan; see also Macmillan, *Riding the Storm*, pp. 336–41).

[3] In his nationwide broadcast on January 4 Macmillan would propose a nonaggression pact with the Soviet Union. Clearing away the "rubble of old controversies," he said, could lead to a summit meeting that included the Soviet Union (*New York Times*, Jan. 5, 1958); for his subsequent message to the President on January 2, 1958, see no. 508.

[4] The reference to Indonesia at the end of this sentence was deleted from the final outgoing cable (see Eisenhower to Macmillan, Dec. 26, 1958, AWF/I: Macmillan). Indonesian workers' groups had recently taken over Dutch enterprises as relations between the Netherlands and Indonesia deteriorated over the latter's claim to West New Guinea (see State, *Foreign Relations, 1955–1957*, vol. XXII, *Southeast Asia*, pp. 511–71; see also NSC meeting minutes, Dec. 6, 13, 1957, AWF/NSC; and Telephone conversations, Dulles and Alan Dulles, Nov. 29, Dec. 7, and Dec. 8, 1957; Dulles and Herter, Dec. 8, 1957; and Dulles and Cumming, Dec. 12, 1957, Dulles Papers, Telephone Conversations). The Netherlands prime minister had called upon the NATO heads of government to coordinate their policies in the area in order to prevent a Communist takeover (State, *Foreign Relations, 1955–1957*, vol. IV, *Western European Security and Integration*, p. 235). For a reference to the Indonesian situation in the communiqué see *U.S. Department of State Bulletin* 38, no. 967 (January 6, 1958), 13; for developments see no. 662.

502

EM, AWF, Name Series: Disposition Presidential Gifts

TO FRANK J. DONOHUE

December 27, 1957

Dear Mr. Donohue: First I want to thank you for coming to my office yesterday, with Mr. Ruschmeyer, to review my 1957 income tax liability.[1] I am so deeply indebted to you for the many instances of your kindly courtesy that I am almost embarrassed. At any rate, I do assure you of my lasting appreciation of your interest in my personal affairs and your helpfulness in seeing that they are properly handled.

One of the matters we have often informally discussed is that of disposing, legally and ethically, of any gift that has or may come from the Head of any foreign government, to me as President of the United States. In this letter I have tried to outline the gist of our agreed arrangements for carrying out this purpose, so as to assure ourselves that no misunderstanding can occur.

A basic fact is that the proffer of any such gift cannot be rejected by a President. To do so would cause resentment and misunderstanding on the part of the donor; it would become practically an "international incident." Yet such gifts manifestly do not belong to me as an individual. Consequently our agreement has been that I should make disposition of them in such way as to avoid any personal advantage accruing to me, and so that, eventually, they will be available to the public.

We have planned that these types of gifts are to be segregated from all others. They are, or will become, the property of some non-profit organization, the principal beneficiary being the Eisenhower Foundation at Abilene, Kansas. In this way these "President's" gifts will be available to the public but will, in the main, be concentrated in one spot, because of their availability to visitors. There are two ways in which this plan operates. One is by outright gift, already made, or to be made in the future. The other method is by disposal by bequest under the provisions of my will, long since made.

The preferred alternative is disposal by bequest rather than by immediate gift, even when the items are already located, on loan, in the Eisenhower Foundation. To dispose of such things by bequest will allow me, during my lifetime, to designate some alternative non-profit institution as the beneficiary. At the same time it will give to the Executors of my estate sufficient leeway to make certain that any item of special local interest could be treated separately, but always with some non-profit organization as the beneficiary.

Of course, all of the Orders, Degrees and personal gifts which, under general authorization of the laws in force during World War

II and during the years immediately thereafter, came properly into my possession, have been for many years part of my estate or already given away. A few of these have been gifted, as family keepsakes or memorabilia, to members of my family, and where necessary, required gift taxes have been paid. But in any case, these items, while bequeathed to the Abilene Foundation by my will, are completely separate from all those that come to me from heads of Governments during the period of my Presidency.

It is to these "Presidential" items that my special interest attaches. It is my hope that the Eisenhower Foundation will make one particular corner or room of the Museum available in which to concentrate these particular items. I have in mind such valuable things as the swords from Arabia and Morocco, jewels presented by Ceylon, and a number of items from the Emperor of Ethiopia.[2] I suppose there are others, but they can easily be identified when occasion necessitates.

With renewed thanks and warm personal regard,[3] *Sincerely*

[1] Donohue and Walter Ruschmeyer were certified public accountants with the firm of Haskins and Sells in New York City. A draft of this letter with Eisenhower's handwritten emendations is in AWF/N: Disposition Presidential Gifts.

[2] The Moroccan sword, received in November 1957, the Arabian sword, the jewels from Ceylon, and gifts from the Ethiopian Emperor are housed at the Eisenhower Museum in Abilene (Accession sheets, Dwight D. Eisenhower Presidential Museum). For another example of the disposition of a foreign gift see no. 395.

[3] Donohue would reply on January 6 that Eisenhower's letter clearly expressed "the substance" of their discussions, and that Haskins and Sells "shall be guided by it" (AWF/N: Disposition Presidential Gifts).

503 *EM, AWF, International Series: Norway*

TO JAMES J. WADSWORTH [*s.* HAGERTY] *[December 30, 1957]*
Top secret

For Wadsworth (thru State): President feels there is some misunderstanding implied by your message.[1] President listened with interest to Andvord's opinion that certain developments in USSR gave evidence of some political weakness in high places. President talked with Andvord only as an old friend, and stated if Andvord had any specific information or special convictions that these could be sent to President through President's personal secretary. While President stated he was interested in any move that gave real promise of lessening tensions, he expressed no opinion on matter. He did not, repeat did not, talk to Prime Minister or Foreign Minister except in briefest fashion and without mentioning anything related to message. There was no thought that anyone should act as an intermediatory.[2]

[1] Four days earlier Wadsworth, U.S. deputy representative to the United Nations, had told Secretary Dulles that during an alleged conversation between Eisenhower and Norwegian government officials at the recent NATO conference, the President had said that he was prepared to "take any step" that would lead to a "genuine lessening of tensions" and had told the Norwegians that they "could get in touch with him by having their ambassador in Paris contact [a] certain individual in the White House." Soviet officials in Oslo had subsequently informed the Norwegian prime minister that their government was interested in bilateral discussions with the United States in order to reduce tensions in Europe. Wadsworth asked Dulles if the President was interested in having Norway explore the idea further with the Soviets, and if so, what channel should be used (Wadsworth to Dulles, Dec. 27, 1957, AWF/I: Norway). After Dulles had indicated that he had no knowledge of Eisenhower's conversation with the Norwegians, State Department officials had asked the White House for clarification. Eisenhower had written this response at the bottom of a message asking James Hagerty if he could get the President to confirm that the conversation had taken place (Howe to Goodpaster, and Minnich to Hagerty, Dec. 30, 1957, *ibid.*).

[2] For background on Rolf Otto Andvord, former Norwegian ambassador to the Soviet Union and ambassador to France since 1948, see Galambos, *NATO and the Campaign of 1952*, no. 593. Although Dulles had met briefly with Norwegian Foreign Minister Halvard Manthey Lange at the NATO conference, we have found no record of Eisenhower's conversation with either Andvord or Prime Minister Einar Gerhardsen (see State, *Foreign Relations, 1955–1957*, vol. IV, *Western European Security and Integration*, p. 220). For Gerhardsen's visit to Washington in May 1958 see no. 694.

504 — *EM, AWF, Administration Series*

To Raymond J. Saulnier — *December 30, 1957*

Memorandum for Dr. Saulnier: I have studied carefully Chapter 1 of the Economic Report. On the text I have made a number of pencilled notations which are not intended as revisions; rather they merely raise questions for your attention. There are small portions of the text that are repetitious which may indicate a few deletions.[1]

I have also read Chapter II, but on this I have made no notes. It seems to me it is possibly more detailed and voluminous than is required—however, you may find that this is necessary for clarity.[2]

[1] On December 27 Chairman of the Council of Economic Advisors Saulnier had sent Eisenhower a draft of the annual Economic Report, noting that he would be "particularly grateful" if Eisenhower would read Chapter 1. "I have tried in Chapter 1," Saulnier said, "to present a balanced view of what we are striving to do in economic policy, and to show how our policy actions in 1957 were designed to achieve our

goals." Eisenhower had written on the letter: "Saulnier, I have made a no of notes on Chapt I, not as revision but as thoughts which I'd like to talk over with you." Saulnier's draft is not in AWF; for background see Saulnier, *Constructive Years*, pp. 96–116.

[2] Eisenhower would meet with Saulnier to discuss the Economic Report on January 10, 1958 (Ann Whitman memorandum, Jan. 10, 1958, AWF/AWD). The final report would be delivered to Congress on January 20, 1958 (U.S. President, *Economic Report of the President, 1958* [Washington, D.C., 1958]).

505 — *EM, AWF, Dulles-Herter Series*

To John Foster Dulles — *December 30, 1957*

Dear Foster: Again a year's end is upon us. Together we have spent twelve months in the onerous, demanding, often confining but always rewarding, work of the Federal government. So I want to try once more to tell you of my lasting appreciation of the great service you are rendering. To you and your associates I am deeply indebted for invaluable support and assistance. Specific instances are without number. They serve only to remind me of the real gratitude that I owe to all of you individually and collectively.

Above everything else, I want to thank you for your dedication to our country's welfare and for the unswerving loyalty which have characterized your work in our country's behalf.

As, together, we approach the New Year, to continue tasks already begun and to tackle those that will be new, I experience that lift of spirit that comes from the realization that I am surrounded and assisted by able and firm friends. My confidence in the future stems, in great part, from my knowledge that the Administration is rich in its possession of men of character, ability and integrity.

With best wishes for the happiness of yourself and your family, and for continued success, *As ever*

P.S.: In view of the intimacy of our long friendship, this letter may seem to you a bit on the formal side. It is not meant to be so. I am simply trying to make of record an expression of my grateful thanks.[1]

[1] This same letter, with some minor variations, was sent to members of the Cabinet and to White House officials (see the related correspondence in AWF/A, AWF/N, and Hagerty Papers). On January 3 Dulles would reply that Eisenhower's letter gave him "encouragement and inspiration . . . for the New Year" (AWF/D-H).

506

EM, AWF, Dulles-Herter Series

TO JOHN FOSTER DULLES
Personal

December 31, 1957

Dear Foster: I am in receipt of your memorandum of the 28th regarding a possible trip by you to South America.[1] I urgently believe something should be done![2] Could we use Dick? Then plan a summer trip for you—when climate is better?

Or, just possibly, I might, next summer do *part* of the tour. Could I do *some,* to supplement your own journeying, or would I have to make the rounds?[3] *As ever*

[1] Dulles had enclosed a memorandum he had received from Assistant Secretary of State Roy R. Rubottom, Jr. Rubottom had recommended that Dulles schedule a visit to the southern tier of countries in South America (Brazil, Paraguay, Bolivia, Chile, Argentina, and Uruguay) as soon as possible because of changes in the governments of those nations and deteriorating economic conditions (Rubottom to Dulles, Dec. 26, 1957, AWF/D-H). "I feel there is a real need," Dulles told Eisenhower, "as I have never gone to most of South America. On the other hand, there is the Baghdad Pact meeting the end of January, the SEATO meeting in March and NATO again in May." Eisenhower had handwritten all but the first sentence and the complimentary close of this letter at the bottom of Dulles's message (Dulles to Eisenhower, Dec. 28, 1957, *ibid.*).

[2] Ann Whitman misspelled "urgently" when she transcribed Eisenhower's handwritten message.

[3] Eisenhower had originally used two question marks to end this letter. After reconsideration, Dulles would tell Eisenhower that a Latin American trip combined with his other commitments "might give an impression of too much travel and too much absence from Washington," particularly when Congress was in session. He had, however, approved Milton Eisenhower's visit to Panama and Central America in June (Dulles to Eisenhower, Jan. 7, 1958, Dulles Papers, White House Memoranda Series). Vice-President Nixon would visit eight South American countries in April and May 1958; Milton Eisenhower would visit six Central American countries in July 1958; and the President would visit Brazil, Argentina, Chile, and Uruguay in 1960 (see nos. 658 and 968; and State, *Foreign Relations, 1958–1960,* vol. V, *American Republics* [1991], pp. 222–48, 249–66).

507

EM, AWF, Name Series

TO ROBERT BAUMLE MEYNER
Personal and confidential

December 31, 1957

Dear Governor Meyner: Some weeks back George Allen told me that you had expressed to him, informally, the desire to have a chat with me at some convenient moment in the early part of this year.[1] I assure you that I would enjoy such an opportunity.

In view of the practice of our columnists to draw unwarranted or distorted and unfortunate political implications from any such meeting, when political figures of opposite parties are involved, I would suggest that our talk be "off the record." If you would merely drop me a note, addressed in care of my personal secretary, Mrs. Whitman, I think we would have no difficulty with such a possibility.

Incidentally, the months of January and February should be very busy ones for me (the latter month includes plans for a visit to Georgia).[2] I would therefore suggest that we plan for a talk for some time in March.[3]

With best wishes to you and yours for a Happy New Year, and warm personal regard, *Sincerely*

[1] Meyner (LL.B. Columbia University 1933) was the Democratic governor of New Jersey. In 1947 he had served as senator and in 1950 as minority leader in the New Jersey senate. Eisenhower's old friend George E. Allen had spent December 4 and 5 with the President at his Gettysburg farm. Later this evening he and his wife would attend the Eisenhowers' New Year's Eve party.

[2] The Eisenhowers would visit Milestone Plantation in Thomasville, Georgia, February 13–23 (see no. 578).

[3] On March 4 Eisenhower and Meyner would meet privately at the White House for more than one hour (see Meyner to Eisenhower, Jan. 24, 1958, and Eisenhower to Meyner, Jan. 28, 1958, both in AWF/N). Eisenhower's memorandum describing the meeting is no. 592.

508 — *EM, AWF, Dulles-Herter Series*

To John Foster Dulles — *January 3, 1958*

Secret

Memorandum on letter of Prime Minister Macmillan dated 1/2/58:[1] I have noted certain specific suggestions of possible action that Harold has discussed in his long cable.[2] They are quoted in order:

1. "One course is to say that we stand on the four Power partial disagreement proposals."[3]
2. "We may, on the other hand, be prepared to go further than the four Power proposals."
3. "In addition to this, we must also have a view about the so-called policy of disengagement."[4]
4. "We must remember that we might be drawn into the wider problem of demilitarization or neutralization."
5. "We (ourselves) must surely work out an agreed policy for our two countries on all these issues."
6. "The Russians will also agree to inspection for this purpose, be-

cause they can do this without any of the disadvantages that would follow a whole system of inspection and control applied either to the manufacture of weapons or of fissile material."[5]

7. "From my own government's point of view, we could not accept the abolition or suspension of tests in the present state of our knowledge. . . . If you were prepared, after a revision of the Atomic Energy Act to make your knowledge available to us, our position would be different. . . . We would at least improve the chances of stopping the nightmare of all the other countries coming along with their tests."
8. "There are suggestions that we ought to aim at total nuclear disarmament. I think there would be great dangers if this idea were canvassed."
9. "We ought to clear our minds about these fundamental proposals because we are now approaching a point when it may not be possible to rely any longer on throwing the blame upon the Russians for the breakdown of negotiations." (This is a suggestion directed toward psychological factors and propaganda efforts).
10. "The only thing I would very much dislike is a special meeting of the Assembly of the United Nations."
11. "If the Russians will not cooperate in the new disarmament commission of the United Nations, we ought to renew our offer to talk direct." (Harold suggests first a meeting by Ambassadors to discuss an agenda, then a Foreign Ministers meeting, and finally, if necessary, a Summit meeting.) On balance, Harold believes that the "Ministers would be drawn from the NATO and Warsaw Pact countries, but would not be regarded as "representing each Pact."
12. "If our two governments could reach clear and agreed views on all these subjects, I myself would not shrink from what is called a Summit meeting, at the right moment."
13. "What it comes to is, are we prepared from the moral and political point of view to say: disarmament, to be fair and honest, must keep the balance?"
14. "We must, of course, produce an interim reply to Bulganin to keep things quiet."[6]

I have these other general comments:

A. When speaking about "total nuclear disarmament," Harold ignores our conviction that this kind of disarmament cannot be achieved with certainty. In other words, both the Russians and ourselves have publicly stated that bombs already manufactured can be so concealed that no known inspectional system could uncover them.

B. I think he is quite right in his implied conclusion that if our countries—all the Western Nations—should stand irrevocably on the "four Power partial disarmament proposal" we will be weakening our position in the cold war. As Harold points out, we have already indicated, in the NATO meeting, that we are ready to study other proposals.[7]

He is obviously toying with the possibility of a series of meetings, one of which might finally become a "Summit meeting." I think this subject will probably require more study on our part than almost any other. It is easy to get entangled in such a proposition but not so easy to get out of it.[8]

C. These two facts put upon us quite a burden of developing some new ideas—if we are both to become "flexible" in the study of other proposals and at the same time gain a propaganda advantage by being first in the field.

D. In some instances, I am not quite certain what Harold really means—for example, at the bottom of page two when he says "I am still a little uncertain as to where Adenauer really stands."[9] At another point he says "test inspectors would live in a desert." My own feeling is that test inspectors would have to be in a number of places with all of their equipment of every kind, if we are to determine that no tests have in fact taken place.

E. I think that the policy of "disengagement" would lead to some very great difficulties even though I recognize that the idea, in the abstract, appeals to me.[10] In my talk with Chancellor Adenauer he seemed most emphatic in his continued opposition to any thought of general neutralization or demilitarization.[11] However, assuming that we do *not* mean demilitarization of Germany, it would certainly be most difficult for SACEUR to establish an area in which his troops were armed in one fashion and another area employing different weapons. There is of course some sense to what Harold says about a possible "balance of advantage" in some measure of disengagement, if for no other reason than we would have secured a considerable degree of effective inspection.

In any event, my immediate reaction is that the disengagement theory should not be part of any new proposals that we might advance.

F. You and I recently spoke about nuclear tests with the renewed recommendation against their elimination.[12] This one I think we should look at very carefully and for my part I should like to see us get a law that would permit the British to have access to whatever weapon information that was necessary (a possible exception would be to give them certain weapons on the theory that these would substitute for any required information).[13]

G. The subject that we have promptly to study more intensively than any other is that of procedure.[14]

[1] Macmillan's letter from the London Public Record Office is dated January 1.
[2] The prime minister had been "brooding" about the future and had told Eisenhower that he would send him a long letter before beginning his commonwealth tour (see no. 501). Macmillan was concerned about disarmament and the support of the free world and the uncommitted countries. Disarmament discussions, he said, had always been "largely propaganda exercises" based on the assumption that the Soviets would never agree to Western proposals. He suggested that the United States and Great Britain should reevaluate their position, because the Soviet Union might be more willing than before to negotiate an agreement (Macmillan to Eisenhower, Jan. 1, 1957, FO 371/135279; see also Lloyd to Caccia, Jan. 1, 1957, *ibid.*; and Dulles to Lloyd, Jan. 3, 1958, AWF/D-H).
[3] See n. 7 below.
[4] The policy of disengagement contemplated establishing a neutral or partly demilitarized zone in Central Europe; see n. 10 below.
[5] Macmillan is referring to inspection as it applied only to the suspension of atomic weapons testing.
[6] For more on the December 10, 1957, letter from Soviet Premier Bulganin see the following document.
[7] On the disarmament proposals presented to the Soviet Union in August 1957 see no. 364. The decision to study other proposals was included in the communiqué released at the conclusion of the NATO meeting (see *U.S. Department of State Bulletin* 38, no. 967 [January 6, 1958], 13; see also State, *Foreign Relations, 1955–1957*, vol. IV, *Western European Security and Integration*, pp. 232–42, 244–48).
[8] For continuing correspondence regarding a summit meeting see no. 575.
[9] Macmillan was referring to Adenauer's position against the neutralization of the Federal Republic (see State, *Foreign Relations, 1955–1957*, vol. XXVI, *Central and Southeastern Europe*, pp. 341–42).
[10] The idea that both the NATO nations and the Soviet Union should remove or partially disarm (disengage) their forces from a central zone in the middle of Europe, leaving the area as a buffer between East and West, had been presented in various forms since 1952. Some proposals had included the reunification of Germany, which was unacceptable to the Russians, and others had included neutralization of the area, which the West Germans had rejected (see, for example, former British Prime Minister Anthony Eden's plan for demilitarization of the area in Galambos and van Ee, *The Middle Way*, no. 1523; see also Michael Howard, *Disengagement in Europe* [London, 1958], pp. 26–38, 54–62; and Hugh Gaitskell, "Disengagement: Why? How?" *Foreign Affairs* 36, no. 4, [1958]). Sentiment for some form of a disengaged zone had intensified after the Hungarian uprising (see Galambos and van Ee, *The Middle Way*, no. 2044). On October 2, 1957, the Polish foreign minister had presented to the United Nations a proposal (the Rapacki Plan) to establish a denuclearized zone in Poland, Czechoslovakia, the Federal Republic of Germany, and the German Democratic Republic. "The acceptance of the Polish proposal . . . offers certain advantages," Macmillan had written. "For example, the three Communist countries concerned are more than twice the size of West Germany, and the introduction of inspection into this large area would be an obvious asset" (Macmillan to Eisenhower, Jan. 1, 1958, FO 371/135279; see also State, *Foreign Relations, 1955–1957*, vol. XXV, *Eastern Europe* [1990], pp. 671–77; Macmillan, *Riding the Storm*, pp. 464–65; James L. Richardson, *Germany and the Atlantic Alliance: The Interaction of Strategy and Politics* [Cambridge, 1966], pp. 53–56, 233–36; and Timothy J. Botti, *Ace in the Hole: Why the United States Did Not Use Nuclear Weapons in the Cold War, 1945 to 1965* [Westport, Conn., 1996], pp. 99, 110).
[11] When the two men had met at the NATO heads of government meeting in December, Eisenhower had told the German chancellor that "nothing could be more wicked for Germany and the world than neutralization of Germany." Neutralization

would produce one result, he said, "absorption by the communists" (State, *Foreign Relations, 1955–1957*, vol. XXVI, *Central and Southeastern Europe*, pp. 345–47).

[12] Eisenhower had told Dulles that he thought it might be advantageous "to propose a suspension of testings with adequate safeguards." Dulles, however, was concerned that the British and the French, lacking the technical knowledge of the United States, "might want to go on testing unless we gave them all our information" (Memorandum of Conversation, Dec. 26, 1957, Dulles Papers, White House Memoranda Series).

[13] For background on the proposed amendments to the Atomic Energy Act of 1954 see no. 409. For developments on this issue see no. 628.

[14] In a note to Dulles referring to this memorandum, Eisenhower had written: "I doubt that it has any slightest value, but I send you a copy anyhow. I suggest you find a nearby wastebasket" (Jan. 3, 1957, AWF/D-H). For Eisenhower's answer to Macmillan see no. 514.

509 — *EM, AWF, Dulles-Herter Series*

To John Foster Dulles — *January 3, 1958*

Dear Foster: I am not certain that you had a copy of a recent note sent to me by Cabot Lodge. I quote its text:

> "There is no doubt that Bulganin's letter made a big impression at the UN. The so-called 'uncommitted countries seemed to agree with it and thought his points were reasonable. The countries on our side thought it was clever.[1]
>
> "I certainly wish we could get things organized so that we could make frequent specific offerings liberally peppered with sweet talk—for which the world, as I judge it here at the UN, has an apparently insatiable appetite.
>
> "This should not necessarily mean new policy decisions (useful though they undoubtedly are), but a technique of 'ringing the changes' on the policies we already have. We should be the ones to make the advances.

It seems to me that what Cabot is referring to are procedures and methods at the United Nations, rather than guidance, as to substance, from the State Department. I see some advantage of wrapping our proposals in different packages occasionally and tying them up in different colored ribbons.

I have already acknowledged Cabot's note.[2] *As ever*

[1] In his December 10 letter to Eisenhower, Soviet Premier Bulganin had decried the measures taken by NATO which, he said, would intensify the production of armaments and increase "preparations in general for war." Appealing for joint efforts to end the cold war, Bulganin had proposed that the Soviet Union, Great Britain, and the United States agree to a cessation of testing of all types of nuclear weapons be-

ginning on January 1, 1958, for at least two or three years. He proposed that the three countries refrain from placing any kind of nuclear weapons within the territory of East and West Germany. This decision, he said, could lead to the creation in Central Europe of "a vast zone with a population of over one hundred million people excluded from the sphere of atomic armaments—a zone where the risk of atomic warfare would be reduced to a minimum." He also called for a non-aggression agreement between the countries of the Warsaw Pact and NATO (Bulganin to Eisenhower, Dec. 10, 1957, AWF/I: Bulganin; Lodge's letter is in AWF/A).

[2] Eisenhower would use these same ideas in his reply to Lodge: "In other words," he said, "you are concerned with the wrappings of the packages that we have to sell. I am very much in favor of variety in this matter" (Eisenhower to Lodge, Jan. 3, 1957, AWF/A). Dulles would tell Eisenhower that he also agreed with Lodge's point of view (Dulles to Eisenhower, Jan. 3, 1958, AWF/D-H).

In discussing his reply to Bulganin with Dulles, Eisenhower would describe the Soviet premier's letter as "a masterpiece of needling" and not "the best piece of propaganda. We should be just as firm but get it more positive and have more hope in it" (Telephone conversation, Eisenhower and Dulles, Jan. 3, 1958, Dulles Papers, Telephone Conversations). For developments see no. 514.

510

EM, AWF, International Series: Ghana

To Kwame Nkrumah

January 3, 1958

Dear Prime Minister:[1] Since acknowledging the receipt of your letter of November twelfth, my advisers and I have given the most careful attention to the viewpoints and suggestions which you have advanced regarding the Volta River scheme.[2] As I think you know, this Government has followed with deep interest since their inception the extensive studies which have been made of this challenging project.

I, of course, fully appreciate the importance which you and your Government attach to the need for economic development and diversification in Ghana, and I know that I need not assure you of the friendly and sympathetic interest of the American people and Government. I have had a number of conversations with the Vice President since his return from the Independence Ceremonies and he has described to me the hopes and aspirations which guide your Government and people under your leadership.[3] It is obvious that these worthy aspirations can best be realized under the conditions of a strong, prosperous and stable Ghana.

As you are aware, we are not only interested in this vital task of Ghana's economic development and diversification, but desire to help in such ways as are within the limitations of our resources and other heavy commitments throughout the world. It has been in this spirit that we have undertaken, at your request, to send a technical survey group to Ghana to examine several specific project fields of potential economic development, the outlines of which have already been suggested by your Government.[4] It is my sincere hope that this team may be able to assist in drawing up practical projects capable of implementation in a manner which will contribute to the diversification which you seek.

In your letter of November twelfth, you have made specific reference to the possibility of obtaining a loan for the Volta River project from our newly created Development Loan Fund. In so doing, you have suggested in effect that such an indication of willingness by the United States Government to make a loan might provide the necessary stimulus to bring the scheme to life.

There is no question as to the desire of this Government to be helpful in the economic development of Ghana. At the same time, there are definite limitations on our lending activities imposed by the availability of funds for such purposes. Thus, in the case of a project of the magnitude of the Volta, we would have to have assurance not only that the project is economically and commercially sound, but also that the total financing which would be required to bring it to fruition is obtainable. In this connection it is apparent that the active participation of the aluminum industry and its ability to provide the requirements for the mining and manufacturing part of the project are essential to the success of the total project. I do not know how far you have been able to proceed in obtaining firm indications of intention to participate by the aluminum industry or in obtaining the necessary assurances of financial support from private sources, international institutions and other governments. Until such time as the project may reach the stage where Ghana has reasonable assurances from these sources, it is difficult for us to appraise the economic feasibility of the project, particularly in its financial and commercial aspects. When you have these assurances concerning the establishment of an aluminum industry this Government would be pleased to explore further with the Government of Ghana the possibility of assistance in financing a part of the project, such as a portion of the hydroelectric installation.

I hope that the foregoing suggestions may be helpful to you in your further efforts to interest private enterprise in the feasibility of this project. Meanwhile, I wish again to emphasize our general desire to be of assistance in Ghana's economic development program. If there are other specific project fields of a more limited nature than the Volta Scheme which you believe might be useful for our Technical Survey Group to examine, or should you perceive advantage in a more general survey of Ghana's essential development needs, we would be glad to consider broadening the terms of reference of the Group to make this possible. I hope that you will feel free to discuss any further questions you may have on these matters with our Ambassador to Ghana who is thoroughly familiar with the consideration we have given them here.[5]

Again, let me say how gratified I am at the spirit of determination to progress which prompted you to raise this matter with me. You can always be assured that Ghana's aspirations to a peaceful, prosperous and stable development, which is of such importance to its people, to Africa and to the free world, will command the sympathetic attention of this Government.[6] *Sincerely*

[1] The State Department drafted this reply to the Ghanaian prime minister.

[2] For background on the Volta River project and Nkrumah's November 12 request for U.S. aid through the Development Loan Fund see no. 440.

[3] On Vice-President Nixon's trip to Ghana see no. 11.

[4] "As a first step," Nkrumah had told Eisenhower, "perhaps consideration could be given to sending representatives of your Government to Ghana as soon as possible to discuss with us how best the project might be undertaken" (State, *Foreign Relations, 1955–1957,* vol. XVIII, *Africa,* p. 386).

[5] Wilson Clark Flake, former counselor of the embassies of South Africa and Italy, became U.S. Ambassador to Ghana in June 1957. Acting Secretary Herter had suggested that Flake, who was then in Washington for consultations with State Department officials, hand deliver this message to Nkrumah. "I believe it would help make the Ambassador more effective . . . if he were in a position to say he has discussed this matter with you personally" (Herter to Eisenhower, Dec. 30, 1957, AWF/I: Ghana; see also State, *Foreign Relations, 1955–1957,* vol. XVIII, *Africa,* p. 387).

[6] In his response (Jan. 17) Nkrumah would tell Eisenhower that U.S. interest in the project had given "us all fresh heart," and he would, as the President had suggested, "pursue the matter through the normal diplomatic channels" (AWF/I: Ghana).

Nkrumah would discuss the Volta project with Eisenhower during his visit to Washington on July 23–26. At that time Eisenhower would tell the prime minister that if the Ghanaian government could interest private aluminum companies in the project, the International Bank, the Export-Import Bank, and the Development Loan Fund might provide the remaining financing. The United States, Eisenhower said, would not forget Nkrumah's interest in the project (State, *Foreign Relations, 1958–1960,* vol. XIV, *Africa* [1992], pp. 645–53; see also Eisenhower to Nkrumah, Mar. 4, 1958; Nkrumah to Eisenhower, Mar. 7, 1958; Eisenhower to Nkrumah, July 28, 1958; Nkrumah to Eisenhower, Aug. 1, 1958; all in AWF/I: Ghana; and Reference Paper, The Volta River Project [July 19, 1958], *ibid.*).

In September 1959 Nkrumah would report his country's progress in eliciting proposals for the establishment of an aluminum smelter (Nkrumah to Eisenhower, Sept. 17, 1959, AWF/I: Ghana). Eisenhower asked to be kept informed (Eisenhower to Nkrumah, Sept. 25, 1959, AWF/I: Ghana). For developments see no. 1605.

511 *EM, WHCF, Official File 8*

TO WALTER HENRY JUDD *January 4, 1958*

Dear Walter:[1] Only one aspect of your January second telegram—which, incidentally, I warmly appreciate—gives me the slightest concern. That is your statement that "some in the government" are engaging in an organized attack against Secretary Dulles.[2] Presumably you mean people now in this Administration. This is the first I have heard of any such activity. If you can document it, please do. I should like to learn the identity of any such person.[3]

Foster has now, as always before, my total support and confidence. I cannot imagine how anyone, anywhere, could doubt that fact. His traits of character—as well as his intellectual honesty and diplomatic knowledge—all make him as nearly indispensable as a human ever becomes.

Knowing that he shares my respect and regard for you, I am sending him a copy of your telegram.[4]

With warm regard, *Sincerely*

[1] For background on Congressman Judd, who had been appointed in August 1957 as a delegate to the Twelfth United Nations General Assembly, see Galambos and van Ee, *The Middle Way*, no. 193.

[2] Judd had told Eisenhower that he was "profoundly disturbed" by the attack. "If alleged inflexibility means refusal to succumb to communist blandishments and threats," he said, "then please God give us more of such inflexibility" (Judd to Eisenhower, Jan. 2, 1958, same file as document).

[3] We have found no further correspondence from Judd on this matter.

[4] "I am deeply moved about what you say concerning me," Dulles would answer, "and will do my best to live up to your estimation" (Dulles to Eisenhower, Jan. 13, 1958, AWF/D-H; see also Harlow to Dulles, Jan. 9, 1958, same file as document).

512 *EM, AWF, Administration Series*

TO ARTHUR FRANK BURNS *January 4, 1958*

Dear Arthur: I was amused by your report of the difficulties encountered by the members of the American Economic Association in regard to their invitation to two Russians to read papers before the recent Convention of your Association.[1] And I do hope that your associates gained a certain tolerance for the difficulties of progress in the field of international relations, particularly with the Soviets.

When I left Washington I had not yet received the book based on your Fordham lectures. And, since I did not have an opportunity to read but a few of the ones you sent me in mimeograph form, I assure you that I look forward to the entire, published version.[2]

May I also thank you for keeping me informed of your current thinking on economic matters, and tell you once again how much I value your occasional reports?[3]

With warm regard to you and Mrs. Burns, *As ever*

P.S. I should like to know whether you were able to dispel any of the economic gloom in which your professional brethren apparently were living.

[1] Former Council of Economic Advisors chairman, Burns had written the President on January 2 (AWF/A) to report on events at the American Economic Association convention. The association had sent invitations through the Russian Academy of Science to two scientists. The Russians had not replied until shortly before the meeting, when the invitation was accepted on behalf of only one of the desired men. The Soviets substituted an unknown person in place of the second scientist, and gave as the title of his speech something "which bore some such propagandistic ring as The Economic Aspects of Peaceful Coexistence." After several delays which necessitated difficult rearrangements in the program, the Russian scientists never appeared. "You can imagine the consternation of the professors!" Burns wrote. "For the first time in many a month they had some kind words for Foster Dulles and the State Department." See also *New York Times*, December 18, 29, 1957.

[2] On *Prosperity Without Inflation*, a collection of Burns's lectures delivered at Fordham University in October 1957, see no. 216.

[3] Burns had written Eisenhower that the atmosphere at the Economic Association Convention was one of "gloom" about American economic prospects. "There is surely room and need," Burns said, "for concern about the current recession, but I had the feeling that my professional brethren were overdoing things." See also nos. 204 and 429.

513 *EM, AWF, Name Series*

To William Edward Robinson *January 5, 1958*

Dear Bill: While I agree with your comments regarding the irresponsibility of some—by no means all—of the people in the newspaper business, I am somewhat astonished at the vehemence of your convictions. Incidentally, I had much the same thing said to me by one of my friends who listened to the yearly round-ups of world affairs given by some of the reporters stationed in other world capitals.[1]

I am trying to work your specific suggestion into the State of the Union speech.[2]

Seemingly I have lost personal contact with you this holiday season, something we must remedy as soon as I get over the next few hurdles.

With all the best to you personally for a fine New Year, and warm regard, *As ever*

[1] Coca-Cola Chief Executive Officer and long-time friend Robinson had written on December 30, 1957 (AWF/N) to express his distress with the many newspaper articles, editorials and cartoons that in the wake of Sputnik criticized the United States for its failure to keep pace with the Soviet Union in science and technology. Robinson wrote that one of his friends "was commenting rather triumphantly that *The Daily Worker* was going to have to cease publication. My comment was that it was no longer necessary to the communist cause since the American press was doing the job." "Is there any justification for a Sputnik to create a cacophony of petulant and frantic voices which are intent on substituting fear, terror and dissension for the nation's natural virtues?" he asked. "Why can't these hairshirted quick-bleeders compare the forty-year history of the communists with the last forty years in the United States?" For background see nos. 389 and 396.

[2] Robinson had urged Eisenhower to use the State of the Union message "to remind the world of the characteristic courage, confidence and faith of the American public," while condemning "those who would substitute panic, fear and terror as appropriate motivations for our people." "This is not only a time for reaffirmation of our confidence and our faith; it is also a time for casting out the evil spirits," Robinson said. On the January 9, 1958, State of the Union Address see no. 526. See also *Public Papers of the Presidents: Eisenhower, 1958*, pp. 2–15.

514

EM, AWF, International Series: Macmillan

To Harold Macmillan — *January 5, 1958*

Cable. Confidential

Dear Harold: I thank you for your letter of January 2 with its intimate insight into your thinking about the problems with which the Soviets confront us.[1] It is indeed useful for us thus to "think out loud" to each other when, as is too much the case, we cannot sit down and chat together.

I do not have time before your departure to make a full and considered reply in the exact terms of your letter.[2] But it happens that Foster and I had during the New Year period been thinking hard about these problems in terms of replying to Mr. Bulganin's letter.[3] Yesterday Foster gave Harold Caccia, for transmission privately to you and Selwyn, the full, although still tentative, text of what I have in mind to say. This covers in large part the same field as does your letter and will in that sense serve to give you our thinking about the subject matter of your own letter.[4]

There is one other point which you particularly emphasize, that is whether, if nuclear tests are suspended, we can give you all of the information which we will have garnered from our tests. The answer to that is that we shall seek from the Congress broad discretionary authority to do that. I hope we shall get it; but that is by no means certain.[5]

Until Foster read me the message he received this morning from Harold Caccia, I was somewhat disturbed by the passage in your broadcast of yesterday which suggested making a fresh start with the Russians by negotiating a pact of non-aggression.[6] We would, I think, have very considerable difficulty with that. Already leading Foreign Relations Committee Senators, Republican and Democratic, have questioned the wisdom of this approach and there would be grave doubt that we could get Senate ratification. It is widely felt that if the Soviet word is dependable we already have a non-aggression pact in the United Nations Charter provision against the use of force. If their word is not dependable, why do we seem to accept it as such by repeating the same words over? Will not this create a false sense of security and be used in some quarters as an excuse for reducing our security efforts? One immediate reaction from an important quarter here is that if Western Europe thinks that a non-aggression pact with the Soviets has value, then we can pull out our United States forces there.

No doubt this passage in your broadcast has been overemphasized by our press and radio commentators and too much separated from the context. I am glad, however, to have your assurances that the suggestion does not represent any revision of your thinking on the Russian problem and that otherwise you would have consulted with me first. If you could do anything to shift the emphasis it would, from our standpoint at least, be helpful and in the interest, as you put it, of making sure that we "keep together".[7]

I send you my best wishes for a successful trip to the East and shall look forward with great interest to learning the impressions you derive.

As you doubtless know, Foster is going to the Baghdad Pact meeting later this month. This is responsive to Selwyn's strong urging and will I hope be helpful in indicating our support of and interest in the Pact, even though, for what still seem to be good reasons, we are not formal members.[8] *Faithfully yours*

[1] Macmillan's letter, with Eisenhower's handwritten marginal notations, is in AWF/I: Macmillan. For background see no. 508.

[2] Macmillan would leave on a five-week tour of the commonwealth nations on January 7 (see Macmillan, *Riding the Storm*, pp. 384–414).

[3] Soviet Premier Bulganin had written to both Eisenhower and Macmillan on December 10. See no. 508 for background.

[4] Two days earlier Dulles had sent Eisenhower a draft of a suggested reply to Bulganin to be discussed "on a very private basis" with Macmillan. After Macmillan had

had an opportunity to make suggestions, Dulles said, the draft would be shown to the NATO council and then sent in final form (Dulles to Eisenhower, Jan. 3, 1958, Dulles Papers, White House Memoranda Series; see also Telephone conversation, Dulles and Eisenhower, Jan. 3, 1958, Dulles Papers, Telephone Conversations). Eisenhower's reply to Bulganin is no. 521.

[5] On amending the Atomic Energy Act of 1954 see nos. 409 and 628; see also Telephone conversations, Dulles and Strauss, January 2, 1958; and Dulles to Caccia, January 4, 1958, Dulles Papers, Telephone Conversations.

[6] In a nationwide broadcast on the preceding day Macmillan had proposed "a solemn pact of non-aggression" between Western nations and the Soviet Union as a first step toward resolution of differences (see Party Political Broadcast by the Prime Minister, Jan. 4, 1958, PREM 11/[2462]; and Macmillan, *Riding the Storm*, pp. 461–64). After the broadcast British Ambassador Caccia had told Macmillan that Eisenhower was "getting het up" and that the President "would have hoped that such a proposal should not have been made in public without some warning, or better still, prior consultation." Caccia suggested to Macmillan that he send Eisenhower "some personal and reassuring message" (Caccia to Macmillan, Jan. 4, 1958, PREM 11/[2462]).

The Foreign Office had instructed Caccia to tell Dulles that Macmillan was distressed by the thought that he had upset the President. Macmillan's point, Caccia reported, was "that mere verbal agreements were inadequate by themselves" to secure peace. The press had given the suggestion of a non-aggression pact "undue prominence" and the idea did not represent a revision of British policy (Foreign Office to Caccia, Jan. 5, 1958, *ibid.*; see also Telephone conversations, Dulles and Herter, Jan. 4, 1958; Dulles and Caccia, and Dulles and Eisenhower, Jan. 5, 1958, Dulles Papers, Telephone Conversations).

[7] Dulles had asked Caccia to request that the British minimize the proposal for a pact: "There was no chance at all of Senate approval, and it would be tragic if the United Kingdom and the United States were at this stage to appear at variance on such a point" (Caccia to Foreign Office, Jan. 5, 1958, PREM 11/[2462]).

[8] The meeting would be held in Ankara, Turkey, from January 27–30 (see State, *Foreign Relations, 1958–1960*, vol. XII, *Near East Region; Iraq; Iran; Arabian Peninsula* [1993], pp. 32–33).

For developments see the following document.

515 — *EM, AWF, International Series: Macmillan*

To Harold Macmillan — *January 6, 1958*

Dear Harold:[1] Your note was most gratifying to Foster and me because of the similarity in your and our views on the Bulganin letter and because it has reassured us on the real meaning of one passage in your Saturday speech.[2]

We have been most interested in your weekend political preoccupations. You have had your share of tough breaks, and I am filled with admiration for your handling of them.[3]

I hope your trip will be a great success.

[1] Eisenhower's handwritten draft of this message is in AWF/I: Macmillan. Ann Whitman telephoned the text to British Ambassador Harold Caccia, who copied it in longhand. Whitman had relayed Secretary Dulles's request that Caccia do everything possible to get the message to Macmillan before he left on his tour of the commonwealth countries the following day (Ann Whitman memorandum, Jan. 6, 1958, AWF/AWD; and Caccia to Foreign Office, Jan. 6, 1958, PREM 11/[2462]).

[2] Macmillan's note to Eisenhower said that he had been working on his draft reply to Bulganin and that the Prime Minister's approach was consistent with the President's (Macmillan to Eisenhower, Jan. 6, 1958, AWF/I: Macmillan). Eisenhower's reply to the Soviet Premier is no. 521. For background on Bulganin's December 10 letter see no. 509.

On Macmillan's controversial speech see the preceding document. The prime minister apologized for any disturbance the speech might have caused. "The reference to a non-aggression pact has been high-lighted by the press in a way which I certainly did not intend and which the context does not support," he wrote. "I am sure there is no real difference between your thought and mine on this; if I were not, I would of course certainly have got in touch with you before the broadcast."

[3] Inflationary pressures and economic instability as the result of a weakened pound had plagued the British economy throughout 1957. Although the government had raised the bank interest rate in an attempt to stabilize the pound, efforts to balance the budget had resulted in the resignation of several officials, including the chancellor of the exchequer and the economic and financial secretaries to the treasury (Macmillan, *Riding the Storm*, pp. 342–74; and *New York Times*, Jan. 7, 1958). Dulles had described Macmillan's "bad weekend" to Eisenhower. Foreign Secretary Selwyn Lloyd had appealed for U.S. help "to try to underplay the situation," and Dulles had spoken to Treasury Secretary Anderson about the matter (Telephone conversation, Eisenhower and Dulles, Jan. 6, 1958, AWF/D).

In Eisenhower's original draft, this sentence had included the words: "I am astonished that in view of your week end political preoccupations that you should attempt a speech at all."

516 — *EM, AWF, Name Series*

To Milton Stover Eisenhower — *January 6, 1958*

Dear Milton: I had exactly the opposite reaction as a result of our conversation the other evening to the one that was expressed by you in your note of the third.[1] I felt that you had been most helpful, not only in informing me of some of our nation's educational needs, but in suggesting some different handling of the particular recommendations by HEW.

Unfortunately governmental plans and programs represent a technical as well as a philosophical view of such problems; indeed they reflect self and group interest as well.

So I think our three-cornered conversation the other evening did a lot that should be helpful both to Jim Killian and to me.[2]

With respect to the possibility of a Central American trip, I would very much like State to look into it. I do not want to put any burden on you this summer, but I cannot fail to believe that such a visit would be helpful.[3]

As you know, the summer season is particularly bad in Panama, but in the other Central American countries I think that the altitude would do something to alleviate the discomfort of the hot weather.

In any event, I shall find out either directly or from you what the State Department's views are.

All the best, *As ever*

[1] Eisenhower's brother Milton had written on January 3 (AWF/N) to note that he felt "discouraged" by his failure to make his main point during the previous evening's discussion with the President and Dr. James R. Killian, Jr., on the government's role in education. Milton said that he believed "that the government could, by using the right criteria in its scholarship, fellowship, and other programs not only achieve its own security purposes, but could also stimulate educators to bring about basic reforms needed in education quite apart from security considerations."

[2] Killian had been appointed Special Assistant to the President for Science and Technology on November 15, 1957 (see no. 396). In the wake of Sputnik Eisenhower had acknowledged the need to develop American science and education to keep pace with the Soviet Union (see nos. 447 and 448). In his January 9, 1958, State of the Union Address, Eisenhower would list education as one of eight areas in which federal action was "imperative." He called for HEW to "encourage improved teaching quality and student opportunities," and for a "five-fold increase" in the funds available to the National Science Foundation to stimulate education and research. The President urged "state and local governments, private industry, schools and colleges, private organizations and foundations, teachers, parents, and—perhaps most important of all—the student himself" to redouble their efforts on behalf of education (see *Public Papers of the Presidents: Eisenhower, 1958*, pp. 2–15. On the struggle to launch a federal program to support higher education in science and the humanities see Divine, *The Sputnik Challenge*, pp. 47–58; and Clowse, *Brainpower for the Cold War*, pp. 55–65.

[3] In his letter Milton had said that he had forgotten to mention his discussion with the State Department regarding a possible goodwill visit to the five Central American countries and Panama the summer of 1958. He noted that while it did not seem to be a good time to visit the Caribbean, conditions seemed favorable to visit Central America and Panama, and that he already had personal invitations from three of the presidents. For Milton's account of the trip see no. 947, and his memoir, *The Wine is Bitter*, pp. 208–28.

517 — *EM, AWF, Administration Series*

To Richard Milhous Nixon — *January 7, 1958*

Dear Dick: Since the State of the Union is, I am afraid, going to block out of my mind such an important matter as your birthday on Thursday, I send you this note to be sure that I extend to you my warmest felicitations on your anniversary and best wishes for your happiness, health and success in the years ahead.[1]

At the same time, may I say once again how grateful I am for your understanding and help over these last difficult weeks?[2]

With warm regard—and Happy Birthday! *As ever*

[1] Nixon would turn forty-five on January 9. On this same day Eisenhower would deliver his State of the Union Address (see no. 513).

[2] The President had suffered a cerebral occlusion on November 25 and had traveled to Paris to attend the NATO meeting in mid-December (see nos. 477 and 501).

518

EM, WHCF, President's Personal File 1751

To Edward C. Thayer

January 7, 1958

Dear Mr. Thayer: I was so pleased and complimented by the excerpt of the letter you wrote your mother in January, 1918, that I asked Bobby Cutler for your address so that I might tell you personally what a lift your comments of so long ago gave me.[1] It's difficult at any time of life to judge oneself, and I find it particularly hard to remember what I might have been like at twenty-eight.[2] At any rate, it's nice to know that I did not make too bad an impression upon the Reserves at Fort Leavenworth!

With many thanks for letting me have the original letter,[3] and with best wishes for a fine New Year, *Sincerely*

[1] Thayer (LL.B. Harvard 1917) was an attorney with the firm of Rackemann, Sawyer and Brewster in Boston. While looking through his mother's effects, he had come upon the letter and sent it along with the excerpted paragraph describing the President to Special Assistant Cutler (Cutler to Eisenhower, Jan. 6, 1958, same file as document). In January 1918 Thayer had been one of a group of provisional second lieutenants stationed at Fort Leavenworth and trained by Eisenhower. According to Cutler, Thayer thought the President "might be diverted by this 40-year old appraisal" of himself. "Probably there are not many living people who can look at an estimation of themselves made by a Yankee forty years ago which makes such agreeable reading," Cutler had written.

Thayer's letter had referred to Captain Eisenhower as "one of the most efficient and best Army officers in the country." He is "a corker," Thayer continued, who "has put more fight into us in three days than we got in all the previous time we were here. . . . He knows his job, is enthusiastic, can tell us what he wants us to do and is pretty human, though wickedly harsh and abrupt" (*ibid.*). For Eisenhower's account of his three-month assignment at Fort Leavenworth see his memoir, *At Ease*, pp. 132–33.

[2] In fact, Eisenhower had been twenty-seven in January 1918.

[3] Thayer had inquired if the President would like the original for his archives (*ibid.*).

519 *EM, AWF, Administration Series*

To Sherman Adams *January 8, 1958*

Dear Sherman: Another "year" is about to begin for you, and on this, your birthday anniversary, I want once again personally to express to you my admiration of your steadfast loyalty and tremendous contribution to the functioning of the White House staff, to the work of the entire Administration and to the people of America.[1] I hope someday someone will write a book that will put in proper perspective the great strength and integrity that are so characteristic of you, and that—because you are you—have influenced so greatly *all* the functioning of the Administration. Until that time I can only thank you.

I have wandered from my subject, but I primarily want only today to extend my warmest felicitations and wish for you and your family the best of everything in the years ahead.[2]

With personal regard, *Sincerely*

[1] Adams was born January 8, 1899. For another example of the President's esteem for the Assistant to the President see no. 393.

[2] For developments on the Eisenhower-Adams relationship see no. 753.

520 *EM, AWF, Dulles-Herter Series*

To John Foster Dulles *January 11, 1958*

Dear Foster: I note from a recent memorandum that some members of your staff seem to feel a responsibility for fixing some special time for President Coty's possible trip to Washington.[1]

On three different occasions President Coty emphatically told me he could not plan such a trip at any particular time. He had several reasons: (*a*) political—and he intimated winter months would be pretty bad for him; (*b*) climatic—he is very fearful of extremely hot weather. In fact, he said his health was not sufficiently rugged to undertake such a trip except under the most favorable climatic circumstances. He did once say that he thought the middle of May or early June might be nice. And (*c*) preoccupation with the hope of amending partially the French Constitution.[2]

My invitations to him were made as sincere and warm as I could make them in my limited French or through the means of an interpreter. But finally we agreed that the invitation should be kept constantly open until such time as he and I had the opportunity to work out between us a suitable date.[3]

So unless there have been some developments of which I know nothing, I believe that the most I should do is to find an opportunity to assure President Coty once more of our readiness to welcome him and his daughter to Washington.[4]

With warm regard, *As ever*

[1] A French cabinet crisis had forced President René Coty to postpone a planned state visit to Washington in June 1957 (see no. 152). We have been unable to locate the memorandum Eisenhower mentions.

[2] Conversations with Coty had occurred during the heads of government meeting in Paris in December 1957 (see no. 501).

[3] At the close of the NATO meetings Eisenhower had thanked Coty for the "heart-warming welcome" he had received from the French people and invited the French president to visit the United States at any time during the following three years (Eisenhower to Coty, Dec. 19, 1957, AWF/A, NATO Briefing Papers). Coty had replied that he would be delighted to visit the United States as soon as the French political situation had stabilized enough to avoid "the bitter disappointment" of the previous June (Coty to Eisenhower, Dec. 27, 1957, AWF/I: France).

[4] Eisenhower would assure the French president that he understood his difficulties and that an invitation to visit the United States would remain "constantly open until such time as it may be feasible to work out a mutually convenient date" (Eisenhower to Coty, Jan. 16, 1958, *ibid.*). For developments see no. 563.

521

EM, AWF, International Series: Bulganin

To Nikolai Aleksandrovich Bulganin *January 12, 1958*

Dear Mr. Chairman: When on December tenth I received your communication, I promptly acknowledged it with the promise that I would in due course give you a considered reply.[1] I now do so.

Your communication seems to fall into three parts: the need for peace; your contention that peace is endangered by the collective self-defense efforts of free world nations; and your specific proposals. I shall respond in that same order and make my own proposals.

I.

Peace and good will among men have been the heartfelt desire of peoples since time immemorial. But professions of peace by governmental leaders have not always been a dependable guide to their actual intentions. Moreover, it seems to me to be profitless for us to debate the question of which of our two governments wants peace the more. Both of us have asserted that our respective peoples ardently desire peace and perhaps you and I feel this same urge equally. The heart of the matter becomes the determination of the terms on which the maintenance of peace can be assured, and the confidence that each of us can justifiably feel that these terms will be respected.

In the United States the people and their government desire peace and in this country the people exert such constitutional control over government that no government could possibly initiate aggressive war. Under authority already given by our Congress, the United States can and would respond at once if we or any of our allies were attacked. But the United States cannot initiate war without the prior approval of the peoples' representatives in the Congress. This process requires time and public debate. Not only would our people repudiate any effort to begin an attack, but the element of surprise, so important in any aggressive move, would be wholly lacking. Aggressive war by us is not only abhorrent; it is impractical and impossible.

The past forty years provide an opportunity to judge the comparative peace records of our two systems. We gladly submit our national record for respecting peace to the impartial judgment of mankind. I can assure you, Mr. Chairman, that in the United States the waging of peace has priority in every aspect, and every element, of our national life.

II.

You argue that the danger of war is increased because the United States and other free world nations seek security on a collective basis and on the basis of military preparedness.

Three times in this century wars have occurred under circumstances which strongly suggest, if indeed they do not prove, that war would not have occurred had the United States been militarily strong and committed in advance to the defense of nations that were attacked.

On each of these three occasions when war came, the United States was militarily unprepared, or ill-prepared, and it was not known that the United States would go to the aid of those subjected to armed aggression. Yet now it appears, Mr. Chairman, that you contend that weakness and disunity would make war less likely.[2]

I may be permitted perhaps to recall that in March 1939, when the Soviet Union felt relatively weak and threatened by Fascist aggression, it contended that aggression was rife because "the majority of the non-aggressive countries, particularly England and France, have rejected the policy of collective security", and Stalin went on to say that the policy of "Let each country defend itself as it likes and as best it can . . . means conniving at aggression, giving free reign to war."

Now the Soviet Union is no longer weak or confronted by powerful aggressive forces. The vast Sino-Soviet bloc embraces nearly one billion people and large resources. Such a bloc would of course be dominant in the world were the free world nations to be disunited.

It is natural that any who want to impose their system on the world should prefer that those outside that system should be weak and divided. But that expansionist policy cannot be sanctified by protestations of peace. Of course the United States would greatly prefer it if collective security could be obtained on a universal basis through the United Nations.

This was the hope when in 1945 our two governments and others signed the Charter of the United Nations, conferring upon its Security Council primary responsibility for the maintenance of international peace and security. Also, by that Charter we agreed to make available to the Security Council armed forces, assistance and facilities so that the Council could maintain and restore international peace and security.

The Soviet Union has persistently prevented the establishment of such a universal collective security system and has, by its use of the veto—now 82 times—made the Security Council undependable as a protector of the peace.

The possibility that the Security Council might become undependable was feared at the San Francisco Conference on World Organization, and accordingly the Charter recognized that, in addition to reliance on the Security Council, the nations possessed and might exercise an inherent right of collective self-defense. It has therefore been found not only desirable but necessary, if the free nations are to be secure and safe, to concert their defensive measures.

I can and do give you, Mr. Chairman, two solemn and categorical assurances:

(1) *Never* will the United States lend its support to any aggressive action by any collective defense organization or any member thereof;

(2) *Always* will the United States be ready to move toward the development of effective United Nations collective security measures in replacement of regional collective defense measures.

I turn now to consider your specific proposals.

III.

I am compelled to conclude after the most careful study of your proposals that they seem to be unfortunately inexact or incomplete in their meaning and inadequate as a program for productive negotiations for peace. You first seem to assume that the obligations of the Charter are non-existent and that the voice of the United Nations is nothing that we need to heed.

You suggest that we should agree to respect the independence of the countries of the Near and Middle East and renounce the use of force in the settlement of questions relating to the Near and Middle East. But by the Charter of the United Nations we have already taken precisely those obligations as regards all countries, including those of the Near and Middle East. Our profound hope is that the Soviets feel themselves as bound by the provisions of the Charter as, I assure you, we feel bound.

You also suggest submitting to the member states of NATO and the Warsaw Pact some form of non-aggression agreement. But all of the members of NATO are already bound to the United Nations Charter provision against aggression.

You suggest that the United States, the United Kingdom and the Soviet Union should undertake not to use *nuclear* weapons. But our three nations and others have already undertaken, by the Charter, not to use any weapons against the territorial integrity or political independence of *any* state. Our profound hope is that no weapons will be used by any country for such an indefensible purpose and that the Soviet Union will feel a similar aversion to any kind of aggression.

You suggest that we should proclaim our intention to develop between us relations of friendship and peaceful cooperation. Such an intention is indeed already proclaimed as between ourselves and others by the Charter of the United Nations to which we have subscribed. The need is, not to repeat what we already proclaim, but, Mr. Chairman, to take concrete steps under the present terms of the Charter, that will bring about these relations of friendship and peaceful cooperation. As recently as last November, the Communist Party of the Soviet Union signed and proclaimed to the world a declaration which was designed to promote the triumph of Communism throughout the world by every means not excluding violence, and which contained many slanderous references to the United States.[3] I am bound to point out that such a declaration is difficult to reconcile with professions of a desire for friendship or indeed of peaceful coexistence. This declaration makes clear where responsibility for the "Cold War" lies.

You propose that we broaden the ties between us of a "scientific, cultural and athletic" character. But already our two countries are negotiating for peaceful contacts even broader than "scientific, cultural and athletic". We hope for a positive result, even though in 1955, after the Summit Conference, when negotiations for such contacts were pressed by our Foreign Ministers at Geneva, the accomplishments were zero.[4] It is above all important that our peoples should learn the true facts about each other. An informed public opinion in both our countries is essential to the proper understanding of our discussions.

You propose that we develop "normal" trade relations as part of the "peaceful cooperation" of which you speak. We welcome trade that carries no political or warlike implications. We do have restrictions on dealings in goods which are of war significance, but we impose no obstacles to peaceful trade.

Your remaining proposals relate to armament. In this connection, I note with deep satisfaction that you opposed "competition in the production of ever newer types of weapons". When I read that statement I expected to go on to read proposals to stop such production. But I was disappointed.

You renew the oft-repeated Soviet proposal that the United States, the United Kingdom and the Soviet Union should cease for two or three years to test nuclear weapons; and you suggest that nuclear weapons should not be stationed or produced in Germany. You add the possibility that Poland and Czechoslovakia might be added to this non-nuclear weapons area.

These proposals do not serve to meet the real problem of armament. The heart of that problem is, as you say, the mounting *production*, primarily by the Soviet Union and the United States, of new types of weapons.

Your proposal regarding Central Europe will of course be studied by NATO and the NATO countries directly involved from the standpoint of its military and political implications. But there cannot be great significance in de-nuclearizing a small area when, as you say, "the range of modern types of weapons does not know of any geographical limit", and when you defer to the indefinite future any measures to stop the production of such weapons.

I note, furthermore, that your proposal on Germany is in no way related to the ending of the division of that country but would, in fact, tend to perpetuate that division.[5] It is unrealistic thus to ignore the basic link between political solutions and security arrangements.

Surely, Mr. Chairman, at a time when we share great responsibility for shaping the development of the international situation, we can and must do better than what you propose.

In this spirit, I submit some proposals of my own.

IV.

(1) I propose that we strengthen the United Nations.

This organization and the pledges of its members embodied in the Charter constitute man's best hope for peace and justice. The United States feels bound by its solemn undertaking to act in accordance with the Principles of the Charter. Will not the Soviet Union clear away the doubt that it also feels bound by its Charter undertakings? And may we not perhaps go further and build up the authority of the United Nations?

Too often its recommendations go unheeded.

I propose, Mr. Chairman, that we should rededicate ourselves to the United Nations, its Principles and Purposes and to our Charter obligations. But I would do more.

Too often the Security Council is prevented, by veto, from discharging the primary responsibility we have given it for the maintenance of international peace and security. This prevention even extends to proposing procedures for the pacific settlement of disputes.

I propose that we should make it the policy of our two governments at least not to use veto power to prevent the Security Council from proposing methods for the pacific settlement of disputes pursuant to Chapter VI.[6]

Nothing, I am convinced, would give the world more justifiable hope than the conviction that both of our governments are genuinely determined to make the United Nations the effective instrument of peace and justice that was the original design.

(2) If confidence is to be restored, there needs, above all, to be confidence in the pledged word. To us it appears that such confidence is lamentably lacking. That is conspicuously so in regard to two areas where the situation is a cause of grave international concern.

I refer first of all to Germany. This was the principal topic of our meeting of July 1955 and the only substantive agreement which was recorded in our agreed Directive was this:

> "The Heads of Government, recognizing their common responsibility for the settlement of the German question and the reunification of Germany, have agreed that the settlement of the German Question and the reunification of Germany by means of free elections shall be carried out in conformity with the national interests of the German people and the interests of European security."

In spite of our urging, your government has, for now two and one half years, taken no steps to carry out that agreement or to discharge that recognized responsibility. Germany remains forcibly divided.

This constitutes a great error, incompatible with European security. It also undermines confidence in the sanctity of our international agreements.

I therefore urge that we now proceed vigorously to bring about the reunification of Germany by free elections, as we agreed, and as the situation urgently demands.

I assure you that this act of simple justice and of good faith need not lead to any increased jeopardy of your nation. The consequences would be just the opposite and would surely lead to greater security. In connection with the reunification of Germany, the United States is prepared, along with others, to negotiate specific arrangements regarding force levels and deployments, and broad treaty undertakings, not merely against aggression but assuring positive reaction should aggression occur in Europe.

The second situation to which I refer is that of the countries of Eastern Europe. The Heads of our two Governments, together with the Prime Minister of the United Kingdom, agreed in 1945 that the peoples of these countries should have the right to choose the form of government under which they would live, and that our three countries had a responsibility in this respect. The three of us agreed to foster the conditions under which these peoples could exercise their right of free choice.

That agreement has not as yet been fulfilled.

I know that your government is reluctant to discuss these matters or to treat them as a matter of international concern. But the Heads of Governments did agree at Yalta in 1945 that these matters *were* of international concern and we specifically agreed that there could appropriately be international consultation with reference to them.

This was another matter taken up at our meeting in Geneva in 1955. You then took the position that there were no grounds for discussing this question at our conference and that it would involve interference in the internal affairs of the Eastern European states.

But have not subsequent developments shown that I was justified in my appeal to you for consideration of these matters? Surely the Hungarian developments and the virtually unanimous action of the United Nations General Assembly in relation thereto show that conditions in Eastern Europe are regarded throughout the world as much more than a matter of purely domestic scope.[7]

I propose that we should now discuss this matter. There is an intrinsic need of this in the interest of peace and justice, which seems to me compelling.

(3) I now make, Mr. Chairman, a proposal to solve what I consider to be the most important problem which faces the world today.

(*a*) I propose that we agree that outer space should be used only for peaceful purposes. We face a decisive moment in history in relation to this matter. Both the Soviet Union and the United States are now using outer space for the testing of missiles designed for military purposes. The time to stop is now.

I recall to you that a decade ago, when the United States had a monopoly of atomic weapons and of atomic experience, we offered to renounce the making of atomic weapons and to make the use of atomic energy an international asset for peaceful purposes only.[8] If only that offer had been accepted by the Soviet Union, there would not now be the danger from nuclear weapons which you describe.

The nations of the world face today another choice perhaps even more momentous than that of 1948. That relates to the use of outer space. Let us this time, and in time, make the right choice, the peaceful choice.

There are about to be perfected and produced powerful new weapons which, availing of outer space, will greatly increase the capacity of the human race to destroy itself. If indeed it be the view of the Soviet Union that we should not go on producing ever newer types of weapons, can we not stop the production of such weapons which would use or, more accurately, misuse, outer space, now for the first time opening up as a field for man's exploration? Should not outer space be dedicated to the peaceful uses of mankind and denied to the purposes of war? That is my proposal.

(*b*) Let us also end the now unrestrained production of nuclear weapons. This too would be responsive to your urging against "the production of ever newer types of weapons". It is possible to assure that newly produced fissionable material should not be used for weapons purposes. Also existing weapons stocks can be steadily reduced by ascertainable transfers to peaceful purposes. Since our existing weapons stocks are doubtless larger than yours we would expect to make a greater transfer than you to peaceful purposes stocks. I should be glad to receive your suggestion as to what you consider to be an equitable ratio in this respect.

(*c*) I propose that, as part of such a program which will reliably check and reverse the accumulation of nuclear weapons, we stop the testing of nuclear weapons, not just for two or three years, but indefinitely. So long as the accumulation of these weapons continues unchecked, it is better that we should be able to devise weapons which will be primarily significant from a military and defensive standpoint and progressively eliminate weapons which could destroy, through fall-out, vast segments of human life. But if the production is to be stopped and the trend reversed, as I propose, then testing is no longer so necessary.

(*d*) Let us at the same time take steps to begin the controlled and progressive reduction of conventional weapons and military manpower.

(*e*) I also renew my proposal that we begin progressively to take measures to guarantee against the possibility of surprise attack. I recall, Mr. Chairman, that we began to discuss this at our personal meeting two and a half years ago, but nothing has happened although there is open a wide range of choices as to where to begin.[9]

The capacity to verify the fulfillment of commitments is of the essence in all these matters, including the reduction of conventional forces and weapons, and it would surely be useful for us to study together through technical groups what are the possibilities in this respect upon which we could build if we then decide to do so. These technical studies could, if you wish, be undertaken without commitment as to ultimate acceptance, or as to the interdependence, of the propositions involved. It is such technical studies of the possibilities of verification and supervision that the United Nations has proposed as a first step. I believe that this is a first step that would promote hope in both of our countries and in the world. Therefore I urge that this first step be undertaken.

V.

I have noted your conclusion, Mr. Chairman, that you attach great importance to personal contact between statesmen and that you for your part would be prepared to come to an agreement on a personal meeting of state leaders to discuss both the problems mentioned in your letter and other problems.

I too believe that such personal contacts can be of value. I showed that by coming to Geneva in the summer of 1955. I have repeatedly stated that there is nothing I would not do to advance the cause of a just and durable peace.

But meetings between us do not automatically produce good results. Preparatory work, with good will on both sides, is a prerequisite to success. High level meetings, in which we both participate, create great expectations and for that reason involve a danger of disillusionment, dejection and increased distrust if in fact the meetings are ill-prepared, if they evade the root causes of danger, if they are used primarily for propaganda, or if agreements arrived at are not fulfilled.

Consequently, Mr. Chairman, this is my proposal:

I am ready to meet with the Soviet leaders to discuss the proposals mentioned in your letter and the proposals which I make, with the attendance as appropriate of leaders of other states which have recognized responsibilities in relation to one or another of the subjects we are to discuss. It would be essential that prior to such a meeting these complex matters should be worked on in advance through diplomatic channels and by our Foreign Ministers, so that the issues can be presented in form suitable for our decisions and so that it can be ascertained that such a top-level meeting would, in fact, hold good hope of advancing the cause of peace and justice in the world. Arrangements should also be made for the appropriate inclusion, in the preparatory work, of other governments to which I allude.

I have made proposals which seem to me to be worthy of our attention and which correspond to the gravity of our times. They deal with the basic problems which press upon us and which if unresolved would make it ever more difficult to maintain the peace. The Soviet leaders by giving evidence of a genuine intention to resolve these basic problems can make an indispensable contribution to clearing away the obstacles to those friendly relations and peaceful pursuits which the peoples of all the world demand.[10] *Sincerely*

[1] The State Department draft of this letter is in AWF/I: Bulganin. Eisenhower had consulted with Secretary Dulles, AEC Chairman Strauss, and British officials before approving it. The President told Dulles that he could make minor changes without asking him, but the letter should make clear that the United States wanted to know when the Soviets would start honoring the promises they had made (Telephone conversation, Eisenhower and Dulles, Jan. 11, 1958, AWF/D; see also Dulles to Eisenhower, Jan. 3, 1958, AWF/D-H; Telephone conversations, Dulles and Whitman, Jan. 3, 1958; Dulles and Eisenhower, Jan. 6, 1958; and Dulles and Strauss, Jan. 7, 1958, Dulles Papers, Telephone Conversations). For background on Premier Bulganin's letter (in AWF/I: USSR and AWF/I: Bulganin) see no. 509. On British involvement in the response see no. 515 and Macmillan, *Riding the Storm*, pp. 464.

[2] Bulganin's letter had criticized the close ties existing among the NATO countries and had stated that NATO forces were mobilizing for war.

[3] The declaration, which reaffirmed the revolutionary nature of the Communist movement, was issued after a meeting of twelve Communist countries in Moscow from November 14–16. Referring to the United States, the declaration stated: "On the pretext of 'combating communism' they are angling to bring more and more countries under their dominion, instigating the destruction of democratic freedoms, threatening the national independence of the developed capitalist countries, trying to enmesh the liberated peoples in new forms of colonialism and systematically conducting subversive activities against the socialist countries" (Royal Institute of International Affairs, *Documents on International Affairs 1957*, ed. Noble Frankland [London, 1960], pp. 527–39; see also State, *Foreign Relations, 1955–1957*, vol. XXIV, *Soviet Union; Eastern Mediterranean*, pp. 186–87; and NSC meeting minutes, Nov. 25, 1957, AWF/NSC).

[4] On the 1955 Geneva Summit Conference and subsequent meetings of the foreign ministers see Galambos and van Ee, *The Middle Way*, nos. 1523, 1607, and 1623.

[5] Bulganin had proposed that the Soviet Union, Great Britain, and the United States agree not to keep nuclear weapons in East or West Germany. He made no mention of eventual reunification.

[6] Chapter VI of the United Nations Charter outlined the conditions under which parties to a dispute might bring their grievances before the Security Council and outlined the procedures the council might use to settle such disputes.

[7] For background on the Hungarian uprising in October 1956 see Galambos and van Ee, *The Middle Way*, no. 2044.

[8] On the Baruch Plan for the peaceful uses of atomic energy see Galambos, *Chief of Staff*, nos. 902, 946; and no. 192 in these volumes.
[9] On Eisenhower's personal meetings with the Soviet leader during the 1955 Geneva Summit Conference see State, *Foreign Relations, 1955–1957*, vol. V, *Austrian State Treaty; Summit and Foreign Ministers Meetings, 1955*, pp. 478–80; and Eisenhower, *Mandate for Change*, pp. 517–18.
[10] Before this letter was sent, Eisenhower had received additional correspondence from the Soviet leader (Jan. 8), calling for a summit meeting that would consider a moratorium on atomic weapons testing, the renunciation of the use of weapons of mass destruction, and the creation of a nuclear-free zone in Central Europe (Royal Institute of International Affairs, *Documents on International Affairs 1957*, ed. Frankland, pp. 51–62; see also *U.S. Department of State Bulletin* 38, no. 972 [February 10, 1958], 211; and *New York Times*, Jan. 10, 12, 1958). "I believe I have dealt with the substantive matters which it contains in my message of January twelfth," the President would respond. "Should further study of your letter indicate that additional response is appropriate, I shall communicate with you at a later date" (Eisenhower to Bulganin, Jan. 18, 1958, AWF/I: Bulganin; see also Dulles to Eisenhower, Jan. 17, 1958, *ibid.*; and Telephone conversation, Eisenhower and Dulles, Jan. 15, 1958, AWF/D). For developments see no. 574.

522

EM, AWF, Administration Series

To James Rhine Killian, Jr.
Memorandum

January 13, 1958

Recently there was reported to me a statement, purportedly made by Mr. Ernest Breench, of the Ford Motor Company, to the effect that "we" have had for some time the ability to launch a satellite and that such launching had been prevented by the government, presumably by me.[1]

I am not exactly sure whether the word "we" above was supposed to designate the government, the Ford Company, or some other organization. But the statement, made in November at Hot Springs, probably during a meeting of the BAC, apparently represented the urgent views of Mr. Breench. Since Mr. Breech is a responsible businessman and obviously thought he had some information that has apparently been withheld, I would like to have you ask him, either by telephone or by a note, so that we may know what he was really talking about.[2]

[1] Ernest Robert Br*eech* (CPA, University of Illinois at Urbana, 1921) was chairman of the Ford Motor Company. In 1955 he was a member of the government's panel on the impact of peaceful uses of atomic energy, and had served as vice-chairman of the Business Advisory Council (BAC) since January 1957.
[2] Presidential Science Adviser Killian would respond on the following day (AWF/A). He explained that he had contacted Breech by telephone and learned that Breech's

conversation had been with Defense Secretary McElroy. Breech had expressed concern that Aero Utronics Systems, a Ford subsidiary, which had been created to undertake government work and which had participated in the development of the Farside rocket, was not being adequately used for missile development. Killian added that he had found "no evidence that Mr. Breech was expressing any statement that there had been an effort by the government to prevent the launching of a satellite, or that he would make such a statement in the future." Eisenhower would meet with Breech on January 27 at a White House luncheon organized to discuss economic development and security problems (see Eisenhower to Breech, Jan. 28, 1957, and other correspondence in WHCF/OF 150-A). For background see no. 455; for developments see no. 524.

523 — *EM, AWF, Name Series*

To William Alton Jones — *January 13, 1958*

Dear Pete: This morning I had a telephone talk with Bill Rogers, the Attorney General. He has the same impression that I do—namely that the Petroleum Advisory Council, as a voluntary organization, has been of great value to the country and to the government.[1] I told him that there had been some talk about imposing, upon the Council, certain regulations concerning chairmanship and agenda and that there was some feeling that this would probably disrupt the Council. He is going to make a very close analysis of the whole thing and tells me that already there has been arranged a meeting with some of the members of the Council—I think he said that you were one of those included—to be held next week.

I do not know from what source the difficulty stems, but I am quite sure that an airing of the whole problem will be all to the good.

It was fine to have you here for the weekend, even though Sunday afternoon seemed to present to you and George a very muddy track and slippery going in general.[2] Saturday evening and Sunday evening seemed to see you both going very well indeed.[3]

With all the best, *As ever*

[1] Eisenhower was referring to the National Petroleum Council (NPC), an 85-member advisory committee established by President Truman in 1946. The NPC was intended to serve as a channel of communication between the federal government and the petroleum industry. It also studied problems of oil policy as they arose (see Galambos and van Ee, *The Middle Way*, no. 2027; see also Chester, *United States Oil Policy and Diplomacy*, p. 21; and Nash, *United States Oil Policy, 1890–1964*, pp. 186–87).

[2] On January 10 Eisenhower had telephoned Cities Service chairman of the board Jones to invite him to Washington for a weekend of bridge (Eisenhower to Jones, Jan. 10, 1958, AWF/D). George was probably Eisenhower's friend George Allen, a frequent bridge partner.

[3] Jones would reply on January 15 (AWF/N). He would apologize for not being able to attend the Attorney General's meeting but noted, that he had already expressed his views to Rogers and was "hopeful that the matter can be worked out to everyone's satisfaction." "There is no doubt in my mind but that the Council has rendered some valuable service," he added, "particularly during periods of stress, and it would be a mistake to let it fold up."

524 — *EM, AWF, Administration Series*

To Sherman Adams — *January 13, 1958*

Dear Sherm: Herewith a note from Cabot Lodge, who is responding to my request at the last Cabinet meeting for a written memorandum from anyone who has some practical ideas for helping handle the Five Year Trade Agreement Extension Bill.[1]

I had been under the impression that in the job of martialing [marshaling] outside support for this program we were grouping it with the mutual security project.[2] It would appear that Cabot would separate the two.

Cabot believes that Paul Hoffman would be the most effective leader of the project for mobilizing women's clubs, labor organizations and a number of other groups that he names in paragraph four. Paul was, of course, very successful in getting this kind of support for the Marshall Plan.[3]

The question I am really concerned with is whether the two programs should be handled separately or, if Eric Johnston is supposed to be the grand marshal of the whole affair, then Paul Hoffman might be used by Eric to work on the trade extension work.[4]

You might like to show this note also to Foster and to Chris Herter.

As ever

[1] Lodge had written on January 11 to offer his recommendations for handling the Trade Agreements Extension Act of 1958 (AWF/A). He suggested that Assistant Secretary of State Christian Herter be appointed to oversee the congressional campaign to pass the bill. Lodge added that the best arguments for the bill were that foreign trade was profitable and advantageous to the United States; that foreign trade saved the United States money that it would otherwise have to pay to protect its trading partners from Communism; and that foreign trade greatly increased the solidarity of the noncommunist world, making all countries "more immune to communist penetration." See Cabinet meeting minutes, January 10, 1958, AWF/D.

[2] For background see nos. 60, 75, and 76.

[3] Lodge had suggested that the White House appoint Paul Hoffman to oversee the organization of public support for free trade among "women's clubs, labor organizations, business groups engaged in foreign trade, church groups, groups interested in foreign relations, and so-called service clubs." Lodge saw the organization of public support for the trade bill as "an essential part of an effective program. In fact,"

he said, "without this the legislation might not pass." Hoffman had headed the Marshall Plan program from April 1948 to September 1950 (see Alan R. Raucher, *Paul G. Hoffman: Architect of Foreign Aid* [Lexington, Ky., 1985], pp. 64–79).

[4] Johnston, president of the Motion Picture Association of America, had been chairman of the International Development Board since 1952 (see no. 230). On January 9 the President had spoken with House Speaker Rayburn about appointing Johnston to head a committee to mobilize opinion on mutual aid programs. Noting that Senate Majority Leader Lyndon Johnson had already approved such an appointment, Eisenhower agreed to accept the Speaker's recommendations as to the Democrats who would be included on this committee (Ann Whitman memorandum, Jan. 9, 1958, AWF/AWD).

Eisenhower would answer Lodge on January 14, 1958 (AWF/A), thanking him for his suggestions but noting that the nucleus of an organization had already been set up in the Commerce Department. "This does not preclude, of course," he added, "outside help, and I shall keep your ideas very much in mind." On January 30 the President would address Congress on the Reciprocal Trade Agreements Program (see *Public Papers of the Presidents: Eisenhower, 1958*, pp. 132–35). He would argue that a five-year extension of the trade agreements, "unweakened by amendments of a kind that would impair its effectiveness," was essential to American economic interests, security and foreign relations. For developments see nos. 534 and 691. See also *Congressional Quarterly Almanac*, vol. XIV, *1958*, pp. 58–60, 165–79.

525 *EM, AWF, Administration Series*

To John Hay Whitney *January 13, 1958*

Dear Jock: Many thanks for your note from Thomasville and, also, for your letter of the sixth. (Incidentally, I did read carefully Harold Macmillan's talk, made before he departed on his Commonwealth tour. I agree entirely with your comments.)[1]

This is the first time I knew of your intention to bring the mounted turkey to Washington.[2] I had assumed that you intended to keep him (at Greenwood Plantation) as an example of the fine turkey country in South Georgia.

I am glad that you liked the State of the Union talk. While, as usual, extremists on each side of any question discussed will be completely dissatisfied, the fact is that most people of solid judgment and common sense will probably try to seek permanent and satisfactory solutions. The typical demagogue likes those that are hysterically proposed and as quickly abandoned.[3]

Reverting again to thoughts of Greenwood, I hope, one of these days, to participate in a dove shoot. I have not done so in something over thirty years. But I rather suspect that the season does not quite coincide with the opportunities that I normally have for visits to Georgia.[4] In any event, it will be interesting to hear about your big day when you and Betsey stop by here.

It just occurs to me that I had better ask Mamie whether or not she and Betsey have agreed on the exact timing of your visit. It will be fun to see you both.[5]

Love to Betsey and, as always, the best to yourself. *As ever*

[1] Whitney had written on January 10 (AWF/A) from his Greenwood Plantation in Thomasville, Georgia, to compliment Eisenhower on his State of the Union Address delivered January 9 (see n. 3, below). Whitney's earlier letter had reassured Eisenhower, who was then preparing to deliver his message, that "the small speech difficulty you are conscious of would be unnoticed in anyone else." He cautioned, however, "they do watch you for it and will do so in public speeches." (The President had suffered a stroke on November 25; see no. 477.) Whitney had suggested that the President read Macmillan's national broadcast of January 4 "not for content but for style." Macmillan's talk, Whitney said, was "comfortable for the speaker and, while not playing down to the public, everyone can understand every word. It may be a bit 'fire-sidey' for a State of the Union, but I do believe it should be examined for other occasions." On Macmillan's speech and Commonwealth tour see no. 501.

[2] Eisenhower apparently was referring to a wild turkey he had shot in February 1957; see Rowley to Baughman, February 13, 1957, AWF/D. The turkey's neck is "rather like that of a high-mettled race horse proudly arched," Whitney had written. "I imagine the artist felt you should have a king of birds and so applied a little poetic license" (Jan. 10, 1957, AWF/A).

[3] Whitney said the speech was "just plain tremendous." It "hit all the really vital issues hard and smack in the middle. . . . I believe the people will now know their jobs and really help you to make Congress get on with it" (*ibid.*). Eisenhower's speech dealt with defense reorganization; an accelerated defense effort; mutual aid and trade; scientific cooperation with allies; research and education; spending and saving; and efforts to achieve peace (see the following document).

[4] As it turned out, Eisenhower would hunt doves while vacationing at the Augusta National Golf Club on December 29, 1959.

[5] Later this same day, following a conversation with Mrs. Eisenhower on the telephone, the President would send another letter to Whitney indicating that both January 17 and 18 were convenient for the Whitneys to visit the White House (AWF/D). The Whitneys would visit the White House the evening of January 17 and Eisenhower and Whitney would meet again the morning of the eighteenth. Eisenhower's January 18 thank-you letter to the Whitneys is in AWF/A. Whitney would reply that they "appreciated it being 'just family' and . . . enjoyed every minute. . . ." He would also wish the President "Good luck" with the upcoming congressional session (Jan. 20, 1958, AWF/A).

526 — *EM, AWF, Administration Series*

To Arthur Larson — *January 13, 1958*

Dear Arthur: I don't think that I have adequately—or, indeed, can adequately—express to you my appreciation of your contribution to the State of the Union Message, or of your patience with my many changes in your drafts.[1] (At heart you must understand that I am an editor; no written text appeals to me until I have inserted my own particular mannerisms of style).

Seventeen complete drafts—and many smaller revisions—of a document as long as this one is a colossal task; I am truly grateful to you and your staff for the long hours and hard work that it entailed.

So many gratifying letters and telegrams have come to my desk in the last few days about this talk that I am asking that they be collected and sent to you. I think they will convey to you, better than any words at my command, the real debt I owe to you.[2]

With warm regard, *As ever*

[1] Larson, former director of the United States Information Agency, had served as special assistant to the President since the end of October 1957. He had joined U.N. Ambassador Lodge and White House Press Secretary James Hagerty, among others, in helping to draft the State of the Union Address (see Ann Whitman memorandums, Jan. 6, 7, 8, 9, 1958, AWF/AWD; see also Arthur Larson, *Eisenhower: The President Nobody Knew* [New York, 1968]). See *Public Papers of the Presidents: Eisenhower, 1958*, pp. 2–15.

[2] Eisenhower had delivered the State of the Union Address on January 9, 1958. He had spoken on behalf of a balanced program of military strength and foreign economic aid and trade, and he had called for action on eight items to "focus our resources upon the two tasks of security and peace" (see *New York Times*, Jan. 10, 1958). The President had asked for defense reorganization; an accelerated defense effort to secure advance warning against missile and bomber attack; mutual aid increases; a five-year extension of the Trade Agreement Act; increased scientific cooperation with NATO members; increased funding for education; reduced spending in nonessential areas; and greater efforts in such "works of peace," as scientific and educational exchanges with the Soviet Union. Among those who had complimented the President were James Mitchell (see Eisenhower to Mitchell, Jan. 9, 1958), Emmet Hughes (Eisenhower to Hughes, Jan. 10, 1958), Lucius Clay (Eisenhower to Clay, Jan. 13, 1958), C. D. Jackson (Eisenhower to Jackson, Jan. 13, 1958), Dillon Anderson (Eisenhower to Anderson, Jan. 16, 1958), Sigurd Larmon (Eisenhower to Larmon, Jan. 9, 1958), and William Robinson (Eisenhower to Robinson, Jan. 10, 1958). Eisenhower's letters of acknowledgment are in AWF/A and AWF/N.

527 — *EM, AWF, Ann Whitman Diary Series*

[MEMORANDUM] *January 14, 1958*
Secret

C. D. Jackson has been talking to the Secretary of State about the idea that the Secretary might now be more valuable as my Special Assistant and Advisory and a younger man take on the duties of Secretary of State.[1] I find that C. D. Jackson now wants to talk to me about this kind of thing.[2]

[1] After learning that Jackson and Dulles had discussed the proposal previously, Eisenhower had been reluctant to talk with Jackson without informing Dulles. Meeting with Dulles earlier this same day, Eisenhower had suggested the creation of a cabinet position with responsibilities for all foreign policy, including the international issues that were usually handled by the Commerce, Agriculture, and Defense Departments. There was a need for "a tighter organization" of external efforts related to the cold war, Dulles told Eisenhower, and he suggested that the President ask Jackson if he would agree to return to Washington (Dulles, Memorandum of Conversation, Jan. 14, 1958, Dulles Papers, White House Memoranda Series; and Telephone conversation, Dulles and Eisenhower, Jan. 14, 1958, Dulles Papers, Telephone Conversations; see also Ambrose, *Eisenhower*, vol. II, *The President*, p. 444; and H. W. Brands, Jr., *Cold Warriors: Eisenhower's Generation and American Foreign Policy* [New York, 1988], pp. 127–37).

Ann Whitman reported that she had asked Eisenhower "if it was not an effrontery on the part of C. D. to suggest such a thing." The President replied that Jackson and Dulles "had a long-time warm relationship" and that Dulles welcomed any ideas that Jackson felt were important (Ann Whitman memorandum, Jan. 14, 1958, AWF/AWD).

[2] After talking with Jackson, Eisenhower would tell Dulles that he thought Jackson would take a position as assistant secretary of state (Telephone conversation, Eisenhower and Dulles, Jan. 15, 1958, AWF/D, and Dulles Papers, Telephone Conversations). Jackson later told Eisenhower that their meeting had recharged his batteries. "I do hope you will be able to solve the Foster situation soon," he wrote. "I know that he is eager for some kind of solution which would give him time to think about the incredible problems which face our foreign policy. I am also confident that you would like such a solution" (Jackson to Eisenhower, Jan. 17, 1958, C. D. Jackson Papers). For developments see no. 555.

528

EM, WHCF, President's Personal File 1419

To Ernest Nason Harmon *January 14, 1958*
Personal

Dear Ernie: Thank you for your note.[1] You hit neatly on one source of my current problems—that every scientist considers himself a top military strategist, every military man knows what priority scientific developments should take, and every politician knows all the answers. But a lot of the suggestions I do get are well meant, and they spring from a sincere desire on the part of worried people to be of help.

I shall keep in mind your offer; at the moment lack of qualified manpower is not apparent but I shall not forget that you are available. And I do greatly appreciate your willingness to be of service.[2]

With warm regard, *Sincerely*

[1] Major General Harmon, president of Norwich University since 1950, had retired

from the Army in 1948 (for background see *Eisenhower Papers,* vols. I–XI). On January 11 (same file as document) he had written that he sympathized with the "terrible pressure" Eisenhower was undergoing. The launching of the Russian satellites, Sputniks I and II had produced increasing anxiety and disagreement among military, political and scientific experts about the capabilities of the American satellite programs (see nos. 390, 394, and 447).
[2] Harmon offered to do anything at any time. Not for "pay or glory," he said. "It would just be kind of nice to do something for my country again."

529

EM, AWF, DDE Diaries Series

To Alfred Maximilian Gruenther — *January 15, 1958*
Notes

1. The article is critical but not constructive.[1] I cannot find any single thought in the entire column that suggests any practical means of correcting the situation.
2. The main difficulty, one not mentioned by Cy, is that in the Soviet there is only *one* source of propaganda. Among the independent nations there are thousands, and many of them mutually contradictory.
3. I don't know what the man has against Dulles, the wisest and in many ways the strongest international statesman I know. He refers to Dulles as a "tragic-comic" figure. Publicly and privately many of the world's great figures have expressed their respect for Dulles but press representatives, including Cy, seem to have no thought that in the attempt to destroy Dulles they are at the same time destroying themselves. The testimony of Adenauer, Macmillan, Fanfani,[2] Mendares,[3] and others, seems to me to be more valid than does this type of criticism.
4. With no other apparent purpose than that of writing a plausible story, Cy contradicts himself. He is critical at one point because the West bills the struggle as between "Democracy and Communism." This of course implies that men are not particularly concerned with political systems or with differing ways of life. But in another place he says "men do not fight for living standards but for a way of life." If this last thought is not a recognition of the struggle as ideological, then what is it?
5. Finally, what bothers me is the attitude of a man for whom, some years ago, I had a considerable respect—I mean not only as a person but as a thoughtful writer. I have a feeling that he is becoming just another columnist.[4]

[1] Cyrus Leo Sulzberger, chief foreign correspondent for the *New York Times,* had criticized the United States for relinquishing the initiative in the propaganda contest with the Soviet Union. The United States had lost the allegiance of the uncommitted nations as well as the attention of its own people through carelessness and stupidity, he had written. Moscow was taking the lead in the quest for peace (C. L. Sulzberger, "Why We Are Losing Out in Propaganda," *New York Times,* Jan. 15, 1958; Sulzberger would include an expanded version of this same article in his book *What's Wrong with U.S. Foreign Policy?* [New York, 1959], pp. 59–81; see also Cyrus Leo Sulzberger, *The Last of the Giants* [New York, 1970], pp. 443–44).

In a letter accompanying these notes Eisenhower had asked Gruenther to write Sulzberger: "He is a friend of yours and I hope that you can find the time and the inclination to send him a letter to tell him just how stupid he is beginning to appear" (Eisenhower to Gruenther, Jan. 15, 1958, AWF/D; see also Ann Whitman memorandum, Jan. 15, 1958, AWF/AWD).

[2] Amintore Fanfani, a former professor of political economy, was secretary of the Italian Christian Democratic Party. He would become prime minister of Italy in July 1958.

[3] Adnan Menderes was prime minister of Turkey.

[4] For developments see the following document; for more on Eisenhower's relationship with Sulzberger see Galambos and van Ee, *The Middle Way,* no. 956.

530

EM, AWF, Administration Series

To Alfred Maximillan Gruenther — *January 15, 1958*

Dear Al: I approve every word of the letter you wrote to Cy.[1] There is one item I should have included in my little list of suggestions which had slipped my mind at the moment. If you get an answer from Cy, you might advert to the following:

> Khrushchev is now insisting that there should be a Summit meeting without any preparatory moves.[2] We have always insisted on proper preparation and consequently some of the "critics" within the independent countries have called us negative and lethargic.
>
> Now here is the payoff. On May 10, 1957 Khrushchev was quoted in the *New York Times* as saying that a necessary prelude to a profitable Summit talk was that all subjects to be discussed should have good advance preparation.[3]

I hope that you have a nice trip to Detroit.[4] I shall be looking forward to seeing you.

Just a few minutes ago I came back from my press conference and I think it went off satisfactorily. The principal subjects were the American economy and the exchange of letters with Bulganin. Only a short time was consumed in talking about military reorganization—and there was a question or two about my health.[5] *As ever*

[1] For background see the preceding document. Gruenther had told Eisenhower that he was as "burned up" about Sulzberger's foreign policy column as the President had been. He had also enclosed his reply to Sulzberger, which had incorporated Eisenhower's suggestions and even some of his language. "If you can think of any additional insults," he asked the President, "let me have them please" (Gruenther to Eisenhower, Jan. 15, 1958, AWF/A).

Gruenther good-naturedly had told Sulzberger to "withdraw every kind thing" he had ever said about him. "Your article is devastatingly critical, but I cannot find a single thought that suggests any practical means of correcting the situation." He raised the question of Secretary Dulles's role in drafting both Eisenhower's State of the Union message and the President's reply to Soviet Premier Bulganin, both of which Sulzberger had praised. "Don't you think that Mr. Dulles perhaps had a role in the preparation of both these documents? Can he be the stubborn dunce that you paint him?" Gruenther chided (Gruenther to Sulzberger, Jan. 15, 1958, AWF/A, Gruenther Corr.).

Eisenhower would send Dulles a copy of Gruenther's letter to Sulzberger. "Al and Cy are warm friends," Eisenhower said, "so you will understand that his letter of censure had to be written in a vein of humorous sarcasm" (Eisenhower to Dulles, Jan. 15, 1958, AWF/D-H).

[2] A letter from Soviet Premier Bulganin to the heads of nineteen nations on January 9 had called for a summit conference within the next several months to discuss outstanding issues (see *U.S. Department of State Bulletin* 38, no. 972 [February 10, 1958], 211; see also *New York Times*, Jan. 10, 12, 1958).

[3] In a postscript to Sulzberger, written after receiving this letter, Gruenther would tell the columnist about Khrushchev's May 1957 statement. "It seems to me that this is a theme that you might well use, and you can be assured that you are on the side of the angels because the information came from the NEW YORK TIMES. Certainly there could be no better Bible!" (Gruenther to Sulzberger, Jan. 15, 1958, AWF/A, Gruenther Corr.).

[4] Gruenther would leave on this same day to speak at the convention of the Society of Automotive Engineers (see Biggers to Eisenhower, Jan. 16, 1958; and Eisenhower to Biggers, Jan. 18, 1958, both in *ibid.*).

[5] For Eisenhower's news conference see *Public Papers of the Presidents: Eisenhower, 1958*, pp. 90–100.

531 — *EM, AWF, Name Series*

To Douglas McCrae Black — *January 15, 1958*

Personal

Dear Doug: In view of my understandable difficulties with some individuals who refuse to see the reasons for preventing publication of certain statements of the utmost sensitivity and, indeed, the most vital importance to the safety of our country, I could not possibly sign the suggested statement as it is written.[1]

Moreover, in view of the fact that I am still in active political life, and because any statement that I would make would necessarily be subjected to conditions and explanations, I personally think that the signing should be limited only to ex-Presidents.

I do not mean, of course, to encourage any of these people who make it their business to interfere with the access of others to truth and knowledge. Moreover, it goes without saying that I support the general purpose and program to be climaxed by National Library Week. Nevertheless, for the reasons I have given, I hope that you will drop the matter of sending to me an invitation to participate.

One of your gift books to me had an unusual appeal—the one about Charles Russell, containing many reproductions of his best paintings. I read every word of it and found it completely absorbing. Of course its attraction for me may have some connection with my persistent liking for a really good Western.[2]

Give my love to Maudie[3] and, of course, warm regard to yourself.[4]

As ever

[1] Black, president and director of Doubleday & Company, had written Eisenhower on January 13, 1958 (AWF/N) on behalf of National Library Week. Jointly sponsored by the American Library Association and the National Book Committee, Library Week was intended "to emphasize the importance, in our society, of the printed word." Black noted that the program had the support of libraries, newspapers, magazines, television and publishers, and more than forty state committees were already preparing local programs "to focus attention on the function of libraries and the importance of reading." Black had asked the President to sign a statement supporting the program, "together with President Hoover and Mr. Truman, as the three living Presidents" (see *New York Times*, Mar. 16, 1958).

White House Press Secretary James Hagerty, concerned with the publication of such secret material as that in the Gaither Report, had advised Eisenhower not to sign the statement which, he said, stated "in effect that anything ever written should be made available to everyone" ([Ann Whitman] memorandum, n.d., AWF/N, Black Corr.; on the Gaither Report see no. 463). The statement is not in AWF.

[2] Eisenhower was referring to *The Charles M. Russell Book: The Life and Work of the Cowboy Artist*, by Harold McCracken (Garden City, N.Y., 1957). Charles Marion Russell (1864–1926) was a sculptor and painter who specialized in depicting the American West. Black had included with his letter several books, and said that he would continue to send him others "from time to time, to give you some much needed relaxation."

[3] Black's wife, the former Maude Bergen.

[4] Black would respond on January 20, 1958 (AWF/N). He would say that he felt sure that Eisenhower would "support the general purposes and program of National Library Week. The specific suggestion that was made is only one means of evidencing support, and I fully appreciate your reasons for finding it inappropriate." In a handwritten note, Black would add: "Your letter is *not* in my files. Its contents and the fact that you wrote it are known only to me—and so it will be."

To Robert Tyre Jones, Jr. *January 15, 1958*

Dear Bob: It is a red letter day for me when I get from you two messages at the same time. This answer will be to both.[1]

Already I am intrigued by the new book, even though it has not yet been received. Your thumbnail sketch of the author and John Lardner's review of the book assure me that I will really have some interesting bedtime reading.[2]

Now as to your idea of giving one of my so-called "paintings" to Golf House.[3] First you must understand that my opportunities these days for playing with my paints are very irregular. So, the foremost job that I would have would be the selection of a suitable subject and the next would be the time and patience to do it in recognizable, if not adequate, fashion. There are only three pieces that I have attempted that pertain to golf: first, the copy of the Tommy Stephens portrait of Frances Ouimet; secondly, one of yourself; and the third one is of my grandson. It is now hanging on the top floor of Mamie's Cottage.[4] I have never been successful in depicting any typically golf scene and have burned up everything of this kind I have attempted.

If by chance I do succeed some day in producing a presentable and appropriate piece, I think my best bet would be to follow the procedure that we did in the case of the Ouimet picture—I presented it to you and later you, with my permission, presented it to St. Andrews. Incidentally, if you have any photograph or anything else (for example, some old picture of yourself) that appeals to you, I would appreciate a suggestion.

I have no objection to your telling Mr. Dey that I might at some future time make this kind of an attempt, but please give him no assurance of accomplishment. There are too many uncertainties in the way. In fact one of these is more than an uncertainty; it is a very definite hazard involving my lamentable lack of ability!

Give my love to Mary. I hope the two of you will have a fine winter. If I am lucky enough to get back to Augusta just after the Masters, maybe I shall also be lucky enough to find the two of you there—at least for a short time.[5] *As ever*

[1] Jones's letters, written on January 13, are in AWF/N.

[2] Jones had written that under separate cover he sent Eisenhower a copy of a book by Fred Russell, entitled *Bury Me in an Old Press Box: Good Times and Life of a Sportswriter* (New York, 1957). Russell, wrote Jones, has an "understanding of sports, a remarkable sweetness in his appreciation of other people and an irrepressible humor which I know you will enjoy." Author John Lardner, a columnist and correspondent for *Newsweek* since 1939, had written the review for the *New York Times* (Dec. 22, 1957).

[3] Jones had enclosed a letter he received from Joseph Charles Dey, Jr., executive di-

rector of the United States Golf Association since 1934, inquiring whether Eisenhower would be willing to present a painting to "Golf House," home of the USGA (Nov. 22, 1957, AWF/N).

[4] On the portraits of golf champions Jones and Francis D. Ouimet (winner of the 1913 U.S. Open) see Galambos and van Ee, *The Middle Way*, nos. 98 and 846, respectively. "Mamie's Cottage" was the Eisenhower home at Augusta National Golf Club (see no. 122).

[5] The Eisenhowers would vacation in Augusta, Georgia, April 25–28.

533 — *EM, AWF, Administration Series*

To Arthur Larson — *January 17, 1958*

Dear Arthur: Perhaps the Mencken book will give us a few speech ideas, but then I suspect the better nature (at least I hope I have a better nature) of both of us would repudiate them.

At any rate, I know I shall enjoy "A Carnival of Buncombe." I can imagine the editing was a task that Malcolm Moos thoroughly enjoyed.[1]

With my thanks and warm regard, *As ever*

[1] Malcolm Charles Moos (Ph.D. University of California 1942) taught political science at the Johns Hopkins University. The author of numerous books on American politics and foreign policy, Moos had also been a delegate to the 1956 Republican Convention. Moos had served as a White House consultant since the fall of 1957. The Johns Hopkins University Press had published *A Carnival of Buncombe*, a selection of political essays by H. L. Mencken (Henry Louis Mencken, 1880–1956), and edited by Moos, in 1956. Mencken, a commentator on literature, politics, and mores, was renowned for his imaginative prose style and caustic views of life. On Larson's role as White House speech writer see no. 526.

534 — *EM, AWF, Administration Series*

To Paul Gray Hoffman — *January 18, 1958*

Dear Paul: Thank you very much for your note and for the copy of your address that accompanied it.[1] I read it thoroughly and I applaud your readiness to think courageously and specifically about difficult obstacles that confront us as we reach for the dream of a just peace.

I make only one comment about detail. In the middle of page six there is a paragraph beginning "In determining our own position . . ." With respect to the first two questions you propose in that paragraph, I personally think we are not only ready to answer in the affirmative, but that we have already, through our faithful adherence to the United Nations Charter, done so.[2] With respect to the fourth question, I think there is no difficulty about defining "government of their own choosing."[3] Obviously we mean any government freely chosen by the majority of its citizens. But in question three you have really posed a difficult problem.[4] One of these difficulties comes from an apparent contradiction of terms. Communism could, I think, be defined as a doctrine of complete socialism, but *including the clear determination to employ any means, including force and international war, to bring about a destruction of other forms of government.* Consequently we should not favor on a reciprocal basis giving to proponents a full opportunity to promote Communism, because Communism cannot be divorced from the readiness to use violence.

I do not believe this is quibbling.

I have another question of a more general nature. You point out the great advantages of using the United Nations as a forum in which fruitful negotiations might be carried on. I think it would be necessary to define procedures to be used. Manifestly nothing but chaos would result if we should attempt to debate important details of major questions within the General Assembly, even though all nations should have some real sense of participation. I realize that you did not have an opportunity to describe details of applicable procedure.[5]

Give my love to Dorothy.[6] *As ever*

[1] Eisenhower's State of the Union Address and his reply to Soviet Premier Bulganin's message had given the United States the initiative in the search for world peace, Hoffman had written. Both had prompted him to send Eisenhower a copy of a speech on peace prospects that he had delivered on January 14 at the New School for Social Research (Hoffman to Eisenhower, Jan. 15, 1957, AWF/A). On the State of the Union Address see *Public Papers of the Presidents: Eisenhower, 1957,* pp. 2–15; Eisenhower's letter to Bulganin is no. 521. For more on Hoffman's involvement in Administration policy see no. 524.

[2] Hoffman had asked, first, if the United States would guarantee that it would neither attack the Soviet Union militarily nor support such an attack by any of its allies. Second, he asked if the United States would guarantee not to support in any way the violent overthrow of any government regardless of the form of that government (Paul G. Hoffman, "Prospects for Progress Toward Peace," Jan. 14, 1958, AWF/A, Hoffman Corr.).

[3] Hoffman had asked: "(4) Are we prepared to state precisely what we mean by 'government of their own choosing.'?" He apparently thought that the United States needed to define the concept of self-determination so that this major American goal in international affairs might be understood clearly.

[4] "Would we favor, on a reciprocal basis, giving to proponents of any ideology [the opportunity] to propagate their faith by non-violent means?" Hoffman had asked.

[5] Eisenhower sent a copy of the speech to Secretary Dulles, who found it "interesting" (Eisenhower to Dulles, Jan. 18, 1957; and Dulles to Eisenhower, Jan. 20, 1957, both in AWF/D-H).

[6] Hoffman's wife was the former Dorothy Brown.

535 *EM, AWF, Administration Series*

To Kevin Coyle McCann *January 18, 1958*
Personal

Dear Kevin: I have been studying your proposal for an exchange of students on the basis of ten thousand such individuals. I find that we have had long negotiations with the Soviets on this matter, including the detail of the number of students to be involved.[1]

The Soviets originally proposed that the number be limited to five. We got it up to twenty for the first year and forty for the second. Moreover, the Soviets wanted to insist that their students should be divided into "blocs" of their own selection. Apparently they wanted to keep the students in groups so that the individuals could watch each other. But by negotiation I think that we are successful in getting the authority to allocate them at our discretion.

In view of this start, I am wondering whether it would be wise to push them, at this moment, as much as would be implied by your suggestion. On the other hand, I believe that if once we could get the first twenty, we might then propose the far more dramatic action you have suggested.[2] *As ever*

[1] McCann, who had returned to his position as president of Defiance College on February 1, 1957, had proposed "a massive and continuing interchange" of young men and women attending the universities of the United States and the Soviet Union. He had discussed the plan with Milton Eisenhower, who suggested that it be presented to the President in the form of a draft letter to Soviet Premier Bulganin, "expressed with stark simplicity." Both men were unable to present the proposal to Eisenhower in person, McCann wrote, "So I send it to you unescorted and unwarmed by Milton's or my conviction about it" (McCann to Eisenhower, Jan. 16, 1958, AWF/A; and Draft of Possible Letter to Premier Bulganin [Jan. 16, 1958], AWF/A, McCann Corr.; see also Milton S. Eisenhower, *The President Is Calling* [New York, 1974], pp. 358–59).

Administration officials had considered student exchanges with the Soviet Union since the Geneva Summit Conference in July 1955. The East-West Contacts division of the State Department had presented a proposal in October 1957 for the exchange of one hundred students with the Soviet Union for a six-week period. Also in October negotiations had begun in Washington between U.S. and Soviet officials on the subject of technical, scientific, and cultural exchanges (State, *Foreign Relations, 1955–1957*, vol. XXIV, *Soviet Union; Eastern Mediterranean*, pp. 193–94, 200–208, 218–19, 259–68; see also NSC meeting minutes, Feb. 18, Mar. 25, 1955, AWF/NSC; and *U.S. Department of State Bulletin* 38, no. 960 [November 18, 1957], pp. 800–803).

[2] After meeting with the President on January 24, Milton Eisenhower reported that Eisenhower liked McCann's idea but "felt it would be a grandstand play in view of the negotiations that have been carried on" (Ann Whitman memorandum, Jan. 24, 1958, AWF/AWD). For developments see no. 552.

To Sinclair Weeks *January 18, 1958*

Dear Sinny: We have a lot on our legislative plate this year and I am rather reluctant to start any new fights in which important members of my own Cabinet cannot see quite eye to eye.[1]

In theory I have always favored secret ballots for any important question that must be settled by the unions. On the other hand, Jim Mitchell has constantly pointed out to me the practical results from secret balloting that he believes would be damaging to collective bargaining.[2]

Certainly if we analyze the secret ballot, we are compelled to note that it brings up some constituent factors—for example, the timing of balloting with respect to preliminary or final decisions made by a union. In this particular item alone I think there is great room for difference.

In any event, because of these puzzling points—and the further factor of the already crowded legislative program—I have agreed that we should not bring it up at this moment.

Repeating that my instinctive reaction to any such proposal is affirmative, I still have not yet been persuaded that even a successful legislative effort to make the secret ballot a feature of our labor laws would work to the best advantage of the country.[3]

With warm regard, *As ever*

[1] In preparation for his January 23 labor message to Congress, Eisenhower had discussed with his Cabinet various legislative proposals to curb union abuses and protect individual workers (Cabinet meeting minutes, Nov. 12, 1957, AWF/Cabinet). Concerned about disclosures of corruption and racketeering revealed during congressional investigations of the labor unions in 1957, the President sought to promote a labor program that emphasized greater protection for the rights of union members (see *Congressional Quarterly Almanac*, vol. XIV, *1958*, pp. 674–86; for background on the intra-Cabinet split on labor policy matters see R. Alton Lee, *Eisenhower & Landrum-Griffin: A Study in Labor-Management Politics* [Lexington, Ky., 1990], pp. 25–29). Eisenhower's reference to his crowded legislative agenda may have been made with his defense reorganization plans in mind (see nos. 540 and 630; see also *New York Times*, Jan. 24, 1958).

[2] Secretary of Labor James P. Mitchell.

[3] In his special message to Congress on labor, Eisenhower would call for the election of union officers by secret ballot at least once every four years, the registration of all pension funds, and annual financial statements from all unions. The President did not ask to have strike votes conducted by secret ballot (see *Public Papers of the Presidents: Eisenhower, 1958*, pp. 118–24, and *New York Times*, Jan. 24, 1958). For developments see no. 734.

537 *EM, AWF, International Series: Philippine Islands*

TO CHARLES EUSTIS BOHLEN *January 18, 1958*

Dear Chip:[1] This morning Floyd Akers came in to report on his visit to the Philippines, and to bring me the gifts that President Garcia had sent.[2]

Floyd's enthusiasm knew no bounds, both as to the country itself and as to the fine job you are doing there. He was particularly impressed by your general grasp of the affairs of the Islands. He had a wonderful time and is highly appreciative of your courtesies to him.

He tells me, incidentally, that President Garcia is anxious to visit this country at an appropriate time; I suspect that you will handle that matter in the normal diplomatic channels.[3]

At any rate, I did want you to know of my personal gratitude for your attention and assistance to Floyd.

With warm regard, *Sincerely*

[1] Bohlen, a specialist in Soviet affairs, had been U.S. Ambassador to the Soviet Union from April 1953 until April 1957, when he became ambassador to the Philippines (for background see Galambos and van Ee, *The Middle Way*, no. 118; see also Charles E. Bohlen, *Witness to History 1929–1969* [New York, 1973], pp. 309–36, 441–56; and T. Michael Ruddy, *The Cautious Diplomat: Charles E. Bohlen and the Soviet Union, 1929–1969* [Kent, Ohio, 1986], pp. 140–41).

[2] Automobile executive Floyd DeSoto Akers had represented Eisenhower at the inauguration of Carlos Polestico Garcia as president of the Philippines on December 30. Garcia, vice-president at the time of President Ramon Magsaysay's death in March 1957, had completed Magsaysay's term of office and had won the presidential election in November. For background on Akers see Galambos and van Ee, *The Middle Way*, no. 1608; see also Ann Whitman memorandum, Jan. 18, 1958, AWF/AWD).

[3] Eisenhower would write Garcia on this same day. After thanking him for the gifts, he told the Philippine president that he had reminisced with Akers about the "pleasant memories" he had of his country (Eisenhower to Garcia, Jan. 18, 1958, AWF/I: Philippine Islands). Garcia would visit the United States in June. For developments see no. 605.

538 *EM, WHCF, Official File 72*

TO WILLIAM FIFE KNOWLAND *January 20, 1958*

For a long time I have personally been considering a plan for establishing a "First Secretary of the Government." Such an official would, of course, have the task of coordinating all the activities of the State Department, the USIA, the ICA, and would assist in establishing policies, under the President, to guide international activities of Defense, Commerce and so on.[1]

To my mind there would be many great advantages to such a plan. When we have an opportunity, such as a breakfast, I should like to talk to you about the matter.[2]

[1] In the spring of 1957 Eisenhower had begun discussions about the creation of a post for a "Secretary for International Coordination or First Secretary." This official would serve, he explained later, as "a Deputy Chairman of the National Security Council. During the intervals between the President's meetings with the Council such an assistant would be, day-by-day, engaged in the task of making sure that agencies having any connection with foreign problems were all working together to carry out the President's decisions" (Eisenhower, *Waging Peace,* pp. 634–35; see also Arnold, *Making the Managerial Presidency,* pp. 211–14). Eisenhower appears to have attached this note as a postscript to a January 20 letter to Senate Minority Leader Knowland. The letter, which is not printed here, concerned a proposed bill to establish a National Freedom Board (Eisenhower to Knowland, Jan. 17, 1958, same file as document; Signatures, Jan. 20, 1958, AWF/D). For background see no. 527.

[2] Eisenhower would meet with Knowland for about forty-five minutes on January 23 and may have discussed the matter at that time (see Ann Whitman memorandum, Jan. 30, 1958, AWF/AWD). See also no. 527. For developments see no. 555. See also the report of the President's Advisory Committee on Government Organization, "Organization for International Affairs," Feb. 9, 1958, AWF/A.

539 — *EM, AWF, Gettysburg Series*

TO ARTHUR SEYMOUR NEVINS — *January 20, 1958*

Personal and confidential

Dear Arthur: Assuming that you have returned to Gettysburg, may I ask you about recent newspaper accounts of payments in the past couple of years made by the government to my farm?[1]

My farm is run as a residence with no income whatsoever asked or received by me. I have no agreements with any other persons that would justify them to receive governmental monies which could presumably reimburse them for any expenditure for which I am responsible.[2]

For some days I have been awaiting a convenient time to talk with you about the whole matter but just today noted a new comment in the press to the effect that I have just received another thousand dollars.[3] If by any chance this report is correct please take immediate steps, if at all possible, to return the check, with statement that payment is not desired. We can then go over past accounts to see what steps I should later take to straighten the affair out.

I have always opposed any agricultural payment by the government to me and so far as I know have never received a single dollar of such payment. My entire effort has been to avoid any connection with the government or with others who have, without any formal agreement, used my ground, not as a farm, but as a residential property. These individuals have endeavored to observe the same complete separation of interests.

I am on my way to Chicago and shall try to contact you by telephone; but failing that will send you this message which I have written on the airplane.[4]

With warm regard, *As ever*

[1] Nevins had been in Thomasville, Georgia. On January 8 the *New York Times* had reported that the President's Gettysburg farms received soil bank payments in excess of $2,000 for retiring thirty-two acres of corn land from production in 1956, and for keeping fourteen acres out of wheat in 1957.

[2] The Eisenhower farms had received an additional $1,120 from the Federal Agricultural Conservation Program, a program the Administration sought to abolish in 1956. For background on the Administration's farm program see Galambos and van Ee, *The Middle Way*, nos. 1748 and 1841, and no. 345 in these volumes.

[3] On January 27 the President would join Nevins and two certified public accountants in an off-the-record meeting at the White House. Following the meeting Eisenhower would decide to file amended income tax returns for the years the soil bank payments were received (Telephone conversation, Eisenhower and Allen, Jan. 27, 1958, AWF/D). Apologizing on January 29, Nevins said he hoped that the matter of soil-bank and other farm supports would be settled so that Eisenhower would be "spared any further annoyance." Nevins said he regretted that he did not "foresee the possible trouble that the press could stir up on this subject." He also intended to "forego any government supports" until the President was out of office (AWF/Gettysburg; see also Nevins, *Five-Star Farmer*, pp. 129–30, and Ann Whitman memorandum, Jan. 8, 1957, AWF/AWD).

[4] Later this evening, before some 5,000 Republicans attending a fund-raising dinner sponsored by the United Republican Fund of Illinois, Eisenhower would ask Republicans to keep the national security issue out of this year's "political chess game." The address, broadcast by radio and television networks of the National Broadcasting Company, would open the party's fight for victory in the 1958 congressional elections (see *Public Papers of the Presidents: Eisenhower, 1958*, pp. 114–16, and *New York Times*, Jan. 20, 1958).

540 *EM, AWF, Administration Series*

To Charles Douglas Jackson *January 21, 1958*

Dear C. D.: You misunderstood one point I intended to make when I called your attention to the fact that I would be on this job only three years more.[1]

I don't give a hoot what my particular successor thinks about my ideas on military organization, or on what success I may have in bringing about a reorganization. What I meant was something entirely different. It is that staffs and Congress go on forever. It happens as the head of the entire Defense establishment I stand between staffs and Congress. If the organization is going to be sound and durable, I must be able to lead, persuade, cajole and of course to some extent compel appropriate parts of these continuing organizations to go on.[2]

Thanks very much for your letter. *As ever*

[1] Jackson, publisher of *Fortune* magazine and former Presidential Assistant, had written on January 17, 1958 (AWF/A) to discuss his January 14 meeting with Eisenhower (see Ann Whitman memorandum, Jan. 14, 1958; see also no. 527). Jackson said that during their discussion of the reorganization of the Defense Department "one item came up on which I did not have the nerve to argue with you at the time, but after thinking it over I felt that I ought to mention it." The President's State of the Union Address, Jackson said, gave the impression that all the details of the defense reorganization had already been worked out. "It is now somewhat of a let-down for this member of the public to discover . . . that it is Neil McElroy who is going to come up with a proposition, and disconcerting to hear that McElroy, who obviously has not been in the job long enough to be able to have experienced firm ideas on this subject, is turning to Messrs. Twining, Bradley, and Radford, all three of whom do not have exactly shining records as far as controlling inter-Service rivalry is concerned."

Eisenhower had remarked that since he would be in his job for only three more years, he did "not want to do anything in this area which might not be viewed as the right solution" by his successor. Jackson wrote that his response to Eisenhower's comment should have been: "Mr. President, in the mind of the American people you are not only the nation's Chief Executive, but the nation's foremost soldier, and the one man in the whole country who knows more about the Defense Establishment and what ought to be done about it than anybody else. A command decision from your mind is what we are all looking for. We don't have any faith in committee surveys and recommendations, particularly if the committee is composed of the interested parties. And as far as pleasing your successor is concerned, to hell with that. He will be able to take care of himself."

On the State of the Union Address see no. 526.

[2] For background on the defense reorganization plan see no. 401; for developments see no. 630; on efforts to convince the public of the need for defense reorganization see Eisenhower to Larmon, January 28, 1958, WHCF/OF 3-VV.

541 — *EM, AWF, Name Series*

To Robert S. Hartley — *January 21, 1958*

Dear Bob: Here is a page advertisement from a small Texas paper that interested me. It has to do only with steer feeding, and I wonder whether you know about the product that they call "Synovex."

Possibly the veterinarian might be well informed on it if you have not looked up the matter.[1]

Sometime when I am up at the farm, I will talk to you about it.[2]

Incidentally, I notice also that the ad says you can write to the Squibb Veterinary Department to get more information. *Sincerely*

[1] Developed in 1956 by Syntex, S.A., in Mexico City, Synovex, a growth agent for cattle, was marketed by E. R. Squibb & Sons. The advertisement is not in AWF. For background on Eisenhower's participation in the care of his Aberdeen Angus herd see, for example, Galambos and van Ee, *The Middle Way*, nos. 1101, 1714, and 1984.

[2] The President would telephone Hartley, his Gettysburg herdsman, on January 23 (Telephone conversation, AWF/D). The Eisenhowers would visit their farm in Gettysburg March 28–31.

542 *EM, AWF, Administration Series*

TO BERNARD MICHAEL SHANLEY *January 22, 1958*

Memorandum. Personal

Some days ago you spoke to me about an intention of asking some of my friends to be helpful in financing your campaign for the Senatorial post now occupied by Alec Smith.[1] Of course there are always two parts to a campaign, the primary and the election itself.

In this first part, I cannot in any way indicate, even by implication, any preference as among those individuals who will be seeking nomination by the Republican Party.[2] Consequently, in requesting funds to assist in the primary, I feel that you must go on your own steam—that is, you will not seek help from people except those who are your *own* friends and who you have reason to believe will be sympathetic.

Of course, I suppose that anyone seeking the nomination would want to describe some of the details of his own political experience, whether it would be in the White House, in Congress or anywhere else. To this there can certainly be no objection.

With respect to the election campaign, I think that any personal solicitation of funds directed to people who are my friends should contain a statement about as follows:

> "In spite of my long friendship and intimate official association with the President, I am very anxious that my request for assistance should not be interpreted as imposing upon his friendship, or used, in any way, as a lever intended to influence your action in the matter. My only excuse is that knowing of the friendship between you and the President, I felt it proper for

me to pledge to you my unswerving determination to support him in every possible way if I am successful in winning the office I seek."[3]

[1] Shanley had resigned as Eisenhower's appointments secretary in November 1957 to run for the New Jersey Senate seat of Howard Alexander Smith. Smith, who had served as Republican Senator from New Jersey since 1944, had not decided at that time whether to seek reelection in 1958 (see *New York Times*, Nov. 7, 8, 1957).

[2] Eisenhower would announce his refusal to support any candidate for Senator in the New Jersey Republican primary race at his news conference on February 5 (see *Public Papers of the Presidents: Eisenhower, 1958*, p. 149).

[3] Eisenhower had accompanied this formal memorandum to Shanley with a note saying: "Dear Bern: In order that there can be no possible misunderstanding between us as to your approaching any friends of mine for campaign contributions, I have made a memorandum for the record which I think expresses my meaning as clearly as possible. I send you a copy" (Eisenhower to Shanley, Jan. 22, 1958, AWF/A; see also Ann Whitman to Shanley, Jan. 23, 1958, AWF/A). In a letter written January 30 (AWF/A), Shanley would thank the President for the memorandum: "Naturally, as you are aware, I will do nothing to embarrass you in any way in this present situation."

Eisenhower would console Shanley on his loss of the New Jersey Republican primary election to Robert Winthrop Kean in an April 22 letter (AWF/A). "You ran a good race," he said, "and it was too bad that the principal contests had to be between two men who were so enthusiastically supporting the Administration" (*New York Times*, Apr. 16, 1958). Kean would lose the election for Senator in November (*New York Times*, Nov. 5, 1958).

543 — *EM, AWF, DDE Diaries Series*

To Cortlandt Van Rensselaer Schuyler — *January 22, 1958*

Dear Cort: After leaving Paris I made a mental note, in the midst of my preoccupations, to write a personal message to you. This feeling was inspired by a number of things, among which was the fact that we have been friends for a long time. Another was that I had seen so much less of you and Wy than I had hoped that I felt that to that extent at least my visit to Paris had left an unsatisfactory feeling.[1]

Moreover, I wanted to tell you that, in my opinion, you have been one of the indispensable wheel horses of the NATO organization. I say this with even greater feeling because of the fact that I personally held for a short time the position of SACEUR and I am consequently more familiar than most with the complicated nature of your problems, as well as their vital importance.[2]

Every once in a while Al and I have the opportunity to indulge in a visit of a half hour or so. Invariably your name comes up for mention and it has become almost routine for one or both to express a feeling of lasting appreciation because of your dedicated and efficient service in one of the toughest spots in our whole military organization. Frankly, I hope that you will stay on in your post at least as long as I am in mine.[3]

As I say, I should liked to have had more time for a completely personal chat with you when I was in Paris, and do hope that if you are contemplating any trip to this country, no matter when, you will make some effort to contact my office with a view to setting up an engagement.[4]

Give my affectionate greeting to Wy and, of course, warm regard to yourself. *Sincerely*

[1] Schuyler had served as Chief of Staff to both Supreme Allied Commanders, Europe, Alfred M. Gruenther (1953–1956), and his replacement, Lauris Norstad, at SHAPE (see Galambos and van Ee, *The Middle Way*, no. 1786). Eisenhower had visited Paris from December 13 to December 19, 1957, to attend the NATO Council Meetings (see nos. 493 and 501). "Wy" was Schuyler's wife, the former Wynona Coykendall.

[2] On Eisenhower's service as SACEUR see Galambos, *NATO and the Campaign of 1952.*

[3] Schuyler would respond on February 5 (AWF/A). He had been thinking of retiring at the end of 1958 to "avoid a later situation in which both SACEUR and his Chief of Staff could be leaving about the same time." There were also "one or two minor personal considerations" involved. "However," he said, "these factors are of no consequence whatever in the light of your feeling that you still need me here. That being the case I shall, of course, now give no further thought to the retirement matter. Should new considerations arise at any future date I shall take no action in this respect without again consulting you." For developments see no. 1013.

[4] General and Mrs. Schuyler had attended a luncheon for Eisenhower on December 15.

544 *EM, AWF, Name Series*

To Willard Stewart Paul *January 22, 1958*

Dear Stewart: Sherm Adams showed me your recent letter about the possibility that I might find real use after next June for the two properties that you have purchased to help meet the future needs of Gettysburg College.[1] I am deeply touched by your thoughtful suggestion, particularly as it carries with it the idea that I should make some permanent use of offices within the building known as the "Old Dorm."[2]

Up until this moment my visits to Gettysburg have been confined almost exclusively to weekend periods and in most cases I have not been pushed for office space. While I had originally intended to do a great deal more commuting between Gettysburg and Washington than I seem to be able to fit into my schedule, the fact is that my trips are not only short in duration but widely separated as to time.

Quite naturally I would like to be identified, in some definite way, with Gettysburg College. With the thought that I might even during the next three years have a more definite need for office space in the town than I now have, I shall ask an Aide, one of the Secret Service men, and, possibly, in addition a Signal Corps officer, to make a little survey to see what would be required. After they make their survey they can possibly have a talk with you, as well as with me.[3]

In any event, I have been looking forward for some time to a real visit with you. Possibly we can set up an engagement one of these days.[4]

With warm regard, *As ever*

[1] Lieutenant General Paul (USA, ret.) had been president of Gettysburg College since 1956. He had commanded the 26th Division in Europe during World War II and had been Personnel of the Army Director (G-1) while Eisenhower was Chief of Staff. For background see *Eisenhower Papers*, vols. I–XVII. Paul had written to Sherman Adams on January 17 (AWF/N) that Eisenhower had approved a plan to install a suite of rooms for his use as an office in Gettysburg (see n. 2 below). In the meantime, wrote Paul, the President could make use of two houses next to the football practice field. The houses could be reached from Eisenhower's farm and the airport without going through town, and there was space for a helicopter landing.

[2] Paul had decided to renovate the oldest building on the Gettysburg College campus. "Old Dorm" had been used as a hospital during the Civil War.

[3] Paul had suggested that Adams have the buildings surveyed. As it turned out, the plans for the office building at Gettysburg would be "dropped" (Telephone conversation, Eisenhower and Mamie Eisenhower, Jan. 28, 1958, AWF/D). For developments see no. 1242.

[4] The Pauls would visit the Eisenhowers at their Gettysburg farm on December 30, 1958.

545 *EM, AWF, Gettysburg Series*

TO ALLAN A. RYAN *January 22, 1958*

Dear Allan: You know how grateful I have been for your loan to me of Ankonian 3551 for use with my cows and those of the Angus cattle belonging to the Allen-Byars partnership.[1] Ankonian has been invaluable.

You will recall also that in allowing me to have his use, you listed, on the records of the Angus Association, my name as a one-third owner, so as to permit me to use artificial insemination on the relatively few cows I have. But knowing all along that I should not impose indefinitely on your generosity, I have at times felt almost guilty because of the length of time that I have kept him at the farm. As soon as I can get the necessary papers from Gettysburg, I shall arrange for the re-transfer and re-registration and, within a reasonable time, will have him trucked back up to the Ankony farm.[2]

With your consent, the actual date of shipment may be somewhat delayed, while I am making necessary arrangements for a replacement.[3]

A special—and it seems to me compelling—reason for effecting the transfer of registration at this particular time involves a sale the Allen-Byars partnership is planning in late April.[4] Some of these cattle carry the service of Ankonian 3551. So long as my name appears on the registration records, the sale catalogue would of course, in these cases, list the "Eisenhower Farms" as a one-third owner of Ankonian 3551. This would defeat the special care I have observed always to assure the complete separation of my cattle from those of my future partners.

These men are just as anxious as I that there be no official or business connection among us, so long as I hold my present office. Consequently I have never sold any animal or taken any income of any kind from the disposition of calves and steers, or from culling my tiny herd.[5]

I mention this particular situation just to emphasize my concern about timing of the transfer so as to prevent any misleading information to be included, no matter how innocently, in the catalogue that will undoubtedly soon be prepared. Since, even without these special circumstances, I have felt it proper and only decent to return Ankonian 3551 this year, my present decision merely sets up a need for promptness in my action.

Again I repeat that I could not possibly feel a greater sense of gratitude to you for your kindness and that of Mr. Leachman.

I have been very proud of the animal and I am sure that by the time I can actually give my own attention to the breeding of fine Angus, I shall feel an even deeper gratitude to you because of the improved types of quality heifers that I shall have at the place, all due to your kindness.

Please convey to Mrs. Ryan my warm greetings and, of course, the very best of everything to yourself. *Sincerely*

[1] For background on the herd sire see Galambos and van Ee, *The Middle Way,* no. 1888, and no. 15 in these volumes. On the Allen-Byars partnership see Galambos and van Ee, *The Middle Way,* no. 1101, and no. 70 in these volumes.

[2] Ryan would reply (Jan. 27) that he had spoken with farm manager Arthur Nevins and they would comply with Eisenhower's wishes regarding Ankonian 3551. On January 29 Nevins would report that he had mailed the registration certificate and an

application for transfer of Eisenhower's one-third interest to Ryan at Ankony Farms. The transfer date was fixed at December 15. Nevins said he also had confirmed with Ryan the purchase of a one-third interest by the Allen-Byars partnership (see also Whitman to Nevins, Jan. 23, 1958, and related correspondence, all in AWF/Gettysburg).

[3] For developments on the replacement see no. 697.

[4] The Byars and Allen sale would take place on April 26 (see Memorandum in AWF/Gettysburg and Telephone conversation, Eisenhower and Nevins, Apr. 23, 1958, AWF/D).

[5] For background on Eisenhower's arrangement with Allen and Byars see no. 70.

546

EM, AWF, Administration Series: People-to-People

To Charles Edward Wilson — *January 23, 1958*

Dear Charlie: I was glad to receive your letter on the People-to-People Program, together with a copy of the memorandum to your Trustees and Directors, and also to learn the results of the meeting you had with the Vice President, Ambassador Allen, and my staff on Wednesday.[1] I can well appreciate that the way must seem uncertain in view of the lack of financial support, even though the idea and the objectives of the program are accepted by so many people who are already dedicating themselves to the work of the many committees. In discovering and developing the right structure for the People-to-People project, there is no alternative to persevering efforts of the kind you are making—all based on the principle that this must be a truly private effort, with governmental ties limited to liaison only, but with a constant readiness on the part of my associates and myself to help in any legitimate way we can.[2]

In this connection, I agree with the thought that has been expressed to me that the undertaking of a major "impact" project by the whole organization might give purpose and direction that could well have a beneficial effect on the willingness of those to whom we must look for solid support. The proposal to hold an assembly of world-recognized individuals in the Arts and Humanities would seem to be, in many ways, an ideal example of such a project. I understand you will be actively looking into such an idea in the coming weeks.[3]

As you and your associates develop your proposals—along these or other lines, I hope you will continue to stay in close touch and let me know at any time of ways in which I can be of help.[4]

With warm regard, *As ever*

[1] Wilson, president of the People-to-People exchange program, had written on January 22 following the meeting (AWF/A, People-to-People). Initiated by Eisenhower in September 1956, the program had been operating as a private organization since September 1957. At that time Eisenhower had met with trustees of major foundations in an effort to obtain financial support for the project (see nos. 283 and 380). On January 20 Wilson had submitted to the trustees and directors of the People-to-People program a "feasible plan" for transferring the operation of the program from "government to private auspices" (AWF/D).
[2] Wilson wrote in his January 20 memorandum that requests for funds had been turned down by three major foundations, several minor ones, and most of the 500 largest American business corporations (for background see no. 380). Wilson said that the current structure of the organization was the obstacle to raising funds. People-to-People contained forty-two autonomous committees largely composed of volunteers who were involved in other business or professional activities. These volunteers could not be expected to raise funds and employ and supervise staffs to carry out their plans, he stated. Wilson wanted "to use the rich and valuable experience of the program chairmen at the policy level and relieve them of the burden of fund-raising and administrative responsibility. . . ."

At the policy level, Wilson wrote, a dozen or so groups should meet monthly or bimonthly and make recommendations quarterly to the board of trustees. These groups, he went on, should be composed of volunteers representing business, hobbies, education and culture, patriotic service, the professions, communications, religious groups, youth groups and women's groups, farm and labor, sports, and civic organizations. The professional staffs in Wilson's proposed organization would concern themselves with: research and evaluation; program development for national organizations; industry and commerce; public information; local community organizations; public relations; international relations; awards; and fund raising.
[3] Assistant to the President Sherman Adams had suggested this idea to the President following the meeting with Wilson (Ann Whitman memorandum, Jan. 22, 1958, AWF/AWD; see also no. 197).
[4] In November 1961 the People-to-People program, with the financial assistance of the Hallmark Foundation, would incorporate with its headquarters in Kansas City, Missouri. Eisenhower would serve as the first chairman of the board of trustees (Abbott Washburn, "Why Did President Eisenhower Put So Much Faith in People-to-People Contacts?" *People*, Summer 1990; *New York Times*, Nov. 9, 1961). See also no. 1402.

547 — *EM, AWF, Name Series*

To John Michael Budinger — *January 23, 1958*

Dear Jack: I find myself the fortunate recipient of three letters from you. But most importantly, I want to congratulate you, and the directors and members of the Blind Brook Club, on your election as President.[1] That fact alone renews my desire some day to have another game there.

Still on Blind Brook matters, I appreciate the kindness of the Board of Directors in electing me to Honorary Membership for the calendar year 1958. And much as I should like to attend the dinner party in honor of Ike Harvey, I know you will realize it will be impossible.[2] I hope, however, that you will extend my greetings and best wishes to all who join with you on that occasion, and that you will give Ike a special salute for his fine work and long term of service.

Now as to your suggestion of an "economic high command." In a sense we have a group that operates as such a body. I hold fairly regular meetings with the Secretary of the Treasury, the Chairman of the Federal Reserve Board, the Chairman of the Council of Economic Advisers and Dr. Hauge (who, as you know, is my Special Assistant on Economic Affairs.) We discuss informally all the problems that confront us. But your suggestion goes even further than our discussions and offhand I would think it has much merit. I shall get some of my "experts" to give me their opinions.[3]

With warm regard, and again congratulations on your new job!

As ever

[1] Bankers Trust Senior Vice-President Budinger wrote frequently with suggestions on the President's management of economic affairs (see no. 484). In one letter written on January 20, and two on January 21 (AWF/N), he discussed affairs at the Blind Brook Country Club in Port Chester, New York (for background see Galambos and van Ee, *The Middle Way*, no. 1541).

[2] Budinger's January 20 letter had invited Eisenhower to attend a dinner party to honor outgoing club president I. J. Harvey, Jr., president of the Flintkote Company, manufacturers of asphalt shingles and roofing materials. The January 21 letter had advised Eisenhower on his honorary membership in the Blind Brook Club.

[3] In his second letter of January 21, Budinger had complimented Eisenhower on the State of the Union Address (see no. 526). "I was pleased to see you put so much stress on the economic aspects of our position," he wrote, "but I am wondering if on the economic front we are properly organized, both defensively and offensively." Budinger suggested that the United States needed an "economic high command" to ensure that the various economic and financial agencies of the government not go in "different and often opposite directions." "I was very much impressed with the measures taken by the European Economic Communities to effectuate their long term aims and purposes, with which I think we eventually may come in conflict unless we coordinate our economic activities with our western allies," Budinger wrote. On Eisenhower's interaction with his economic advisers see, for example, no. 572.

548 *EM, AWF, Name Series*

To James Campbell Hagerty *January 24, 1958*

Memorandum

We hope that there will be numerous occasions for making announcements in the field of scientific achievement. Many of these, of course, will be directed toward improvement of weaponry for our forces.[1]

I have two suggestions:

a. I assume that each of the Services that has an important part in this kind of achievement will want to make its own statement. But I do hope that wherever possible these will be made by the Secretary of Defense in person.

b. At the same time, I think that very quickly after one of these experiments has been successful, we should have a White House statement prepared. Its particular purpose would be to relate the discovery to peace. It seems to me that within 24 to 36 hours after a significant event of this kind, we should be able to get out something that would be slanted strongly toward:

1. the need and opportunity for peaceful negotiations in the international field, and
2. the peaceful uses of the natural laws that have now been harnessed for defense purposes.[2]

[1] Eisenhower may have been anticipating two planned satellite launches, both using military missiles. The Navy's Vanguard program, which having failed to launch its satellite in December, had scheduled another attempt for January 18; the launch would subsequently be postponed until January 28. The Army, using the Jupiter-C rocket with the Explorer satellite, had postponed its scheduled launch from January 29 until January 31. Although the troubled Vanguard program would again fail to orbit its satellite, the Army would succeed in launching the Explorer, the first American satellite, into orbit on January 31 (see *New York Times*, Jan. 28, Feb. 1, 1958; see also Divine, *The Sputnik Challenge*, pp. 71–72, 93–96, and Levine, *The Missile and Space Race*, pp. 68–69). For background on the intense controversy over the U.S. failure to match the success of the Soviet Union's Sputnik satellite, and the competition among the services to be the first to launch a satellite, see Robert J. Watson, *Into the Missile Age, 1956–1960*, History of the Office of the Secretary of Defense, ed. Alfred Goldberg, 3 vols. to date (Washington, D.C., 1982–97), vol. IV (1997), pp. 171–97 (hereafter cited as Watson, *Into the Missile Age*); and McDougall, *The Heavens and the Earth*, pp. 141–76.

[2] On February 1 Eisenhower would issue a very brief statement regarding the successful satellite launch. Noting that he had been informed that the United States had just successfully placed "a scientific earth satellite in orbit around the earth," Eisenhower said only that the launching was "part of our country's participation in the International Geophysical Year." He promised to share all information received from the satellite with "the scientific community of the world" (*Public Papers of the Presidents: Eisenhower, 1958*, pp. 140–41; see also Ann Whitman memorandum, Jan. 22, 1958, AWF/AWD).

549 *EM, AWF, Name Series*

To Julius Earl Schaefer *January 24, 1958*

Personal

Dear Earl:[1] Except in its details, your suggestion for a better integrated education for our young men in the Service Academies was made by me to Admiral Nimitz as long ago as 1947. He and I really got steamed up on this purpose, which we had outlined to ourselves in principle. It turned out that we were defeated by staffs that found in the idea such insuperable technical and administrative difficulties that we had to give up.[2]

Of course at that moment we had only two Academies, and our first thought was to avoid the construction of a third one, so that by transferring candidates back and forth between the two we would get practically the same basic education for all.[3]

Your suggestion takes cognizance of changed conditions; now it may seem more appealing than it did ten or eleven years ago. In any event, you may be sure that I shall bring it to the attention of Secretary McElroy and some of his associates.[4]

The other day my friend Al Gruenther was in Wichita, but he told me that he did not get to see you. I am sorry because he is one of my very fine friends.

With warm regard, *As ever*

[1] Schaefer had been vice-chairman of Boeing since 1938 (see Galambos and van Ee, *The Middle Way*, no. 1316). His January 22, 1958, letter to Eisenhower is in WHCF/OF 3-WW.

[2] See Galambos, *Chief of Staff*, no. 1271. Retired Fleet Admiral Chester William Nimitz had been serving as special assistant to the Secretary of the Navy since 1947. As Chief of Naval Operations he had served on the Joint Chiefs of Staff with then Army Chief of Staff, Eisenhower.

[3] On the establishment of the Air Force Academy see *ibid.*, no. 1697, and Galambos and van Ee, *The Middle Way*, nos. 980, 1584. See also John P. Lovell, *Neither Athens Nor Sparta? The American Service Academies in Transition* (Bloomington, Ind., 1979), pp. 45–56, 59–69.

[4] Schaefer had suggested a six-year program of military training. The first two years, at West Point, would be used to educate students in the customs and traditions of the Services, and to teach land warfare and philosophies, as well as basic academic subjects. The third and fourth years, to be served at the Naval Academy, would stress modern naval warfare, with an emphasis on mechanics, engineering and the sciences. The fifth and sixth years, at the Air Force Academy, would emphasize air strategy and techniques, along with an academic program of advanced engineering and scientific subjects. The graduates of this program, Schaefer wrote, "would be well-rounded, technically trained military men and citizens . . . with the capability to specialize in any field to which they might be called. More particularly, they would be better prepared to understand and appreciate the broad concept of duties that would fall to administrators, and later to formulators of national policy. Certainly this would

be true for our present age of dynamically changing functions involving space and speed." There is no correspondence with Secretary McElroy on this issue in AWF.

550

EM, AWF, Name Series

To Hastings Lionel Ismay
Personal

January 25, 1958

Dear Pug: I was indeed pleased to receive your note, written from the Barbados. And I was keenly interested in some of the news you were able to give me and in the explanation of the circumstances surrounding the writing of Brookie's book.[1]

Of course whatever Brookie could possibly have said about his other war associates is not so important as what he says about his own wartime Chief.[2] All of us got impatient, at times, with some of the mannerisms, the idiosyncrasies and even the demands of Winston. But I had supposed that all of us felt that these were of no consequence as compared to his great contributions to the war effort and, for myself, I never lost an unbounded admiration and personal liking for him. I could not imagine myself as being guilty of writing anything, ten years after the war was over, that could be construed as disparaging the accomplishments of the wartime Prime Minister.

With regard to the book itself: For some years my reading time has been severely limited. So when I pick up a volume that seems to me to be unbalanced or to reflect prejudice and, as you suggest, mental and physical fatigue, I simply ignore the book and go on to something else.[3]

As you know, I developed, during the course of the war, quite a liking for Brookie. I tried to work with him cooperatively, and was delighted when, on March 24, 1945, as we just succeeded in forcing our "power" crossing of the Rhine, he came to me and said in effect, "Thank God you stuck to your plan. I was wrong and I cannot tell you how happy I am that you had the faith and persistence to see it through."[4] At that moment it was no longer merely a question of liking him; I now felt that he had become a really big man. I prefer to think of him as he was on that morning, as he and Winston and I were watching what we clearly saw as the end of the Hitler regime, than to think of him as an embittered individual who has allowed himself to be used for belittling others and himself to appear to be something less than generous.

It is really wonderful that you are coming along so well, and I know how much you and Kathleen[5] must be enjoying the rest and recreation you are getting. Incidentally, if I knew the identity of "one of your trusted NATO staff" I would thank him for the compliment he paid me in his letter to you, which you relayed to me. It gave me a lift.[6]

With warm regard, *As ever*

[1] Ismay, who had retired as NATO Secretary General in May 1957 (see Galambos and van Ee, *The Middle Way,* no. 271, and *New York Times,* May 17, 1957), had written (n.d., AWF/N) to thank the President belatedly for his Christmas card. He had reported on his own health; on his recent meeting with Churchill ("deaf now, and rather frail; but the indomitable will power and profound wisdom are still there"); and the beginning of work on his memoirs.

"Brookie" was Alan Francis Brooke, First Viscount, Baron Alanbrooke of Brookeborough, British field marshal and chief of the Imperial General Staff during World War II (see Chandler, *War Years,* no. 2397). Ismay had commented on Sir Arthur Bryant's *The Turn of the Tide: A History of the War Years Based on the Diaries of Field-Marshal Lord Alanbrooke, Chief of the Imperial General Staff* (London, 1957). Calling the book "little short of tragedy," Ismay had wondered "How Brookie could have been so sick as to hand over his diaries—written late at night when he was exhausted, depressed, and self pitying—defeats me! If I had indulged in committing my nocturnal thoughts to paper," he added, "I would have quite often written most scurrilous things about our beloved Chief—and been sorry and ashamed of myself next morning. Brookie himself realizes his error, and is I think very sad about it. So I hope that the Second Volume will be less of a travesty."

[2] Alanbrooke had called Churchill "a wonderful character, the most marvellous qualities and superhuman genius mixed with an astonishing lack of vision at times, and an impetuosity which, if not guided, must inevitably bring him into trouble again and again." Churchill's "most remarkable failing" was his inability to "see a whole strategical problem at once. His gaze always settles on some definite part of the canvas and the rest of the picture is lost." Summing up, Alanbrooke said that Churchill was "quite the most difficult man to work with that I have ever struck, but I would not have missed the chance of working with him for anything on earth" (Bryant, *Turn of the Tide,* p. 723).

Alanbrooke was equally hard on Eisenhower. "It must be remembered that Eisenhower had never even commanded a battalion in action when he found himself commanding a group of Armies in North Africa," Alanbrooke said. "No wonder he was at a loss as to what to do, and allowed himself to be absorbed in the political situation at the expense of the tactical. I had little confidence in his having the ability to handle the military situation confronting him, and he caused me great anxiety. . . . He learnt a lot during the war, but tactics, strategy and command were never his strong points" (pp. 527–28). See also *New York Times,* February 17, May 19, 21, 1957.

[3] See also no. 933.

[4] Eisenhower recalled this episode in *Crusade in Europe* (p. 372). Alanbrooke would later dispute Eisenhower's version of events in the second volume of his memoirs. "To the best of my memory," Alanbrooke would write, "I congratulated him heartily on his success and said that, as matters had turned out, his policy was now the correct one; that, with the German in his defeated condition, no dangers now existed in a dispersal of effort. I am quite certain that I never said to him, 'You were completely right,' as I am still convinced that he was completely wrong" (Arthur Bryant, *Triumph in the West: A History of the War Years Based on the Diaries of Field-Marshal Lord Alanbrooke, Chief of the Imperial General Staff* [Garden City, N.Y., 1959], pp. 332–33).

[5] Ismay's wife was the former Laura Kathleen Clegg.
[6] Ismay had added as a postscript: "I have just this moment received a letter from one of my most trusted NATO Staff of which the following is an extract about the Council Meeting: 'President Ike was very inspiring and did a magnificent job.' I knew you would." On the NATO meeting see no. 493.

551 *EM, WHCF, President's Personal File 308-A*

To Arthur Krock *January 25, 1958*
Personal

Dear Arthur: Thank you for your courtesy in sending me excerpts from Mr. Hickey's letter. I acknowledge a feeling of great compliment in what he had to say.[1]

Some time you and I may, perhaps, have a chance to discuss the possibility he suggests that the thinking and action of an individual might subconsciously be shaped by the great respect and admiration such an individual might have for another.

Speaking in general, I think such an influence would certainly be felt. But when such a thought is made definitely specific and personal to me, I cannot escape a feeling of humility bordering on embarrassment.

In any event, both my son and I share Mr. Hickey's enthusiasm for Freeman's biography of George Washington. Both of us likewise liked his biography of Lee and his volumes entitled "Lee's Lieutenants."[2]

Again let me say I deeply appreciate your passing on to me a thought that could not fail to give me a heartwarming lift.

With warm regard, *Sincerely*

P.S. I am taking the liberty of writing Mr. Hickey a little note of appreciation.[3]

[1] *New York Times* columnist Krock had enclosed the excerpts with his letter of January 21. E. James Hickey, an attorney from Rochester, New York, had written to Krock (Jan. 7) to express his approval of Krock's January 3 editorial defending Eisenhower against mounting criticism. Hickey told Krock that while reading Douglas Southall Freeman's six-volume set *George Washington: A Biography* (New York, 1948–57), he found himself "struck time and again by the similarity of character traits between Eisenhower and Washington." Hickey said he believed that Eisenhower "subconsciously or otherwise patterned his life" after the first president. Hickey's opinion had been prompted by Krock's reference to an interview in which Eisenhower said he believed that the "greatest American leaders in time of peril" were Washington, Lincoln, and Robert E. Lee. Hickey also wrote that he recently read that Eisenhower described Washington as "the greatest individual produced in the history of the English speaking peoples."

[2] These were the Pulitzer Prize-winning *R. E. Lee: A Biography*, 4 vols. (New York, 1934–35) and *Lee's Lieutenants: A Study in Command*, 3 vols. (New York, 1942–44).
[3] Eisenhower would write to Hickey on this same day. See also Hickey to Krock, and Hickey to Eisenhower, January 27, 1958. All correspondence is in the same file as the document.

552

Dulles Papers,
White House Memoranda Series

TO CHRISTIAN ARCHIBALD HERTER — *January 27, 1958*
Personal. Eyes only

Dear Chris: I am more than happy to make a statement about the agreement contemplating certain exchanges with the Soviets in the cultural, technical and educational fields. I would be even happier if we could implement a program of getting some of these contacts based upon thousands rather than upon scores.[1]

One thought that occurs to me is this: agreements on a quid pro quo basis are one thing, but suppose we should just issue an invitation that would go up to the order of five or ten thousand, where there would be no obligation on the part of the Soviets to reciprocate beyond the degree to which they desired. The only thing we would need would be the consent of their government to allow these students to study in one of our universities for a year.

Please do not by any manner of means circulate this to anybody in your Department. I have already talked about it informally with Foster, but the difference between a unilateral invitation as opposed to a head for head exchange may have some appeal to the Communist officials.[2]

With warm regard, *As ever*

[1] For background on student exchanges see no. 535. Earlier this same day Eisenhower had called for a vast expansion of the exchange of students from Communist countries. At a ceremony to celebrate the tenth anniversary of legislation providing for the government's information and cultural exchange programs (the Smith-Mundt Act), Eisenhower had endorsed these exchanges as "a sure way to increase understanding and secure a just peace" (*Public Papers of the Presidents: Eisenhower, 1958*, pp. 125–26).

After the ceremony Eisenhower had endorsed a suggestion that the United States admit Russian students whether or not the Soviet Union reciprocated. He also suggested that private contributions finance the visits (Ann Whitman memorandum, Jan. 27, 1958, AWF/AWD; and *New York Times*, Jan. 28, 1958).

[2] On this same day after negotiations between U.S. and Soviet officials, the two nations issued a joint communiqué that established a program of student exchanges between Moscow and Leningrad universities and American schools. Twenty students

from each country would participate in the program in the 1958–1959 academic year, and this number would increase to thirty in 1959–1960 (*U.S. Department of State Bulletin* 38, no. 973 [February 17, 1958], 243–48).

On January 30 Eisenhower would tell Kevin McCann, who had brought an exchange proposal to the President's attention, that he might offer scholarships to the Russians "within two weeks" (Ann Whitman memorandum, Jan. 30, 1958, AWF/AWD). For developments see no. 618.

553 *EM, AWF, DDE Diaries Series*

TO SHERMAN ADAMS *January 27, 1958*
Memorandum

Senator Thye has addressed to me a personal communication about the dairy situation in Minnesota.[1] In order to assure that I personally received the message, he transmitted the letter directly to the Usher.[2] You will note his final paragraph requests a conference with me. I assume that you had better set this up, but please be sure some staff officer is included in the appointment who is knowledgeable in this field.

Attached to this letter is one Ezra Benson independently submitted. I think you will want to read both.[3]

As quickly as you will let Mrs. Whitman know of a convenient time for Senator Thye to visit me, she will draft a note asking him—or alternatively you can telephone his office.[4]

[1] Republican Senator Edward John Thye of Minnesota had long protested Administration efforts to lower price supports for dairy products (for background see Galambos and van Ee, *The Middle Way*, no. 787). His concern stemmed from Secretary of Agriculture Ezra Taft Benson's December 1957 announcement that federal price supports on dairy products were to be cut as deeply as the law allowed, effective April 1, 1958. The move had aroused bitter opposition across party lines in Congress, prompting demands that Eisenhower fire Benson (*New York Times*, Dec. 19, 1957).

[2] J. Bernard West was the White House Chief Usher.

[3] Benson's letter is not in AWF.

[4] Eisenhower would meet with Senator Thye, Sherman Adams, and White House aide Jack Z. Anderson for sixteen minutes on January 31. Anderson, who had served as special assistant to the Secretary of Agriculture from 1955–1956, and Governor Adams had briefed Eisenhower on the milk support price issue in preparation for the meeting with Thye (Anderson to Whitman, Jan. 31, 1958, AWF/D). Rejecting the Administration's position, Thye would tell the President that while milk production was up because of improved feeding methods, farmers were "working their way out" of their overproduction dilemma by reducing their herds. He would say that the announced reduction in the milk support price "would mean a loss of twenty-five cents per hundred weight to farm producers" and would place "the Republicans and the Administration in a defenseless position politically."

Eisenhower would reiterate his support for Secretary of Agriculture Benson's position on cutting price supports. Responding to Senator Thye's statement that Congress was likely to pass legislation freezing support prices, the President would say that any such plan by Congress would be "a serious blow to the free enterprise system." As predicted, in March Congress would pass legislation outlawing cuts in farm price supports for 1958. Eisenhower would again defend Benson's position and veto the legislation (see Eisenhower to Thye, Mar. 13, 1958, and other papers in WHCF/OF 1; *Congressional Quarterly Almanac,* vol. XVI, *1958,* pp. 269–71, 335; and *New York Times,* Mar. 22, 1957).

554 *EM, AWF, Administration Series*

To Arthur Ellsworth Summerfield, Jr. *January 27, 1958*

Dear Bud: Thank you for your note about the little talk I gave in Chicago. Incidentally, the reception there pleased Mrs. Eisenhower and me enormously; everyone seemed to go out of his way to make us feel welcome.[1]

Heidi is definitely an asset to life in the White House.[2] She cavorts on the South Lawn at a great rate, with such important projects as chasing squirrels and investigating what might be under bushes. She is beautiful and well-behaved (occasionally she tends toward stubbornness but is then immediately apologetic about it). And she is extremely affectionate and seemingly happy. I am constantly indebted to you both for giving her to me and for arranging with Mr. Kellogg to train her.[3]

With warm regard, *As ever*

[1] Summerfield's note is not in AWF. On January 20 Eisenhower had spoken at a dinner for the United Republican Fund of Illinois (see no. 539). The President listed the three objectives of the Republican party: security and a just peace; the American system of private enterprise; and doing "for people what needs to be done, but what they cannot do for themselves" (*Public Papers of the Presidents: Eisenhower, 1958,* pp. 114–15). On the reception see *New York Times,* January 21, 1958.

[2] Summerfield had given Heidi, a Weimaraner puppy, to Eisenhower in August 1955 (see Galambos and van Ee, *The Middle Way,* no. 1545).

[3] Marion Knight Kellogg (LL.B. Yale 1928), a leading Weimaraner enthusiast, had been recommended to Summerfield by the president of the National Weimaraner Club. In 1956 Kellogg had retired from law practice in Detroit to lecture on international law at the University of Virginia (Summerfield to Eisenhower, June 25, 1956, AWF/Gettysburg).

555 *Jackson Papers*

To Charles Douglas Jackson *January 28, 1958*
Personal

Dear C. D.: I have just read the letter you wrote to Sherman Adams. It seems to me to fail to be responsive to the proposition I had in mind.[1]

In the simplest possible language, my proposal was that you take a position under Dulles in the State Department as Under Secretary of State. While it would probably be an euphemistic title, your duties would be to head up the cold war effort. This would, of course, include studying and keeping abreast of every possible proposal, friendly or unfriendly, in disarmament.

Admittedly this plan would assume the authorization by the Congress of a second Under Secretary of State. Some years ago we had two of these, but in recent times only one.

In our conversation I pointed out to you that my "ideal" organizational change would be to create a post which I would call "The First Secretary of the Government." This officer—who in this case would be Mr. Dulles—would be responsible to the President for coordinating and directing the efforts of the State Department, the USIA, the ICA, and the international activities of the Departments of Commerce, Agriculture, Labor and Treasury. He would be relieved of the chore of meeting with Committees and long hours of detailed discussion and argument—he would be given time to think.

Even with this scheme of mine, I still think there should be within the State Department an officer specifically charged with the responsibility for carrying on cold war activities, including disarmament. However, it would probably, under this proposition, *not* be necessary to create a new post of a second Under Secretary, because presumably the new Secretary of State and his Under Secretary could handle this function since they would be relieved largely of responsibility of representing the President at international conferences, of formulating basic policy and of making final decisions in all the major elements of diplomatic procedure.

In any event, why could you not, after Foster comes back, come to see him or me once more and see whether there isn't some virtue in the idea I have discussed?[2] I have no notion of making you simply a Presidential representative, with vaguely defined duties and responsibilities, nor have I ever dreamed of you as an individual who was begging disarmament favors from the Kremlin.

I am not sure when Foster will be back, but I suppose it will be toward the end of the week.[3]

With warm regard, *As ever*

[1] For background on Eisenhower's proposal to create a position within the State Department for Jackson see no. 527; on the President's proposal for a first secretary of government see no. 538. In his January 27 letter to Adams, Jackson had declined a suggestion by Adams that he consider a post as presidential assistant for disarmament matters. He had a "personal distaste" for disarmament, Jackson had said. The United States had done more than any other nation to promote the reduction of armaments, and he opposed any further "unilateral American sweetening of the disarmament kitty." Believing as he did, he could not honestly take a position where he would be "identified publicly" as the man responsible for promoting the Administration's disarmament position. He also believed that the time had passed for effective work to be done by a presidential assistant "with vague terms of reference, nebulous responsibilities (except for disarmament), and no authority except what he can cajole out of his betters" (Jackson Papers).

[2] Dulles was attending the Baghdad Pact Council meeting in Ankara, Turkey, from January 27–30.

[3] "I have a certain feeling of embarrassment in replying to your January 28th letter," Jackson would write," because while I have a normal desire to absolve myself, at the same time I do not want to add anything to the crossed-wires department." His letter to Adams, he said, was in response to a different proposition made to him earlier by Adams (Jackson to Eisenhower, Jan. 31, 1958, AWF/A). For developments see no. 603.

556 — *EM, AWF, DDE Diaries Series*

To John Foster Dulles — *January 28, 1958*

Dear Foster:[1] I received a cable this morning and intended answering it at once. Thereafter I learned that Chris Herter had already drafted a message. I approved it, but did suggest the addition of a paragraph in which I urged that you impress upon Selwyn Lloyd the very unfortunate consequences of any government, unilaterally, pushing out into a new direction toward objectives and procedures that have not been agreed among a number of us. I think that the difficulties and misunderstandings thus created would be particularly important to our two countries, which have made so many efforts to concert our views and actions.[2]

I am relieved that the Communist terrorists apparently made nothing more than a futile gesture against you and the American delegation at Ankara.[3]

Take care of yourself. *As ever*

[1] Acting Secretary of State Herter sent this message from the President to Secretary Dulles, who was attending the Baghdad Pact Council meeting in Ankara, Turkey (see Eisenhower to Menderes, Jan. 13, 1958, AWF/I: Turkey).

[2] After meeting privately with British Foreign Minister Lloyd, Dulles apparently had notified Eisenhower that Prime Minister Macmillan intended to respond favorably to a January 8 letter from Soviet Premier Bulganin urging a summit meeting. "I fear

that Macmillan under powerful domestic pressures from the left is trying to run a little too fast with the summit ball," Dulles had said (Dulles to Eisenhower, Jan. 27, 1958, AWF/D-H; see also Ann Whitman memorandum, Jan. 28, 1958, AWF/AWD; on the Bulganin letter and the proposed summit see no. 521); for Macmillan's opinion on the U.S. reaction to his proposals see Macmillan, *Riding the Storm*, pp. 387–88, 402, 466–67).

Dulles would show this message to Lloyd and subsequently would explain the U.S. position. A summit meeting could be justified only if there were a "reasonable expectation" of results, Dulles said. And the results "must be more than merely a superficial declaration of generalities and the deceptive appearance of friendly and trusting relations. . . ." Dulles asked Lloyd not to pursue the matter further until Bulganin had answered the basic questions Eisenhower had asked in his January 12 letter to the Soviet leader (see no. 521). Dulles also decried Bulganin's tactic of writing simultaneous letters to individual leaders of the Western nations and receiving separate replies, which contained "inevitable divergencies which the Soviets can exploit" (Dulles to Lloyd, Jan. 29, 1958, AWF/D-H).

[3] Shortly after midnight on January 27, subsequent to Dulles's arrival in Ankara, two bombs had exploded, resulting in minor damage to the U.S. embassy warehouse and to the American Publications Bureau. Later that day the Turkish National Assembly had condemned the acts as a Communist plot designed to destroy Turkish-American friendship (*New York Times*, Jan. 28, 1958). Dulles himself remained unruffled by the bombings. "I slept through it all," he told Eisenhower, "although most of our party heard the explosions. Fortunately no great damage was done and there was no personal injury to anyone." Dulles had also told Eisenhower that the Turkish prime minister believed that the bombings were "a communist demonstration against the Baghdad Pact and particularly against me" (Dulles to Eisenhower, Jan. 27, 1958, AWF/D-H).

For developments regarding the summit proposal see no. 575.

557 — *EM, AWF, Administration Series, Emanuel Corr.*

To William Pierce Rogers — *January 28, 1958*

Dear Bill: Reference our conversation this afternoon, I give you a little memorandum on the question of Immigration visas for Bernard A. Murphy and Manuel Guerra. A note to my office from Mr. O'Connor of the State Department provides the following information:

> "Murphy has appointment on 24th for his medical and issuance visa if qualified.
>
> "Guerra is chargeable oversubscribed Portugese quota. Application indicates his occupation to be butler. Letter from sponsor indicates Guerra to be employed as cook in sponsor's home. Occupation and position offered would not appear to qualify Guerra as First Preference applicant but suggest sponsor communicate with Immigration and Naturalization Service in this

regard. Sponsor's son in England notified of difficulties regarding quota chargeability of Guerra and has indicated he is seeking another applicant not chargeable to oversubscribed quota."

If there is any proper way of handling the matter I would be most appreciative.[1]

With many thanks, *As ever*

[1] Eisenhower had telephoned Attorney General Rogers regarding a request by the Eisenhowers' long-time friend Victor Emanuel. Rogers had agreed to assist the President and Eisenhower said that he would send him this memorandum (Telephone conversation, Jan. 28, 1958, AWF/D; see also Whitman to Eisenhower, n.d., and Whitman to Rogers, Jan. 28, 29, 1958). Emanuel, chairman and president of Avco Manufacturing Corporation, had encountered a problem securing immigration visas for domestic workers to care for his ailing wife. The two men currently worked for Emanuel's son in Great Britain (see Emanuel to Allen, Jan. 17, 1958, and Whitman to Allen, Jan. 28, 1958). For background on Emanuel see Galambos, *Chief of Staff*, no. 1488, and *Eisenhower Papers*, vols. XII–XVII.

Roderic Ladew O'Connor (LL.D. Yale 1947) was Administrator, Bureau of Security and Consular Affairs in the Department of State. He had noted along the margin of his memorandum that there was little that the State Department could do unless the Immigration and Naturalization Service (INS) approved Guerra's petition for preferential admission to the United States (O'Connor to Morgan, Jan. 23, 1958).

On January 30 Eisenhower would thank Rogers for "promptly and efficiently handling the matter." The President would also notify Emanuel. Rogers's actions appear to have been successful; Murphy and Guerra would arrive in the United States on April 4 (see Emanuel to Murff, Apr. 5; Emanuel to Swing, Apr. 5; and Swing to Whitman, Apr. 14). The President would thank the commissioner of Immigration and Naturalization Services on April 15. All papers, as well as additional correspondence, are in AWF/A and AWF/A, Emanuel Corr.

558 *EM, AWF, Administration Series*

To Arthur Ellsworth Summerfield, Sr. *January 30, 1958*

Dear Arthur: I can't tell you how much I appreciate the heartwarming note, and the lovely roses, that you and Miriam sent to me this afternoon.[1] Your thought of me helps greatly.

Arthur's death causes a great void in the Eisenhower family circle. He was our "big" brother—always dependable and always devoted.[2]

With warm regard, *As ever*

[1] Postmaster General Summerfield's note is in AWF/A. His wife was the former Miriam W. Graim.

[2] Arthur Bradford Eisenhower had died on January 26 at the age of 71. For background on his failing health see nos. 1, 4, and 439. On January 29 the President had attended the funeral services in Kansas City, Missouri (*New York Times*, Jan. 27, 30, 1958). For developments see no. 742.

559 — *EM, AWF, Name Series*

To Robert Tyre Jones, Jr. — *January 30, 1958*

Dear Bob: My new set of Spalding clubs has just arrived. Ed Dudley arranged with Mr. Tait to have the swing weights slightly less than in my previous set which, of course, immediately gave me the idea that all my difficulties would be immediately rectified. I haven't had an opportunity to practice much of late and while these new clubs feel very fine, my wrist muscles are so weak that I can't claim the superior prowess that I thought would result. However, I do think that in general the weights are better. Certainly the clubs are very handsome and I am, as always, grateful beyond words.[1]

With warm regard, *As ever*

[1] In 1956 Spalding had begun producing woods and irons under Jones's name (see Galambos and van Ee, *The Middle Way*, no. 1980). For background on golf professional Dudley's offer to have a set of Spalding clubs made for the President see no. 499. On this same day Eisenhower also would thank Dudley and Don Tait of A. G. Spalding and Brothers, Inc. (both in AWF/N).